"What a book. It is interesting, fun to read, and full of knowledge! Norbert has summarized his deep knowledge, combined it with great storytelling, and even succeeded to involve his great interest of bicycling. This book should make any innovation library, at least if you want to win!"
— Peter Palmér, Senior Manager, Transformation Office, Scania, Sweden

"*Winning Innovation* is a fascinating novel that describes the adventure of implementing lean innovation in an Italian bike company. While textbooks on lean are often dreary to read, this book makes lean easy to understand and pleasant to read. A page turner that will help you implement lean innovation in the most gratifying way."
— Jean-Claude Kihn, former Chief Technology Officer of
The Goodyear Tire & Rubber Company

"Every element of Winning Innovation applies to any industry, especially healthcare. What resonated for me was the need to establish clear goals, a culture and system that empowers people to bring ideas forward, and the visibility to know if you are winning or losing. The novel illustrates that with a leadership vision, respect for individuals, and a process to innovate rapidly, organizations can excel at what they already do while looking to the future and staying ahead of the curve."
— Anne Musitano, Operational Excellence Administrative Director,
Akron Children's Hospital

"I like that *Winning Innovation* was written as a novel, weaving the practices required for a successful innovation system into a unique and easy-to-read story. Key innovation principles are presented and applied by a cast of real-life characters as they encounter new situations and challenges, many of which we are likely to encounter on our own journeys working in all areas of innovation. The book is comprehensive from start to finish, covering a full spectrum of characteristics necessary to deliver winning innovations and showing how an innovation transformation and culture change can lead to a lot more value for an owner, company, and everyone connected to it."
— Todd Kooken, Vice President, Technology and Solution Strategies, Lincoln Electric

"In his book, *Winning Innovation*, Norbert Majerus brings his vast knowledge of product creation to life. He weaves together his experiences in transforming companies and intimate knowledge of bike racing to create an accessible read. The stories and characters make it clear that, while tools and processes are important, people need to be the center of any attempt at transformation. Not only that, but the compelling storyline lays out steps that any organization can replicate to produce dramatic improvement in innovation. I highly recommend this read for any leader involved in bringing new products or services to market."
— Durward K. Sobek II, Vice Provost of Academic Affairs and Professor of Industrial &
Management Systems Engineering, Montana State University-Bozeman

"In today's fast-paced business environment, leaders need to develop innovative ways to drive organizational success. This requires a shift in mindset — away from traditional management practices toward more agile and collaborative approaches. In *Winning Innovation*, Norbert Majerus takes you on an exciting and interesting R&D transformation journey, as the business novel explores a lot of the ups and downs everyone experiences when working in research and development (R&D). It shows that for successful business transformation, organizations must focus on people, communication, and processes."
— Sannah Vinding, Executive Director Product Development and Marketing VCC,
Mind the Innovation Podcast Producer, and former LPPDE Chair

"*Winning Innovation* gets to the heart of what drives any successful transformation—people. If you make people visible, they'll make you valuable. More than innovation principles, the book illustrates how the most effective companies embrace both the source of an idea (the people, regardless of their stature or position in the company) and their solutions to create value. *Winning Innovation* is a lesson in how to change a culture, starting with leadership, and the importance of diversity and inclusion to make this happen."

— Billy Taylor, CEO, LinkedXL

"Business novels are risky propositions: they need an engaging plot as well as a worthwhile educational message. *Winning Innovation* hits the mark on both counts, providing a fun story with an insightful education in the way that lean thinking propels innovation. If you enjoyed The Gold Mine, this book is for you."

— Dan Markovitz, Author, *The Conclusion Trap*

"*Winning Innovation* is a delightful, inspiring, and fun novel of an innovation transformation, from its complicated beginning to a happy ending. This captivating lean love story illustrates real challenges and rewards along the journey. It describes not only principles needed but how to change a culture: developing leaders to care for a "business family" and empowering, educating, and enabling employees. *Winning Innovation* shows that the future of lean is more than profits and efficiency; it's about creating an innovative, sustainable company that delivers value to shareholders, employees, and society."

— Myrna Flores, President and Co-founder of the Lean Analytics Association and Executive Director at Imperial College of Business School

"Reading Norbert's book, I was able to learn how LPPD (lean product and process development) can drive innovation both in the product itself and in the operation of R&D organizations. In particular, I think that *Winning Innovation* will give you an insight into how various LPPD principles can successfully lead to innovative solutions on new product development. Norbert is a real LPPD expert, and he is a great LPPD teacher."

— Sungyul Kim, LPPD Lead, and Ken Joongkil Kwon, Program Manager and LPPD Lead, HP Printing Korea

"This is a really compelling business novel about innovations and building the culture and processes behind them: a story about company transformation, which is enabled by people transformation. *Winning Innovation* is easy to read, but filled with Norbert Majerus' vast knowledge and experience with well functioning practices and tools in the field of innovation."

— Juha Tammi, General Manager, Lean Association of Finland

"For nearly one decade I have had the privilege of learning from Norbert. He loves to tell stories, and *Winning Innovation* does that while teaching. In this work Norbert combines his passion for cycling with his compassion for innovators. As he asserts from the beginning, it is all about the right environment for the people—an innovation ecosystem. Transforming an organization to innovation excellence takes years of determination and to start. This novel inspires one to start the journey by telling the story of transformation. It is a light to guide your journey."

— Larry Navarre, Lecturer, School of Management, Kettering University

"In *Winning Innovation*, Norbert Majerus invites readers to follow a company's transformation to implement an innovation system and an innovation culture. The leaders' challenges and how they navigate their learning process and succeed gave me many déjà vu moments. In the book, the bike company's journey really shows the importance and interrelations of all principles to build a winning innovation system. Teams create innovations with agile processes, effectively closing knowledge gaps and then working according to takt time, on one project at a time, to significantly reduce cycle time and free up resources."

— Christer Lundh, Chairman, LPPDE

Winning Innovation

Winning Innovation

How Innovation Excellence Propels an Industry Icon Toward Sustained Prosperity

A Novel by
Norbert Majerus with George Taninecz

Routledge
Taylor & Francis Group

A PRODUCTIVITY PRESS BOOK

First published 2022
by Routledge
605 Third Avenue, New York, NY 10158

and by Routledge
2 Park Square, Milton Park, Abingdon, Oxon, OX14 4RN

Routledge is an imprint of the Taylor & Francis Group, an informa business

ISBN: 978-1-032-13990-6 (hbk)
ISBN: 978-1-032-13989-0 (pbk)
ISBN: 978-1-003-23183-7 (ebk)

DOI: 10.4324/9781003231837

Typeset in Garamond
by Apex CoVantage, LLC

Contents

Foreword

A lean enterprise is all about innovation. In fact, the whole point of any lean transformation is supporting innovation. This is why lean production centers around quality and flexibility: new products must convince customers on quality right away, and flexible processes must make it easier to build new products on existing lines so as to lower the manufacturing costs and make products more affordable as they are released. On paper, the problem is simple. Sustained business success rests on a steady flow of innovations that hit the spot with customers in terms of features, quality, and price—and leave a healthy profit.

In real life, however, this is a formidable challenge. First, real innovation means innovation that works for customers. As Mo, a leading character in Norbert's novel, discovers for himself, it is one thing to dream up a chainless bike and even to build working prototypes; it is quite another to deliver the product to a mass audience at quality and price targets. Innovation is not simply about having bright ideas and getting them executed by the organizational machine; it's about fixing every single little thing so that the innovation finds its natural audience.

This means that a truly innovative company is one that sustains a constant flow of ideas throughout the organization and, principally, across the functional silos that unavoidably build up. As Junior, the CEO of Norbert's bike company, learns the hard way, silos and hierarchies are necessary to make any organization work, but they also steer resources to the wrong projects and suppress the necessary flow of conversations from which true innovation springs. A fantastic insight that is well demonstrated in the book—as only storytelling fiction can do—is the importance of "who talks to whom" as the foundation of innovative thinking. This can't be organized mechanically; it needs to be fostered by the right culture and conditions.

Which brings us to the third aspect of transformation, skillfully brought to life by Norbert's storyline and characters: it's all about people—people, with their potential and their limits, their style and their backgrounds, their knowledge and their preferences. People interact daily, choose whether to join the transformation or fight it, whether to support other people's innovative ideas or bury them under criticisms, and, as Norbert shows so well, the same person can be at the same time brilliantly insightful on some things and a complete jerk on others—people.

Yet, a flow of ideas will never happen mechanically—ideas only exist as people breathe life into them. For ideas to become realities, people must come together and share, experiment, and learn. The truest leadership role is to create the conditions for this to happen, by better clarifying the goal posts and the purpose of the common effort, and then by daily encouraging teamwork, challenging individuals to give their best, and recognizing and rewarding them for it. But where does one learn to do that?

Here again, Norbert's book is an essential read. Through the story, he details the practical tools to get started beyond the overall intent and to get innovation going. Then he explains precisely how to build robust processes to structure enduring innovation beyond the early wins (and disappointments) and to step by step improve the business as a whole. This very complete approach to the tools and processes of a value-based organization is a key strength of the book that makes it a must on fostering and supporting innovation from the inside.

In this fantastic tale of lean innovation turnaround, Norbert brings the transformation process to life with charming characters and an engaging storyline while also getting into the nuts and bolts of the principles, tools, and processes needed to make it happen in the real world. I heartily recommend this great read to anyone interested in *winning innovation*.

Michael Ballé
Paris

Acknowledgments

I want to start by thanking Taylor & Francis Group and Michael Sinocchi, publisher at Productivity Press, a division of Taylor & Francis, for giving me the opportunity to publish this book.

Thanks to Michael Ballé for writing the foreword and all the people and organizations who endorsed the book.

I owe special thanks to George Taninecz, who wrote this book with me. George was a lot more than a co-writer: he also was my coach.

I appreciate all the work of Juan Quirarte, who did the illustrations.

I would like to thank a very large community of colleagues and experts in innovation, operational excellence, lean, agile, and six sigma for teaching and coaching me throughout and after my career as an engineer.

Gratitude to all the organizations with which I've worked: the Shingo Institute, Association for Manufacturing Excellence (AME), Lean Enterprise Institute (LEI), Lean Product and Process Development Exchange (LPPDE), American Society for Quality (ASQ), Product Development and Management Association (PDMA), Innovation Research Institute (IRI), Lean Analytics Association (LAA), Lean Frontiers, Product Development and Management Association (PDMA), and many more. Thanks for their role in sharing, publishing, and educating.

A special thanks to the organizations who gave me an opportunity to share what I learned about lean, operational excellence, and innovation. Thank you for letting me experiment, learn, and grow. Special thanks to those who provided feedback on what I shared and taught. A lot of that feedback is reflected in this book.

Thanks to all my clients for challenging me to find new ways to help them.

But most of my gratitude is to all the folks who want to learn more about the subject of innovation excellence and chose—among many options available today—this book as a source for inspiration.

Norbert Majerus

Authors

Norbert Majerus

Beginning in 2005, Norbert implemented a principles-based lean product development process at the three global innovation centers of The Goodyear Tire & Rubber Company. For more than a decade, he was Goodyear's lean champion in research and development.

In 2016, Norbert published his first book, *Lean-Driven Innovation*, which received the Shingo Research Award. Also in 2016, with Norbert's guidance, the Goodyear R&D organization applied for and received the AME Excellence Award.

Norbert, born and raised in Luxembourg, has a master's degree in chemistry from the Universität des Saarlandes, Saarbrücken, Germany, and worked most of the disciplines and held various roles in the Goodyear innovation centers in Luxembourg and Akron. Norbert holds 60 patents and trade secrets in the United States alone and has a master black belt in six sigma.

Norbert has taught workshops and has given keynotes at many conferences in the United States and other countries. Since retiring from Goodyear in 2017, he continues to share his extensive lean expertise via norbert majerus consulting ltd. He is a Shingo Academy Fellow, an AME assessor, and serves on the board of LPPDE (Lean Product and Process Development Exchange). Norbert can be reached at norbert.majerus@gmail.com.

George Taninecz

For more than 20 years, George, as president of George Taninecz Inc., has helped executives publish award-winning books that illustrate applications of lean thinking. He also supports companies and associations with white papers, articles, and case studies on the deployment of lean in manufacturing, healthcare, and other industries.

George also is vice president of research for The MPI Group, a research and knowledge-development firm, where he creates research, benchmarking, and maturity-model tools that enable organizations to assess their performances, gauge best practices, and define paths for improvement. He also manages innovative thought-leadership projects for MPI clients.

George was a communications specialist at McKinsey & Company in the firm's manufacturing practice and worked at *IndustryWeek* magazine as a managing editor and director of the America's Best Plants program. George can be reached at george@taninecz.net.

Introduction

Loud rock music blasted from Pete's oversized speakers. I was fixed on a video of an old cycling race that was playing on a small screen in front of my winter bike-training class. To my left were a bunch of young bike racers who certainly would have dropped me if we were training on a road. To my right were riders who struggled like me. Although I'd seen the video of the Giro d'Italia at Pete Gladden's training class often enough to remember every single stage winner, it helped me focus as the 18-minute drill reached its climax. When the drill ended, we spent our three-minute break mostly panting and laughing at jokes my friend John cracked from the back row. As my eyes wandered from the video to the falling snow outside, it hit me: My next book would be a business novel that lets me combine my passion for cycling, innovation, and operational excellence. I'll place the action in northern Italy and combine beautiful scenery with the exhilaration of bike racing. There will be great food and wine, and maybe I can even work into the plot my passion for skiing.

By the end of the winter training, the complete book had come together in my head. Maybe the old Greek philosophers were right when they said that exercise stimulates the brain. The story would address all principles of lean innovation—from lean startup to mass design, from knowledge management to standard work, and from respect for people to humble leadership—and I'd illustrate the principles with compelling examples. I'd also show the complete innovation process, from the formation of an idea to counting the money.

In my more than 40 years of experience in industrial innovation, it always bothered me that innovation did not seem to have a well-defined process. Stifling creativity usually was cited for the cause. But after seeing how operational excellence is used today in myriad industries and applications, including hospitals and banks, I gained the courage to apply it to innovation. The result is a surprisingly simple process of innovation excellence that actually fosters creativity.

There was so much I had learned since my first book, *Lean-Driven Innovation*,[1] such as applying lean thinking to the creative part of innovation and the process of lean technology creation. But I was most excited to finally demonstrate that achieving excellence and sustainability is about more than process. I wanted an opportunity to describe my experiences with change management in more detail, including the simultaneous implementation of lean processes and systems alongside the cultural transformation of people—and *Winning Innovation* has given me the platform to document this best practice.

When I teach change management and transformation, I ask the class—mostly lean experts leading or participating in a transformation—about their main focus and the metrics they use to track their progress. I consistently find that 90 percent of the answers are focused on the process. Then I steer the discussion toward behaviors, culture, and leadership engagement and ask what is more difficult to change, the process or the people. The answer is unanimous: the people. I get the same answer when I ask what is more important, the process or the people: the people. Then when

I ask the class why they don't focus their metrics on what they say is most challenging and most important, I have their attention.

In my class I also share how I started my first transformation focused primarily on the process, and I was frequently annoyed by associates and leaders alike. And when I thought the time had come to focus on the people, I found the people and cultural transformation a lot harder than if we had addressed people and process concurrently. I knew this would have to be a critical element of my story.

Over my many years in innovation and operational excellence, I was fortunate to learn from experts, famous authors, and humble practitioners. One of the most important things I learned—from Jim Womack (*Seeing the Whole*[2])—was that the biggest results of a lean transformation are achieved if the initiative is deployed across the entire enterprise. I was able to validate Jim's observation many times in a large company; however, the real results are a little delayed and disguised in a large company because of the breadth of the deployment. For this reason, I chose to place the *Winning Innovation* story at a relatively small company to clearly illustrate the enterprise effect.

Another advantage of choosing a smaller company is that I was able to tell a fast-paced story, one that illustrates just how quickly a transformation can take place and how rapidly it can generate results. The roadmap I present for this journey is easy to understand and replicate. My story is about products and services with R&D as the main driver, and it illustrates how innovation excellence is deployed to create revenue and growth (not to reduce costs). The principles—being universal—apply to every company and business and can be scaled up to the largest of companies.

The story also shows how even a competent, industry-leading organization—like many companies I know—needs a catalyst (not necessarily a burning platform) to pursue innovation excellence. Once deployed and embraced, innovation excellence then dramatically transforms the company's ability to innovate and how it operates overall.

Most important for me is that this book finally allows me to share a lot of personal experiences and hard-learned lessons that I wish I had acquired earlier in my career. I hope this book will spare readers the long, painful learning curve that I experienced. I probably chose to become an engineer to avoid dealing with people; throughout my career, no technical challenge was too big, but the slightest people challenge set me back. That all changed when I started to lead a large innovation excellence transformation. I had learned many leadership principles and behaviors earlier that did not work for me, but it was the *lean behaviors* that eventually made the difference. As I taught those behaviors to associates and leaders—respect and care for people, humility, engaging everyone in the change process—I quickly became a believer. Responsibility, ownership, and accountability now have totally different meanings for me.

This book is pure fiction. Any resemblance to actual persons or companies is purely coincidental. As a business novel, it gave me an opportunity to picture myself in at least four different roles that arise during an innovation excellence transformation. Some elements of these roles were based on positive as well as painful experiences in my career, while others are ideal traits for positions that I wish I had held: a wide-eyed innovator who refuses to let the system beat him, a change agent who once again must overcome workplace distrust and apprehension, a knowledgeable R&D leader who deftly sets the right technical and organizational innovation course, and an executive who finally discovers genuine care for employees through his own people-centric transformation.

Telling stories was also a lot of fun. I enjoyed taking recollections from my long career in both innovation and change management and placing them in the plot in order to explain actual initiatives and their outcomes, illustrate key principles, and tell a realistic story. All this made the plot natural and exciting.

I hope reading this book is as much a joy to read as it was for me to write. An experienced transformation leader may criticize me for making all this look too simple—that I did not put enough setbacks or trouble in the story. Trust me, I had my share of trouble and challenges in my career and an abundance of stories to tell. But when I taught soccer, I didn't teach players how to twist their ankle or break their leg, nor did we practice how to lose games. I taught skills, tactics, and strength conditioning for success, and we had fun and very few injuries. Winning was a consequence of good skills and fitness; setbacks were a natural part of learning, and most of my players continued playing through college and beyond. I hope readers will have the same experience: learn the right principles, have fun, dream about how things will be one day, and consider their own mistakes and setbacks a normal part of their learning.

I considered summarizing and highlighting the principles that come up in the story after every chapter, but George Taninecz said I was thinking too much like an engineer. He convinced me that the story and the context in which the principles appear illuminate the book's key learnings—without them being explicitly spelled out and recapitulated. I've come to agree with George: readers need the opportunity to reflect and process the principles for themselves as they encounter them and consider how to apply those that are right for their own work and life.

With an authentic blend of business, innovation, and action, I believe *Winning Innovation* will appeal to a practitioner, an executive, a leader, or the owner of a company, those deeply immersed in innovation as well as those with little or no experience. Enjoy the story, reflect and learn, and good luck with your own transformation.

Norbert Majerus

Notes

1. Norbert Majerus, *Lean-Driven Innovation*, CRC Press, Boca Raton, FL, 2015.
2. Jim Womack and Dan Jones, *Seeing the Whole*, Lean Enterprise Institute, Brookline, MA, 2002.

Chapter 1

Chain Reaction

If Fausto Davanti were alive and walked into the company he founded in 1960—Davanti Nella Gara—he wouldn't notice much of a difference. And that was a problem.

Fausto Davanti was a two-time winner of the Tour de France in the 1950s as well as three Giri d'Italia, two Vueltas a España, and so many classics that he'd lost count. He had saved the money he made as a pro cyclist and invested it in a small bike shop. Fausto's nickname on the racing circuit was "Davanti Nella Gara," which means leader of the race or, literally, "ahead in the race," a position that he often held. His nickname would be the beacon for his company. It soon followed that Fausto's talents were not only in the bike saddle; he was an intelligent man with a great vision and excellent business sense. When he retired in 1995, he had built one of the world's leading bicycle companies, supplying pros and amateur racers with the best bikes in the world. In addition to the business, Fausto Sr. also had created one of the best pro cycling teams, the pride of every employee in the company.

Through his tenure as owner and CEO, Fausto expanded the company into other bicycle markets, including touring and recreational bikes. These efforts met with moderate success, but enough to slightly boost revenues. Today the company has annual sales of nearly 500 million euro, albeit flat in recent years. Davanti Nella Gara now markets bikes in many countries around the world, selling through all the common channels, but relying heavily on bike stores and multibrand dealers. It assembles most of its bikes in a Davanti-owned, state-of-the-art plant in Taiwan that employs about 300 people. Davanti's top-of-the-line frames are made in its own plants, other frames are sourced from a premier factory in Taiwan, and components are purchased from leading component manufacturers around the world.

The original shop that Fausto Sr. started in Fumane, Italy, north of Verona and near the foothills of the Alps, was converted into a plant for custom race bikes and bike tuning for the top racers in the world. Davanti has invested heavily in carbon fiber-reinforced bikes (commonly referred to as "carbon bikes"), a technology preferred by all bike racers because of their light weight and superior performance. The Fumane site also houses prototype and testing facilities with technical capabilities unsurpassed in the industry. It remains the company headquarters and R&D center, and employs about 200 people.

Since Fausto's retirement, his son, Fausto Davanti Jr., has run the company. "Junior," as he is called in the company, has spent most of his life walking or running (as a child) through the halls of the Fumane site. He shares his father's love of bikes and business sense, although he never was a great bike racer and often questions his own leadership skills. Still fit and despite the many business demands he faces, Junior finds enough time to ride on a regular basis. He rarely misses the

DOI: 10.4324/9781003231837-1

weekly company ride, where he joins 30 to 40 employees crowding the beautiful roads through the countryside.

On this day, Junior, his black hair streaked with gray, wishes he was out riding or, at the very least, enjoying the fruits of his own retirement. Instead he's concerned that his own path from the company will never emerge, the wear easily visible on his face as he heads into a conference room for an R&D presentation.

***

Today is a big day for Maurice Pensatore. He will meet with Junior and the leadership team to present his business plan for a new idea that he believes will revolutionize the bicycle industry.

"Mo" was very lucky to land his dream job with Davanti Nella Gara, where he works in the research and development department. He and about 100 other engineers and technicians develop new model bicycles, which they prototype in the Fumane plant and test in its state-of-the-art lab and on the roads with pro and amateur racers and testers. Mo had submitted a bike concept through the company's new idea submission system, believing it deserved his company's attention and was surprised that this day has come. For a few weeks, he'd heard nothing about his proposal.

Due to stagnated sales at Davanti Nella Gara, the owner and CEO had challenged engineers and technicians to become more innovative. When introducing the idea submission system, Junior said, "My dad used to ride a bike 70 years ago that looked almost like what we produce today. We need to think outside the box and come up with some new ideas." Since Junior's announcement about six months ago, the organization had not produced anything significantly new in terms of ideas, a point that Junior made quite clear to his chief technical officer (CTO), Emilio Indiretto, at the latest leadership meeting. Emilio's response was to storm back to his office, pull out a few ideas that he had personally discarded, and prove to Junior that his innovation system was a waste of time. Mo's idea was one of the ideas temporarily resurrected.

Mo's supervisor, Ricardo Capace, had immediately liked Mo's idea when he saw it a few weeks ago: "Wow, that's a unique way to eliminate one of the biggest problems affecting cyclists today," he exclaimed when glancing through the proposal. Ricardo likes to focus on opportunities; he believes there is always time to address potential problems and likes to leave the details to those best equipped to deal with them. It's one of the reasons he hires talented and enthusiastic engineers like Mo.

But when Emilio—Ricardo's boss—initially reviewed Mo's submission, he stopped reading after the first paragraph. Emilio figured it would take years of development and that he and Junior would be retired long before the idea could get to market—it would have virtually no impact on the company in the foreseeable future and no impact on his own status and compensation. Another reason for Emilio's initial rejection is his preoccupation with his pet project—a new derailleur/chain combination dubbed "Darvin," which most believed Davanti was developing jointly with Coppimechanica, the leading Italian bicycle component manufacturer. Darvin is shrouded in secrecy. Only Emilio and his inner-most circle seem to know what is going on, even though the project consumes a lot of engineering and testing resources.

Mo didn't understand why his idea had sat idle, and no one explained the delay. He simply heard nothing and waited. From the moment the idea came to him weeks earlier, there was little else he thought of. Well, almost little else.

***

Mo had been out riding on a beautiful early March weekend near Fumane, the chill of spring replaced by blooms of pansies and primrose and radiant new green shoots everywhere. In the lowlands, all remnants of an unseasonably cold winter had finally disappeared, allowing Mo to get in his first, good mountain ride of the spring. Having just turned 30, Mo still rode his bike to work often and, if he had enough time to train, he would love to participate in races again, especially if the circuit included high altitude roads through his favorite Alps. He never made it to the professional racing level; that was more of a dream than a goal. He had put his engineering career ahead of sport, and his best racing days were past him. Mo graduated with a degree in mechanical engineering from the University of Turin and followed up with an MBA from Politecnico di Milano. His studies and then work left him little time for training and local weekend races, but Mo was OK with that and prouder of his engineering accomplishments than his racing career. He had combined his passion for bikes with his professional goals, and he was thrilled to work for the best bike manufacturer in the world.

As Mo reached the higher altitudes, he could still see banks of snow and, in the distance, skiers on the slopes. Mo put on a warmer jacket after he had climbed the first hill and whiffed down the slope toward the valley. The cool spring air felt great, and he was ready for another climb, which he executed in the same fashion; he looked forward to the last descent that would bring him home. He was riding with his head so pointed to the ground that he almost did not see her as she called out: "Hey, champ, can you help me?" He came to a stop, turned around, and saw the young female rider who was grounded. He unclipped both pedals and shuffled back toward her. "I just upgraded to the most expensive chain—can you believe this?" she spewed, holding up a greasy, broken chain. "It lasted less than 1,000 kilometers!"

Mo just shook his head, took off his gloves, and started dumping the contents of his saddle pouch. He was surprised that the last piece to fall from the pouch was his chain repair kit, which actually would work for the bike in front of him.[1] Within minutes, Mo had repaired the chain and earned the woman's respect. "Wow, that was fast. If you hadn't shown up, I don't know how I would have gotten back. I really should have my own repair kit for this type of ride. By the way, I'm Marie," she said, extending her greasy hand and shaking Mo's greasy hand. "How did you get so good at this stuff?"

"It's Mo," and he explained what he did for a living and his job at Davanti. Marie was impressed. Mo wiped his hands on his pants—already permanently stained—and the two riders put their gloves back on.

"Thank you," said Marie, shaking hands once more—glove on glove. Marie explained that she was registered for bike races in the coming weeks, so she was training on those circuits as her work schedule and locale allowed.

"Good luck in the races. I hope to see you again," said Mo sincerely as he got back on his bike and pedaled away. Marie took her time to get ready and eventually pedaled in the same direction as Mo, who was out of sight, but not for long. She soon spotted him, quickly gained ground, and was one loopback away. "Thanks again! See you soon!" she yelled as she passed Mo, who was surprised and upset that she had overtaken him so quickly. Due to the long winter, he was more out of shape than he'd thought.

As he watched Marie speed away from him, he believed he would see her again. He also thought about her broken chain. There had to be a better means to transfer power from the rider to the wheels. As most bike riders, Mo was sick of chain and derailleur problems. There is nothing messier than a bike chain, and the derailleur must have been invented for no other reason than to trouble riders. Mo knew that a lot of bike innovation in the last 30 years was aimed at improving the chain drivetrain, but little had been done to replace it. Bikes had gone from three gears to 33, and the switching mechanism went from cable to electric and hydraulic—all still dependent upon the annoying chain and the derailleur.

As Mo peddled into town, he thought of other more progressive machines, which are similar to bikes but not reliant on a chain. Sure, he thought, even motor bikes are driven by chains, but many consumer-market machines use a direct-drive mechanism. Those applications face weight challenges just like bikes, and they rely on sophisticated new materials to solve such issues—many even using carbon fibers, just like bicycles. The hand tools Mo often used had gears and direct-drive mechanisms as well. There might be something to this. As he entered Fumane, he passed his friend Marco Marrone on the street, waved, and raced home to document his thoughts.

***

Mo had spent nearly a week preparing a detailed technical presentation for his idea, including a business plan, finally using some of the skills learned in his MBA studies. He made assumptions about the newer mechanisms he was suggesting to use. His buddy Marco, who worked in the Davanti marketing department, provided sales and revenue projections, but Mo was not convinced that Marco's numbers were based on anything realistic. Mo's biggest problem was the folks in finance and accounting: They gave him little help. They said that Mo had failed to provide solid financial input data, and, because of that, they would not put their "good name" on what they believed to be an ill-fated financial study. So Mo did his own financial assessment based on what he learned at school, but he wasn't optimistic he'd ever get accounting's endorsement.

Mo was surprised to find out, however, that when exploring patentability, Davanti's contracted legal services liked his idea. "Mo, there may be potential patents linked to this project; we'll begin exploring the patent applications," exclaimed Federico Ricco, the owner of the firm, factoring in his mind the billable hours he would accumulate and genuinely pleased there would be some patents coming out of his biggest client. "I'm happy that you're happy," countered Mo. "Wish me luck."

Today, riding his race bike into work, Mo mentally rehearses his project's 40 PowerPoint slides. He had seen them so often, he'd memorized every single word. He parks his bike in the bike lot, which is nearly twice as large as the Davanti lot for autos. Most bikes are left unlocked: who would steal a bike from the parking lot of a bike company?

Mo grabs a coffee in the cafeteria and then heads to his desk, partitioned in an office with five other engineers. He exchanges greetings with his colleagues and at 10:00 am, after several pit stops, heads to the conference room, where Junior has scheduled his customary Monday morning executive meeting. Mo is the first to arrive, and while setting up his computer, executives begin to come in. Busy and engaged in their own discussions or smartphones, most do not notice Mo. Occasionally he catches someone's eye and nods or says, "Hello," but, for the most part, he is invisible. Eventually Junior arrives and everybody gets quiet.

"Well, Mo, I'm really excited to hear your story," Junior says. "It is about time that we launch some real innovation again, ideas that would even make my dad proud."

Mo kicks off his presentation with an in-depth technical overview of a direct-drive mechanism and its application to a bicycle. He speaks as though he's talking to a room of engineers and shows detailed cutaways of direct-drive gear mechanisms found in hand tools and other machines, such as ski lifts he rode during the winter. He also shows drawings of how he would connect the pedals to the gear box—a key part of Mo's concept is the solid-drive shaft that connects the gear box to the rear bike wheel. Mo has spent significant time on the engineering drawings of the proposed mechanism and explains each in great detail to the executive team.

Finally, glancing up from his computer, he looks toward the executives and pauses. "Any questions?" No one says anything, instead nodding as if they see this every day. Mo wonders if they even understood what he had just described—a *direct-drive bike*.

"OK, I'm going to run through some of the market projections for the new drivetrain," Mo says to break the silence. Now the executive team perks up, clearly hearing language they are more likely to understand, and a lively discussion ensues. Mo wonders if anybody really grasped the benefits of his proposal because they're skeptical about the marketability of the innovation. But he also knows that even projections for conventional bikes meet the same kind of resistance. Time to push on.

Mo begins to click through the PowerPoint slides that describe the financial aspects of the project; he's proud he could complete this area on his own—thanks to his MBA—and believes it to be reasonably sound analysis. He does not expect the agitated and depressing discussion that follows, led by the finance and operations executives. They question everything: procurement pricing, availability of materials, manufacturability, warranty costs, etc. For 15 minutes, everyone interrupts everyone. As the VP of manufacturing, Constantine Rendere argues that such a bike cannot be made on the existing Taiwanese assembly lines or in the prototype lab. Mo notices that Junior is staring with frustration at the ceiling. Mo tries to answer the few cost and pricing questions that are asked, but nobody waits for him to finish. Emilio frequently interrupts him and asserts, "Nobody really knows that." It's the same answer he frequently gives to anyone who asks him any technical question. The executives are not impressed.

After looking at the clock three times in five minutes, Junior rises precisely at 11 am. "That's enough for today. We'll get to the other business later this week." As Junior leaves, everyone else rises in unison. Despite the raucous ending to the presentation, all are now jovial and quickly follow Junior out of the conference room.

"What the . . ." thinks Mo. He's devastated. Emilio left without even acknowledging Mo's effort. Maybe ignoring him is part of Emilio's plan, whatever plan that might be.

Mo goes back to his desk, files away his presentation—for good? That afternoon he has a hard time getting his mind around his other projects and decides to knock off early. He dashes down to the locker room, changes into his spandex shorts and a tight jersey and jacket, grabs his race bike, and hits the road for the mountains. A solid, aggressive ride will be just the thing to wind down and provide a good night sleep after this depressing experience. By the time he reaches higher elevation, he's talking to himself. "What a bunch of morons. What do they understand about my idea—or any idea—anyway? And why would Junior give them the authority to evaluate any innovation. That's ridiculous?"

***

The next morning, Ricardo shows up at Mo's desk and asks how the meeting went. "You know, I'm not sure it could have gone much worse," says Mo. "They were uninterested in the actual innovation and brutal with the market and financial projections. Junior quickly lost interest in the meeting and, I'm afraid, the idea itself."

"Did Emilio give you any support, any good questions?" asks Ricardo.

"Nothing," says Mo flatly.

"I'm not surprised," says Ricardo. "All Emilio cares about is his new Darvin project. He's pushing the project as if we work for Coppimechanica." Mo is quite familiar with the company; Davanti has excellent relationships with the three major global component makers, but Coppimechanica, the only Italian manufacturer, has been their favorite supplier since the times of Fausto Sr.

Ricardo and Mo discuss the recent flurry of new race bicycle innovations—electric and hydraulic shifters, a switch from two or three front chainrings to one, adding more cogs in the rear—with Coppimechanica leading the way. "Best I can tell, this is the latest in the series, and they enlisted

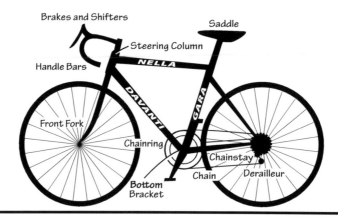

Figure 1.1   Davanti Nella Gara Bicycle.

Emilio and Davanti because the new mechanism needs a frame modification, which is our specialty," adds Ricardo. "As usual, only Emilio knows the details of the deal that was struck."

In a competitive industry where non-disclosure agreements (NDAs) are common, it's convenient for Emilio to block questions that are asked of him by pointing to the NDA with Coppimechanica. It's *believed* that the Darvin contract calls for Davanti to get an exclusive on the final product, which could include a new cog, chain, shifter, and derailleur. Ricardo knows that the project is getting all priorities and the support of Davanti's best engineers, despite Ricardo's objections. "Emilio has never been comfortable with new ideas, but I think right now he lets nothing that might need resources get in the way of Darvin," sighs Ricardo.

"So now what?" asks Mo.

"It may take time," counsels Ricardo. "Junior and Davanti need new ideas, not the same old stuff that rattles out of tired engineers and that his executive team can understand. This is just the first stage in a very long race. You need to get ready for the next. They've now seen your idea. You need to sell them on the benefits, and you need to think about how you can engage them."

Note

1. The kit includes a small hand tool and a replacement chain pin or replacement chain link, depending on the chain brand. The tool is used to remove broken links in a bicycle chain and reattach the two ends.

Chapter 2

Junior's Sicilian Dream

The morning had turned difficult for Junior. He had again witnessed his colleagues tear apart another promising idea. He did not feel like having lunch in the company cafeteria, so he walked down the street to enjoy a spinach frittata and latte at his favorite cafe. While there, he bumped into his old college friend, Marcel Ricco, and the two agreed to move their monthly meeting up to that night over drinks and good food.

Once back at the office, Junior's afternoon did not get better. He spent the rest of the day with the marketing folks discussing yet another forecast of declining sales. He finally bid his marketing team goodbye, nearly pushing them out of his office. Closing the door behind them, Junior looks at a portrait of Fausto Sr. opposite his desk, exhales heavily, and asks, "So, pop, is this what it was like for you?"

On his desk sits a folder with Mo's direct-drive bicycle presentation along with a few others that he believed had potential. Maybe they could be something, he wonders. But how to turn a file of papers into a marketable product? He'd forgotten how, if he ever knew in the first place. He stuffs the folders into his desk, gives a glance to Fausto Sr., turns off the light, and leaves his office.

***

Junior pulls his Toyota Camry up to Trattoria di Giorgio, parking behind Marcel's Maserati Quattroporte. His difficult day has turned into a lovely spring evening. He wanders in and finds Marcel at a small table on the veranda, with a view of a vineyard covering nearby hills. Marcel is a successful business entrepreneur, who grew his startup food equipment business into a holding company that includes manufacturing plants and related service companies. You couldn't walk into a restaurant in Europe without bumping into some of Marcel's equipment or his service providers. The company also specializes in marketing innovation for products and services—helping acquisitions with innovation is where Marcel made his mark. He is adept at buying small, competent-but-struggling companies and turning them into profitable entities in his own holding or selling them for a multiple of the purchase price a few years later.

"Fausto, over here," waves Marcel. "I took the liberty of ordering you an Aperol. Am I correct?"

"Perfect," replies Junior. "It's good to see you again. It's been too long. You seem to be doing well as always."

"I am at that," counters Marcel as a young waitress arrives with drinks and bruschetta, cheese, and prosciutto. "How are things with you? Did you get your innovation initiative under-way?" Marcel had suggested the idea submission process to help his friend's company with innovation.

DOI: 10.4324/9781003231837-2

Junior raises his glass and touches it to Marcel's: "Cin cin. And I'd rather not get into that today."

"Junior, it can't be all that bad. Innovation is supposed to be fun. Something must have come from it by now. Remember the cost of innovation delay—the cost of not doing it. It can be the difference between retiring in Fumane or getting your villa in Sicily!" chides Marcel.

"Oh, I know, I know. Here we are making the Ferrari of bicycles; my dad should have raced cars and I'd be driving a Maserati by now and having my drink looking at Mount Etna. . . . The innovation initiative is up and running and delivering some ideas, but my executive team critiques them into the ground. Our engineers walk away directionless and hopeless, at best. A few have quit."

"Fausto, why would you ever have your executive team assess engineers' ideas? This isn't *Shark Tank*. That's OK for a TV show, but in a company you don't raise such difficult technical assessments to the level of the least technical competence. Feeding your staff technical details must be way above their heads."

Junior's eyes widen, surprised by what he's done and how little sense it makes when he hears it said aloud: "Yes, why would I do that? Frankly, I don't understand many of the technical details either." He's surprised how with a sentence or two, Marcel can rearrange his thinking.

At their last meeting a few months ago, Junior spoke to Marcel about the future of Davanti Nella Gara and his own future as well. Junior wants to explore a sale of the company soon and retire to the Sicilian mountains. But he also wants to make sure he can honor the wishes of his late father and keep Davanti Nella Gara bikes winning races and keep the brand alive and well. Junior has two daughters—one a pediatric physician and the other a lawyer. Both are married and neither they nor their husbands have any interest in running the bicycle company. Junior's wife Martina is a ceramic artist and instructor, often traveling to teach workshops throughout Italy. With friends and colleagues across the country, she's happy to follow Junior's path to retirement wherever he wants to go.

"I know you want to sell Davanti, Junior. That's clearly your vision, or maybe you'd call it your objective. But what is your goal?" asks Marcel.

"That's easy. I want to sell for as much as I can. But I also want to respect my dad's wishes: keep our race team winning races and keep our operations intact here in Italy."

"Your brand is worth some money," reminds Marcel. "It's a start toward your retirement dream, but it won't get you what you deserve. What other equity do you have in the company?"

Junior has a hard time with that question: Most of Davanti's patents have expired, and many competitors in many countries have caught up to Davanti's technology. All of the Davanti improvements made in the last 10 years have been incremental carbon-fiber frame modifications, most to take advantage of new materials. The latest Davanti frame looks, indeed, like the one his father rode 70 years ago, and not even their most advanced computer tools have suggested anything different. The assembly plant in Taiwan is not worth much more than the real estate it sits on; Marcel told him as much last year. Junior sips his Aperol and stares toward the hills. "I'm thinking . . ."

"Well, let me help you *think*," says Marcel. "Your goal should be to at least double the value of your company in the next couple of years. You have equity, you're just not tapping it. The fastest way to increase value in your company is to use the expertise of the very engineers you're destroying. Use their talent and experience as well as all the knowledge you accumulated in the last 50 years to develop some innovative products and to produce a more diverse and innovative product portfolio. Everybody—especially you, my friend—can be successful with innovation. It's the fastest way to get what you want and deserve."

"At the pace we're innovating, I'll be 90 years old before we get the first thing to the market," counters Junior.

The comment hits a nerve with Marcel, who scoffs, sips his drink (a Campari on ice), and slyly looks at his friend. "Fausto, you have *plenty* of time, and this can be done *quickly*."

"I don't follow."

"Let me share a secret with you: My business success comes from the fact that I figured out how to do innovation right and *fast*. It's known as 'innovation excellence.' With lean thinking, my companies can do four projects in the time others do one. When our competitors go to market with their knockoffs, we're already another innovation or two ahead of them. Innovation speed is a huge asset for all of us."

"That's really no secret Marcel, but *how* you innovate so fast is," says Junior matter-of-factly. "We went to the same schools together. We didn't learn it there. Any way you could share that with your old friend?"

"That's why I recommended you start the innovation initiative; to prime the pump," says Marcel. "Obviously, you need much more help than that."

"So what *are* you doing Marcel? You've done this for so long, I think you've forgotten how difficult it is for others to figure out," implores Junior. "Please, you've mentioned innovation and lean, and I know what lean means. I drive a Toyota, after all, and our plant in Taiwan is as lean as it can be. But what does lean have to do with innovation?"

"Our innovation processes and systems follow the same principles we learned from Toyota, but there are many more. Our people understand the principles behind the processes, and they know how to manage those processes for optimum value," says Marcel, trying his best to describe innovation excellence in a simple way for Junior.

"So where do I find the people to get this going? Where are such experts?"

"That's a good question. The really good ones are hard to find. And after many years of trying to bring people experienced with innovation excellence into my company, I finally realized that's not the way to go about it. It's better to educate your own people and develop your own experts."

"Really, Marcel? Seriously? I don't have the time or patience to become an innovation expert and then the time to teach others. You had help at some point, right? I need to jump start this now!"

"OK. True. I didn't do this on my own," says Marcel, trying to calm his friend. "I had people who believed in what I was trying to do and ran with it. I may be able to loan you one of my associates, who started off with me as a project manager many years ago. Over the years, she learned as much as possible about lean innovation and became one of our lean champions. She's worked with several of our acquisitions, and she continues to be a steady and motivating voice within the company and for me. I may be able to send her on a short sabbatical to Davanti. If she agrees, I will ask her to stop by Davanti and look around. Is that OK with you?"

"Absolutely."

"But it will cost you, my friend."

"I'll consider it an investment in my future. Thank you. That wasn't so hard now, was it? How about another drink?" asks Junior. "I'm suddenly feeling hopeful."

Chapter 3

From Mind to Lab

On Saturday morning, Mo is up early and has breakfast on his apartment balcony. It's unseasonably warm. He chews on an energy bar—a habit from his race days. He enjoys a cappuccino, freshly brewed with his new expresso machine, and listens to the local news coming from his living room TV. He hears "female bike race" and thinks this must be one of the events for which Marie had been training. He gets up from his chair and watches the broadcast. He learns that the race is in Bardolino, along Lake Garda and backed by the Italian Alps, and will start in a few hours. "Hmmm. Maybe I can see Marie. What else have I got to do?" Mo finishes breakfast and decides to attend his first female bike race. A few hours later, he's absorbed in the pre-race bustle of Bardolino.

Anxiously strolling amid the small crowd, he suddenly sees a wide smile and bright eyes staring at him. Although it's been weeks since their brief encounter, he immediately recognizes Marie.

"Hey, it's chain-fixer Mo!" exclaims Marie, dressed in racing garb. "It's really nice to see you again. What brings you here today?"

"Oh, I've got some errands to run in town, and I realized a race was getting ready to start. By the looks of things, this must be one of the races you mentioned," says Mo, hiding his plan to find her. "Good luck."

"Thanks. Maybe I'll see you after the race."

Mo plans to watch only the first of four rounds of the race; each round consists of a pass through town. About 40 minutes after the racers set out, they return to town on their first lap; the field is still grouped, but a few riders have already dropped back. Mo has trouble spotting Marie in the tight peloton and does not see her among the trailing riders either, so he decides to wait for the second passage to see if he can locate her.

When the riders enter Bardolino the second time, the peloton has exploded. He's pleased to spot Marie, who is in a second small pack with another five or six riders. Mo isn't going anywhere now. The third time through town Marie has lost a lot of ground. At the final, she's near the rear of a distant pack.

Mo walks to the finish line and finds Marie. She is leaning on her bike, sweaty, totally exhausted and frustrated. "This was not my day," she says as Mo steps toward her. "No legs, but if I could afford a Davanti bike, maybe I'd be on the podium now."

"Or maybe you should come here more often and train on these mountains," suggests Mo.

"That's probably not a bad idea either," admits Marie. "How about a latte for fixing my chain? Give me a few minutes; I'm going to shower up and I'll be right back. Wait here."

DOI: 10.4324/9781003231837-3

A half hour later, Mo and Marie are sitting in Caffe Speranza, a local coffee shop. Marie has changed into shorts and a t-shirt. She is more attractive than Mo remembered, and it makes him a bit nervous.

"Marie, what do you do when you're not racing?" asks Mo.

"I work for a Swiss accounting firm. My last name is Vigneron. I have an apartment close to Geneva, but at the moment I'm working out of Lugano in Switzerland. About three hours from here. It's beautiful, much like it is here."

Mo finds Marie intelligent, and he learns that she is well educated. She frequently travels to client locations for work, where she sometimes lives for three to six weeks. Despite long hours, her job allows her to race throughout Europe, and she has no immediate plans to slow down.

"Enough about me," Marie finally insists. "What have you been up to? What are you working on at Davanti these days?" asks Marie, still fascinated that he works in the bike industry.

"It's Mo Pensatore," he says, then reluctantly explains his project and what happened after their first meeting: "You know, I've fixed dozens of bike chains on my bikes over time. And I'm sick of it. Every biker is sick of it. The day we met, it came to me: A bike without a chain. Where does it say that a bicycle must have a chain? So many other machines rely on direct-drive mechanisms, so why not a bike?"

"That's radical, Mo. I like it. Can you do it?"

"Can I? Yes. Will I? I don't really know. I submitted my idea to our innovation initiative, and this past week I got a chance to present my findings and business plan. Then poof," Mo says, making a motion of a bomb exploding. He pauses, drinks the last of his latte, and explains the difficulties. "No one really understood the idea, but they buried it anyway. Worse of all, our CEO, who I always thought had an open mind, gradually lost interest as the haggling wore on. Eventually, they all got up and left. . . . I don't think leadership likes it enough to fund it. But I honestly can't say where it stands."

"That seems like an awful way to nurture a great idea," says Marie, her brow furrowed and an angry look on her face. "Why can't they see beyond the numbers stuff. You've got an amazing idea, Mo. How many other good ideas do you think they've buried?"

Mo had taken the fallout from his presentation personally and hadn't considered that it might be more about the executive team than him and his idea. Marie's question got him thinking. He had spoken to other Davanti engineers who similarly had submitted ideas for the innovation initiative, and, though maybe not as ground-breaking as his, most seemed like excellent advances in bicycling science. What came of those? "You've got a point, Marie. How many other good ideas within Davanti are tucked away on a shelf or in a desk."

"It's easy to toss a file in a drawer," says Marie. "Why not come up with something that isn't so easy to file away?"

"I don't follow?"

"You mentioned that your CEO has an open mind, so why don't you make a bike that he and others can actually ride?"

Mo nods. "I need to *show* them something they cannot ignore." Marie finishes her latte, and they text each other their cell numbers. "We'll chat soon," says Marie with a smile as they get up to leave, and then texts him a smiling face emoji.

"Yes. Yes. I hope we do."

***

Monday morning, Mo asks to speak with Ricardo, and mid-morning he heads toward Ricardo's office. On the way he runs into Gus the security guard, who is escorting a woman that Mo guesses is in her mid-50s.

"Good morning, Mo," says Gus.

"Good morning, Gus," says Mo, who then turns to the woman. "Good morning."

"Good morning," says the guest. "It's beautiful here in Fumane."

"Yes, especially in the spring," replies Mo.

"I'm Sofia Saggio," she says, extending her hand. "I'm here to speak with Mr. Davanti."

"Hello. It's nice to meet you. I'm Mo Pensatore. . . . Gus, I can walk Signora Saggio to Mr. Davanti's office. I'm heading that way."

"Thanks, Mo," says Gus, who heads back to the lobby.

"Do you mind if I ask what you do here?" asks Sofia.

"Not at all. I'm an engineer. You know, tinker with bicycles, come up with great ideas," he jokes, realizing how stupid that sounds.

"And how is that going?"

"Uh, it has its ups and downs."

When they reach Junior's office, Mo says, "Here you are. It was nice to meet you. Enjoy your day. Addio."

Mo continues down the hall to Ricardo's office. When he gets there, the door is open. "Come in, Mo. Sit down. I am anxious to hear what's on your mind."

"Ricardo, I want to give Junior and the non-technical folks something they can actually understand. Maybe that way I can engage them to provide feedback or at least ask meaningful questions."

"How do you propose to do that?" asks Ricardo.

"I want to show them a working prototype. I think if they can ride it, they can critique the device and not my business plan," says Mo.

"Forget about the business plan. You were out of your league there. Provided they like the prototype, they'll figure that out without anybody's help."

"And Emilio?"

"If Junior likes the bike, Emilio will like the bike," replies Ricardo. "You need to focus on what you can control. Why don't you talk to Luca in the lab? He knows more about prototypes than anyone here."

"I'd like that."

"Well, let's go find him," says Ricardo, who gets up from his desk.

Luca Notte, in his 50s, is the lab supervisor and has worked for Davanti his entire career. He often eats lunch with Mo, who shares leftovers from family dinners, especially desserts. Luca is particularly fond of Mrs. Pensatore's cannoli. Many employees in Davanti have tasted and love the cooking of Mo's mom, and spots next to him in the cafeteria on Mondays are a hot commodity.

Luca knows more about bicycles than anyone Mo knows. Mo has always enjoyed and learned from his interactions with Luca, who is exceptionally intelligent, inquisitive, and open-minded. Ricardo and Mo enter the lab; Luca is pounding away on his keyboard. Luca looks up, pleased to see them both.

The prototype factory is a mix of the most modern technology imaginable with old-world bicycle building. Partitioned off in one clean corner is Luca's office with a number of computers; the rest of the area is filled with machining centers, welding stations, fiber-winding equipment, curing presses, painting booths, and many workbenches and bike assembly stations covered with wheels, gears, chains, and parts of every kind.

The smell of machine shavings and oil mixed with vapors from freshly cured bike frames is in the air, although it could be coming from Luca's slick-backed hair.

"Luca, Mo here would like to talk to you about a new idea for a bike. Got a few minutes?" asks Ricardo.

"Of course, just give me a second to shoot off this email. . . . There. I'm all yours," says Luca. "Tell us about the idea, Mo," says Ricardo.

Mo walks over to a whiteboard and begins to draw up the mechanism he envisions to power a bike. "It's for a direct-drive bicycle," says Mo, pausing to take a deep breath. "I think it's easier to see it than to talk it to death, but I'll fill you in on some of the key functionality as a I go." Mo continues to draw and describe the device, much as he did in his executive presentation. This time, however, he has an audience that grasps every detail and understands the benefits. "I don't see why it can't transfer power equivalent to most modern chain-drive mechanisms without the potential for breaking and stranding riders."

Luca listens intently, nods often, and then calls over to Vincente Romo, who is bent over a bike, getting it ready for the Davanti team and an upcoming race. "Hey, Vinnie. Come over here and take a look at this."

Vinnie's father was Fausto Sr.'s chief mechanic at the peak of his racing career, which has endeared him to Junior. Vinnie learned about bikes from his dad, and he developed the same passion for bikes and the sport as Junior and his dad. In his younger days, Vinnie also raced. Today he enjoys the respect of the Davanti engineers and riders for his practical work and knowledge, and they trust his instincts. He is the go-to resource for all hands-on bike questions, and many Davanti employees even bring their personal bikes into the shop, which Vinnie tunes and repairs on his own time. When he's in a good mood, he'll offer ideas on how to soup up their rides—to the dismay of the patent organization, of course, fearing all of the undocumented intellectual property that he's giving away.

Vinnie's clothes are clean, although incredibly wrinkled and about 20 years out of style, emphasized by the fact that Vinnie looks much younger than his age. Nearing retirement, he has a reputation of being short on words, which makes him appear unapproachable at times. The other lab techs barely notice as Vinnie leaves the bike he's working on at the far side of the room, takes off his lab apron, and ambles over to the whiteboard. He stares at it with Luca and Ricardo for a few minutes, occasionally touching a spot of the board, getting ready to speak, and then continuing to study it.

Mo senses the questions on Vinnie's mind and discusses a few problems that he's sure the lab veteran has already solved. Vinnie confirms a few technical details about the bike—describing them more succinctly than Mo did for Luca—and they share a few additional ideas, finishing each other's sentences.

"So what do you think of this, Vinnie?" asks Luca.

"I can build that—I think. I never made one before. But, come to think of it, maybe no one's ever made one before," says Vinnie with a laugh.

***

Sofia arrives at Junior's office, which is fronted by his administrative assistant Anna. "Excuse me, I'm Sofia Saggio. I am here to see Mr. Davanti."

"Good morning. He's been expecting you. This way, please," says Anna, cheerfully and professionally, and directs Sofia to the door behind her. "Can I get you anything? Coffee? Latte? Espresso? Water?"

"An espresso would be great, grazie."

Junior's door is open, and he sees her arrive. He stands and greets her. "You must be Sofia Saggio. Please, come in. Have a seat. I've been looking forward to meeting you. Marcel has so many good things to say about you. So how would you like to start. Maybe a quick tour of the complex?"

"Let's chat a little first, if that's all right? Marcel has told me a bit about you and the company, but I'm still in the dark about much of what you do here. I'm not a bicyclist, and I don't follow the bike news or sport." Sofia takes a seat opposite Junior's desk, and his assistant Anna brings her the espresso. "So tell me a little more about your company, Mr. Davanti. I understand that your father founded it with the money he made as a pro racer. You must be very proud of him."

"That is a painting of my dad," says Junior, pointing to the wall opposite his desk. He picks up a picture frame on his desk and shows it to Sofia as well. "Here is Fausto Sr. in yellow after winning the Tour de France. . . . You can call me 'Junior.'

"Today we make the best race bikes that money can buy," he continues, and gives a brief history of Davanti Nella Gara and its current market positions.

"Let's move on from the current state of affairs at Davanti. What would you say is the company's future? What do you want this company to be in a couple of years, Junior? What is your vision or your objectives, your goals?"

Junior takes a moment to consider the question and then declares proudly, "Our goal is to keep making the best bikes in the world, and winning races just as we always have."

"Really, that's it," she responds nonchalantly.

"No, of course not. We have all kinds of plans." Junior stands and walks toward his assistant's desk. "Anna, can you bring me a copy of our business plan?"

Marcel has explained Junior's retirement ambitions, and Sofia is surprised to hear his conventional response. "So tell me, do you want to be the one leading this company as it continues to make great bikes? Would you like to boost the sale price of the company? Would you like to find the right new leadership that will help sustain the company after you're gone?"

"Well, 'yes' to all," says Junior with a bit of irritation and a long awkward pause. Anna breaks the silence by handing him a four-page document, which he passes on to Sofia with a smile. "I would be glad to explain it to you in sufficient detail."

Sofia glances at the front page: "This says 'Company Confidential.' Are you OK with me looking at this?"

"Well, in our business, you cannot be too careful. That helps to remind everyone here of who we are and how we got here. Our competitors watch us like hawks. Everybody wants to get their hands on the industry leader's trade secrets and business plans. But to answer your question, please study the document."

Sofia takes a closer look at a document full of incomprehensible technical and financial jargon. "Who have you shared this document with?"

"Only my direct leadership team. They communicate with the associates on a need-to-know basis."

"This reminds me: I'm happy to sign a nondisclosure agreement with your company. I have no plans to work for your competitors. . . . But back to your objectives and goals. Let me ask you a more difficult question: You could make the best bikes and lose money, no?"

"Yes, I suppose that's true. In fact, I know that's true. It's happened to a few of the other old Italian bicycle firms," realizing how foolish he must have sounded.

"Marcel tells me your objective is to retire in a couple of years and that your goal is to maximize the value of your company over the next two years," she says.

"That's true, but I also want to make sure I respect the wishes of my late father and assure the future of the Davanti name and this site."

"Great goals, but have you thought about how you will accomplish that? What is your strategy to accomplish those goals?"

"Marcel mentioned that this is where you can help?"

"Help, yes, but you own the company. I understand your implicit objectives and goals, but who else? Do you want to share those with your associates?"

"It's my company, and those are my objectives and goals."

"But don't you count on all your associates to help you accomplish those goals?"

"Absolutely. And I pay them all well to make us a great bike company, make money along the way, and move me toward my goals. What good would it do to tell them that I am planning to sell the company? Some would jump ship in a heartbeat and go work for our competitors, telling them my plans. Others would fight for turf. Is that what you suggest?"

"Those are fair points. It's easy to announce a corporate transformation if the company is in deep trouble. In your case, it will be a little more difficult. You've given me enough about your implicit plans to work with for now. Let me learn a little more, and I'll think about how to get the associates engaged in supporting you on this. You may not be willing to share everything with them, but you've still got to provide direction."

"True. I agree. I'll think this over as well. You see, though, it's not as black and white as it appears. But I think I have an idea."

Chapter 4

Riding an Idea

All week long, an anxious Mo had been frequently stopping by the lab to see what Vinnie was up to. He could follow Vinnie's tinkering, even though Vinnie said little when he saw him. Vinnie continued to tune up race bikes during the day, but Mo noticed more and more parts showing up at Vinnie's workbench, including a gear mechanism from a hand drill. "I took this out of my cordless drill. I'll have to order me a new drill," Vinnie had said.

Mo also had noticed an old-style steel frame with steel pedal arms, a used rear wheel with an internal three-gear mechanism, and a large collection of steel gear wheels in many sizes and configurations. "Do we really need 20 gears in this first bike?" Vinnie had asked. "I can get nine right now, three from the drill and three from the rear wheel hub.[1] Do you think that will do as a start?"

Mo was excited to have more than three gears. "Sure."

"Well, then, I will do some welding tonight when the other guys go home," said Vinnie.

By Friday, Mo was tired of running back and forth from his office to the lab and decided to attend to his regular assignments and keep them from falling behind. He left a little early on Friday to get ready for a party at his parent's house on Saturday to celebrate their 40th wedding anniversary.

He stopped by a shop on the way home to pick up engraved wine goblets he'd ordered for his parents—nothing terribly expensive but meaningful—and then grabbed a pizza and beer at one of his favorite parlors, La Pizza di Zio. He would normally head out and meet friends on a Friday night, but once at home, the week caught up to him. He dozed off at his laptop while searching for upcoming female bike races in hopes to meet up with Marie again. He woke up well after midnight, thinking about a shift mechanism for the bike.

***

Midday Saturday, Mo heads to his parent's villa that overlooks Lake Garda in the resort town of Peschiera del Garda, which is less than an hour's drive from Mo's apartment. Mo's dad was a director with an Italian automotive manufacturer, whose revenues were far greater than Davanti. The company had its ups and downs, but Mo's dad always did well financially. Mo's mom supported her husband and raised Mo, an older sister Catherine, and a younger brother Benito. Both of his siblings received excellent educations—just like Mo—and found good jobs. Catherine is a VP at a small bank in Verona, and Benito works in purchasing for the same auto company from which his dad retired. Mo's dad would have liked to see all his children join him in the car company, but that was never an option for Mo. He needed to make his own way in life, and, because of that, was considered somewhat of a black sheep in the family.

DOI: 10.4324/9781003231837-4

It was another spectacular day at the lake, with puffy white clouds casting random shadows over the brilliant blue water. A light breeze was filled with the smell of the lake and hyacinths. Mo parked his Fiat, grabbed the gift, trotted up the steps to the villa, and bounced in the front door: "Ciao!"

Mo was greeted by Catherine and her six-year-old daughter Lisa. "Hello, little brother. Why didn't you bring your girlfriend with you?"

"I keep working on it, but these things take time," says Mo, giving his niece a hug. "It's nice to see you, too, sister."

Catherine's husband has seen this ritual off and on for years, depending on Mo's current dating status, and he hands Mo a glass of wine: "Give him a break. He's got high standards."

"I'm pickier than your husband," says Mo to his sister, jokingly.

"Good one, brother," laughs Benito, who enters the room to see who has arrived.

Relatives—a few uncles, aunts, and cousins—have already started the party in the dining room. Mo's mom comes out to the entry, gives Mo a hug, and scolds the group: "You kids behave now. It's a party. Come, let's go to the patio." His dad slaps Mo on the shoulder. "Welcome, Mo. It's good to see you."

The group heads to the patio. A warm breeze is blowing into the villa through wide screen doors. On the deck, Mo sees three large tables arrayed with antipasti trays (cheeses, salumi, fruit, and many of his mom's homemade specialties). His mom has spent most of the week cooking the dinner with the help of their housekeeper, and Mo has spent most of the week looking forward to enjoying it.

Mo eats dinner with his parents at least once a week and usually takes home more food than he can consume in a week. But beyond the food, he genuinely loves and respects his parents, even if his dad gives him a hard time about his "hobby" of a job. Everyone is chatting simultaneously as they find places to sit at a large, antique dining table. The covered patio protects guests from the unseasonable glare of the sun, and the fantastic weather and special day have warmed everyone's spirits. When all are seated, Mo stands between his sister and brother, holding up his glass. "Saluti," he says. "To mamma and pop. Congratulations on 40 years of marriage. To another 40 years!"

Mo's mom and dad toast their guests and then share a kiss. His mom rushes back into the kitchen, and, along with the housekeeper, begins to bring out the first dishes for the guests to pass: freshly baked focaccia, squash tortellini in cream sauce, and potato gnocchi in red sauce. "Mangiare," encourages Mrs. Pensatore when all the food has arrived. Mo's dad brings out local Verona wines and fills the guests' glasses.

Mo, his siblings, and guests immediately rave about the food. "Best ever, mom," shouts Benito. Mo's mom is so busy attending to her guests that she has yet to sit. Eventually, her husband takes her by the shoulders and leads her to her seat. "Finally," says Catherine. "Please mom, take a break." The break is short. She soon rushes back in to get fried rabbit with rosemary potatoes and pork shanks in red wine.

Hours later as the meal winds down, Mrs. Pensatore and the housekeeper bring out her famous tiramisu, accompanied by biscotti, cannoli, espresso, and Vin Santo. Mo grabs his dessert and moves to the open seat next to his dad. "Pop, retirement agrees with you," says Mo. "I've never seen you look so relaxed."

"It's hard not to be relaxed on such a beautiful day," Mo's dad replies. "I could not be happier. How about you? How's that hobby of yours?"

"Dad, *work* is actually pretty good right now. I've got a . . ."

Lisa, Catherine's youngest daughter, and Benito's son jump into their grandfather's lap and interrupt the conversation. "Nonno, nonno," the kids scream. "Take us for a boat ride."

"It's too early in the season for that, little ones," he answers as he hugs his grandchildren. "When the lake warms up, we will go. Come, let's see what nonna has for you." Mo's dad gives him a look of "Oh, well," and heads off with the kids.

Mo stays the night at his parents and the following day enjoys a breakfast that is as good as the anniversary dinner. Before leaving, his mom loads his car with party leftovers as well as a focaccia she baked that morning. He'll need to work out after this weekend, or he'll never be able to keep up with Marie—if they ever get to ride together again.

***

Before heading to the lab on Monday morning, Mo goes to his desk to catch up on emails and see if any new, unexpected assignments have landed in his lap. It wasn't unusual for Emilio to circumvent Ricardo and toss a project on an engineer at the worst possible time. Many of Mo's colleagues were strapped with "urgent" Darvin assignments while they were trying to manage their own projects.

Suddenly, Vinnie sticks his head into the office. Mo's fellow engineers are surprised to see Vinnie out of the lab. They are equally surprised to hear him talk. "Mo, you have to come to the lab." As quickly as Vinnie appeared, he's gone.

Mo glances at his colleagues, shrugs his shoulders, takes a last glance at his computer screen, and then heads to the lab.

When Mo gets to the lab, Vinnie is pedaling down the aisle on the direct-drive prototype. The bike is a hodge-podge of components. Mo smiles and begins applauding. Luca joins Mo in the applause. Vinnie clearly understood Mo's ideas and even expanded on them.

Vinnie brings the bike to a stop, and Mo can see all of Vinnie's craft: He took an old steel frame and welded the three-gear mechanism from his drill to the V-shaped frame just above the pedals. On the left side of the bike where the gear box was originally connected to the drill motor, he welded a steel gear that connects with another steel gear on the pedal axle. On the right side of the gear mechanism, Vinnie had replaced the straight drill chuck with a 90-degree version. He had used the steel wheel with the internal three-gear hub in the back of the bike, but he had replaced the chain cog with a conical steel gear. He had made a shaft with a matching conical gear for the rear and had inserted the other side of the shaft into the chuck in the front.

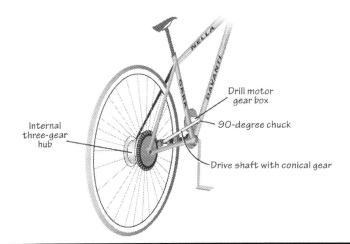

Figure 4.1   Direct-Drive Prototype.

"Vinnie, it's fabulous," says Mo, realizing just how talented Vinnie really is. "But will it work for more than a few laps around the lab?"

"I rode it more than 100 kilometers over the weekend," says Vinnie. "Of course, I'm no tour racer, but I still bike pretty hard, and I could not break it!" Mo was surprised that Vinnie could ride even 50 kilometers at his age.

Mo felt like it was Christmas when he touched the bike for the first time. "May I?" he asks Vinnie. Vinnie nods, and Mo jumps on the prototype and immediately notices how immediate the reaction is—no more delay for the chain to straighten and engage.

"Today I will install a better shifter for the drill mechanism and ride the bike on the group ride Wednesday," says Vinnie. "We'll both ride it. How's that?"

"That's a great idea. With any luck, maybe Junior will ride with us this week."

Mo is certain he'll wake up at any moment and realize he's been dreaming. Then he smells the oil and bicycle tires and knows he's really in the lab and that he and Vinnie will soon be riding the prototype direct-drive bicycle on the road and maybe up hills into the Alps.

***

The company ride usually began in the northwest corner of the Davanti bicycle lot. If the weather was favorable, there'd be dozens of employees pedaling about. This Wednesday, another warm day, the lot is busy, but no one is pedaling. They're all in a circle around Vinnie, Mo, and the prototype.

Junior walks his bike up to the crowd, ready to join the ride. Normally, he'd have everyone's attention. Today, no one has even noticed that he arrived. "Hey, what's going on?" asks Junior.

An employee turns slightly, not enough to see that it's Junior, and says, "Hold on, would you? He's explaining the new direct-drive gear box." The employee looks back to see who interrupted the demonstration: "Oh, geez, I'm sorry Mr. Davanti. I thought . . ."

"No worries, son," Junior says, kindly. "Let me take a look."

Junior walks through the group and gets next to the prototype. Mo, who had been explaining Vinnie's work, stops talking. "Well, what do you know," says Junior curiously.

"Hello, sir. Do you like it?" asks Mo.

"I've not seen it go anywhere yet," replies Junior, hinting that it's time to ride. "Let's see if this thing can make it through the ride."

"You heard the chief, let's ride," yells another employee.

For about 30 minutes, riders take turns getting near Vinnie on the prototype and Mo next to him, who takes mental notes as he watches how the bike performs on the ride. Just before they plan to break, Junior is riding between Vinnie and Mo. "It looks effective," says Junior.

"Only one way to find out," yells Mo. At the midway break site, Vinnie pulls a tool out of his jersey pocket and swaps out the pedals and seat from Junior's bike to the prototype. Most of the other riders are still talking about the prototype when the CEO heads off up the road.

The pack catches up to Junior, who is clearly enjoying himself. He can feel that the bike responds faster than would a normal chain-drive, and, despite having been put together from old parts, is reasonably comfortable and cohesive; the shifting is flawless. Climbing is a little slower because of all the heavy steel components. The group normally does not slow down when Junior or any *more seasoned riders* fall behind, but today everybody waits—curious to see if the new bike makes it up a hill. Although Junior never was a good climber, he ascends a hill without problems and does not disappoint the riders; Vinnie picked the right gears to make the climbing painless.

As the bikers head back to town, the entire valley and Fumane can be seen below—an array of homes and shops amid the lush spring trees and flora. Junior can make out the sand-colored buildings of Davanti Nella Gara and feels as good about the company as he has in months. "Maybe this bike can be the first of many new innovations for Davanti," he thinks.

Back at the Davanti bike lot, Mo helps Vinnie return Junior's equipment to his bike. Mo, who has only taken a few laps around the parking lot on the prototype, looks at Junior and holds his palms up, silently asking the question that is on everyone's mind.

"Molto bene!" says Junior. "I know a good thing when I see it. The ride was excellent. We'll talk soon. Molto bene."

***

At work on Thursday morning, the complex is buzzing. Word of the direct-drive bike rapidly has spread. Emilio has called Ricardo to his office and wants to know more about the bike.

"It's a crude but effective prototype," says Ricardo.

"I've seen it. Crude, yes. We'll have trouble making the drive contraption fit on most styles of bikes," counters Emilio.

"Maybe, but we have lots of room in those big bottom-bracket houses we design these days to hold this kind of drive," suggests Ricardo.

Emilio tersely justifies the size of the frame with the need for stiffness. His negativity takes another tack: "I'm concerned how we'll make 20 gears for something like this. We don't have suppliers for anything close to this. Vinnie can't make them all in the lab."

"Yes, I suppose that will need to be answered," says Ricardo, already growing weary.

"And what about . . ." Emilio continues, before Ricardo cuts him off: "You can't assess a new idea unless you start working on it; only when you learn enough can you evaluate and manage the risk. Please have a little patience. There are many questions that still need to be answered, of course, but that's what R&D is about, Emilio. We're talking about a very rough prototype, not a product that's ready for market. We've got a wealth of talent and technology out there to solve these problems."

"I've seen this before," counters Emilio harshly. "Before long, we have our valuable talent involved in a project that drains our resources and goes nowhere."

"We'll have to make sure we stop the work on this project—or any project—as soon as we learn that the idea is not going anywhere," counters Ricardo.

"Maybe we should stop it right here. Don't even think about asking for resources to develop it. We're pretty loaded right now with the new project-management software deployment and our high-propriety projects. Initiatives like this one just cause distractions among the staff."

Ricardo does not respond. He knows it's usually a waste of breath to argue with Emilio.

In his office, Mo considers many of the same technical issues as Ricardo and Emilio, but from a more inquisitive perspective. Many colleagues had asked him questions all morning about the bike and suggested unique ideas for version 2.0. Seeing and riding the prototype had brought a surge of new ideas to him as well as Vinnie and Luca, things that they'd never considered. If it had been a perfect prototype, no one would have offered any recommendations—and, thus, no need for improvement. "Hmmm. Is this how R&D is supposed to work here?"

***

Junior, in his office, smiles and stares at his father's portrait on the wall. "I think you'll like this, poppy. Pay attention."

Sofia is the first to enter Junior's office.

"Junior, I'm surprised to get your invitation to this meeting," she says. "I'm curious. What's up?"

"Thank you for coming on short notice. I'd like your observation of something, which, in more ways than one, could be exciting for Davanti. It may be the start of a new way for how we innovate here and turn ideas into revenue. By the way, did you have a chance to take our new direct-drive bike for a spin?"

"You know my bike-riding skills—or you probably don't. I don't want to destroy the prototype before it can be developed. Seeing it was enough for now."

Soon Emilio arrives along with his favorite project manager Gina Turno, followed by Mo, Luca, and Ricardo in unison. Vinnie was invited, but asked Luca if he could pass; this type of meeting has always made him uncomfortable and would often kill his output for days. Luca knew that Junior's invitation was a courtesy to Vinnie's hard work, and he told him not to worry about declining.

Emilio sits down rigidly at Junior's meeting table and is anxious to hear what's coming, especially after seeing the group that has arrived with him. Mo is mostly all smiles: "This cannot be a bad thing," he thinks. Ricardo and Luca act like they've been in this situation many times before, which they have.

"Thank you for coming, everyone. I'll be quick and to the point. We're here because Mo, with the help of Luca and Vinnie in the lab, developed a prototype for a chainless bicycle—a direct-drive bike." Emilio gives a slight roll of his eyes. Mo continues to smile. Ricardo and Luca show no emotion. Sofia, despite knowing little about bikes, knows that bikes usually have chains, and she, too, smiles.

"Junior, I've seen the prototype," says Emilio. "It's good work."

"I rode it yesterday," says Junior. "It was surprisingly responsive, and shifting is easy and very smooth. I think our customers, whoever they might be, might feel the same way. So what prevents us from getting this *product* underway without delay?"

Gina nods. She is intelligent, attractive, and known for her rigorous organizational skills. Without Gina's project-management capabilities, Emilio would not be CTO for long.

"I'd like this group to meet weekly here and update me on all details of your work going forward—procurement of components, test results, manufacturing options, market projections," orders Junior. "Provided I like what I hear, I will give approvals quickly in those meetings to keep this thing going as swiftly as possible. Any delay in development will cost us. I'm actually afraid that someone might have seen it on the ride yesterday before we get a chance to package it up securely in patents."

"I got legal started on the patents a few weeks ago, Mr. Davanti; I believe we're covered for most aspects of the prototype," says Mo. "I'll ask Federico to give you an update."

"Thanks for bringing this up, Mo—and, please, call me 'Junior.' All we need now is a patent issue to derail this product. You remember what happened to one of our component manufacturers a few years ago. Nearly wiped out the company. We must give this aspect our utmost attention. And Emilio, I expect you to assign your most competent project manager to this project and assure that all resources and priorities are provided."

Emilio looks at Junior and says nothing.

Sofia sits quietly, taking it all in.

"That's it for now. Let's create the best direct-drive bicycle possible," gleams Junior, pleased that he has rallied the team.

All but Sofia leave Junior's office.

"Junior, that was interesting," says Sofia. "Can you tell me just what that was about?"

"We can't waste a day getting this bike to market, getting any innovation to market," says Junior, surprised that Sofia would not understand that. "Marcel has told me as much."

"Yes, I agree wholeheartedly. None of the innovations to come from Davanti should run into unnecessary delays. But you, as CEO, directing the effort won't make that happen. Probably just the opposite. What will you do with the 10, 20, or 30 next ideas you like? Are you going to direct those projects, too?"

"I am doing what I see as necessary to get *this* innovation to market as quickly as possible," replies Junior shortly.

"I know you are. It's just, well, not likely to turn out well, regardless of how powerful and effective you can be. Your role is to create an environment where innovation can thrive; ensure that the right talent, processes, and maybe funding are in place; and help wherever you can. There are dozens of ways you must lead the innovation efforts of your company, but this isn't one of them."

"Thank you for your opinion. But I managed this company for almost 20 years. Please don't tell me how to do my job. Now, if you'll excuse me, I need to get back to work."

***

Junior is fuming all morning, and just before lunch he's decided he's had it with Sofia and that he should let Marcel know. It's the right thing to do. He dials Marcel's number and is glad he picks up.

"Marcel, good morning. Well, it's still close to morning," says Junior.

"Fausto, I was expecting your call," says Marcel.

"You what?"

"Yes, I think I know why you're calling. You can't believe Sofia disapproved of your meeting this morning, and now you've had enough of Sofia. Am I right?"

"Yes," says Junior, perturbed that Sofia got to Marcel first.

"Did you really consider what she told you this morning? Think about it, my friend. You're the CEO. You're not a project manager or even the CTO. You have a right to know what's going on, but you should not have to tell your experts what to do. If you're working at that level, you'll be in the weeds so low you'll never see where the company is going and be able to guide it. And who is the most competent to make technical decisions or manage a project anyway?"

The look on Junior's face changes from bitter to bruised. "I'm listening," he says. "But you, of all people, know that I don't have much of a runway left before we start losing cash. I've finally seen an opportunity for innovation at Davanti. Making things happen quickly should be my role now, right?"

"As CEO, your role in making things happen is to develop a vision and set clear objectives. I understand your objectives and goals very well, and you'll find the right words to communicate them. And I know you can lead the rest of the organization in coming up with the right strategy to accomplish them and do it fast."

"Go on."

"Every associate should clearly understand how they contribute to accomplishing your goals. Give them a True North and engage them to follow the direction without you pushing them along the way. And let your engineers and project managers do what they do best. That's why you hired them."

"And that's it. I point in the right direction and just sit here and watch things happen?"

"No, of course not. At times you'll be directly involved—breaking down barriers, providing the resources they need to succeed, and coaching your associates, if needed. All of that is a hell of a job in itself, by the way, without you trying to direct a product team. And if you feel you can help your associates on occasion, you should; I'm sure they'll appreciate it. But don't take the lead on everything."

"I don't see anyone else stepping up to lead it."

"Not if you're always in the way."

"Maybe you're right. I'll think about it. Thank you, Marcel."

Note

1. 3 gears x 3 gears = 9 gears.

Chapter 5

Innovation Excellence Begins

The meeting invitation was titled, "Davanti Objectives, Goals, and Strategy." Anna had scheduled the meeting for late Monday afternoon in the Davanti conference room. As Junior walks there, he remembers the mess they'd made of Mo's direct-drive bicycle presentation weeks earlier. "There'll be no more of that," he thinks, and hopes that he'll never witness another such farce. He turns to see Sofia, walking behind him, and stops to greet her.

"Sofia, good afternoon."

"Good afternoon, Junior. You look like a man on a mission."

"I am, thanks to you," he says, pausing to get his composure. "I regret my boorish behavior the last time we spoke. I apologize. I've got a lot to learn, and I better be prepared to occasionally look foolish."

"Please, think nothing of it. Your intent was good. Your commitment is everything. You would not believe how many times I've seen a leader fall back to managing the day-to-day stuff they are familiar with rather than tackle the tough 'transformation stuff.' It has to start at the top, and you will understand it and embrace it. I have no doubt."

"Thank you for the positive reinforcement. It comes at the right time. . . . Now, let's get this meeting started and see where it goes. I invited you so you can see how we're doing things at Davanti."

The two walk into the conference room. Inside are Emilio and all the other senior executives in the company from sales, finance, marketing, manufacturing, procurement, supply chain, and human resources.

"How are we all today?" asks Junior of his colleagues.

"Couldn't be better," says Anika Suhaanee, human resources director. "And with the great weather we've had, I'm looking forward to finishing my spring planting tonight." The others nod in agreement, looking forward to the end of their day as well.

"Before we get started, I want to formally introduce Sofia Saggio," says Junior. "I think you've all met her by now, and some of you may have spoken at more length with her. Sofia has done wonders at my friend's companies, and she's agreed to help us develop *innovation excellence processes*. You might think that those three words mean that this only applies to R&D, but it really involves all of us and will require the support of all of you, which you will soon see."

The executives look side to side at each other.

"Sofia challenged me to develop objectives, goals, and a strategy that could successfully carry Davanti Nella Gara into the future. I told her some dribble about wanting to build 'the best bikes in the world,' and she rightly threw that back at me. We could build the best bikes and still

DOI: 10.4324/9781003231837-5

lose money doing it. She pressed me about that and asked about my vision—or, more precisely, my objectives for the company. I've given that some extensive thought and concluded that new innovations should align with and support our values and culture. Therefore, I think our objective should be to increase the value of Davanti for all stakeholders."

Leandro Nero, the VP of supply chain, asks, "Who are our stakeholders?"

"Good question. They are our customers, of course, but also our suppliers and our associates—that includes you and me." The executives nod politely.

"Why some new objective? Aren't we already increasing the value of the company?" asks Emilio. "What happened to our mantra from last year: 'We safely make the best bikes in the world.' We make the best bikes, don't we?"

"Of course, and that's necessary. But will it sustain Davanti? Our growth has slowed, and, I believe, how we go about our business is no longer sustainable. Joe, please tell them what you've been telling me."

"Our market is saturated," says Joe Bersaglio, marketing VP. "There has been no increase in high-performance bike sales for a couple of years now. There has, however, been more competition, which has eroded volume and prices and our profits along with them. How long can we sustain the same course?"

"And we can't go any further on reducing the cost," argues Constantine Rendere, manufacturing VP. "Our operations are already lean, and our automation is the best in the business. There's no place to go."

"You're both right," exclaims Diana Rialto, procurement VP. "That tells me we need new stuff. We need to innovate. You would not believe how many new materials and components I get pitched every day by our vendors. Why aren't we doing the same thing—offer innovation at a premium price?"

Most of the executives again nod in unison. Emilio, however, frowns and looks as though they've taken a corporate problem and made it his problem. "So it's an R&D problem again," bites back Emilio. "We've tried game-changing innovation many times. And before you know it, we have dozens of new projects that take all our resources and go nowhere. We can't afford that again. And who even knows if we could sell any of those new things anyway. We're a conservative company built on safety and quality—we shouldn't rock that boat or take such risks."

"It's not an R&D problem," says Junior flatly. "It's a Davanti problem, and we each have a role in how we tackle it. I want you all to think about this challenge today. You all know the situation we're in, whether you choose to believe it or not. We need an objective and goals that will move us into the future, one that everybody agrees with—and then we'll need to find a strategy for how to achieve the goals. It's as simple as that."

"You've already given us the objective, and it sounds like you may have the strategy or solution as well," confronts Claudia Contanti, VP sales. "Is this why you brought in your friend here, under the disguise of an innovation program? And why the sudden focus on the value of the company? How will that help the rest of us?"

Joe jumps in. "Hold on, Claudia. I think Junior is right. We have to do something different, and that includes a new focus. Am I the only one who sees the writing on the wall? I appreciate the fact that Junior is asking us to find the right solution and path forward."

"Yes, Joe, thank you," says Junior, grateful for a sympathetic ear. "If I had wanted to define my own goals, would I have brought all of you here? I think that increasing the value of the company should be our objective. It affects all stakeholders. It focuses us on the best common denominator. It can make us competitive and assure all of our jobs, our salaries, the Fumane site, the prosperity of our suppliers, and, above all, the satisfaction of our customers. Sofia has experience with innovation excellence and its major concepts, such as lean, but whatever we do must line up with our values, strengths, and where the company should go. And Claudia, I don't have the goals or the solution."

"What do you want from all of us?" asks Leandro Nero, VP of supply chain.

"If you all agree on the objective to increase the value of the company for all stakeholders, I would appreciate your ideas about the resulting goals that can achieve that. Then we'll eventually need a strategy for how to achieve those goals. And one more: Communicate this to all our associates and ask for their input. Let them know that their ideas are welcomed."

"And please remember that our associates are also stakeholders," reminds Anika.

"We'll put this on the agenda of our next staff meeting," concludes Junior. "Please have your input ready by then so we can figure out a plan and execute it."

The groan in the room is nearly palpable. Most don't feel the urgency or see the reasoning behind Junior's request. "Maybe this, too, will pass," they think. Sofia wishes she had a euro for every time she's seen that look.

Junior also recognizes the ambivalence among his staff. He'd like to tell them everything—including his personal goals—but his gut says don't go there. It's difficult enough getting buy-in as it is. Maybe that will change, he wonders, but for now he's determined he made the right move.

***

Junior and Sofia meet on Tuesday afternoon. "So what do you think about yesterday's session? Looks like I got their attention. I should have done this a long time ago."

"Yes, you had their attention," replies Sofia, trying to appear positive. She's already angered Junior once and decides to coach more gingerly. "You told me before the meeting that you'd show me how things were done at Davanti. So you're delegating things going forward? I'm curious what they'll come back with next week."

"I have confidence in the process and in them. . . . Let's go to the lab to see what's happening with the chainless-bike prototype."

"Yes, let's do that. But can we first discuss your products?" she asks. "As you know, I'm no bicyclist. So tell me about your bikes. Tell me about all of your products, bikes or not. Walk me through Davanti's product portfolio?"

"A product portfolio?" Junior replies, his brow furrowed as he looks at Sofia. "You mean our brochures and catalogues with our product offerings?"

"No, Junior, it's more than a document. It's part of a pragmatic approach to innovation."

"I guess I don't understand. We have the best brochures money can buy that describe all our products in great detail," says Junior, opening a desk drawer and pulling out a copy. "They describe our innovations on every page."

"A portfolio is not just about what you sell today," says Sofia. "Yes, Davanti has products and services it's creating and selling for revenue. It has—or should have—technologies that make those products and other new products possible. And it has—or should have—an innovation engine that enables the creation of both new technologies and new products. A product portfolio is the balance of those three with proper planning, good risk management, and a process that brings the right products and services to market when needed. It should be the power behind Davanti's income today and what sustains the company in the future."

"Well, I'm aware of what we're making and what we plan to make," replies Junior bluntly. Sofia again struck a nerve. "I leave most of the product-planning details to Emilio and Joe, who keep me informed. If something significant happens, I know about it. Well, I *usually* know about it."

"Actually, you don't need to know all the details of all products or services that Davanti sells. That's not what I mean. You are responsible to put in place the processes and systems that ensure your products can achieve your goals. Those processes (or lack thereof) resulted in what was designed and sold today (current portfolio) as well as what will be designed and sold next year and the next (future portfolio). Done well, they'll establish the right diversity and balance in your product portfolio to deliver optimum value and support future revenue and growth."

"Diversity and balance. That's what my financial advisor keeps telling me about my personal investment portfolio."

"That's a great analogy, Junior. I hope you're doing a better job on your investment portfolio than your product portfolio."

Junior stares at Sofia as if he's looking into a deep abyss.

"It's not as challenging as it sounds. I'll set up a small team to begin to figure this out, and, with their help, get a good approximation of your current and future product portfolio in a few weeks. OK with you?"

"That sounds fine. If anyone resists, let me know."

***

After meeting with Junior, Sofia sent a meeting notice to Mo, Ricardo, Gina, Marco, Luca, Giovanni Santucci (a manufacturing engineer), Stella DiCaprio (a sales manager), and representatives from procurement, finance, and supply chain. They had been identified by leaders and functional heads to be members for what she called the "Change Management Team." This cross-functional group will help her get the Davanti transformation underway and support it down the road with their business, technical, and cultural expertise.

"Welcome everyone," greets Sofia on Wednesday morning. "I formed this team because I need a group of experts who can lay out the path for big changes at Davanti based on innovation excellence. You're going to help create a new process for how Davanti develops and sells goods and services, but, more importantly, you will help create profound change in your company's culture—you will inspire and help engage leaders and associates to accomplish Davanti's objectives and goals."

"I know nothing about change management or this innovation excellence stuff, if that's what we'll be working on," says Stella. "How can I contribute?"

"Good question," replies Sofia. "Most of you are starting from the same point. Of course, Giovanni was part of the plant transformation, and that will help down the road. We'll first discuss Davanti's business and common activities. Then you'll be trained in innovation excellence and change management; you'll probably be joined in those sessions by leadership. I'll have details on this soon."

Marco looks at Mo and mouths, "Oh my."

"You were selected because you deeply understand Davanti's business and technology, and you certainly represent your departments well. I've also been told that you have the respect and the trust of your peers and Davanti leadership. That gives me hope that you can influence both upward and downward. I've met most of you, and I see individuals who are open-minded and willing to change direction on this journey, if needed."

"So we're all working for you now, Sofia?" asks Gina.

"Not really. This is a part-time assignment in addition to your current responsibilities. I talked to all of your supervisors about the need for some flexibility, but you may also want to discuss your day-to-day assignments with them. We certainly can work around any conflicts that may come up, and your supervisors may be able to lighten your loads. Everyone sees this will require some extra effort from all of you. This can be a lot of fun, but you also need to brace for setbacks and maybe frustration at times. And not everybody will be thrilled when you involve them in the creation of a new innovation process. Thus the reason for some change-management training."

No one seems pleased by Sofia's answer, but they don't object either. Being part of defining and shaping the future of the company still sounds better than getting directives handed down to them.

"Please let me know if you're willing to go to battle with me on this transformation or if you'd rather pass. . . . No hard feelings if you feel you're not the right person for this. But if you are a 'go' now, I expect you to hang in there for a while. Please also feel free to enlist other folks from your departments as needed. So is everybody in?" Sofia makes eye contact with everybody and asks for a verbal "yes" as if they were sitting in the emergency exit row of an airplane. Everyone affirms their participation.

"Thank you for the commitment," says Sofia earnestly. "Oh . . . I think we should have a name for this team. What do you suggest?"

"Given the challenge, how about Ninjas, Houdinis, or Supermen and Superwomen," suggests Marco jokingly.

"Maybe famous cyclists of the past, some of Fausto Sr.'s competitors," offers Giovanni.

"Why not be more inspirational and look at famous innovators?" steers Sofia. "Maybe the Italian ones, like DaVinci."

They quickly make a list of Italian innovations, from pasta to pianos, shoes, violins, sports cars, espresso machines, and batteries.

"Were batteries invented in Italy?" asks Luca.

"Yes," says Ricardo confidently. "Alessandro Volta invented today's electric batteries."

"I vote for him," says Gina. "We can be 'Volta.'"

The rest of the team agrees.

"I hope this will *spark* many great ideas," adds Marco, and the group groans at the pun.

"On that note, let's take a five-minute break," advises Sofia, "then we'll get started on the challenge of the day."

***

As most of the Volta team dashes out to the cafeteria for a coffee, Mo checks his phone, which had been silenced, and sees a text from Marie.

"Racing in Bussolengo in 2 weeks. Trial the course Saturday?"

Mo quickly responds. "Yes."

"Let's meet at the duomo at 8:30. Bring tools?"

"No problem."

***

"Our first job is to identify and put some hard numbers behind Davanti's entire product portfolio, current and future," instructs Sofia. "We'll account for everything—products, services, joint ventures, licenses. With this data, we can establish a baseline and, going forward, tell if the Davanti products have a chance to contribute to our eventual objectives and goals. And since every product addition affects every other product, it will help us assess tradeoffs and conflicts."

"This doesn't seem so unusual," says Ricardo. "I think that among all of us we should be able to compile a spreadsheet for everything out in the stores and in the pipeline."

"Why do we need to create anything?" asks Marco. "Why not use our product roadmap—current and future to get started."

"I didn't know we had a roadmap, Marco," says Sofia. "Let's take a look."

Marco pulls the Davanti product roadmap up on his laptop, hooks the computer up to a projector, and shows it on the 60-inch video screen.

"We've used these for years, and we've learned many lessons since we started this product planning exercise," notes Marco. "You can see what we launched in past years, what we currently have in the pipeline, what they will replace, and when."

Sofia looks at the chart with great interest: Every product is neatly color-coded. And for each product, its launch date and approximate lifecycle are recorded.

"See, we stagger all the launches," comments Stella, getting up and pointing to the screen. "We learned that the hard way. We can't launch everything at the same time and then go in a lull for three years. The market can't handle that, and we run out of resources. Although we do try to time a lot of products for the Eurobike show."

"These slides are a pipe dream," says Giovanni. "It's what's supposed to happen. All wishful thinking. We argue over this plan at the start of every season, we are late for every launch, and we continue to pile launches on top of each other. It creates havoc in the plants every spring."

"It's the best view we've got," says Marco defensively.

"That may be, but it also doesn't show the massive losses due to late launches," interrupts Stella. "And that's not just manufacturing's fault. I can't remember the last time we had a technical release on time or even within six months of the due date. We just give the sales away to our competition. I think we're so predictably late now that our competitors have that built into their launch strategies."

"That's not exactly right, either," says Ricardo. "We've all played a part in this."

"I think all of you are speaking the truth and pointing out things that a new process can help to fix," says Sofia. "We've got some great opportunities here that can make a real difference for Davanti." She points to the delivery dates on the screen. "Imagine if all of these dates were actually on time. What else can we learn from the roadmap?"

The team analyzes the roadmap and concludes:

■ Most products are incremental improvements—no revolutionary products, just more of the same.
■ There are no service offerings or licensing revenues.
■ Although there is a well-defined launch schedule, there does not seem to be a defined end date for most products in the market.

"So why do we leave the old product in the lineup when we launch a new one; what's the point of that?" asks Matteo Catena, the supply-chain representative on the team.

"Dealers like that. They get to sell the old-model bikes at a discount," replies Marco.

"Have we ever calculated the cost of keeping all these product codes in line for so long?" asks Matteo.

"It's not as bad as it seems. Our fixed cost is recovered, so we can discount them and still make some money," says Marco.

"But what about inventory, cost of changeovers, logistics?" asks Matteo.

"Hmmm. We never calculated that," says the finance rep Charles Okeke. "And I do not want to see the results; I may have to do something about it if I see the results."

"And what about the effect on new sales?" asks Sofia. "You're keeping an old product that you sell at a discount when you could be selling a new product at a premium."

"Not good business," Gina chimes in. "Am I the only one who understands that?"

"This portfolio isn't unusual," says Sofia. "However, the good news is we've set a very low baseline for our work. It will be easy to improve as we move forward, and we can do it fast."

Gina asks the question that is suddenly on everyone's mind: "How many of the products in our current portfolio are making money?"

"If they launched on time, maybe they *would* make money," answers Stella.

"I can share that information with you," says Charles. "But I do not think you will like it?"

"Why?" asks seemingly everyone in the room.

Charles shifts uneasily in his chair. "We have made money on less than 50 percent of the products we launched in the last five years. And that is the case regardless of how I allocate overhead or whatever creative accounting I can come up with. And whenever I present the data to the leaders, they do not believe my data and criticize our antiquated accounting practices. They deny the obvious . . . and I have no idea why."

The team members look incredulous.

Sofia would love to explore the root cause a little deeper, but she fears another round of finger-pointing and excuses. "That is water over the dam," she quickly adds. "I like to look forward and see how to make sure we only launch products that meet the business case, which for Davanti is to contribute to the value and growth of the company or at least make money."

"How do *you* suggest we do that?" asks Luca. "Do you have a magical spell that makes bad projects smell different than good ones? Working on the right stuff among everything that could be worked on is the biggest challenge of any R&D organization?"

"No magic fairy dust," answers Sofia. "I usually use net present value or NPV. It may not be the ultimate wisdom, but it's certainly good enough for Davanti to get all projects on a common denominator and help us understand the likely value of the portfolio."

"Please explain," requests Stella.

"It is not so complicated," says Charles. "Net present value is the difference between the present value of cash inflows and the present value of cash outflows over a period of time."

"Come again?" says Giovanni.

"Maybe I can try," says Sofia. "Let's say we expect to have a product in the market for one year. So we take all the cash that we expect to collect on the product minus the cash that will be spent on the product and one-time expenses, like R&D cost, tooling, changeover. That would be the NPV for the product."

"OK, understood," replies Giovanni.

Sofia starts to write a formula on the whiteboard and continues to explain NPV: "But if the product stays in the market for more than one year, we have to account for the depreciation. So we divide the expected collectable cash by a factor to account for the depreciation." She completes the formula and looks at the team.

$$NPV = \underset{\text{Year 0}}{\left(\underset{\text{in}}{Cash} - \underset{\text{out}}{Cash} \right)} + \underset{\text{Year 1}}{\frac{\underset{\text{in}}{Cash} - \underset{\text{out}}{Cash}}{(1+d)}} + \underset{\text{Year 2}}{\frac{\underset{\text{in}}{Cash} - \underset{\text{out}}{Cash}}{(1+d)^2}} - \underset{\text{Investment}}{Initial}$$

d = depreciation factor

Figure 5.1 NPV Formula.

"The math-savvy among you will understand that the denominators of this formula will go up fast as the years accumulate," says Sofia.

Ricardo chimes in, "The NPV deteriorates fast over time, and growth is only possible with increasing sales and profit."

"Is that what we call 'diminishing returns?'" asks Luca.

"You could look at it like that," says Sofia. "But the way I think about it is that there quickly comes a time for a product when a decreasing margin joins with rapidly growing depreciation."

"Which should tell us it's time to replace the product in the portfolio with a new one with a higher NPV," finishes Marco. "And I guess the higher NPV comes from the higher price we can ask for the new product."

"Precisely," responds Sofia. "And with an NPV for existing products, we can then truly assess the viability of proposed products for the future. The idea is that as a new product gets to market, its NPV should be much higher than the product it replaces, thus boosting the NPV of the entire portfolio."

"Sofia, we launch a lot of products for prestige and advertising," says Marco. "We know before launch that they we won't make much money on those."

"We do account for those," notes Charles. "We depreciate some of that cost as marketing expense."

Rene Noce, procurement manger, looks surprised at what he's been hearing. "I understand that there are a few prestige products that we need to sell regardless of their NPV or margins. But for all other products shouldn't we at least recover our investment—like R&D, distribution, advertising? Can we make sure we stop launching any new products unless we're sure that we'll recover our investment?"

"That seems simple and yet elegant," says Giovanni. "Where do we start?"

"Charles' numbers tell us that past profits on some past products probably have been abysmal," says Sofia. "We don't need to dig deeper there; it's history. Let's focus on the future, look at what we'll launch in the next five years, and how products will affect each other. Stella, can you take the lead on this and, with the help of Marco, Giovanni, Charles, and Ricardo, estimate the NPV for all the products that we are currently selling and the ones that we are planning to launch in the next five years? Don't try to be excessively precise, but do be consistent in your assumptions. If we get a good relative comparison between our projects, I'll be happy, and you'll have some powerful information. Let's then meet later this week to see what it looks like."

***

While Junior had agreed to not "lead" the direct-drive bicycle project, he was still very much interested in seeing that it moved along rapidly. Sofia had reassured him that she would talk to Mo about prototype 2.0. Sofia had been given a small, vacant office down the hall from Junior, which has a large window overlooking the bicycle parking lot.

Late Wednesday afternoon, Mo knocks outside of Sofia's open door and sticks his head inside. "Hello. You asked to see me? Is this about Volta?"

"Yes and no, Mo. Please come in and have a seat." She stands by the window and points to the parking lot in front of her window. "I don't think I've ever seen so many bikes in one spot."

"Which one is yours?"

"Oh, no. I don't bike. Well, at least not yet. Looking at this makes me want to try."

"I'd be happy to help you get started. You know, find the right bike that you're comfortable with, etc."

"Thanks. I will seriously consider that. Now, I'd like to hear about your new bike idea. How is the direct-drive project?"

"Did Junior ask you to keep tabs on me," Mo asks harmlessly.

"Sort of. But think of me more as a coach. Please tell me what your plans are."

"I've done a fair bit of research on the direct-drive mechanism to determine more of the technical capabilities and limitations. I called the drill manufacturer that makes the gear mechanism that Vinnie put in the current prototype. I asked an engineer there about the testing applied to the drill, and she was very open about what occurs—we buy a lot of their drills. Of course, she doesn't know what we're going to put it through. And, unfortunately, I don't know if it will hold up because I can't get any testing capacity. Gina has locked up literally all the testing capacity for the month with Darvin."

"Let's not worry about the testing resources at this time. I'm more worried about you and your idea."

"I don't follow. You've seen the prototype, you understand the concept, and you and everyone else understands its potential."

"Guilty on all counts, Mo. Your idea to replace the chain seems revolutionary. The problem is you showed me one idea. We need 100 more ideas to replace the chain. The right one may be yours or it could be something entirely different."

"How many solutions to a chainless bike can there be?"

"I have no idea. Neither do you. But we need to rapidly explore as many possibilities as we can. It could be more than 100."

"It would take forever to develop and test even 10 ideas, let alone 100. That would be a huge waste of time."

"I agree that testing that many prototypes could be a huge waste. But what has Davanti to lose if we can efficiently gather and critique many possibilities in their simplest forms?"

"I wouldn't know where to begin, Sofia."

"But I do. I suggest we try something new for Davanti: a hackathon."

"Is that legal," Mo asks facetiously.

"It's not only legal, but it's also a lot of fun, especially for someone with your sense of exploration and investigation. You'll enjoy it."

"OK, just what is it?"

"Hackathons started in the software industry, where a large group of programmers would collaborate to develop a new program in a very focused one- or two-day event. The purpose is to focus on a customer pain point and rapidly formulate as many ideas as possible to solve that problem. Then we narrow them down to a handful of innovative but practical concepts that could become the basis for an engineering effort."

"Well then, let's get hacking."

"I'll make some calls, and we should be able to begin next week."

Chapter 6

100 Ideas

The Volta team meets in the same conference room where a week earlier they kicked off their effort. Stella and her group have posted their NPV portfolio calculations on the walls around the room. They've also posted a financial summary of all current bike lines.

"Does this show what I think it shows?" asks Gina. "We make 80 percent of our profits from the three premium race bike lines, which only account for 40 percent of our volume."

Marco stands up next to the board and points to information on the premier line. "Something else is pretty clear. More than 90 percent of the profits from that line are from the latest models. Do we really need a 10-year-old model in the line that we cannot afford to make any more?"

"The current portfolio is a mess," states Charles. "Some projects *launched* with a negative NPV and never made it out of the hole. Others were launched so late that the value opportunities had eroded by the time they reached the market. But, fortunately, other projects were good and more than made up for the bad ones. And it gets worse—based on our NPV calculation, about half of the future portfolio will likely not make money either."

"We can't show this to Junior and the leadership team," says Gina. "They'll go ballistic and deny everything. I don't want to be the one to deliver the bad news."

"They need to hear it," says Rene. "They're as responsible for it as anyone."

"I think the leadership team will be more receptive to this than you think, especially if we make a proposal and not let them come up with their own solutions," suggests Sofia. "It's true that some people like to shoot the messenger, but I can help you deflect those bullets. We can only blame this on the process or the lack thereof."

"It's no wonder our profits are declining," marvels Marco. "We could have predicted that if we had done these calculations earlier. So what do we do now?"

"This exercise will help us avoid working on projects that make no money," says Ricardo, "and we can redeploy those resources to opportunities that create higher value and revenue."

Gina shifts in her seat and hopes nobody will talk about the Darvin project, which has been calculated to have a marginal NPV at best, provided Davanti gets exclusive rights.

"And we also have to worry about volumes," says Marco. "We must have something in the stores to sell or the dealers will drop us."

"We should start with a couple of simple standards," suggests Sofia. "One, remove at least one product for every new product we launch. Two, cut the losses and replace the money losers. Three, balance the portfolio with traditional, innovative, and diverse products and services. Four, set standards for NPV and criteria like needed volume, obsolescence, image, or prestige. And as we work with this, we can add other standards."

"You're right; image means something," says Marco. "Winning the Tour de France carries so much prestige. Everybody wants to ride the bike brand of the winner—if they can afford it. I'd hate to drop that bike just because of low NPV."

"You know, the dealers will kill us when we take the old product out when we launch the new one," says Stella.

"Why not let the dealers know well ahead of time when we launch and give them plenty of time to get orders in for the old products," says Matteo. "We could make this work to our advantage with the dealers, if we give them time to plan ahead."

"That only works if we meet launch dates in the first place," counters Stella. "Otherwise, dealers won't have any Davanti bikes in their shops."

"So what should a good portfolio look like?" asks Charles. "Are we focused on Davanti profits and growth?"

Sofia walks to an open whiteboard and begins to write. "As noted, it should be diversified, like an investment portfolio. Here's two guidelines to get you started:

■ Aligned with Davanti objectives and goals
■ 40 percent of sales from products less than two years old"

The team gathers around the board, exchanges ideas, and eventually comes up with a few more guidelines:

■ Good mix of higher risk/higher return and lower risk/lower return products
■ Appropriate returns from service, licensing, partnerships, and joint ventures
■ 10 percent additional sales every year from new bike lines (e.g., mountain, time-trial, electric bikes, etc.)
■ Online sales increases of 15 percent every year

"This looks OK to me," says Charles. "Just don't ask for an accurate financial assessment at this time."

"This is a good start," says Sofia. "I'd like to add two more for consideration that cut across all of these: The products can't take away sales from each other, and there should be synergy; the value of two products together in the portfolio should be higher than if they were individual products in separate portfolios. For example, if we create an appropriate service, we use bike sales to promote the service and we use the service to increase bike sales."

"I like that idea," exclaims Stella. "Why haven't we thought of this sooner?"

"Excuse me for dampening the excitement, but where do all the ideas for the new products and services come from?" asks Charles. "We do not have 40 percent new products and certainly no high-risk/high-gain products in the pipeline."

"We're going to spend quite some time on that question in the near future," says Sofia calmly. "There will be brainstorming, hackathons, idea submission initiatives, displays, studies. Trust me, we'll have more ideas than we need."

"Great. We'll need more leadership executives to shoot them down," jokes Mo. "Trust me. I know."

***

Mo and Marco head to Bruno's Birreria-Ristorante after work to grab a beer and a burger. They were thrilled when Bruno's opened, the first of many craft breweries to spring up in and around Fumane. The beers—from traditional Italian pilsners to over-the-top, ultra-hoppy imperial

IPAs—are top-notch, and the burgers and sandwiches as good as any in town. They both find street parking near Bruno's and walk in together. The Thursday night crowd has yet to show up, and they grab two seats at the bar.

"Hello, boys, good to see you again. What will it be tonight?" asks Marianne, one of their favorite bartenders. She's generous with free tastes and occasionally throws in a "gratis birra."

"Ciao, Marianne," says Marco. "It's nice to be back. I'll have the Bruno's IPA."

"Likewise, Marianne," adds Mo. "Nice to see you again."

"Do you want menus as well?"

"No, I think we know what we'll be getting. That is unless Mo has some crazy idea, which he tends to do these days."

"OK. I'll be back with your beers."

The bar is dark wood with a copper top. Seating and tables are similar in style. Opposite the bar are large windows into the brewing area through which patrons can see the stainless 1,000 liter–capacity brewing system. The air smells of grains, hops, and burgers.

"What a day?" says Marco.

"No kidding. I really like what's happening at Davanti. It feels like we're part of something important, something meaningful. More than just work. You know what I mean?"

"Absolutely. I'm thrilled to be part of it. Never thought I'd be involved in an innovation project."

"How do you feel about tomorrow, when we meet with the big guys?"

"I think it will be good for us, regardless of how they take the news. We're doing stuff that's never been done in Davanti and, whether they realize it or not, will make us a better company down the road."

"Yeah, I agree."

"Here you go, two IPAs," says Marianne, placing two large glasses filled with amber and suds in front of them.

"Grazie, Marianne," says Mo. "Can we please get a couple of burgers? I'll have the basic with the works."

"Same. And fries."

"I'll put that in for you."

Mo and Marco touch their glasses in a toast and take a drink.

"So what's new with Marie? Are you going to see her again?"

"Yes. She races next week in Bussolengo, and I'm going to tune up her bike this weekend."

"Yeah, right. Tune up her bike. Sure, whatever you say."

"No, really. I mean . . . oh, forget it. Your mind's in the gutter," Mo takes a long drink. "I hope that burger comes out before I finish this beer. I'm starving. All the thinking today has built up an appetite."

"No kidding. And we want to stay sharp for tomorrow. . . . But another beer won't kill us."

***

The Volta team invited Junior and the executive team to the conference room to review their portfolio work. They also removed all but a few of the room's chairs, encouraging the leadership to conduct the meeting as a standup as they review information on the walls.

"Let's see what you've been working on Sofia," says Junior as he looks for a seat. "Where are the chairs?"

"We want everybody to have a chance to focus on the information on the walls," replies Sofia. "This way you can see it all at once and go back and forth without having to flip through

PowerPoint slides. And this information is so fresh, we had no time to pull together a slide presentation. It's important that you see it as soon as possible."

"This will be a short meeting," says Junior. "It will end when we're tired of standing. I like this."

"The right product portfolio and a process to create it is the most effective first step toward reaching objectives and goals and a good place to start our lean initiative," explains Sofia. "I asked the team to look at the current product lineup as well as future products that have already been slotted; for each group, they calculated the NPV."

Most of the executives have heard of NPV, and those that have not won't admit it.

"You all should have a pretty good idea of how the *current* product lines are doing, so we don't need to rehash that. What the team really wants you to understand is that only half of the current products are profitable, and that will likely not improve with the *new* products that are planned."

The executives don't look too surprised, as they've seen the pattern before, and wander around the room to look at the NPV details. Emilio looks closely at the Darvin numbers and glances over to Gina, who shrugs.

"We can't change the past—but we can learn from it for the products that we're about to launch next year and the following years," adds Sofia.

"So where do we go from here?" asks Junior.

"This situation is not that unusual," replies Sofia. "I've seen it with many companies with which I've worked. Many companies launch new products with the wrong assumptions and usually with delays, but few understand how to remedy that situation. You're in good company."

"And the remedy?" asks Constantine, VP of manufacturing.

"It seems very easy to me," Stephano, VP of finance, says casually. "We just stop work on the bad projects and focus on the better ones, provided we can figure out which is which."

"But we invested so much money in these projects already," argues Emilio. "We may as well finish them."

"That's not a good idea," cautions Sofia. "If it's a bad idea, it won't get better if you invest more into it—and you will invest more. It's like your investments made with your own money. If you lose money on a bad performing stock, you wouldn't invest more money into it to make up for the loss. You're better off selling the bad performer and moving that money to a better performer to make up for the loss. Stella, please go over the NPV details of the projects currently scheduled for launch."

Stella points out that based on the NPV of the new products, the Davanti revenues are predicted to decline even further. Now the executives begin to fidget.

"But the good news is that on many of those we can do something about it," adds Stella.

"I don't trust this group's numbers," says Emilio, immediately bringing glares from the Volta team. "We've never relied on these types of calculations, and yet we've been very successful. What makes us think this NPV or whatever you call it is accurate? Who knows if it has any validity in predicting revenues for the coming years? Anything can happen. We in R&D have always developed the right products. But marketing keeps adding features, and we can't predict all the problems that will occur when we start manufacturing. Then the costs spiral out of control. We just need to . . ."

"No, that's not the problem," says Stephano. "Every time marketing proposes a new product they make the numbers—whatever numbers they use—look good so we approve the funding. But in the end, they never live up to the assumptions. The cost always comes in higher than expected because engineers add so many design complications that make them difficult to manufacture. Why do we have to go through that with every product?"

"And don't forget that sales immediately drops the price of the new product to meet their volume targets," adds Constantine, "and then they ask manufacturing to reduce the cost. At least with the NPV we have a consistent number. We can validate it with our history and learn to trust it."

The members of the Volta team have been standing quietly, taking it all in. They wonder how this company could have survived this long.

Junior looks disgusted—not by the NPV numbers or the work of the Volta team, but by the infighting of his leadership team. "Sofia, what are you drawing?"

"I understand how you all feel," she says. "Denial and passing blame are not unusual reactions to this kind of information. But no single person or department is at fault here. It's the processes and the culture at Davanti. They make it hard to succeed."

Sofia turns away from the whiteboard and reveals three overlapping circles.

"You can have the best idea for a new product," says Sofia, pointing to the left circle, "but if it can't be sold, it's useless. And even if you could sell it, it's still useless if it can't be produced at an advantageous cost. Successful innovation can only happen in the overlap of the three circles. At Davanti, the three currently work independently and in sequence; then the overlap is created by making compromises. You each work on your piece and 'throw it over the wall' to the other, often missing the needed overlap entirely, which leads to struggles and countless adjustments, redesigns, and scope changes to get back into the feasible area. All of these cost time and money and result in compromised product performances, late launches, and the fingerpointing we just went through. How many times did it happen that the product could not be manufactured, had to be redesigned, and when it finally was produced the cost was too high and an immediate cost-reduction program or a new marketing approach had to be developed?"

"Too many to count," says Constantine.

"Agreed," says Emilio and supply chain VP Leandro in unison.

"With good collaboration, projects start in the overlap area and stay there through the launch," she says.

"So we make our compromises earlier rather than late," chides Joe VP of marketing. "What will that accomplish?"

"It's a lot easier to work out problems in the early stages of the design when you still have all the freedom," says Sofia. "Changes are a lot easier and less expensive at that stage. Consider what it costs to make a change after tooling has been purchased."

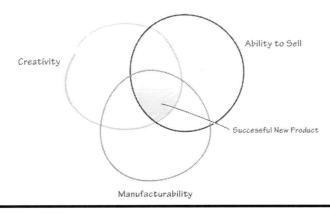

Figure 6.1 Winning at the Intersections.

"Does that mean we have to get manufacturing involved when the idea is still more a dream than a product?" asks Constantine. "That seems like a lot of waste, too."

"Constantine, you complain that we throw stuff over the wall to you, and now you don't want to remove the wall," teases Emilio.

"Don't forget sales," says Claudia Contanti, VP sales. "We need to see the final product to know if we like it, and if we don't . . ."

"This won't come naturally at first," interrupts Sofia, "but it also won't require everyone's involvement with every step of the process. What is important is that everybody agrees with the assumptions and targets for performance, price, cost, sales, things like that. As projects progress, adjustments may be needed, and they need to be understood and agreed upon by everybody, including stopping a project as early as possible if required. No more unilateral decisions by departments. Good collaboration requires some adjustment. I don't think we can achieve that in this meeting."

"If not today, Sofia, then when?" asks Junior.

"Soon. In situations like this, I often run an exercise to let people experience what it really means to help each other for the sake of delivering customer value. It's fun. You'll enjoy it. I will work with Anika and maybe we can run it at the next staff meeting."

"I'm looking forward to it," says Junior, making eye contact with everyone on his executive team. "I'm sure everyone here is as well."

"So we'll learn how to work together," continues Sofia. "But let's get back to the product portfolio and see what a good portfolio should look like. Stella will show you what we'll be working on."

The group walks with Stella to a flipchart that the team had prepared a day earlier, and she explains the thinking behind the suggested portfolio—everything from new bicycle lines and other innovative products to online sales and services—and the standards and guidelines they developed.

"Mountain bikes? Really?" asks Constantine.

"Services? That's new," says Joe.

"We'll all be retired before we could get any of this done," says Emilio, not taking any time to digest the information. "And who's going to pay for all the people needed to do this? We would need to triple our staff."

"If we reassign the people from the bad projects that we stop, that would be a start," says Stephano.

"Constantine, you've applied lean in production," says Sofia. "There are many other lean principles that we'll look at to increase efficiencies in R&D and other Davanti functions. Resource efficiencies emerge in countless ways once we move through the transformation. But we can't get all this done in one day."

"When we thoroughly deployed lean principles in the plant, we gained capacity equivalent to about half a factory," says Constantine confidently. "I wish we would have had product to fill that capacity. But I can't predict what will happen with this initiative?"

Junior walks in front of the group: "Except for the resources to do all this work, what does everybody think about the ideas for the new portfolio and the standards the team has suggested?"

None of the executives seem to object. They appear to have exhausted themselves in the face of data and reason and the long time on their feet. Most concerns were about how this could be done, how it might affect them personally, and if this could ever be done in time for them to see the results.

"I'd like to thank the Volta team for their work," says Junior, who looks forward to a chair and sitting down. "We all should thank them as well as Sofia. I'm excited about the opportunities ahead. I don't see us making bikes like my dad anymore."

***

Mo found a lot in Bussolengo near the duomo around 8:30 am on Saturday and pulled his bike from the rack on his car. It would have taken him at least two hours to bike from Fumane (and then two hours to return home), and he did not want to lug his tools on the bike. The weather also was anything but accommodating. A cool drizzle had been falling all morning and, if not for the opportunity to see Marie, he would have remained in bed much longer. He texted Marie his whereabouts and waited for her to show up.

Marie soon appeared on her bike. She had parked near a bicycle shop east of town and planned to look at new bike parts later, especially if Mo could not work his magic on her current ride. "Ciao, Mo!"

"Ciao! You've picked a wonderful day to ride," he jokes while setting up his little bike stand. "Let me grab my tools and see what we can do with your bike before we get going."

"Grazie."

Mo begins by clearing the crud from the chain, chainring, cog, and derailleur of her bike, while Marie holds an umbrella and describes the upcoming race and route to Mo.

"Wow, look at this," says Mo, showing her the rag he is using to clean the chain. "You are spending 20 percent of your energy in dragging this gunk through your drivetrain."

"Yeah, I'm clearly not too good about maintenance. I have so little time to ride, I don't want to waste it cleaning my bike."

"I think your attitude will change after today."

Mo cleans all the drivetrain parts, shaking his head quite often over what he discovers, and then he quickly adjusts her shifters, derailleur, brakes, and tire pressure. He ends by greasing all moving parts on her bike.

"I didn't know that pedals needed grease, too," says Marie.

Mo does not respond, but just smiles and shakes his head.

"Maybe I should have met you a few years earlier," says Marie, when Mo signals that he's done.

"I couldn't agree more. But after today, I'll teach *you* how to clean and grease your own bike."

Mo puts his toolbox back in the car, zips up his rain jacket, jumps on his bike, and follows Marie as she heads down the route for the upcoming race. She is amazed at how easily she's flying along, with Mo doing his best to keep up. After completing one full lap of the race circuit, she pulls her bike to the side and jumps off. The drizzle has turned into a steady rain.

Mo soon arrives and stops beside her: "Everything OK?"

"Everything is fabulous. The bike rides great. Thank you," she says and kisses him on the cheek. "So do you plan to come to the race?"

"I'd love to, but I'm heading to the Liège–Bastogne–Liège pro race next weekend. It's my turn to support the Davanti race team and listen to the rider complaints—most are prima donnas and wonder why we engineers are unable to fix all their problems. But I shouldn't complain, it's a great learning experience for an engineer. Nothing can compete with direct observation of customers, and the pros are our most demanding customers."

"Sounds like fun. Big race and a first-row seat to watch it."

"It should be. . . . I know you'll do great in the race, seeing how your clean and greased bike ran today. But let me know how it goes."

"Of course I will. . . . Another time through the route?"

Mo looks to the sky and back at Marie. "I think that's it for me today. . . . How about dinner one day? I can come to Geneva, or wherever you'd like."

"I'd like that. Let me check my schedule and my whereabouts, and then we'll set something up. Arrivederci."

"Arrivederci."

Mo and Marie bike in opposite directions as the sky lets loose with a torrent.

***

Sofia had spent the weekend arranging the hackathon at Davanti and was pleased that her old friend Nelly Gedanken was available to facilitate the event. She has relied on Nelly, a creativity consultant, to lead events across Europe in the past decade.

Nelly shows up at 7:00 am on Tuesday with a truck load of stuff—scissors, cardboard, glue, duct tape, string, balsa wood, markers, wire, sticky notes, pipe cleaners, masking tape, rubber bands, and more. The room looks like a craft store. Sofia worked with Ricardo, Luca, and Joe from marketing to hand-pick attendees—mostly engineers, lab technicians, and marketers, which included Mo and Vinnie. Ricardo also had sent an invitation to other departments, asking for volunteers to RSVP their willingness to get involved. They even have representatives from a supplier and a nearby dealer, and, to everybody's surprise, a local bike racer showed up after Marco twisted his arm.

Vinnie arrived, wheeling in a collection of bicycle frames, pedals, wheels, gears, and, essentially, anything he could lay his hands on from the lab surplus and squeeze into a pushcart. Luca had to pry Vinnie out of the lab and only his curiosity motivated him to check out "this hackathon thing." They use a large conference room near the lab that is frequently empty, giving the group good access to the lab if necessary. Sofia had catered in coffee as well as an assortment of the best pastries in town. At half past the hour, about 20 other attendees begin to arrive, most of whom head straight for the drinks, bombolini and cornetti.

Sofia eventually gets the group's attention and introduces Nelly. "Welcome to Davanti's first hackathon. I think we're all going to have a great time here today and do something very powerful for Davanti. For how that will occur, I'd like you to meet Nelly Gedanken, who's facilitated dozens of these. Nelly . . ."

"Hello everyone. Some of you may be familiar with hackathons, and for others this may be completely new. Here's what today's hackathon is about. Your customers have a problem: bike chains and derailleurs. Our objective today is to come up with as many ideas as possible for alternatives to chain-driven bikes."

"You said our customers have a problem. Who's our customer. Racers? Weekend riders?" asks the bike racer.

"Let's say it's everyone who's ever ridden a bike. So if you can imagine all Davanti customers rolled into one, that's who it is. We're going to use the persona 'Marie,' and she actually started Mo thinking about his direct-drive bicycle."

Mo gets up and explains how Marie had busted her expensive chain after fewer than 1,000 kilometers on it and could have been left stranded on an Alps pass had he not shown up. "And just this past weekend I cleaned a pot of crud out of her chain and derailleur. Why do we put up with this, and how much more time and effort will we spend perfecting a technically inferior system like this?"

Mo is surprised when the group hoots and cheers in agreement as if at a soccer match. But then again, they all ride bikes and have an easy time empathizing with Marie.

"Let's get started," says Nelly as she splits the room into quarters. "How can we help Marie? We want at least 100 ideas from every team in the next 60 minutes. As you work out your ideas—write them on a sticky note, read them aloud, and put them on the walls. And no restrictions. Think outside the box and go crazy. Anything goes. We're not manufacturing it today, we're imaging it."

Nelly understands that imagination is often the limiting factor when it comes to generating ideas, and she is well aware that some people, like Vinnie for example, are uncomfortable with exercises like this. That is why as a facilitator she tries to make people comfortable in this uncomfortable environment where they are expected to share crazy thoughts and sometimes look like fools.

Working in four diverse teams—with members defined by numbers when they walked in—they get to work, and Nelly and Sofia hear ideas being discussed, laughter, and shouts of excitement. Then they hear somebody say, "Are you crazy? That will never work!"

"Everyone. Your attention for a moment." Nelly uses a small megaphone that she brought to get her voice heard. "We're not here to judge ideas—at least not yet. As I said, anything goes. We're after volume at this time."

As people write down their ideas, place them on the walls, and read them, they both motivate and razz the other teams and challenge their colleagues. Mo notices how many ideas trigger others on the same team or other teams; there is a fascinating idea chain reaction going on.

Occasionally the voices in the room get quiet and members take a break on their own. When Nelly senses things getting too quiet, she shouts out a question: "How would Superman solve this problem? How would Google or Apple have helped Marie out?"

Eventually Nelly tells the teams to forget all physical or scientific restrictions. "Give us the most outrageous ideas, but make them legal and practical. Anything goes!" Now the teams really go wild and begin placing notes on the easel that read "Teleporting" and "Solid rocket boosters."

After an hour, the walls are plastered with notes; the teams had lost steam, and Nelly gives them a break for more coffee and pastries.

The teams casually talk about their ideas during the break, and then Nelly calls them to the center of the room. "OK, OK, everybody. Now is the time to assess these ideas. We'll use a method called 'DOT voting' or 'Dotmocracy.' Each of you will be given five blue dots to put on your most creative and innovative ideas and five green dots to put on your most practical ideas. Get your dots, and start voting."

After all the dots are placed, each of the four teams gathers their 10 sticky notes that had received the highest total number of dots. "These are 40 interesting ideas; great work," says Nelly. "Now please explain your ideas to the other teams to get their feedback, and then we'll go through the same DOT-voting process again to distill this down to the best ideas in the room."

After the second round of voting, Nelly asks for the 10 finalists   most of them with blue and green dots on the same idea. "Remember that for Steve Jobs the best ideas were always the ones that would demo the best. With this in mind, I now ask every team to pick one idea from the finalist list. I want you to visualize that idea as if you had to *sell* it at a trade show to a customer or to your leadership for funding."

The idea of pitching leadership brings some reality to the room.

"Let's first break for lunch, and then we'll start visualizing the finalists," instructs Nelly. Sofia has wheeled in carts with an assortment of sandwiches, salads, and waters. There is a lot of laughter and fun during lunch. It looks like people are starting to enjoy the exercise. Even Vinnie is now comfortable and happy he was able to contribute. After lunch, Nelly pulls the group back together.

"You've got a variety of materials to help you build something. Pull in anything you need. And you may have noticed that you have *real* bike parts, too. I know prototypes are the most popular with engineers, but why not make a skit, a sales presentation, or compose a song. The most creative and best crafted presentation wins a prize at the end."

While the teams have fun illustrating their ideas, Sofia notices how the visualization adds clarity and agreement among the team members and how they all embrace an idea that may not have been their own. "Having something to show is only a part of this exercise," comments Nelly when Sofia shares her observation. "Team building is another."

"Have you ever had a team build something together to reach consensus on non-technical challenges, like organizational or behavioral disagreements?"

"*Wow*, that is a great idea, Sofia. We should try that together one of these days."

"I'll let you know when the right opportunity comes up."

The teams spent at least an hour and a half working on their illustrations, after which Ricardo, Joe, Claudia, and Sofia judge the presentations and award a winner.

Claudia turns to Joe while they're judging, amazed at the outcome of such a short exercise: "I could almost sell these prototypes. Many address all the criteria we're looking for—creativity, clarity, practicality, presentation." One of the teams had chosen to glue a series of cardboard gear wheels on the chainstay (the two tubes that run from the bottom bracket to the rear fork) of an old frame that Vinnie had brought in. The small gears made the connection between a cardboard gear, like the one Mo used, and the rear wheel. Another team had glued an old chain right on the rim of an old wheel and built a cardboard and balsa wood mechanism to connect the pedals with an old cog to engage with the chain; the wheel even moved when they turned the pedals. Another team's brief comedy sketch illustrates the benefits of their idea.

All of the attendees watched as the judging occurred. Mo is almost as excited as when he saw for the first time the prototype that Vinnie had built and thinks, "So there actually were many more ways to eliminate the chain." Some prototypes were so clearly visualized that he almost felt like climbing on one of the bikes and riding it.

To the winning team, Nelly awarded drinks and pizza on the house at the nearby Bistro del Strada, the gastropub down the street from the Davanti facility. The winning team started their celebration in the conference room, and Mo and the other teams joined them in the Bistro. The chainless-bike ideas kept flowing into the night over pizza, wine, and beer.

***

The following morning Sofia, Ricardo, and Mo grouped the top ideas from the voting into three platforms: direct-drive bikes, similar to Mo's idea; bikes that were in some way powered by a hydraulic mechanism; and bikes using unconventional wheel and gear arrangements, such as pedals attached directly to the front wheel (like a tricycle) and powered by a rider lying on his back. Ricardo assigned investigators to each platform. Mo was assigned to the spinoffs of his original idea.

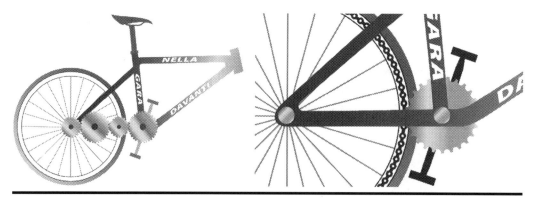

Figure 6.2 and 6.3   Hackathon Ideas.

Mo spent the rest of Friday recording (sketches, photos, drawings) all the mechanisms that had been proposed in his platform. He was surprised by the volume and variety of ideas that were comparable to his own (although he still felt his to be superior). These included several direct-drive shaft mechanisms, various designs for gear wheels mounted on a frame, and even designs that integrate gears on the rim of a bike.

Tomorrow Mo will head to the Liège–Bastogne–Liège and join the Davanti support team. Since he'll be gone all weekend, he grabs his jacket and rushes out of the office for a Friday evening dinner at his parent's villa. He'll get there just as the meal is readied: chestnut fettuccini with porcini mushrooms, oven-roasted squab with rosemary, and tiramisu for dessert.

***

The Liège–Bastogne–Liège is one of the more challenging one-day races on the European pro spring bicycling circuit (Les Classiques). For more than 100 years, riders have raced through the Ardennes region of Belgium. The 250-kilometer race begins in Liège, travels to Bastogne, and then ends back in the Liège industrial suburb of Ans. The course is notorious for its many steep climbs—rising approximately 4,500 meters—and unpredictable spring weather: a true test of riders and equipment. Although it's early in the season, the Davanti-sponsored team is the one that everybody has their eye on today.

Bike and component manufacturers use "The Bataille des Ardennes" as another opportunity to gauge their products prior to the season's big multistage races, and they send their best engineers and technicians to observe products in action. No matter how much and often testing is done, the final and truest assessment is a race, which always uncovers that which testing never could. The race is a business treat for Mo, and this year Vinnie also has been assigned to attend to bikes before the race. And what better opportunity can engineers and technicians have to observe and interact with their most demanding customers—the best pro racers in the world.

Mo had flown to Brussels and driven to Liège on Saturday and stayed at a hotel many blocks away from the race starting line. Sunday morning, after an espresso and checking email and social media, Mo heads to the starting line. Already a mammoth crowd is making it difficult to navigate the narrow streets of the Liège city center and, unfortunately, the weather has turned bleak: a mix of snow showers and sleet.

Mo walks past plaques and monuments, including a tank, that commemorate the British liberation of the city from the Germans near the end of World War II. After about 15 minutes, he is thick in the pre-race bustle and eventually squeezes through jostling fans to get to the team area near the narrow historic square. He is fortunate to ride today in one of the Davanti team cars that will keep him as close as possible to the action through the entire race, although he has to assume the job of a "water boy" and pass out the cold water bottles to the domestiques who supply them to the leading racers. But the cool weather will make that job easy today. In the car, Mo also can listen to the race radio and the communication of the Davanti directeur sportif Johan Leffe with the racers. There is no better place to be for a race, especially on a day like today.

As he fights through the crowd and heads toward the team canopies, he spots Vinnie, who had come to town a few days earlier to fine-tune bikes. He'd spent the early morning doing final adjustments for the Davanti team riders. "Hello, Mo," Vinnie yells.

"Good to see you, Vinnie. Where are the team cars?"

"This way, follow me," and the two meander through the crowd. "You know, I was race mechanic for many years. I loved traveling from race to race. I'd do anything to be involved. I even handed out lunches to riders—and ate many of them myself when the riders passed up the food. But eventually I couldn't keep up. My ability to dash out of the team car, fix the bike of a stranded rider, and then push him back up to speed eventually wasn't good enough. So now I do the pre-race stuff."

"Nowhere else is there such a high cost of delay as in a race," Mo commiserates.

"So true. Every second counts."

"Hey, I think I see my friend Rollo from Coppimechanica. Rollo!" yells Mo, waving across the crowd. Rollo waves them over to where the team buses, sponsors, support crews, journalists, photographers, and TV cameramen have gathered and where warmup rollers are set up for the riders. Mo and Rollo have worked on some successful Davanti/Coppimechanica projects together, and it's a treat for them to not only take in a race and meet bikers—all on their companies' travel accounts—but also to look at all the new stuff their competitors are sporting this season.

Many of their colleagues from other bike and component manufacturers consider the Davanti and Coppi folks arrogant. Mo and Rollo wear the stereotype proudly; the others can only wish for the race success the two Italian firms have enjoyed through the years. Mo has gotten to personally know many of the pro cyclists, especially those from the Davanti team, as he worked on design changes for their bikes. One such rider is Mo's favorite, Augustine Rossa, who is in excellent early-year form and favored to win the race. He is highly respected for his athletic abilities. His nickname is "Testa Rossa" (red head) or "Rossa" for short, not because he is as fast as the famous Ferrari model but because his shaved head becomes all red when he gets angry, which happens frequently.

By the time Mo gets to Rollo, he realizes he has very little time to get to the Davanti support car. "Rollo, so good to see you," says Mo. "But I'm afraid we'll have to catch up after the race. I am in danger of losing my ride."

"I'll look for you later. Please keep an eye on those chains and derailleurs for me, will you. Così lungo."

Mo pushes his way through the soaked crowd and joins the Davanti support team: the directeur sportif, who sets the strategy during the race; the training coach; a doctor; a therapist; two in-race mechanics; and two soigneurs, who take care of the riders (food, clothing, massages, etc.). Mo knows most of them and waves as he hops in his assigned car, which will follow the riders. Most of the others head straight to the ravitaillement or the finish line. Domingo Pucci, the assistant sports director, is driving Mo's car, and a mechanic is in the passenger seat. Mo shares the back seat with the mechanic's toolbox and the water cooler. In the trunk of the station wagon is a small warehouse of spare parts, including wheels with tires, chains, and cranks; there are four spare bikes on the roof of the car. The team car is in constant audio contact with the key riders, especially Rossa. They even have displays showing key riders' GPS positions, speed, and signals from heart-rate monitors worn by the riders.

The snow has turned to all rain in town, but it will be wet snow at the top of the Ardennes mountains. Most riders wear long pants and capes—most are used to this weather; some have grown up and trained in this part of the world, while others have learned to put up with it over years of riding European spring races. Still, Mo wishes they'd had the unseasonably warm days of a few weeks ago.

From the support vehicle, Mo watches the local mayor send the riders on their way: Despite the bad weather, the square is packed. It's a mosh-pit of locals wildly cheering on their favorites and riders pumping hard on their bikes as they exit town.

Not much happens in the first leg of the race and the field is packed together. As they approach the midpoint in Bastogne, riders cross many of the routes taken by Sherman, Tiger, and Panther tanks during the Ardennes Counteroffensive (Battle of the Bulge) in the winter of 1944–45. The field is still grouped—taking it easy on the dreaded wet pavement—and stays that way until they exit

Bastogne and head back toward Liège. As they pass the tank in the main square in Bastogne, Mo realizes why this place was the location of the decisive battle in WWII: the terrain must have been an order of magnitude more challenging to the armed forces in the harsh winter of 1944–45 than it is today for the riders.

The rain and snow have made it difficult for any team or rider to make a move, and Johan advises the Davanti riders to be patient and to look for an opportunity between Spa and Sprimont. It's there that Rossa gets into a breakaway with the help of his teammates, and the small group maintains their lead until Liège. During the final ascent into Ans, Rossa breaks away from five others in the lead group and crosses the finish line nearly 20 seconds ahead of his followers.

As Rossa hits the finish, everyone in the Davanti support vehicles is shouting and slapping high fives. It's another impressive victory for the Davanti team and a promising sign for the rest of the young season. When the support car stops in Ans, Mo imagines seeing his direct-drive bike crossing the finish line.

When Mo exits the team car, he joins Vinnie and the other mechanics to collect the bikes and ask the riders for their feedback. The engineers normally learn a lot from their customers (riders) after a race, but today the feedback is scarce. There were no incidents during the race, and the riders are anxious to clean up, go to the ceremony, and head to a warmer place as fast as possible. After the riders leave, Mo helps Vinnie and the other mechanics inspect the bikes and prepare them for shipment back to Fumane.

With the bikes stored away, the technical team gathers under the Davanti canopies (the only dry place around) to sum up the race. One mechanic reports that Rossa had complained about his derailleur, but when he asked for more details, he simply barked, "Fix it. That's your job." The mechanics agree that if Rossa had not complained about the derailleur, he would have complained about something else. Nevertheless, the mechanic communicated the issue to a Coppimechanica rep, who examined Rossa's derailleur and found no problem. Vinnie tagged the bike and promised to take another look at the derailleur back in the lab.

As Mo finally walks out of the team area, he spots Rollo, who is totally soaked, and goes over to catch up.

"Rollo! Another win!"

"Yes. Congratulations, Mo. I looked at Rossa's derailleur, and everything looks fine to me. And please let me know when there's an empty seat in your team car for me."

"I will do that. Congratulations to you, too. Everything worked perfect today. Those changes we worked on made a difference."

"Yes. I think we could have done even more if it weren't for the new drivetrain work draining my team's time."

"Tell me about it. Even I can't get anything tested because of it. . . . So tell me, Rollo, are you working with other customers on that project or is Davanti the only one? When will it launch?"

"As far as I know, we thought it was a good idea to get Davanti involved originally because the new system needed a frame modification. But that's changed. We made it fit standard configurations now. As far as I know we'll offer it to all bike makers next season."

***

Before heading to his car, Mo texts Marie: "How did your race go? Our Davanti team rider—Augustine Rossa—just won the Liège–Bastogne–Liège race."

Chapter 7

Challenging Changes and Chains

At Junior's staff meeting on Monday morning, the race is top of the agenda. Sofia can't help but notice how excited the executives are, describing how they'd watched the race on TV over the weekend. They are all die-hard, bike-racing fans and probably would have discussed the race regardless of the winner, but Rossa's victory has them in a crazy buzz. It's as if they've all had one-too-many lattes. Sofia had watched the end of the race to see who had won and has started the habit of checking the pro racing circuit on Sundays—to prepare for just this kind of meeting.

After 15 minutes of racing replay, Junior gets the group back to business: "We'll have more usable information on the race later this week when we hear from the techs and the mechanics. But all in all, it was a great day. So enough with the past. Let's now talk about the future. How have your discussions about objectives, goals, and strategy gone? Were you all able to get input from your organizations? I've received no reports yet, so I'm hoping you've brought them to this meeting."

As he tries to make eye contact, everyone is either staring at the ceiling or at their laptops—except for Anika from HR. "I'll tell you how it's gone. It's gone nowhere and won't, at least not as long as I'm here. I had a meeting with my associates and explained that now *your* objective is to increase the value of the company and that you expect everybody to figure out how it should be done."

"And what did they think?" asked Junior calmly when Anika paused.

"They wanted to know what happened to our core values, like safety first, perfect quality, and superior race performance."

"Obviously, no change there, but maybe we should incorporate that in how we define 'customer value' as well as address value to our employees. Good point. Maybe you can help Sofia address that."

"Junior, frankly, I want no part of this. This is another one of those perennial initiatives where everybody gets excited but nothing gets accomplished except distracting people from work. Just talking with my staff about this started a firestorm. I had an army of people in my office all week. They don't understand why you suddenly want the company to be worth more, and they're concerned, even scared. Why change something if it's not broken? Rumors are flying out there about your new friend here," Anika says, pointing to Sofia. "What is she really up to? People think the

DOI: 10.4324/9781003231837-7

worst and wonder what you're hiding. So no, I can't support something like this, whatever it is supposed to turn into. And no, I don't have a report!"

Junior says nothing, but is not happy with the bold rebuke.

Sofia breaks the silence: "Anika, I appreciate your concern and candid feedback. Let's talk after the meeting. I want to better understand your concerns and the angst that your associates are experiencing."

None of the other senior executives have much to say, but they are more apologetic with their approach. For example, Constantine from manufacturing asked for more time because most of his team works halfway around the globe. "And once I sat down with this—taking it seriously, mind you—I realized that it's more complicated than I imagined. It was a lot easier when we implemented lean in manufacturing. We had a consultant with a very clear roadmap that we followed."

Stephano in finance was similarly caught off guard by the depth of the assignment: "The assignment seemed simple enough, and I thought I understood what you were looking for Junior. But, to be quite honest, I've come to feel like I'm on a court playing a game that I never learned or practiced."

Junior obliged both with more time as well as Claudia (sales), Diana (procurement), and Leandro (supply) when it became clear that no reports were even close to ready. He was grateful not to have a full mutiny on his hands and then quickly changed the subject to more immediate business issues.

***

After the executive meeting wraps up, Sofia and Anika are still seated in the conference room.

"Anika, what can I do to help you?" asks Sofia.

"Well, have you considered going back to where you came from?"

"Yes, I have. I almost always do when I'm put in this position. But I eventually remember that being on the frontline of change is like wearing a bullseye on your back. Whether it's warranted or not, I will face criticism. I expect that and respect feedback."

"Then why do it?"

"Junior asked for my help because of Davanti's flat sales and dwindling profits, which is a direct byproduct of Davanti's inability to innovate and introduce new products and services fast enough. I want to help him—and you and your colleagues as well, not only with Davanti's current challenges but in building a company that can sustain success into the future and assure the jobs at this site."

"This just feels like another one of Junior's wishful ideas. We've seen many of these, and we're tired of the interruptions. And every time this happens, Junior has only a partial idea of how to proceed. So he ends up delegating the real work to the rest of us. Why make it such a big deal about a new strategic direction when that only makes people insecure and causes fear?"

"I can't change what's happened in the past," says Sofia. "But how can I help you and others today."

"Well, today it's 'increase the value of the company' and so on. Honestly, I don't understand this business stuff about flat sales. Junior always thinks it's worse than it is. We've proven him wrong many times before, and we can dodge this one if we let it blow over. And if it's a real problem, he'll do something about it. It's his company, after all."

"A transformation is only as effective as the individuals in the company who aspire to achieve it," stresses Sofia. "Without real, honest engagement of all associates it's just words on paper. Junior can't do this alone, even if he wanted to."

"You're not listening. We've seen this 'cheerleading' before. Every time a fad pops up in business, we jump on board and present it to the associates with an event. It sort of reminds me of a pep rally, with ice cream and balloons. Like spring perennials, the 'big idea' pops out of nowhere and wilts away just a few weeks later."

"Do you really think Junior's desire for all departments to get on board is such a fleeting activity? Don't you see benefit in Davanti being a more innovative company?"

"Yes, maybe there is a need. Innovation is one angle we haven't tackled before. And I do respect Junior, although it may not sound like it. I know he's earnest in what he's trying to do."

"So what can I do to alleviate your concerns and to help you and the Davanti associates overcome their fears and help Junior? How would you like to see this done?"

Anika senses the conversation has turned, and she's not quite sure how it happened. She pauses and then says, "We could start with an appropriate communication to all staff about who you are, what you do here, and an honest description of what this is all about—one that everybody understands. And we also could let the folks know how this all aligns with the core values of the company and how it helps everybody."

"Anika, I like that idea. I'm sure you've given this some thought already. What should the communication look like?"

"Shouldn't that come from Junior?"

"From what I see, you understand the concerns throughout the company much better than Junior, so I think you're in an excellent position to draft the communication. You can be a huge ally to Junior in doing so and help him to grasp and address the fears of your colleagues. Maybe he should deliver the message in a town hall meeting—but no ice cream or balloons."

"OK, I admit that can work, and it would underscore the importance of what Junior wants to do," says Anika, again surprised she's agreeing with Sofia. "But I still don't understand why Davanti needs to become an Apple or Google."

"I appreciate your candid feedback on this. I guess I totally underestimated the reaction of the Davanti associates. They're fortunate that Davanti has people like you who are concerned about them and listen to them. Thank you."

***

Before lunch Sofia receives an email from Anika. Attached is an excellent communication that Junior could probably deliver verbatim to Davanti associates. It's a document that only an experienced HR person can write. It shows empathy with all associates about a significant looming change and spells out *what* is going to happen, *how* it is going to be deployed, and what could happen if it's ignored.

Sofia heads to Anika's office, knocks, and sticks her head inside. "Thank you for the email. It's excellent."

"Anything you have to add to it?" asks Anika.

"Maybe, but I'd like to tell you a story first: Last week I decided to buy my first bike. I thought if I work at Davanti, I should own a bike like everybody else here. I think the exercise will do me a lot of good, but you won't see me riding to work just yet. So Mo gave me some suggestions to get me started."

"I hope you bought a Davanti Nella Gara."

"Yes, once I got over the sticker shock. It also helped that the salesperson did a great job! He explained to me *why* I need a Davanti bike, rather than a cheaper ride from a competitor. He convinced me that people are more likely to spend time on their bike if they find it fun and comfortable to ride. He said good bikes are like good shoes—you appreciate them more as they age.

You don't get that experience with most bikes. And he also mentioned that some cheaper bikes log more miles in or on cars driven to repair shops than being ridden. He said that I will pass the Davanti bike to my grandchildren. From that experience, I learned that the people selling Davanti bikes are trained to start with *why*."

"I brought that training into Davanti," beams Anika. "We use it to train all the folks who interact with customers, and we also invite our dealers to the training. I'm glad it works. But, wait a minute, there's more to your story. . . . You're suggesting I should add some *why* to the communication. Like why this is so important to Junior and to Davanti, to everybody. I will work on that, but it will need Junior's touch and vision."

***

As Mo is wrapping up his Monday morning, he realizes he had not heard back from Marie. He'd lost track amid the celebration after the race. He searches the results online and sees that she was in the breakaway group with five other racers and took third in the sprint. He thinks of texting again, but instead calls: "Marie, congratulations!"

"Thanks. Mo, it's nice to hear from you. I'm sorry I didn't reply to your text. I was rushing to get packed up and home after the race, and, when I did, I just collapsed and slept until this morning. I really gave it my all yesterday. But I should have gotten back to you."

"No problem. I'm just pleased to see your results."

"Well, more like our results. The weather wasn't so good, but the terrain suited my style well. And the cleaned and tuned-up bike was a huge difference. I can't thank you enough. I should hire you as my race mechanic."

"Like I said, you're going to start doing your own mechanic work from now on. I'll help you get started. I've accumulated extra tools over the years."

"If this is what happens with maintenance, I'm all on board."

"I'm glad it went well. I was worried when I didn't hear from you."

"My mistake. Next time I'll text that I won."

"You do that. Say, I'm running late and need to grab some lunch before an afternoon meeting. Let's talk or text again soon, OK?"

"Sure thing. Bye."

"Goodbye."

***

Junior and Anika had worked out details of the town hall address to employees, and assistant Anna had scheduled the meeting in the yard between the HQ offices and the prototype building. The weather had changed considerably from the weekend, now with blue skies and pleasant breezes. Italy's wonderful spring weather has kicked in.

Virtually every single Davanti employee in Fumane was standing on the cobble stones that separated the Davanti buildings, listening carefully as Junior delivers the communication that Anika jumpstarted. With his usual charisma, Junior captivates the audience, frequently quoting his father and reiterating the company's long-held values.

"My father believed strongly in values like safety, quality, and perfect performance. I believe that as well. I also want to emphasize that all this should occur in a workplace where everyone's contributions are respected and expected. . . . We are the best in the bike business, and we know how to win races, but I'm afraid our pursuers are catching up fast. We have to do something different if we want to stay ahead, and it has to be more than just pedal harder. Let me put that in business terms: Davanti has recently faced a lot of headwinds and stiff competition. Our growth has slowed due to fallen sales and declining revenue. Winning races is no longer enough to excel in business."

The employees are silent and motionless, hanging on Junior's every word.

"I'm concerned about the company, our customers, our suppliers, and all of you. We must ensure that all of you and your children have a job at Davanti or in the Verona community. So what would we do if we were racing? We'd make sure that we beat the competition wherever possible, right? We'd set goals—win stages, win tours, win the team competition. We'd develop a race strategy to achieve our goals and make sure everybody understands and supports the strategy. Then when on the road, we'd execute and adjust as the race unfolds."

The crowd nods, following along with race analogy.

"In business, we need to similarly *define winning*:[1] We beat the competition if we increase the value of the company by creating value for all stakeholders—me, you, our suppliers, dealers, customers. Right? And we set our goals accordingly and develop the strategy for the business. We'll need to articulate the specific methods how we will do that, but, for starters, we'll focus on value and innovation. We can't win this race by doing the same old things over again. You and I will learn about innovation excellence in the coming weeks, and we'll figure this out together. We have unbelievable talent and technology at Davanti. We need to leverage it for a greater variety of innovative and profitable products and services."

Junior pauses, and seems to make eye-to-eye contact with every employee. "If every rider on our Davanti team did his own thing, we'd never win a race. But if we define winning, have a race strategy, and every rider understands his role and helps one another, we'll kick butts like last weekend."

The employees erupt with applause and shouts.

"That will not only get the winner over the finish line, but reward support riders and the rest of the peloton. . . . We can do the same here within Davanti. Everybody understands what winning is and what we're trying to accomplish. And then we align, collaborate, and work hard to achieve our goals. And if company and business conditions change as we execute, we make the appropriate adjustments just as the racers do."

Anika looks over the crowd as Junior talks. She can easily see that he has their full attention. The speech appears to be working so far.

"As all of this became clearer to me, I realized a huge omission on my part. I fear we've not given you the systems and processes you deserve and need to win. Today, you are great riders without a great support team. I don't want you to work more or harder. It's about making all our work easier and more effective by implementing superior processes. And we want you to work on the things that make a difference so that you don't waste your talents on things that eventually are ignored in the market."

Junior pauses and takes a sip from a bottle of water.

"I know change makes everybody insecure. Nobody likes change, especially when things seem to be going well. I see the looks on some of your faces. Let me say, Davanti Nella Gara and what we believe in has not changed and it will not change. . . . But we must make the necessary changes now in how we work to sustain both the company and our jobs. If we wait too long, we'll face a situation one day that neither you nor I will be able to fix or survive."

No one thinks of applauding now. They recognize a level of gravity on Junior's face that's rarely been seen.

"We have the time and the talent to make this work. And I've brought in an innovation expert, Sofia Saggio, to help us along the way. She is your biggest advocate," says Junior as he points her out in the crowd. "She's worked for many years for my friend Marcel, helping many good companies to become great companies by becoming innovators in their industries—companies with far less talent than I'm looking at right now. She is here to keep me true to my word. You will continue to see her walking the halls, offices, shops, and labs. Not to point fingers, but to observe and help us all implement innovation excellence processes that will deliver our future. Her role is as straightforward as that: an ally and guide."

Sofia gives a reassuring wave to the employees.

"I really want to know what you think about this, so I'm going to stay here for a while to answer your questions and listen to any concerns one on one. You've certainly listened to mine today. And you are always welcome in my office at any time. No appointment necessary. Thank you for your time."

Many in the crowd head back to their offices, but about two dozen employees take Junior up on his offer and go to speak with the CEO. For about an hour, Junior patiently answers questions and calms nerves. He's pleased with how things have gone, but he's wondering what Sofia thought of it all.

***

"So how did it go?" asks Junior of Sofia, who's sitting in front of Junior's desk. He earnestly wants feedback on his performance.

"I'm impressed. Marcel has always spoken highly of you. I'm seeing why every day."

"Thank you. I've always been able to get people's attention. But I'm frequently afraid it's just words. I don't feel that I've made things happen in the past. You once said I need to be an enabler. How do I do that?"

"You began to do that today. You let the employees know why change is needed; you pointed in the right direction; and you described their role in the change process. You showed genuine concern, you removed some fear, and you replaced it with motivation—I think they want to help you and Davanti. But a favor: Regardless of what we run into, we've got to stick with this. If what we're doing is not good enough, we'll improve it—not replace it with a new initiative."

"OK, I understand that now. . . . Here's what's been bothering me for some time now: How do I turn motivation into innovation. We've got great staff, engineers, and technicians. But where are our *innovators?*"

"You have 200 innovators here and 300 in Taiwan. They're just waiting to be set free."

"Huh?"

"The idea generation program helped a little, but not how you intended. Sure, it got Mo's idea pulled from a drawer and into the prototype lab. But, more important, it showed you and me that the processes that foster innovation on a daily basis at Davanti do not exist. Is Mo's idea really the only exciting concept out there that could be developed? I doubt it. There are systemic hurdles that inhibit creativity and ideation within Davanti. Now that you know that, you can find and remove them. Your first step in helping associates to be innovators is to remove those obstacles and create an environment where innovation can flourish. The best way to turn motivation into innovation is to have an innovation process that all your associates can be successful with."

"You can't set a process for innovation. Sofia, innovators work like artists or Italian chefs. They need total freedom and can't be limited by a process. Am I right?"

"No. Artists don't just think stuff up, throw it against the wall, and see what sticks and how it looks. There is a process—or can be—for anything, even the most creative endeavors. Even four-star Michelin chefs have a mise en place process that removes variation or risk from mundane techniques and frees time for creative cooking. Artists and how they systematically prepare paints, paper, and tools do the same."

"I can understand that to a point, but . . ."

"This can be tough to grasp without doing it or seeing it. I think we've come to the point where you and your staff need to go see what innovation excellence looks like. See it in action at a company. Seeing it work will ease everybody's concerns and help them understand their role in the new process and organization."

Junior jumps to his feet. "I'm ready. Say when."

"Let me work with Marcel on that. We'll take you and your leadership team to one of Marcel's companies in the area. I'll give it some thought and organize a visit. Possibly Marcel can join us and help all of you understand your specific roles in what we'll see."

"I'll reach out to Marcel and ask that he joins us, and I'll follow your guidance for the visit. Thank you."

***

Mo shows up in Sofia's office late Tuesday afternoon with drawings of the ideas for the hackathon platform for which he was assigned.

"Sofia, I was able to knock these drawings out in no time, but I wonder if I can ever get anything like this built or tested."

"And why is that?"

"Like I said the last time we talked: all the prototype and test resources are consumed by Gina and the Darvin project. Every single one. How can we do innovation without build and test capacity? If you want 40 percent of revenue from new products, why not reserve 40 percent of resources for them?"

"That's an interesting thought, Mo."

"So let's do it."

"I doubt we need that much capacity in the early stage of new ideas. But I'm concerned by what you're telling me about the resource allocation. If I go talk to Luca, can he shed light on what happens?"

"He's the man, Sofia. He told Ricardo, who subsequently told me."

"OK, I will see him after our meeting."

"And one more Darvin detail that I learned from a friend at Coppimechanica. He believes the project doesn't need a frame modification, which opens the door to all our competitors. If that's true, we may have wasted our time thinking we're the exclusive partner. That's above my pay grade. Emilio would know."

"Thank you, Mo. So let's see the drawings."

Mo points to Sofia's computer, where a dozen or so drawings sit in her inbox. She opens the first. "Wow, I couldn't do something like this in 20 years."

"It takes practice."

"I'm sure it takes talent as well."

Sofia clicks through the other drawings, each unique to the hackathon ideas and as technically perfect as the first. "Impressive. . . . So, Mo, do you know why we grouped the mechanisms you drew into one platform. Well, not we. It was actually Ricardo's suggestion."

"Of course; they all share the same core mechanism—the drill gear."

"I guess that wasn't so hard. But now I have a more difficult question: What is the most critical question about that mechanism? Of all the assumptions that you made, what would be the first one you want to verify—the one that could make or break the whole thing?"

"Are you asking what concerns me the most?"

"If you had only one experiment to run to prove or disprove your idea, what would it be?"

"I can come up with a dozen."

"Let's say you want to build a house. What would be the first thing to consider?"

"Finding a site and getting it prepped, I guess?"

"What about a contractor, a drawing, maybe a permit, and some financing?"

"Yeah, those, of course. Maybe for me it would be how much money I can borrow? If I can't get enough of a loan, there'll be no house."

"So let's apply the same go/no-go logic to your bike idea."

Mo thinks about the metaphor for a moment, translating it to his bike idea. "OK, I get it. Here it is: I keep wondering if that thing is strong enough to take the forces that a cyclist would put on it under all circumstances—climbing, sprinting. Or will it simply break. The forces and torque that racers can develop are incredible. I had considered this and called the people who designed the drill mechanism. They had no concern about the torque in the work context for which it was designed: drilling holes and torquing screws, which happens under constant input from a DC motor without any side forces on the axles. Biker-generated torque and forces are all over the board during the course of a race. The drill manufacturer can't help me with that, and, of course, I didn't tell them what we want to use it for."

"Are you concerned about sharing your concern or disclosing your idea?"

"Neither. I just don't want them to laugh about what we're working on these days."

"Mo, you just told me that if the motor-gear mechanism can't take the rider forces, none of the projects in your platform can go forward. Why spend the time and money to build and test the mechanisms you drew up at this time and scrap them later?"

"Fair point. We need to address the gear strength hurdle, or we don't have a project. I think I follow you."

"Yes, Mo, we need to find a way to manage this risk early, fast, and inexpensively. With this approach, most ideas will fail fast, but some will withstand the risk thresholds. And if they do, we deal with the next critical question, whatever it may be. Only after the risk is manageable do we spend the resources to advance the technology."

"That's so simple, it's genius!"

"I had a good coach. . . . So how do you proceed?"

"I don't know. I'm afraid it will take time to answer the strength question, even if I can get some testing capacity."

"Really? What if I challenge you to come up with the fastest and cheapest way to answer that strength question?"

"The development of the right test alone will take at least six months. We've never done anything like this?"

"Mo, you've done an excellent job leveraging the knowledge of your friends in the company and on the outside. Coming up with a test for a critical question to assess an idea often takes more creativity than the idea itself. You'd be surprised where solutions emerge. Can you answer your question in a couple of days for pocket change?"

"I understand why I shouldn't waste time on this, but why should I limit my efforts to pocket change. We have the resources at Davanti to do this right."

"The fact that the resources are there is not the reason you should use them. I want you to think like lean startups that have limited resources. And if everybody thinks this way and minimizes the resources they use, we'll be able to evaluate a hundred ideas for the price of one."

"OK. I get it. I'll try."

***

Mo spends much of Tuesday afternoon talking with the colleagues in his office and other Davanti engineers and technicians. Despite the late hour in Taiwan, he texts the company's overseas testing engineers for ideas. To a person, they agree with Mo's initial response to Sofia: it will take a long time to develop and run a strength test of the direct-drive mechanism.

He thinks about the test on the ride home, that night while watching a soccer match, immediately as he awakes in the morning, and the next day as he rides back into the office. "How can this be done cheaply and quickly? There must be a way. Time to reach out a little further."

As soon as Mo gets to his office on Wednesday morning, he dials up Rollo at Coppimechanica.

"Rollo, hey, it's Mo over at Davanti."

"Still basking in the race victory?"

"Only for a while. The feeling has been replaced by work anxiety, which is why I'm calling."

"Sure. What can I do?"

"Well, you've always been able to answer a lot of my questions about drivetrains and assembly, but this time I have a more unusual question."

"True, so shoot. You know you can trust me, Mo."

Mo pauses, wondering if Rollo will think he's lost his mind.

"I came up with an idea for a new bike-drive mechanism and even developed a prototype."

"Geez. I wasn't expecting that. Is Davanti now trespassing on our turf? How's it work?"

"I'll show you when the time is right, Rollo. And then you might just laugh at me. But today I need to come up with an efficient, low-cost test that will gauge the device's ability to withstand the forces that a professional racer will put on it. If the mechanism isn't strong enough, no other testing is necessary. That's my biggest concern about the bike, and I'd like to address it sooner than later."

"Mo, I've got one word for you: Chainbuster."

"Chain what? Is that some kind of test you guys developed?"

"It's not a test. It's a him. Karl Obermeyer. He was on the German four-man bobsled team in the Turin Olympics. He was a pusher on the team—the last one to jump in."

"I thought the last to jump in is the brake man."

"He was that as well. Rumor has it that during his team's gold medal win Karl was so exhausted from the great push that he became dizzy when he jumped in and couldn't find the brake until they crossed the finish line. Nothing slowed them down. He works here as a technician now, and he does our chain- and drivetrain-strength testing."

"I still don't follow. How's he testing the chains. Does he operate your test machine?"

"Mo, he's enormous, all muscle. He will literally ride a bike until he breaks the chain. He always breaks the chain. It's just a matter of when it breaks. And if the chain was strong enough, he would break something else on the bike."

"When can he be here?"

"I'll talk with him and give him your information. I am sure he'll do it. You're our best customer. But make sure you treat him well—he loves to eat. His appetite is as big as he is."

***

That afternoon in the cafeteria, Mo is grabbing a Pellegrino from the refrigerator. Emilio is at the counter getting a cup of coffee.

"Hello, Emilio. Can I ask you a question?"

"Sure, Mo. Anything."

"Have you ever heard of the Chainbuster?"

"Of course. . . . What? Are you planning to have him test your bike?" asks Emilio, beaming with the thought of Karl destroying the prototype. He's thinking, "That will be a quick end to your project," but says, "Good idea, Mo, and good luck."

***

Rollo immediately had coordinated arrangements with the Chainbuster, and Wednesday evening Mo meets Karl at the Hotel di Ulivo, where he's put the former bobsledder up. Karl has muscles upon muscles, and it looks as though his shirt and jeans won't contain them. He's too old for the Olympics now, but still incredibly fit.

The hotel's restaurant is one of the better dining spots in Fumane, and Mo is certain Karl will appreciate the many menu options and size of portions. Mo orders a bottle of a local Valpolicella to kick off their conversation as well as an assortment of appetizers: calamari, olives, and bruschetta.

"Thank you for the work, Mo. What am I supposed to test? Are you guys now in the chain business, too?" asks Karl as the waiter pours the wine.

"It's a bike with a new gear mechanism. Nothing like you've ever seen."

"Oh, I've seen about everything. And I've broken everything."

When the appetizers arrive, Mo can't imagine they'll need more food, but Karl devours most of them within minutes. The waiter quickly moves in to take their entrée orders, fearing that a hungry Karl could be a liability. Karl orders an asparagus and spring greens salad, chili and garlic spaghetti with mussels, and a rack of suckling pig with purple potatoes. Mo opts for a house salad and asparagus risotto.

Mo is still eating as Karl finishes off his pork and waves to the waiter to bring a dessert menu. Karl orders sbrisolona, a crumbly cake, and Mo orders a grappa for them both. He wonders if all the food and drink will take Karl off his game or only make him more effective. Either way, he's fine with the outcome. At least he'll have an answer to the critical prototype question.

***

Thursday morning, Mo and Ricardo meet Karl outside the hotel. They pull the prototype off a rack on the back of Ricardo's convertible Alfa Romeo. They plan to follow Karl to bring him and the bike back if needed—after all, he will likely break the bike.

Mo cannot ignore the expression on Karl's face when he sees the bike—a mix of "who came up with something like that" and "this will be easy to break." After some bike adjustments and some road descriptions and directions, Karl takes to the road.

For more than an hour, Ricardo and Mo follow Karl as he ascends into the Alps. He started slowly, but is now pounding away on the bike. His intent is clear: he wants to break the gear mechanism like he breaks chains. The more it does not break, the more perturbed he becomes and the harder he presses into the pedals. Following close behind, they can hear him grunting and panting.

On a serpentine ascent, they momentarily lose sight of Karl and then hear what they fear the most: a terrible loud crack followed by the sound of a crash. Quickly driving around the turn, they see Karl on his butt, kicking the bike away from him. Ricardo pulls over, and Mo jumps out wearing a safety vest and putting up a triangular warning sign to protect them from any traffic.

"Karl, are you OK? Are you hurt?" asks Ricardo, who gets to Karl first.

"The f#^&% pedal," Karl screams, and he stands up with the pedal in his hand and gives the bike one good, last kick.

"Please stop kicking the bike," pleads Mo as he assesses the damage and realizes that Karl broke the pedal.

"You should have used a Coppi pedal. This is a piece of crap."

"Have you ever broken a pedal before a chain?" asks Ricardo.

"It's always the chain. I break chains. I don't break contraptions like you have on that bike, whatever you call it. No chain has ever taken so much pressure as I gave that thing today."

"Karl, we can replace the pedal and give you more time today."

"No, no. They don't call me Contraptionbuster. I could use a beer instead."

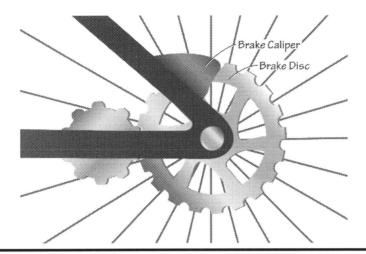

Brake Caliper
Brake Disc

Figure 7.1   Brake Disc Used as a Gear.

They load the bike onto the car, and Mo squeezes into the back seat of the Alfa, letting Karl ride shotgun.

"I do have one question," says Karl, still surprised by the durability of the mechanism. "Why did you add another gear wheel in the back? Why didn't you just notch the brake disc and use it to power the rear wheel? Is there any reason why you can't use it as a gear?"

Mo considers the idea: Modern bikes use disc brakes like cars or motorcycles. When activated, a caliper presses a brake pad against the sides of a metal disc attached to the center of the wheel, which causes friction and slows the bike. The outside edge of the disc, however, serves no purpose. Since the disc is already on the bike, if notched it could also be used as a gear and would likely be strong enough to withstand the pressure from pedaling.

Mo is flabbergasted. Ricardo stares at Mo, speechless. "We'll do that tomorrow, Karl. That's a great idea!"

"The name is Karl Anthon Obermeyer. Be sure you spell it right on the patent application. Now let's get those beers."

Note

1. Phrase coined by Billy Taylor, founder of the business-improvement company LinkedXL and the former director of manufacturing for The Goodyear Tire & Rubber Co.

Chapter 8

Lost in the Shadows

Mo and Ricardo each had a beer with Chainbuster back at his hotel, then they had to beg off and stay sober enough to work.

On the way back to Davanti, Ricardo comments: "This was a fast and easy way to answer your first critical question. Challenging people to come up with a fast and cheap assessment not only saves time and money, but it gets folks like you to think outside the box."

"I agree on all counts."

With the first critical question addressed, both are anxious to share the result and eager to develop the project further. As they discuss their next move, Mo receives a text from Marie.

"In Milan tomorrow. Dinner? LMK[1]"

"Yes. When and where?"

"BBL[2]"

"Everything OK?" asks Ricardo.

"Yes. I think everything is just fine. This is turning into quite a day."

***

The leadership team shows up Friday afternoon in the Davanti conference room and finds assigned seating.

"We will have some fun today," says Sofia as she hands out envelopes to Junior and his staff. She had requested the leadership team meeting, and she grouped them into two groups of five. Anika was the odd person out, and she'll observe. All are happy they've reached the end of a challenging week, but they don't look ready to have "fun," especially when it comes to a project from Sofia.

"Do not open the envelope until I have explained the game," Sofia instructs. "It's called 'Silent Squares.'[3] The goal is for everybody on a team to assemble a square puzzle—five completed puzzles per team. But you can't talk or use non-verbal communication. You're not allowed to ask a team member for a piece that you think you need, but you can offer a piece from your own puzzle if you think that it could help somebody else." She glances around the room. No questions—they all look like bike racers on the start line.

"Open the envelopes and get started."

Everybody has two to four puzzle pieces of various shapes (triangles, rectangles) and sizes in their envelope, and they rotate them around to see what fits. A few executives—Emilio; Diana Rialto, VP procurement; and Stephano Stanco, VP finance—are able to complete their puzzles with the pieces provided in the envelope, but others struggle to make anything work and jealously

DOI: 10.4324/9781003231837-8

look at their neighbors with a completed puzzle. "I don't think you've given us all the necessary pieces," says Constantine Rendere, VP manufacturing, somewhat in jest but wondering if it's true.

Then silence, except for a few groans of frustration. The people with a completed puzzle see no reason to stay involved—they are done after all, and it's not their fault that the others have not figured it out. Emilio, with a completed puzzle in front of him, has his phone out and is working on emails. He glances around the room, as if to say, "Might as well do something useful since Sofia wants to waste everybody's time."

The people who are not able to complete their puzzle look helpless, and Sofia has to stop some non-verbal communication as they get increasingly frustrated. Some shake the envelopes, hoping for missing pieces to fall out, but there is nothing to be found. Suddenly, one team seems to make progress. Diana takes her completed puzzle apart and starts offering pieces to her colleagues. Others do the same, only now realizing they're not done until everyone on their team has completed a puzzle. If they see an opportunity, they offer the right pieces to their struggling colleagues, showing them the piece they may want to consider. After a few more minutes of silent collaboration, Diana and her colleagues have five completed puzzles in front of them. They exchange high fives, adding to the frustration of Emilio's team, which includes Junior; they are still waiting for inspiration or something to happen. A few minutes later, Sofia pauses the exercise and puts the failing team out of their misery.

"How does everybody feel?" asks Sofia.

"What was this about?" asks Emilio. Sofia ignores the question.

"Strangely good," says Stephano, who was on the team that had completed five puzzles, "considering that we just spent 10 minutes pushing little pieces of paper around. I eventually realized, like Diana, that the game was about *all* of us being successful. We all had to help each other to accomplish that, so I started to break down my own completed puzzle and offer the pieces to the other folks to help them."

"And how did you feel doing that?"

"Well, I was hoping that if I help them, they'd help me later put my puzzle back together and things will work out for all of us—and that's pretty much what happened."

Leandro, who was on the Emilio team, shares how helpless he felt: "If we had been a race team, we would have performed miserably. Maybe we need to learn from the race team how to help each other."

"So maybe we can now help our colleagues on the other team," suggests Sofia.

Emilio starts throwing the pieces from his puzzle on the table and very quickly everybody follows suit. Quickly the second team had five finished puzzles as well.

"This was ridiculously simple, but it's a great exercise," says Anika. "It shows a deep cultural issue at Davanti. We compete against each other instead of helping each other to compete against those out there who want our market share."

Junior, deep in thought, says nothing.

"Sofia, will you help me to develop collaboration training around this exercise?" asks Anika. "Maybe one day we can eliminate the fingerpointing and blaming others for problems that we can only resolve when we help each other."

Junior nods in agreement: "And one addition. Tell them to help each other first before they expect me to intervene and fix their problems. It's not about who in Davanti wins. It's about making the customer win."

The executives, all with a look of guilt, are surprised by Junior's blunt comment.

"I really enjoyed this exercise," says Stephano. "These simulations are fun and a very effective way of learning. I've seen simulations used to illustrate lean principles, but I didn't know they can be used to help people change behaviors."

"We've had good results with simulations in our lean training in the factory," replies Constantine.

"And we should use as many of them as possible in the office, including those that teach human interactions," adds Anika. "And we'll use them to train all associates, not only executives."

"That's it," concludes Sofia. "Thirty minutes that can change the way Davanti operates for 30 days, a quarter, a year. Thank you for attending and your engagement. Enjoy your weekend."

***

After the executive meeting, Sofia heads to the lab. She's scheduled a small window of Luca's time. The lab appears busier than usual, and there are racing bikes everywhere. Luca gets up from his computer and walks over to greet her.

"Sofia, welcome to the lab. It's your first time here, no?"

"No, I've been in now and then, just quietly observing. It's fascinating. What's going on today? It looks more hectic than I remember."

"It's the heart of race season for us. Every member of the Davanti team gets a special bike and a few spares if something breaks for almost every race. And a lot of other teams that Davanti doesn't sponsor also ride our bikes. Riders are extremely demanding, and they want the bikes as soon as possible so they can trial and fine-tune them on the road. But I don't let anything out of here that is not 100 percent tested and certified. When the Davanti name is on it, it must be perfect."

"So everyone in here is working on bikes for the next races?"

"No, no. Some are working on development projects, quality control, customer concerns. . . . Those require much more time and testing."

"Like Darvin? I understand that is supposed to be the next revolution in biking."

"That is certainly one of the development projects. Or, I should say, *the* development project. It takes a lot of our resources. In fact, right now it takes almost all of our resources not devoted to the current race season. I just hope it's worth it."

"How are the resources assigned?" she asks, not wanting to implicate Mo and his complaints about a lack of testing capacity. "What is the process?"

"The engineers write and submit orders on their computers, and we build their prototypes and test them. And we're always low on capacity. We could use twice as much. But, even if we had that, the engineers probably would ask for twice as much building and testing. That's their nature."

"So are there standards for what gets built and tested first?"

"Sort of. If a project is deemed important, it gets a lot of capacity. Pretty much free rein. If the project is less important, it just waits until it becomes important or drops off the list."

"What makes one project more important than another project?"

"Everything is sorted out through our priority system."

"And how does that work?"

"Twice a week, all of the functional managers and project managers come here for a meeting, and we fight over every slot of the schedule that I manage. But, here's the thing, as soon as they all go back to their office, I get calls from the real powers in the company to change the schedule. Emilio frequently sends me an email and tells me what has to go to the top of the list—he has the last word. We all work for him. It's funny, but we've gotten used to how he'll prioritize things. So there are fewer arguments in the priority meetings, but more frustration. Like right now, everybody knows that Darvin is first. But I have to say, anything that has to do with safety, quality, customer satisfaction, etc. still eventually gets to the top of the list."

"Well, I'm glad to hear that."

"And sometimes Junior calls and asks for stuff to get moved up. He's the one guy who doesn't have to ask Emilio first."

"And why is the Darvin project so important?"

"Ah, yes. All I know is that it's the No. 1 project in Davanti now. Gina makes that very clear in every meeting, and she makes it clear that she has Emilio's backing on that. Despite that, she's fun to work with and really an excellent project manager. All the technicians get along well with her, and she always brings in goodies. But it would be fun to work on some other projects now and then."

"You mean like Mo's project."

"We were very happy when Mo brought something new to the shop. We're all a bit jealous of Vinnie who got to build it, but we kept it well under the radar."

"There will be more of that one day. Davanti will have innovation processes that rival its bike-racing abilities. We'll make that happen."

"We're ready and waiting."

"Thanks for your time and the information, Luca. I've got to be running."

***

Sofia is rarely in her office, preferring instead to walk the complex, talk with individuals, ask questions, watch how people work, and take notes. As the end of the workday nears, she stops by the office that Mo shares with other engineers. Mo is hunched over his keyboard. He sees her walk in and saves what he's working on. Sofia takes a seat next to his desk.

"Mo, you were absolutely right about the lab capacity. It's a classic case of shadow engineering. And it seems to be the only type of engineering at Davanti."

"I know about shadow boxing, but I've never heard of shadow engineering."

"Shadow engineering is what happens when there's no clear company and product strategy. Everybody does what they think is the best—for the company, for their department, and/or for themselves. If there's a conflict, the strongest win, and if something goes wrong, there's always somebody to blame."

"Yes, that's what it's like."

"Davanti seems to have unwritten rules about safety, quality, and customer satisfaction, but beyond that, project decisions are made in the shadows. I'm sure that excellent projects die on the vine without any chance of advancing."

"You think Gina and Emilio aren't following the Davanti playbook?"

"I can't fault Gina or Emilio. I don't imagine there is a 'playbook,' as you say. Emilio has Junior's trust, and he may think that pumping all the resources into Darvin is best for the company. As for Gina, she's supporting her boss. And he picked the right person. Luca says she knows how to get things done."

"Yes, that's for sure. . . . I think we're all a bit guilty of shadow engineering," says Mo, looking at his colleagues around the room. "We all on occasion have done and said whatever was necessary to keep our projects moving. And trust me, at Davanti people are more creative in finding ways to work around the system than inventing new products."

The other engineers in the office look over at Sofia and have a "guilty as charged" look on their faces.

"In the absence of a good strategy, a product-planning process, and standards, this will happen. It's also a work environment in which the Emilios and Ginas of the world will thrive. Sometimes people like Gina get promoted because leadership thinks they're awesome managers. But when they get in a situation that calls for collaboration and sharing of resources, they don't do as well, and leadership can't understand why. Managing is not always about getting things done, but getting the right things done. I don't fault Gina—or you and your colleagues—but this needs to change."

"Good luck, Sofia. As long as I've been here, that's the way it's been done. I'm sure Luca told you as much as well."

"When the time comes to invest real money and time into the new projects—the kind of funding that can make or break a company—we'll need a process we can trust to lead us to the right decisions."

"You really see us doing that any time soon? I mean, you think Emilio and Gina are just going to give up their power?"

"It will be a challenge but one worth the effort. And I think it will happen. I don't quite know how yet, but we must make it happen."

***

Friday after work, instead of meeting Marco for beers as is their typical weekend kickoff, Mo heads to Milan to meet Marie. She had texted him the time and place: 8:00 pm at Sapori, one of the hot new restaurants on the city's west side near the Politecnico di Milano. Mo looks forward to revisiting the sites of his college days and to catch up with Marie.

He pulls up to Sapori and valet parks. He's anxious to see Marie and doesn't want to waste time looking for parking on a busy spring Friday evening. The area is overflowing with college students, hipsters, and young couples out on dates. Mo doesn't quite feel old, but he also doesn't feel like a collegian anymore.

Before walking inside, he spots Marie at a nice table for two near the front window. He dashes in the door. Marie greets him with a kiss on the cheek. "Hmm, that felt like a kiss my aunt would give me," thinks Mo.

"I'm glad you could come, Mo. I've been thinking about you."

Mo now thinks, "That sounds better."

"I was thinking that I really needed to do something to show my thanks for how well I did in the last race. The tuneup on my bike was great. It's run like new. Unfortunately, even when it was new it was never that good. You know, it's still no Davanti."

Mo doesn't quite know where this is going and tries to play it cool. "You don't need to do anything. I was glad to help. I wish we could have had a nicer day and a better ride together."

"Thanks to you, Mo, dinner is on me. I insist."

"No, no, nothing of the sort. I tell you what, we'll split it. Remember, if not for you, I wouldn't have come up with the direct-drive idea. And it was your idea to make a prototype for Junior. See, we're a pretty good team."

Marie seems a bit embarrassed by the comment and is glad to see the waiter arrive.

They order a Chardonnay produced near Milano. When the waiter leaves, they awkwardly discuss the menu, until Mo finally says, "How's your work, Marie?"

"It's good," she says, relieved to discuss something without emotions involved. "I was scoping out a new project for my company today. I may get assigned to it, or maybe not. My current assignment will wind down in a few weeks and I need to land somewhere."

"What have you been doing."

"Mostly post-merger integration execution."

"That's a mouthful."

"Yes. And it's not any easier to do. Most M&A looks good on paper. The numbers, you know. But then you get into the culture of companies and it's like oil and water. If I do my job well on the front end with due diligence and research, there usually aren't too many surprises. For this latest gig, that's not been the case."

The waiter returns and opens and pours their wine. Mo offers the taste test to Marie, who declares it "delicious. I think we're ready to order."

They both opt for a cup of the stracciatella, an egg drop soup, and order light entrees of seafood: roasted amberjack with almonds (Marie) and braised octopus with pea shoots (Mo). They quickly finish off their first glass of wine, and Mo pours them another.

"And you, Mo. How is your work?"

"It's as good as it can be. The prototype survived a critical strength test this week. And, just between you and me, I'm working with a team to develop a better innovation process within Davanti. This is really what I signed up for years ago, and it's coming to fruition."

"I'm happy for you, Mo. It sounds like an amazing place to be right now."

"It's not without its problems, but it has been amazing. . . . And I got to see the victory last week at the Liège–Bastogne–Liège. So it's been a pretty good week."

The waiter arrives with their soup, which they both enjoy as Mo describes the race. The waiter soon arrives with their entrees, sooner than either Mo and Marie expected. They shrug, "Thank you."

"I've looked forward to seeing you, Marie. I was glad to get your text."

"Likewise, Mo. It's been nice to see you again."

"I'd like to get to know you better, Marie. Maybe I could join you more often on your training rides; I've thought about getting back into racing myself."

Marie slowly tastes her amberjack and has a drink of wine. She puts the utensils on the table, and sighs slightly. Mo's smile turns to a frown.

"Mo, you're a great guy. And it's been good getting to know you. But I'm sort of getting over a difficult relationship. Two weeks before you fixed my chain, I split from my long-time boyfriend. He moved out of our apartment and back to his home country. We'd had problems for a while. At first I thought it was due to my work travel. You know, trying to make our distance-relationship work out with daily texts and calls. But it was more than that. More complicated. He grew up in a different culture. Although we spent many vacations in his home country together, I never really adapted to those customs and behaviors, and vice versa. Then when we'd get together, we'd just argue about not being together. It was difficult for me and still is. Sometimes I wonder if I tried enough and was too set in my ways; other times I think the relationship would never have worked regardless of what he or I did."

Mo's frown deepens.

"And, fortunately, my racing has been the distraction I've needed. I'm not ready for another relationship. I'm sorry if you feel differently. I was afraid of this." Marie quietly begins crying, unable to hold back the tears.

"It's OK, Marie. I understand."

"We can still remain friends and keep in touch, right?" asks Marie, putting her hand over Mo's, sad that she's hurt someone she now regards as a friend. "Is that OK?"

"Absolutely. I want to know how your racing goes. There's a lot of season ahead."

"And please come to my races. Beyond my parents, I don't have a lot of fans right now."

The waiter interrupts and asks if they'd like to see a dessert menu. As much as Mo wants dessert, he wants more to just get away. "Nothing for me, thank you."

"Nothing for me, either. Just our checks, please."

***

Mo spent most of Saturday morning sulking around his apartment. By noon, though, he'd had enough and changed into his bike clothes. It was a beautiful early May day. Maybe a ride would set his head straight. He texted Marco to see if he'd like to join him, and they agreed to meet up near the Sporting Club Fumane and ride into the Alps in the afternoon.

They both hit the club at precisely the same moment and neither breaks stride as they head north. After about an hour of cycling, they break for water.

"You were flying, Mo. I could barely keep up."

"Sorry about that. I was trying to outrace a memory."

"Uh oh, that sounds like your date last night was not so good."

"Yeah, that's pretty much it. Marie is the right girl at the wrong time."

"Damn, that's too bad. Don't give up, though. Did she cut you off completely?"

"No, but I've already got friends and relatives. You know what I mean."

"Do I. I'm spending my Saturday with you, right. But maybe she just needs some time. You never know. Tell you what. I'll race you back into town. Loser buys the beers," says Marco to Mo, who is lost in his thoughts and does not even seem to hear Marco.

"Mo! Hey! The way you're riding today, that's me saying I'm going to buy you beers. Get it? Let's get rolling."

***

Early Sunday, Mo heads to Lake Garda for brunch at his parent's villa. His mom wanted to take advantage of spring vegetables hitting the local markets and promised him a feast. Although he wasn't quite up to it, he could not refuse. Along the way, Mo stops at a farm stand for a bouquet of white and blue irises and stunning yellow peonies. He brings his dad, who has a passion for thrillers, the latest Dan Brown novel.

"Ciao, mama," says Mo through the open window of his Fiat as he parks. His mom is sitting on the front steps, enjoying the nice day and waiting for Mo.

"Ciao, Maurice. You're early for once. I'll need to get back to the kitchen."

Mo gets out of the car and grabs the flowers.

"No rush, mom. I brought these for you."

"Che bello! Oh, Mo, I love them." She jumps to her feet, grabs the flowers, and gives Mo a big hug. By the look in his eyes, she senses something is wrong. "Are you OK, Mo? You don't seem yourself today."

"Just tired from a long week, mom. I'm fine."

"Come, come. I need to get these in water. Go say hello to your father. He's in the back working on the garden and patio containers."

Mo walks around the side of the villa and surprises his dad. "Hey, old man."

"What? Oh, Mo. You shouldn't do that. I'm not as young as I used to be."

"Sorry, pop, I couldn't resist. . . . Wow, it's really beautiful out here today. You can see all the way to the opposite shore."

"Yes. Could not be better. If only I was fishing, but your mom's making me work. She wants to finish planting her tomatoes and herbs this week."

"And it's your job to do the heavy lifting, right? I know the drill. At least the garden is a little smaller than what I worked as a kid. You remember?"

"Yes, you're right. I should be grateful it's only this. She keeps asking for more space and more planters. . . . How are you, Mo?"

"Così-così, pop. Been better."

"Well, maybe lunch will perk you up. Let's go in and see what's cooking."

Mo and his dad approach the patio screen door, and the kitchen smells come wafting toward them. "Boy, that smells amazing. I can't wait to see what she's cooking. She says it's a surprise. Something she's never made before."

Inside, Mo's mom is at the stove, stirring a pot.

"We thought your brother was going to come," she says. "But he said the boys had too many things lined up this weekend. Maybe next week they'll come. He says 'hello.'"

"He doesn't know what he's missing," says Mo's dad. "Exactly what is he missing? It smells great."

"We're having sweet peas with spring onions and prosciutto; ricotta gnocchi with morels; and bread made with wild leeks. That's the morels you're smelling."

"Mom, it smells wonderful. Thank you. You shouldn't have gone to so much work—it's just me today."

"I also asked your father to pick up a few flavors of gelato for dessert. Now that it's warmer, the gelato tastes so good, don't you think?"

"Come, have a seat, Mo," yells his dad from the patio.

"Pour a glass of wine for you and your father and relax. You do look tired. You've been working too hard. Tell that Mr. Davanti to lighten up."

"Sure, mom, whatever you say."

Mo heads to the patio, where his father has a bottle of chianti and three glasses.

"Let's have a glass of wine and see what's bothering you. Is work going all right?

Mo is surprised that his father doesn't rib him about his "hobby," and walks over and sits next to him. "Dad, work has been good. We've developed a prototype around a new idea I had. And it actually works. Even the owner rode it. We tried to break the new drive mechanism on it this week, and we couldn't do it. This could be something pretty big for Davanti and the biking industry."

"That's wonderful, Mo," exclaims his father as he hands him a glass. "Saluto."

"Saluto, pop. . . . Don't mind me, I'll be fine."

"I know you will."

"I've also been getting some new project management duties. And I've got a question for you."

"Please ask. Anything."

"Well, we've got this consultant at the complex who's trying to help us develop innovation excellence processes. She says we actually lack any innovation process and standards, so we waste a lot of time, resources, and talent. The end result is that we're not good at creating new ideas, and we're even worse at turning ideas into products. . . . Do you have any experience with stuff like this? You know, lean, innovation, and similar things?"

"Oh sure. Lean became a big deal in the '90s in the automotive industry. You know, our leadership and management began to learn about the Toyota Production System and the lean ideas from *The Machine That Changed the World*.[4] And soon after that many consultants and some former Toyota employees started knocking on the doors of all car manufacturers, including ours."

"Yeah, I've heard of that."

"We embraced it in production at all of our manufacturing locations, and it really helped us eliminate a lot of waste and increase value to our customers. The objective is to not do anything in production and the supply chain that the customer won't pay for. It had a huge impact on quality and productivity. By the time I retired, we were pretty good at it in manufacturing all around the world as were most automakers. We had no choice."

"Did it work in R&D?"

"That's another story. I've never actually seen it work R&D. We had a few R&D managers try to transfer some of the lean principles from our production facilities, but they applied it with a focus on cost reduction and as if design engineers were line workers. Manufacturing and innovation processes are not apples-to-apples. As you know, a lot of what you do in R&D is creative work. Our R&D engineers became frustrated, and they believed that lean was stifling their creativity and upsetting their work. We never got the initiative out of the starting block in our R&D organization, and, quite frankly, I believe it would be challenging to apply lean to innovation."

"I think we're using lean in our Taiwan plant," says Mo. "But this is unrelated to that, which sounds like that could be a good thing. The consultant who's helping us has an entirely different innovation tack. She says R&D drives the bus to revenue and profits, and all departments should align with R&D when it comes to innovation. She's helping establish a corporate process to do that. I'm going to get more training on it in the coming weeks."

"That's a unique perspective of R&D's role. I get it."

"So, dad, what were the problems in R&D that could have benefitted from lean? I always thought your company launched great new products that your customers liked."

"Sure, we had a good idea what customers were looking for in a new car, and we had a good product strategy and excellent portfolio management. And each model launched was pretty close to on time, which is critical—but at an enormous expense. A lot of features and improvements were cut at the last minute, and all available engineers worked on launches. It seemed like everybody was working on the same old problems, and the plants had to do whatever they could to cover the gaps during rampup and launch. All that overtime and expediting adds up. We would constantly throw resources at the biggest, latest panic. It's how we did things. If you constantly work in this mode, you have no time to work on real innovations and new technologies. You just put a bandage on it and run to the next launch."

"That sounds familiar," says Mo, taking a sip of wine.

"One thing we did do right, however, was that we created a true global organization, with global functions and global auto platforms; and every platform had a chief engineer in charge of it, and all contributing functions supported the chief engineer. I think that the chief engineer idea also came from Toyota; not sure where we got the idea for the platforms. Each platform consisted of different models that shared common traits. But I'm sure we didn't use them as effectively as others. Everything got reinvented for every platform and model—not much learning or even common components were reused. Nobody trusted anything that anybody else had designed or developed. The number of drawings we produced and tests we conducted were mindboggling. Every engineer seemed to do their own thing, so we'd run the same tests for multiple engineers. In hindsight, it was a lot of waste, but we could never spend the time to figure out how to prevent it because we were so busy with launches."

"That also sounds a lot like Davanti. I will let you know if we find a solution. . . . But I've never heard of platforms or chief engineers . . ."

"Let's save that for another time. You've got a lot of interesting things going on—keep it up. But for now, let's relax a bit and enjoy the day. You need to get your mind off work for a while, and I need a break—after lunch your mom will have me back in the garden."

"Good idea, pop."

"And chin up. Whatever is bothering you, this, too, will pass."

Mo was pleased to get a little positive reinforcement from his father. This weekend it's what he really needed.

"Come in you two; everything is ready."

Notes

1. Let me know.
2. Be back later.
3. "Silent Squares Simulation," Lean Construction Institute.
4. James P. Womack, Daniel T. Jones, and Daniel Roos, *The Machine That Changed the World*, Harper Perennial, New York, 1991.

Chapter 9

Seeing Is Believing

"Welcome to Fusilli," says Marcel, holding his arms out open as a delegation from Davanti Nella Gara enters the bright, airy lobby of one of Marcel's companies. "Fausto, it is a pleasure to have you and your team here."

Junior is joined by his executive staff, the Volta team members, Sofia, and functional and R&D project managers. Many of the Fusilli staff standing with Marcel are excited to see their former innovation excellence coach again.

"As some of you may know, Fusilli invented the machine to make the famous pasta almost 100 years ago," explains Marcel. "They dominated the pasta machine industry for more than 80 years, providing the best pasta machines in the world. But over time they could not sustain their company by only making pasta machines. My group acquired them about eight years ago, and the first thing we did was remove obstacles that hindered innovation. We built on their strengths, like design excellence and manufacturing quality. We kept all their staff and transformed the company from the inside out into a successful, innovative supplier to the food industry." A few from the Davanti clan nod, having heard of Fusilli's transformation but not knowing how it occurred.

Marcel leads the group into a huge, open-format office environment in which a couple hundred employees are at work. He walks the group over to a large digital monitor that shows the amazing Fusilli financial results obtained through his tenure as well as trends in some key performance indicators. The results speak for themselves. Stephano, the VP of finance, is most impressed with the flat R&D budget and flat staffing through Marcel's tenure and Fusilli's growth. Junior is thinking, "No wonder he drives a Maserati and I drive a Camry."

"And you attribute all this to innovation excellence?" asks Stefano.

"Innovation excellence was more of a catalyst and then a roadmap. What I showed you are the results of the good work done by people in this room." He turns to look at all the people in the room. "The principles of innovation excellence are necessary, but they are not sufficient."

"Is this all your staff?" asks Anika from HR.

"Yes, everybody works in this one room. The corporate leaders have a small desk like everybody else. Actually, you never know where to find anybody. People always move their desks to huddle with their current teams."

"But where do you have your meetings, conference calls, etc.?" asks Anika, obsessed with the layout.

"If you look around, there is plenty of social space and quiet areas, some of it is even sound-insulated. We also have a loft," continues Marcel, who points to a ladder and a person sitting on top of a small cubicle, deep in thought with a laptop on his knees. "Sometimes they have to get

DOI: 10.4324/9781003231837-9

above the crowd to be creative. We have additional work areas outside on the patio. And you can also see that nobody has more than 50 meters to a food station."

"Can you tell us more about your products today?" asks Joe, VP marketing. "What's different?"

"Today we're still a leader in food-processing equipment, but far beyond pasta makers. We make machines for a range of foodservice applications, from home kitchens to restaurants and small food factories. We sell our own Fusilli brand, of course, but we also make the equipment for many popular food-equipment brands with which you are all familiar."

"I've seen your restaurant-quality equipment," says Constantine from manufacturing. "They're well-made, impressive machines."

"And we've moved beyond machines. We also created several new value streams, like our 'Chef Facile' line. The initial idea was to develop kitted meals that included ingredients, recipes, and, of course, our equipment. That would enable cooking-impaired folks like me to create wonderful meals in a short time with minimum effort. Not a radical idea, but far from our sweet spot. Then we quickly discovered the business opportunity at fast food restaurants and other food services. Our latest addition is our institutional line, where we enable corporations, churches, schools, even prisons to serve superior meals at a very low cost and with a minimum effort or training. We just expanded the package size."

"But how did you go from food equipment to food?" asks Junior.

"With the new building and set up here, our associates started to experiment at the food stations, wondering first how to improve some of the equipment that makes the food, then realizing that the food could be just as interesting and lucrative. Apple and Google aren't the only ones to spoil their employees with gourmet food around the clock. But in our case, it has had other huge benefits."

"That makes sense," says Anika. "You've created a space and culture without restrictions."

"Yes, that's true. But I want you to talk with the people who create the value here. I'd like you to meet Colette Bucco, the leader of our Chef Facile value stream. Colette is a chef by education."

Colette rises from her desk and waves to the group: "My job is extremely simple: I create value by engaging our associates, aligning their work and efforts with the objectives and goals of the company, and then helping them to be successful. Along the way, I develop future leaders for all positions in my value stream."

The group gives her a puzzled look, trying to figure out just what that looks like day to day.

"OK, that was a little business-speak. Let me tell you about my standard work: In the morning I walk around and talk to associates, finding out how they're doing and how I can help them. I participate in their huddles, look at their metrics, remove obstacles, and coach them as they innovate and solve problems. After lunch, I meet with my peers, the other value-stream leaders. We share our experiences and learnings from the morning and help each other. Then I huddle with support organizations as needed. For example, I'll discuss technical issues with R&D and review financial metrics with sales. Here, too, I listen to their concerns and help wherever I can, and they help me. At 4:00 pm, me and my value-stream colleagues talk to Marcel, if he is available."

"So you get your marching orders at the end of the day," says Claudia, Davanti VP of sales.

"No, not at all. Quite the opposite. That is when we tell Marcel where he needs to help us."

"So who do you ask for advice about the business you're running?" Claudia asks.

"The people best positioned for that are the people working for me and my peers. They usually have the best answers."

"But how do you know what your customers want?" asks Joe. "You seem to serve such a diverse market."

"That's a great question. We develop everything for 'Remy.'"

"The rat in the movie *Ratatouille*?"[1] asks Mo, thinking he's made a joke.

"Precisely. As you know, Remy aspires to be a chef but he has absolutely no skills? We figure, if we can help Remy, we can help anybody. He is our persona. My staff interacts literally every day with the Remys in this world, wherever they are, in house kitchens, in corporations, on soup lines. Some Remys actually work here. And then we make lots of things and let Remy try them. Our developers observe Remy, and then they improve, change, or drop the concept. Our success rate is pretty low. Most new ideas fail but . . ."

Emilio, who has a taste for the negative, interrupts: "How can you be successful if most fail?"

"Not all fail. Most, but not all. We try so many product ideas to make sure we do not miss the best. Even with a small percentage of success, we come up with many really promising innovations. And once we know we have a winner, we assign a team to develop the product."

"And you can afford that?" Emilio asks sarcastically.

"Can we afford not to? Our experiments are very cheap and very fast—that is why it works. Would you rather we make goods and let them suffer their fate on the market after all the investment in production, distribution, and sales?"

Emilio doesn't answer. The other Davanti folks look impressed, wondering if she's bluffing or if that is really how they work.

"If there are no more questions, I'd like you to meet Fabio Monti. He is responsible for talent development here."

"Colette, thank you for your time this morning," says Junior, and the Davanti group gives her polite applause.

"Hello," starts Fabio. "I help all my colleagues by making sure we always have the right person in the right position at the right time. We accomplish that with training, coaching, and recruiting. As you can imagine, given our various value streams, we have an extremely diverse workforce—market researchers, engineers, chefs, nutritionists, food scientists, technicians—and they come from more than 15 different countries."

"Do people like to work here?" asks Anika. "It seems a bit, umm, unstructured. You know?"

"Good point. Many applicants are shocked when they see the place when they interview. For that reason, we let promising recruits shadow our associates for a week or two with pay, and then, if they're still interested, we make them an offer. Our job acceptance is about industry average, but our retention rate is far above average."

"What does the org chart look like here?" asks Anika.

"We operate in a matrix. Our associates report to project or value stream managers in addition to functions."

"If people have more than one boss at Fusilli, how do you assess performance?" asks Ricardo.

"Everyone that our associates interact with—including peers, lab technicians, admin—give input on their performance. We value innovative thinking, collaboration, and behaviors that support our culture. Our associates thrive on reflection and feedback from customers, suppliers, and colleagues as well as coaching from their leaders and mentors."

Fabio entertains other questions from the Davanti folks. It's obvious to them that he supports a highly different culture than what they've been living. It's also clear—and a bit daunting—that this culture did not appear overnight.

"Any openings today?" asks Stella, sales manager on the Volta team. The others laugh. "Just asking."

"Yes. We are hiring constantly because we're growing constantly. . . . Well, with that, I've been asked to guide you to the food stations where you can grab something and take a break before meeting with others here. This way, please."

After the break, the Davanti folks split into small groups and spend most of the day talking to associates from all levels. When they've seen and heard as much as they can absorb in the day, they are walked back to the lobby. Marcel arrives to send them off.

"Marcel, thank you and all Fusilli associates for spending the day with us," says Junior.

"You're welcome. We love telling our story." Marcel makes sure everybody has his business card with his email address and phone number. "Please email me if you saw something today that we could improve or if you have an idea that will help us. And all of you, please take a salmon souffle kit on the way out. This way you can try Fusilli at home. And be sure to tell us about your experience with the kit and if you liked the outcome. Arrivederci."

As the Davanti group walks out of the building and toward their cars, the discussions start:

"I can't believe this."

"I never imagined you could do this."

"Did you see the number of new products in testing? That can't be right."

"I wouldn't believe this if I hadn't seen it with my own eyes."

"I can't imagine this will ever work in Davanti."

"I hope I'm retired before something like this ever gets deployed."

"We make bikes, not cannelloni."

Anika is in intensive discussion with Sofia. She carpools back to Davanti with Sofia and as soon as they get in the car, she asks: "When can we start the training?"

"Glad you asked. I will get you my contacts tomorrow. I normally start with a program called, 'What leaders need to know about innovation excellence.' Then I engage the leaders—you, Joe, Stephano, etc.—in the training of all the associates."

"That's a great idea. Let's get a budget on Junior's desk before the end of the week so we can get started. I may have some more questions. For instance, in your experience, is it better to use outside resources or should we use our own trainers at Davanti? Well, I think I know the answer already: use outside resources to get started and develop our own trainers down the road."

"You're learning fast, Anika. I normally get better results by training key internal staff the principles, and, once they've thoroughly grasped the concepts, we make them instructors. You can run into problems by completely relying on outside teachers who don't know the work and the culture. My trainers will handle the initial training and then follow up by certifying Davanti trainers; then you won't see them again."

"I love that approach. It's not only the best way to start the culture change but also the only way to sustain it. This will be the way people work at Davanti: leaders will coach new associates, and we'll need very little formal training or outside help after a while."

***

Back at Davanti, Junior follows Sofia into the building. "Sofia, excuse me. I'd like you to join Marcel and me for dinner tomorrow, if you're available. We're going to his favorite spot in Verona. I want to thank you and him for organizing the visit to Fusilli. It was excellent."

"I'd love to. Is it Tavolo del Contadino, by chance?"

"Yes."

"Thank you for asking me."

***

Tuesday evening, Junior, Sofia, and Marcel are seated at a table in the corner of Tavolo del Contadino, a small but charming restaurant that prides itself on farm-to-table ingredients. Many local crops are now hitting the markets, and the menu reflects the wide variety of produce available.

"Wonderful choice," says Junior as his second course arrives. They all had the pasta of the day as a first course—orecchiette with squash blossoms. Marcel and Sofia are having grilled trout with fresh herbs; Junior has opted for a pork stew with sweet and hot peppers.

"This trout tastes like it was caught today," says Sofia. "It's amazing."

"Yes. I always have a hard time not ordering the trout here. But there are so many other wonderful dishes. And you, Junior. How is your stew?"

"Wonderful," replies Junior, motioning to the waitress that he'd like another glass of Brunello. Marcel and Sofia are sharing a bottle of Pinot Grigio with their trout.

When the wine is poured, Junior lifts his glass. "Thank you for the tour yesterday. It was very inspiring."

"Inspiring? Is that all?" asks Marcel.

"Maybe I should call it 'overwhelming.' Everybody at Davanti asked me if something like this can happen on my watch. I told them 'yes,' but I'm not sure I believe it yet. . . . By the way, we didn't meet the president of Fusilli. Was he or she out of town?"

"Yes, Fausto, it can happen on your shift. And as for the president, I've been running Fusilli up to now. That's why Colette and others meet with me at the end of the day. But I'm thinking about appointing a leader soon. Are you interested?" he chuckles.

"I have my hands full at Davanti."

"Yes, you do. I understand that Sofia and her new friends at Davanti have started planning the training. You understand that should begin at the top. You and your staff will be heavily involved in training the associates."

"Those are some expensive trainers. . . . I'm betting they won't all like it. I wouldn't if I were them."

"You are one of them," counters Sofia.

"You're kidding, right?"

"I'm not. You're going to be trained and then training as well. But it's not like you and your leaders do all the work. We start with outside trainers who develop Davanti's own internal innovation excellence experts. You and your executive team won't be full-time trainers, but you and the others will show up during the training, teach a piece of the class, and answer questions. It's as much about showing commitment and support as teaching."

"I can't teach, and I don't want people like Emilio ruining this out of the gate. He hasn't bought into this thing at all."

"My good friend, let me teach you a few lessons," says Marcel seriously.

"Lesson #1: You may lose a person or two from your team through this. So I hope you have good succession planning. If you can't trust a colleague to support you and Davanti, then why are they there?"

Junior looks weary and has a sip of wine.

"Lesson #2: You teach behaviors first—beliefs follow the behaviors. But I don't want to give you lectures in psychology. Just trust me on that. Once your leaders start teaching the principles of innovation excellence and change their behaviors accordingly, beliefs will change like leaves in autumn.[2] Sofia will make sure you are all up to the task. When the training gets rolled out, please stop by personally to every session, even if it's only for 10 minutes or so."

"I think the last time I was taught behaviors was when I was a child. How many more lessons are there?" asks Junior, annoyed.

"How many can you handle without being overwhelmed again?"

"OK, a few more."

"#3: Reorganize before starting the transformation."

"Now you've lost me. I thought I was supposed to engage everybody in innovation excellence?"

"That's the ideal," says Sofia, "but it's not always possible. We learned that it's hard to engage folks if you're changing or even eliminating their jobs. Although we're not planning to reduce staff, I suggest we get the reorganization out of the way first."

"Reorganize to what? I have no idea what we're supposed to look like—even less than I did a month ago."

"Sofia will help," calms Marcel. "She knows enough about Davanti now, and she's done this many times. You don't have to get it perfect right away—you can engage your folks later to get it right. Sofia can draft something up, and we'll look at it together. I don't expect it to be very difficult in your case."

"I'll trust you on that one, Marcel."

"And lesson #4: Build on your strengths and address your weaknesses and gaps with the right innovation excellence initiatives."

Junior shakes his head, and has another drink from his Brunello. "I feel like you've thrown me into the ocean and forgot to teach me how to swim."

Marcel chuckles and takes a sip from his Pinot Grigio. "I will include the swimming lessons when I send you the bill."

Junior chokes a bit on his wine, gives Marcel a stare, but says nothing.

***

After work on a cloudy Wednesday, a modest group of Davanti employees has gathered for the weekly bike outing in a light rain. Among them are Mo and Marco. Junior also shows up in a big rain jacket before they set out. He needs the exercise, but he's also hoping to hear what may be percolating among employees as the changes at Davanti are starting.

"Hello, Mo. Hello, Marco," says Junior.

"It's good to see you, Junior," says Marco.

"Beautiful day," says Mo sarcastically.

"Oh, it could be worse," replies Marco. "We're cyclists. There is no bad weather, only bad clothing."

"How do you like our chances for the Giro d'Italia," asks Mo of Junior and Marco. "We're off to a great start, no?"

"I'm expecting great things," says Junior. "I feel like the team has been on a roll. Everyone, from technicians to riders, is continuing to get better. I like the team's chances for a great finish."

"I'm going to agree with the boss on this one," chimes Marco. "Rossa has been a monster. I don't see him letting up in any way."

The other employees in the lot are beginning to pedal away.

"Well, let's ride like we're in the Giro," says Marco, and begins to bike away. The three sprint to catch up to the group and head toward the Alps.

***

The road is starting to flatten, and Rossa can now see the end of the grueling last ascent of the seventh stage of the Giro d'Italia. From there it will be an easy, short decent to the finish line in L'Aquila. Rossa is sure he'll wear the leader's jersey for another day, and, if things continue as they have, he may wear it through Verona in the 21st and final stage.

Rossa, the top rider on the Davanti team, is hugely popular in his native Italy. His team has fought off all attacks by archrivals so far, and he's built a 29-second advantage in the overall standings. The first seven stages of the Giro, since the start in Bologna, have brought the bikers down the western coast of Italy, across the country to San Giovanni Rotondo, and then back inland to L'Aquila, the capital of Abruzzo, near the Apennine summits and heavily damaged by an earthquake in 2009. Rossa is pleased with his performance and especially proud of his Davanti teammates, who have supported him with passion. His fans are gathered on hillsides, cheering and waving Italian flags in his honor.

Rossa is in a chase group behind the three stage leaders and just under two minutes ahead of the peloton. The three leaders do not concern Rossa—they are far behind in the overall standings. But clinging to his rear wheel are his two main rivals, currently second and third in the overall standings. He's confident of his position and expects to stand at the podium again today, putting on a fresh maglia rosa to thunderous applause amid a sea of Italian flags and supporters. As he shifts to a more comfortable gear, his daydream turns into a nightmare.

The chain on Rossa's Davanti bike has slid off. "Oh no," he screams. He cannot comprehend how this could have happened, and he's unable to get the chain back on while still on the bike. He jumps off and grabs the chain, yanking to get it back on the chainring. It doesn't budge; it's stuck in the derailleur now and he cannot rip it free. "$@%^&*?!)*#&," he rages.

The riders in his breakaway group speed away. Rossa drops the bike and throws up his arms, totally helpless while he looks for the support car, which he realizes is still stuck behind the peloton and over a minute away. No teammate is in sight with whom to trade bikes. "So much for the $@%^& lead," he yells. His head is now as red as a ripe tomato, and out of frustration he grabs his Davanti bike with both hands, raises it above his head, and throws it into the ditch in disgust—unaware that a cameraman on a motorcycle is filming the action, and his incident is shown live on most European TV stations, including the main Italian station.

When the peloton catches up to the blazing red Rossa, a teammate finally trades bikes with him. Rossa finishes the stage in the peloton, but he lost the leader's jersey and fell to fifth place in the overall standings.

***

The next day, the headline in the *National Italian Cycling* magazine reads, "Ultimo Nella Gara" (last in the race). An editorial in the magazine asks if this incident is indicative of Davanti losing its edge on the pro cycling circuit. The writer claims that many competitors have caught up to Davanti's technology, and he points to the vulnerability this has placed on the riders: The racers are squeezing fractions of a second from personal equipment tuning and custom components. Equipment these days has become so sensitive that anything and everything can break at any time, and races are too often decided by equipment performance—or the lack thereof—and not rider performance. The editorial concludes by wondering if the incident may have cost the most popular Italian rider his victory in this year's Giro and the Davanti team its best rider.

Late morning Junior walks into the Vicenza office of his friend Guido Marchioni, CEO of Coppimechanica. Guido and Junior have been friends ever since Guido took over as chairman a few years ago. Coppi has supplied parts to Davanti since Fausto Sr. was leading the firm, and it made the chain and derailleur on Rossa's doomed bike.

"Well, Guido, you're lucky the name of your company was not evident on the bike as it was laying in the ditch with the cameras focused on it."

"I agree, but you have my full support on this Fausto. The drivetrain is already in Germany with the company that was contracted for the tuning. They will let us know later today if the equipment had anything to do with Rossa's misfortune. Here at Coppimechanica, we watched the race video a hundred times. Do you know that Rossa activated both the front and rear shifters simultaneously under full chain load?"

"Isn't that common practice among riders?"

"It works 999 times out of 1,000, but we still tell them 1,000 times not to do it."

"Yes, I know. The equipment has become so terribly sensitive."

"The riders want it that way. They go for every nanosecond they can get, and there are rules and consequences that come with that."

The Coppi PR director knocks and sticks his head in the door: "You guys need to see this." He grabs a remote and turns on the TV in Guido's office. He finds a recording of an interview that Rossa gave to the Italian sports station only minutes ago, prior to the start of today's stage. In the interview, a contrite Rossa apologizes for his behavior and apologizes to his sponsor and his team. "I made the mistake that cost me the leader position in the tour. We've got great equipment with Davanti, and I promise our fans that there are enough stages left for me to recover. I will be the most aggressive rider every day until the end of the race. I know I can still win it."

"Well, that helps, but the damage is still done," says Junior.

"Maybe that editorial writer was correct after all," suggests Guido. "Maybe we're pushing the limit of our equipment too much."

"Maybe we will get race rules one day about that."

"Or maybe we, the manufacturers, should write our own rules."

"That will be a long time coming."

"Yes. Until then, let me get you some lunch."

Junior and Guido leave the Coppi headquarters and walk across the street to a contemporary, casual eatery. They each have a light lunch of an Italian-style niçoise salad with sparkling water; both have busy afternoons, and Junior has an hour drive back to Fumane. They finish with espressos and, as the waiter arrives with the check, Junior changes the topic from Rossa to Darvin.

"Talking about pushing the limits of our equipment, how is the new drivetrain project coming? We sure seem to do a lot of testing for it."

"Oh, we're getting ready to launch it next season. Thanks for all the help. It turns out it needs no frame modifications after all, so it will be widely available . . ."

"Widely available to whom?"

"To all bike manufacturers."

"Seriously? I was hoping for a little exclusivity for all our efforts."

"Well, I will make sure we give you an appropriate deal. It's the least I can do for our friends at Davanti. And you'll certainly get first notice of the release date so you can have your products ready to go."

"That's better than nothing, I guess," says a glum Junior.

***

On the drive back from Vincenza, Junior hardly notices the countryside, lush with ripening vineyards and other crops taking off in the late-May warmth; all he can think about is Rossa and Darvin. Junior calls Monica Totti from his car. Monica works for an Italian communications company, specializing in sports, and she has been handling all of Davanti's PR duties for the last 10 years.

"Fausto Davanti, I was expecting your call today."

"Well, I guess you, like everyone else, saw the news."

"He is called 'Testa Rossa' for a reason. But at least he apologized today and admitted his mistake."

"Yes, it was good to see that. So I just had a meeting with Guido Marchioni from Coppimechanica, and we talked about Rossa and saw the recent video. Can you write something from both Davanti and Coppi, thanking Rossa for his apology and wishing him good luck in the remainder of the Giro?"

"No problem, but since he admitted it was not Davanti's or Coppi's fault, shouldn't we throw 'Ultimo Nella Gara' back in the journalist's face? He was wrong to blame the bike—even if he was right about the problems the racers are experiencing."

"I've got no animosity toward the journalist or the magazine. Readers figure that stuff out by themselves. I like to take the high road: I just want to repeat that Rossa admitted his mistake, publicly absolve his behavior, and let our fans know that he—and Davanti—are still a contender in the Giro d' Italia, regardless of what anyone says or writes."

"Very good, Fausto. You will have my draft when you get back to the office."

***

At the end of his busy day, Junior sits quietly at his desk. He stares at this father's portrait. One more task before he heads home. He calls to Anna and asks her to get Emilio. A few minutes later, Emilio walks in.

"Emilio, please, have a seat." Emilio slides into a chair across from Junior's desk. He's not sure what to expect. Could it be about Rossa and the Giro? Is it about his objectives and strategy stuff, which he still has not given to Junior?

"Emilio, I'd like to have a copy of the agreement we have with Coppi for the Darvin project?"

Emilio stares back at Junior for a moment, glances around the room, and stands. "Pardon me."

***

Junior is usually one of the first to Davanti headquarters each day, and this morning is no different. The sun has barely risen when he's greeted at the door by security.

"Good morning, Mr. Davanti."

"Good morning, Gus. Have a good day."

He walks to his office and notices lights on in Emilio's office as well as Anika's. When he enters his office, he sees a folder on his desk. "Ah, the Coppi contract," he thinks. Junior opens the folder and finds a single piece of paper: Emilio's resignation letter. His VP is apologetic for the "misunderstanding" regarding the Darvin project and for any embarrassment his behavior has caused for Junior and Davanti.

Junior sits down, reads the letter again, and opens his laptop to see if there is any other surprising news to start his day. Amid dozens of email, he finds nothing unusual, and walks to the cafeteria for a coffee. As he passes Emilio's office, he sees boxes piled on the VP's desk. Farther down the hall, he passes Anika's office. The door is closed, but he can see her talking with Emilio. Junior considers going in, but something tells him that he should let this take its course.

By 10:00 am, Emilio has left the building. Soon thereafter, Anika stops by and explains that Emilio has officially resigned. She says he seemed quite comfortable and content with his decision, and chose not to leave any contact information. "I am pretty sure he's already deployed his golden parachute, and I have a hunch where he will land."

Notes

1. *Ratatouille*, produced by Brad Lewis (2007: Walt Disney Pictures and Pixar Animation).
2. Arnoud Herremans, *LPPDE 2016 North America*, Philadelphia, 2016.

Chapter 10

New Way of Working

The Volta team is talking about the experience at Fusilli as well as Emilio's exit as they wait for Sofia. The news of Emilio spread instantly through Davanti and has been the talk of the day. The team also is having some fun with the agenda for today's meeting: *SWOT.*

"So when will we get the riot gear?" asks Gina.

"I've always wanted to be on a SWAT team," says Marco.

Sofia enters the room, hears the comments, and moves toward a flipchart. "Sorry folks, but there'll be no law enforcement action today. She spells out the acronym and what it represents:

- Strengths
- Weaknesses
- Opportunities
- Threats

Everyone looks disappointed. "Where's the fun in that?" asks Mo. "A real SWAT mission would have been much more exciting. But, then again, I don't know what a SWOT mission is."

"That's actually a good lead-in. I was just going to explain why I like to do this exercise at this period of the innovation excellence journey: In a major transformation, like the one Davanti is about to embark on, there really is no tried-and-true recipe for what to do. Every company is different, and the worst thing a company can do is to try to emulate another company. I know you were all impressed with Fusilli, but Davanti is not Fusilli."

"You can say that again," says Rene Noce, a procurement manager on the team. "And food is more popular in Italy than bicycles."

Sofia gives him a glance, and then continues: "There is no 'one size fits all' for an innovation initiative. For example with lean, so many companies tried to blindly imitate Toyota. But in doing so, they sometimes trade what they're good at for the Toyota tools as well as the Japanese terms. Years later—after not getting the results they'd hoped for—they realize that their company wasn't making cars and their culture wasn't Toyota's culture. Many executives are then sorry that they threw out a lot of their own best practices in favor of Toyota versions. Like most other companies, Davanti has its own strengths that we should continue to leverage. And they won't necessarily conflict with innovation excellence and the new principles we'll apply to overcome Davanti weaknesses, exploit opportunities, and shield the company from competitive threats."

Everyone nods in agreement.

DOI: 10.4324/9781003231837-10

"So, first, what do you think are the strengths of Davanti?" Sofia waves Marco toward the flip-chart. "Anyone? Marco will record the Davanti strengths." As Marco gets up, he flexes his bicep to illustrate the category.

The team members proudly rattle off a long list of Davanti strengths as Marco tries to keep up. The strengths are as overarching as "HQ location" and as detailed as "pre-race tuneup technicians." Marco eventually groups similar ideas into the following buckets:

- Safety, quality, high-performance culture
- Experience and knowledge about bicycles
- Excellent people/talent with good skills, especially hands-on experience
- Camaraderie and loyalty
- Cycling race performance and enthusiasm for the sport
- Lean manufacturing plant and principles (ideas called out by Giovanni from manufacturing)
- Supplier management and collaboration (Rene from supply chain provided a range of best practices)

Marco points to the board, bows, and then returns to his seat, after which Sofia asks Mo to take over the flipchart and record weaknesses. He stands, and pulls his bicep downward, mocking Marco's motion. The team members take a bit more time, carefully considering their answers. Eventually a list begins to grow, with ideas grouped to the following:

- Lack of product diversity/stuck in a rut
- Anti-innovation culture
- Getting things done/delivering on time
- Launch panics and shortcuts
- Arrogance, NIH (not invented here) syndrome
- Super slow and overly bureaucratic
- Too many changes and reworks

The last bucket gets the group to bickering: Giovanni accuses R&D of making unnecessary and costly late changes to products, and Gina and Mo counter that manufacturing is too rigid in their work habits to accommodate necessary innovation. Marco adds that both functions make it difficult to develop a cohesive marketing strategy for new products because they often don't know precise product cost until it comes out of manufacturing. The rigid viewpoints and the lack of respect for each other's thinking remind Sofia of her interactions with the leadership team; leader attitudes have clearly been embraced by their staffs.

"OK, OK, I think we've got the weaknesses adequately addressed," says Sofia loudly. "Although we might want to take 'Camaraderie' off the strength list after this discussion. . . . Let's talk about opportunities. What are the circumstances or moments that can give Davanti a competitive advantage? Stella, would you please write these out?" Stella makes no effort to mimic Marco or Mo's behavior as she moves to the flipchart. The team calls out their thoughts:

- Win all the big races every year
- Expand carbon know-how into other fields (medical devices, aerospace, fitness industry, other sports)
- New ways of marketing bicycles
- Other lines of bikes (mountain, electric bikes, scooters)

- Services related to the cycling sport
- Licensing other product lines like clothing and components

"Excellent list of opportunities. Nice work. OK, Charles, how about you take over and list the threats."

"It figures that someone from finance would deal with the threats," jokes Luca.

"You all look like a threat to me," replies Charles as he gets ready to write:

- Best racers switch to other bike manufacturers
- Competition surpassing Davanti (racing performance, sales, brand awareness, etc.)
- Reaching limits of carbon fiber-reinforced bike technology and no technologies to follow
- Increasing customer demands and complaints
- All eggs in one basket
- Diminishing financial returns

After a minute of quiet, Sofia prods the group. "Really? That's it? Are any of you worried about the future of the company? About your jobs with Davanti? About keeping a job in northern Italy?"

The looks on their faces say, "No," they've never considered those as threats. "Should we?" asks Gina. "Do you know something we don't?"

"No. Just surprised it wasn't mentioned."

"So, Sofia, what will *you* do about the weaknesses and the threats?" asks Luca.

"Me?"

"Well, that's why you're here, right? To turn this all around. Fix our weaknesses. Help us turn away threats."

"Not quite. I'm here to engage all you and your colleagues in a program to capitalize on strengths and opportunities, overcome weaknesses, and defeat the threats. Every action we take going forward should address one, if not all, of the items we just put on the board."

The team is quiet.

"To wrap this up, I'd like a volunteer to type these up. We'll review them from time to time and adjust as needed."

The team now recognizes that they are, indeed, on a mission.

***

"Junior, I'm happy you always have time for me," greets Sofia, stepping into the CEO's office. She looks at the portrait of Fausto Sr., and it's as if she's looking at a slightly older Junior.

"It would be a big mistake to ignore you, Sofia. I like what you've started here. When I got your email about Emilio's replacement, I cancelled the meeting with my VPs about the Primo Veloce project."

"The Primo Veloce project?"

"It's our latest and greatest. A new bike that should really get the attention of amateur racers. Or so we hope."

"Then why did you cancel the meeting? Am I more important than your major project?"

"Oh, no. . . . I mean, yes, I guess. In reality, I am tired of these meetings. I'm like a judge in a court of law: they all plead their case and then I must rule. But usually I just calm them down and try to make a decision that makes everybody happy. It's always the same. Come to think of it, I think I've made many bad decisions in the past by putting their happiness and conflict avoidance ahead of company revenues."

"Are you asking for my help with the PS project?" Sofia asks anxiously, worried that it's one more task on a growing list of assignments.

"No, no. That's under control as best as can be for now. Let's talk about Emilio's replacement."

"Who did you have in mind? Who is on your succession plan?"

By now, Sofia is used to Junior's deer-in-the-headlights look. "He must still think I'm from another planet," she wonders. But she also knows that he has started to trust her.

"I take it you have no succession plan. Another one for your to-do list, but let's embark on that after the reorganization."

"So do we reorganize first, or should we replace Emilio right away? We need to fill that role quickly."

"I agree, Junior, so who do you have in mind?"

Junior shakes his head and bites his cheek. "I should have seen this coming. Emilio never seemed to like you. I think his replacement should align with what you're trying to accomplish. R&D is certainly the key driver in your initiative, right?"

"It is not *my* initiative nor is it just an *initiative*. It is a *Davanti transformation*. Please remember this as you discuss it with employees. But you are correct. Emilio's successor will play one of the most critical roles, besides you, of course. Are you asking for my recommendation?"

"I guess I am."

"I recommend Ricardo Capace for the role."

"He hasn't been here very long. Please convince me that he's the right choice."

"I've had a chance to work a little with Ricardo. He's on the Volta team. He's also been here long enough to have developed a good level of experience with bike technology. But I'm most impressed with the way he engages people, and, most importantly, he seems great at collaborating with the rest of your organization. And if it weren't for Ricardo, the chainless-drive idea might still be locked away in Mo's head or PowerPoint slides; he helped Mo keep it alive."

"Go on. I'm listening."

"I think most people here didn't realize it, with the exception of Anika and maybe Emilio, his *former* boss, but Ricardo actually has the right background for what we're trying to accomplish. He graduated from ETH[1] with a master's degree in ME. Then he got an MBA from the EPFL,[2] where he specialized in research and innovation management. Then for 12 years he worked for one of the medical industry leaders in lean product development."

"That's all very new to me. How did he end up here?"

"I asked him that only recently when I was walking through his area: His wife took a position as department head in a local hospital; she's a physician. To support his wife's career, they moved their family here. Ricardo needed a job as an engineer, and Davanti had an open position that accommodated him, at least temporarily. He was probably a little overqualified. You should know that Ricardo saw Davanti as a transition. He wasn't happy with Emilio's management, and he would have left for the first reasonable opportunity. He's not only the right person—but if he weren't promoted, you'd also be filling his role as an engineering supervisor anyway."

"So you're telling me we had the right person all along and didn't even know it."

"Davanti has many right people that nobody knows about. We'll find more Ricardos, but, for now, I guess we're just very lucky. And when you're lucky, you just take what you get and run with it."

"Well, then let's run with Ricardo. You've convinced me. Please tell Anika to get this set up quickly. I'd like to present the offer to Ricardo today, if possible. And let me know of anything I can do to get him up to speed in his new role."

"Ricardo will be pleased."

"And one more thing, Sofia. Marcel suggested that you draft a proposal for the pending Davanti reorganization. I look forward to seeing that."

"I've given it some thought. I don't think it will be very difficult. But I'd like Marcel to explain the rationale to you first, if that's OK?"

"Absolutely. It's always enjoyable, enlightening—and humbling—spending time with Marcel."

***

Sofia walks into Anika's office with a cappuccino in each hand.

"You know how to get on my good side," says Anika.

"I try."

"By the way, based on what you've told me, I pulled together Ricardo's promotion package and gave it to Junior. His assistant Anna is setting up a meeting as we speak."

"Thank you," says Sofia as she hands a drink to Anika and sits. "I have another subject I'd like to discuss. . . . Please tell me how Davanti has done change management in the past?"

"Well, as I mentioned, Junior comes up with something, we wait until it blows over, and then it's back to business as usual," says Anika half-jokingly. "Something tells me it's going to be different this time."

"It will. And given your answer, let me ask in a different way: What *should* change management look like at Davanti?"

"Thanks for asking my thoughts. I learned a lot about change management from my former employer, but I've never really had an opportunity to apply it here. Many people think change management is just corporate-speak for managing a major project, a single initiative, like implementing a new software system. But that's just project management. Good change management is so much more, and so much more interesting. It's about *people*, process, and culture—not just about Gantt charts and tools. In many organizations, engineers and other professionals lead such transformations, and they're ill prepared for the challenges of engaging people and transforming a culture. Of course, we're loaded with engineers here."

"Well said. I've seen many transformations fail because people didn't understand what you just explained."

"I've seen it as well. Good change management starts with a clear objective and direction from the top—and we're working with Junior on that. And you created a team of experts, which also is necessary. What is it called again, 'Volta,' or something like that? And I assume you're leading the transformation, at least for now. Would you mind if I sit in on your meetings—only to learn? And then as soon as I know enough, I can help you appoint a Davanti coleader to work with you, if that's OK."

"You're welcome to join Volta, but not as an observer. As a contributor. And please help me groom my successor. This will be much more sustainable with an *internal* leader who has the respect of the Davanti associates. So what's the next step in the change-management process?"

"Leadership support, I guess. We have that from some. That, too, is typical; the others will follow where the rest is going. I think we just got rid of our biggest opponent. And then the next step is communication. Not a one-time communication: Junior started that, and other leaders are starting to speak more regularly with associates. And, of course, the most important element: training. We've told associates why we're doing this, and now we must give them the necessary training so that they can understand *how* to do it—the principles that will be involved. That will engage them and enable them to shape the process and steps, especially those that affect them."

"Wow. Anika, you know this as well as I do. I assume you also were involved with the lean transformation in the plant."

"To the extent possible from Fumane."

"I believe that transformations are an 'inside-out' change. When associates know why we do this, when they understand what is in it for them, and when they know how to contribute, they'll drive it—not because they were told to do it but because they want to do it. And, of course, if they build it, they'll want to sustain it as well."

"Yes, I could not agree more."

***

While Sofia and Anika are discussing how to change Davanti's culture, Junior is taking action to change the state of R&D in the company. Junior stands when he hears Ricardo greet Anna outside his office and then welcomes him in: "Ricardo, hello, please have a seat."

Ricardo looks comfortable but cautious. As an R&D manager, he'd never been to Junior's office but knows something is about to happen.

Junior hands him a folder labeled, "Ricardo Capace, R&D Director," and asks him to open it: "We want you to lead Davanti R&D. From what I've learned, you are precisely the person to do it. This summarizes what you'll want to know about the position. Please take a moment to look it over."

Ricardo looks carefully at the two enclosed pages and sees that it's a highly competitive offer; when Emilio was in charge, Ricardo had received a few external offers, but nothing close to this. "First, it's generous, Mr. Davanti. Second, I very much want to lead Davanti's R&D department and transform how we innovate. I certainly accept this promotion in principle, but, if I may, I'd like to speak with my wife and get back to you and Anika in the morning."

"Absolutely. Take the time you need. And please, call me 'Junior.'"

"Certainly, Mr. Davanti. Uh, I mean, Junior. That may take some getting used to."

***

As Sofia and Anika continue to talk about change management, their discussion shifts to leadership. "Leadership support alone won't make this happen," Sofia explains. "Leaders also have to change, or the culture change won't happen. Their behaviors set the example for the rest to follow. It will take time, which is why we've got to start now."

"What do you suggest?"

"It's all part of training. You're familiar with what psychologists call 'cognitive dissonance.' I find it useful when engaging and transforming leaders."

"I remember it as the conflict in the brain between beliefs and behaviors. Right? How do you use that to change leaders?"

"The common thinking is that you train, indoctrinate, and lecture people so they change their beliefs—and when they change beliefs, they will change their behaviors accordingly. In our case, if they believe the principles of innovation excellence will work, they'll support the principles and eventually act accordingly."

"Yeah, that's how I learned it. It's why we train so much."

"Here's the shocker. It actually works the other way around: change behaviors and the beliefs will follow. I know this sounds backward, but it's worked for me many times."

"Really? How do you suggest we go about it? Walk behind the leaders and do situational coaching when they're not behaving how we want?"

"There will be coaching, but we'll start with a training session called, 'What leaders should know about innovation excellence.' It describes the reasons companies embark on a program like this, shows results that leading companies achieve, and sets reasonable expectations for what can be achieved at Davanti. It also explains key principles and illustrates them with examples and short exercises and simulations. The session ends with what is expected of leaders to make the initiative successful. All principles covered will suggest ideal behaviors we want from the leaders."

"I'll get that training planned for next week, but that just seems like more lectures. How will it affect their behaviors?"

"Once the leaders know the basics, we start training associates—aka 'Innovation Excellence Bootcamp' or 'Innovation Excellence 101.' And we ask each leader to teach a small piece of the bootcamp. As they teach the principles, they begin to practice what they teach and change their behaviors. It's difficult to teach something that you don't practice yourself. Eventually you see their beliefs changing."

"Hmmph. And that really works?"

"With your help we can make it work, Anika. I'll need your help in explaining to the leaders why we need them to do the teaching as well as coaching them about their new tasks. And after the training, we'll continue coaching them and look for additional ways for them to be involved. Of course, some will take more coaching than others."

"What about Junior?"

"He's part of it. Marcel made that clear to him."

"I'm surprised but pleased to hear that."

"How else can I help you get the training underway?"

"I think I understand the content needed from the training program from the information you provided: innovation, lean principles, collaboration, respect for people, and topics like that. I think that's a good start, and not so technical that it will worry the executives. It also lines up with Volta's SWOT analysis that you shared with me."

"Good. Anything else?"

"I believe in just-in-time training—it should be situational, shortly before people will use what they learn. Typically, I like to start with overviews, principles, etc. for everybody, and then do the deeper dives as they get engaged in different programs and activities. Sometimes we have to repeat certain parts, but less so than with other approaches."

Sofia nods in agreement: "We'll advance from mindset to skillset and then to toolset. Start with the reasons why we do it, follow up with principles, and then identify and deploy the tools they need. Many companies make the mistake of teaching the tools first. Associates can't determine where to use them and quickly lose interest."

"Sofia, I want this to work, but I also want people to be interested in learning. I want the training to be engaging and fun—not lectures, endless pages of internet reading, PowerPoint presentations. We used a lot of simulations, activities, interactions, and games in the plant. People learned as much from each other as they did from the instructors."

"Excellent. I couldn't agree more. Let's also include a class on managing people in a lean, innovative organization and make it appropriate for both leaders and associates. It reminds leaders of desired behaviors and shows associates what to expect."

"I'm surprised how much we agree. I guess you can say I'm shocked. But I'm glad we do. . . . Unless you have a better suggestion, I'll review training programs available with Ricardo, and then make the initial purchases. I'll also ask Ricardo to brief leaders on the programs prior to the classes to put them at ease."

"That sounds like an awesome plan, Anika."

"Thanks. But, as you know, change management is more than training. At the appropriate time let's talk about the next steps, especially that of engaging all the associates."

"We will do that," concludes Sofia, glancing at her watch. "Now, if you'll excuse me, I've got to run. Ciao."

"Ciao."

***

For 10 minutes, Junior has watched three VPs in his office argue back and forth about Davanti's upcoming bike launches, the new Primo Veloce (PV) amateur racing line and redesigned Primo Sempre (PS) pro line. He hasn't so much as said a word, even when they ask for his thoughts or pose a question.

"We need the replacement of our current amateur PV line as soon as possible," says Joe, VP marketing.

"We have at least two lines in that space already," counters Leandro, VP supply chain. "Why can't we just integrate PV improvements into one of those lines?"

"We can't just put the new 'PV' name on an old, tired line and expect better NPV," says Stephano, VP finance. "Junior, please, your thoughts."

Junior looks at the three VPs and rolls his eyes. "Here we go again," he says under his breath. "Clearly the collaboration exercise has not sunk in yet."

Joe chimes in before Junior can answer, "We cannot . . ."

"Enough," says Junior, rising out of his chair. "I'm now going to leave my office and close the door. When I'm gone, put an end to this by understanding each other's viewpoints. Then respect each other and assume everybody has a positive intent behind their position. And then I want you to start helping each other. Got it?"

The VPs are speechless.

"I'll ask Anna to make sure you don't leave until you've figured this out. *Let the customer be your judge, and the company goals your guide.* And please spread the word—this is how we'll work from now on!" As Junior leaves his desk, he remembers: "Oh, and don't take too long, I need my office back soon."

Notes

1. Eidgenössische Technische Hochschule Zürich, Switzerland.
2. École Polytechnique Fédérale de Lausanne, Switzerland.

Chapter 11

A New Organization

Marcel sticks his head into Junior's office. "Fausto, this doesn't look much different from the last time I was here. How long ago was that? You had a celebration of some kind, and I came for a reception. The mayor and the local dignitaries were here. It must have been an anniversary."

Junior waves Marcel in and stands to greet him. "Come in. Yes, it was our 50th anniversary—that was more than 10 years ago. Thanks for coming out today. I don't know what we would do without your help and, of course, the help of Sofia."

"Always glad to help an old friend. But remember, we only do the coaching. You have to lead the initiative, and *you* and your associates hold the key to its success."

"Yes, of course. I get it. I really do now. . . . Can I get you anything before we head to the conference room and meet up with Sofia?"

"No, no, I'm fine. Thanks. Let's get going."

The two walk down the hall and into the Davanti conference room. Sofia waves them in and asks, "Are we ready to get to the theme of today's meeting: the best organization for Davanti?"

"Yes, yes, please begin," says Junior.

Sofia briefly covers the transformation activities that have gotten underway within Davanti—including creation of the vision and objectives, the SWOT analysis, and a portfolio analysis. She points to posters that show the progress made and sets the stage for today's discussion. The three stand, looking from one poster to the next.

"I've been looking forward to the SWOT analysis—sort of," says Junior. "I'm especially concerned about the weaknesses."

"We'll get to those," says Marcel. "But know that you get better returns by first focusing on your strengths. You want to quickly capitalize on your strengths, which will be the fastest way to generate more innovative products, services, licenses, spin-offs, etc., and more revenue, of course. And innovation excellence can really enhance strengths and restrain leaders from thinking they need to start over with entirely new principles, systems, and practices."

Sofia summarizes the strengths and notices the pride on Junior's face. "Finally," he thinks, "Marcel hears something good about Davanti." But his face quickly changes as Sofia talks through an extensive list of weaknesses.

"You can see for yourself; our list of weaknesses is just as impressive as our list of strengths," cautions Sofia.

"It always is," says Marcel calmly. "Don't be too upset by that. You've taken the first step to do something about them. For me, the biggest weakness or waste in a company is to not recognize

DOI: 10.4324/9781003231837-11

or do anything about your weaknesses. I've made a lot of money buying such companies. I turn them into real winners by helping them bank on their strengths and turn around their weaknesses. Right, Sofia?"

"Frequently, Marcel. I'd say you have a Midas touch if I didn't know how much hard work and dedication you put into it."

"And you as well, Sofia, which is why you're at Davanti," says Marcel.

Sofia smiles and then summarizes the opportunities and threats. After a few questions, Marcel gives Junior a confident nod: "Everything you do from here on out—organization, goals, strategy—should be designed to leverage Davanti's strengths, address gaps and weaknesses, and/ or capitalize on opportunities while you keep an eye on your threats."

"That will happen," says Junior confidently.

"I know your objectives, and it's not hard for me to predict your goals," says Marcel. "I now know your strengths, weaknesses, etc. It's all very similar to what I've seen in some of our acquisitions, so I have a very good idea what innovation excellence will do for you. So let's take a look at the organization Sofia recommends."

Sofia and Marcel talk quietly in front of a flip chart; the first page is blank. He asks her a few questions, and she replies with one-word answers that are cryptic to Junior.

"Will you include me in your discussion soon?" asks Junior.

Marcel smiles when Sofia tears the blank page from the flip chart, revealing something that to Junior doesn't look at all like an org chart. After giving it a good look, Marcel likes what he sees: "This will help Davanti accomplish what it needs to do. I think Sofia has Davanti figured out pretty well."

"Probably better than me," says Junior, with an uneasy look on his face as he keeps staring at the chart before him.

"Let me start by saying that the changes in personnel and positions are minor," says Sofia. Junior exhales and appears a little more at ease.

"But before we talk about the new organization, let me explain how you ended up with the organization you currently have," says Marcel.

"It's the one we've always had," says Junior, "since my father started the company."

"Yes. Your current organization is largely functional, and that was typical for traditional companies back then and still is today. Functions date all the way back to universities of the Middle Ages, starting with Bologna,[1] which organized their teaching by specialties or disciplines. When industry started many hundred years later, they recruited from universities and so, naturally, followed the same pattern. A functional organization served them well and it allowed them to generate specialized knowledge—like engineering, finance—and manage that knowledge effectively. And it continues today when experienced functional professionals teach new employees."

"So what's that got to do with Davanti?"

"Things have changed, Junior. Products are launched today far more rapidly, and their complexity demands involvement from many different disciplines over their lifecycle: design, manufacturing, distribution, etc. But as you may know, every function sees the product or the project through its own lens and culture, and leadership reinforces that behavior by rewarding people for their functional contribution and personal accomplishments—not for their collaboration and efforts to reward the customer. And if something goes wrong, everybody blames everybody else, and you can never understand what the real problem is."

Junior listens intently to his friend and nods in agreement. "Yes. That's pretty much how it's been working here. Go on. I think we're getting somewhere."

"A product or service can only be successful today if all functions focus on creating the best possible customer value regardless of functional or personal priorities."

"Agreed," responds Junior. "I know enough about lean to know that everything is focused on creating value for the customer."

"In your case it's relatively easy," says Marcel. "You really only need one product director or value-stream leader at the moment. But I hope you create a few additional value streams down the road, and then each would have dedicated directors—this is like the position that Colette, whom we met at Fusilli, holds. The product directors are responsible for the P or L of their value streams from design to manufacturing and sales. They 'buy' services from the functions. For example, they pay for R&D, contract out production to your manufacturing organization, they pay for financial forecasts and analysis, etc. This also serves as an incentive for all the functions to be competitive with outsourced options."

"You know, Marcel, we do outsource some services."

"Of course. I agree with your decision to outsource IT, legal, and PR because of the relatively low volume of work required. But the others—finance, manufacturing, sales, marketing, supply chain, R&D, HR—should feel that they need to compete for business as well. One day, you may outsource more or maybe less . . . but that's a subject for another day."

Marcel pauses. "Where was I? Oh, yes. Today your functions train people, collect and manage knowledge, set standards. Right? And they must continue to do that."

Junior nods.

"In an innovation excellence organization, full- and part-time staff in the functions also are assigned to support value-stream directors and project managers."

Marcel points at a matrix drawing on the flip chart. Value streams and the new product projects within them run horizontally, and functions are represented vertically.

"You see why we call it a 'matrix,'" adds Sofia.

"I get it now," says Junior. "It makes sense, especially for product work. But not all our work is managing products. We have other crossfunctional work—like the lean transformation Sofia is managing or the implementation of the new corporate computer system. How are those managed in the matrix?"

"Great observation, Junior," says Sofia. "Those activities are projects as well." She traces her finger across the horizontal line "Large Projects" on the matrix. "Large projects work the same way,

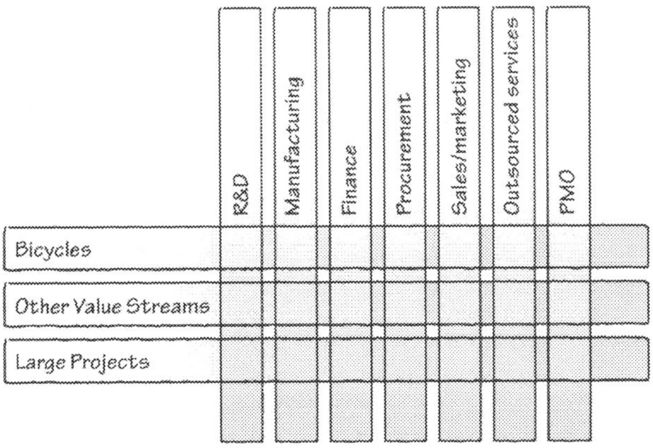

Figure 11.1 Davanti Organizational Matrix.

except they may be smaller in scope, shorter than a product-line project, and managed by a project manager rather than a value-stream director."

"We already have project managers at Davanti."

"Yes, but they report to a function, and they'll do what's best for the function," says Sofia. "We recommend that project management *itself* be a function, like finance or sales, to ensure Davanti develops knowledge and talent around project management. The PM function would then be responsible for project management knowledge and standards and assign project managers as needed. And, of course, they provide the same training and coaching to the project managers that functions provide to their staffs." Sofia points to the vertical line on the matrix chart titled "PMO" for project management office.

"Let me get this straight: people who work in a matrix work for *two* bosses?" asks Junior.

"Correct, Fausto," says Marcel. "They find out *what* to work on from their product director or project manager. The function they also report to develops the standards on *how* that work is done. The functions are responsible for the people and talent, and the project managers control the budget."

"We primarily pay based on performance. How would that work?"

"Performance may still be the primary way to evaluate staff, Fausto. Keep that up. But with a matrix organization, you'll want to get feedback from both superiors and maybe other staff with whom an individual works. And you may want to add a few other criteria to promote desired behaviors, things like collaboration and respect for people. Sofia can take your HR director to Fusilli to observe how it's done there. I'm confident you'll develop an appropriate system for Davanti."

"I can see this working here," considers Junior. "It's different, but not a radical shift."

"But let's not forget, Junior, it will take cultural adjustments and changes in behaviors to make it work, including your own," counsels Marcel. "That's the hard part compared to implementing new processes."

"We're already making those adjustments," responds Junior. "I think Sofia would agree. . . . Thank you, Sofia. Informative as always. So let's get on with the reorganization. So what do I do tomorrow?"

"Sofia has a list of tasks that she'll help you with—like picking the right people for the product director or the director of the project management office. And you may want to think about consolidating a few functions when you reassign folks. After you identified the right people, I suggest you get everybody directly affected by the reorganization in a room, *you* personally explain why *you* chose this organization, and *you* lay out *your* expectations. And don't count on Sofia to help you out; she won't be at that meeting. Maybe you can also share the business trends and results from the SWOT analysis to explain *why* you chose this organization. You'll need to get their buy-in for the new organization, since it will be the vehicle to execute your strategy and achieve your goals."

"I'm confident I can handle this."

"And please listen to comments and feedback. You may get a few ideas to fine-tune the organization. Sofia will keep a close eye on things for a few weeks. The personnel changes likely won't upset the apple cart, but it will take people some time to get adjusted to working in a matrix. There will be a few problems, but I think you can solve them as they arise."

"What if they tell me that they don't like the organization? People at Davanti won't be shy. To what extent should I try to accommodate them?"

"The key is that you give them a chance to voice their opinions, express concerns, and make suggestions, which may be very valid. Make sure you listen to all of them. If you get good ideas, just implement them. If you get resistance, listen and acknowledge their objections, but don't get bogged down in long discussions and don't make promises and commitments to feedback that you disagree with."

"Marcel, since you keep telling me that R&D drives the bus to successful new products, how does R&D fit into this? What's different?"

"First, congratulations on selecting a new leader. It sounds like he understands everything you're trying to do, especially with R&D."

"Again, I thank Sofia for that find."

"The organization of your R&D function could mimic your corporate organization. Every project has a project manager, who is responsible for budget, deliverables, managing the team, etc. Those managers will report to the product director as well as R&D. I'm guessing your new manager will understand this structure."

"We'll discuss the new set up with Ricardo soon," says Sofia. "But I, too, have a feeling it will be familiar to him."

"Well, how do I thank you Marcel for all of this. It all makes so much sense that I can't understand why we didn't come up with this by ourselves years ago."

"You're not alone, Fausto. Executives are too busy solving day-to-day problems that they rarely find the time to focus on what really matters."

"Marcel, how can I repay you?"

"I will start billing you for Sofia's time," says Marcel. "And maybe one day you'll let me partner with you on one of your new value-stream startups—I'll tell you when I see the right one."

"I didn't know I was doing startups. I'm not even sure what they are. But if I've got one, you are in, my friend."

Junior and Sofia walk Marcel out of the conference room and out to his car. They see him off, and Junior turns to Sofia: "Let's talk tomorrow so we can start putting names with the matrix. No time to waste."

***

Mo joins Ricardo in Sofia's office. She had asked for an update on Mo's project and wanted to know the next steps they were planning. The two walk in together, chatting about the latest racing gossip, and see Sofia once again staring at all of the bikes in the Davanti lot.

"Is your bike out there?" asks Mo.

"No, I'm not quite up to riding to work," Sofia says. "Maybe by the end of the season."

"I'll keep asking."

"So, Mo, I think you did an excellent job answering the most critical question on your project," says Sofia. "Your use of the Chainbuster test left no doubt about the strength of the device."

"Even Emilio would have agreed," says Mo. "However, my heart was beating as hard as Karl's during the last ascent. And the added bonus was that Karl gave us an excellent idea to use the brake disc as the drive wheel."

"Yes, I think that is definitely worth taking a look at," encourages Ricardo. "That will save weight and make the design easier."

"So what is the next critical question?" asks Sofia. "And, Mo, understand that we're using your project as a pilot to develop a new creative process for Davanti, so we want to be thorough and document our steps."

"I thought you've used this process before?"

"Yes, at other companies. The same principles apply, but the work here is a little different, and we need to learn from the folks at Davanti what works best for them."

"OK, I'll remember that. I've been keeping good notes. So what's next?"

"Remember the conversation we had about building a house and the steps you go through. Well, just like that, every time we answer a question we stop, reassess, and pivot—or move to the next question until the risk is low enough to invest in the development of the technology."

"OK, I can see where we're going—the next most critical question," Mo pauses. "I can't decide between weight and friction. I think the two are somewhat related."

"I understand weight as a critical question. Nobody wants to drag extra weight up a hill. But tell me about friction," requests Sofia.

"With all the disadvantages associated with a bike chain, it has one huge advantage—it consumes very little energy. A well-lubricated and -tuned chain drivetrain (chain, chainring, derailleur, and cogs) consumes about 5 percent due to friction. But, of course, that can go up to 20 percent quickly if not properly maintained and greased."

Ricardo leans forward and asks, "So you want to make sure the direct drive is in that ballpark for friction losses?"

"Yes, but the prototype is far from it. This also is a very difficult question because we used a 'random' gear mechanism. A different mechanism could be better or worse. I'm afraid we'll only know if we start developing one with the right partner—that will take a lot of time and effort. But you keep telling me that you only learn if you try, so we need to try and learn."

"Looks like an opportunity for a small sprint team," says Sofia.

"I don't follow. You mean racing sprints."

"Sort of. So let's consider bike races. Since I've started watching races on TV, one thing that puzzles me is that sometimes the racers ride 200 kilometers at a measured pace and then sprint at maximum effort for the last kilometer or so to decide the winner. As far as I'm concerned, the same result could be accomplished if they raced only five or 10 kilometers, and then they could have five or more stages in a day and reduce the days of the Tour de France from 21 to 10."

"Whoa, no!" exclaims Mo. "Sofia, this lean stuff has gotten to you. Some things are better off not leaned out."

"I was being facetious about the five-kilometer stages, but not about the many focused and concentrated efforts we should look for at Davanti. I suggest we create a sprint team to help you with the friction question and maybe also with the weight question."

"So we sprint against each other?"

"No. You collaborate as a team with a focused, quick effort on each question: the sprint. The whole team is in a series of sprints together. Some people call these 'scrum cycles,' and the process is sometimes referred to as 'agile.' But since we are a bike company, after all, sprint seems appropriate. But the key principles are the same: how can we answer the friction and the weight questions as fast as possible with minimum effort?"

"OK, so how quickly can we pull together a team?"

"Maybe Serfino and Alexandra can help," says Ricardo. "The project they're working on just got canceled as we start to lean out the portfolio. Let's ask them."

"That would be great. We really only need to know if the friction and the weight of the direct-drive bike can be in the ballpark of a traditional race bike. Further improvements will be made if we decide to invest in its development."

"And you said friction and weight are *kind of related*. What do you mean?" asks Sofia.

"Yes, in the sense that if we reduce the weight, I think we'll also reduce the friction."

"I generally don't recommend combining critical questions," warns Sofia. "But because they're related, it seems to make sense to combine them. Please, give it a try."

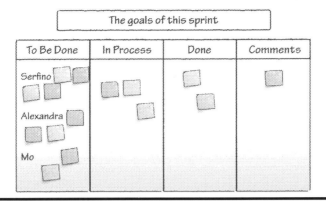

Figure 11.2   Sprint/Scrum Board.

"Anything else?" asks Ricardo.

Sofia walks up to the whiteboard and begins to draw.

"Sprint teams find this visual useful. It's a sprint board. Mo, you and your colleagues should consider using one as you investigate these two questions. The three of you will decide the goals for each sprint and how long it will take to get the answers you need. As you lay out the work that you need to do, you put every task on a sticky note, and you put all the notes under the 'To be done' column to start off."

"OK, so far," says Mo.

"Sprint teams like to meet every day for a few minutes in front of the board to discuss progress and plans for the day and move the notes as work progresses—first to 'In Process' and then to 'Done.' They also record obstacles or new challenges that come up and help each other. If needed, you all can meet with Ricardo every couple of days, as he may be able to remove any obstacles you encounter and help you to stay on track."

"And when all sticky notes are in the "Done" section?"

"Then your team makes one of the following recommendations:

- *Plan another sprint*—you may have made progress and learned new things, but you may not have fully answered the critical question.
- *Freeze the idea*—you cannot bring the weight and/or friction of the bike into the desired range and you may stop the work, at least for now.
- *Change direction*—maybe you'll determine that the current mechanism won't work, but you found a better idea to eliminate the chain.
- *Move to the next critical question*—since you've determined you can get weight and friction in line with a racing bike, it's time for the next critical question to be addressed."

"Who's the boss of this team?"

"Sprint teams are often self-directing. The boss is the objective you agree upon—determine if weight and friction can be brought into the acceptable range. Sometimes teams use rotating leadership, and there may be times where a team needs a designated leader because of the complexity and scope. But in this case, I'm sure you can collaborate with Alexandra and Serfino without a formal leader."

"Absolutely. We've all worked together before. Of course, we've never sprinted together before, but I'm sure we'll run fine."

***

Mo has followed the female amateur races closely online, but he finds no mention of Marie Vigneron in the results. Sitting at his desk after a long day, he gets the courage to send her a text: "Marie, how is the racing going? I don't see you in any standings?"

Mo gets up and walks around the office, wondering if he'll get a response. To his surprise, his phone pings within minutes.

"Been busy at work—latest assignment more difficult than expected. Not training like I wish."

"Hope you get a break and can race again."

"I won't miss the upcoming race in my hometown. Will you come support me?"

"Absolutely!"

"Thx. I'll send details."

***

As Junior heads out of the Davanti office, the early summer sun has almost set. The hills around Fumane glow orange. He sees a few bikes and cars still left in the lot, but most of the employees have gone for the day. He wishes he could have been relaxing on a patio somewhere all day, but he's pleased with the work that's been accomplished today inside of Davanti.

"It's beautiful, no?" comes a voice behind him.

He turns to see Sofia, also leaving after a long day. "Yes. We're fortunate to see this every day or at least on the days the weather is clear."

"Yes. . . . So, Junior, have you recovered from the reorganization shock?"

"More than recovered. I'm revitalized. I can't tell you how many times I heard my functional leaders argue about product issues and blame each other. Why didn't I think of a product leader? It creates ownership and limits the leverage that function leaders hold, and it forces them to focus on the product and the customer. I love it."

"Have you thought about individuals for those roles? Do you think you have the talent in Davanti, or do you want to go outside and hire somebody?"

"Good question, Sofia. I think we have the talent. You'll need to coach them up. I think it will be easier to teach a Davanti person about innovation excellence than teaching a person from the outside the ropes of running a bike business in the Davanti culture. Right?"

"I'm happy to help with the coaching. There are times to go outside, but I agree with an internal choice. So who did you have in mind?"

"I'd like to see Joe Bersaglio from marketing as the first product director. He's got a good perspective of the end-to-end product stream and certainly knows our customers. It seems natural."

"That sounds like a good choice."

"I'd also like to tweak our organization chart a bit: combine sales and marketing for now, especially given the new role for Joe. I think we also can combine supply chain and manufacturing, since they're already very much aligned on their functional targets. That would free up Leandro Nero, the VP of supply chain, to take over the new PMO function; he could report to me for now. He's been here for at least a decade and has had a lot of project management experience. And I was thinking about asking Marco Marrone to take Joe's old position as marketing leader; he would report to Claudia."

"That, too, sounds reasonable, Junior."

The sun has nearly set, and Junior realizes that Sofia probably wants to be on her way as does he. "I've got some other ideas, but I don't want to hold you up much longer. . . . Just one last thing. I plan to congratulate Ricardo for accepting the position, but I'd like to have a broader discussion with him about his role. Would you please join us for that?"

"Yes. Happy to do that. Please have Anna include me on the meeting notice."

"Thank you, Sofia. Enjoy your evening."

"You as well, Junior."

Note

1. University of Bologna, founded in 1088 and the oldest university in the world.

Chapter 12

New R&D Culture Emerges

Mo has met every morning with teammates Serfino and Alexandra for 10 to 15 minutes since he and Sofia discussed the sprint board. The three have tried to answer the two new critical questions of weight and friction. They now stand and review their sprint board, which is propped up on Mo's desk. Today, Friday, they're joined by Sofia and Ricardo.

At the top of the board is the sprint question: *Can a direct drive achieve the friction and weight targets of a chain drive?* They estimated 10 days to answer the question. They started with about 20 sticky notes in the "To do" column, estimating all were needed to answer the sprint question. Today, three days into the sprint, two of the tags have already reached the "Done" stage and six notes are in the "In Process" column.

"I got a bunch of tradeoff curves yesterday from a company in Japan," says Mo. "Not sure yet what to with them. After our meeting, I'll talk to staff there and try to understand what they mean and how we can use them."

"We dropped one vendor from China," says Serfino as he moves the corresponding note from "In Process" to "Done." "They're not interested in working with us on the project."

"I wish I had time to test some of the units from a US company as they suggested," says Alexandra. "But the timing is out of our scope. . . . But, Mo, tell me more about those tradeoff curves. My contact mentioned something similar and said he can model what we need if I can provide a few more parameters."

They go through several more tags and make some notes on the sprint board for followup.

"Looks like you're making good progress," says Ricardo. "Let me know if I can help you in any way."

"I know what happens if we can meet the targets for friction and weight," says Alexandra. "But what happens if we can't?"

"Well, then we'll either freeze the project or we pivot," says Ricardo.

"We're going to need a large freezer if you want at least 90 percent of projects to fail in this phase," says Alexandra. "Why not just cancel them?"

"Give or take, 90 percent is pretty accurate," recalls Sofia. "And virtual freezers hold a lot of projects. And we freeze the projects because some new solution or need may emerge later."

"How do you pivot then?" wonders Serfino.

"Consider everything you're learning as you seek answers," says Sofia. "So maybe the drive doesn't work for race bikes, but would it work on electric bikes? Pivot is just a different term for a change in direction."

"I'll let you get back to work," says Ricardo, looking at his watch. "You know where to find me."

DOI: 10.4324/9781003231837-12

"Yes, me as well," says Sofia. "Let me know if I can help."

***

Mo and Ricardo are in the office on Saturday morning, both landing in the cafeteria to jumpstart with a cup of coffee.

"Did you go home, Ricardo, or were you here all night?" jokes Mo.

"Yes, it was a long day, but it did eventually end. And what about you, what are you up to on a Saturday morning?

"I just came in to grab my notes on tradeoff curves to help Alexandra. I don't plan on staying long."

"Well, I'm glad to see you. I was impressed the other day when Karl Obermeyer suggested to use the brake disc as a gear. What else can we do to get more ideas like that for the concepts that you're working on?"

"I thought that's why we had the hackathon?"

"That was a while ago. Anything else since then?"

"Well, I brought the subject up a few times at lunch, but, although interested, I'm not sure anyone really understood what I was talking about."

"Do you remember what you had to do to visualize your first idea?" asks Ricardo.

"Yes, of course. But can I put a bike on a lunch table? Maybe I can park it in a corner or maybe at the entrance where everybody can see it."

"Did you keep all the props that the teams built in the hackathon?"

"Yes. I get it. We'll use those, too. Maybe I can talk Marco into helping me put a little display together—he's really good at that."

"Excellent. Displays help people visualize, and I'm always amazed how many new ideas they trigger. And it seems like the more simplistic the display, the more suggestions they spawn."

"We're on it. Have a good day and enjoy the rest of your weekend, Ricardo."

"You as well, Mo. Any plans?"

"Marco and I are going to bike north this morning to Castelletto, provided the weather permits."

"That's a nice ride along the lake."

"Yes, and then tomorrow it's off to see my parents to put some weight back on."

"Oh, yes, the Sunday dinners. I've heard about them. Enjoy."

"Ciao."

***

Monday morning, Junior is in the office early as is Ricardo. Junior heads toward engineering, where he walks across the still empty area and surprises Ricardo, who has his back to Junior and is typing furiously: "Ricardo, I . . ."

"Oh my, I didn't see you there," says Ricardo as he spins around. "Mr. Davanti, good morning."

"It is a good morning, Ricardo. And please, call me 'Junior.'"

"Yes. I've got to get used to that."

"Congratulations on the promotion. I'm really pleased that you've officially accepted and excited to have an engineer of your caliber lead R&D. We're fortunate to have you. I wish we had been using more of your talents prior to now."

"Thank you. You'll get everything I have now."

"If there is anything I can do in the short term, please let me know. Longer term, Sofia has some strategic plans we'd like to work on with you. We'll set that up shortly."

"Excellent, Junior. I've got many tactical ideas already in the works, but strategy will be key."

"I agree. Well, have a good day and a good week."

"You as well."

***

Monday afternoon in the cafeteria, Mo shares leftover calzones with his lunch buddies. This dining crew has now grown to include Vinnie, Serfino, and Alexandra.

"Wow, the mozzarella in this is amazing. And you say your mom made this?" asks Vinnie.

"Yes. I don't think there's anything she can't make."

"Maybe she should knock on the door at Fusilli—it may be the start to a great career," chuckles Marco.

"The sausage is nice as well," says Luca. "Your dad made that, right?"

"Yeah, pop loves to make sausage. As much as I love to eat it."

"When do we get to go to Sunday dinner?" asks Luca.

"No, no, no. That's family time."

"So, Vinnie, do you think we'll put somebody on the podium this year in the Tour de France?" asks Marco.

"If Rossa doesn't throw his bike in a river, I think we have a chance. He caught up well in the Giro and still got a second place after his little episode."

"And he's been resting since," adds Alexandra. "I didn't see him on the list of any of the smaller prep races for the Tour."

"We sure prepared a lot of bikes for him," says Vinnie. "He has the best bikes we've ever made. They didn't trust the German tuning company any longer; all moving parts on the bikes were tuned here in Fumane."

"I understand we beefed up the frame where the front derailleur is mounted," notes Marco.

"Yes. They had cracks in that area in the last two races. I believe it will work. We don't want another Giro PR disaster."

"I've also heard that Johan had some tough meetings with Rossa—threatened to send him to anger management school in the offseason," says Serfino. "I was riding in the team car a few weeks back, and I think the tone between Johan and Rossa has changed. Johan doesn't listen to his whining anymore; he just switches the radio off when Rossa starts."

"You know how Johan can see the readout of the racer's Garmin in the car—speed, cadence, and heart rate. Maybe they should get a readout of Rossa's head temperature, too," jokes Marco. "Oh, geez, look at the time. I've got to roll."

The rest of the luncheon group realize they're running late, get up, recycle their trash, and then head to their desks. Mo and Marco walk out together.

"Mo, you're not very talkative today. What's up?"

"Oh, just thinking about my work. That's about all I've got to think about these days. No personal life. If I didn't have work and visit my family, I'd have no life whatsoever."

"That's not true. You're still riding, right. No, this is more than that. When you say, 'personal life,' you mean Marie."

"Yeah, I guess I do."

"So what's your plan?"

"You really want to know?"

"Sure, let's hear it."

"So what does it take to get a demo Davanti race bike these days?"

"Ha. You mean besides an act of God. It rarely happens, and the demand is incredible. We're getting to the peak of the race season, my friend! You think Ferrari gives out their race cars to anybody that wants one."

"What about getting a bike for your friend?"

"Are you saying you want to race again?"

"No. I'd like to lend one to Marie for her next race. We still text occasionally about her races. She could be a lot better if she had better equipment. It was just a thought."

"I might be able to work something out. Sales gets some bikes that they lend to dealers, and in the past I've been able to get my hands on one of those."

"Wonderful. I owe you one, Marco. Please make it a 54-centimeter frame with a Coppi drivetrain, Zip wheels, and the smaller handles."

"Wait a moment."

"You promised!"

"OK, OK. When do you need it?"

"I'd like it by the end of the next week, so I can get it to her early Saturday. Her next race is the following day."

"Well, at least we're not in a hurry. I'll see what I can do."

***

Junior is at his desk, working through ideas for the reorganization meeting, and he appears to be enjoying it, when his assistant Anna sticks her head in his doorway. "Mr. Davanti. Don't forget to attend the associate innovation excellence training that will be starting soon."

"I was wondering what that was on my calendar. Can you ask Sofia to stop by?"

As he is waiting for Sofia, Junior reflects on the training he recently received along with his leadership team, the Volta team, and all the managers. The training—"What leaders should know about innovation excellence"—was taught by a representative from Politecnico di Milano. For the first time Junior understood the full scope of the transformation. The instructor walked them through innovation excellence principles and showed them examples of how other companies have applied them. It was obvious to Junior and most of the Davanti leaders where they would apply them within Davanti and the benefits they could expect. The teacher also did a great job explaining the leadership roles and responsibilities in the transformation and how their behaviors must change. Junior felt energized by the class and was looking forward to helping spread the innovation excellence message through his company—although he did not quite understand how he'd do that. He begins to write a note to himself when Sofia enters his office with Anna.

"How many of these all-day classes do I need to attend?" asks Junior. "I'll get nothing else done."

"Relax, Junior. Marcel asked you to *drop by* as many classes as possible—just 10 minutes to demonstrate your support. You don't attend the entire class."

"Yes, thanks for reminding me of that. But what do I do when I get there?"

"The instructor expects you and will ask you at the appropriate time if there is anything you'd like to share with the group. It would be nice if you explained to them why you want them to pay attention. Also encourage them to ask you questions that may come up. . . . You'd better get going."

Junior looks at the clock, grabs his smartphone, and hustles out of the room, leaving Sofia and Anna staring awkwardly at Junior's empty chair.

***

"Hello, Mr. Davanti, welcome to Innovation Excellence 101," says Giacomo Quercia, the trainer, when Junior enters the room. "Glad you could join us for a few minutes. Anything you would like to share with the class before we get started?"

Junior says hello to everyone and briefly explains why Davanti needs a change in culture and process. He encourages everyone to contribute to the success of the transformation, starting by giving the training their utmost attention. Then he sits down and asks if he can observe the class for a few minutes.

The instructor continues and begins to describe waste in an office setting. Junior asks if he can comment. "Please do."

Junior stands. "You know, if I go into a plant, I can see the work as it progresses. I can pretty much see what adds value and what causes waste as a product moves down the line. But if I walk in the office, I only see people at their computers. If they all look busy, I think everything is OK. But they could be wasting their time and the company's time with what they're working on. Work in the office is invisible, which also makes it very hard to see if it's moving or if it's stopped. Waste is even harder to see. The whole project could be a waste of time." He then gives a few other Davanti examples of office value vs. office waste.

The class is surprised that Junior knows so much about lean, and a few ask followup questions regarding the examples he provided. One attendee is concerned about doing too much that is considered waste and fears he'll be judged by that. "Please bring it to your supervisor's attention after your supervisor takes the training, and if things haven't changed in a few months, please come see me," says Junior. He not only answers all the questions and concerns thoughtfully, but also invites participants to schedule more time with him if they'd like to discuss any concerns further. Eventually he sits down again and listens with fascination. Twenty minutes later, he gets a text from Anna: "Mr. Davanti, they're waiting for you in the conference room."

"Excuse me. Enjoy your day everyone. I've got to run, or I'll be wasting people's time in our conference room."

As Junior leaves the training room, he vows to attend more classes. He enjoyed the interaction with the participants and has always liked explaining principles in his own terms. And he's got plenty of Davanti examples he's witnessed through the years. "This is going to be better than I thought," he thinks.

***

Mo and Marco spent Monday afternoon working on a direct-drive display and setting it up at the entrance to the cafeteria. By Wednesday afternoon, they are surprised by how many people stopped at their display and even more surprised at some of the great feedback and good ideas they received. And it wasn't just from engineers and technicians. Even employees in HR and finance offered valuable contributions. If people didn't talk with Mo or Marco in the cafeteria, they found them at their desks or sent emails with their suggestions. Mo acknowledges receiving all the suggestions as he gets them and records the good ones—some he can use on his project, and others he'll share with colleagues and Ricardo.

In the short time since Sofia arrived in Fumane, the ideation atmosphere within Davanti has evolved dramatically. The use of displays was an idea that previously would not have occurred. Nor would the use of hackathons and brainstormings, which were being employed by other engineers on other projects. Ricardo and Sofia also revamped the idea-submission system after people realized that their ideas did not end up in a trash basket. They digitized the system and purchased a

Facebook-type app where people can throw out their ideas and others can comment and spin them further—sort of a brain-blogging. But the most important achievement is that so many more associates at Davanti are engaged in the creative process.

Ricardo and other leaders provide simple feedback to those who submitted or tried an idea, thanking the individual and asking clarifying questions if needed. Of course, not every idea that came in was worth consideration—as is usually the case with every idea submission system—but thanking people and showing interest in the suggestion keeps people motivated to try again, even if a suggestion wasn't pursued.

The bureaucracy of evaluating dozens of new ideas was one of the problems that Emilio and the VPs had with the original idea-generation system. Ricardo immediately implemented new methods that encouraged the systematic evaluation of reasonable ideas and simplified the process. For example, if an idea was relatively easy to implement, the creator was encouraged to simply do it. If further help or resources were needed and the creator could engage two peers to support the idea, R&D would fund the implementation or the building of a small illustration or prototype. At that point, it was easy for a sponsor to pick up the idea and start with the critical questions. Overnight, Davanti had eliminated layers of unnecessary complexity and created an engaging idea-generation and -development process.

Ricardo also started using "creativity kits" to spur the development of ideas. Employees who come up with an especially promising idea receive a kit, which includes pertinent reading material, flash cards to broaden their thinking, and information on how to visualize and prototype an idea. But the most important content in the kits is a debit card and internal service tokens. The card can be used to purchase some items without having to go through the dreaded purchase-order process. The tokens can used to buy services from the prototype plant and testing lab without additional approval.

New R&D ideas are organized into groups and platforms; Ricardo keeps a list posted at his desk, which includes concepts such as:

■ *Gyro bike:* A gyro mechanism like the one used on Segways reacts to the movement of a rider, such as braking when the rider leans forward or turns when the rider leans to a side. A stabilizing mechanism would make it easy and safe to ride.

■ *Alternative-powered bikes:* Arms and/or legs provide thrust at the same time, such as a kayak bike whereby power comes from a rider, who sits as if in a canoe and performs a rowing and pedaling motion.

■ *Hydraulic-drive bikes:* Pedals drive a small hydraulic motor. Pressurized fluid powers a hydraulic motor in the hub of the wheels. This idea would allow two wheel drive bikes, an idea popular for mountain bikes and time-trial cycles. The project could be partnered with a major hydraulic motor company to develop a high-torque, low-flow motor.

■ *"Safety" bike for city use:* The bicycle scans for cars and pedestrians, brakes on its own, and includes fall-proof provisions. The idea is to partner with a self-driving car company.

■ *Capsule commuter bike:* The rider sits in a low-weight, self-supporting shell like the carbon-fiber, self-supporting shell of a blimp. This concept reduces drag and consumes minimum energy.

■ *Other ideas:* New generation of powered scooters and skateboards, mechanisms for power steering, carbon-fiber helmets, and inner-city bikes powered by rubber bands that are wound prior to riding.

For the most promising ideas, the engineers or technicians who submitted the ideas begin working with small crossfunctional teams on determining the most critical questions and planning small assessments, experiments, prototypes, and studies, just as Mo is doing on the chainless bike. Mo, Ricardo, and Sofia provide appropriate coaching.

Most of the resources in R&D who work on new ideas are coming from the discontinued projects (e.g., Darvin), and Ricardo expects more available resources as the work on the product portfolio continues.

Late Wednesday Ricardo shares his list with Sofia, who is surprised how fast and easy it has been to get Davanti employees engaged in the creative phase of the innovation process. They must have been holding these ideas for years, waiting for an opportunity. She emails Junior that if the evolution continues, he'd soon have his 200 innovators.

Junior's reads the email and calls Sofia: "Thank you for the email, Sofia. But who knows if these ideas will work?"

"You'll only find out if you let people try them. And now we do, it costs very little, and we'll adjust as needed. . . . And get this, Junior, employees are beginning to submit ideas for other Davanti functions as well."

"Really?"

"Yes. Of course, some leaders have a hard time accepting ideas submitted by staff outside of their department, but we're dealing with that. Stephano has taken the lead in personally thanking anyone—inside or outside his own organization—for their input of a non-R&D idea, and he follows up for idea clarification if needed."

"Things are certainly changing quickly. I'd better get used to this."

***

Mo, Serfino, and Alexandra had each received a lot more data about weight and friction for the direct-drive bike than expected, most of it in the form of tradeoff curves and tables. For example, tables listed weight by the number of gears and weight by different materials. Some tradeoff curves showed friction as a function of load or speed and the friction associated with different gear materials. Other curves showed torque and friction for different gear ratios.

The engineers, who had not used tradeoff curves prior to their sprint, were impressed by their usefulness. And a US company that Alexandra was working with had supplied data from their computer-simulation effort for conditions close to those that she had specified. With all that data, the three bike engineers were able to come up with reasonably good approximations and calculations related to their two critical questions. They updated their sprint board and shared the results with Ricardo during Thursday morning's sprint huddle.

"We should have curves like this for all the bikes we're designing," Serfino suggests, and Ricardo agrees. He had used tradeoff curves in his previous job.

"I think we have all the information we can get from the suppliers," says Alexandra. "Originally we wanted to order a few mechanisms and test them ourselves because the operating conditions we're interested in were not covered by supplier testing. But then we realized that we could extrapolate the curves to learn what we needed to know. To play it safe, we discussed the results with the suppliers. They said they've never developed anything for the range we are interested in, but they didn't consider our operating range impossible either—maybe not for 20 gears right away, but that's not critical for us at this time."

"I agree," says Ricardo. "We can cross that bridge later. Are all three of you confident that we can get the friction into the ballpark?"

The three engineers nod in agreement.

"And what about the weight?" Ricardo asks.

"We were kind of surprised when we learned that stress can be distributed very evenly among all the gears—unlike a bike chain where every single link must carry the full load," says Mo. "This would allow the manufacturers to design some of the gears very small and with light-weight materials. The assemblies would be quite small and light, but with more gears there is more weight in the overall mechanism."

"Just like on a traditional bike—the more cogs the more weight, right?" says Ricardo.

"Kind of like that," comments Serfino, "but a little more weight per gear than on a traditional bike. We might need to consider a solution like that used for trucks or tractors: two gear boxes, each with four gears, providing a combination of 16 gears. We were also thinking that we could make the gear boxes easily exchangeable. When racers ride in the mountains, they use a different gear box than in flat stages. When they get tired or need to attack, they get a different gear box from the team car—or they carry one in the back pocket of their jersey."

"That sounds pretty futuristic, but I like the thought of it. I trust your professional judgement on this."

"Now what?" asks Alexandra.

"Sounds to me like you're saying we should move on. I'm impressed that you reached that conclusion without building prototypes and testing. Did you give any thought to the next critical question?"

"I think it's the patents," says Mo. "Junior wants to know what the patent situation is and to make sure we don't infringe on any major patents. He's always been focused on ethics, but I'm sure he remembers what happened to one of our component suppliers a few years back—a lost patent-infringement suit nearly bankrupted them."

"Mo, what's your opinion on the patents? You've probably already done some research?" asks Ricardo.

"Yes, I did. I don't expect a showstopper, but we need a little more information from our legal experts. I don't think my personal opinion will put Junior's concerns to bed. I suggest we make that our next critical question."

Serfino and Alexandra agree.

"OK, see if legal can answer your patent question in a few days, and let me know if I can help you," offers Ricardo. "And one more thing. I like the codename you came up with for the project: Leonardo. I think Leonardo DaVinci would have had a blast working here."

***

Friday morning Mo catches up on other projects, for which he still has some responsibility. His priority for the day, however, is to talk with the lawyer, but it's unlikely that he's in the office as early as Mo. He'll give him an hour or so and until then organize the rest of his day.

At 9:00 am sharp, Mo uses the office landline and calls the lawyer's office. He is surprised that Federico's assistant patches him through. Federico is known for long delays in responding to calls, and Mo is unprepared to speak.

"Hello. Federico Ricco here. Hello?"

"Um, uh, hello, Mr. Ricco. This is Maurice Pensatore at Davanti Nella Gara."

"Yes, Mr. Pensatore, how can I help you?"

"Well, you may recall the project we talked about a month ago. It's really taken off, and we're going to need you to address some of our concerns about patentability and infringements. Junior is especially anxious to get this piece of the project resolved quickly."

"I understand, and I'm happy to help you."

"Out of this call, I'm going to send you a zip file with all the project details and updated drawings, but you already have most of this in my patent application. We'd like to hear back from you on the patents by Monday if possible."

"Mr. Pensatore, in the best of worlds that is nowhere near possible. It will be weeks of research. My staff and I will need to assess all prior art, review any existing patents that may be comparable, and then actually draft a comprehensive report. This is no small undertaking."

"But you were already exploring some of the applications based on our last discussion. And we don't need all you're describing. All we need is a quick assessment focused on the most critical aspects. And you've had the drawings. I assure you there are no substantive changes since then . . ."

"And if Davanti has a lawsuit five years from now, we'll be very sorry and wish we had done a better job on this."

"Federico, the device is not even designed yet. We just need to understand if we should move on with design. We just need a quick assessment to tell us to proceed or not."

"Maybe you do superficial work in engineering. We do nothing like that here with legal matters. And things that are only partially designed are the hardest to assess and take much more time."

The two have been getting more aggressive in tone and talking faster. Mo is ready to strangle the guy, thinking: "What doesn't he understand about this simple request. He has no appreciation for the cost of time and risk management—he's focused only on absolute risk elimination and getting paid for all of the hours to get there."

"Mr. Ricco, please consider our request," pleads Mo. "Mr. Davanti is personally involved in this, and he is the one most concerned about the patent situation. I'll call in two days to see where you're at."

"Please call whenever you'd like, Mr. Pensatore. Goodbye," says Federico, who then hangs up.

Mo slams the receiver down, startling his colleagues who are getting their days started. He gets up and leaves the office for a walk and another coffee.

A few hours later, Mo is surprised to see Junior show up at his office. What's more, he doesn't look particularly happy. "What did I do?" wonders Mo.

"Mo, let's take a walk." Mo gets up and the two head out of the office and down the hallway.

"Our patent lawyer called. He asked me what *my* patent concerns are and what *I* want from him," says Junior.

"I explained to Mr. Ricco what your concern is, and I asked him for a quick assessment. I told him that to proceed with the project a quick assessment would be good enough—for now—but he says it will take weeks if not months. We reviewed the patent situation earlier, and a good lawyer should be able to reply in a couple of days. If he has the computers and access to EU and US patent databases, this is really quite straightforward. All we need is a rough idea of patentability or infringements at this stage of the project. Why is that so difficult?"

"Mo, he explained all of that to me. But that's not the problem. You need to sell this project on its own merits and get help and results without pulling me into this. If you use my name, they call me and put me right in the middle—like a referee between you and the lawyer. I'm sure you can handle this part of the project without me."

"Of course, Mr. Davanti."

"But if you really do need my help, *you* can call me any time. You and I should talk instead of people calling me about you."

Mo pauses for a second. "You're absolutely right. I should have tried this differently, Mr. Davanti. But, as a matter of fact, I think I do need your help *now*. My hands are tied with Mr. Ricco. Could you please get back to him and ask what it would take to get an answer in two days? After all, this is not a parliamentary investigation."

"I'll see what I can do, and please call me 'Junior,'" says the CEO, who pats Mo on the shoulder and heads back to his office. Mo heads to the cafeteria for yet another cup of coffee.

***

Junior steps out of another training session, pleased with his part but also happy with the enthusiasm of the attendees. As he walks past Anika's office, he sticks his head in.

"Anika, excuse my interruption, but I'm curious how you think the innovation excellence training is going."

"It's all on schedule. The leadership session is well behind us, and now we're quickly getting staff developed around the basics."

"I'm loving it. And how are my staff doing?"

"Some seem to have a very easy time participating in the classes, and they really enjoy it."

"But?"

"Others are a little anxious, and Diana has not signed up to participate. She doesn't feel as if she knows enough about lean or innovation."

"You know, don't push her on it yet. We've got enough leaders participating, and the others will get better.

"Constantine, Leandro, Stephano, and some members of the Volta team—like Mo, Gina, and Rene—have scheduled themselves for additional classes, and the teacher Giacomo is grooming them to take over the class in the very near future."

"Great news. Thanks, Anika," says Junior, and he disappears from her office.

***

Mo's work week was exhausting and at extremes of good (the visual display and voluminous feedback) to the bad (the wrangling with legal and reprimand by Junior). He'd also spent another good part of Saturday at the office working to catch up on his secondary projects, such as the revamping of the Davanti Primo Sempre pro racing line. It was also a good way for him to keep his mind off Marie.

By Saturday afternoon, Mo has had enough of work and heads home. He changed into his riding gear and headed toward the Alps, riding hard until sunset. It was a prelude to summer, with temperatures topping 30 degrees C in the valley. The weekend road was full of bikers, and all of them seemed happier than Mo.

Arriving home after dark and nearly five hours of riding, Mo showers, changes, and then warms leftovers provided by his mom. He didn't bother to figure out what he wanted; he tosses a few containers into the microwave, opens a beer, and watches Hellas Verona lose to Palermo on a penalty kick. He wonders what Marie is doing.

***

Mo sleeps in late on Sunday, and takes his time getting to his parents' Lake Garda villa. He's still thinking about Marie. It's a beautiful early June afternoon—in contrast to Mo's mood—and starting to get warm as Mo drives west. Once at the villa, he walks up to the front door, knocks, and then walks in. He sees his parents and sister Catherine seated for a late lunch on the patio. His mom begins to get up to greet him.

"Mom, please, you don't need to get up."

"Where have you been, Maurice? I was beginning to think something happened to you."

"I'm sorry. I should have called. I was doing some laundry and stuff around the apartment. I lost track of time."

"That's not like you, brother. You're an engineer, after all. Punctual."

"Glad you're here, son," says Mo's father.

"Where's Eric?" asks Mo.

"He's camping with the kids and other fathers and children from our neighborhood. They've had great weather."

"I wish they were here with us," says Mo's mom. "It's Sunday, and we should be together. Benito, too. He's always doing something."

"Soon, mom, don't worry," says Catherine apologetically. "We'll all get together very soon."

"Mo, have a seat. We've got a beautiful pasta salad with fresh greens, tomatoes, and herbs from the garden. And your father has grilled some fish that he caught yesterday. . . . What can I get you?"

"It looks wonderful, mom. Maybe a little pasta salad for now."

Mo's father looks suspiciously at him, knowing that his son is always hungry, and instructs his wife to give him the fish as well.

His sister, too, senses something—she can hear fleas sneeze: "Mo, my friends tell me that you'd be quite the catch. Maybe you should move on from this one and get back in the water."

Mo takes the plate from his mom and gives his sister a grumpy look.

"You know, with online dating you could have a date by tonight. A good date, too."

Mo's mom and dad have no idea what Catherine is talking about. They have a computer and email, but that's the extent of their digital life.

"The girls at the bank use online dating like I use the web to buy clothes. Click on what I want, try it out, and send it back if it doesn't fit. I hear that some kids today are ending a relationship while at the same time they're confirming their next online date, and . . ."

"Maybe that's why I wouldn't date your friends," says Mo, clearly irritated. "Enough with the online dating. . . . I've had a long week, and I'm just looking to relax a bit. So let's please change the subject and relax."

"Excellent idea, Mo," says Mr. Pensatore. "Try the fish. It's trout. I think it turned out great. Of course, I would say that: I caught it and grilled it. I was pleased your mother let me contribute today. . . . Mamma, please pass Mo the wine. He looks like he could use it."

"Pop," says Mo, rolling his eyes and cooling off. He would never address his parents harshly, and deep down knows they're all trying to help. "Sure, pop, let's have some wine. What is that, a Soave?"

The family finishes their lunch with cappuccinos and homemade cookies. They all sit quietly, enjoying the warm breeze off the lake and the beautiful view.

"Thank you, mom and pop. Another fine day and meal," says Catherine. "And Mo, thanks for the company."

"Yes. Thank you," adds Mo.

After helping his mom and sister clear the table, Mo announces that he really must get back to Fumane. "I'm sorry, but that's it for me today. I really need to get going."

"Not without some leftovers," says his mom, who's already begun assembling a package of food.

"Thank you, mom," he says, and walks over and gives her hug.

"Maurice. Things always work out for the best in the end. Don't you forget it."

Chapter 13

New Organization, New Goals, New Direction

On Monday morning, Junior receives via email a four-page letter from Federico Ricco: The first three pages are filled with nothing but disclaimers. The fourth page lists all the sources that were consulted in the assessment and more disclaimers about the drawings provided by Mo. At the bottom of the fourth page, nearly obscured by intermittent legal jargon and lawyerly meanderings, the report discloses, "After due diligence and considering all cited disclaimers . . . we cautiously decided at this time that based on all the information available to us and cited above . . . and due to the fact that the two-day timeline did not allow for a more detailed assessment . . . it is our cautious conclusion that we do not see any significant infringement and we expect good patentability at this time."

"At least they'll only bill us for two days of work," thinks Junior. Then it hits him: "We should be doing this with every request to the lawyers, and maybe for all our other service requests as well. How much have we been spending on excessive patent investigation for ideas that eventually failed subsequent critical questions and fizzled out? And, what's more, we should work like this with our *own* functions as well. How much time do we spend perfecting things beyond what we really need?"

Junior sits back in his chair and winks at the portrait of his father: "I think I'm getting this lean stuff, pop." As he talks to the portrait of his father, he notices Sofia walking down the hall and toward the cafeteria. He quickly jumps up and calls to her. "Sofia, Sofia. Uno momento. I just had a Eureka moment."

"OK, so let's hear it. You usually don't grab people walking down the hall."

"So we streamlined the legal review of Mo's project to get some early indication of patentability. What would have taken weeks and painstakingly overdone at great cost, we got done in two days."

"That sounds good."

"Good? It's great. Do you know how much we normally pay in legal fees for this type of work?"

"I can only guess."

"But it's not just the money. . . . So I'm thinking, maybe this works with everything. The less time that engineers spend doing their work, the lower our total engineering costs per product. And if it can work for testing, it can also work for accounting and marketing. I think we've been adding large chunks of time to every project, and staff are filling the time allotted to them. We

DOI: 10.4324/9781003231837-13

lose precious time and pay extra on top of it. Isn't that what lean means, getting rid of all this self-inflicted waste? I think I'm getting it."

"I think you are, too, Junior."

Junior looks at his watch and realizes, as the functional leaders show up, it's time for the staff meeting to start. "I should not make my staff wait. We'll discuss this further."

"I am looking forward to that," says Sofia. "I'm going to grab a latte, and then I'll be right back."

***

As the executives walk in, they talk about the recently completed Tour de Suisse.

"With Rossa on break, our young Pasquale Barto sure put up an impressive show," says Joe. "If it hadn't been for the climb up the Col de Torrent, he may have been on the podium. He sure blew everybody away in the time trials."

Junior sits at the table and gets everyone's attention: "OK, let's move from Tour du Suisse to the tour of Fusilli. I tried to give everybody an inspiration with the visit. How did you like it?"

"It was a real eye opener," says Stephano. "You really think we can pull that off here at Davanti?"

"It was inspiring, Junior," adds Diana. "But they're light years ahead of us."

"I agree. But some things may be right for Davanti today, and we've got to try," responds Junior.

"Junior, all my phone calls are confidential," says Claudia from sales. "Do you really expect me to make them in the open with everybody listening in? Will you also join us in that big room?"

"Let's not get ahead of ourselves with office layouts. Think about what really mattered at Fusilli. The processes. The engagement of leaders. The involvement of everyone. The clear responsibilities. We don't need a new floorplan to get that going."

"I think I see where you're heading, Junior," says Leandro of supply chain. "We've already started. The training is a great first step. I'm on board."

"I really enjoyed the training," says Constantine." It was a great adaptation of what we implemented in manufacturing. In the plant where you can see the bike progress from beginning to end, it is easy to see waste. But the training really opened my eyes to see the waste in the office where the work is not visible."

"Likewise," says Joe. "I'm most impressed with the lean startup principles and how risk is managed—small experiments along the risk scale will allow us to engage in many ideas without making them monster projects and breaking the bank."

"I know we can apply many lean manufacturing principles to the product development part of the process," says Ricardo, speaking for the first time with the staff who are now his peers. "I've seen it happen. There needs to be standard work like in manufacturing. When that happens, product development will become fast and predictable—no more late launches."

"I see no reason for delaying that part of the implementation," says Leandro.

"To some extent, we've already started," counters Ricardo.

"Excuse me, but let's think a bit more about Fusilli," says Anika. "I took away from the visit and the training that everybody—leaders and associates—need to be engaged in the change. Let's start there, go slow, and get it right."

"Good feedback, everyone," says Junior. "It sounds like we understand where Sofia has been wanting us to go."

"Before I agree with anything, I need to know what we're going to sell next year," says Claudia indignantly. "Ricardo wants to cancel all these 'marginal products' as he calls them. That's 25 percent of our volume, and we may lose some dealers in the process. I wish I could sit here and entertain your dreams, Junior, but they're turning into nightmares for me."

"We all understand your concerns, Claudia," replies Junior casually, trying to diffuse her anxiety. "Together—sales, marketing, manufacturing, supply chain, R&D—we'll find a way to replace the income from the cancelled projects. Maybe even make more. Have you considered that possibility?"

Before Claudia can rebut, Stephano jumps in: "Junior, I was impressed with Fusilli and, sure, we're not ready for the big open office, but I really liked their emphasis on value streams. As an organization they know how to collaborate to make money."

"Precisely," says Junior. "I'm glad you brought up the subject. Our value streams will require all our support and collaboration. . . . If that's all for Fusilli, let's get to our finance report."

***

Mo, Marco, Luca, Vinnie, and Gina are eating lunch outside on the Davanti patio. Mo texted them Monday morning that he had ample leftovers from his parents: yesterday's pasta salad as well as other entrees his mom had tucked in. So no one brought or bought lunch, although Gina brought some of the pastries she baked over the weekend. Vinnie joined them—but only because Mo personally invited him and baited him with leftover lasagna.

The beautiful late-spring day has everyone in a good mood, even on a Monday. They're anxious to hear Vinnie's assessment of the Davanti racing team. He had just returned from race mechanic duties at the Critérium du Dauphiné in France and the Tour de Suisse, which take place between the Giro and the Tour de France. Some riders, like Rossa, skip them to recover, but for others they're an opportunity to prepare as well as put their name on the list of Tour contenders. Johan skips most stages of these races as well to attend to business in the office; assistant Domingo Pucci fills in as the team director.

"When Rossa's not there, Pasquale Barto is the king of the hill," says Vinnie "He leaves no doubt that he can be the lead rider and that he deserves the support from the team to win the Tour." Vinnie marvels about how big and strong the young Pasquale is and how his form is peaking at just the right time.

"I even had to swap a bike for him because he cracked the frame," continues Vinnie. "I bet he will beat Rossa in every time trial in the Tour. The other riders notice, and he's convincing the rest of the team to support him instead of Rossa. He and Rossa don't get along, and he's convinced that with the right support he can do better in the Tour than his team rival. Riders told me that he even talked to friends from other teams to get their support."

"Vinnie, you must be a good listener; you picked up a lot of stuff," says Marco. "What does Johan say? Will he put his foot down? This could mess with team chemistry?"

As Vinnie shrugs his shoulders, Luca chimes in: "Just like work. Your peers and team members are your worst enemies sometimes. They'll try to get ahead, even at your expense."

"Oh, we're not that evil, are we Luca?" says Mo.

"They're a highly competitive race team," comments Gina. "They're paid to win. Whereas the animosity within Davanti is the result of our reward and promotion system. I hope they have a better system for the team."

"Yeah, I guess they couldn't win a race with our office system," chuckles Mo. "I'm sure Johan will have this fully under control when the Tour starts."

"I am sure he does," adds Marco. "But I'd be curious how he deals with it. And, Vinnie, I'm not ruling Rossa out."

"I agree with Marco on both counts," says Luca. "Johan runs the show, and Rossa's still the man to beat. Hey, I need to grab a coffee and head back to the office." The others agree, help Mo pack up what's left, and head back to work.

***

On Wednesday morning, the executive team is gathered for a six-hour retreat in Bardolino, about a half hour west of Fumane. Junior wants their complete attention for this important day when he unveils the new organization. He didn't want staff dashing off to take calls, answering emails and texts while they pretended to be engaged, or treating this like another day at the office. As Sofia had suggested, an off-site would emphasize the importance of their task—or so he hoped. Staff began arriving shortly before the 10:00 am start. Lunch would be brought in at midday, and then Junior was taking everyone to a nice restaurant at the end of the day on the way back to Fumane.

As Junior walks into the main conference room of the center—a converted monastery overlooking Lake Garda—his colleagues grab a final cup of coffee and head toward their seats. For some, the meeting won't be a complete surprise; Junior has discussed new positions with the few whose jobs will change, and they greeted the news with pleasure. Anna sent out the agenda, in advance:

- The new organization
- Comments about the new organization
- Development of Davanti goals
- How to meet Davanti goals

As everybody settles in, Claudia looks around the room. "Shouldn't Sofia be here? I mean, she started all of this."

"I don't want you or anyone here to think that this is the organization *she* designed," says Junior forcefully. "This is my organization. Better yet, it's our organization, it's Davanti's organization."

"Fair enough," counters Diana from procurement.

"So let's get with it. In our previous discussions, it became clear that we have to innovate our products and services. But in addition to rethinking *what* we produce and sell, we also have to innovate *how* we do it. I know that many prosperous companies have held their inflation-adjusted budgets, especially their R&D budgets, flat for a decade or more. Same with staffing and capacity—flat. Yet somehow they do more with the same amount or less. They're not smarter than the people in this room. So how can we do that?"

"So is this what it's all about?" asks Claudia, rhetorically. "We've already moved manufacturing offshore. Who's next? It takes virtually nothing to move office functions to China or India."

"Sure, there is amazing talent in China and India," notes Anika. "But that's not what you're talking about? Is it, Junior? More offshoring?"

"No, just the contrary. We need to get better at what we do and how we do it. That alone will sustain Davanti and the Fumane site."

Now Junior has everybody's attention. He repeats the Davanti vision—"increase value to all stakeholders"—which by now everybody knows. He covers the trends in the business numbers, results of the SWOT analysis, the portfolio weaknesses, his frustration with his past role as a referee, and the personal inspiration he gained from the Fusilli tour and involvement in the innovation excellence training. "I'm not who I was a few months ago. Davanti is not what it was months ago. But to do more, we all have to change."

Then he shares his computer screen on a large monitor in the room and displays the new organizational chart in the matrix format. He starts by explaining that nobody has been cut, demoted, or their roles given less importance. "If anything, today you are all more important—and empowered—than at any time in your careers."

He notes that Ricardo is filling the R&D position, and then points out Joe's new role as product director, which he characterizes as a value-stream director. Joe nods, aware of the assignment prior to the meeting. "Joe works for our customers, and he can only argue with himself when he has to make a product decision," jokes Junior. "Joe is responsible for the full bicycle value stream, and he buys services from all of you. I hope we'll soon have additional new product lines, and then we'll create additional product-director positions."

Junior then explains that the project management office (PMO) is a new function, and clarifies the activities of the PMO; he repeats what Sofia had described (i.e., the PMO function ensures Davanti develops knowledge and talent around project management). "And I'm happy to announce that Leandro has accepted a new position to head up the PMO. He knows our business, our culture, and how to manage projects, and I hope you all support him in his new and difficult role."

Leandro smiles and nods to all, happy with the assignment and the challenges ahead.

"We also created the position of a continuous improvement director, which is currently held by Sofia," continues Junior. "She'll groom her successor in due time, and we'll decide then on a reporting line."

Junior pauses to gauge reaction: "We also eliminated two existing vice president positions: supply chain will report to manufacturing and marketing will report to sales. As you see, with new roles for Joe and Leandro there's no job losses with either of those moves."

Everyone easily follows along, although Claudia, who was briefed about the sales/marketing combination, looks increasingly irritated as Junior continues.

"The biggest change I want to tell you about is the creation of a matrix organization. This type of organization can best support the value streams and the projects. Every major new product and every R&D or corporate initiative will be managed by a project manager. The project managers have responsibility for deliverables and their budget, and they buy services, including personnel, from the functions. They report to a value-stream director like Joe, to Ricardo, or to the leader responsible for a major new initiative, also called 'sponsors.' They also report to the PMO. They are accountable to the leader or sponsor for what they do and to the PMO for how they do it."

"This is a big change, Junior," comments Anika. "How do you know you got it right?"

"I believe it's the right direction. I'd rather we try to do the right thing and improve it as we go than be perfect at doing the wrong thing as we have in the past. I'm sure we'll fine-tune this in the near future, but I think it will give us a good start. And the fact that all my direct reports have director titles now doesn't mean your positions are less important or less compensated. It articulates our desire for a flatter organization. OK, I've talked enough. Comments, questions?"

"I think the organization really puts the focus where we need it: Creating value for our customers," says Stephano. "They pay the bills."

"We had enough problems when people had one boss; reporting to two bosses adds four times the problems," complains Claudia.

"It's not difficult," interrupts Constantine. "We run the plant in a lean matrix. I'm happy we found a way to bring it to the office. It will work very well."

"Are we getting more staff from your friend to fill the open positions," asks Claudia, intent on expressing her disapproval whenever and wherever possible.

"Good question, Claudia," says Junior. "I forgot to mention the two unfilled positions: Marco Marrone will be our new marketing manager and, as you and I discussed earlier, report to you Claudia. Matteo Catena will manage the supply chain and report to Constantine. My friend, as you call Sofia, will coach them to fit into the new organization. I think it's easier and less disruptive to teach our Davanti folks lean behaviors than to hire a lean expert and teach the expert about Davanti technology and culture. So that is the new organization. What do you think?"

There are many questions and comments for about a half an hour—most of them constructive. From their context, it shows that Junior's staff understands why Davanti had to change, they understand the new organization, and they are ready (albeit with concerns for some) to help Junior to get there.

***

While the executives were discussing the matrix organization, the center's staff had quietly begun to wheel in serving carts with lunch and beverages: first up is an antipasto salad, followed by a choice of roasted chicken, beef tips, or grilled cauliflower with side dishes, and ending with Italian cream cake and coffee. The group breaks for lunch, finishes their meal, and Junior gives them 20 minutes to look at emails and check voicemails. He's pleased to see them regroup in timely manner without announcing any "emergencies" to which they must attend.

"OK, so now it gets interesting. I want everybody's input. What should be our goals? What's our definition of winning? And when we figure that out, we'll begin to discuss how we win. Of course, we may not get all this done today. . . . I hope you all have had some time by now to discuss possible Davanti goals with your own organizations. The training sessions should have given everybody great input for that."

"I got some great ideas from my staff," says Stephano. "I'll get us started . . ."

Each of the executives suggests goals, and Leandro lists them out, grouping some and drawing a line through others. Occasionally they jump to the "how" to reach them, but Junior gets them back on track. After much discussion, they formulate the following goals:

- Continue to improve safety, quality, and bike performance
- Increase revenue and profits by at least 15 percent year over year
- 40 percent of sales from new products or services (less than two years old)—half of those sales from non-bike manufacturing/sales
- Develop a highly engaged workforce
- Create a never-ending continuous-improvement culture

Junior says, "This is a good list, and I think these are aligned with our vision. What do you think?"

Diane is the first to answer: "I think the business items certainly support the growth and the value of the company. And it's obvious that they can't be accomplished in the traditional Davanti company. We must have a change in our culture, and I'm glad we included that in our goals."

"I believe the new organization will provide the focus needed," says Joe. "It certainly gives me more responsibility, but it doesn't give me or anybody else more talent and money. We still need to figure out how to do more with less to meet the product goals."

"My staff and I can sell anything that comes out of that list," says Claudia. "But I have little faith that we'll *ever* get those goods and services. So far, we've only cut projects. Even before we started killing projects, we never got half of what we wanted from R&D."

"Claudia, you'll get enough new products and services," says Ricardo. "I can promise you that. But I won't promise that you get *everything* you or anybody else wants. Together we'll wisely pick those products and services that contribute the most to Davanti goals and have the staff to deliver them on time."

"And just where will the non-bicycle products come from that we're supposed to sell? Will you also develop those, Ricardo?" pushes Claudia.

Ricardo looks at Junior and then to Claudia: "I'm going to table an answer until we have a little more clarity about that new value stream."

"And how are we supposed to change the culture," adds Claudia, now clearly on a rant. "That doesn't just happen. Will Sofia do that?"

"One person alone can't change the culture," says Junior. "Sofia will provide guidance on how to move in that direction and coach us along the way. We all need to do it. And with that, I'd like your input into how we'll accomplish our goals. How will we win?" Junior is exasperated by Claudia's attitude, but he's not letting it slow him down.

"I think we can accomplish some of these goals by just stopping the losers and the bleeding," says Stephano from finance, pausing but clearly with more on his mind.

"Go on, Stephano," encourages Junior.

"When I met with my organization," Stephano continues, "they wanted to know if strategic support supersedes traditional activities, such as paying salaries and bills, generating reports required by law, filing tax documents, and creating P&L statements as well as budget-vs.-actual spending reports."

"Stephano, of course not. What are you getting at?"

"I'm guessing you still want the monthly financial reports we generate for you and the leadership team to manage the business, like income statements, cost reports, forecasts, etc."

"Of course. What's your point? That's how your organization adds value and supports the company's strategy and contributes to meeting our goals."

"Junior, you've mentioned value, so let's talk about it. I brought copies of some reports we issue monthly." Stephano plops two inches of paper on the table. "Most of you get these in electronic format, but it is more impactful if I show the paper stack." He reads off a few titles that to most in the room sound like financial jargon.

"I don't review any of those," says Junior. "Please tell me that somebody else at Davanti needs them."

All the executives stare at Stephano and then at Junior.

"I thought so," says Stephano. "I will stop those reports and maybe other ones. Please call me if you miss any of them. We'll use our time and resources only to provide what adds value as specified earlier and support all the other departments and their roles and goals. For example, Joe asked for help to develop a more accurate method to assess NVP for future projects, and Ricardo would like help to develop a simple method to calculate something he calls 'cost of delay.'"

Junior nods in full agreement, and all eyes are on him again. "Thank you, Stephano. You and your team understand what we're trying to do now."

"I took away from the lean training that we need to take a good look at our suppliers," says Diana from procurement. "We need to develop more of a partnership and collaborative working relationship with our main component suppliers to help them improve their quality and performance to us. We have, however, spent far too much time and effort approving the many minor suppliers that come and go. I'd rather we spent some of that effort into developing fewer and better local suppliers in the region that stick by us and that can help us with flexibility and speed."

"Anything else, Diana?" asks Junior.

"Yes. My staff wants to be more directly involved with our innovators and help them find the right partners for their new ideas. They're catching the innovation bug like everyone else."

Anika suggests that HR is looking to eliminate waste from some administrative processes and automating others, all of which will free up her staff. "We need to apply HR where it can really matter. Lean management and culture need a change in people behaviors on all levels, and I want to make sure we have the right resources for training. And since that training cannot be done in the classroom, we need to up our coaching resources."

"Is that how you'll develop an engaged workforce?" asks Claudia.

Anika looks surprised: "People don't put an engagement score on their resume, and we can't replace the disengaged, so we need to learn to respect and motivate our associates. I can certainly help all of you—with direction, training, and coaching—so we can accomplish that."

For the next few hours, the rest of the directors describe similar actions they plan to take, describing how they and their staffs have begun to root out legacy wastes, thus freeing up time and resources to support the product value stream and the other initiatives. Even Claudia indicates ways that her sales staff can better support Ricardo's group, such as formally sharing insights they typically gather during sales calls—but in the past never bothered to give to the engineers. And she has not had a chance to work with Marco yet, but says she will support both Joe as the value stream leader and Ricardo as the new R&D director. Junior is pleased with most of their attitudes about the assignment and the outcomes.

"Out of this meeting, I'd like you all to review the corporate goals we've discussed with your associates. Help them understand the goals and get everybody engaged in how each person can do his or her part to accomplish them. We need to define how we'll all win together. That is, we need to synthesize all of your input into a common corporate strategy. That will be our roadmap to guide us on our journey and enable us to meet our goals.

"The innovation excellence principles will help us improve, but please don't assume they are the only way. And as my friend Marcel reminded me, I'll remind you: in accomplishing our goals we want to first leverage our strengths. How will we exploit our strengths *and* drive us toward meeting our goals?"

"What about the rest of SWOT?" asks Diana. "The WOT?"

"The principles we're learning and other ideas, both within and outside of Davanti, will help us overcome our weaknesses, deflect some threats, and capitalize on some of the opportunities we listed. . . . We've accomplished a lot today, and since it's getting late and you all look a little weary, we'll get to those another day. I'll ask Sofia to work with all of you in the coming weeks to finalize our corporate strategy—and then we'll review it in an upcoming staff meeting."

"It looks like we all could use a drink," says Constantine. "Unless, of course, Junior has more for us today."

"No, I think that's a fine idea, Constantine. Thank you, everyone. Take a little time to get caught up on your emails and whatnot, and then let's meet at Casa della Festa in the bar at 5:00 pm."

***

On Thursday morning, at the request of the Leonardo team, Ricardo joins their huddle.

"So are we done now with Leonardo's critical questions?" ask Mo.

"You and your teammates make the call," replies Ricardo. "You answered three or even maybe four critical questions already. What do you think? If it was your own savings money, would you invest it in this project now?"

"Wow, the project couldn't survive a week on my savings, but I get your point," says Alexandra. "We've reduced the technical risk. But will Leonardo be in the Tour de France next year? That is what we're designing for, right? We have no idea what it would take to get the pro bike race governing bodies to allow bikes like this next year or ever."

"Can we ask them?" suggests Ricardo.

"I have no idea whom to ask?" says Serfino. "And would they—whoever they are—even look at a prototype."

"And I'm not sure the lawyers would be happy if we disclose that much information about the project either," adds Mo. "I assume the governing body would want to see years of experience, but we can't get racers using the bike without their approval. It's a chicken-and-egg situation."

"I guess we can ask people with more knowledge about the subject," suggests Alexandra.

"Whom do you suggest?" counters Serfino.

"We have a professional race team, and both Mo and I have spent some time with Johan Leffe, the team director," says Ricardo. "Maybe he can advise us in this matter. He's been in racing a long time, as a pro racer and a team director, and I understand he also sits on the rules and regulations advisory board. Why not give him a call?"

"He must be terribly busy right now—the Tour de France will start in a week," says Mo.

"You won't reach him *during* the Tour."

"That's for sure. I'm going to contact his office right away," says Mo.

***

"So, Junior, what's on your mind? What's so urgent?" asks Sofia, arriving in his office.

"Well, since I locked the VPs up in my office, I'm not being scheduled for as many meetings. I think my referee days are finally coming to an end. I have time to think again, and I'm still thinking about the work the lawyers did for us a few days ago."

"Was the quick job the lawyers did good enough?"

"It certainly was in this case; others may take a little longer."

"There is an important concept that we learned from lean startups: 'Good is good enough.' For lawyers and engineers in traditional, conservative companies there is only one definition of 'good': everything has to be perfect in every stage of a project. And if time is available, engineers will always find a way to fill that time."

"I thought that's what got us to the quality we have today. But I can see where perfection is not always required, like in the lawyer case."

"Actually, the reason for filling every minute available with work is not always rooted in the desire for perfection—often it's risk avoidance. Companies occasionally make mistakes, and then they overreact. They make new rules, and those rules eventually get applied to everything and never removed, which makes for a risk-averse culture."

"And what's so wrong with that?"

"It is an obstacle to innovation, for one, and you spend a lot of time and money on work that is not needed in the early stages of your development."

"Well, we no longer have the luxury of unnecessary spending."

"You want to think like startup entrepreneurs, who don't have a lot of funding. Many are run based on the owner's personal savings, so they're extremely frugal when it comes to developing a new product or service. They can't afford to spend anything that's not absolutely needed, and they're very creative in how they can get by with the minimum of means. They work with very crude and cheap prototypes at the beginning and only test incrementally as the product matures. This also saves them precious time. Once they're committed to the product and come closer to launch—and only then—do they build more advanced prototypes and conduct more extensive testing."

"Huh. I imagine that long ago my father might have done the same thing. But it was a very different company then."

"Yes. Larger companies, like yours now, have resources, prototyping capabilities, funds, etc. at their disposal. But that doesn't mean they need to use them for every project at every stage of development. Anything more than what's absolutely needed at a given time is a waste. Remember Mo's prototype that you rode?"

"That was pretty crude, but good enough to show us that there was something to the idea."

"Exactly. But would you give it to a rider in the Giro?"

"Of course not. We'll need a much better prototype and a lot of safety and quality testing first."

"Right, but it only happens when needed and in the amount needed. The lean principle that applies here is waste elimination—overprocessing, to be more precise. You learned in the training that waste is everything that takes up space, consumes resources, or costs money that customers won't pay for. For example, customers want a safe bike, and they'll pay for appropriate safety testing. But I'm sure that Davanti performs testing that customers would frown at if they could see it in an itemized bill."

"Go on."

"Lean seeks to eliminate the eight cardinal wastes, including overprocessing. Overprocessing is prominent in non-manufacturing settings as are some of the others. You know them: waiting, defects, inventory, overproduction, motion, transportation, underutilization of knowledge and talent."

"At least we don't have waiting in the office. When I walk through the office, I never see anybody sitting around waiting as if for a bus or train."

"Junior, as you know, the most challenging thing about wastes is that they're often hidden so well that you can't see them. That's especially true for an office: you don't see the work; you only see the people. Everybody looks so busy because you overload them—when they wait for something for one project they jump to another project."

"Well, at least we got that right. We've eliminated waiting."

"Not quite. The engineers aren't waiting, but the projects wait."

"Go on . . ."

"Do you know what every hour of project waiting time costs Davanti?"

"You tell me. I can't imagine it's much. If it was I'd know about it."

"Let's assume you have this awesome new bike, and people are clamoring to get their hands on it. In fact, they'll pay you a premium for the high-margin product. If the launch of that bike is delayed, how much revenue and profit would you forfeit every day while you wait?"

"Wow. That could be a lot. But I'd personally make sure that would never happen."

"Really. How many of those projects do you have right at this moment?"

Sofia sees the bewildered look on Junior's face to which she's become accustomed.

"I assume you moved projects ahead in the past. Did you do that at the expense of other projects? Was it based on a gut decision? Might you have put a project with a low cost of delay ahead of one with a high cost of delay without knowing it?"

"Cost of delay came up in the organization meeting. I have the feeling this isn't the last time I'll hear about it."

"You will. In short, it's the potential profit for a project divided by the number of days for that profit to be achieved. Add in any daily fees or penalties that come up as the project drags on, and you get the COD for each day of delay."

"That's simple enough, but," says Junior, cut off by an alarm on his phone. "Oh, I lost track of the time. I'm late for my next meeting. And you don't have to tell me—I'm paying the salaries of all those folks waiting for me. Now that's really a cost of delay."

***

Johan Leffe had been a Belgian pro racer whose career was ended by a severe accident. He decided to pursue his passion for the sport as a coach and worked his way up to the directeur sportif/team director, which is essentially the head coach of the Davanti racing team. He has a small office in

Geneva, which he shares with Veronique, his capable assistant. Johan is not only the technical director of the Davanti team, but he also manages the bike racing operation.

Johan spends most of the race season in the main team car and on the road because all other business—signing new riders, finding sponsors—usually happens in the offseason. While Johan is on the race circuit, Veronique runs all business in the office. She is a fervent race fan, and there is a rumor that it's Veronique who finds and recruits the new talent for the Davanti team while Johan drives the team car. Johan has an excellent in-season race support team (technicians, therapists, soigneurs, a doctor) with little turnover for years, which helps with the administration.

Davanti is the team's primary sponsor and pays for salaries, equipment, and support. Other cosponsors cover some administrative costs. For accounting purposes, Davanti writes off the race team expenses as advertising cost, but only a few people know the real cost. Davanti also donates bikes to racers from other teams who do not have a bike company as their sponsor. About 40 percent of all pro riders are atop a Davanti bike—that's a lot of ads racing around the globe.

Despite the contributions from other cosponsors and fervent support from Junior and all Davanti associates, many times Junior considered dropping the race team because it consumes a lot of Davanti's annual budget. But at the end of the day, his dad's legacy, prestige, and the passion prevail. And as long as Davanti can demand a premium price for every bike it sells, Junior can afford the team. But it doesn't mean the support costs don't keep him up at night.

Junior allows Johan to manage the team as he sees fit. He, Stephano, and other directors, such as R&D, occasionally meet with Johan in the offseason. Junior's primary concerns (other than team costs) are that engineers receive the right design input and that the team avoids bad press; he reminds Johan at every opportunity that there will never be a Davanti doping scandal. Junior has zero tolerance for breaking *any* rules. His father Fausto won races the old-fashioned way—with talent, training, and respectable behavior—and he expects that of every Davanti team member under contract.

In Johan's office, Veronique picks up the phone when Mo calls. He explains the reason for the call and expects his request to speak with Johan to be politely turned down. But instead he hears, "You are in luck. Johan plans to stop by today. He may have time to call you back Monsieur Pensatore. But after today, he'll be splitting time with the team and his family. They won't see him during the Tour de France unless they come watch a stage."

"In that case, let me leave my cell number. He can reach me any time at his convenience."

***

Mo is getting ready to head to lunch when his cellphone rings; he sees "Johan Leffe" as his number appears on the screen: "Monsieur Leffe, thank you for calling me back."

"A small favor for the bikes you design for us. So what can I do for you?"

Mo explains his project, and Johan listens with great interest. "So based on your experience, what are the chances the governing bodies would ever approve a new drivetrain like this for the race circuit? Without pro racers endorsing this new technology, we likely won't generate sales."

"As long as the equipment is safe, the international bike association will approve what the racers want—that's the bottom line," says Johan. "And the new technology has to be made available to all of them who want it. I assume you know that. . . . So what do the racers say about your new idea?"

"I don't know. How would I know?"

"Ask them. The Davanti riders are sworn to corporate secrecy by their contract."

"Just ask them. You mean after the Tour. They're busy training now, right?"

"No, not today. Why don't you bring a few samples and show them. They're all together in our training center in Grenoble now on light-duty cycling pensum. After dinner, they hang out killing time. Come out tonight, and I'll give you a half hour to talk to them."

"This is awfully nice of you, Monsieur Leffe. Thank you."

"No problem. See you at 8:00 this evening in Grenoble."

Mo, too excited to eat, skips lunch and spends an hour packing all the components into his car. It's at least a five-hour drive to Grenoble, and Mo wants to give himself plenty of time. Meeting the Davanti riders is all he can think about.

When he arrives at the training camp around 6:30 pm, he draws a lot of curious looks by riders and staff alike. Many had seen Mo at their races, and some wonder if he's brought a secret weapon.

Mo's heart is pounding when Johan introduces him after dinner: "Mo Pensatore is a Davanti engineer, and he and his colleagues design those bikes that you guys use to win races," says Johan. All the pros applaud, and Mo blushes.

Mo shows the prototype and describes how Vinnie built it. The racers look skeptical; many are thinking it won't reach the first kilometer mark in a race. Mo invites them to try it out, but he gets no takers. Then he briefly talks about the advantages: no broken chains, no derailleur malfunction, etc.

"I like the concept," says Rossa, but few others offer comments or have questions.

"What if these bikes are a lot better than those of your competitors?" asks Johan. "There's a very good chance that may be the case. Only Davanti has this technology." He has their attention now.

"I'll ride anything that gives me a fraction of a second on the finish line," comments one of the riders.

"Would any of you ride a bike like that in a major competition?"

"If it's faster, of course," chimes in Pasquale.

"Will it have a larger spread of gears?" asks Rossa. "I'm tired of the limitation of the current derailleur. I want fewer gears and more difference between them."

Mo takes careful notes as other riders ask similar racing questions.

Johan looks around the room: "Everybody wants it if it helps them win. So who's first to try?" All hands stay down; still no takers.

Mo's initial enthusiasm fades to disappointment, and he understands quickly that his presentation is over when Johan stands to discuss the next day's training program. Mo thanks the group for their time, wishes them good luck in the Tour, and packs his demo pieces, most of which were not shown.

"Well, that was fast," says Mo when Johan pauses the meeting to walk him out.

"Don't read too much into that. These guys avoid every risk possible—even ones that don't make sense to most people. They all get their own bikes, and everybody thinks he has the best. They put all kinds of talismans on their bikes, and they think switching bikes is like cheating on their girlfriends. But remember, if there's something better out there, they'll kill to get it—but only after someone else tries it first. And, Mo, one more thing. Have you considered proving the technology on the amateur circuit? Let the amateur racers spread the news. And then when you have something more refined and field-tested to try, I'll get you back here again."

"Thank you for the advice. I'll remember that."

Rather than the long drive back to Fumane, Mo drives a few hours east and checks into a small hotel near Bardonecchia. There he goes over his notes, organizing his displeasure for a debrief with Ricardo the following morning.

***

"So how did it go?" asks Ricardo.

"After listening to them and talking with Johan, I think we found our no-go answer. For the pros, the project is dead."

"I guess this idea needs a pivot. Even if an assumption can't be verified, it's not the end of an idea. We only learned that the road we were on is at an impasse—there are other roads if we can make a turn."

"Johan was very clear that those guys kill for fractions of a second—they just don't want to be the first ones to try something new. Johan said there could be other options to prove the technology."

"Like what?"

"Amateur racers and aspiring pros are thankful for any free Davanti bike they can get. They ride under the same conditions as the pros. We can learn from them what we need to know to develop the drivetrain. Johan was very clear that if the pros see the slightest advantage, they'll want the bike, and, if they want it, the authorizing body will approve what the racers want."

"So that's your new direction. Focus on the amateur circuit and their feedback to develop the concept, and if it shows promise, show it to the pros again."

"Maybe we keep the Davanti name off the first bikes out there, just in case one lands in a ditch," jokes Mo.

"Ditch or not, it will show that Davanti is innovating. . . . How will you get in touch with amateur racers?"

"Well, we've got 30 or so amateurs that meet every Wednesday in the parking lot. That's a start. And I'll talk to Marco about how to move forward as well. He's pretty tapped into the amateur circuits around here."

"That sounds like a pivot plan to me."

Chapter 14

A New Approach to R&D

Mo spent his weekend reflecting on the conversations with Johan, the racers, and the pivot with his project. He attended a men's amateur race near Verona on Sunday and was able to speak with a race organizer and a few riders after the event. Just hearing the name "Davanti" and the possibility of getting involved in the design of Davanti bikes got the racers excited. Mo couldn't divulge any details of the project, of course, but he was pleased by the impressions that Davanti bikes had made on riders.

On Monday and Tuesday, he followed up on some leads that Marco provided—leaders from local bike clubs as well as a few riders who Marco knows from the ProSeries, a second-tier tour with races in Europe, America, Asia, Africa, and Oceania. Mo is sure he'll have little trouble finding volunteers to ride prototypes once legal signs off, and he's confident he can find racers to give him the *right* input for the design and maybe critique his next prototypes under race-like conditions.

Mo has also been reading a lot about lean startups and best practices in product development, many of which he intends to use for the Leonardo project. He plans to combine some methods that he learned in school, like design of experiments (DOE), with quick learning cycles—a build-test-learn process that would include quick assessments by a few racers.

By Wednesday, optimism about the pivot has given Mo the courage to press his luck in another direction. Marco confirmed that he has a Davanti demo race bike that will fit Marie. Mo picks up his smartphone, and sends a text: "Are you signed up for the race in Champel?"

"Yes. I'll be racing. Why do you ask?"

"I'll be in town."

"OK. Maybe I'll see you. Ciao."

It's not quite the response Mo was hoping for, but it's good enough. He gets up and heads to Marco's office to pick up the bike.

***

Mo takes Friday afternoon off and after lunch heads to Champel with the bike on his Fiat's rack. As he gets on E70 headed west, he stops for gas and to text Marie.

"Will be in town today. Can you meet me at the Mercure hotel, east of Champel, at 1900?"

"Why?"

"I brought something to spice up your ride."

"What is it?"

"You just have to see."

DOI: 10.4324/9781003231837-14

"OK" followed by a frustrated face emoji.

About four hours later, Mo is driving northeast on A40 and nearing his exit for a Mecure hotel. He's excited, but he's definitely learning to temper his enthusiasm—for work and life. He takes the ramp that gets him to the Rue des Jardins, from which he makes a left into the Mercure parking lot. He parks and stands next to his Fiat with the Davanti bike on the roof.

Marie can't miss him as she pulls into the lot and an adjacent parking spot. She cautiously steps out of her car, and gives Mo a friendly hug. "It's nice to see you. I see you brought your bike—too bad you can't participate in the race, Mo. But I can show you some nice tours here for you to ride."

"I didn't bring my bike. I brought *your* bike."

"You what? Are you kidding? I can't afford a bike like that."

"Don't worry about buying it. It's a Davanti demo, to your specs, and it's insured."

"You brought this for *me*. For the race?"

"I was hoping it would give you a little boost. After all, you want to do well in your hometown race."

"I can't believe this. Can you fit it for me? Maybe tomorrow? I'd like to take it for a short ride before the race."

"That's why I came a day early. I'm hoping you have enough time to get used to it."

Marie gives Mo another hug, this one more emotional than the first. She starts to speak, but then stops and stares at the bike. "It's beautiful . . . I can't . . . Wow. I can't wait to see the looks on the faces of my club mates. Can I take it home tonight?"

"Sure. Let's get it on your rack, and then I'll meet you in the morning. Just say where."

Mo switches the bike over to Marie's car, and helps her secure it. Marie, over-the-top happy, gives Mo another hug, then says goodbye and heads out of the lot, waving repeatedly and beeping her horn as she drives off.

Mo waves and smiles. He thinks about checking in, then sees a brewery sign just across the street and a patio bathed in late-day sun. It's time to celebrate with an IPA.

***

The next morning at 9:00 am, Mo meets Marie at the parking lot near her favorite training route. Mo has his toolbox, and it only takes him a few minutes to install her seat and pedals and adjust the bike. She takes a short spin around the lot, grinning widely, and, after a few more minor adjustments, plans to meet others from her bike club for a short ride to loosen their legs before tomorrow's big race. Marie is very grateful and excited, but a bit more cautious today.

"Mo, I can't thank you enough. This really is amazing. I can't wait to give it a good test."

"Then you'd better get to it. I'll look for you tomorrow. Good luck," says Mo, who then heads to a coffee shop to get a late breakfast and catch up on emails and work.

Marie quickly gets used to the new bike on her bike-club ride. In the afternoon, she texts Mo: "Wow. Can't wait for tomorrow!"

***

Mo heads out early the next day and gets to the starting line in the high-end Geneva suburb. It's perfect summer weather for a race, with a light morning breeze and not a cloud in the sky. He is unable to talk with Marie before the start of the race, but he sees her warm up with six women from her local club. They look good in their pink jerseys, which remind Mo of the leader's jersey in the Giro d'Italia.

The race is scheduled to pass three times through the town. Mo decides to watch from the top of the first ascent and drives to the location before the racers head out. On the first and second loop, the field remains packed. But on the third loop, Mo spots a pink jersey heading up the hill ahead of the field; the rider has completely broken away now, and his heart starts pounding. He recognizes her—Marie has left the rest of the riders behind. Mo sprints alongside her, cheering like the fans on the mountains of the Tour de France. He hopes she can keep her lead to the finish line.

Mo jumps into his car, and he makes it to the finish line before the riders. Marie survived a late push and wins the race to the applause of her friends and family.

Marie's parents are the first to congratulate her, followed by her teammates after they cross the finish line. They're all exhausted but extremely happy. Mo soon makes his way to the celebration.

"Congratulations," says Mo.

"Oh, my. Mo, thank you so much. I want you to meet my parents—they are my biggest race fans."

"As they should be."

"Maman, papa, this is Mo. He works for Davanti Nella Gara, and he got me the demo bike for today's race. It made all the difference and helped me win."

"Nice to meet you, Madame et Monsieur Vigneron. It wasn't all the bike. Marie's a good racer."

"Good to meet you as well, Mo," says Mr. Vigneron.

"It must be exciting to work for a bike company like Davanti Nella Gara," says Mrs. Vigneron. "What do you do?"

"I'm an engineer. I was on the team that designed the bike Marie rode today."

"Nice work. That's a good-looking bike," says Mr. Vigneron.

Marie gives Mo a big hug. "Can I keep it?" she asks with a sheepish grin.

"I think my friend Marco will come here personally to repossess it if I don't turn it in Monday at 8:00 am."

"I understand. I was just kidding. It's too bad that Davanti can't make this possible for other bikers. You know, people like me who can't afford one."

"What do you mean?"

"It would be months of salary for me to own one. Why can't I rent one now and then? Or any of us?"

"That's a great question . . ."

"Thanks again, Mo. I need to get going and cleaned up," says Marie as she gives the bike a kiss. "I'll miss this, that's for sure."

"Goodbye, Marie. I hope to see you soon."

"Me, too. Ciao."

As Mo walks back to the car with the winning bike, a tall young racer in a pink jersey stops him. She is dragging an older bike.

"Hey, Davanti, any more single engineers at your company? Can you set me up with a date? I need a new bike, too."

***

Junior and Sofia walk into the engineering area and see Ricardo waiting for them at a large table in the corner of the room. Junior smiles; he loves to see everyone hard at work.

"Ricardo, let me again say how happy I am to have you on my staff," says Junior.

"Thank you for the confidence, Mr. Davanti," Ricardo replies.

"Now, remember, my staff call me 'Junior.' . . . So this meeting reminds me of Fusilli, out in the open. I'll have to get used to that. But at least we have chairs."

"I have a few more by my office," pointing to his desk in the middle.

The engineering area is being transformed into a big open room, with the managers dispersed among the engineers. On the perimeter is room to construct quiet areas of various sizes, some fenced off by sound dampening partitions. Flat-screen monitors are already on some of the meeting desks, allowing staff to connect their computers and share information. There also are tables for meetings in areas where they do not disturb people—many with partitions around tables so they can be used as obeyas for major projects.

"I expected you to move into Emilio's office?"

"No, I prefer to sit here with the staff—close to the action. We're using Emilio's office for conference calls, meetings with customers and suppliers, and discussions where privacy is needed."

"Did you come up with this after the Fusilli inspiration?"

"I worked in an area like this before, but I let my staff decide on the layout. They have to work here, so they may just as well set it up. We still have some arranging to do."

Junior looks surprised: "Good idea. . . . Sofia tells me that you learned about lean and innovation excellence from your former employer. And by the way, how is your wife doing at her new job?"

"She's doing very well; looks like the relocation really worked out well for both of us."

"So tell me about your plans. How will we reshape R&D?"

"We must create an R&D organization capable of supporting the Davanti goals we formulated the other day, and it must align with the new corporate organization. Toyota says that 95 percent of a new car's profits are decided by the engineers in R&D during the design of the car. We can argue the exact percentage for Davanti, but I'll make sure the returns are as high as possible, and we'll use the principles of innovation excellence to maximize it."

"Please explain, Ricardo," requests Sofia.

"Many companies use lean to cut the cost of R&D, but those companies are rarely successful. I'll show you in a minute how we establish R&D efficiency—but before we work on efficiency, we use the principles to maximize what R&D can do to create value and help the business make money and meet other company goals. I consider R&D an investment, and Davanti is entitled to a return."

"I like the sound of that," says Junior.

Sofia notices a very pleased expression on Junior's face that seems to say, "Why didn't we promote this guy earlier?"

"When I came to Davanti I was very impressed with our performance and quality, but I wasn't happy with the product portfolio, among other things. Now I'm excited to work with Joe and the rest of the team to get it right. You know one of the biggest challenges in R&D is picking the right products—and if you don't know how to do that, you'll end up working on everything that anybody in marketing wants. Eventually you sort them out when they clog the system, dropping projects that you've wasted a lot of money on. Going forward, before we spend real money on a project we'll have a good idea how much money it will make."

Junior just smiles, thinking, "I hope he can deliver half of what he promises. But I will remind him later if he forgets."

"We'll align the work with our available resources, and if Joe or other product directors for future value streams need more work, we'll have to first find the resources. We'll design the process for flow, so everything moves all the time—no project waits. I'll also discuss launch times with Joe. In the past, we had a panic every year because everything is launched at the Eurobike show."

"But that's where we have to launch," interrupts Junior.

"Of course, but we don't have to do all the work a month before the show. We can pull some work ahead so it doesn't all pile up in the weeks before the show. Overburdening and work imbalance are very wasteful. We need to correct those before we really see the impact of removing the other cardinal wastes."

"I'm hearing a lot about wastes. I'm glad you are as well."

"Absolutely."

"So tell me, Ricardo, I haven't seen a budget yet for all the new projects you started. Emilio was always looking for more money when projects kicked off. It often seemed warranted."

"We need to do a better job of managing the resources we have before putting our hand out for more. For now, we've reassigned some engineers from canceled projects to the new work; others are working to develop the new processes. And as we eliminate more waste, we'll gain more resources. Many world-class companies held their R&D budgets flat for 20 years or more after they implemented innovation excellence—that's my goal for Davanti."

"I'm glad to hear that. Thank you, Ricardo. But that does remind me: Claudia is in my office three times a day telling me about cancelled projects and lost volume, upset dealers, loss of reputation . . ."

"She still thinks that it's better to sell a lot of bikes at a loss than to get our portfolio straightened out and profitable. We promised her more bike volume—but they need to be the right bikes that create value and make money. We're moving up the Primo Sempre pro line and the Primo Veloce amateur line to early next year. Claudia is part of the planning team, but she obviously doesn't trust the process yet."

Junior is not convinced that will keep her out of his office. "If you need help with Claudia, let me know."

"Thank you, Junior, but I'm sure this will work itself out."

"You mentioned that R&D efficiency was not your first priority. But can't the innovation excellence principles be used for that as well?"

"Yes, Junior. Before we ask for more money, we'll definitely eliminate waste and increase efficiency to create more capacity and space. But I'll focus our R&D changes foremost on becoming much faster."

"Wonderful. We really need that. I'm tired of hearing how much faster our competitors are."

"Development speed is a huge asset. We can make so much more money if we're the first one on the market. And when we develop a new product faster than our competitors can copy our old one, then we've really made the leap. But let me share one of the best-kept lean secrets with you: when you get faster by applying lean principles, you get more efficient at the same time. It's as if the efficiency was free, a byproduct of speed."

"I like the sound of that, but will speed hurt our quality?"

"We don't achieve speed by cutting corners. Innovation excellence, when applied correctly, will actually improve quality. I will prove that to you at the right time."

"I never got anything for free in this business. We didn't hire you to be a magician."

"Look at it this way: What do we do to get faster? We create flow, collaboration, alignment. We eliminate waste. We reuse knowledge. We stop unnecessary work (aka overprocessing). We avoid stop-and-go. We don't need to cancel projects anymore. We eliminate changes and rework. *All* of those principles will create speed *and* efficiency. I've seen companies double or even triple their R&D capacity."

Junior considers all that Ricardo has said and shakes his head. "Hmm. Maybe you're a magician after all."

"No, it's not magic—just good innovation excellence thinking and experience. But those aren't the only changes we'll make."

"What do you mean?"

"We're going to implement three innovation excellence processes."

"Three?"

"Yes. Let me explain," says Ricardo as he stands and walks over to a whiteboard. He grabs a marker, draws out three process arrows in a row, and then explains them from left to right. "They look like this:

- The ICP—idea creation process—is what took place when we prototyped Mo's idea. This process allows us to create and assess a very large number of new ideas in a very short time and with few resources. We have many other ideas in this process now. When an idea is ripe for further investment, it enters the . . .
- TCP—technology creation process. This is where we focus on closing the knowledge gaps and developing the technology needed for one or many products in a lean fashion. For this, we'll use fast and efficient processes, including set-based concurrent engineering. When we're ready to develop the products, we get to the . . .
- PCP—product development process—where the products are created using current and new knowledge. Here is where we design all the frames, styles, component levels, etc. and get ready to launch the products in a process that almost looks like manufacturing."

Junior studies the board for a moment, looks to Sofia and then back to Ricardo.

"As you may imagine, there are different requirements for the different processes," continues Ricardo. "For example, the ICP is about trying many ideas, and most will fail. But with PCP, failure is certainly not an option; we should have reduced the risk up to the PCP to prevent unpleasant surprises."

"This is the first I've heard of the three processes, Ricardo. Where do they stand today?"

"The deployment of the ICP is going well, and I hope we'll soon have our first idea ready to deploy in TCP. We have plenty of projects entering the PCP, so Sofia and I decided to implement innovation excellence in the PCP next."

"Our plans for the PCP are well-documented," says Sofia. "I call it the 'Goodyear process,' which was well publicized in 2016.[1] It's similar to the manufacturing process we use in our plant, which shows results quickly and makes it relatively easy to engage associates."

"It will also help that the PCP, which consumes 70 percent of our resources, has the highest return—the highest impact. And with faster speeds in the PCP, we'll also get our friends in sales the volume they need."

"You'll need to prove to me that you aren't superman," says Junior, impressed but somewhat skeptical that all this can be accomplished. "That's a lot to take on, and, for now, you certainly have my support. I hope you razzle and dazzle the rest of my staff next week when you show them your plans. They're not easily convinced."

***

Sergio Monticello, a young lab technician, stops by to see Mo. "Do you have a moment to look at something, Mo? I think I've found something you could use on the direct-drive mechanism."

Mo looks up from his desk: "Give me just a second to wrap this up." Mo pounds away on his keyboard for about a minute.

"What do you have?"

Sergio shows him literature on a device used in key-hole surgeries—a thin, flexible, carbon cable fitted through a nylon tube. "Doctors insert the flexible tube through tiny incisions, twist the carbon cable, and activate cutters or grinders on the other end, either by using their hands or a mechanical drill," explains Sergio. "This could be used to transfer the torque from the gear mechanism to the rear wheel. They say it has extremely low friction and it can handle very high torque, which is required for orthoscopic procedures. They even use it to cut tendons. Maybe we could even bend it enough and make front-wheel drive cycles. Oh, and it only weighs a fraction of the shaft that Vinnie put on your first prototype."

Mo briefly scans the documents and looks disinterested: "This thing probably costs more than a bike alone. And, besides, we're already looking at a hydraulic motor drive. It also has a flexible supply line and could be used for front-wheel drive bikes."

"But . . ."

"You'll have to excuse me, Sergio, I'm late for a meeting."

Mo hands the papers back, gets up from his desk, and walks out of the engineering room, leaving Sergio wondering what that was all about.

***

After lunch, Mo is leaving the cafeteria and runs into Ricardo, who is entering for his lunch. Ricardo stops him and asks to speak with him for a moment.

"Sure, Ricardo. What can I do for you?"

"Let's have a seat over here," says Ricardo, pointing to a table away from the bustle of the room. "Did Sergio talk to you about his idea. You know, the surgical shaft?"

"He did. I told him those devices are prohibitively expensive for what we're doing and that we're already exploring front-wheel drivetrains with the hydraulic option."

"He shared with me what you told him. He was surprised by your reaction."

"He caught me at a bad time, but I'm glad he understands the problems with his idea."

"Mo, do you remember how people reacted to your first idea about Leonardo?"

"Of course, but my first idea was a lot better than the surgical device. There's no way . . ."

Ricardo holds up both hands, giving Mo a stop sign: "How do you know that? Nobody can know yet if there is a way or not for the surgical device to work on a bike."

Mo gets the sense that this conversation is about more than a surgical drive: "I'm listening."

"Let's make a little game out of this. Tell me, what's the worst part of his solution?"

"It costs a fortune?"

"OK, so let's turn this around for a second: How could we overcome that hurdle?"

Mo pauses, looking around the cafeteria as if the answer can be found among his fellow employees. "Well, like many medical devices, the prices are probably horribly marked up to cover potential liabilities."

"Yes, which means that even if the medical devices are produced in large volumes, they're still expensive," adds Ricardo.

"Right. But I'd bet the materials themselves aren't that expensive. Maybe we could patent a non medical application and let others manufacture it?"

"Mo, you've just shown me that there was an answer to what you thought was the worst thing about Sergio's idea."

"OK. I get it. Maybe I was too busy to give Sergio the time this deserved. I could have managed that better."

"Mo, you're a good engineer. But I think you can be more than a good engineer. You can be a good leader. You're already on that path. But just like becoming an engineer, you'll have to work at leadership . . . and sometimes set aside your own ideas while you listen to others."

"Yes, I agree. I think I've learned the lesson. Thank you. So what do I tell Sergio?"

"Tell him, 'Thanks,' and ask him for more details. With some quick assessment, your team can determine if this is a concept to add to the Leonardo project."

***

It's happy hour on a beautiful summer day at Bruno's Birreria-Ristorante, with its large, garage-style doors wide open. Mo and Marco sit at the bar. They each order a Hefeweizen, the perfect complement to the warm breezes blowing through the brewpub.

"Good choice, gentlemen; nothing like a hint of lemon on a sultry day," says bartender Marianne with a wink and a flirt.

Mo and Marco are momentarily mesmerized by Marianne, then turn to each other and touch glasses in a toast.

"Congratulations on your new assignment, Marco."

"Thanks. And likewise, Mo. We're doing alright."

"Yes, we are."

"I'm looking forward to working with Joe in his new role. I'm not quite as sure about working for Claudia. That could be a challenge."

"You'll figure it out. Just a little of upward coaching and influencing."

"Maybe, we'll see. Thanks for bringing the bike back promptly. Looks like Marie did well."

"Well? She won the race. And you know what comes next: she'll want a bike for every race, and so do her teammates."

"Friendship can only get you so much. At least you got to see her again."

"I've attended a few amateur races recently, and I don't see many Davanti bikes," says Mo, waving to Marianne so they can order some snacks.

"No wonder. Look at our price tag."

"But why do we only *sell* bikes?"

"You want us to give them away?"

"No. But there are many other ways to collect money for bikes."

"Like?"

"Lease. Rent. Maybe Davanti can finance them, like car companies, who make tons of money through their credit organizations."

"That's an interesting thought. Maybe on the sales side Davanti is as conservative as the development side."

"And think about what, if anything, we do with the demo bikes once they have a few scratches—we can't use them for demo anymore. What will happen to all bikes that return from the Tour de France this year? The pros get new bikes every race, and I bet some of those get retired. Some get retired without ever having been ridden at all. What could we do with those?"

"Excellent questions," says Marco as Marianne asks what they'd like.

"Two orders of frites, please," says Marco.

Marianne punches the order in: "You got it. I'll keep an eye on your beers, too."

"Marco, let's add the ideas to our big list of new ideas," says Mo. "Or should we just do something about this. You know, run with it? Who would we assign to this?"

"Does it have to be someone in R&D?"

"I don't see why it needs to be. There's as much about this idea that's not R&D. Any ideas?"

"We recently hired a new associate—Rebecca Sabrese—who's really interested in getting engaged with the innovation initiative. She has a solid sales and marketing background, and she knows the customers, the dealers, and the supply chain. She used to manage a small multibrand bike store. I'll see if she'd like to take this on."

"Great. We may be on to something."

"So tell me more about Marie. What did you two talk about besides the bike?"

"We didn't have much time to talk. She was with her parents after the race. And, of course, I needed to get back with your bike. . . . But it was good to see her. I think she felt the same about seeing me."

***

Sofia walks into Junior's office well past the end of a typical workday. Late afternoon sun drenches the office, and a particularly sharp beam of light illuminates the painting of the senior Fausto. Junior's assistant Anna went home more than an hour ago, so nobody announces that Sofia has arrived. Junior, glued to his monitor, is startled to see her, although she was expected.

"Oh, I didn't hear you come in," says Junior. "Thanks for the late meeting. I didn't think I could put this off another day. These wastes and the money associated with them keep me up at night."

"I agree, Junior. Then let's talk more about eliminating them."

"As I said, the lawyers really opened my eyes to waste, and I'm thankful that you're helping me put things into perspective. When I first learned about lean, I didn't see waste in the office; now I see it everywhere, and the more I see the more it upsets me. And it's not just overprocessing and waiting, I also see waste in motion, transportation, and with defects and rework. But I'm having trouble with a few of the waste concepts."

"Such as?"

"Inventory. We eliminated the warehouses in manufacturing, and there are no warehouses in the office. And I can see overproduction in the plant, but where is it in the office?"

"In the office, the lines between those two wastes can be blurred—so just let me give you a couple of examples: The most prominent form of office inventory is work in process. People often get assigned many projects and tasks for a period of time to assure they're busy. With engineering work, which is quite complicated, they really can only concentrate on one single thing or task at a time. So engineers with many projects let others sit while they concentrate on one, then when that one is completed or delayed, they move on to another. This form of stop-and-go multitasking leads to a lot of work in process—waste—which is inefficient and leads to more mistakes. And this also means that the money you've invested in those unfinished projects has not yielded a euro of return, just like bikes sitting in a warehouse."

"OK, that was helpful. So tell me about overproduction. It's not as if we can produce too much in the office and keep it in a warehouse. We aren't even getting done what we're supposed to deliver."

"You can't see overproduction in the office because that waste is virtual and stored in computers. Bikes that were designed and never sold and projects that were half completed when they got cancelled were clearly overproduced, right? Or consider engineers working on project components that later get changed."

"Sure. I get it. What should I know about knowledge and talent waste?"

"Davanti spends millions every year on R&D, right?"

"Almost 30 million."

"For that money, R&D creates knowledge, like how to design or manufacture better bikes, how to solve technical problems, how to ascertain what customers really want, how to win races. . . . Some of that knowledge is reused. Obviously, your bikes are better today than they were 10 years ago, but much of what went into designing the bike is still in the heads of engineers. The knowledge retires one day when the engineers retire. If that knowledge is not passed along, many engineers will have to reinvent what was already known."

"And talent waste?"

"Remember when I told you that you had 200 innovators? Was I correct?"

"You sure were. All we had to do was stop killing their ideas."

"And we also now have associates contributing their talent and knowledge in many other processes and activities beyond R&D."

"The more I understand you, the more upset I get. Why didn't we see all these wastes for all these years? We really could have used that money for much better things."

"Junior, at least we're working to eliminate them now. Imagine if we weren't. Remember, as Marcel said, the biggest waste in a company is to ignore all the opportunities for improvement: 'No problem is a big problem,' as Toyota luminaries have been known to say."

"Yes, we know we have problems. And too much waste is one of them."

"And we're doing something about them. We've trained the associates, and they're working on the wastes: Joe and Ricardo started eliminating one of your biggest wastes—developing and making bikes that didn't sell or that didn't make money. And they've also stopped those projects that linger for years and will never get finished. Stephano has stopped the reports that nobody was reading. And you not only have 200 innovators, but you're on the way to having 200 innovation excellence experts—they're working to eliminate all the waste we just talked about and much more."

"OK. So how do I help? I can't sit here and stare at pop all day."

"Waste elimination on all levels is part of lean and innovation excellence. It will save money and time, improve cash flow, and boost your bottom line. But there are bigger opportunities with innovation excellence that also can improve your *top line* and create a better company as well. Remember how Ricardo uses innovation excellence to help the business create revenue and the company achieve its goals?"

"Yes, and I'm beginning to understand how that the same approach could help us achieve our corporate goals sooner and be a better, more profitable company—and get me to retirement sooner. I'm all in. How do we do that?"

"We make Davanti *faster*—but not like a fast train that once you set it on its tracks, you can't stop or redirect it. We also make Davanti *agile*. Davanti competes in a business where things change every day: customers change their preferences, new technology comes on the market, there are disruptions in the economy, there is political change. . . . When I came here, the process at Davanti was to set concrete targets for bikes and extend the time to meet all those targets regardless of anything that happened during a bike's development. Sometimes the product was obsolete before it was fully designed."

"Yes. I know, I know."

"In an agile process, you work in small steps—in the business just as in R&D—and after every step, you assess the results and the situation: what did you learn; is the challenge more difficult than we thought; what happened in the market; are there new components available, new releases by our competitors, or better opportunities for our investment? And then you decide to stay the course, to change direction, or you may decide to freeze a project. And if you do this right, you've invested the minimum when you stop or freeze a project."

"Waste, speed, agility, value, delivery. The list keeps growing. What else is covered by innovation excellence?"

"People have crammed a lot of stuff under the innovation excellence umbrella or lean as it's been narrowly defined. In fact, it encompasses a lot more than was discovered at Toyota many years ago that came to be known as 'lean.' You and your associates learned all the key principles, but not everything is right for every company. One size of transformation doesn't fit all. There may be things at Davanti that are as good as they can or should be. Davanti is different from Fusilli, and Fusilli is not like Marcel's other companies. There is no secret recipe. The associates now know the principles, they know the work, they see the problems, and they will pick what is needed to improve their work. If they don't find it under this umbrella, they'll find it somewhere else or develop it themselves."

"You keep telling me what everybody else will do. What do I do?"

"Fair enough. *You* will finally have time to add value and do what matters most for Davanti. You already set the company on the right track by creating a vision, setting goals, and engaging associates. You're developing a strategy, aligning the organization, and removing many obstacles. I can see the culture changing—you're building an environment based on empowerment, trust, and accountability."

"And now?"

"Now your role is to help everybody be successful. Help them deliver to Davanti goals and accomplish their own personal goals. You lead the development and growth of people—develop a successor for yourself; coach everybody to do the same. Junior, every day you have to set the example that you expect everybody in the company to follow. Most associates now believe that innovation excellence—unlike past initiatives—isn't going away. They're also beginning to believe that change and continuous improvement are here to stay. You need to reinforce that every day in everything you say and do."

"I think I'm starting to get the full picture now. Thanks, Sofia, for another great lesson. Just wondering: how many more lessons are there?"

"How many more can you handle?"

"Let's leave it at that for today. You know, when I brought you in here, Sofia, I thought you would change *everybody else*. Never could I have imagined the extent that I would have to change as well."

Note

1. Norbert Majerus, *Lean-Driven Innovation*, CRC Press, Boca Raton, FL, 2015.

Chapter 15

New Davanti and
R&D Strategies

The Tour de France is the biggest bicycle event of the season, with nearly 200 riders racing for the yellow jersey. The race—with 21 daily stages and only three days of rest—is one of the most-watched sporting events in the world, with millions along the roads and many more watching the race on TV.

The Davanti team is once again one of the favorites, with a reenergized Rossa leading the way. Directeur sportif Johan Leffe has been determined to take a hard line with his team's star, and Rossa responded well to the coaching. Both he and Johan expect nothing but a win for Davanti.

This year's race, as every other since it began in 1903, ends in Paris. This year, "La Grande Boucle" kicks off in the Grande Place, the central square in Brussels, Belgium, with an individual time trial. The organizers chose this prologue because the first week of the Tour passes through the northern flatlands of Europe, where most stages are determined in a sprint finish. All riders get assigned the same time as the winners in those stages, thus creating no separation in the "classement général" by which the Tour winner is determined. The Brussels time trial will split riders up by at least a few seconds, which adds a little more action to the flat stages.

A US rider—a time-trial specialist—wins the prologue, and Rossa comes in 11th place. It's an excellent placement for him. Time trials are not his specialty, and they are where he's often lost valuable time that cost him a victory in multistage races. It's a good sign and a very good start for him.

***

Junior has dedicated his Monday staff meeting to the development of the corporate strategy. Most of the directors appear in an exceptionally good mood for a Monday, excited by the start of the Tour and because most have already provided their strategy suggestions to Junior. New to the gathering are Marco and Matteo; they sit quietly, while others chat about their weekends and the Davanti team performance in the Tour.

Junior walks in, gives all a wave, and claps his hands together. "We finalized the corporate goals recently, and I think by now we're aligned well enough to take a similar approach to finalizing our corporate strategy. I understand these meetings about organization and strategy are not everybody's favorite. I hope this will be the last for a while."

Many directors nod emphatically.

Junior notices the reaction and smiles: "Thank you all for sending your suggestions. I asked Sofia to summarize them."

DOI: 10.4324/9781003231837-15   137

Junior shows the summary on the large monitor. The ideas range from creating value for the customer faster than the competitors to respecting employees and making innovation part of the culture. As the executives review the list and discuss what each of these means to them, they start to detail the pieces of strategy to achieve Davanti's goals. Sofia writes them on a whiteboard, and, after much writing and rewriting, she steps aside to reveal two major strategic themes:

Create World-Class Products with a World-Class Process Built Upon

■ Safety, quality, and performance
■ Customer focus
■ Speed and agility
■ Innovation

Create a World-Class Culture Based on

■ People engagement
■ Relentless improvement of process, people, and products
■ Embracing the need for change at all times
■ Trust and respect

Leandro is the first one to give two thumbs up to the formulation of the strategy: "It looks sound. I can support this. My function can support this." Others nod in agreement, except Claudia, who says, "I'll believe it when I see it."

Junior seems pleased, but Sofia can't tell if it's because he thinks it's a great strategy or because it only took one meeting—or both. "I will post the strategy to the vision and the goals in front of Junior's office," she announces. "As we develop metrics associated with our strategy and goals, I'll post them as well. . . . Please use these as a guide to develop your own functional strategies."

"This isn't cast in stone," adds Junior. "You can talk to me about this any time. And we'll revisit it from time to time. But these are just words on a piece of paper unless we align and execute accordingly. This is not my strategy; this is Davanti's strategy. It is your strategy. Proper execution also requires proper alignment. With your help, most associates were engaged in this process, so the strategy we've agreed to should not come as a surprise. I think every associate should be able to articulate vision, goals, and strategy in their own words and relate them to the work they do. But what's more important is that all associates understand that this deployment is not a roll-down. This rolls both ways: associates must understand that the people in this room are responsible to help them be successful. So all obstacles and needs must roll up and get addressed appropriately. And I hope some reach my level—and if not, I will go find them."

"Junior, as far as deployment and alignment," says Constantine, "in the plant we used the x-matrix[1] to formulate our strategy, and we also used it to deploy and align."

"I think that's a great idea, Constantine," says Sofia. "I also like that tool. Please offer help to your colleagues who would like to learn about it and coach them in the use of it. I chose not to use it in the first round at Davanti; people sometimes concentrate too much on the tool, and the tool drives the thinking. However, I certainly support your use of the x-matrix for clarity and to facilitate alignment and deployment."

"That's really it then for the corporate strategy," says Junior. "Thank you all for supporting this difficult task. If you need assistance with your functional strategies, please reach out to me or Sofia. Ricardo has been working on the R&D strategy, and he's planning to share that on Wednesday. You may find it helpful if you're having a hard time formulating your own."

***

"Invention is the mother of necessity," says Sofia as a new hackathon begins.

"Excuse me, Sofia," interrupts Ricardo. "I think you have that backward."

"No."

"What about all those college courses on this subject—were they wrong in describing need as the mother of invention?" asks Ricardo. "We learned how engineers design products in response to specific needs or customer problems. You know, in response to an oil embargo, the Germans in World War II made gasoline from coal, which was plentiful. We were taught that you find a customer problem or pain point, then develop a persona and empathy for the persona. And then you come up with ideas to solve the persona's problem. We did it in the last hackathon, did we not?"

"Yes, that is what we did. That's one way of doing it. It's how Mo's project developed: he discovered a customer problem—the bike chain—and he's trying to solve that problem. But I, in fact, said exactly what I intended."

"OK. Now I'm all ears."

"Consider all of the innovations where something gets invented and afterward the need is created for it. As Henry Ford said, 'If I had asked customers what they want, they would have said faster horses.' Steven Jobs didn't develop the iPhone based on a marketing survey. Today I can't live without it; a few years ago, I was perfectly happy with my flip phone and laptop."

"So you think Davanti should be inventing products that have no market?"

"I think there's a lot of money made in innovation when solutions are created out of technical *opportunity*, and then consumers are found and convinced that they must have the product . . ."

Sofia picks up a stack of Post-It Notes. "The inventor, Art Fry, got this idea when his bookmarks were falling out of a choir songbook. He quickly developed the appropriate glues to make them stick in his songbook. He used materials he and his colleagues had developed in the lab for a different application. Although Art personally needed the notes, he and his 3M colleagues had to create the market necessity around what became a multibillion business."[2]

"I wish they'd taught that in my innovation classes. I guess nobody ever asked for electric bicycle shifters either. But micro motors and lithium batteries made them possible, and now bikers love them. I'm sorry I ever doubted you."

"So here's the challenge of today's hackathon," says Sofia. "What Post-It® Notes does Davanti have? What are the great ideas here for which there is yet no need? Think about technologies, like the use of carbon fibers in sports articles or services similar to those used to support race teams. What knowledge is within Davanti that has never been exploited."

Sofia looks around the room. In attendance are Ricardo, the Volta team, and representatives from other functions. She could have listed items from the SWOT exercise but didn't want that to be the sole focus of the hackathon. She preferred that Nelly expand the group's thinking as wide as possible.

Nelly is well prepared as usual and begins to prompt the group with numerous questions. Within a few hours, the associates have come up with hundreds of ideas, from moon bikes to artificial limbs and rickshaws. After a few hours of divergence, she converges on some promising concepts—portable town scooters, applying race know-how to the servicing of airplanes on the fly, ski bikes, robotic artificial limbs, and solar-powered city transporters—and gets teams working on illustrations and simple prototypes.

Whereas some teams perform skits or give presentations to communicate their ideas, Ricardo's team builds a prototype for a ski bike, which looks like a real bike, but with blades instead of wheels. And to better convey the idea, they show how a rider with short ski blades on their feet would ride it. It even included mechanisms—like snowmobile tracks or solid rocket boosters, using snow as a propellant—to get back up the hill.

At the end of the hackathon, some teams pull out smartphones, take photos of their work, and leave the props behind to be trashed. Nelly notices, however, that Ricardo is taking the ski bike prototype with him. "Are you going to ride this to work when we get the first snow?" she asks.

Ricardo is surprised she noticed. "No. I'm going to take it back to my office and see if we can generate more ideas around it. Maybe I can find a volunteer to develop the first critical question for it."

***

Tuesday evening, Mo is getting ready to watch the replay of the day's Tour stage when his phone rings. It's Sofia. "Why would she be calling so late?"

"Hello, Mo?"

"Yes. Sofia. What's up?"

"We need your help. I've been biking with Nelly this evening, and her bike broke."

Sofia had invited Nelly for a ride after work. Nelly likes to ride with family and friends, and she was looking forward to spending some quality time with Sofia after the day's hackathon. The two left work early and drove out to Sofia's favorite bike trail near Fumane. They had plans to bike for a few hours, taking advantage of the long daylight and beautiful weather, and then have dinner on their way back at one of Sofia's favorite pizza places. Their fun ended abruptly shortly after 7:00 pm when Nelly's chain got stuck between the front two chainrings. Although they both pulled as hard as they could, all they got were dirty hands. They started walking and, exhausted, soon realized that they would not get back to their cars before dark. Sofia figured a resourceful person like Mo could help.

Although she explains the problem in layman's terms, Mo immediately understands their dilemma. Sofia describes their location—a trailhead with a parking lot that they just passed.

"I'm on my way. It's not too far."

Within 20 minutes, Mo reaches the parking lot and sees the pair of weary bikers sitting in the grass.

"Our hero!" says Nelly as she rises.

"It's a good thing you were in a convenient spot with good cell service," says Mo when he gets out of his car. "You two could have been out all night." He goes to his trunk and takes out his tools. He fixes Nelly's bike in minutes.

"Wow, that was fast," says Nelly. "I couldn't have done that even if I'd known how."

"You know, it's getting late. Instead of riding, why don't I take you back to your cars?"

"You don't have to twist my arm," says Sofia.

They load their bikes on Mo's rack and head back toward Fumane. On the way, they pass the pizza parlor where Sofia had planned to stop. She and Nelly ask Mo to join them for dinner, and he gladly accepts the invitation.

The cheery, rustic, roadside restaurant is filled with the smells of wood-fired pizzas. A large, ancient oven is at the back of the room, and all tables have a view of two chefs performing their craft. They find a table and are quickly met by a server who takes their order: a pitcher of house red wine and two large margherita pizzas.

Over dinner they have a lively discussion about food, bikes, the Tour, and, eventually, innovation.

"So beyond hackathons, what other tools do companies use to stimulate ideas?" asks Mo.

"Some companies use 'open innovation,' which is like having a hackathon with the millions of people out there in cyberspace. Social media, of course, is also great tool to enhance the creative process. We've had companies use their internal social media to gather input."

Nelly describes other means to stimulate innovation and how they're used for incremental, breakthrough, and disruptive innovation. She also tells Mo about innovation strategies such as blue ocean and lean startup.

"Why aren't we using those?"

"I think some of this is already part of Davanti's innovation process. You started in the right place, and you're on the right track."

"So how can I—me, personally—learn to be more creative?"

"Many schools teach creativity classes, but most are focused on creating art. There are good programs that teach industrial creativity, but I like to tell engineers that practice and habits are critical to those who aspire to improve their creative thinking. Get in the habit of always looking for many ways to solve problems, including thinking outside the box. Look for stimulus: Go to an art show, a museum, a flea market. Try to understand how things work, take things apart, stimulate your curiosity. Practice thinking like an artist, a bike racer, a pilot, a croupier at the casino, a mom with six children . . ."

"I don't even want to think about what it's like to have six children."

"The point is to get comfortable at thinking and behaving differently, even if peers may laugh at you. Remember, you spent 20 years in school to learn to think like everybody else, and that's a habit that's hard to break. Most companies have spent 50 years to get everybody to think the same way, and then they wonder why creativity died. Many companies have uniform and boring offices. Others, like Google, make the work environment stimulating and encourage people to break their habits. Google even uses ConferenceBikes for brainstorming.[3]"

"ConferenceBikes? I thought I knew every bike type that exists."

"Six riders are positioned in a circle around a seventh rider in a steering position. As all seven pedal, power is transferred to the wheels.[4] People can be more creative during exercise and movement, and the bikes encourage collaboration."

"Do you think we're ready for that?"

"One day. Who knows, maybe Davanti will enter the market for such bikes. . . . For me, the most effective way to establish a creative environment is to simply remove barriers and generate a place where creativity can happen, where it is encouraged and appreciated. Many diverse opportunities emerge from there. I also encourage companies not to limit where creativity can flourish. I've seen a lot of creative processes, even in accounting and HR."

Mo is fascinated with Nelly's approach to creativity and could listen for hours. But eventually Sofia reminds them that they still have to get back to their cars and then drive home.

Sofia and Nelly quickly divvy up the check and walk out to Mo's car. He drives them back to the trailhead where they started their ride and helps them with their bikes.

"Ciao, Nelly. I hope to see you again soon. Sofia, I'll see you tomorrow. Good night."

As Mo drives home, he reflects on how much more he still has to learn about innovation.

***

Junior has called together the directors for a Wednesday morning meeting in the conference room. The email calendar invitation is titled "R&D Strategy and Organization."

Junior starts by setting the right tone: "I've been with this company since my dad brought me here when I was a little boy. And I think I've learned more about R&D in the last few months than in all the years before. For me, R&D was always something that companies did. It was, I thought, a 'cost of doing business.' I'd walk into their work area and see nothing, except for expensive computers running expensive software and a bunch of busy, highly educated engineers and scientists. As much as I wanted new products, all I focused on was how much money we spent on R&D. I felt it was best to leave R&D alone and not ask questions—I might not understand the answers. But now I know that R&D is not a cost, but it's an investment that pays dividends in the form of revenues and profits."

Junior reaches down, grabs a pitcher of water, and pours himself a glass. He casually takes a swallow.

"I'm really happy that, with the help of Sofia, we have found the right person in Ricardo to lead our R&D effort. But I also believe it's important that we all—myself included—get engaged a lot more and collaborate with R&D to create the *right* products and ensure that what we develop is of value for our customers and meets our corporate goals. I've asked Ricardo to share how he's restructured R&D and the R&D strategy with all of us in detail. This is how R&D will drive us toward our goals."

"I always thought the main job of R&D is to spend the money we allocate to it and then ask for more when something new comes up," chides Stephano, director of finance.

"And I thought it was R&D's job to make life miserable for manufacturing," jokes Constantine, director of manufacturing.

"Neither of you are correct," says Ricardo cheerfully. "First, I'd like to thank Junior and all of you for trusting me with this responsibility at Davanti. I can understand your past frustration with R&D. It's hard to put a value on a drawing or a spec, and, I have to admit, R&D work is often shrouded in secrecy, sometimes justified and sometimes just for convenience or power."

Ricardo then expands on the role of R&D, just as he had discussed it with Junior. He summarizes R&D's objective—"Help the company meet its objective and goals in collaboration with all other functions"—and explains how it is aligned with the corporate objective. He talks about R&D goals around safety, quality, performance, innovation, and people engagement, and shows how they will contribute to the corporate goals. "And, of course, our new organization and our strategy were inspired by the corporate examples as well."

The executives nod. Many are pleased to hear *any* news coming from the R&D function.

"I engaged a team of senior R&D engineers in formulating the first draft of our strategy," says Ricardo as he reveals the following flipchart:

- Provide constant flow of the right innovative products at the right time
- Leverage innovation excellence principles to become better, faster, and more efficient
- Build a world-class technical organization (talent, knowledge, and processes)
- Create a culture based on innovation, respect, and collaboration.

From there he describes the three innovation processes—ICP, TCP, and PCP—and how they'll be used to ensure enough ideas are considered and that the best concepts are efficiently developed and launched.

"That's enough of me talking for now. Tell me how the new R&D organization can serve you and Davanti better."

"I have a hard time believing that 40 percent of our bike sales in the future will come from new products?" asks Diana. "How?"

Junior gives her a brief glance, and then looks to Ricardo, who explains that he first wants to fully exploit Davanti's strengths and know-how. For that, he offers some of the ideas to boost innovation in the current bike portfolio, with products like more affordable Davanti sports bikes and mountain bikes, maybe even electric city bikes. "Beyond that, we expect to have new products other than bicycles."

"We can sell bikes," says Claudia. "But how can me and my staff sell 'other' stuff when we don't know what it is? Do you even know what that is?"

"It's a fair question. For example, we've started discussing opportunities to leverage Davanti's technology and brand name for non-bike products. There are opportunities for our carbon-fiber know-how in other sports, in aerospace, or the medical field. And we can leverage the Davanti name on bicycle accessories, like clothing and components."

"Wow. Are we joining the fashion industry now? I always wanted to move to Milan," says Leandro.

"No," laughs Ricardo. "It's just one example—an obvious one that we've been missing out on for decades. We should all be wearing Davanti-branded clothing, especially when we're working with the race teams and at public events."

"I like that," says Junior. "Keep going."

"I'm sorry I can't share your excitement, Junior," warns Claudia. "This looks like Christmas for the marketing guys and maybe some others here, but not for me. In the past we couldn't get a fraction of all we really needed out of R&D. And now, suddenly, we're going to get mountain bikes and all this other stuff? Ricardo sounds like he's on the political campaign trail, making promises and omitting the part where he tells us how he'll pay for all of this? And I still can't believe we'll have enough to sell next year."

"Claudia, we've been working with you and Joe on short-term opportunities to cover the lost sales volumes and keep cash flow up the next two years," reminds Ricardo. "It doesn't always take a new product to do that, sometimes a face lift, fixing some problems, and updating existing products can quickly close that gap. That's already underway. I'm confident that *together* we'll meet short-term volume and profitability targets."

"She also asked how you'll pay for it all," interrupts Diana.

Unfazed by the negativity of the director of procurement's followup question, Ricardo answers: "I'm not here asking for more money. With Joe's help, we already eliminated some marginal new products, and those engineers were reassigned to the new opportunities we identified. With Sofia's help, we'll continue to eliminate process steps that add no value. And as we strive for speed, we'll gain enough efficiency to carry us for a long time with our current budget allocation."

"Interesting," says Stephano.

"It's not so much the product ideas that worry me, but the sheer number of new ideas that you plan to explore," says Anika. "It could be hundreds. How do you plan to staff all those projects?"

"Anika, I understand your concern. We all agree that the more diverse ideas you explore the higher your chances for success, right? At Davanti, you and your leadership colleagues have rightly been concerned about supporting new ideas because, in the past, every idea resulted in a protracted project—regardless of if it was a good idea or not. There were always too many projects underway, and many fizzled out after years of development. Innovation is about considering as many ideas as possible, but they can't all develop into projects. We're borrowing a page from Eric Ries' *The Lean Startup*[5] book: startups don't have a lot of resources, so they have to be very creative about how to assess their ideas and apply the little resources they have."

"But we're not a startup," counters Anika.

"No. And since we're Davanti, we think we have deep resources and funds. However, that still doesn't mean we have to use any more than a startup would use. We can assess 100 ideas for what we previously would have spent blindly supporting one single idea. The key is not to stick with a given idea any longer than is absolutely necessary. We must eliminate bad ideas as fast and efficiently as possible and keep moving the good ones on a path for investment."

"So you're saying we're going to fail fast," says Claudia. "How does that help us succeed?"

"You got that right, Claudia," adds Diana. "Most startups fail. We're a large company, and we have a lot to protect, like the Davanti name for starters. We're risking our reputation with a lot of this innovation stuff."

"For real startups, it's a matter of succeeding or failing," agrees Ricardo. "For us, if ideas fail fast, then we've invested close to nothing in them. Few if anyone outside of Davanti will ever hear of these so-called failures. And remember, we can learn a lot from even the bad ideas. It's good risk management. It's important that we reduce the risk of the new ideas fast and with the minimum means before we decide to invest real money in them."

"I understand what we do when we determine an idea is bad," says Stephano, "but explain what happens with the good ones?"

"Excellent question. That's a challenge for any R&D organization—the selection of the right things to work on. Many companies rely on gut instincts with close to no information available. That's very risky. The bottom line is that we won't know until we start working on them. And we do that in the fastest and most efficient manner during the idea creation process, which, by the way, we're piloting with Mo's chainless bike."

"And who decides when it's time to invest real money on an idea?" asks Constantine.

"For that, the idea has to pass a firewall and enter the technology creation process."

"Who makes the firewall decision?" asks Anika.

"The associates working on the idea make recommendations to a multidisciplinary team of gatekeepers. If the gatekeepers agree with the recommendation of the engineers, the funds for the second phase are approved."

"And then?" asks Diana.

"Then a project manager is assigned, and our associates determine what technology and knowledge we already have for the project and work on the gaps that need to be closed. They follow a fast and efficient process that, among other techniques, includes the principles of set-based concurrent engineering."

"How is it that we've never heard of this?" asks Claudia. "Are we that far behind the times? If this was a good idea, others would already be doing it."

"Some companies are; many are not. We haven't used it at Davanti yet because we're waiting for the first project to go through the gate so we can deploy the pilot process. I can explain the details of set-based better with an actual project example in about a month. But let me say here that the TCP focuses on the development of technology and knowledge that could apply to many products—not just the one entering the TCP. Only in the last phase, the product development process, do we design the products."

"And who makes the decision about those products," asks Stephano, sensing that the time for the big investment has arrived.

"The PCP is guided by the needs of the product portfolio. Products are pulled into the PCP using existing technology or new technology released from the TCP. And I need to stress that the technology could be developed based on a new idea or a need identified by the portfolio. The process starts with another gate," explains Ricardo. "This time Joe's team holds the gate keys because the product director and his team allocate the funds for the final products—not only for the development but also for the tooling, launch, etc."

"Wait a moment," interrupts Diana, noticing a venture into procurement's territory. "Isn't it a little early to worry about tooling? What if we cancel the R&D project later?"

"At PCP, we have the information that we need to get a good NPV assessment, and we can begin to estimate an ROI; no project should be canceled or significantly changed after passing this gate. PCP consumes 70 percent of R&D resources, and we would waste a lot of money if we didn't launch the product to the scope and timeline on the table."

"Have we forgotten how much money we wasted in the past when we canceled projects late in the game," reminds Stephano. "I mean, *wow*. This alone could pay for Claudia's cash flow projects."

"The time for failure is before passing the PCP gate. Failures are expected in the idea creation process and maybe even in the technology creation process. But there cannot be a failure after money has been spent in the last phase, the product creation process. And in the PCP, we work almost like a lean manufacturing plant."

Constantine's face lights up: "I was always told that this lean manufacturing stuff can't be used in the office. Well, what do you know? But, of course, some things, like standard work don't apply to the creative process, right?"

"If applied correctly, it does. We want people to use their creativity for new products and services—not to bypass the best way we've documented to do things. Unless they can prove a better way, we even want engineers to follow standards, especially in the product development phase. Of course, in the creative phase there is a lot more latitude."

"I can't believe my ears," says Constantine, and the group chuckles.

"The good news is that we have enough projects that can enter the PCP gate at this time, including the products needed for cash flow. So we'll have a team pilot this phase right away."

"I'm looking forward to the first gate meeting," says Joe. "You certainly have the support from me and my team!"

"One more important point before I get to the organization: R&D must create profitable value streams, not just new and innovative products. We can have the greatest idea in the world, but it's of no value to Davanti if we can't sell the resulting product or efficiently manufacture it."

"It's why manufacturing always sent new products back for redesign," adds Constantine.

"So what will you do about that? What we've been doing is hardly efficient."

"No, it's not. Sending stuff back is a waste. Do you recall Sofia's overlapping circles of innovation excellence, sales and marketing excellence, and operations excellence? We must *start* where the circles overlap and stay in that zone. In the past, every function did its own thing at Davanti, and then we forced the circles to overlap by making compromises and changes."

"I remember those days" says Junior. "As soon as we launched the product, we started a cost-down program and then we had to upgrade the components because we didn't meet our sales targets."

"That will change," continues Ricardo. "Before we design a product, all degrees of freedom are open to the needs of all functions—marketing, manufacturing, procurement, and even the supply chain or finance. The changes are easy, fast, and cheap early on because nothing has been designed; nothing needs to be redesigned."

Everyone nods in agreement.

"But this goes both ways," stresses Ricardo.

"Stop right there," exclaims Claudia, motioning with both hands. "You mean I have to make a decision before I can see a completed product? Sales needs to see a final product before we can know if we can sell it."

"Same in manufacturing," adds Constantine. "We can't afford to assess or even develop manufacturing technology for anything that won't be a final product. Anything else would be a total waste. I thought this process was lean."

"Now wait a moment," interrupts Junior. "Listen to what you're saying. How many years have I listened to your complaints that if you had known about this new product a little earlier you would have had a chance to provide input and a lot of problems could have been avoided. Here's your chance to voice your concerns at the earliest stages—and in a formal, organized, constructive manner."

"But Junior," tries Constantine.

"And, Constantine, with this new approach you'll also be able to identify and communicate the level of investment needed by manufacturing," continues Junior. "Your operations will be ready with upgrades when the product reaches manufacturing, not like today when we start that effort after R&D is done and then lose valuable time."

"I like this idea," says Stephano. "We'll finally have visibility of how we spend our money in R&D. I really like it."

"Thank you, Stephano," says Ricardo. "But let me warn you all. Early engagement also comes at a price: if a project gets funded at the entry gate, everybody has skin in the game, and everybody must support the project from there on out. There's no saying later, 'If I had known about this . . .' We don't expect industrialization right away for every good new idea—just an early firewall assessment. As the project develops, however, the activity and investment will increase."

"If nothing else, the crossfunctional gate meetings are a great way to keep everybody aligned and engaged throughout the project timeline," offers Anika, director of HR.

"Correct, Anika, and we'll later add in less-formal events, like integration events. I'll describe those when the first project reaches that stage."

The group pauses to consider the changes they've heard, each realizing that something very different is underway within Davanti. Junior breaks the silence: "Before Ricardo describes the new R&D organization, let's all catch our breath. I've texted Anna to have some coffee, water, and snacks brought in, and they should be here momentarily. We'll convene in 20 minutes."

***

"Who knows, maybe we can get some of those gourmet food stations like at Fusilli," says Constantine as he walks up to Stephano carrying a crostini and an espresso.

Stephano looks around the room at his colleagues and sips at his coffee. "I feel like we're a bunch of birds who landed on a shaky branch. Should we trust the branch or our wings?"

Constantine laughs: "Well, we know Claudia certainly trusts her wings. And, to be honest, the branch shook for me when Ricardo said he doesn't need more money."

"Yes, we need to see about that. But he certainly has brought a lot of transparency to R&D. With Emilio, R&D was a black box. Every annual budget was based on the year before plus some technical rhetoric to justify an increase that nobody understood. I hope that we're about to base our budget on real products and projects soon. Then we'll see if Ricardo can keep his budget flat, but I hope that requirement doesn't apply to our own budgets as well."

"I saw the lean savings in the plant. If 70 percent of the R&D work is managed like a manufacturing operation, then he may be right and won't need more funding. And armed with the right knowledge, I bet we can reduce our own budgets, too. Look at the wastes you've already cut from finance."

"Well, I'm not committing to anything just yet."

"Fair enough."

"I do like that Ricardo is opening up the creative process. I mean, why was creativity and innovation always an R&D-only privilege? Even us bean counters have good ideas sometime."

"I like that as well. My folks in the plant suggested a lot of great product ideas in the past, only to have them fall on deaf ears. I think a more open innovation process has far more advantages than disadvantages. My group will be pleased to hear this, and I'm sure they'll contribute."

"It looks like we're still on the branch," surmises Stephano. "We'll need to get comfortable with the idea that it shakes from time to time."

"Chirp. Chirp."

***

Unlike meeting breaks of old, everyone is sitting and attentive at the 20-minute mark. Ricardo and Junior are anxious to give more news to the executives.

Ricardo welcomes the group back, and then moves right into the topic: "The new R&D organization is patterned after the corporate organization—it's a matrix. Every major project will have a project manager, with a reporting line to Joe for alignment and product objectives and to Leandro and the PMO for execution and the best quality of service. The R&D function will provide the appropriate staff to the project managers, armed with the latest technology, knowledge, and tools.

"Is that consistent across the three processes?" asks Constantine.

"Product creation and technology creation projects—if you remember, the second and the third innovation processes—are managed by a project manager, but in the creative phase we give our inventors more flexibility to promote innovation and entrepreneurship on their own."

"That seems logical," replies Constantine.

"Our philosophy for the organization is pretty simple:

- *Flat and responsive*—We've had an organization that was very deep and slow. In some areas there were two or more positions between an engineer and my position, which gave a lot of people a sense of control and power. No more. We now have one layer.
- *Flexible and agile*—We need to be able to quickly respond to changing market demands, new technologies, and new ideas.
- *Focused*—We need to move work from multitasking to monotasking, which will improve quality, speed, and productivity.
- *Collaborative*—I will use this word once again. We need to support each other and work together for common goals.
- *Engaged, empowered, respected, and trusted associates*—We will treat associates as we wish to be treated, and we'll respect them but hold them accountable for agreed-upon deliverables."

"How does all of this flatten the company?" asks Diana. "I don't follow."

Ricardo walks to the whiteboard and sets up an org chart that he has developed.

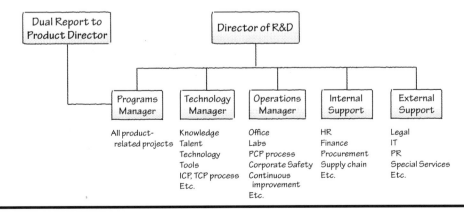

Figure 15.1 The Flattened R&D Organization.

"We'll have only three managers, who will oversee the following teams:

- *Programs*—The programs manager is responsible for all R&D projects in the PCP. The PCP project managers report to the programs manager and the PMO office. The most important task of this manager right now is to work with Joe and his staff to get the project portfolio right and to execute projects to deliver on time and to targets.
- *Technology*—This position manages the talent in R&D with the help of HR, and is also responsible for technology development, knowledge management, patents, and other technical matters. And until we find a better solution, this position also oversees the ICP process and individuals working to move their ideas along. TCP project managers report to this position and the PMO. The most important initial task of this position is to document and organize all knowledge Davanti has in our associates' heads, drawers, and databases and to establish an efficient knowledge management process.
- *Operations*—This manager is responsible for all technical processes, including the R&D processes, testing, and the prototype shop. In addition, he or she is responsible for R&D transformation activities and continuous improvement as well as corporate safety. The most important project right now is to manage the current R&D transformation with Sofia.

The operations manager and the technology manager will report directly to me; the programs manager reports to both me and Joe. For all other support, we count on the corporate functions, like finance, HR, procurement. They're the experts at what they do, and we'd gain nothing trying to duplicate such services within R&D. And we'll tap into outsourced services like IT and legal as we need them. One more important point: Anika has assigned a staff member to engage associates in creating a dual- or technical-ladder career path for Davanti associates; we'll pilot that in R&D and maybe expand it to other functions."

"So dual-reporting alone wasn't complicated enough?" snorts Claudia.

Anika stares intently at Claudia: "The two are quite different. Davanti has experts, certainly in R&D, with world-class skills in the bike business. Their contributions are at least as important and valuable as contributions of a leader. But they either don't aspire to be a leader or don't have the time or interest to develop the skills to become a leader. In order to retain such experts, we must offer them an upward career path at Davanti just as we provide for leaders."

"I have such people in my organization, too," says Stephano. "Anika, please keep me posted on this one. It would be good to reward the non-leaders."

"I agree; same in manufacturing," says Constantine.

"So where do all these R&D people work?" asks Diana.

"The teams will be collocated as much as possible—at least the large ones," explains Ricardo. "And they can design their own work areas, within certain rules. We may even have permanent teams and move the projects to them. Associates on the smaller teams may want to move their desks as they get assigned to different teams. My desk is right in the middle of everybody else, and I plan to stay there. I don't need much space."

"I hope we don't all have to work like Fusilli," comments Diana. "I can't work like that."

Ricardo leaves that comment unanswered and quickly changes the subject: "And by the way, here are the names of the three new managers: Bart Amico (programs), Bolaji Ajaya (technology), and Carolina Petrale (operations). They know bikes, and they know Davanti. I'll have plenty of opportunities to teach them the ropes of innovation excellence." Ricardo walks over to the org chart and writes the managers' names on it.

"Here, again, we're talking about the same people we've had at Davanti for a long time," notes Junior. "We've had good people all along—just bad processes."

"I've never seen an organization quite like this," says Anika. "We should expect issues. Many people will have a different role, and they may perceive it as one of lesser importance."

"Yes, there will be issues," concedes Ricardo without hesitation. "Although there are no layoffs or financial consequences, some people like the power of their old positions, and for many that will go away. To help address that, the more senior associates will get an opportunity to manage bigger and more important projects; some may choose the technical ladder."

"But they still won't wield the power they once did," adds Anika.

"That's right. In the new organization, people will have more engagement and responsibility, and power is replaced with collaboration and empowerment. So some people who crave the power may not be happy. Some people also will be unhappy because their projects have been discontinued. When I roll this out in a town hall meeting, I'll touch on the new leadership roles and behaviors, but we should expect some to complain or decide to try their luck elsewhere."

"As with every major transformation, that has to be expected," says Anika. "But I think that together we can work our way through this. I'll make sure I post openings in other parts of the organization and help those who want to consider a different role. And we can avoid some issues by giving people the chance to question and comment in the town hall."

"Will Sofia create the new processes you described?" asks Matteo, the new supply-chain manager.

"We'll look to her for suggestions and coaching, but when I get your approval for the new organization today, I'll engage the R&D folks to design the Davanti version of the three innovation processes. They understand the work they do, and they have to live with the processes. We'll provide more specific innovation excellence training as we get up to speed. I went through it with my previous employer, and I found it to be interesting and motivating."

"Ricardo, I respect your intentions," begins Diana. "But I've been at Davanti for a while. You need to be a wizard to pull this off without a huge budget increase."

"I can help to answer that," says Junior. "You don't believe Ricardo can do it without more money. That's your right. But he hasn't asked for any more funding. First of all, I have a lot of respect for our Davanti associates and Ricardo and their capabilities. And I've seen very encouraging things happen already. Second, I'll relay what Ricardo told us about managing projects: 'You won't know if a project works unless you try—experiment in small steps and then either keep progressing forward if results are positive or pivot or freeze the project if it doesn't go in the right direction.' I'd like to give Ricardo and his R&D team the benefit of the doubt and the opportunity to experiment with this new R&D organization. I'll personally keep close to this transformation, and I think we'll all learn a lot from what happens in R&D."

All eyes are on Junior, then they shift to Ricardo.

"Thank you for the support, Junior," says Ricardo confidently.

"So unless there are objections, I say we approve what Ricardo has presented and start a new chapter for Davanti R&D," says Junior, surveying the room.

"I'm on board," says Constantine. The others also agree.

"Ricardo, put this plan in motion."

Notes

1. An x-matrix is a one-page strategy planning, deployment, and tracking tool. An "X" near the center of the document forms four quadrants, which typically list long-term objectives (three to five years), annual objectives, improvement projects, and key performance indicators (KPIs) and owners responsible for the KPIs.

2. "History Timeline: Post-It® Notes," 3M.

3. "Google Is Using the CoBi for Team-Building," ConferenceBikes.

4. The ConferenceBike was developed by Eric Staller and is sold by ConferenceBikes.

5. Eric Ries, *The Lean Startup*, Crown Business, New York, 2011.

Chapter 16

Transformation Metrics

Claudia is the last to enter a small conference room near her office, which also serves as a work area for her sales staff. As usual, she's dressed conservatively but stylishly and carries an oversized coffee mug. It's her first staff meeting since marketing was folded into her department. Marco, the new marketing manager, and his colleagues are anxious to get a sense of direction. Having witnessed Claudia's relentless pushback in Junior's staff meeting, Marco doesn't know what to expect.

Claudia closes the door and gets right to business: "For the new people on my staff. First, welcome. Second, I want to stress that what happens in this room stays in this room. That goes both ways. What you say to me stays with me. I believe in open conversation, and I believe that dead fish must be put on the table so the odors can get resolved."

Marco nods in agreement.

She sits and continues: "I need to discuss a very smelly fish today. I'll be blunt. I don't like what's going on at Davanti right now. This innovation excellence stuff is too much too soon. I'm also not a fan of 'Miss Innovation,' but I guess everybody knows that."

Marco doesn't move a muscle.

"All I can see is a big cash hole and a tarnished reputation for Davanti. And we'll be lucky if that's the worst of it. I'm concerned about my own career and all of yours as well. I can't believe that Junior still supports this."

"Excuse me, Claudia," interjects Marco. "We've seen at Fusilli that this approach can work. It can . . ."

"That's my other problem," counters Claudia quickly. "Let's be clear. Fusilli is a company owned by Junior's friend Marcel. I don't want to work for Marcel, and I think that's what this is all about. Before long, Davanti will be another puppet on his list of acquisitions and he'll be running us, too."

A moment of silence as the group considers her hypothesis. Claudia's staff looks calm and relaxed; they're used to this kind of talk. Marco is not, and he presses on, nonetheless.

"So you don't think we can pull this off at Davanti?" asks Marco.

"Since you've asked: I respect Junior, and I suppose that if this was to be successful, I could come around to support it. But I'm convinced it will ruin the company before it has a chance to work. It's his company but my career. Unfortunately, I'm the only one with the guts to ask the difficult questions. Everybody else seems to cuddle up to Sofia like little puppy dogs. So if any of you have similar concerns, please share them with me. I'll make sure they're heard by the right people."

Marco realizes it's fruitless to counter her further. Some of Claudia's staff ask a few questions about the transformation, clear that Claudia has not shared many details beyond what they heard at Junior's initial town hall meeting. Claudia answers each question as quickly as possible, and then moves on to the normal agenda of the sales meeting, going through accounts and action items for the week. She asks Marco to provide details of marketing activities, which he succinctly does, having expected Claudia to request an update from him. He closes with a request of his own: "I believe there's a lot that me and my marketing colleagues can learn by working more closely with you all. Similarly, I hope you'll get some insights from us that can help you in your work. Please ask any of us how we can assist."

"Thank you, Marco," says Claudia. "So with that, let's get on with it."

***

Junior and his wife Martina walk up to the entrance of a small hillside restaurant, Ristorante sul Collina, located in San Petro in Cariano, about 10 minutes south of Fumane. Their arrival coincides with that of Marcel and his partner Luci. As most of their monthly get-togethers, Junior and Marcel opted for dining with a view: the restaurant's garden-like patio offers a glimpse of the Romanesque La Pieve di San Floriano, built in the 11th-12th century.

"Martina, Fausto!" greets Marcel. "Good to see you again. Come, let's go in."

"Likewise, my friends," replies Junior. "It's good to see you and Luci as well."

Junior's wife loves hanging out with Luci. Marcel did not remarry after his divorce, but Luci has been by his side for about five years. She gets along well with Marcel's adult daughter, a surgical nurse for Doctors without Borders who is currently working in Africa. In fact, she gets along well with everyone.

Luci is Marcel's age, shares his passion for skiing, and has an education in history (specifically, the Italian Etruscan period). She no longer digs for relics but has put her energy into oil painting—large colorful works, mostly featuring human faces, animals, and nature. The detailed paintings take her weeks to complete, after which she commissions multiple handpainted copies as well as prints. She keeps or donates the originals and earns a fine living selling the copies and prints through her studio and gallery in Milan. When not with Marcel, Luci lives in her apartment overlooking the Mediterranean sea near Genoa.

Luci talked Martina into painting her ceramics, and they frequently explore techniques and styles together. Martina has brought a recent creation to the restaurant for Luci to critique, and they quickly pick up a conversation about their latest pursuits. Marcel and Junior begin talking business.

"How are things going at Davanti? You and Sofia seem to get along now. No complaints?"

"Things are good, Marcel. But I suspect you know that. I told Sofia yesterday that I learned more in the last three months with her than in my whole career. What did we really learn in business school? We both went to the same school, remember? They didn't teach this stuff."

"Business schools study successful big companies, and they teach what they learn from that study. They also tend to move pretty slowly, and things change very rapidly these days. It will be some time until they catch up with what I learned and you are learning. That's good for us and can keep our businesses on the leading edge."

"I'm grateful that you're pulling me to the edge with you, even if I was initially kicking and screaming as you and Sofia tried."

"I'm happy to teach you. You're a good student and making progress. Not everyone who tries this stuff gets it or can stick with it. In fact, most don't."

"Thanks, Marcel. I really think everything is going exceptionally well."

"What makes you think so? Your metrics?" asks Marcel.

"Well, maybe the metrics, but they're not specific to what we're undertaking now. . . . I see where you're going. Something's still missing?"

"Fausto, there are many metrics that will give you a solid understanding of how Davanti is doing in this transformation. You'll get a true sense of the value you're creating for the company and for yourself. But I'm not going to bore you with a lesson tonight. I'll leave the details to Sofia. She's pretty good with that stuff. She teaches me a thing or two from time to time."

A waiter approaches and recognizes Marcel. "Mr. Ricco, so good to have you back. How can I get you and your friends started this evening?"

"Antonio, let's begin with some Fritto Misto and a pitcher of house Frascati." Marcel looks at Martina, Luci, and Junior: "Are you all fine with that?"

"Sounds wonderful, Marcel," says Martina.

"Yes, that will be nice," agrees Junior.

"Very good, Mr. Ricco. I'll put that in," says Antonio, setting four small, paper menus on the table. "And here is a list of the house specials for today. I'll take the rest of your order when you are ready. But please take your time and enjoy the view."

Marcel turns his attention back to Junior: "I understand you've done well establishing your goals. Sofia shared them with me."

"Yes, we did, much better than the first attempt," says Junior. "The trip to Fusilli set the stage, and then our off-site meeting reinforced the need for us to change how we operate."

"The important difference was that you stopped delegating and started engaging your staff."

Junior realizes that Sofia must have shared more details with Marcel than he would have expected.

"It worked the second time because you respected your associates and engaged them in the process. You showed them what good looks like, you trained them (and yourself), and then you pointed them in the right direction. In fact, you almost had to hold them back—they would have run without you!"

"I understand the difference between delegating and engaging now, but what does that have to do with respect? I respected my parents and teachers, my kids respect me, and I respect friends like you, Marcel. Help me out?"

"You showed respect to your associates by not telling them what to do but rather helping them figure it out. You respected that they can play a decisive role in the transformation. You provided them with the education they needed to know on their own what to do. You respected them for their intelligence and experience by asking them to help you formulate the goals and how to accomplish them. And guess what?"

"What?"

"They probably knew better than you what to do and how to get there," interjects Marcel. "I was in that position many times before. I wasn't born like this."

"You're right again, of course," says Junior.

Antonio quietly walks to their table and deftly sets the pitcher of wine on the table with four glasses without interrupting the conversation.

"I have to compliment you on a job well done, my friend," says Marcel.

"Thank you. I appreciate the positive reinforcement."

"Getting a strategy defined isn't easy, if done right. Next we'll help you with the deployment of it. But before that, you'll need to set your new metrics. They come after objectives, goals, and strategy and will help you measure your progress."

"I've always kept a very close eye on the financials, P&L statements, sales, revenue, cash flow, cost . . ."

"And keep doing that, Fausto. Those are still necessary. A few new balanced metrics, however, will be needed to indicate how well Davanti is progressing toward the goals and the objectives of the transformation."

Marcel pauses and pours wine for each of them. "Now let me toast you for successfully reaching your first milestones: you established a True North, you formulated goals, and you aligned your organization. Let me put your next step in racing terms. The team is now at the start of the race. They are well trained and prepared. They know how to win. They're well organized and everybody knows their role. So now it's time to win the race!"

He raises his glass in a toast. "Saluti."

"Saluti," replies Junior as the ladies join in on the toast; they don't quite know what they're toasting but by the expression of their partners they realize it must be worthy.

***

Wednesday afternoon after the company's weekly bike ride, Mo and Marco sit in the long shade of the setting sun at the edge of the Davanti bike lot, rehydrating from their water bottles. Marco stares at the bottle between his feet.

"Marco, you don't look so happy today. What's on your mind?"

"You know, I really enjoyed working with Joe. I still get to do that given his new role, obviously, but it's not the same. What's not the same is Claudia isn't Joe. She's a good salesperson, but as a leader I really can't figure her out. As long as me and the marketing team fit into her agenda, she seems fine. One attempt otherwise and she just shuts us down, especially if she thinks we're helping Sofia. I wonder how and why her staff are so loyal. At least most of her staff strike me that way."

"I'm sorry to hear that."

"Yeah, I wish it was different. For example, we started helping some engineers with critical marketing questions for their new ideas. Claudia was furious. She thinks we're wasting time on products and services that will never exist. When some of the ideas do emerge as real products, however, we'll be scrambling to understand them and rushing with promotional resources. Stuff like that."

"Well, at least you can still talk with Joe occasionally."

"Yes, but that's not as easy as I thought, either. When I start supporting Joe's work, I suddenly get pulled back to a marketing task assigned by Claudia. And then vice versa. The matrix is confusing me, frankly. It's pretty chaotic right now."

"Maybe you should chat with Sofia. She's been through this process a number of times. She might have tips on how to make it easier on you."

"Good idea. I'll do that. . . . Well, enough about me. How about you, Mo? What's been happening with the direct-drive?"

"My project is going well, although we had to pivot recently. But that may be for the better. We're going to the gate soon. As for the rest, we'll see."

"You don't look so happy about it."

"I'm concerned about getting a PM assigned to it, who could then change things. Only time will tell, I guess. And like what you told me about Claudia, the matrix has me unsure of who I report to next. So far, I'm working fully with Ricardo, but that will change soon, I'm afraid. Ricardo has talked about the new organization, but he's still working out the specific assignments. Everybody is nervous, and some are concerned about their jobs."

"Well, from what I hear in the executive meetings, no one should be concerned about losing their jobs."

"Easy for you to say."

"Yeah, I know. Say, what's your plans for August?"

"Not much. I had hoped to spend some time with Marie, but she's traveling with her parents. It would have been nice to ride the route of a Tour stage with her, but that won't be happening. I might hook up with some college buddies for a week, get in some biking, and help my dad at the villa. He has some house projects he wants to take on. And you?"

"I'm planning to visit my parents in Rome. It's been a long time since I've been home, and I really need to spend at least a week or two with them. . . . So are you going to watch the Tour highlights tonight?"

"You bet. The race has been pretty tight so far, and we've seen some great sprint finishes. Fortunately, no ponchos yet as well. I'm surprised that the weather has been so good. Long sleeves were only needed in the Bretagne."

"I'm surprised that the standings are still pretty much what they were after the prologue."

"Some days I have to agree with Sofia," considers Mo. "You could get the same results with short sprints all in one day."

"No way," declares Marco, getting up off the grass to stretch his legs. "The first week is for the sprinters and the millions of fans that line the roads in the northern part of Europe. And don't forgot that most of the sprinters are on Davanti bikes."

"Yes. And it looks like Rossa is holding up well. The entire Davanti team is doing well."

"They really haven't been challenged yet—wait for the mountains to start," cautions Marco. "Have you seen the red Omega team? Most of them did well in the prologue, and they've been really aggressive recently. You always see at least six red jerseys in the front of the peloton. Their riders are from around the globe. I'm sure we'll see more of them. Yet I never heard of Omega before this year or their sponsor."

"I read that they spent a lot of money to get two European aces and a seasoned directeur sportif—all recruited for this year for a shot at the Tour," says Mo. "That's all you need to know. What's not to like about them, other than they don't ride Davanti bikes and they're not our team?"

"Do you plan to attend any stages?" asks Marco.

"I had hoped to ride in the team car, but that's a hard assignment to come by for the Tour. I'll probably watch the whole thing on TV."

"I have a pass left for Paris," says Marco proudly.

"For the Champs-Élysées?"

"Yes, and a closeup for the ceremony. Would you like one?"

"Would I? Of course. Say, might you have two?"

"I was afraid you'd ask that. You owe me double."

***

Junior walks down to Sofia's office early Thursday morning. He expects to find her in, even though most employees won't arrive at Davanti for another half hour or so. He's surprised to see her office empty, but the lights on.

"Junior. Are you looking for me?" comes Sofia's voice from down the hall. She's carrying a coffee from the cafeteria. "We really need to get those Fusilli food stations set up. It's a long walk for coffee."

"I'll make that a priority," jokes Junior.

"What can I do for you?" asks Sofia as she enters her office. Junior follows and they both sit down at a round table for four.

"I've been thinking about the metrics that Marcel mentioned. I can't wait to get started. What metrics should I drive besides the financials, P&L statements, sales, revenue, cash flow, cost, etc.?"

"Business results are the consequence of a good vision/strategy, a good process, and good people. You must be concerned about getting those three right—if you get them right, the good results will follow. You don't drive results, and you can't wait until financials roll in to take action—by then, it's too late to affect them."

"I don't follow."

"Say you're watching the Tour de France. They flash the current positions and the time differences of the riders at the bottom of the screen. You know who is in the lead, and you see how far behind the chasers are. Imagine if that information wasn't provided."

"I'd have no idea what's going on. I'd have to wait for the finish to know what happened."

"What else do the flash updates tell you?"

"People like me can assess reasonably well who is likely to win a stage, what attacks are likely to happen, and what the overall standings will be."

"Right. You don't have to wait until the end of the race. You have a pretty good idea at any time, and it gets more likely the closer you get to the finish, right?"

"OK. You're telling me that, for example, I shouldn't wait until the end of the selling season to find out if we met our sales and income targets. If I know what's going on sooner, I can make adjustments just like the coaches of the racers."

"Yes. A good metric, Junior, is a leading indicator. It helps you to understand what *will happen*, not just *what happened* in the past. A good example for a leading safety metric is near misses—they tell you where accidents are likely to happen in the future."

"Go on."

"Metrics should also have a direct line of sight to a corporate goal. If a department measures their contribution to the growth of the company, that's a good metric. But if they measure only their internal efficiency, their metric could conflict with delivering on the corporate goal: for example, they might reduce the cost of their operation at the expense of on-time delivery and company revenue."

"Is that the balance that Marcel talked about?"

"Yes. It shows how some metrics affect others. You already know that if you push speed too much, quality may slide. So it's a good idea to concurrently watch the metrics that affect each other so you don't optimize one thing to the detriment of another. I also tell people that metrics should be actionable. You can hold R&D accountable to deliver their contributions on time and on target, but if you make profitability their responsibility, they alone could not implement appropriate countermeasures."

"This all seems very straightforward. Anything else?"

"Don't emphasize trivial metrics. I've seen companies track office supplies or the number of photocopies the associates create. What's the real return on metrics like that?"

"OK."

"And one more important attribute. Metrics must drive the right behavior. Let's assume sales has a target of number of bikes sold."

"Well, that's their job, so they're responsible for the number of bikes sold."

"Then what do they do if sales are dropping?"

"They could drop the price and/or spend more on advertising."

"But what if the root cause for sliding sales is the availability of the product or poor customer satisfaction?"

"So what should the metric be?"

"You could still look at volume, but there should also be a metric for revenue or even profit per bike or maybe even customer satisfaction, so you understand the real problem and promote the desired behavior accordingly."

"OK, I understand the rules you've laid out. But *what* do we measure? We always considered safety and quality the most important."

"Yes, they should dominate the hierarchy and not be traded off for anything else."

"And my dad told me to always keep an eye on cost."

"Let's assume you have a perfect, low-cost product in your portfolio," replies Sofia, sipping her coffee, which she has ignored until now and realizes it's lukewarm. "But you don't have any to sell. Or what if you have a bike at the right cost that nobody buys for reasons other than the price. In either case, how much money will you make?"

"Sounds like cost is tricky. Maybe delivery of the right product at the right time, place, and price should be next on the list."

"Yes, that's a good way to frame it. . . . Are there other measures that align with Davanti's strategy, such as value to the customer?"

"We already get excellent input from the pros," counters Junior, "and we've been using that data for years. So we've got value covered."

"Well, I've seen the feedback from the pros. It is good input. But pros don't pay for their bikes—what about the rest of your customers?"

"You mean consumers. They buy what the pros ride. And we've done feedback forms, and we usually only get responses from a few unhappy customers. That input is not very helpful. What more could we be doing?"

"Does your sales staff call buyers soon after their purchase to discuss and record their satisfaction? And when was the last time you stopped by the multibrand dealer here in town and asked how people like Davanti bikes?"

"OK. What else have I been missing?"

"Let's leave bikes for a minute. In a transformation like we're on now, what do you think is more difficult—getting the process piece implemented or getting people engaged to make it successful?"

"The people part, of course."

"So what metric will Davanti use to understand the most important and most difficult piece—the people engagement?"

Junior thinks for a while and shakes his head. "I don't know. Maybe Anika could help with that."

"Why not ask the people?"

"Who? Me? Ask them what?"

"Everybody who manages people should ask them how they're doing, how they feel about the work they do and the company they do it for. You can also supplement that with third-party surveys to get to the stuff that people won't tell you to your face. I can work with Anika on that."

"Thanks," says Junior, with a smile. "And how will I measure the results of your innovation excellence, Sofia?"

"Excellent question, Junior. First, it's not my 'my innovation excellence,' as you well know."

"Of course. I hear it so often, I had to try it myself."

"Many companies measure how many folks have been trained or how many continuous improvement initiatives they start, but that measure rarely correlates to real results. Innovation excellence should help everybody do a better job and contribute to revenue, profit, and growth. If you don't see the difference in the top and bottom lines, you and me haven't done our jobs. But it may take a little while to see the results, so we look at leading indicators like value of the portfolio, development speed, on-time delivery, innovations."

"Sofia, we've resurrected innovation in the company, and I'm sure it will contribute to our goals."

"I do, too. And proof of that will help push things further. So please give the metrics more thought and reach out to your associates for input. I'll ask the Volta team to get a proposal for us as well—they've uncovered a good set of metrics in their work. Then we can discuss how you're planning to review metrics with your staff and how action items get created. There's nothing more wasteful than creating and tracking a metric that nobody looks at. And don't drown yourself and others with metrics. I've seen companies track 30 or more metrics, which overwhelmed them to the extent that the measures were ignored, and nothing ever changed."

"I won't let that happen. Sofia, thanks for your time this morning. This will keep me busy."

"My pleasure. Reach out if you need more advice or examples."

"I will."

"In a few weeks, after you get this under your belt, we'll talk about gemba walks."

"Gemba what?"

"It's a way for you and others to talk to people, follow up on the strategy deployment, stay apprised of all the improvement initiatives, and keep a pulse on people engagement. They'll also help you figure out how to help everyone add value."

"That seems like a pretty big lesson."

"Yes, which is why it can wait. Rome wasn't built in a day."

"It would have been if you'd been there!" says Junior with a grin.

***

Thursday afternoon, Mo leaves the office early. It's his birthday, and he's driving to Peschiera del Garda to meet his family for dinner. He had wanted them to meet at one of his favorite restaurants, Filigrana, which is about a mile from his parent's villa. Since it's customary in Italy that the celebrant foot the bill, that seemed to be an ideal spot. Mo's mom, however, insisted on making one of Mo's favorite dishes, and he couldn't refuse her. He did insist on bringing a cake and the wine to honor tradition, and he got everyone to agree that there would be no gifts.

Promptly at 6:00 pm, everyone arrives simultaneously at the lakeside villa. It's a warm summer evening. Everyone greets Mo with shouts of 'Buon Compleanno,' and Mrs. Pensatore hustles everyone on to the patio where a large antipasto platter awaits. "Come, come. Mangiare."

Mo's sister Catherine serves the wine, a Super Tuscan, which pairs well with rabbit in mustard sauce. Not exactly a dish for a summer night, but it's what Mo requested and his mom obliged. Brother Benito helps his mother bring out the entrée, a side of green beans and herbs, and a freshly baked ciabatta. When Catherine and her mother are seated, Mr. Pensatore offers a toast: "To Mo and another year of health and happiness."

They all raise their glasses, "To Mo," and then begin to sing "Tanti auguri a te."[1]

Everyone eats and enjoys the moment and each other's company; the kids plead for the cake to be served, a chocolate ganache from a favorite bakery of the family. Mo cuts the cake and serves his nieces and nephews and parents first. The kids devour their cake. Mo and his parents have espresso and homemade apricot liqueur with their dessert, taking their time to enjoy every last bite; his siblings pass on the drinks and soon begin to gather the children for the drive home.

"I'm sorry we need to run, Mo, but they've got camp in the morning," says his brother-in-law Eric.

"No problem. I understand. Thank you for coming and bringing the kids. It's good to see everyone."

"It's good to see you, too, Mo," says Catherine. "Well, off we go. Now you and dad can talk that lean talk again. Maybe next time I'll listen in. I've heard people at the bank talk about it. Sounds like something we should be doing."

After the siblings leave, Mo and his dad help in the kitchen and then spend some quality time on the patio. The summer sun is still well above the horizon, making the hills and the lake bright yellow and orange.

"So dad, last time I was here you were telling me about platforms and chief engineers. Do you remember?"

"Of course. We were very successful with product platforms. We even had global platforms."

"How did that work for your company?"

"Rather than developing every car model separately, we developed more generic platforms—like a common building block that could be applied to many cars. We started making many models—a sedan, a coupe, a station wagon—based on the same platform. Next we made a car for every brand off the same platform, and eventually we made several car lines off the same platform, like a smaller and bigger brother. Global platforms became our best-kept secret—with them we were able to spin off cars for all kinds of applications in all our countries and markets. To consumers they looked like different cars, but for us they were changes to a spec."

"Wow, dad, that must have been a huge savings in the development cost."

"Not only development cost—the tooling, purchasing, and manufacturing savings were enormous, and we drastically reduced quality problems. It made us a truly global organization. Even all R&D functions were global—some leaders were in Italy, and others were in Brazil and even China. Our global thinking led to global processes and tools. These gave us the same advantages that we saw with global product platforms. Any improvement made in one place could be leveraged globally."

"I'm going to talk to our new R&D director about the platform idea. This could be huge for Davanti, although it would be an order of magnitude smaller than what you're talking about."

"Something else I should mention: Every major platform project had a chief engineer in charge. They had a huge responsibility and were personally accountable for many projects aspects, like the specs, delivery, major investments."

"What was the difference between the chief engineer and a project manager?"

"We had project managers, too. I was one. We managed a project with a small scope compared to the chief engineer. However, we didn't have the influence, power, or respect of a chief engineer."

"What brought this about at your company?"

"I'm not sure about the global platforms, but I'm pretty certain we got the chief engineer concept and other lean ideas from Japan—and, unfortunately for us, they were quickly adopted by the whole automotive industry. They put all of us back on a level playing field."

"I really appreciate you sharing this with me. Thank you. I hope we'll find time to talk about this some more soon. This was not part of my training at Davanti, and I'd be surprised if even Junior has heard about these ideas. They could give Davanti a competitive advantage. Who knows when others in our industry would catch up."

"Mo, here I thought all you did at Davanti was play with bikes. I'm coming to find out that you're learning a lot about business and industry lately."

"I have no choice. And thanks for teaching me, dad."

"You're welcome, Mo. There's plenty more to tell."

"Well, I should chat with mom and get ready to go."

"And Mo, next time tell me a little more about what you're doing at Davanti."

"I'll do that. Promise."

Mo gets up and walks into the villa as the sun is setting. He spends a few minutes with his mom while she finishes her apricot liqueur. She looks happy but tired.

"Mom, you worked too hard on my birthday. Next year, we're all going out. OK?"

"Yes. I won't argue with that. . . . But I've got some great idea for dishes for our next get-together."

"I figured as much. I love you, mom. Get some rest tomorrow."

"I love you, too, Mo."

Mo says a last goodbye, leaves the villa, and gets into his car. His phone alerts him of a text. It's Marie:

"Happy Birthday, Mo."

"How did you know?"

"We're friends on Facebook, remember? I've been reading all the well wishes for you today, and I wanted to add my own."

"Thank you. I hope to see you soon."

"Me too."

Note

1. A lot of wishes to you.

Chapter 17

New R&D Function Takes Shape

"My good friend Fabian Tuzzi did most of the thinking behind this," explains Gino Latieri to Ricardo, Luca, and Sofia. "He was the engineer and the inventor, and I built pieces for him several years ago when Emilio and his police weren't watching. When Fabian retired last year, he left a lot of pieces behind. I picked them up because I think Fabian deserves that I show them to you. I've actually tinkered further with some. You know, to have something to think about in the shop."

Ricardo is intrigued by what Gino—a 40-year-old technician who has spent his entire career working in the Davanti prototype shop—has to show the group.

Gino begins his description with a lesson in traditional carbon-frame building: "We assemble frames from a multitude of engineered sheets of resin-impregnated carbon fibers. The pieces are layered on a hollow, plastic core in the shape of the frame, and then the assembly is cured in a mold under pressure."

Ricardo and Luca nod knowingly; Sofia furrows her brow, but she appears to follow along.

"But here's the thing," continues Gino. "Only a few critical pieces of the frame—like the bottom bracket and the steering column—really need such a sophisticated, resource-intensive process. So Fabian and I had purchased cheap, extruded tubes made from short, carbon-fiber-filled plastic. We reasoned they'd work well enough to connect the critical bike pieces. We assembled the frame in the same manner you'd weld extruded aluminum tubes together to make an aluminum bike. The aluminum welding is easy, but it's a little more challenging to connect the four plastic tubes to the carbon fiber-reinforced bottom bracket. But we eventually succeeded."

Gino proudly shows the group the bike parts: "As you can see, we cut the bottom bracket and the steering column from standard carbon fiber-reinforced bikes. We know how to make those, and they're the really critical parts on a bike. We knew that if we can connect them to cheap, mass-produced tubes, we can make an awesome bike for a fraction of the cost. And if we learn to also make the steering columns and bottom brackets themselves out of the cheap material, we add another level of savings. Last week, I got one of the R&D innovation boxes with a debit card, so I bought more tubes. I haven't received them yet."

"Did you do any testing?" asks Ricardo.

"We built a couple complete bikes. We couldn't get access to the lab back then, but we rode over five hundred miles on our prototypes. We left our personal bikes with the guard for letting us take the prototypes home. The bikes are still in inventory. I will use the tokens in the innovation box to test them in the lab now."

DOI: 10.4324/9781003231837-17

"So how did the bikes perform on your rides?"

"We wouldn't win the Giro on them, but they performed better than expected. We were able to beef up critical joints to get decent durability. The ride is the best characteristic: less stiff than what the pros ride, but we never intended to make them for the circuit. We also were surprised by the durability—we had a few breaks, but they were caused by poor craftsmanship more than anything else. Like I said, working with these cheap tubes was pretty new to us."

"So I'm looking at a light-weight bike concept here that rides very well, has likely good durability, and costs a fraction of a race bike," summarizes Ricardo.

"Precisely. We thought it was a good way to make affordable sports bikes, mostly for recreational riders, but maybe even for entry-level racers. You know they sell very good, welded alu bikes for less than 1,000 euro, and we felt we should be able to make a carbon bike for the same price, but with less weight and a much softer ride."

"Looks like you answered some critical questions already," says Ricardo, "and you obviously spent almost no money on it—you had none to start with."

"And we also made progress on the next most difficult part, the steering column," he adds, proudly holding up a prototype made entirely of extruded tubes.

"We eventually learned to use cyanoacrylate glue to hold the pieces together temporarily—you know, like tack welding. Then we wound the carbon tape around that and cured it in one of the bike molds at night when nobody was around. But, as I said, we didn't get very far with that piece and never started working on the even-more-difficult bottom bracket made all from extruded tubes."

"This is a classic example of stealth engineering," exclaims Ricardo to Sofia and Luca. "I wonder how many more of these projects we have at Davanti. This is what people do when they're underchallenged."

"So, Gino, what is the worst part of your invention?" asks Luca.

"Well, we still have to learn how to make bottom brackets out of extruded tubes, but I really don't think that should be a showstopper. Worst case would be that we have to make them the way we make them now, just in smaller molds."

"Aren't affordable touring bikes one of the opportunities on your list, Ricardo?" asks Sofia. She has been trying to keep up with the conversation but did not understand much about the technology discussed.

"They certainly are, and I think Gino and his friend may already have answered enough critical questions to take this to the gate and the next level. This could really boost Davanti sales and revenues next year, and it would be a perfect opportunity to pilot the new technology creation process."

Gino's eyes widen.

"Gino, have you talked to any engineers about this?" asks Ricardo.

"Hmmm. I had these pieces sitting out here for a few days. Many stopped by and asked me questions about them."

"Anybody in particular?"

"Come to think of it, Mariano Disota came back several times asking me questions."

"Do you mind, Gino, if we ask him to take a closer look at this? Would you be willing to share with him what you know about this bike?"

"I would love to."

"Excellent. Thank you again, Gino. This will be interesting for you, I'm sure. We'll let you know about the next step because we want to keep you involved in this project. And thanks again for sharing this with us."

As Sofia and Ricardo leave the lab, she says, "We could organize an idea-generation event, like a blogstorming or a hackathon, to help Gino with some of the more difficult problems. And Gino has plenty of samples for the show and tell."

"I'll assign one of our more experienced project managers to this and send a few engineers to set-based training. And since Gino already answered the critical questions, we've got our pilot project for the TCP process. We should help participants prepare the information they'll need for the first gate meeting. We won't have a lot of solid data, but nobody knows yet what to expect at the first gate meeting—it will be a little experiment in itself."

***

Ricardo walks up to Mo's desk. Mo is busy at work as his colleagues begin to file in. "Mo, how about a coffee or espresso?"

Mo is surprised: "Yeah, sure. I finished mine about an hour ago. Thanks."

They walk quietly down to the cafeteria. Mo is unsure of what to say, and Ricardo wants to save his comments for when he can deliver them precisely as needed. They make their way to the caffeine stations and load up on two large coffees. "How about we take a break for a minute?"

"Sure."

"I'm pretty busy right now and didn't have a lot of time to spend with you on the direct-drive project. I wish I could have given it more attention."

"Ricardo, you're the reason it's still alive. Period. And I've been busy myself. The Volta team is more time-consuming than I thought it would be, but I'm learning a lot from the team."

"Mo, we appreciate that you embraced some of the extra tasks we recently assigned, like helping the Volta team with the definition of the metrics. And you've done really well on your Leonardo project. Despite having some things to learn—don't we all—I think you're cooperating well with people. I've enjoyed working with you, and I think you can do with less coaching now."

"If you say so. Your guidance is always helpful, Ricardo."

"I'll still be there for you as a mentor. And you may need that soon, since I'm offering you the position of a PM—starting tomorrow. I will announce it today when we discuss the new organization."

"Wow, Ricardo, I don't know what to say. Well, thank you. Seriously, so much is changing around here I'm sometimes not sure if I'm moving down or up. I couldn't be happier."

"We want to keep entrepreneurs with their ideas if possible, and you'll do well as a PM. You have the technical and soft skills to succeed. It will be fun watching you handle the role."

They both pause for a moment and sip their coffees, Mo realizing the details are to come and Ricardo anxious to put Mo in the midst of it.

"So will Leonardo be the only project I manage?"

"Leonardo is part of it. But most promotions come at a cost: We want you to manage the complete direct-drive project, including the hydraulic option and the other devices that came out of the hackathon. And, of course, you'll oversee the development of the drive shafts, including Sergio's option. You'll report to Bolaji Ajaya, who's being assigned as the manager of the technology creation process."

"That'll be great. I've worked with Bolaji on a number of projects. He's sharp and doesn't take any shortcuts. I like his intensity. Sort of matches mine."

"I'm glad to hear that, Mo."

"And that's not all. You may also pick up some continuous-improvement projects soon. Well, you and everybody else, really."

"No problem. I like where Davanti is heading. It's good."

"And one more point: with this new responsibility, you'll need time to prepare for the gate meeting of the extended Leonardo project. We've got a different near-term opportunity that we're going to use to prototype the TCP, so that affords you time for more formal learning. We're going to send you to my alma mater in Lausanne for a couple of workshops on innovation excellence and lean project management. Anika in HR is working out the details."

"That's great news. This is all very exciting, Ricardo. Thank you."

"Enjoy your coffee and your day. I have to excuse myself now and talk to a few more folks before we roll out the new R&D organization this afternoon. Good luck with your new assignments."

Mo raises his coffee and gives Ricardo a nod. As he watches Ricardo exit, a million things run through his mind—including that Lausanne is closer to Marie than the Davanti headquarters in Fumane.

***

Mo had texted Marie earlier in the day to share the news about his promotion, but she had not replied. He's putting leftovers in the microwave when his phone rings; it's Marie.

"Mo, congratulations on your promotion. I wanted to phone rather than text you back. That's great news."

"Thanks, Marie. I appreciate the call."

"It's wonderful that you'll get to spend some time in Lausanne. The city is beautiful."

"I'm looking forward to it. I hope we might get together when I'm there. . . . How are you doing?"

Silence on the other end.

"Marie, are you there?"

"Yes, I'm here."

"Are you OK?" More silence.

"Marie, is there a problem? Can I help you with something?"

"No, I'm fine."

Marie resists telling Mo what's bothering her. She instead asks him questions about his promotion. Mo eventually realizes that she's clearly upset by something and not really listening to his answers."

"Marie, please tell me what's going on. I can tell something is wrong."

"Well, it *would* be great to see you in Lausanne if I was still going to be stationed in the region."

"Have you been assigned somewhere else?"

Marie finally explains that her current client did not like the analysis she pulled together on their business, and the CEO called her new boss, who is the account executive and a new partner in her firm. Marie's contact from the client team shared with her that the CEO requested a different account manager. She tearfully tells Mo that her company thrives on unparalleled customer service and assesses the performance of its staff largely based on client feedback: "Being removed from an account is almost as bad as getting fired."

"It can't be as bad as that. Have you talked with your boss about it?"

"I'm afraid to. He's new, and I don't know him that well."

"Why would you be afraid? It sounds like you did everything by the book and what your company expected of you."

"Of course I did. And the results of my analysis are what they are."

"So you shouldn't worry about speaking with him. If another colleague gets assigned to the account, the results will be the same unless somebody embellishes them."

"I think I should just email my boss, apologize, and accept the consequences." She keeps repeating that she really likes her job and is proud of her professionalism. Mo keeps listening and again encourages Marie to call her boss and ask what—if anything—she could have done differently.

"If you made a mistake, your boss should tell you and coach you. If not, he should support you and your work."

They go back and forth for another minute, and then Marie agrees to make the call. Mo has given her the confidence to finally believe she did nothing wrong in her analysis and that the whole thing could be a misunderstanding.

"Mo, thank you for talking me through this. You helped a lot. I didn't know who else to call. It's just a relief to talk about it."

"That's what friends are for. Thanks for calling me. Let me know what your boss says, OK?"

"Yes. Goodbye."

***

"Welcome to the first product creation process gate meeting," announces Ricardo, showing a graphic of the three innovation processes separated by gates and pointing to the gate in front of the PCP. He explains that the projects discussed today do not need a TCP gate meeting since they use existing technology and why it's important to have this PCP gate meeting at this time. "These products are ready for the gate, and we're discussing them today so they will be ready for launch at the end of the year. I will represent R&D at all gate meetings. I'll also coach and assist Marco, who will chair the PCP gate meetings and represent marketing."

The others in the meeting—which is the first step toward approving projects and turning them into products—are essentially Junior's executive team: product director Joe Bersaglio, Leandro Nero from supply chain, Claudia Contanti from sales, Constantine Rendere from manufacturing, Stephano Stanco from finance, and Diana Rialto from procurement. Although Junior's staff are allowed to send a representative to these meetings, today all attend in person. Some of the engineers and the project managers responsible for the projects to be reviewed are also in the meeting and available for questions that may come up.

"If this is this anything like the gating processes I've run across, I want no part of it," says Joe adamantly. "At my former company, we used gates to kill projects. We killed many, and then we'd watch our competitors launch what we killed."

"Our gate meetings are not intended to kill projects, Joe," Ricardo says calmly. "Why would we kill projects this late in the process after we've begun to invest time and some money in them? Our work in ICP and TCP will freeze or pivot projects before they get to this gate. But, as noted, we have no new technology involved today. And our gate process is simpler, more intuitive, and less taxing than what you may be used to—and it's mostly intended to align functions for proper execution."

"OK," replies Joe. "I see the difference now. I'm on board and welcome the opportunity to look at the latest data with the whole team."

"So let me get this straight: we, the gatekeepers, make the important decisions now?" remarks Claudia. "Emilio used to make these decisions and run them by Junior. I'm not qualified to assess the technical stuff that goes into the bikes."

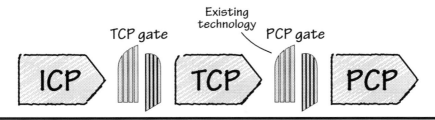

Figure 17.1   Innovation Gates.

"The team members that developed the project are the technical experts," explains Ricardo. "They know much more about the technical details than anybody in this room. During the ICP, the TCP, and, in this case, some prep work for this meeting, they've done sufficient testing and experimentation to assure us that this project is ready for the PCP. They believe there is no *technical* reason why the project should be rejected by you or anyone. You won't be evaluating its technical merits."

"Then just what do we do here?" asks Claudia.

"This meeting serves the following purposes," explains Marco. "It ensures that:

- Funds, capacity, and legal-compliance requirements are in place.
- The product to be created aligns or still aligns with Davanti goals and strategy based on the latest data.
- Support of all functions is assured. After the gate meeting, everybody's full support is expected for the scope and timeline that we approve today."

"Well said, Marco," approves Ricardo.

"We sent all the pertinent information to you ahead of this meeting," adds Marco, "or at least as much as we had. I know at least some of you have verified it with the experts in your area. These projects that we'll review today were pulled from our old portfolio, but their scope was changed significantly since their inception. There will be more and better information with further projects, since those developing them will know in advance the information required for the gate meetings. Going forward, we all have to make sure that we only request information for gate meetings that we really need—we don't want the meetings to become an administrative burden on our associates."

All nod, but most are still suspicious.

"Today we're approving two projects for full development and launch," says Marco. "That means that we decide to spend the money for styling, design, tooling, industrialization, advertising, launch cost, etc. Remember, we call this gate 'success assured' because the project team has decided that all information is available that supports the business case for the product."

"So no late surprises?" asks Constantine.

"Not as far as meeting all business requirements and timing," replies Marco. "But bad things can still happen. We can have a financial crisis, a supplier may default. But if a major change in the scope happens, we all will be aware of it."

"As you may remember, we canceled several projects because of poor returns," continues Marco. "These two projects will make up the loss of volume, cash flow, and revenue, and it's why we moved them up in the timeline."

"OK, so let's get gating," urges Stephano, anxious to talk about the projects.

"The first affects our premier race line," says Ricardo. "It's our top of the line—the Primo Sempre (PS) product. The team is convinced that the product performance is still more than good enough to compete. But since we need to create some marketing excitement, we'll do a face lift: new styling, reinforce a few parts of the frame, and update the bike overall with the latest components. That will allow us to have the bike available for the next race season at a very moderate price increase."

"I'm a little nervous about that," notes Diana. "We've never done a 'face lift' before. Are we cheating? Deceiving the customers?"

"The automotive industry and many others have done this for years," says Joe. "Our competitors do this. It all comes down to the way we advertise the product and what we promise."

Marco projects a summary of all pertinent data: volume targets, NPV, test results, financials, cost, etc. After some additional discussion about the changes and the direction the ad campaign will take, there are no objections to the project.

"The second project that we bring to the gate today is the new amateur racing Primo Veloce (PV) line," says Ricardo. "This one is a new design, and it was scheduled to launch in two years, but we need to move it up to next year. Both products will be ready to launch at the Eurobike show in January."

"So we're doing two years of work in the rest of this year?" asks Constantine, concerned that the brunt of that effort will fall on manufacturing.

"The development team is confident that it's possible," says Ricardo. "Several of the engineers who worked on canceled projects have joined this team now. And we've simplified the requirements with marketing as well."

"Will the new innovation excellence process help?" asks Diana.

"I'm sure it will help, but we're not banking on that yet," answers Ricardo.

"I'll certainly be happy to get the volume I need," says Claudia. "I hope the profit projections aren't as fictitious as the timeline."

Marco walks the group through the pertinent data, and after more questions and comments, he summarizes that both projects are approved as presented in the meeting and goes over the support required by each function. As the group leaves the room, most wonder what they just signed up for.

"So I see that I'll need to have some sophisticated excuses ready as these move forward," Constantine tells Ricardo with a wry smile.

"Or you could just let us know what additional help you need," advises Ricardo. "We just agreed these are important projects. Those that support them will get the help they need."

"I'll get back to you on that. You can count on it."

***

Late in the afternoon, Ricardo has called together the R&D staff for a town hall meeting in the engineering area. He's let them know that they will find out how the R&D function will be different going forward, and everyone in the function is anxious and in attendance. Mo stands near the back, alongside Vinnie, who has surprised all by his attendance. Everyone takes some comfort to see that Junior is present as well.

"Thanks for coming today," says Junior. "You all know Ricardo. He's going to lead R&D to becoming a world-class, innovation excellence organization."

The group applauds.

"Davanti has had many good years without being really challenged by competition, but those good times may be coming to an end. Our competition has caught up on technology and to our capabilities—so we have to beat them on a higher level. I believe we develop the best products at Davanti. But if we want to remain competitive and profitable, we have to also become the best at how we do it. Let the competition try to match that."

The group applauds louder and longer.

"Davanti recently formulated new and very aggressive objectives and goals, which are needed to secure the future of the company and the Fumane site. All functions, including R&D, have been asked to align their strategy to help us meet the corporate goals and to create the right organization to accomplish that task. And, in my opinion, there is no other function more important than R&D when it comes to achieving our goals."

Junior pauses to look around the room, taking in the faces spread throughout the room.

"I understand everybody's concern. Change is never easy. So I encourage you to voice your concerns to Ricardo, Anika, or even to me. And with that, I turn it over to Ricardo." Junior walks to the back of the room and stands against a wall.

"Thanks, Junior. I like how you explained why we must become the best at what we do and how we do it. I'll also stress that we need to do it right here in Fumane. When manufacturing operations move to another country with lower labor costs, it costs a lot of money to build or retool a factory. What does it take to outsource engineering jobs? Internet is in every country, computers and workstations are cheap, and the talent is abundantly available in many countries with much lower engineering costs. So what do we do to ensure that we in Italy can compete with anybody in the world on creativity *and* efficiency?" Ricardo pauses and lets this sink in.

"How can we get more creative, more agile, faster, more efficient, and more productive? The clock is ticking."

Ricardo briefly shows the corporate vision and goals on a large portable screen behind him and on all monitors in the engineering area. "This is our True North. We are here to help Davanti achieve those goals." He then shows, as he did with the leadership team, how the R&D objectives and goals align with the corporate vision. Many in the room, having participated in their development, are familiar with the chart and objectives regarding constant flow of the right products at the right time; speed and efficiency; world-class technical organization; and a culture of innovation based on respect and collaboration.

"I'm not telling you today how we'll do this—other than to say that we're not implementing innovation excellence to cut costs or even jobs. It's to become a better organization and help the company create revenue and achieve its goals. You'll all be engaged to help define *how* we do that. Today I want to introduce you to the new R&D organization that will help us achieve those goals and to hear your questions and feedback."

Many appear to believe Ricardo and applaud politely, but others think, "We've heard such things before."

"I also want to point out that I didn't come up with this new organization on my own: It's inspired by the new corporate organization and has been reviewed and endorsed by the leadership team. And, like the R&D strategy, most of the ideas came from a team of R&D managers, project managers, and engineers." Ricardo shows the names of the individuals he had consulted and thanks them for their time and effort.

Next on the screen, Ricardo shows the five characteristics of the new R&D organization (flat and responsive, fast and agile, focused, collaborative, and engaged/empowered). He speaks to all of them and summarizes, "These will help us promote innovation and entrepreneurship. We're moving technical responsibility to where it belongs—to the technical experts. We'll only take on as much work as we have capacity for, and we'll try to allow engineers to focus on only one project at a time. We'll be flexible and agile in dealing with change, and we'll pursue collaboration with Davanti functions rather than redesign and rework. Finally, we'll build a culture based on respect, empowerment, trust, and accountability."

The engineers appear to like what they hear, but most will withhold judgement until they see all of this in action.

Ricardo explains the R&D matrix organization and how most people will report to a project manager and a functional manager. "I know project management is not new for many of you, but your work will be much more organized and standardized." Then he pauses for questions and comments.

Alexandra is concerned about her increased responsibility and accountability that a flat organization seems to bring with it.

"We had a deep organization before, and the command-and-control structure gave us a sense of achieving good quality," says Ricardo. "In reality, the layers spent most of their time sorting out conflicting requirements and managing engineering changes. There will be more upfront clarity around project value and requirements in the future and fewer engineering changes, if any. But I understand your concern about more responsibility. The younger engineers will have mentors, more senior folks who coach and help them. You will always have your functional manager or project manager who can verify your recommendations. And let me clarify accountability: associates will only be held accountable for what they and their superiors have agreed on."

"With so few layers in a flat organization, how can we advance?" asks Serfino.

"First of all, there will not be less compensation. Careers should not be defined by rank and office space but by responsibility, competency, contribution, challenging work, and rewards."

The question also gives Ricardo an opportunity to introduce the technical ladder: "We're also going to create a technical career path or ladder. To date, Davanti R&D associates had only one opportunity to advance their career—that was through a leadership ladder that led to management. As you've pointed out, the leadership ladder will get very small and short. The technical ladder will allow talented engineers, who don't aspire to be a leader, to reach the same level of pay and status as a director by developing deep technical expertise and contributions to the company. Those contributions and expertise can be in many areas: engineering, computer simulations, even project management, and this will be available to engineers, technicians, and support staff. We'll soon publish the requirements for the different levels and how to apply for these career options. And unlike the leadership ladder, technical advancement will rely heavily on nominations and recommendations from peers, customers, suppliers, etc. A higher level in the technical ladder also means additional technical responsibilities, like maintaining product or test standards, mentoring young engineers, conducting training, and serving on technical councils. I know some of those terms may not be familiar to you, but we'll have communications and training to explain them."

Peter Baggio, an engineer, complains, "I've been here for many years, and over time our jobs have become more bureaucratic and complicated. I think all of these paths and activities will make it even worse. When will we have an initiative to make my job easier?"

"Peter, we're all affected, not just you," exclaims Johnny Torto, another engineer. "I've been here longer than most of you. You don't see me complaining. I volunteered to help redesign or create these new processes that Ricardo talked about—they'll not be forced on me. I say we all give this a try, and we all try to make our own jobs easier."

Peter shrugs his shoulders and says, "We'll see."

Mariano Disota wants to know how his performance will be assessed if he works for two bosses.

"We'll still base pay and advancement on performance. But people won't only be assessed for their technical contribution; you'll be expected to collaborate with other functions and help your colleagues. In addition, we'll reward entrepreneurism, innovation, reusing knowledge, making process improvements, finding and solving problems, following standard work, etc. Many more people above and below your level and even customers and suppliers will provide input on your performance, which should create a more rounded view of your contributions. Anika and her team are working on a fair system for compensation and advancements in the matrix."

Ricardo answers more questions about the matrix before showing a diagram of the new organization. He's held off on that because he knows as soon as the names are on the screen, the focus will be on nothing but the names.

He reiterates that "although some leaders in the current hierarchy may lose power, they won't lose responsibility, and nobody will be demoted or suffer a financial loss. And the more senior positions will pick up the more demanding assignments and projects."

The slide shows the three new positions—programs, operations, and technology managers—and Ricardo explains the three roles that have been assigned to Bart, Caroline, and Bolaji, respectively. Then he briefly describes how the organization will work with HR, procurement, manufacturing, and the outside services.

Many look pleased; a few look annoyed.

Ricardo then shows a list of the project managers already appointed, including Mo, Gina, and Stella. Mo is proud to see his name on the list. Vinnie turns to him and gives him two thumbs up.

"And we'll have a special training program for current and new project managers on 'Davanti Project Management,' which will include managing associates and projects. . . . Are there more questions or comments?"

Some engineers comment positively about how the new organization can create clarity and focus and make work easier and more fun. Others say they like the reduction of multitasking and controls. Many agree that responsibility and empowerment are overdue. Most, though, admit they can't quite grasp how it's all supposed to work.

The room soon goes quiet. Junior nods his approval to Ricardo.

"If there are no other questions, let me point out that there are many new positions in the R&D organization," continues Ricardo. "More people will be engaged in idea creation or assessment, knowledge management tasks, continuous improvement, and technology development. As such positions are ready to be filled, we'll post them, so everybody has a chance to apply. And we'll also take applications and nominations for another new position: a project manager responsible for the idea creation process. That position, which I'm currently manning, will report to Bolaji."

Ricardo then turns the floor over to Anika, who explains how people can submit their preferences for assignments in the new R&D organization. She also explains that she doesn't expect everybody to be happy, but she hopes everybody will give it a chance to work. She mentions that there are open positions in other parts of the company if somebody wants to move out of R&D. "My office still has a door, but I rarely close it. Come to me with any concern you may have. And if we can't find the right position for you right away, I'll work with you."

Other questions follow, most about the timing for the changes. Ricardo, too, mentions that anyone should talk to him at any time. "My office is in the center of the R&D organization. I can't say the door is always open because I have no door."

Ricardo looks around to see if there are other questions, and sees Gina wave her hand. Despite losing the power she held under Emilio, she is pleased that she's a project manager and excited by the opportunities ahead.

"We're transforming into a lean company, like a lean startup in many ways. Will we get the perks of lean startups, like free gourmet food, flex hours, and equity in the company? When can I bring my dog to work? Will there be daycare if someone needs it, or can people bring their babies to work?"

"Good questions, Gina. Some of those ideas could fly. Anyone else?"

"Can we install stationary bikes with a space for my computer?" asks Veronika. "Then I can work out while I read email and reports."

"That's an interesting idea, for sure. I'll ask procurement and HR if there are any issues with that. If not, I don't see why that couldn't be made available."

"And how about treadmills—we ride enough bikes after work," exclaims Peter. His colleagues laugh.

Ricardo sees an opportunity to adjourn the meeting on a happy note, and he asks Junior if he has anything to add. Junior just shakes his head and smiles. "Well, that's the new Davanti R&D organization. Your organization."

Suddenly it's nearly 5:00 pm, yet many people remain in the room, huddled in small groups talking about what they've just heard. Others left the room immediately, openly showing their frustration. A few folks thank Ricardo and Anika for the way the announcement was handled and the opportunity to ask questions and voice their opinions. Questions remain on the minds of most, however, knowing that the next morning they will be wrapping up their current work and preparing for reassignment in a transformed R&D organization.

Chapter 18

Bikes without Wheels

When the Tour de France exited the Pyrenees, all talk was about the Omega team. They had shown exceptional form: Their two European aces were in first and second place in the overall standings, but neither had won a stage. As surprising, four other Omega riders—who were essentially unknown in the racing world before the Tour—were among the top 20 in the standings.

The stellar performance of Omega had raised the eyebrows of thousands of race fans as well as riders and Tour organizers. In interviews, the Tour director had made it clear that millions of euros had been invested in new doping test equipment, mobile labs, and medical staff. Testing is the most sophisticated and thorough that it has ever been, he declared, and the Tour intends to never repeat the Lance Armstrong saga. He pointed out that the Omega leaders were being tested every day—both before and after every stage.

Nonetheless, questions and skepticism increase on the circuit.

At stage 16 of the Tour, the Davanti team receives some startling news:

> Justin Lagrange, a young journalist who works for a small French website journal, believed he had uncovered some damning evidence on the Omega team. He noticed a pattern in the performance of their riders: each stage three or four Omega riders and one of the aces would put in a stellar performance. The following stage, a different group of Omega riders and the other ace would excel. Justin made a graph to illustrate his suspicion and shared it with a few close colleagues. He also realized that the Omega team didn't stay in the same hotels or locales as most of the other riders; like Justin, they stayed in less expensive places on the outskirts of the town where a stage takes place.
>
> Justin had been trying to stay at or near the hotel where the Omega holes up. His evening routine was to update his company's website and go for a good, long run. One night he returned as it was getting dark and noticed that a car had picked up one of the Omega aces and another rider. Justin hung out at a nearby outdoor café, waiting to see what happened. An hour or so later the car returned and picked up two more Omega riders. A few hours later the riders returned in the same staggered pattern. He stuck to this routine for three days, and saw the same thing occur each night, with alternate riders involved. The good performances by the Omega riders the next day correlated with the previous night's outings. This was no Uber to a nightclub and back; he was convinced that something was underway.
>
> Armed with his observations and performance data, Justin went to see the head referee and convinced him of his suspicion. The referee passed on the information to

DOI: 10.4324/9781003231837-18

the French authorities, who quickly gained permission to shadow the Omega riders in the evening.

The evening following the next stage, the authorities watched an ace and another rider being picked up from the hotel. They tailed the car and saw them dropped in front of a building that looked like a physical therapy office. There the agents noticed that the riders soon got into a different car behind the building. They followed the second car to a deserted dark parking lot where two RVs were parked. As the riders got into the first RV, the agents received permission to search the vehicles. Inside both RVs were sophisticated mobile clinics along with the Omega riders. Two were in the middle of a process where blood was being drawn, processed, and immediately transfused back, while the two that had just arrived were already getting prepped. Authorities saw that the IV entries were in an area of the riders where the doping controls would never think to check.

The French authorities confiscated the RVs and all equipment, and arrested the Omega staff and the riders.

Rossa and his teammates are getting in their final warmups when the doping news hits the crowd. The Omega team had not shown up at the start of the stage and, after the grace period expired, they were disqualified. "Hey Rossa," yells Pasquale Barto, the up-and-coming Davanti rider. "Omega is out. The whole team was arrested last night. They were doping. The team owner—who isn't identified, don't you know—posted a tweet this morning, denying any wrongdoing, alleging discrimination, vowing to fight any pending suspensions, and demanding the immediate release of his staff and riders. I knew it. I just knew it."

"It's a new Tour," says Rossa. "And we're ready for it."

The day's flat stage ends in a sprint finish with no change in the standings—except for the removal of the disqualified riders. A French rider who had been in third place is dressed in the maillot jaune and accepts the "bises" of the local hostesses. He waves at the crowd to the tumultuous applause of the French spectators.

Rossa has moved up into fifth place and is pleased with his position. The upcoming Tour stages will be difficult climbs into the Alps, a style of racing for which he's famous. After the Alps, there will be a final time trial, and then the Tour will end with the crescendo on Mont Ventoux, before the last stage: the ceremonial ride into Paris.

***

When Mo shows up to the Wednesday evening bike ride, he sees a small canopy set up, much like those Davanti uses when they do race support. Under the canopy and shielded from the summer sun is Vinnie, busy changing pedals and adjusting seats and handlebars at his work stand.

As Mo gets closer, he can see that there is a line of colleagues dressed in bike gear. There is also an assortment of competitor products lined up behind Vinnie, with Ricardo standing behind the bikes.

Vinnie bangs two wrenches together to get the group's attention. "Attenzione," yells Vinnie, and everyone stops chatting and looks at the bikes and Ricardo.

"Thanks for coming to the outing today. I want you and all our associates to understand what we compete against," says Ricardo. "If you'd like, Vinnie will help set you up with a competitor bike today, and you can take them home for a few days as long as you leave your own bike here."

Mo immediately joins the waiting line, and eyes a product from Davanti's closest competitor. When he's finally ready to take a bike, Vinnie pulls out the one he's been coveting. "I knew you'd want this one," says Vinnie. "Have fun."

Mo leaves his bike and hops aboard. "Thanks. Arrivederci."

Most of the other Wednesday riders have started off, and Mo pumps hard to get within distance of them. The bike is surprisingly fast on the downhills, and he wonders if the quality of the rims contributes to that. It's not quite a Davanti bike, but it's clearly a pro racing two-wheeler. "Maybe we're not as advanced as we thought we were," he considers as he finally catches others in the group—many of whom have similar looks of surprise.

***

Mo is watching the daily replay of the Tour de France and spots a few riders on bikes similar to the one he rode earlier in the day. If providing competitor bikes was Ricardo's intent to get his staff's attention, it's working. He's about to call Marco, when a call comes in from Marie.

"Hello, Marie."

"Hi, Mo. I wanted to tell you that I called my boss today." She sounds happier than the last time they talked.

"And what did he say?"

"He had a long talk with the client CEO. He said my analysis was probably accurate, albeit not popular, and the CEO admitted as much. It turns out the CEO was upset with *how* I presented my findings; he would have liked to have been briefed before I shared the results with his full executive team. I wish my contact had told me that."

"The CEO's reaction is understandable."

"Yes. I could have asked a few more questions and read the situation better. My boss gave me some coaching—some really helpful tips—about how and to whom I should present bad news as well as some questions that I should ask of my contacts. He also told me that the CEO accepts my assessment and is fine with me staying on the account. My boss asked if I want to go back or if he should replace me. He's given me a few days to think about it."

"And what did you decide?"

"Mo, I don't know what to do? What do you think?"

"From what I can see, you're a solid professional that serves your clients and your company well. Everybody can make a bad call now and then, but the fact that the client will take you back means they still respect your knowledge and professionalism."

"It just seems a bit weird."

"Yeah, but this could have ended far worse."

"That's for sure. I think my boss wants me to go back, and he'd be disappointed if I didn't."

"Of course he would."

"OK, so I guess I just apologize to the CEO for my approach and thank him for the opportunity to serve his company. Period. And then work hard like I have been."

"It may be awkward at first, but I think it's a good plan, Marie. I wish you the best of luck."

"Mo, again, thanks so much. I'm really blessed to have a friend like you."

***

Thursday morning, Junior sits in his office, clicking through email on his computer to see if any daily alerts had come in from the function directors. He's pleased that he spends less time as a referee and has fewer argumentative meetings these days. He also enjoys having time for more important things—although he's not quite sure what those are yet but certain that Sofia will soon tell him. He feels that he has set the company on the right course and trusts his new organization much more than he trusted the old one. But the old organization had one advantage—*every* problem was eventually dragged into his office. He's now concerned that he may find out about problems after customers, competitors, or journalists. For that reason, he instructed the directors to alert him within 24 hours of any critical issues that negatively affect employees or Davanti have occurred—e.g., safety, quality, customer satisfaction problems. Along with notification of the problem, they were to submit their next course of action and let him know if they needed his help.

Since he started the practice, there were only a few issues elevated to his attention: Constantine reported a near-miss safety incident at the Taiwan plant along with a sound plan to prevent others. A furious bike dealer planned to pull all Davanti bikes from his lineup because of the discontinued models (Junior had to call him personally to explain that new, better offerings were on the way and that the dealer should contact him personally with any remaining concerns). And some Tour teams were reporting tiny stress fractures on bike frames; Ricardo had convened a meeting to explore the problem. This morning, however, he sees nothing unusual and is relieved.

From his computer's message app, he hears the chime and sees a text from Marcel: "When can I see the ski bike?"

Junior calls Ricardo: "Do we have a ski bike?"

"I have a crude mockup from a hackathon at my desk."

"I will be right over."

Junior closes out of his computer, and heads down the hall to engineering. He usually likes to take in the sight of everyone hard at work, but instead makes a beeline for Ricardo's desk. There he sees what Marcel had gotten wind of, most likely from Sofia. "Where did this thing come from? I'm not sure I can describe it. It's a bike, but it's not."

"It came out of a recent hackathon. I brought it over here hoping to find a volunteer to work on the first critical questions. But I've found no takers yet. You're the first to ask about it."

"Can we show this to Marcel?"

"I'd like to see some things tweaked first but, sure, why not. How much time do we have?"

"I'll let you know." Junior answers the text on his phone and describes the concept and the state of its development, knowing full well Marcel's passion for skiing.

"Can I see it?"

"Sure, but you'll have to come here."

"Excellent. I'll be over tomorrow. Eleven am OK?"

"You've got until tomorrow morning," says Junior to Ricardo. "Let me know if you need anything until then. Good luck."

Ricardo works the rest of the day and late into the evening getting ready for Marcel's visit. He asked Gina to help—at least through the visit by Marcel or until he finds a volunteer to take on the project.

Together they'd taken the rudimentary prop from the hackathon and asked Luca's staff to build a little more professional version from better bike parts. By late Thursday, they're both pretty happy with the revised prototype. To bring it all together, Gina found some short skis at a local ski store that keeps a small inventory over the summer. This gave the prototype shop enough material to work with. Before heading home for the night, Gina asks Ricardo about tomorrow's debut: "So what will I tell Marcel tomorrow?"

"Very little. Let the prototype tell the story. Just answer his questions."

***

Promptly at 11:00 am, Gus the security guard brings Marcel to Juniors office. "OK, Junior, let's see this thing. To say I'm curious is an understatement. You know how much I love to ski."

"I certainly do; sometimes I wonder how you find time for work in the winter. . . . Give me a moment to wrap this up. I also want to ask Anna to get us a luncheon reservation, if that's OK."

"Yes, yes, of course. Hurry it up."

A few minutes later, Junior is leading Marcel into the shop. It's his first visit to the shop, and while he takes in all the surroundings, he's absorbed by what looks to be a mini-bike with skis in place of wheels. Junior introduces Marcel to Ricardo and Gina, who sits on the bike dressed in ski gear and wearing ski blades she borrowed from a colleague. "The blades are needed to manage steep and rough terrain, and they also help with mobility at the ski lift," explains Gina. "The bike is so small and light, I can grab it with one hand and take it on the lift."

"I have tried ski bikes before," says Marcel. "I found them to be too heavy, suitable only for a groomed slope. They also were too cumbersome to take on a lift. This thing, I could take anywhere. Do you ski, Gina? Do you think this would be difficult to learn?"

"It gives a skier four skis instead of two," says Gina. "I think it could be learned quickly, and I want to be one of the first to find out."

"Could you build these at Davanti, either here or in Taiwan?"

"Taiwan for sure, but I don't see why not here," replies Ricardo. "There are some components like the ski blades that we'll need to procure, but that's no different for a road bike."

Marcel continues to pepper the trio with questions, and Gina and Ricardo answer them as best they can. Junior finally sees Marcel take a break and offers to get him to lunch. Marcel is obviously impressed, and tells Junior: "Great stuff, Fausto. I've got some questions for you, but we can discuss those over lunch."

As Junior escorts Marcel out of the lab, Gina tells Ricardo: "You got your volunteer for this project—I know a winner when I see one."

Junior gets a ride to the restaurant in Marcel's Maserati Quattroporte, although he feels like he needs a shoehorn to get into the passenger seat. The restaurant—Sole e Pace—is only a few blocks from Davanti headquarters, and it takes Junior longer to get in and out of the car than it does to arrive. The mostly open-air eatery is filled for lunch, but Junior never has trouble getting a table. The owner, Benny Augustine, greets them both warmly and ushers them to a shaded table.

"Grazie, Benny," says Junior. "We're pinched for time. How about two chopped salads and Pellegrinos?" Marcel nods in agreement.

"I'll get those right out," says Benny.

"So how did you find out about the ski bike? I should be embarrassed that you knew something about Davanti that I didn't."

"Sofia texted me about the hackathon and warned me that it was only a crude prototype. She knows my passion about everything that has to do with skiing. And that's more than a crude prototype; I'm glad I came. I really like what I saw today. It's good that it can be carried easily on lifts. I think it's different enough from what's out there that skiers and snowboarders will try it out. It could attract new people to the sport. I wonder how we can promote a product like that."

Benny arrives with salads and waters: "Here you go. I've also brought a little focaccia. Man does not live on salad alone."

"Thank you," says Marcel as he takes a piece of the warm bread. "Fausto, do you think you can develop that thing? I can find people to help you, especially with the skis, if you need it."

"We'll have a working prototype for you before the first snow flies," says Junior with an air of confidence and pride, hoping he's not promising too much.

"And I was very impressed with your staff—Ricardo and Gina. Looks like you are on the right track, my friend."

***

"This is the best Florentine soup I have tasted in a long time," says Sofia. "And you made this from scratch?"

"From the vegetables I grew in my garden," answers Anika.

"You must give me the recipe." Anika invited her new friend to the patio for lunch, which she provides. "Don't tell me you also baked the ciabatta. It's wonderful."

"I did as well. A little appreciation for all I'm learning from you, Sofia."

"And thank you for the great job you did with the training."

"You're welcome, Sofia."

"Something else is on your mind. Am I right?"

"Yes. Before we take the transformation any further, I have a concern to share with you: Claudia's attitude bothers me. She's a very competent sales director, and I don't want her to go down Emilio's path. She'd be hard to replace. But she can become the apple that spoils the whole cart."

"I can see your concern. First, let me say that I don't take her attacks personally. In fact, I appreciate that she is open about everything and she doesn't fight behind the scenes. The rest is her personality. It will take a little longer and more convincing facts to get her on board."

"I'm glad you see it like that. Sometimes I wonder what Junior thinks."

Sofia gives the comment some thought before replying: "I think Junior is a patient person and that he trusts us with the transformation now. He's given it the time necessary to get underway. You know, we were lucky to get him on board so quickly. That's not always the case. Many leaders take a much more wait-and-see approach, which is then imitated by their staff. That kind of delay gives the Claudias of this world a chance to sway their peers and eventually the top leader."

"I feel for Marco in his new role, but I think the other executives have accepted her role as the devil's advocate."

"Yes, and fortunately it's not affected their perception of the transformation."

Anika finishes her soup, packs up the containers, and pauses to enjoy the warm day and fresh air. "It's good to get out."

"Yes. Thank you again."

"So what's the next step? I feel like we're in the middle of our change management program. Have we reached the point where we need to engage *all* associates in all departments to get us over the hump?"

"Yes, the time has come, and we can start that by publicizing any good news about the progress."

"I assume that's what we'll discuss with the Volta team this afternoon."

"Correct. The team will help us prepare the data we'll use to communicate piece by piece to the rest of the organization that we're on the right track, but please help me look for good news in other places, too. Maybe we can quote associates one day about how much happier they are to come to work. The news will help get everybody engaged, which, ideally, will lead to everyone wanting to be involved in improving processes. It's never quite as simple as that, of course, but we've reached an inflection point that can only be activated by widespread employee involvement."

"I think our associates are prepared and ready to contribute. What do you have in mind? I assume we run a pilot first, maybe in R&D, and then we can expand to other areas."

"I think that's a good idea, Anika. Some R&D staff are up to their knees in this—hackathons, improvement events, trialing new ideas, problem solving—but others are beginning to wonder when it's their time to participate. I also think more associates *want* to get engaged. They want to improve their work. And they want to help make this initiative successful. In R&D, we can certainly count on Ricardo's experience, example, and support."

"So when do we turn them loose?"

"Our first projects are moving into the PCP. That would be a good candidate for enlisting associate support for improvements, since most of the R&D associates know that process well. I'll talk to Ricardo about making that our pilot for engagement and get back to you."

"Isn't that a little risky? Allowing associates to redesign a major process on the fly while two critical projects move in?"

"There will never be a perfect time unless we shut the place down. But you're right. It will be challenging. We'll need to carefully plan and monitor this, which we would do anyway. It's really our only choice for success: our current processes may not deliver those products by the end of the year unless we improve them."

"You know, things slow down in August around here—that can work in our favor. How about we grab a coffee and then talk about how we motivate and reward the associates for the extra work we're asking of them?"

Sofia and Anika walk to the cafeteria, pick up cappuccinos, and slowly make it back to the shade of the patio.

"Helping to improve the process can't be perceived as extra work," says Sofia. "It must be understood as the work that everybody does on an ongoing basis. But it helps to show our appreciation to associates—from a simple 'thank you' to formal celebrations."

"Let me work on that."

"Remember that we reward both effort and success. Learning from mistakes and identifying problems is worth celebrating, too. And celebrations can't be perceived as reaching a finish line. Continuous improvement work never ends. Having that mindset is a critical part of culture change. And we shouldn't forget to also thank people for the other work they do every day."

"I'll prep our leaders accordingly."

"Thanks for taking this on, Anika. Recognition will help show respect for people."

"Respect," says Anika thoughtfully, drawing the word out. She recognizes the depth and breadth of work necessary to establish genuine respect throughout an organization.

"Our training addressed the need for a culture based on respect, and there is nothing more necessary to build an engaged workforce, but it takes a lot of effort to get there," says Sofia. "Leaders must openly show respect for everybody. Associates should respect their leaders, fellow associates, and support staff. People have to learn that there's value in diversity—diverse thinking, skills, opinions—and understand that diversity is critical in a healthy culture. People should always assume a positive intent even if an associate may not get everything right or if the associate's opinion doesn't match their own. Leaders have to set the example for this—be humble, recognize they don't know everything, and ask for suggestions before giving instructions. This will take time, coaching, and mentoring. It doesn't need to get completed next month."

"Sofia, we've already started in some ways. Junior's staff meetings are testament to that. And going back to our first encounter, you've always shown me respect. Which makes me wonder: what will we do when you leave one day? How can we sustain this?"

"No change sticks unless the culture changes. Without the culture change, process changes will remain awkward and artificial—plugged onto an organization with no chance to survive past the current generation. Achieving cultural excellence was my plan since the first day I came here. All the training, the new processes, respect for people, the change in behaviors—they all contribute to a better culture. And one of the best ways to sustain improvements is to create more improvement. The desire to always make things better must become part of Davanti's DNA."

"How do we know our efforts to change culture are working? Can we measure it?"

"We could look at results and metrics, but many are driven by things beyond culture. For now, I like to look at behaviors. You should slowly see less frustration, fighting, disrespect, fear, disengagement, anger, mistrust, blame, excuses, carelessness, poor quality, arrogance, and internal competition. Things like that should fade away. In their place we should see humble behaviors: respect for everybody, collaboration, help, trust, concern (for people, company, workplace, and quality), initiative, responsibility, accountability, job satisfaction, pride, listening, patience, care, and even love. Eventually, we'll find appropriate metrics for these, too."

"I'm beginning to see these things now, and I see how we started the culture change months ago, Sofia."

"The best time to start changing behaviors and the culture is the first day of a transformation—there will not be a better opportunity down the road."

"I'm surprised you haven't talked about what this means in terms of specific business results. Isn't that why we're doing all this?"

Sofia sips at her coffee and smiles: "Get the process and the people transformation right, and the results will follow."

***

Marco shows up at Mo's desk just as Mo is getting ready to grab some lunch. Marco has a huge grin on his face and his hands behind his back.

"What's up?" asks Mo. "Why so happy?"

"Happy for you, Mo," replies Marco pulling two VIP passes from behind his back and waving them in front of Mo. "Just as you requested: the last stage of the Tour de France." One pass is in Mo's name, the other has 'Marie Vigneron' printed on it.

"Marco, I knew you'd come through. Thank you so much. Wow, I can't wait to tell Marie."

Mo takes a picture of Marie's pass and texts it to her without a comment.

Less than a minute later, she replies: "What's this?"

"Your VIP pass for the final stage of the Tour de France."

"On the Avenue des Champs-Élysées in Paris?"

"Yes"

"Will you be there?"

Mo answers with a picture of his own pass.

"OMG. How could I pass on that? Thanks, Mo, I'd love to join you!"

The two passes will get Mo and Marie to the most desirable bike event of the year: They will see the last Tour stage on Sunday, with a finish on the Champs-Élysées, followed by the podium ceremonies in front of the Arc de Triomphe. Tens of thousands will cheer on the riders through the eight laps around the obelisk on the Place de la Concorde and the turnaround in front of the Place Charles de Gaulle, with riders vying for a sprinter's most-prized trophy. Mo and Marie will be with the who's who of cycling, alongside heads of state handing out the trophies and in the huge party that follows.

***

Friday afternoon, Sofia has gathered the Volta team for a conversation about the Davanti transformation and the need for it to deliver a quick win. "When you implement a transformation of this order of magnitude, it's critical to rapidly show some positive results," says Sofia.

"When a big change happens, people's first reaction is to deny it and then fight it," adds Anika, who had discussed the meeting with Sofia beforehand.

"And then comes chaos, right?" says Gina.

"Let's try to avoid chaos and call it 'high uncertainty,'" answers Sofia. "It's during this phase that you are likely to find a small percentage of supporters and a handful of open opponents."

"Opponents like Claudia," says Marco. "She's even given you a new nickname."

"I don't mind 'Miss Innovation.' I've been called much worse. And I'm not worried about open opposition—I can deal with that. It's the covert, hidden resistance that caught me off guard in the past. It comes from nowhere. So let's hope we don't have any of that at Davanti."

"So if we have a few supporters and a few opponents, where is everybody else?" asks Mo.

"They sit back, wait for this to catch on or to blow over," says Anika. "They watch other people get on board or join the opposition. It's that large group that we need to focus on now because an early success can get them on board. It not only reassures the associates, but a quick win especially helps with the engagement of leadership."

"This isn't rocket science," says Giovanni Santocchi from manufacturing. "Why can't people just do their job and give it time to work? Revenue and profit are the best evidence."

"That's true, Giovanni," confirms Sofia. "The big support comes when you see the impact of innovation excellence on the top and the bottom lines—increased revenue, reduced cost—but that can take some time to achieve and publicize."

"That's because finance closes the books three months into the new year," says Gina. "By that time, nobody will remember what we did."

"That's right," says Sofia, "and why small wins help the cause. But we can't wait for something good to happen and then spread the word. We need to either plan for something good to happen or look for something that has already happened. Some results are probably there but nobody has noticed yet. And if we can't find any, we may want to accelerate a few initiatives that we know generate savings fast."

"But innovation excellence is more than cost-cutting," counters Mo.

"Of course. Although eventual business results from the initiative are far bigger, cost savings or cost avoidance or capacity increases materialize much quicker, are easier to compute, and can be understood as a transformation outcome."

"So this is the low-hanging fruit that the trainer was talking about," notes Charles Okeke from finance.

"It could be," says Sofia. "Sometimes you bump into it with your head; sometimes the fruit hangs a little out of reach. Here are a few cues that help in the search—the usual suspects as I like to call them. A good place to start is waste. What is typically the largest waste in the office or in R&D?"

Volta team suggestions range from overprocessing to defects and waiting.

"Waiting is often the largest," agrees Sofia. "We need to look at projects or opportunities that wait, and you often can use cost of delay or similar means to quantify that waste. A close associate of waiting is work in process or WIP. That is caused when too many projects are started at once, leading to multitasking, slow processing, and often long delays."

"Other suspects?" asks Charles.

"Overprocessing and overproduction. They're my favorites on the quick-win list, especially in conservative, risk-adverse companies."

"We always order three times more prototypes and testing than we need, just to be on the safe side," says Stella DiCaprio, a project manager. "That's clearly overprocessing, but if a problem comes up, the first thing you hear is 'Did you test enough?' Engineers learn that lesson very fast."

"So what happens with overproduction?" asks Sofia. "You said we make more prototype bikes than we use?"

"They sit in the warehouse for years until we clean the warehouse—and then we scrap them," says Luca. "Lawyers' orders!"

"Well, that's truly wasteful. Another bad example of overprocessing is to pay extra money to finish stuff before it's needed. Do you see that?"

"Absolutely. Ambitious project managers always want things done long before they're needed," says Serfino, who recently joined the Volta team. "It makes them look good." He looks toward Gina, who intentionally looks out the window.

"Wait a minute; we're late on most of what we deliver, so how can we finish anything early?" asks Charles.

"Maybe you're late on one because you deliver something else too early? The worst part with the 'OO' wastes is when we use scarce resources to overprocess or overproduce while something else with a high cost of delay waits."

Finally, Charles can't take it any longer and throws up his arms. "I can't believe what I'm hearing. How are we getting away with that? You could be talking about a million euros here. How can we make money in the first place?"

"The saving grace is often that your competitors are no better at this than Davanti," says Sofia calmly. "But don't bank on that."

"Sofia, what else should we be looking to minimize?" asks Anika.

"Here's are a few more:

- Transportation waste, like expedited shipping. Once you look under that stone, you'll never stop.
- Motion in the office as a consequence of the location of printers and other office equipment. This can get very costly in labs and prototype operations.
- Let's not forget defects, mistakes, etc. Rework is also costly. And mistakes that end up with a customer can be extremely costly.
- Last but not least, wasted talent. Are engineers doing work they're paid for, or are they forced to do work of technicians or administrators? Are they doing technical work, or do they spend time on followup and expediting? Could simple software replace some manual work?"

She encourages them to look beyond the engineering area to find opportunities. "The shop and lab are great places to look first. Work—and waste—are easier to see there, and the lean principles that Davanti has used in manufacturing may apply."

"We're just a small group," says Stella. "How are we supposed to eradicate all of this stuff, some of which we have no contact with or control over?"

"Ask the people who do the work for their input. But we need to be careful and respectful about how we approach them. They may be defensive. They may think that the work they do is important—even if some of it is waste—and they'll fear that eliminating some of their work could mean that their position eventually will be eliminated. Emphasize that we're looking at bad processes—not for bad people."

"I've already had some folks come to me with problems and ideas; there are some colleagues out there who want things to be different," adds Marco.

"As you observe processes and people working, look for these important cues: Whenever things seem to go slow, seem to be complicated, create frustration, or make no sense, take a closer look. I guarantee you'll find something. . . . I could give you some additional signs of trouble, but these will get you going for now. It's good to discover some things on your own. So please engage the associates in your areas; maybe even draw a simple process map together so you can walk the process. And after you walk the process, try drawing a value-stream map—you learned that in the training, but I can assist you if needed."

"This could be a very long list, Sofia," says Gina.

"Out of the gate, it often is. You'll find wastes big and small, so please try to put a price tag on the main issues. Charles, could you please engage one of your colleagues if needed to help cost out these items. Leadership seems to understand things better when they're translated into currency."

"Certainly, Sofia," responds Charles. "I'll run the numbers by Stephano as well, to get his blessing."

"Excellent. . . . Lastly, I would like Mo to head up this initiative. He'll collect the results and summarize them. You may want to split up and work in small subteams. Anika, what do you think about a short communication to the associates explaining why we're doing this; something to give them the confidence to contribute ideas without being afraid of consequences?"

"Sure, Sofia, but I'd like to ask Charles and Mo for a favor," replies Anika. "As soon as you identify a few initial successes, will you share those with me. I'd like to add them to the communication to the associates, along with a few words about what this team has been challenged with."

"No problem," says Mo. "We should have a few examples for you by tomorrow."

"Mo, please keep me posted as well," says Sofia. "Anika, please publish significant results as we find them. It will help to keep everyone's interest high."

***

At the end of the day and work week, Junior walks down to the engineering office. He talks with a number of employees on the way and in the office. Ricardo sent him a list of R&D staff who did something exceptional during the week—e.g., helping somebody, volunteering for continuous-improvement work, submitting a good idea, or reaching a project milestone. Junior knows everyone on the list by face and name, stops at their desks, asks them more details about their work, and thanks them personally for their contributions. Most are packing up for the weekend but pleased to chat with the CEO. Then Junior reaches Ricardo's desk.

"Ricardo, still here I see."

"Yes, for a little while yet. No shortage of things to do."

"So what have you heard since the town hall?"

"Nothing but good things. I'm sure something will come up in the next few days as the new roles take root. And I'm sure we'll need to make a few adjustments."

"Yes, I agree. Some who lose prestige and power will eventually start to squeak. . . . And how is everything else going? How else can I help you?"

"Next week, we start improvement work on the PCP, and I think we may have found the right project to kick off the technology creation process. The TCP implementations will take a little time since we need to engage a lot of the associates in the design of the process. The ICP—the idea part—has gone very well, and we've had great participation and engagement, and Bolaji, the technology manager, is learning how to manage the process. We're getting the new ideas that we need, and we have a lot of engineers engaged in the assessment process. There was a lot of bottled-up innovation in this room. It's finally coming out. We now have more than a dozen new ideas in various stages of the process. We've also frozen about twice as many concepts, but I think that, in addition to Mo's direct-drive, we'll have two or three more moving into the technology development phase soon."

"Wonderful. I'm pleased."

"One thing, though. I could use some of your help with the lawyers. We need to speed up the patent process. We have an enormous waiting line."

"Ah, the lawyers," sighs Junior. "I'm familiar with this. Maybe we just limit the time we give them to file. I can help with that. . . . What else is going on down here?"

"We helped Joe and Marco get the bicycle portfolio right, and we've passed the first two projects through the gate to help deliver the sales volume that Claudia wants next year."

"Oh, good. It looks like she's calmed down a little. Anything else I can help you with?"

"We're working with a couple of marketing folks on the non-bike innovations, like branding, endorsements, clothing—you know, all the fun stuff. It would save me time if we had a point person for that activity. It may be too early to assign a product director to manage this product line or value stream, but just somebody who could start organizing the marketing activities."

"I was wondering what's happening in that area. Thanks for bringing it up. Any recommendations for a person?"

"You know, Junior, how much I like to leverage internal Davanti strengths, but I think this is an area where Davanti doesn't have a lot of expertise. Maybe this is a position where we consider a new person from the outside to bring us the knowledge and experience that we need."

"I agree with you, Ricardo. I'll ask Anika to start the ball rolling."

"Thank you, Junior."

"So tell me, how do you like sitting in the open here? Does the noise distract you?"

"It's not noise. It's activity. This is the place where I belong. We must make it work, and I need to set the example. I think the open environment concept has been misunderstood by many: a noisy disorganized environment doesn't help collaboration and it doesn't stimulate ideas. It's highly beneficial if people learn to respect each other and not do anything they wouldn't want anybody else to do. And that's starting to happen. I see a lot of folks coach their noisy peers, and more and more folks use the perimeter space to hang out and discuss things. Being out here also gives me opportunities to set the example in other ways. They can see how I respect everybody, and one day they'll all respect each other as well. The engineers are now comfortable just walking up and asking questions. And the associates are starting to maintain a respectable work environment. Look at how neat most of the desks are—maybe one day we won't need janitors. So it's been challenging in some ways but overall very good."

"I might have to consider it myself."

"We're planning a few more quiet spaces for meetings and conference calls. And in the next few weeks, we'll create the first obeyas—those will be places where the major project teams meet and keep their visuals and samples. I may request a small budget for this."

"That's fine. 'Obeya.' I heard that term before. Oh yes, Diana was wondering if I knew what all those obeya walls were that she ordered. I look forward to the first obeya tour. Once again, something new to learn. Thanks for that."

Chapter 19

Davanti at the Tour

Monday morning prior to the start of Junior's staff meeting, all discussion is about the Tour de France and the disqualification of the Omega team.

"Looks like they used a substance that Sherpas in the Himalayas have known about for centuries; it's used to help them through long hikes at high altitudes," says Marco to no one in particular. "Of course, the riders didn't chew herbs. The blood doping obviously was more effective."

"Somebody will always be ahead of the Tour doping controls," adds Leandro.

"There are rumors that the team's doping research was funded in a foreign country," says Constantine.

Junior looks uneasy during the conversation of doping, and suddenly everybody in the room braces for a sermon—and here it comes: "Don't get ideas. If we ever feel we must cheat to win, I prefer to lose . . ."

"Junior, please spare us the story about Fausto Sr.," begs Stephano. "Really, we understand and agree."

"OK, I'll skip that, but remember there is zero tolerance for breaking rules and distorting the truth anywhere in my company. I know forecasts and estimates leave a lot of room for interpretation, but not facts and data, including test results. I can live with the bad news, and you know I've never punished the bearer of bad news. But I cannot handle scandals, lawsuits, dishonesty, misinterpreted data, and the like. Period."

"I like Rossa's chances," says Diana. "It sure looks like Johan has gotten him under control this time. What do you think, Junior?"

"I think I'm going to have the best seat at the race when Rossa wins the Tour," says Junior. "I'll be riding shotgun in the team car into Paris next Sunday. "I really can't wait. I think it will be a memorable day for Davanti."

Based on an agenda that Junior's assistant circulated, Leandro starts the staff meeting by giving an update on the PMO. "Project managers and I have recently attended project management training. We learned about classic PM and Toyota best practices, like the chief engineer, and we took a class on lean project management. And most of our project managers have now been appointed. Several of our more seasoned project managers, me included, have also taken on assignments to coach the new project managers. I think we have the right organization and the right support, and we're ready to execute. We asked one of our most senior PMs to write the PM playbook—the Davanti PM standards. About 50 percent of that book will be classic project management and what we learned at Davanti in our 20 years of project management. The rest will be lean PM and other new processes. And then we'll keep updating our standards with all the new

DOI: 10.4324/9781003231837-19

things we learn and develop. All our PMs will keep the book at their desk or have a digital copy. It will be used for coaching and training the new project managers."

"Can I see a copy of that book when it's done?" asks Junior.

"Of course."

Anika takes some time to remind her colleagues to recognize people when they do something right or good. She coaches the leadership team on appropriate methods to express gratitude based on what she and Sofia had discussed. "And nothing will replace the timely and personal expression of gratitude," she concludes.

Joe is up next and announces that with the help of Ricardo's team they have established the new bicycle portfolio. "The NPV of the new portfolio is more than double the value of the old one," he says, getting wide eyes from all. "And if we execute according to plan, we'll easily meet our targets for new product sales, volume, and profit."

"I will bow to you if it happens," says Claudia. "But I don't see how it will. Please don't stretch your estimates; it just sets up false expectations. And remember how the dealers reacted before when you discontinued the old bike lines. They weren't happy."

Joe explains that the dealers liked to keep the old bikes in stock because they'd gotten used to late delivery of the new ones: "That's why we came up with the agreement that before a product line is replaced, the dealers are notified early enough so they can manage their inventory. We're also offering special credits and incentives, if needed. Davanti also agreed to create a small buffer stock of the old bikes, at least for the next two launches."

Joe passes out a new product road map. "As planned, we'll still launch the major products at the Eurobike show in January."

"Thanks, Joe, for the update," says Junior. "I understand we had some quality problems again in the Tour. How bad was it?"

"I will chair the meeting on that subject later today," says Ricardo. "I can brief you after that meeting."

"I'm anxious to hear what you find. . . . So we're getting deep into the innovation excellence transformation. None of you look worse for it. In fact, you all seem quite engaged of late. Thank you for that. But how's it affecting your staffs?"

"We had some employees from R&D inquiring about other opportunities, but more for career advancement than fleeing something unpleasant," says Anika. "Of course, some people are not happy to lose their power positions, and some will have a hard time adjusting to the reorganization. We may lose a few as time goes on."

"I'd rather we lose no one," says Junior. "But we're on the right path, and we need everyone moving in that same direction."

Before the meeting wraps up, Sofia reminds the group of an upcoming meeting to discuss metrics: "Next week we'll meet in the conference room. The Volta team put together key metrics to track Davanti's progress toward its goals. This week, I'm assigning responsibilities for updating the metrics, and all the data will be posted on the conference room walls. It will be a standup meeting, and it will end before the Wednesday bike outing."

***

The Tour de France has not been going well for Davanti's Primo Sempre bike. No riders of that model have been injured, and they've all finished stages without even noticing the problem. But as some of the bikes from early stages were returned to the prototype shop in Fumane for review, the issues are clear: visible cracks right in the area where the front derailleur is attached to the frame.

Everybody with rank and name at Davanti has shown up to Ricardo's meeting to review the problem. Ricardo has created a small obeya room with a sample of the problem bikes and plenty of wall space to pin up facts and data as they become available. They closely examine the bikes on display as if they have solutions to fix the problem already in mind.

"I brought you all out here to see how you can help us solve this problem," says Ricardo. "We're getting ready to launch a face lift of this product, and we need to solve this problem as soon as possible."

"Didn't we solve this problem before?" asks Claudia.

"We thought we solved it," says Joe. "This never happened when we made the bikes here in the prototype shop."

Everybody looks at the director of manufacturing, Constantine. "True, but we made many late changes to this model: we changed the supplier for the derailleur, and we relocated the mounting, just to name two. Did we get all those tested appropriately?"

"I think we should go back to the old derailleur—the frame was developed for it," says Diana from purchasing.

"No, I disagree," says Matteo from supply chain. "All it takes is the old mounting screws. We're pushing the weight savings too much with the new titanium ones."

The back and forth of random solutions continues, until they run out of excuses and people to point a finger at. Ricardo intends to move this group in a different direction: "Thank you for all your suggestions. But the wide spectrum of ideas tells me that nobody really knows what the problem is. So before we chase phantom causes, I suggest we get all the facts and—"

"Who designed this new, lighter-weight attachment anyway?" interrupts Constantine.

Ricardo pauses for a second and continues with a very grave face: "I don't know because that question has the lowest chance to lead to a solution. We must assume that our engineers didn't intend for this to break. They are professionals, and they did the best job they could. We must respect that."

"So what should I ask?" counters an embarrassed Constantine.

"Maybe a better question is: 'Is there a standard design or process, and were those standards followed?' And maybe we could ask, 'Are those standards good enough?' We can build off of those answers for the future. Similarly, 'Were the designers properly trained? Did they know what they needed in order to design such a difficult part? Does Davanti have the knowledge or the tools? Do we have the manufacturing capability? Were the engineers aware of any changes in the manufacturing process?' As you noted, Constantine, just because it was made in the prototype shop before doesn't mean it will transfer to the plant without a problem. Solutions almost always lie in answers to those kinds of questions."

"But how long will that take?" asks Claudia.

"If you speed up a bad process you only get bad results faster, and cutting corners won't get you there either," suggests Sofia.

"What should we all do?" wonders Matteo.

"We can help, support, and coach a team of experts—the ones who know the technology and who follow a standard process to solve this as fast as possible and permanently," explains Ricardo.

Now you can hear a pin drop.

"Who are the experts, and what's the magic process?" asks Constantine.

"We gathered experts from different areas of expertise within Davanti, and they've begun to follow a classic lean problem-solving process," says Ricardo. "It starts with gathering facts: What is the failure mode, when does it occur, where does it occur? Only after we have facts to answer those questions will we be close to knowing what the real problem is."

"I'm glad to hear that," says Stephano from finance. "If I had five lire for every time we fixed the wrong problem."

"Once the problem is identified, the team will determine the root cause or causes, using tools like Five Whys or fishbone diagrams, combined with engineering tools and calculations. Then we'll want to see countermeasures—many countermeasures, not just one solution. And as countermeasures are evaluated and then implemented, the team must verify if the countermeasures were successful or not."

"Yes, the PDCA," comments Constantine. "How silly of us earlier to act like we knew the solutions. Some old habits in Davanti are hard to break. My apologies."

"After they check, they'll know if a countermeasure is working or if they must adjust it and verify again. After the countermeasures have been verified, we ask the experts for a control plan to assure the problem remains fixed. And then we challenge the team to document what they learned and apply it to other applications, if possible. Lastly, the team will propose a new standard—we'll not only solve the problem for this bike but for many future models."

"Remember, we're about to launch the next version of this bike," reminds Matteo.

"Will you keep us posted, Ricardo?" asks Joe, sharing Matteo's concern.

"Certainly. I will add a whiteboard behind these bikes where the team can post their current version of the A3 and any pertinent data as they find it."

"Is this *A3* another one of your inventions?" asks Claudia out of frustration.

"That's a good question, Claudia. For those who've never used or heard of an A3, it's the size of a piece of paper—about 300 × 400 millimeters or approximately 11 × 17 inches—that documents all pertinent information. It will give you the status at a glance. Of course, there's a lot more to it than that, and I'm happy to explain it to you, Claudia, in more detail. But I'm sure if you come here next week and see one, it will explain itself."

***

Dolomiti Cycling is one of the largest multibrand bicycle dealers in the Alpine region. They have stores not only in Italy but also in Germany, Austria, and Switzerland. One store is about 20 minutes from the Davanti headquarters.

"I've driven past this place for almost 10 years and never thought about stopping," says Junior to no one as he pulls into the parking lot. "Why did Sofia have to tell me this?"

Junior gets out of his Camry and walks into the entrance just as any consumer would. He looks around, surprised by the volume and variety of bikes and accessories.

"Good evening, sir, how can we help you?" asks a salesman.

"I would like to look at your bikes for a few minutes."

"Take your time. If I can be of assistance, please ask."

Junior is impressed with the professional display of the Davanti bikes. Competitors' bike displays are equally impressive. Junior also notices the display of a line of accessories that carry a competitor's name.

A startled store manager is walking nearby when he stops in his tracks: "Excuse me. You're, well, you know, Mr. Davanti. What brings you to the store? Can we interest you in a bike from your competitors?"

"Not really. Just gauging the competitive landscape. So tell me, how are those guys doing?" says Junior, pointing at a competitor's bikes.

"We sell a lot of their bikes; they're not as good as yours, but a lot more affordable. But, you know, the Tour de France riders don't shop here."

Junior remembers when he worked as a bike salesman as part of his training. In no time, he has wrapped the store manager in a very informative discussion. He learns that the competitors have a much more attractive dealer package: they offer accessories with a high margin, they finance purchases through lease and credit, and they offer excellent service and training to the dealers.

The manager says that many customers want to ride the bikes the winners use—and those who can afford them will buy them. Junior also learns, however, that average customers can't tell the difference between a Davanti bike and a competitor model when they go on a test ride. "We carry Davanti because it brings customers into the store," notes the manager, "but they usually end up buying someone else's bike."

"Hmmm," murmurs Junior, perturbed.

"But I think that could change. I'm excited about the new Davanti Primo Veloce amateur products that were just announced—those will make a difference for us, and I expect them to sell well. We've been given a little more sales support on those as well, which will help. The new models were announced early enough for us to manage our existing inventory. And thanks for not boosting the price for the PS bike. They would have never sold."

"Even here so close to Fumane, I'm surprised to see so many products that aren't made by Davanti," says Junior.

"We really have no choice. We also carry competitor products because we need to sell mountain and kids' bikes as well. We don't get those from Davanti. Neither do we get components from you."

"That's interesting. Which of our bikes sell the best here?"

"The ones on sale. We take advantage of your model-end discount and order a large quantity of the old models before they get discontinued. We put those bikes on sale, and when we discount them they sell so fast we wish you would still make them."

"Why am I not surprised?" says Junior.

Junior and the store manager talk for another 10 minutes, and then Junior thanks the sales manager for his time and leaves the store.

In the car, Junior is upset and uncomfortable: "I can't believe what I learned here in just 20 minutes. Why don't I get that story from my staff? After all the reminders to be open and honest with me. What am I doing wrong? If they told me, I could help."

And then it hit him: "Maybe they know but believe doing nothing is the right thing because we never encouraged them to take the initiative to change. Maybe their behaviors are a direct byproduct of our culture, organization, reward systems, and traditions. Maybe we aren't encouraging enough new ideas or risk in sales, marketing, and services. Maybe we focus too much on the racers and not enough on the customers who actually pay for their bikes. This lack of innovation and risk-taking is no different than R&D months ago."

As Junior starts his Camry, two customers walk out carrying a competitor's bike.

Junior shakes his head: "I think I need to get out more. To the stores, to the lab, to the plant, to the offices. I need to get a different version of the stories I get in my office. Maybe I can find out what our people struggle with and what prevents them from achieving our goals. I can't help anybody if I don't know what help they need."

***

After Ricardo's town hall meeting, Mo could not wait to call his dad with the good news about his promotion. During the call, Mo's dad repeated that he, too, once was a project manager: "The next time we get together, I'll fill you in."

Tuesday night after work, Mo heads to his parents' villa to catch up with his dad. Of course, he's let his mom know he's coming and hopes to have a nice dinner while he's there. He quickly reaches Peschiera del Garda, parks, and rushes into the home.

"Hello, Maurice," yells his mom from the kitchen. "I'm surprised you're here so quickly."

"I left a little early. Since dad and I will be talking shop, it's almost like I'm still at work."

Mo's dad greets him in the entryway: "Good to see you, Mo."

"Can I get you anything before dinner?" asks his mom. "It will be a little while yet."

"Would you like something to drink, son?"

"I'll have what you're having, dad."

"We still had a bottle of the Super Tuscan that you brought for your birthday. It should go well with dinner. Have a seat outside, and I'll be right out with glasses."

Mo walks through the kitchen and heads toward the patio: "Smells like roasted chicken with braised tomatoes?"

"You've got a good nose. Your father picked some green beans today, and we'll have a salad on the side. He also stopped for some gelato."

"Sounds great, mom. Let me know if I can do anything."

Mo grabs a seat on the patio, and his dad hands him a glass of wine.

"Now dad, tell me about your PM job."

"I was a PM for a long time, and I think it was that time that best prepared me for the rest of my career. I'm happy for you, Mo. Maybe you'll have a similar experience."

Mo describes his new role and tells his father about the Leonardo project.

"Wasn't that project started based on your idea?"

Mo is surprised his dad remembers. "Yes, it was, but the scope was significantly expanded. I was also assigned to a process improvement project. A lot of things are happening quickly."

"Wonderful, Mo. It looks like Davanti appreciates its entrepreneurs. I should have told you more about the chief engineers in my company a long time ago."

"Better now than never. Tell me about your project management experience as well."

"So, first off, I was never a CE, and I think that if I had been a CE, I probably would not be here today; the stress would have killed me. I always respected them for their guts, entrepreneurship, and the way they stood up for the customer. But I probably would not have made a good CE."

"Why? I don't follow."

"We patterned that position after what we learned from Toyota. We picked the best and the brightest and gave them the monster task of writing the specs for the new platforms, and then they were given full responsibility to make it happen. And we also patterned the organization after Toyota to set the chief engineers up for success."

"That sounds exciting."

"The CEs started with a lot of excitement. They were the 'supermen' that they were supposed to be. But a few years later it became obvious that they were burning out fast."

"What happened. Too much responsibility? Not enough staff?"

"A lot of things that are valued at Toyota—like collaboration, observing the customer, considering sufficient options, delaying important decisions—were skipped or minimized in the interest of time. And since we didn't want to go back to the traditional process controls, we invented all kinds of new positions and layers, like regional executives, category managers, global platform directors. They were supposed to fill gaps in the global organization and help with alignment, but they were really just some of the former control levels in disguise. The chief engineers' entrepreneurial spirit was soon replaced with the spirit of compromise. And, quite frankly, I think their projects were too big to manage efficiently in our environment. We were trying to be Toyota without all the systemic supports, organization, and culture that took Toyota years to establish."

"I've heard that story before."

"Toyota put conflict on the table for all to see and resolved it according to the best outcome for the customer. In our company, the fights were initially about internal conflicts, turf issues, and personal power, and the strongest won—and that was mostly whoever represented the vehicle cost. I saw that begin to change prior to my retirement. My friends still within the company and those recently retired confirmed what many of us thought: it took time for Toyota to get this right and it took time for us to get our culture right as well. I think most of those growing pains have subsided.

"So I understand why you're glad you weren't a CE. But you liked being a PM. How was that different?"

"I managed crossfunctional projects for many years. Sometimes they were product-related, sometimes they were process-related. I also managed some HR and financial projects. The scope was smaller than the task of a CE, and the reporting lines were simpler and more direct. Nonetheless, many functional leaders didn't appreciate having crossfunctional managers meddle with their work, and their staffs were often confused. This caused friction and adversity in the company, so we created standards of behavior that included team member satisfaction, conflict resolution, etc. We PMs often had to put employee satisfaction ahead of customer satisfaction or meeting project deliverables. Unfortunately, less-than-good project outcomes became the norm, and management eventually got used to them."

"So, dad, did you *ever* learn to deliver results *and* have happy employees?"

"I learned a lot about managing people when I was a PM. I didn't have the power of a position. I had some authority, but I had to learn to manage as if I had none. That helped me become a much better and humble leader. I built relationships, and I always gave everybody the benefit of the doubt and tried to understand people's real motivation. And I learned to use influence and to engage individuals in finding a solution. Even if I thought I knew the answer, I asked the team for their suggestions first. And I believe I got much better results than my colleagues, but I never really got the appropriate company recognition I probably deserved. I hear that, too, has changed."

"Your approach is a lot like what I've learned about 'respect for people.' Is that something you learned at work?"

"Not explicitly. I learned about respect from your grandparents at home as well as the instructors and mentors I had in school. And I hope we taught our kids the same values. We really didn't talk about it at work. I had to learn a lot on my own. For example, early on I was once asked to take over a crossfunctional project to solve a technical problem. The team was dysfunctional, and when I met the team members for the first time, I thought they were all morons. Everybody had their own agenda. They mimicked the culture of their departments and the behaviors of their bosses. Everybody wanted to score an individual victory and make the others look bad."

"So, dad, how did you manage that?"

"I eventually learned that they were very competent engineers, and I was able to convince them and their superiors that if they pooled their talents and competencies, they could solve our problem in no time and we would all be winners. In the end everybody looked like a hero, and we all were happy. But enough about me. Mo, please tell me more about you and your new job."

Mo fills his father in on the details of the Leonardo project and discusses the sweeping changes underway at Davanti and in the R&D function. As their work conversation winds down, his mom calls them in to eat.

Before they get up, his dad raises his glass. "To you and your promotion. I hope it brings you joy and prosperity."

***

Mont Ventoux sits as a giant in the mostly flat area of the Provence region in southern France. The Tour riders begin to see the dreaded monster soon after the start of the last real stage that may well determine this year's winner. The journey through the Alps on prior days was filled with fierce battles as expected. Despite the intense competition in the Alpine stages and the final time trial, Rossa did well: he is now in third place, only 12 seconds behind the leader. If he could just get 13 seconds ahead today.

Rossa is extremely focused as the Tour winds through the little town of Bedoin at the foot of the nearly 2,000-meter mountain. At the end of town, the road makes a sharp, narrow right turn toward the "Beast of the Provence" that's made Tour winners and losers in the past—and one racer did not make it off the mountain alive.[1]

The field is still packed when they pass the lower-altitude vineyards, but as soon as they reach the steeper terrain in the shadow of the forest, five riders split off. Each in that group is far behind in the standings and nobody cares, except Johan Leffe, who is paying attention to the Davanti rider that split away. Rossa and his two main opponents ride in front of the peloton, shielded by their teammates who do the hard work of creating wind slipstream for their leaders. The three leaders watch each other like hawks—any move by anyone must be countered immediately.

"No, Rossa. Hang tight. We attack above the forest," Johan can be heard over the radio.

The top of the Ventoux is far below the meteorological tree line, but the tip is bare like a moonscape due to deforestation and erosion caused by strong winds. The top of the mountain is dreaded by riders not only because of the high winds but also because of the heat and the repeated serpentines that get increasingly shorter as riders near the finish line at the top.

The five riders in the split-away group gain about two minutes on the peloton in the wooded part of the mountain, and as Rossa emerges from the trees, he asks again when he can attack.

"Too early, Rossa. We only need 13 seconds."

Rossa looks like a horse in the starting block before the Derby. About halfway through the moonscape, he finally hears "OK, whenever you see a hole," and he is ready. It takes him no time to get the inside lane on the next hairpin, and a hard out-of-the-saddle sprint gets him three bike lengths on his two opponents. They are stuck behind a couple of riders, and, when they break free to follow, Rossa is gone. But now alone, he's worried because he knows that his opponents will have the advantage on the next serpentine into the very strong wind because they have the help from their teammates.

After exiting the next hairpin, he thinks a miracle is happening—there's his teammate from the lead group who was asked by Johan to drop back to help him. Rossa's teammate gives it his all, allowing Rossa to ride in his wind slip. When the teammate finally cracks, Rossa can almost see the finish line. Now he understands why Johan held him back for so long. He has just enough left in the tank to keep his pace without his teammate.

Rossa doesn't win the stage, and as he crosses the finish line he's too exhausted to even hear the Davanti support team and the fans on the mountain erupt in celebration, chanting, "Rossa, Rossa, Rossa." They've heard the radio announcers declare Rossa this year's Tour winner. Twenty seconds later, he sees his opponents cross the finish, and then it hits him: he just won the Tour de France.

***

The last stage of the Tour de France starts in one of the small towns on the outskirts of the capital. All riders are in a pack when they enter Paris, and all are assessed the same time. The places in the finish at Champs-Élysées are just for prestige and sprinter points.

Since Johan is not busy until the riders reach Paris, Junior rides shotgun in the team car into Paris. Although the standings are set, the roads are still packed with spectators. It's a nice Sunday, and the fans want to see a final closeup of their favorite riders. Junior enjoys all the banners celebrating the victory of the Davanti rider Rossa, who proudly displays the Davanti Nella Gara logo on his maillot jaune as he rides in front of the peloton as on a victory tour.

Junior also hears the loud cheers for Davanti: "Da-van-ti, Da-van-ti . . ." The victory by Rossa and the Davanti team give a tremendous boost to the Davanti brand awareness, and thousands of fans cheer as the Davanti team car passes behind the peloton.

Junior and Johan look at each other and smile. They're enjoying the victory lap as much as the Davanti riders.

"So tell me how you did it, Johan?" asks Junior.

"Experience."

"I'm not talking about the race tactics. I had nearly written Rossa off, and now he's in yellow riding into Paris."

"Ah, yes. That was the bigger challenge. I had to teach him respect: respect for his team, respect for me, respect for his competitors, respect for his sponsor. So we took it in small steps and came up with daily and weekly behavioral goals. And we discussed them every day, and he got a lot of praise when he met them. And if he didn't accomplish them, I asked him how I could help him, and we formulated a new plan. And we did this on race days and in training. We had the last one this morning. . . . To make a long story short, Rossa has not yelled at a teammate in the Tour. He thanks everybody for what they do for him. He even thanks the domestiques when they bring him water. He treats me with respect and accepts my instructions without argument. He respects his opponents. He respects the soigneurs. He even became fun to hang out with."

Junior's mouth is open, and he doesn't quite know what to say: "It must have been a bigger challenge to make him a better person than getting him to win the Tour."

"I think the two go together."

"You certainly have my respect for a job exceptionally well done."

"Thanks, Junior, just doing the job I love."

"Well, thank you for that. Come to think of it, I hope you documented what you did with Rossa. I'd like you to come to Fumane in the off season and teach the Davanti leaders."

"I've done this so many times, Junior; I don't need notes anymore."

"Consider it booked, my friend: Leadership 101 this winter."

"Ok, but you'll have to excuse me now, Junior, we have a race to finish. Maybe we can get one of our sprinters on the podium today as well."

***

This is Junior's day. Although no Davanti rider placed in the last stage, a Davanti rider won the Tour, and the Davanti team won the team competition—that is all that matters now.

Junior's heart is pounding when the French president and the tour director present the most cherished cycling trophy to the Davanti rider and his team. When Junior watches Rossa on the podium in front of the Arc de Triomphe between his two opponents—joining hands high above their heads—he cannot hold back the tears. He's looking at the exact same picture he has of his dad on his desk. It's not the first time Junior watches a Davanti rider on the podium, but something seems different this time.

After the podium session, Junior is watching Rossa and the team enjoy their victory when the tour director introduces him to the French president: "Monsieur le président, this is Monsieur Fausto Davanti, the sponsor of the winning Davanti Nella Gara team. President De Gaulle presented the winning trophy to Monsieur Davanti's father here—exactly 63 years ago." Junior is so moved he doesn't hear the "quel plaisir"[2] and has a hard time uttering "Merci Monsieur le Président."

Junior spends the rest of the day mingling with all the folks at the bike fest. He graciously accepts congratulations from everyone. Of course, all the suppliers are on hand, including Guido Marchioni from Coppimechanica, who greets Junior with an embrace and thanks him for the business. Junior also wanders around and congratulates the other teams and their coaches and staff. But he spends most of his time personally congratulating all the riders—winners or not—and thanking all Davanti employees who are in Paris, including Mo. And he loves it when riders take a selfie with him.

Thanks to many discussions he had with his dad over the years, Junior knows how difficult it is to achieve today's win. In fact, just finishing the Tour is an accomplishment in itself. He's savoring the moment when Davanti rider Pasquale Barto hands him a flute of champagne. "Thank you, Pasquale," he says and turns his head toward the sky. "This one's for my dad, Fausto Davanti. Saluti, papa."

***

Mo had flown to Paris on Friday night. He wanted to catch up with colleagues Saturday morning and then be sure to greet Marie when she arrived at the Gare de Lyon on the high-speed TGV from Geneva. It was late when Marie arrived; they grabbed a bite to eat on the square in front of the station, and Mo walked Marie to her hotel, which was close to the rail station. Mo took the metro to his hotel at the Place de Gaulle, where he stayed with his Davanti colleagues.

Sunday morning, Mo met Marie at her hotel, and they had breakfast on the terrace of one of the little cafes around the Gare de Lyon. They then rushed to the metro so they could get to the Tour VIP area a couple of hours before the race finish as was required.

They enjoyed the race circus, dispersed in the parks around the Champs-Élysées, and the colorful caravan of advertisement vans, race support staff, and team cars. They saw a British rider win the stage in a sprint and then, like Davanti fans everywhere, screamed loudly when Rossa crossed the finish line leading the peloton. Mo could not believe what he'd seen. Rossa and the Davanti team had done it.

The two enjoyed the award ceremony with the heads of state presenting awards to the riders— best climber, best sprinter, etc.—and celebrated with colleagues and friends when Rossa accepted the Tour trophy. Mo introduced Marie to Junior and Johan, and congratulated them on their momentous day. As they were leaving the celebration, he even ran into Emilio, who was working with Coppimechanica, and said "Hello." Emilio was friendly but uncomfortable.

After about an hour and exhausted, as if they were in the Tour, Mo and Marie walk away from the party, which will last into the night. "Mo, this has been amazing," says Marie. "I can't believe we're strolling past the Place de la Concorde on the day of the Tour finish. It's surreal."

"I feel the same."

They walk across the park to the Louvre, which despite the crowds of the day, looks clean, green, and stunning. They cross over to the Rue de Rivoli behind the Louvre and look for a small café and chance to get off their feet. Most race fans have rushed to the cafés, and they're lucky to grab the last two seats on a nearby terrasse.

"Two Révolution au Paradis, s'il vous plaît," requests Mo of the bartender.

"What did you order for us?" asks Marie.

"It's a French pale lager. It should be refreshing."

"Good. I'm parched. I thought about having a glass of champagne at the Tour party, but after today's heat that seemed unwise. I also figured we'd be enjoying ourselves this evening."

The beers arrive, and they both sip them slowly. Mo looks at Marie, tips his glass in her direction, and she does likewise: "Santé."

"I've got us reservations for Aux Trois Petits Cochons at the foothill of Montmartre. We got lucky. When I called last week, a bunch of cancellations had just come in. Who knows, maybe it was Omega fans."

"That should be wonderful. . . . I like the beer, Mo. How can you know so much about bikes and beer?"

"The two sort of go hand in hand."

"You mean because bikers need to rehydrate so much."

"Yeah, and because some riders, like this one, really like beer."

They slowly finish their beers, grateful to be sitting, and then head for the metro station and get to the restaurant precisely on time. After their long day, they're quite hungry and a little underdressed, but it appears that is the norm on the Sunday of the Tour. There they enjoy a Fume Blanc with a prix fixe meal that could only be matched by the cooking of Mo's mom.

Marie has smoked duck breast with melon carpaccio for a starter; Mo has smoked haddock carpaccio and shredded avocado with a mustard sauce. Marie's main course is grilled king prawns with shellfish sauce, carrots, cardons, and pearl onions; Mo opts for the grilled spareribs and French beans ("We're in France, after all"). The dinner is capped off by an apricot biscuit with mascarpone cheese cream for Marie and lemon tart with meringue for Mo.

After dinner they walk hand in hand up to the Place du Tertre, where they stroll around the artist stands and then to the church of Sacré-Coeur, where they sit on the stairs overlooking Paris as darkness falls on the city and the lights come on.

"Thanks for a wonderful day and a terrific evening, Mo. You sure know how to treat a girl. It will be difficult for you to top this."

"It was all my pleasure," replies Mo. "You're right. It was a wonderful day and a terrific evening." He leans toward her and gives her a light kiss; Marie responds in kind.

"I'll get us a ride so we can head back. We both have early-morning travel home."

"Yes, unfortunately. Don't remind me. Let's sit here another minute, if that's OK. I just want one more look at the lights and to enjoy my time with you."

Notes

1. Tom Simpson, a rider from the UK, died on the ascent in 1967.
2. What a pleasure.

Chapter 20

Chapter 20

The Product Creation Process

Day 1

As Davanti was preparing for its typical late-summer slowdown—common across Italian industry—Ricardo and Sofia gather the Volta team in Emilio's old office.

"With the Tour in the rear-view mirror now, it's time to focus on what's next," says Ricardo.

"You mean the August shutdown?" asks Gina.

"That is part of it," says Ricardo.

"This year it may be more of a slowdown," says Carolina Petrale, the new R&D operations manager. "We'd like to keep a skeleton crew in the prototype shop and test lab to help with the new products we moved up; the offices will be open but largely empty except for this group. Of course, you may have plans, and we understand if you'd rather not be working."

"I'll be here during August," says Gina. "I prefer to take my vacation in winter for skiing."

"Who else will be here at least into early August and willing to contribute time?" asks Carolina. "We can coordinate the dates to make the best use of everyone's available time."

More than half the Volta team raise their hands. Ricardo is happy that, in addition to Carolina, his programs manager, Bart Amico, can join the team during the break. He'd finished a large slate of training, including innovation management, lean project management, and, above all, portfolio management. He will play a critical role in this new process.

"What exactly will we be doing?" asks Giovanni from manufacturing.

"We'll use the slowdown to switch over to a new PCP process. It's a lot easier to do such a changeover when the place is in a lull, and the projects take a break with the engineers absent," interjects Ricardo. "I'm glad we have enough people to help."

"How can we switch over when the process hasn't been designed yet?" asks Bart.

"We're looking for about seven days to get it designed before we switch," says Ricardo, "and then you and your colleagues fill it with the right projects. We really hit the ground running when everybody gets back in September. We'll have a working session here every day. If you commit to be involved but for some reason you can't attend, please try to send a replacement. And you can bring colleagues from your departments with you any day."

"If I remember correctly, the PCP should come after the idea creation process and technology creation process—why aren't we following that order?" asks Giovanni.

"Another good point. That is the theoretical order a new product travels once everything is established: ICP, TCP, and then PCP. But we're still piloting the TCP, and we already have plenty of new products that got underway before the transformation started that are ready now for the

DOI: 10.4324/9781003231837-20

PCP pipeline. These projects either did not need new technology or the technology is already developed. Some of them must launch this year to create volume and revenue. It will help if we get the improved PCP up and running in September, knowing that we may need to make adjustments as the ICP and TCP mature."

The plan makes sense to the team, and each member nods in agreement.

"So if there are no other questions, we'll start today with a value-stream map of the product creation process as we currently know it: from the PCP gate to the production release. You should all remember mapping from the lean training."

The team members start writing the current process steps on sticky notes and pasting them on the wall. An hour later, the value-stream map (VSM) wraps around the room, but people are not pleased with their accomplishment.

"The map is so long because many of the same tags are repeated many times," observes Sofia.

"That's to be expected; we use an iterative process to run our experiments," comments Carolina. "We start with a concept and then we design, engineer, calculate, run models and simulations, make drawings, write specifications, etc. We eventually build prototypes, test them, and after analyzing the results we start over until we hit the targets. Sometimes we can get away with one iteration—sometimes it takes 10 or more."

"Fair enough—are those iterations different?" asks Sofia.

"Sometimes," says Serfino. "For example, a learning cycle—or iteration, as you say—for a product release is typically shorter than one during development when we do more experimenting."

"OK, we can deal with that. So let's map a typical iteration first."

So everybody writes tags again for what they consider the typical activities within an iteration, but the map still will not fit on one wall, despite the large size of Emilio's old office.

"Time for the 80/20 rule," says Sofia. "If an activity happens 80 percent of the time, we consider it always done. If it's 20 percent, think of it as never occurring. So let's remove every activity that occurs less than 20 percent of the time."

Serfino is surprised by the answer: "But Sofia, you don't understand. We need those activities to . . ."

"Don't worry. We're not cancelling the activities. I recognize that they'll still exist. We're just trying to illustrate a 'typical' iteration, not every conceivable iteration."

As the team works to remove activities, the VSM starts to look manageable for the first time. Then Sofia draws a rectangle on the wall: "Now I want you to get all the activity tags into this space."

"That's easy, we'll use smaller tags," says Mo.

"No, smart-ass," scolds Sofia jokingly. "I want you to combine stuff that generally occurs together so we get everything into that space—and no loopbacks yet."

They end up with about a dozen main process blocks that include modeling, engineering calculations, drawing, prototypes, styling, testing, and similar grouped activities.

"Can everybody live with this process?" Sofia asks.

"It's so simple and generic," notes Gina. "You could also use it to make lasagna or paint the house. Of course it accommodates everything we do."

There are other comments from other members, but no one seems to have too much of a problem with the simplified process, especially since Sofia reassures them that no work will be left out when all is said and done.

"I think this is a good time to call it a day," she says. "Tomorrow morning, I would like you to bring as many folks from all areas involved with new products through here as possible—before they break for vacation—and describe the process to them and then ask them for feedback and suggestions."

Day 2

"So how did the walk-through go this morning?" asks Sofia.

Bart points at a wall with at least 20 sticky notes. "Most were excellent suggestions; we had missed a few things and made a few changes already."

"We'll keep all remaining suggestions in the 'parking lot' you've created. Maybe we can get back to some of them later," replies Sofia.

"And as you can see, some others asked to join us today," adds Bart, pointing to a few volunteers who want to be part of redesigning the PCP.

Sofia proceeds to coach the group on how to add data and numbers to the VSM, like resources, approximate times for the different steps, waiting times, inventory, etc. "Don't strive for ultimate accuracy—80 percent correct is enough."

Adding the data takes the group about two hours and often leads to a heated discussion. Sofia can overhear comments like, "How often did *you* design a bike; I do it all the time. I should know."

After a short break, Sofia challenges the participants to identify obvious problems with the current process and, if they find one, create a red note, share the problem with the rest of the group, and then put the tag next to the process step where the problem occurs. She also encourages everybody to place issues from the parking lot on the map. The wall fills fast with red, and when the group runs out of steam, Sofia says, "We'll go around the room now, and you each will pick what you think is the biggest issue with this process."

Mo gets to start: he points out the large waiting time for the prototype lab, and Sofia puts a dot on the tag that Mo has identified.

Gina points out the problems caused with the stop-and-go work mode, which results because every engineer works on too many projects at once. Bart cites the large amount of rework that is required. Vijay, one of the engineers that asked to participate, has an issue with the timing ripples caused by rework: "We don't have capacity planned for correcting something or doing it over. If that happens, it delays everything else."

After the discussion moves around the room twice, Sofia says, "This should be enough to get started, but is there anything we can improve right here, right now?"

The team makes several obvious changes, they update the VSM, and Sofia places the finished tags into a "Done" section that she created on an empty part of the wall.

"I'll type up the remaining red notes, and we'll review them from time to time to make sure we don't forget one. Nice work, everyone. Tomorrow we'll try to remedy some of the remaining problems you just prioritized. But before we do that, we have more homework." Many in the group give an exaggerated groan. "Please go back to your lean training and study the material on bottlenecks, waste, and flow. We don't need to reinvent proven lean principles—we're going to apply them to improve the process. And please invite more experienced associates and project managers to join us tomorrow."

Day 3

Despite the slowdown for most Davanti employees, the group has grown to almost fill the whole office. It wasn't hard to find engineers and PMs to participate—after all, somebody is messing with their process.

Ricardo begins the session by walking the group through relevant lean principles, and they formulate some objectives for the process:

- Removing typical R&D wastes
- Continuous flow—no waiting
- Single-piece flow
- No imbalance or overload
- Fast process

"I hope we won't have to work twice as hard to accomplish all of this," says a young expectant mother. "I've got another task in a few weeks."

"Lean is about working smarter, not harder," offers Ricardo. "We start by first simplifying this process."

"So what is the capacity of this process? asks Sofia.

"Insufficient," says Gina, to the applause of everybody. But all agree that nobody really knows.

"The capacity of the process is the capacity of the bottleneck," instructs Sofia.

"You mean the prototype shop," says Gina.

"Any step could be the bottleneck," says Sofia, "and the bottleneck can change over time."

"But ours currently is the prototype shop, right," repeats Gina. All heads nod.

"Unfortunately, every iteration has to pass through the prototype shop, or at least 80 percent of them," comments Mo.

"That makes sense—bottlenecks are frequently the most popular or capital-intensive steps," says Sofia. "So what is the capacity of the bottleneck?"

"Nine work orders per week," says Luca without hesitation. "We call iterations 'work orders.'"

Everyone is surprised by Luca's answer. "How do you know?" asks Bart.

"I took the total number of work orders we finished so far this year and divided by the number of weeks. Simple as that. I did the calculation last night. I assumed somebody would eventually ask that question."

"Does your number include rework?" asks Sofia.

"I only counted completed work orders. But I would say that at least a quarter had to be reworked, but we don't count them separately. We just do the work."

"So, Luca, are all jobs the same size?" Sofia continues.

"Of course not. We have a few that give us fits, like one a week—especially those new ideas."

"For simplicity, can we count those that give you fits as two iterations and bump up to 10 iterations?" asks Sofia.

"I guess that would be close," reasons Luca.

"So we're operating at 10 iterations a week, and let's assume Luca has 10 slots to accommodate them. How many can we schedule?" asks Ricardo.

"Well, 10 of course," replies Stella. "Why do you ask? Or we could schedule 12, hoping that would get people to work harder."

Many in the meeting hiss with disapproval.

"We want to create a predictable schedule, one that we can always meet, including the iterations that give Luca fits and that, as Sofia said, should account for two slots," continues Ricardo. "Luca has included a fair amount of rework already, but with all the new ideas and new technology coming in, I think we'll have more unexpected problems in the future. Every unexpected issue ripples through our schedule, so I want to avoid that kind of problem and reserve at least one more slot for uncertainty—which brings us back to nine slots that we can schedule every week. And remember, Luca's numbers don't include TCP projects yet. We haven't started the formal technology creation process. I'd like to reserve two slots a week for those projects, which now leaves seven slots for the PCP process."

"Is that enough?" asks Bart.

"We'll find out soon," replies Ricardo. "How many work orders do you have for the next few months?"

"About three times more than we can handle," says Luca, "despite the projects we dropped. I can't believe it."

"I think it's time we create a visual to understand this," says Sofia.

She creates a grid with seven horizontal rows and one vertical column per calendar week for the next 12 months: "This is our planning board. Here is our capacity of seven iterations a week," she says, while adding dates at the top. "Now let's create a tag for every iteration or work order and call them PITs, as in product iteration tags."

Luca reads off the work orders while Mo, Bart, and Gina put the PITs in the week the iteration is supposed to *finish*. They use different color tags for different work content: experiments, product releases, cost-reduction programs, etc. Sure enough, before Luca is half through the list the board is full.

"Here's the thing," says Luca. "You need to know that a lot of these will be canceled. The project managers like to write more orders than they really need—maybe to increase the chances they get those done that they really need. And sometimes even complete projects get cancelled by the business."

"It happens all the time," adds Gina. "And it's not always the bad ones they cancel. But even with potential cancellations, we're nowhere near the capacity we need."

"This was a lot to digest in a short time, but I think I am starting to understand it," says Stella, not quite sure given her marketing background. "Let me put it in my own words: We use the iteration as the common building block for projects. We, the project managers, string as many of them together as we need in a project, and we write work orders for them. But we can only get as many iterations done as the bottleneck, the prototype shop, can deliver. And as we just found out, we

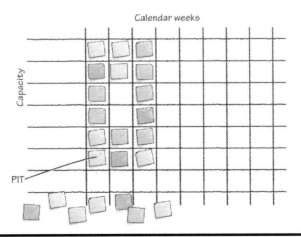

Figure 20.1   Visual Planning Board.

wrote twice as many orders as prototype has capacity for. How about that! Did I get this right? We either have too many projects or too many iterations in every project."

"We could ask to double the capacity, but what are the chances we'd get the money to do that," replies Gina. "But if we keep all the projects and iterations, we'll fall further and further behind for sure."

"At least we can finally see why this happens," says Luca. "And I hope we'll get Joe's team in here to make them understand what a mess they've created for us."

"I had no idea," says Ricardo. "I assumed that since we had capacity in engineering it was the same in the prototype shop and elsewhere. But now that we see this problem, we can solve it or at least try. I'll ask Joe and his PMs to join us tomorrow. I'll let you know when we can meet tomorrow."

Day 4

The Volta team along with Joe, some of his PMs, and some senior associates that Ricardo invited meet the following morning at 7:00 am.

"Thanks for coming in early," says Ricardo. "Sorry for the urgency. We're trying to implement the new PCP process during the slowdown if possible." He then explains to Joe and the PMs the task at hand: aligning new products with available capacity.

A quick look at the existing prototype work orders reveals that some PMs had forgotten to cancel work orders for projects that are no longer in the portfolio. But they'd also not written some work orders for planned projects. A discussion as to why project managers put a few "extra" iterations on the schedule—just in case—took a little longer.

An engineer says that it's easier to cancel a work order than to find a slot if needed. But after Ricardo describes the "buffer" that is built into the schedule, everybody agrees to give it a try and only plan what they know they *really* need.

Bart then explains the purpose of the PIT tags and asks Joe's team and the available PMs to write a fresh PIT tag for every real iteration they know they really need and put it on the board in the week when the iteration is required. After about an hour, they claim that all the PITs are on the board where room is available. Yet they still have many tags in their hands, and there is also a lot of empty space on the wall.

"I don't understand; why aren't you using this space?" asks Sofia, pointing at empty spaces during the winter months, especially from December to March.

"We make our schedules to have enough inventory for the launch dates at the Eurobike show in January," says a seasoned engineer. "Things pile up in the fall, and then we go into a lull."

"Well, that's easy to fix," says Joe. "We can change our project schedules to utilize that capacity; we can pull projects ahead and finish early for a change. So for the sake of this exercise, can you put all remaining PITs in the empty spaces?"

Once all spaces have an iteration, there are still at least 40 PITs without a home.

"Let's use the capacity earmarked for TCP and ICP," comments a rookie from marketing. "Those iterations are not as important as products, are they?"

Ricardo has an indignant look on his face: "I wouldn't mind using that capacity before the ICP and TCP get up to speed, but we couldn't do that long-term. We can't starve those processes. Many companies make the mistake of drawing all resources to their short-term product needs to find out a few years later that the ICP/TCP pipeline is empty, and the short term has run out of good products. So let's not even go there."

"Looks like we either must add capacity or cancel some more projects," says Joe. "I wouldn't have believed it without the planning board. This is hard to argue with."

"Isn't that the truth; it looks like a no brainer," says Carolina. "Am I the only one who could never see this before?"

"No, you and Joe are in good company; I didn't understand it either," confesses Ricardo. "Thanks for the tool, Sofia. It's so simple."

"We'll work on this some more and get back to you tomorrow," replies Joe. "Now that we can see what's really going on, we know what has to be done."

"Thanks, Joe," says Ricardo. "See you tomorrow."

Day 5

At another 7:00 am start, Joe's PMs have already made many changes to their launch schedules and come equipped with tons of data. They have staggered their launches and pulled a few projects ahead—no more empty spaces—and they are convinced that they reduced the iterations to the bare minimum. Nonetheless, after they put the rearranged PITs on the board, there are still 20 left over.

"We could delay a project or two, but then we run the risk of hurting volume or cash flow," says Bart. "So how much capacity is missing?"

They spread the remaining PITs evenly and conclude they need about 15 percent more capacity, at least in prototype.

"So, Luca, what will it take to add the capacity we need?" asks Ricardo.

"It may take a few extra work stands here and there, but I think the majority can be accomplished with temporary staff and overtime; we can run some equipment on two shifts. So I assume we just add another row to the bottom of the visual planning board and go with eight business iterations a week."

"Fair enough," says Joe. "Please let me know how much overtime and temps it will be for the rest of the year. We'll prepare a budget. I can tell you right now, though, overtime and temps cannot be a permanent solution. Sofia, can process improvements provide some of the capacity we need?"

"Of course, and we'll start looking for them as soon as you leave today."

"If we add capacity in the prototype shop, will we also need more capacity in testing and engineering?" wonders Giovanni.

"Good observation," says Sofia. "I was just getting there."

The rest of the group nod as if they were wondering the same thing.

"I'm sure you remember the term 'cadence' or 'takt' from your training. We have just established cadence: the eight iterations per week were established based on the business requirements, and two more per week are set aside for TCP and technology development. And those who paid really good attention in the training will remember that all resources—prototype shop, testing, engineering—must be assigned to meet that cadence. But we have a little more work before we get to that."

As Joe gets ready to leave the room, he remembers a nagging question and asks it: "Sofia and Ricardo, I like what you're doing here. But why does the scheduling stop at the production release?"

"That's when we're planning to dissolve the team for a given product," replies Bart.

"Can we keep the project team together until, say, a year into service? For sure their work will taper down after the product is launched, but it doesn't necessarily disappear. I remember too many cases in the past where engineers wiped their hands after production release; they didn't think problems after that point were their responsibility. Keeping the projects officially active a little longer will keep the right resources available, and we also make a clear statement that engineers share responsibility for their designs well past the launch."

"That's a great idea, Joe," says Sofia, and Ricardo agrees.

"Sofia, can you help us map out the steps after production release so that we can make sure we have alignment when marketing and sales start to play a larger role. Maybe we can improve those process steps as well."

"Of course, Joe, thanks for bringing this to our attention."

"So what's next, Sofia?" asks Mo after Joe and his team leave.

"Tomorrow we'll look for ways to create more capacity. We can start by reviewing the ideas in our parking lot. And for homework, please review what you learned about theory of constraints.¹"

Day 6

"You saw that we need 15 percent more capacity in the prototype shop. Let's see how much capacity we can create there by making improvements to the process," says Sofia. "Any gains will help us eliminate overtime."

"Let's first eliminate the building of prototypes that we don't use," says Ricardo, who reminds them of the large number of prototypes that are scrapped after many years sitting in the warehouse.

The engineers insist they need to order the prototypes for fear of getting second-guessed. "We don't know that we won't need them," stresses Vijay. "It just turns out that way."

Ricardo pauses, taking time to deliver the exact message that's on his mind: "Building inventory is bad enough; building inventory that is not needed is even worse. What if we make a standard, a rule, about what to order in which case, including the samples that are needed? Then if you are questioned, you can blame it on the standard. And if we find a case where the standard wasn't good enough, we improve the standard."

Mo furiously takes notes, putting down his thoughts on the rule, and thinking this will be a good subject for his quick-win team.

"After this low-hanging fruit, let's see if we can apply theory of constraints here," advises Sofia. "We have identified the bottleneck already. What is the next step in TOC?"

"Next we need to improve the bottleneck step itself, right?" comments Gina. "It's what Goldratt called 'optimizing.' Is it time for another VSM of the prototype-building process?"

"Let's not reinvent things here," advises Giovanni. "The prototype process looks awfully similar to our manufacturing processes, and we already optimized them in the plant. Maybe we can transfer what we learned in the plant to this process."

"That is an excellent idea, Giovanni," says Sofia. "We don't need that information from you today, but please put together some recommendations on how we can do that. So let's move to the third step of TOC."

"That would be looking at the subordinate step and identifying the critical items that need to be supplied to the bottleneck on time and in full," says Giovanni confidently. "You know, the specs, need for tools, fixtures, paint drawings." The team spends time doing as their colleague suggests and comes up with a list of improvement activities, to which they assign volunteers.

"When all of this is implemented, maybe Joe won't need to change the budget," says Marco. "I think we created a lot more capacity than the 15 percent we needed."

"Wait a minute," interrupts Luca. "What about the last step of the optimizing process—elevating the bottleneck? I was hoping to get at least some investment out of this exercise."

"Elevating the bottleneck may one day require capital, such as for machine upgrades or expanding the shop, but we should only pursue investments after all other possibilities have been exhausted," cautions Ricardo. Luca's face shows his disappointment.

"Carolina and Luca, could you take the lead on analyzing the testing process the same way we analyzed the prototype process this week?" asks Sofia. "I'll be glad to help you get started. Update Mo on what you find so he can document the quick wins from there, too."

"I think we deserve a vacation after all of this," says Gina.

"I agree," says Ricardo. "Good job, everybody. Just one more day. For tomorrow, we have another homework assignment: we need to learn a little more about the activities upstream of the prototype bottleneck—engineering calculations, modeling, drawings, etc. And I already know that in the absence of a standard, every engineer has his or her own way to do these jobs, but we should come up with a rough average and maybe minimum and maximum times. And one more request: please assess these times as if there was no waiting time and as if every engineer only had one task at one time."

"Are you dreaming?" asks engineer Johnny Torto, who until now has quietly assisted with the tasks at hand. "We'd fool ourselves thinking that were possible. That only worked when there was an edict from Junior or Emilio, and then everybody dropped everything else."

"And what was the result of that?" asks Sofia.

"We got that project done very fast. But when we picked the other projects back up, everything turned ultra-slow again," explains Bart.

"But why can't we do *all* projects as if Junior demanded top priority for each and every one?" counters Sofia.

Everybody is laughing, and they shake their heads.

Ricardo steps in: "Actually, I've seen that happen. And based on what I know about the published Goodyear process, that's how they started. They took the fastest iteration they had done for a project with top priority and succeeded in making all iterations follow the same path at the same speed. But it took them some time to get there. They followed the same principles we're implementing now, especially single-piece flow. Remember that single-piece flow is much faster and efficient than the stop-and-go that we're accustomed to. It all comes down to scheduling. So let's see if we can do it at Davanti and build it into our future-state process. And we'll make adjustments as we learn more."

"But even if we only work on one iteration at a time, some iterations are more work than others," notes Serfino.

"Good point, Serfino," says Sofia. "Why don't we set times for easy, average, and difficult jobs."

"That will work much better," agrees Vijay.

Ricardo assigns a team for each block of work (another unpopular homework assignment) and adjourns the meeting.

Day 7

It's another 7:00 am start in hope of wrapping up the PCP design. As a show of his appreciation, Ricardo has an assortment of pastries, fresh fruit, yogurt, small frittatas, and a portable espresso machine delivered to the office. As the attendees fill plates before taking seats to eat. Ricardo says: "Thanks for taking the time this week and for once again completing the homework. . . . I think we'll all enjoy today's work far more than what we've been working on so far this week."

"Can we get breakfast once a week?" asks Marco. "This is delicious."

"I agree," says Gina. "It's not the gourmet food stations we saw at Fusilli, but it will certainly do."

"I'm glad you like it. You've all deserved it. Now let's get back to the VSM. We've scheduled the building of prototypes for every iteration. There are only two steps after the prototype build: testing and analysis/recommendations. They can be done on a first-in–first-out basis, so we don't have to worry too much about scheduling them. But that's not the case for activities leading up to the prototypes. They're not as easy to sequence. We need to figure out when we must start the engineering work so that we have all information in the prototype shop when needed. And for that, we'll need to establish a 'critical path.'"

"Ricardo, can you go over critical path," asks Charles. "I don't recall that from the lean training."

"Many of the engineering tasks can be done in parallel," begins Ricardo. "For example, assembly drawings can be created at the same time as component specifications are written. But other tasks must be done in sequence: frame drawings can only be done after at least some engineering calculations are completed, and the paint drawings are done after the styling is complete. The critical path represents the activities that cannot be done in parallel. The critical path also establishes the total engineering time required."

With Ricardo's guidance, defining the PCP's critical path is relatively straightforward, but it takes quite some effort and discussion to establish and visualize it. When all the activities are defined, the team starts to add the times. They use the high-priority durations they'd done for homework to calculate a total critical-path time for easy, average, and hard jobs: from three weeks to 12 weeks. Then they review all the PITs on the planning board for easy, hard, and average durations.

"Now I understand," says Serfino. "If my iteration is more complicated, we assign a longer time, and we start it earlier than the easier ones."

"You got it, Serfino, and now we can subtract the critical path time from the need date, and we get the start date for the iteration," explains Ricardo.

"We may want to add a couple of weeks to the total time because we'll lose some time at the handoffs or run into other unforeseen problems," says Bart.

Sofia agrees: "Good point. Let's do that. And then let's make a table with all the start dates for the next six months and see how they stack up."

Mo, Bart, and Marco take turns calling out the start dates, and Gina enters them into a spreadsheet while the rest of team grabs up the remaining goodies. Then Gina sorts the start dates, groups them by week, and projects the results on the wall.

When he sees the result, Ricardo has an incredulous look on his face: "I was led to believe that everything piles up in engineering all the time. This shows the start dates nicely staggered and spaced, just like the tags on the scheduling grid. What happened, Sofia?"

"You're used to a chaotic schedule based on priorities and daily changes. Now that we schedule to a cadence, we get an even flow, and chances are that we keep the same flow through the handoffs, especially since we added a little buffer. But we have to validate all of this when we go live with this process in a few weeks."

"Excuse me, Sofia, but what do we do about the 20 percent of activities that you asked us not to list on the VSM, and what about the loopbacks we skipped?" asks Vijay.

"Good points, Vijay. We have a significant amount of capacity buffer that I think can handle the variability caused by those activities. And I expect some more capacity to be freed up as we improve all our engineering programs, which also will help."

"What else do we need at this time, Sofia?" asks Carolina.

"I think this is all we need to have Davanti's first version of the Goodyear PCP running after the slowdown. Then we'll learn a lot more, and we can engage the engineers in making adjustments as needed. They also will help us redesign and improve all the subprocesses. Lastly, Carolina, please enlist volunteers and start documenting this process. We'll need that for training, and it will soon become our standard engineering process."

"When will we get kanban cards for this?" asks Alexandra.

"Good point," surmises Ricardo. "We could make an experiment with kanban cards in September, but let's not forget we also need training before we get the engineers involved in designing the kanban process and the many subprocesses. So let's not bite off too much too soon."

"But we should be able to draw at least a skeleton of a future-state process at this time," says Sofia. "It will give us a good sense of our accomplishment today."

With Sofia's lead the team is able to sketch a strawman of the future state, and everybody understands that it will evolve a lot over the next few months, especially when teams get to work to discuss the details of all the subprocesses.

"Wow, this looks good on paper, but I'm still curious what it will really take to get all projects executed as if they're running in Junior's express lane," says Stella.

"Let's talk about that in a month, Stella, when we start visually planning resource assignments," suggests Ricardo. "For now, excellent work. Thank you all for hanging in with us on this job. It was a big-time commitment, but I'm very happy with the outcome."

"I like being part of designing my work process; it was well worth it," says Vijay.

"Carolina and I have a few days of work to confirm the schedule with Joe's team, get some software written, and add temporary workers," says Ricardo. "Anika, can you please help with the temps and look for training that we can offer after the shutdown?"

"Of course," replies Anika.

"The rest of you should get on with your personal plans," instructs Ricardo. "If I don't see you before you leave, have a great vacation."

Note

1. Theory of constraints (TOC) was introduced by Eliyahu Goldratt in *The Goal*, North River Press, Great Barrington, MA, 1984.

Chapter 21

Davanti Ramps Back Up

Throughout Europe, many companies had shut down for some period in the summer—the most popular vacation time, with huge traffic jams to and from southern vacation destinations. It was also a logical time for a slowdown of Davanti operations: Everyone feels exhausted after the Tour de France, and Davanti employees, like the racers, look forward to a summer break. Many riders will return for final races starting in September, while others call it a season after the Tour.

For Davanti, the next season starts immediately after the slowdown, with a focus on the fall races, the Eurobike show in January, and then the European Classiques soon thereafter. Some lucky racers will get an opportunity to participate in the "Tour Down Under" near Adelaide, Australia, or in January and February races in the Middle East.

Davanti's curtailed most work in August, yet many employees were at headquarters off and on. In addition to the Volta team and volunteer engineers working on the PCP, a skeleton crew in the prototype shop and test lab was busy with work on the Primo Sempre and Primo Veloce bike lines. The official launch of those two will be at Eurobike show, but Joe, product director, wants the advertisements to be out by November and the bikes available in early December to take advantage of the holiday-shopping season.

Luca was in the office from time to time to check on the progress, but he dedicated the rest of the month to his bees, vineyard, and farm animals. People within Davanti have only heard about Luca's farm—nobody has seen it or sampled any of its produce.

Junior spent time with his family in Sicily, practicing for retirement. He then left for Taiwan with Constantine for his annual plant visit, and since then has been in the office every day.

Bolaji, the new technology manager, spent two weeks in knowledge management training, including a class at the Copenhagen Business School. While at the University of Lagos in Nigeria and when working at companies in Africa and Europe, he'd sought out knowledge about knowledge management and is pleased to have this role. After class, he spent a lot of time talking with colleagues and mentors about how to create a knowledge management (KM) system at Davanti.

Stella went to set-based concurrent engineering training at the Politecnico di Milano and has been seen working hard to apply what she learned to the new sports bike project.

Anika took most of August off, spending time with her kids and her garden. She came in for a day to orient the new hire, Horst Havenstein, who will be the non-bike project manager, building that value stream for Davanti from the ground up. Horst joins Davanti from a major German sport equipment and clothing retail chain.

Ricardo spent some time in the office during the slowdown, even after the weeklong design of the PCP. His kids are off from school, and August is the start of the fall soccer season. He coaches

DOI: 10.4324/9781003231837-21

two teams—one with his son and one with his daughter. He claims he acquired more leadership skills on the field than in the office.

Davanti lawyers were busy during August. They worked on a large pile of patents to file. In months past, they would have been thrilled. But since Junior imposed a time limit on the turn-around for every application, they claim their work is like an assembly line and their billable time greatly diminished.

Mo joined his college buddies for their annual week at the beach; this year they convened in Croatia. Mo also helped his dad make pizza and repair the boat deck, took a couple of days redecorating his apartment, and spent some time in the office making plans for Leonardo and its scheduled gate meeting in mid-September. He has a lot to review given the extended scope of the project, which along with heading up the quick-wins project has kept him busy. He's having some trouble getting his head around the many moving parts. With continuous-improvement projects, there sometimes is no way of knowing where to start.

Mo, Stella, and Marco also spent time with their colleague Rebecca Sabrese, who was assigned to manage the project for renting, leasing, and financing bikes. She has the retail experience from her former employment but needs to learn a lot more about bikes. She had a lot of questions: pricing for used and unused racing bikes, pricing for bikes that were ordered for testing, length of leases and rentals. Mo let her know that when she's ready to rent, he has a customer in Marie: "Who do I make the check out to?"

On the final day before Davanti goes back to full operation, Mo has lunch with Marco and Gina at Davanti. The cafeteria is closed, but Mo's mom is not. As they pour over leftover lasagna and olive salad, Mo says, "I don't know about you, Gina, but I got a lot done here during the slow-down. In previous years we worked on many things and made very little visible progress on any. We always had to wait for somebody to approve or mostly disapprove. This year, I only waited for people when I needed their help or opinion."

"You're right, Mo," she replies. "I can't believe how fast I'm moving on the ski bike. I feel like somebody cut the shackles off my feet. And I don't have to bring in goodies either to get something done—now I bring goodies because I like to bake, and I can't eat it all myself."

As they're wrapping up their lunch, Mo gets a text from Marie: "Looking forward to my first fall race. Practicing a lot. Will you attend?"

"Just say where and when."

"First weekend in September in Verona."

"Should I bring my tools?"

"Please! Start is at noon; see you at 10:00?"

"You bet. See you then."

"Wonderful. Grazie."

***

Ricardo asks the technology manager Bolaji to join him for a walk around the Davanti grounds; it's a pleasant late August day.

"It's good to be back to work," says Ricardo. "Although I'm missing the outdoors."

"Yes, I agree."

"So how was your knowledge management training?"

"Sort of depressing."

"I don't follow. How so? I took similar training a few years ago and found it to be interesting and fun."

"Oh, the training was fun. I especially liked my time in Copenhagen; it's a beautiful city. But with every new thing I learned, I kept thinking of how much money we wasted at Davanti not knowing what knowledge we had and how to use it. Mind you, I'm as guilty as anyone. The teacher made us calculate how much our company spent creating knowledge. I was shocked to see how we wasted it. And the worst part was that we'd create the same knowledge over and over, just to waste it again."

"We've all been guilty. But Davanti probably isn't unlike most other companies. The industry average of knowledge reuse is about 30 percent. I'm not sure what Davanti's average would be."

"Ricardo, I think we have a very strong 'anti-reuse culture' here. Engineers, me included, only trust our own work and our own tests or we find it too cumbersome or boring to educate ourselves to what has already been done. And to be quite honest, we don't make that education easy."

"Yeah, I have that sense as well. So what else did you learn?"

"I was very impressed with the classic stories, how the Wright brothers couldn't develop a plane by trial and error but were able to develop all they needed to know with some very humble means and kite experiments. Got me thinking what they could have accomplished with access to our computers and prototype and testing facilities. Why don't companies like Davanti think like the Wright brothers before they tap into expensive resources? We could test a lot before we design, just like they did."

"Yes, that's a great lesson to apply."

"I also liked the Shell story, when the company could no longer afford all the drilling and they challenged their engineers to find the oil before they tried drilling. I believe that we could engineer some of our new bikes without prototypes and testing—we know where our oil is."

"What else can you bring to Davanti with what you learned?"

"I liked the KM management *process* that was presented: define the knowledge needed; identify the knowledge we already have; find the gaps; and start activities to close those gaps. And then, of course, we learned to capture the new knowledge and put it in usable forms, like tradeoff curves or computer models and simulations, and how to communicate it and add it to the standards so it will never get lost again. I think all of that's applicable here."

"I agree."

"I'm also convinced KM is not limited to R&D—we may deploy it first in R&D, but I hope we can inspire other areas of the company to follow suit."

"Yes. Of course."

"And I had a two-day LPPDE[1] seminar on how to create visible knowledge from what is hidden in test reports, the heads of people, or somewhere else."

"That's new to me. It sounds applicable."

"I'm sure it is, and I took very good notes. I plan on starting that soon so we can put a stop to lost knowledge at Davanti. But they also taught us about knowledge mining—extracting buried knowledge from the company databases. And we did it with simple statistics software, like what we used with six-sigma projects. We even learned about language processing and associated tools and software to create real, visible knowledge from research reports, including anecdotal descriptions. I think we have enough experts at Davanti that we can train in these methodologies to create visible and usable knowledge for generations of engineers to come. And best of all, I figured out where Davanti has the knowledge gold mines."

"Please, go on."

"We have all test data stored on a server, and we can match that with the spec of the bikes or components. I think we'll be surprised with what we find."

"Were knowledge councils and towering experts discussed in any of your training?"

"Of course. That's something else I would like to get started at Davanti."

"Good idea. In fact, many good ideas. You made good use of your time this summer. You should feel good about what you'll be doing for Davanti. Please make your plans, and we'll follow up in a few weeks."

"But now, I have a question for you: how can we get our Davanti engineers to search out existing knowledge before they create new knowledge?"

"That's a common problem, Bolaji. Some companies make it part of engineers' standard work, like the use of checklists, and hold them accountable for it. But I prefer a softer approach, and I'd like your input on that. How can we engage everybody in the knowledge management process?"

"I'll give that some thought."

"Anything else on your mind?"

"Yeah, I was wondering what happened to that engineer we interviewed before I left for my training—the Chalmers University graduate who worked for a Swedish car company? He had an impressive resume and experience with knowledge management. It became clear to me during my training that we really need skills like that at Davanti."

"I'm glad you asked: Peter Hendrikson. Anika made him an offer, and I hope he accepts. I agree with you that we need an outside infusion of knowledge management expertise. I'm optimistic that he'll come on board."

"I'm very glad to hear that."

"In the meantime, what do you think about forming a team to lead the implementation of the KM process? If Peter accepts, he can assist with that and the formal training program. And don't forget—although we're starting the initiative in R&D, we must inspire the rest of the company as well. As you said, they have the same need."

***

Mo arrives in Verona around 9:30 am. It's a cloudy but warm Sunday morning; a good day for a race. He parks on the main square near where the race will begin and texts Marie his whereabouts.

"Will be there in a few."

Marie parked at the local high school together with her team and her coach. They use the locker rooms and showers at the school. As her teammates head to the warmup area, Marie makes a detour to take advantage of her secret weapon: Mo's bike greasing and tuning service. She sees Mo, waves, and smiles: "Mo. My favorite mechanic. How are you?"

"Great. Good to see you, Marie. Are you ready to race?"

"Of course. Once I get my tuneup."

As Mo goes through the routine, they exchange stories about their vacations.

"OK, done. I'll meet you back here after the race, if that's OK."

"Absolutely," says Marie as she gets on her bike. "I hope you'll join me for lattes afterward."

"I'd love to. Good luck."

Mo watches as much of the race as possible from his location on the square. Marie does well, coming in with the main peloton, but she was in a breakaway that eventually collapsed and then she missed the one that succeeded. When she sees Mo after the race, she voices her frustration.

"The bike felt great, and I felt great, but my strategy wasn't so hot."

"That's how things go in bike races. Maybe next time you hit the right breakaway."

"Give me about 20 minutes. I'll meet you at the coffee shop up the street and we can catch up some more."

Over lattes they talk about their careers and personal plans for the coming week. Marie tells Mo that her problems with the client CEO were, to her surprise, easily ironed out, and thanks Mo again for the advice he'd given.

Marie also encourages Mo to get involved in her next weekend race activities. "You know, Mo, you're more than my mechanic. Why don't you think about staying in Modena next week the night of the race. We can go out for dinner and drinks and make a weekend of it. Modena is a beautiful city. I'll even buy you some of their legendary balsamic vinegar."

"You're on. I'll get some balsamic for my mom as well. She'd like that; she loves to cook." Mo thinks that mentioning his mom was a stupid thing to do, but Marie finds it charming.

"She's lucky to have a son like you. You'll have to tell me more about your family."

***

Right out of the summer break, Ricardo starts short one-on-one meetings with direct reports, project managers, and some of the developing entrepreneurs: every other week, they meet in a quiet, comfortable location, usually in the outdoor commons area of Davanti, weather permitting. His first meetings with associates take a little more time than planned, but Ricardo thinks they'll eventually last no more than 15 minutes. He wants to set the example and teach his staff how they, too, should conduct similar meetings. He doesn't have a preset agenda, leaving that up to the other person unless he has something urgent to share. He likes to explore how he can help people and find coaching moments. But he also hopes that these meetings bring things to the surface that cannot be discussed in the few meetings that are still left in the company. Those meetings are often standups and focused on current issues with little time to voice more personal concerns. Although he spends a lot of time walking around the engineering area, the prototype shop, and the lab, he knows that is not enough. He also knows he's dealing with many different personalities and that engineers are not the most extroverted of the human population.

The meetings are set in Ricardo's schedule for the rest of the year; he calls them part of his "standard work." Today he's meeting with Bart, the programs manager. They first discuss some technical issues regarding the portfolio, engineer assignments, the upcoming new products to be released, and the new visual planning system, which is having some growing pains.

"So, Bart, what is the feedback from the PMs?"

"I am glad you asked, Ricardo. There is some frustration. Some of the PMs spent the last 20 years figuring out how to beat the system and their colleagues to get their projects done. We rewarded them for that all those years, me included. It's hard for them to manipulate the new planning system."

"Well, that's the intent. The business sets the cadence and that's it. No more bringing in goodies to get priority."

"I understand, of course. It's just that I have to listen to their complaints. But I think I can help them through most of their issues, and I'm sure they'll find better ways to excel if they so desire. But I have a more fundamental question: why do we start iterations as late as possible? I keep telling my PMs that all iterations must be started in a consistent manner, but the late start makes no sense to anybody."

"Maybe we didn't cover that well enough in the lean training."

"I remember that it's done because the later we start, the more we know. Late start minimizes costly changes and helps cash flow and ROI. . . . And I have to admit, we ordered tooling a few times so early that we had to throw it away later when the designs changed."

"We also know that engineers will always figure out how to fill extra time if we give it to them," offers Ricardo. "So what's wrong with giving everyone *enough* time—though not too much—with a buffer at the end to cover for surprises?"

Bart considers the question before answering: "Nobody is arguing against the buffer. But, you know, after years of starting too early, habits die slowly. What if both the engineers and all information are available early? We could start then and finish early for a change."

"Not so fast. We must consider if those engineers couldn't be better utilized for some other project with a higher cost of delay. We could make exceptions and let them start early, of course, but I would prefer not to do that yet. We should give this time to stabilize, make improvements, establish a good habit, and then see where we are."

"Thanks, I see your point. We should require a certain level of discipline for these principles from the beginning. I'll encourage them to have patience with the approach. It will definitely be harder to reestablish it later if we let it slip now."

"Correct. I understand this is a difficult transition. Some PMs don't like standard work, just like some of the engineers. But please encourage them to speak up if they see problems and if there are ways to improve the standard. That can get them involved. Please keep me posted on this. It's very important."

***

Sofia and Anika have agreed to meet in the Davanti cafeteria for an afternoon meeting. The room is bright and airy, much like the Fusilli working space, and they both think they're more creative there than in their enclosed offices. Anika spots Sofia in a quiet area near the windows.

"Hi. How was your vacation. Sofia? Where did you go again?"

"We flew to Las Vegas where we spent a day gambling before picking up a mobile home. Then we traveled through the American West for two weeks. It was one of the best vacations I ever had. We burned a lot of gas, but we saw so much. Every day I thought we were in another part of the world. Tell me about your August?"

"My vacation was a little less exciting. My garden has never looked so good, and we've been enjoying produce for quite some time now, and more keeps coming every day."

"That sounds delicious. . . . So what's next with our change initiative?"

"I like the work we started with the Volta team for identifying quick wins. As we wait for business results, we can't keep talking about the processes. As with gardening, people like the produce, but they don't want to hear about digging, fertilizing, and pulling weeds. As Mo and his team quantify a few quick wins from the low-hanging fruits, we need to figure out how to best publicize them to reassure people that we're on the right track."

"I agree. What else should we be thinking about?"

"Well, we had decided to engage as many R&D folks as possible in the improvement of their piece of the PCP process."

"Yes, I know. But I keep thinking about how we can motivate them, get them to volunteer."

"I have an idea. I did this at another company, and it may or may not work here: once Horst gets his feet on the ground, let's have him create replicas of Rossa's maillot jaune—with 100 printed on the front and 50 on the back."[2]

"What do the numbers mean?"

"We'll keep it a secret, but some engineers will eventually figure out they're the first goals that Ricardo's team has come up with for the new product development process: 100 percent on time and 50 percent faster. If we tell folks upfront, they'll think we're out of our minds. But after having worn the shirts for a while, they'll begin to consider ways to help us reach those goals."

"When can I have my jersey? But I don't bike enough, I would look silly."

"We'll get some golf and t-shirt versions for people like you and me."

"Great idea, Sofia."

***

Junior was in Taiwan when Horst, the non-bike project manager, was onboarded by Anika and started his assignment at Davanti. He interviewed him prior to the selection, but he hasn't met him as a Davanti employee.

"Welcome, Horst. I regret I didn't welcome you on your first day."

"No worries, Mr. Davanti. Glad to have the opportunity to speak with you today."

"Please, call me 'Junior.' So tell me about yourself and how you'll help Davanti."

Horst explains that the sports-store chain he worked at sold common name brands—mainly top German brands—and also had its own lines of clothing and common sport articles. This even included their own brand of bicycles and bike accessories, many of which were supplied by a Davanti competitor, which surprises Junior. Horst is highly creative and shares some of his ideas to kickstart the new Davanti value stream—merchandising (which he learned in the fashion industry), branding, and licensing—and gives examples of what he's done in the past.

Junior is impressed with Horst's knowledge and experience, but he's surprised and concerned by how little *he* knows about Horst's line of work. Nonetheless, he makes him feel welcome and comfortable. "Come to me any time. I'm here to help. My door is always open."

Horst thanks him and then leaves the office. Junior immediately calls Anna and requests that she get Sofia, who arrives a few minutes later.

"Junior, how did your meeting go with Horst?"

"Do you know how silly I sounded when I told him 'I'm here to help'? How do I help that guy? I know absolutely nothing about that stuff."

"You think Marcel knew about pasta machines when he bought Fusilli?"

"So do I just close my eyes and sign checks and contracts?"

"No, Junior, you have the right to know what the checks are for, what's in the contracts, and how the business operates. But you need to try to learn from him, which you can do by asking him questions. You don't need to be the one with the answers—but you do need to be the one soliciting facts and information."

"How long will that take?"

"Junior, you never stop learning. Marcel has been learning his entire life. Ask questions of all the other experts in the company, too. Ask me. Ask anyone questions to get what you need to know."

"Won't that sound like I'm controlling him or doubting him?"

"It depends on how you ask the questions. There are questions with an intent to learn, and there are questions intended to second guess or control."

"How will Horst know what to do at Davanti if nobody tells him?"

"I'm sure he told you some of his plans. You just hired the best expert you could find for this new value stream, and you offered him a handsome salary, executive privileges, and even a bonus. Maybe you should trust that he knows what he's doing until he gives you reason not to."

"Fair enough. My next meeting is with Stephano. At least I know something about finances."

"I'll bet there's things that even Stephano could teach you."

"Thanks, Sofia," says Junior sarcastically, rolling his eyes.

***

After work on Tuesday, Mo heads to his parent's villa. He has some unfinished business to resolve with his father and a pizza:

Prior to the summer break, Mo's dad had purchased a stainless-steel, wood-fired pizza oven with integrated baking stones. While working with his dad on the boat dock, the two had set it up in the corner of the patio—as far away from the house as possible. His dad is proud of the acquisition, but when it came to making a pizza, there was nothing to be proud of. His inaugural effort resulted in a few charred, inedible pizzas and burned fingers despite a pair of expensive oven gloves. When Benito and Catherine heard about the culinary adventures, they jokingly advised their father to "stick to sausage-making," and they begged their mom to always have enough real food as a backup when their dad planned to make a pizza dinner.

Mo's dad was sure he could figure it out, but after more failed attempts, he called Mo and pleaded with him: "Maybe you can figure this out. You're the engineer in the family."

A few days later, Mo developed a couple of critical questions, including: Will the oven get hot enough? Is there uniform heat, or will the back of the pizza burn before the front is cooked, even with rotating? Is his dad using the right utensils? He headed back to the villa to find the answers.

Using a cheap infrared probe he borrowed from his mom, he affirmed the critical questions. Then to close the knowledge gaps, Mo set up a pizza-making project to determine the correct techniques. With simple experiments using dough-only pizzas, he and his dad figured out how to shoot them into the oven. It took a while, and they learned that they could only get the thin layer of dough off the peel if they used lots of cornmeal between the peel and the pizza; they also had to quickly pull the peel out from under the dough. They further experimented with rotating techniques and found one that seemed to evenly distribute the cooking.

After Mo returned from his beach getaway, they tried their hand with a real pizza. With hungry family drinking wine and looking on, Mo's dad put olive oil, tomato sauce, cheese, and a lot of ingredients on the dough as if he knew what he was doing; reached the peel into the oven as he had practiced with the bare dough; and ripped the peel out with a quick motion. Mo was the first to burst into laughter when all the ingredients scattered around the oven as the dough came out with the peel. Of course, Mo's siblings laughed as much as Mo.

Mo and his dad quickly cleaned the oven and assembled another pizza, determined to get a fully dressed pizza in and out of the oven. They tripled the amount of cornmeal on the peel and succeeded in getting the pizza into the oven. Mo advised his dad to let the pizza cook long enough to increase the odds of retracting it safely. With family anxiously watching—and holding back laughter—Mo's dad proudly pulled out and served a respectable-looking pizza to a starving and slightly drunk family.

"Dad, I'm sorry, but this pizza tastes like burnt tomatoes on cardboard," said Catherine. The others took a small bite, frowned, and put the pizza down. Mo's mom came to the rescue (mortadella sandwiches and broccoli salad). Everyone enjoyed her dinner, and no one left hungry.

Mo told his dad, "I'll come back tomorrow. Get plenty of ingredients, and we'll experiment with some sauce and topping combinations to get a better taste and texture. We'll figure the recipe out."

Davanti Ramps Back Up   ■   217

At that point, Mo's mom had had enough: "If I spent this much time figuring out how to cook things, we all would have starved."

"Mom, you never made wood-fired pizza," said Mo, with his dad nodding in unison.

"No, but I could, and I wouldn't go about it like you two. I would approach it the same way I learned to cook. First, I took cooking lessons from my mother, and then I perfected most of her recipes. Then I added new things to my repertoire. Come see." She motions them to follow her, and she leads them to a cabinet full of cookbooks and files with handwritten notes. "This is how I learned new recipes. Today, I find it easier to search on Google, and it's also much faster. I even find videos that show me new techniques. Did you think I was born a cook?"

Mo and his dad were embarrassed. Why hadn't they thought of using the vast knowledge out there on the web? They certainly weren't the first people learning how to make pizza in a wood-fired oven. The two then spent hours in front of their computers, reading recipes and watching online videos of pizza making. Monday evening, they'd discussed what they had read and planned to put it into action the following evening.

When Mo arrives late Tuesday afternoon, his dad looks confident. He'd even made dough from scratch (he had been buying fresh dough at a local bakery). The family has again gathered and hungrily awaits: Mo and his dad do not disappoint. They make three wonderful pizzas—margherita, sausage and peppers, and a pesto and artichoke—and earn compliments from all.

As Mo works through his third slice of pizza, he asks his mom, "So, mom, where is all your cooking knowledge stored that's not in a cookbook or online? You must have picked up some tricks on your own through the years."

"Oh, yes, especially some of the modifications I've made to my mom's recipes. I've got my secrets. They're up here," she says, and points to her head.

"Do you plan to share them with your children?" Catherine asks.

"You can ask me any time. You know, I can use a little more help in the kitchen nowadays. It would be a good opportunity for you to learn them. You'll never find them on the internet; they must stay in the family."

Mo leaves the table and goes out to his car. When he returns, he hands his mom a notebook with a cover that he marked in bold letters: "Cucina della Mamma Pensatore."

"Maybe you can write down some of your favorite recipes for us. We'd all appreciate that."

"If she writes down all of my favorites," says Benito, "she'll need a few more notebooks."

"I'd love to. Thank you, Mo. Maybe the next time we gather, I'll do the teaching and writing, and all of you practice the cooking."

***

Junior walks into his office on Wednesday morning and finds the yellow jersey on his desk. His assistant Anna comes in as well to take a look. "Must be a gift from Johan," says Junior. "I'll wear this on the ride today. Any idea why he would put 100 on the front and 50 on the back? It's not the 100th Tour anniversary nor the 50th Davanti win. I guess he'll tell me next time I see him."

"No idea at all what the numbers mean," replies Anna.

Then Junior sees Sofia walk by wearing her yellow golf shirt.

"Nice shirt, Sofia," he says as he gets up to walk to his meeting.

Sofia passes Gina, who wants to know where she can get a shirt like that.

"Anna has one for you."

***

Junior rides up to the Davanti group wearing his yellow bike jersey, and a few employees applaud. Ricardo then passes out jerseys to all participants at the Wednesday ride, and everyone cheers. Most riders change immediately, and it's quite a sight to see the sea of yellow leave the Davanti parking lot. The riders, like Junior, think the shirts are meant to celebrate the Tour victory. And since they're free, nobody pays much attention to the bold "100" and "50" numbers. All that matters to the riders is that they're a high-quality garment made by a top German brand.

***

On Thursday, the word gets out that there's enough shirts at Anna's desk for every employee in the company or "as long as supplies last," cautions Anna.

Sofia walks to Anna's desk to see how the supplies are holding up, and Junior steps out of his office.

"I really like these yellow shirts. It looks like every employee has one now. Somehow, I have a feeling you've got something to do with these, Sofia."

"No, it was Horst who had them made."

"I'm sure he had partners in crime."

"OK, Anika and I helped."

"I think it's a great idea—wonderful initiative to rally the Davanti folks around our Tour win. Am I the only one who doesn't know what the numbers mean?"

"They'll reveal themselves in good time as employees get engaged."

"Engaged in what?"

Sofia innocently shrugs her shoulders and walks away. Of course, everyone has the same question as Junior, and wild rumors are flying now about the numbers.

"Thanks for managing the distribution, Anna. If you run into any problems, let me know," says Sofia as her cellphone rings. She sees that it is Carolina Petrale, the operations manager, and picks up.

"Carolina, hi. I'm just down the hall. I'll stop on by in a moment." Sofia walks through a sea of yellow-shirted employees on the way, and finds Carolina also wearing a yellow golf shirt.

"What's up, Carolina?"

"Well, I announced a couple of workshops to improve the engineering processes in the PCP and asked for volunteers to help. We're going to start the workshops with a refresher of the innovation excellence principles and then the teams will start work on the process."

"That sounds great."

"Yes and no. I had to close the list of volunteer applicants after less than an hour. Just too many people. Rumor has it that this has something to do with the yellow shirts. I don't want to turn people down. Any idea what we can do with all those volunteers?"

Sofia calls Ricardo over and Carolina repeats the information.

"We can't turn down volunteers," says Ricardo. "So I have an idea. Let's assign large teams to every subprocess of the PCP, like frame design, tooling, paint drawings, and let them visualize the process, remove waste, or otherwise improve the subprocesses. Then at the end of the day, each team can select a couple of folks to represent them at an integration meeting where they put all the subprocesses together. That smaller group will then continue work on the master process for a few weeks, and we'll call them all back together at milestones and ask for their comments and suggestions."

"Perfect," says Carolina. "Thank you for the idea."

"One last question," says Carolina. "Everyone is asking about the numbers, and I'm starting to lose sleep over them as well. What do they have to do with this initiative?"

"The PCP target for on-time delivery is 100 percent," says Ricardo. "That's the first objective. We're also looking for a 50 percent improvement in cycle time. Mystery solved."

***

While other Davanti engineers and technicians were heading off to beaches, resorts, and campgrounds, Vinnie spent a lot of his time in the shop, helping to get bikes ready for January launches. He did get away for a week with his wife, hanging out in the pretty towns of northern Italy and enjoying the food and wine. He had taken a bike along and would occasionally take advantage of the early daylight and pleasant mornings to do some good riding.

One perfect morning he was pumping hard to get to the top of a hill when he suddenly lost the air in his front tire. He grabbed the spare tube and the CO_2 cartridge, but when he inflated the spare, the assembly blew out. Vinnie had no more spare tubes. He'd forgotten his phone, so he started walking the bike back toward town—not a pleasant thing to do in bike cleats. He knew his wife would be waiting and worried.

As the day's heat was picking up, Vinnie had an idea. He decided that the tire was wasted anyway, so he stuffed it with stiff dead grass, small branches from shrubs, and flowers he found on the side of the road. He rode very slowly—and the ride was harsh—but he made it back to the town, bought a new tire at a store on the outskirts (from where he called his wife), and then rode back to their B&B. Later at lunch with his wife, the grass-tire idea fermented: "Maybe I should stuff a tire with steel wool or a stiff sponge material or . . ."

Vinnie spent that evening on the internet, much to his wife's chagrin: "You know we're supposed to be on vacation." Using his innovation debit card that he carries in his wallet, he ordered a dozen tubeless tires and rims and all kinds of materials that could be stuffed into a flat tire. When replacing his tire at the store, he noticed that the grass and small branches had been ground up and felt moist—the flowers may have acted as a lubricant.

Upon returning to the Davanti shop, he found the materials he ordered and tested them out in tubeless tires. Most were not worthy of a road test, but he found that the stiffest materials worked the best when combined with regular bike grease.

When his colleagues return to Davanti from their summer breaks, Vinnie enlists support for his airless-tire idea. He walks to the engineering room and to Mo's desk.

"Hey, Vinnie, good to see you. How was your vacation."

"Do they make wool out of stiff fibers, such as steel wool?"

"Well, that memorable, huh?"

"No, no, it was wonderful. It's just that I've been working on something."

"So what are you tinkering with now?"

Vinnie doesn't initially respond, waiting for an answer to his question.

"OK. I know of something that might be what you're looking for. Hang on for a moment." Mo taps quickly on his keyboard, and then swings the monitor in Vinnie's direction. On the screen is a material that was spun randomly into a tube shape. It looks like wool. "Says that it's pretty stiff. Is that what you're looking for?"

"That looks about right. Thanks, Mo," says Vinnie as he pulls out a notepad and jots down the information on the screen.

"I can probably get the manufacturer to send us a few cubic feet. We're Davanti after all. Just let me know the shape you'd like."

"That would be great, Mo. When I get to my computer, I'll send you the specs. I owe you."

***

Junior has asked Ricardo, Marco, Sofia, and Joe to join him for an espresso in the Davanti cafeteria, and he describes his recent visit to the local bike dealer. They all listen intently and take notes.

"We've been leaving a large chunk of good business for our competitors. Of course, I don't hold you responsible. This has been going on for a long time, certainly before Ricardo and Sofia got here and probably before Marco and Joe had any voice in the matter."

"A lot's changed, Junior," says Joe. "It could have had to do with how Davanti used to be structured and its incentives."

"The dealer in town carries Davanti bikes to get people in the store, and then they sell them a competitor product because Davanti doesn't offer affordable options or a fuller line," explains Junior. "How is that?"

"Was any Davanti function or leader motivated to get a higher share of lower-price dealer business?" replies Joe rhetorically. "It was never a target that I can recall."

"But I'm surprised that at some time we didn't come up with a product to take a bit of that business."

"We *started* many projects like that over the years—carbon-fiber mountain bikes, high-quality city bikes, low-cost sports bikes," notes Joe. "And we worked on them on and off as you may remember."

"So where are they?" asks Junior.

"In some drawers, computer files, the heads of engineers," replies Joe.

"Why weren't they completed?"

"Maybe it was decided they weren't a good strategic fit at the time or they were never fully developed," says Ricardo. "Since I've been here, I've also seen such projects interrupted many times when we needed all hands on deck to help with problems, launches, and other higher priority stuff. The delays eventually left them to die on the vine. Other initiatives never made it out of the starting blocks. We neither had a business strategy nor a process to move along the idea, the technology, or the product. But that's changed now."

"What would it take to resurrect some of those projects?" asks Junior.

"Which ones?" asks Marco.

"I don't really know, since you and I don't know in detail what we've left to fail," says Junior. "Maybe something that can be developed quickly."

"When we revamped the new portfolio, we considered many new products, but entry-level pricing and having a full line of new bikes were not among them," says Joe.

"So what do you think? Should we have those products like some of our competitors?" asks Junior.

"I think it deserves some thought and some homework," says Ricardo. "We do have some work going on with a new touring bike, but we may have overlooked something important for the other markets. If it can help us increase the value of our portfolio and the value of the company, we need to study it. Simple as that."

"We are doing an excellent job creating capacity in R&D, but I defer to Ricardo if it's enough for what we're talking about now," says Joe.

"We don't necessarily have to develop some of those products ourselves," says Ricardo.

"I don't want our competition to make them for us," says Junior.

"No, it wouldn't be like that," counters Ricardo. "We know how to manufacture those types of bikes. But we could save precious time and resources by finding a suitable partner that could help us with the technology," says Ricardo.

"I've never heard of that," says Junior skeptically.

"We ran across it at Fusilli," says Ricardo. "But let's cross that bridge after Joe is done with his work on the portfolio."

"Good enough. But I have another question: How do we collect more ideas from the dealers? How do we know what they want or need? The dealer talked about being part of a 'dealer council' organized by a competitor. We should consider dealers our customers too."

"Yes. I will get back to you on that as well, Junior," says Joe wearily, further realizing the scope of his new product director responsibilities. "Let's get more people involved in that discussion."

Notes

1. Lean Product and Process Development Exchange.
2. Inspired by a story shared by Billy Taylor, founder of LinkedXL, at the AME International Conference, Jacksonville, 2014.

Chapter 22

Transparency Comes to Davanti

As Junior is going through his emails early in the morning, he notices Sofia pinning a chart to the wall outside his office. A few weeks earlier, this is where she had posted Davanti's vision and the goals. Junior sees her and walks out.

"Good morning, Sofia."

"Good morning, Junior. It's a beautiful morning. I took a different route to work today and passed a huge field of giant sunflowers. It was amazing. Too bad we're inside."

"I know the spot. It is stunning. There are benefits in breaking from traditional routes."

"Frequently."

"I see you've added our strategy to the board. Thank you. Looks like we got this thing figured out pretty well now."

"We certainly have, Junior. Once we got over the initial hurdle, things went smoothly. Now we need to put *you* to work."

"What do you mean? I've been working. And what is there left for me to do? I did the visionary work, inspired the crew, and set this ship on its course. I should now get to sit on the deck and enjoy the cruise."

Sofia laughs: "Not quite. This transformation isn't just putting posters on the wall, Junior. In a lean organization, leadership work is different, but there is no less of it. Sorry to disappoint you."

"I expected as much, but tell me," says Junior, pointing at the wall, "what's this space at the end used for?"

"That is where we'll put the metrics, once we have them defined."

"Ah, yes, the meeting on Wednesday. Right?"

"Yes. I think you'll enjoy it. It's set for just before the weekly ride, so the meeting will end on time."

"I'm sure it will. What could be so hard about metrics?"

***

A few weeks after Marco chaired the first PCP gate meeting, which released two new products to the PCP process, Bolaji Ajaya, R&D technology manager, has assembled a diverse group for the first TCP gate meeting. The outcome from today's gathering clears the way for new ideas to enter the technology creation phase.

DOI: 10.4324/9781003231837-22

Bolaji is joined by project managers and reps from manufacturing, sales, supply chain, and procurement in Emilio's old R&D office. Stephano personally represents finance as does Marco for sales and marketing. Bolaji also invited a couple senior engineers to take advantage of their vast technical experience. Even legal sent a rep. Sofia and Ricardo sit in the back observing and ready to help if needed.

"Thanks for coming, everyone," says Bolaji. "This is the first of many technology gate meetings. Some people call this a firewall, but that term is too scary for me. In these meetings, we make the decision to invest R&D money into the development of the technology for promising new ideas. At this time, we've reduced the risk of a new idea to the point where prudent funding is appropriate. The projects we discuss today are based on two new ideas. But, in the future, the development of new technology also could be driven by a need identified within the product portfolio. We'll follow the same guidelines that we used for the PCP gate, like demanding only a minimum administrative burden. Are we set?"

Everyone nods.

"What products are we discussing today?" asks Giovanni, who represents manufacturing.

"We don't have a specific product yet; the TCP is not about products," says Bolaji. "Today we'll discuss the Leonardo project—the technology needed for Mo's chainless bike idea—and the Marconi project, which started with a bike made out of tubes. We'll review the projects and approve some funding to develop promising technology that can morph into products. We'll only know the products or the product opportunities when we learn more about the technology. If we would pick one particular product today, the best outcome would be that the technology works or does not work for that one product. If we take a broader approach, we may find more and often better opportunities to market the technology. We'll have periodic milestone reviews—called integration meetings—where a crossfunctional group is informed about the progress and the proposed direction of the project. We'll give you more details about integration meetings when we have the first one."

"All I really know about those two projects are their names and the descriptions you just mentioned. Is that enough to make an assessment?" asks Giovanni.

"We're not here to second guess the technical recommendations of the team—we should trust them with the technology," reminds Ricardo. "And we have to understand that although the teams have significantly reduced the risk by answering a lot of critical questions, we still have a lot of gaps, as expected, with innovation in these early stages. But we must make sure that *enough* information is available to assess the risk—there is no innovation without some degree of risk. And if we make a mistake, we all learn from it."

"So what do you expect of us today?" asks Giovanni, still unsure of his role.

"This is an opportunity to ask questions and raise concerns about the team's plans," encourages Bolaji, "about manufacturability, capacity, capability, financial projections. . . . These discussions and assessments are very important early on because the team may have to—and still can—make changes to the plans. But when we are done today, we expect everybody to be behind the projects and give them your full support."

"I really like what we're doing here, Bolaji," expresses Stephano. "We finally made the process transparent. And I appreciate the opportunity to veto a project in times of insufficient cash flow. The transparency also prevents any of us from coming back later saying they never heard about this. But one thing you mentioned: prudent funding. Can you explain that?"

"As you will hear from the PMs soon, we're not launching a million-euro project today. Just as we did in the creative phase, we go one step at a time, except that after this gate the steps are bigger and more expensive. Although we show the total exposure of the project, today we only commit to the first phase of the project, which will last until the first integration meeting. At that time, we may keep moving forward, freeze the project, or change direction based on what we learned up to that point. That's what I mean by prudent funding. And I must make one more important point here: we cannot approve a project if we're not sure we have the capacity that we need or the funds or plans to create it—that is R&D capacity, lab time, plant capacity, etc."

"This alone will save me dozens of trips to Junior's office," replies Stephano. "No more requesting budget changes for surprise projects."

"Do we need to attend every gate meeting?" asks Rene from procurement.

"I would hope if somebody can't make the meeting, a representative can be appointed who reports back to the responsible gatekeeper. The team can certainly answer questions even after the meeting. But if no questions or concerns are raised, we'll assume the missing party supports the decision of the meeting. So if there are no further questions about the gate process, I'll turn it over to Mo and his team."

Mo and his team members give a summary of the results from their creative process and the critical questions they already answered. They also give a brief, layman's description of the technology they are preparing to develop and explain the timeline and the resources needed for Leonardo. Mo then opens the meeting for questions.

"I rode Mo's first prototype, but I never heard about the drive shaft Sergio is proposing," says Giovanni.

Sergio explains the concept in enough detail to make people more comfortable with the idea. Ricardo explains that the shaft concept was tagged on to the Leonardo project at the 11th hour. "If it was a standalone project, it would have gone through its own series of critical questions first. But we were able to integrate it into the overall project without significantly increasing the risk."

At the end of the discussion, Bolaji asks if everyone is comfortable approving the first phase of the project. Stephano is the first to give two thumbs up, and most of the others join in—albeit not with the same enthusiasm displayed by Stephano.

Stella and her team present the Marconi project, which is easier for all to grasp: making a bike with extruded short-carbon fiber tubes just as you would with weld-aluminum tubes. Gino gives a history of the project and explains why the project was already much further along than Leonardo. He also shows them samples and describes how they built and rode a complete bike.

There are fewer questions, and as they near the allocated time to end the meeting, approval comes quickly and with more confidence by all.

Just before the meeting adjourns, the lawyer asks, "Why am I here? We can't file patents yet."

"I'm aware that you can only start filing patents when you get the disclosure of the idea," replies Ricardo. "But we invited you so you understand the scope of the project, and, if necessary, you can advise the team about legal concerns that may exist. For example, given your work for Davanti over the years, you might identify potential infringements and ways to avoid them."

"OK, I think that's a good idea," says the lawyer. "Maybe I can also hurry up the disclosures. We had many cases where the disclosures were submitted so late that we couldn't get the protection that Davanti deserved."

"Well, with the good work of everyone on these projects and a little luck, we'll end up with technologies and products very worthy of protecting," says Bolaji. "And with that, thank you all."

***

For the first Wednesday leadership huddle in the conference room, everybody is standing. In the room are Junior, his direct reports, and some of their staff with binders full of data. While they wait for the meeting to start, they walk around the room, chat with their colleagues, and point at the charts on the wall.

"Welcome to our first huddle," says Sofia. "In case you're not familiar with the term, a huddle is a regular, short, standup meeting where we try to make problems visible to everybody and we collaborate on solutions. Ideally, we solve some problems during the huddle—other problems may need to be assigned to a team. All functions will have their own huddles one day, which along with this one are called 'tiered huddles.' Problems from the lower tiers will roll up to the level where help is available to solve them."

No one seems surprised by the terminology of what they're planning to do.

"But I'm getting ahead: today we'll work on setting the stage for the huddles going forward. We'll discuss the information we need in this meeting so we can quickly see problems and fix them when they're still small."

Sofia pauses and is surprised that nobody asks a question or has a comment. She's convinced that will soon change. She proceeds to introduce Giovanni, who describes his role on the Volta team, and discusses his mini project to help Davanti define its "high-level metrics," as Sofia calls them.

Giovanni is nervous. He looks like the conductor of a big symphony orchestra before the concert. Unlike a conductor, he doesn't know how his audience is likely to respond. He and his team worked hard to identify the most important metrics and the individuals that are responsible for them. He created a sequence of charts all neatly arranged around the room. Most charts have a very visible red or green traffic light on them. Nearly every traffic light is green.

Giovanni explains that they will first review the essential metrics: safety, quality, delivery, cost, and employee engagement. "Then we'll look at progress toward the company goals, and then we'll look at the metrics that track the innovation excellence initiative itself. Every problem related to meeting the goals should be clearly visible."

Still no arguments or questions come from the group.

Carolina Petrale, the R&D operations manager and the global Davanti safety coordinator, points to the first chart that tracks reportable accidents. It shows a calendar grid for the month, and all squares to date are green. "This chart should need no further explanation," she says, and her audience agrees.

"We also track near misses as a leading safety indicator," she adds, moving on to another chart that is a mirror image of the first—all green. Everybody nods, seemingly happy with the report.

Constantine, who is responsible for quality throughout Davanti, steps forward and points at the quality chart—all green. "Any questions?" he asks.

"How can it be all be green if we had a major problem in the Tour de France?" asks Junior. "Is that fixed, by the way?"

"We only track quality problems found in the plant inspection."

"So you're telling me that we manufactured perfect quality all month—100 percent," Junior continues.

"No, our target is 98 percent, and we met it most of the time."

"How can all be green if we made 2 percent bad quality?" asks Claudia.

"Because 98 percent is the target," responds Constantine tersely.

"Constantine, are we getting better on quality, day after day, week after week?" asks Sofia.

"We actually degraded a little because of recent cost improvements. We used to be at 99 percent."

"So you're telling me that we are not at 100 percent, we went backward, and, nonetheless, our indicators are green," says Junior, throwing up his arms in disbelief. Constantine says nothing.

"Who sets the targets?" asks Sofia.

"I set those with the quality inspectors in the plant."

"OK," says Junior, "would it be possible to show us a weekly trend next time—52-week rolling averages?"

"I certainly could do that, but what would be red and what would be green?"

"Maybe when we have that chart, we can discuss the targets and how to apply red and green." Giovanni takes notes.

"Next is delivery," says Constantine, pointing to another chart that is green.

"I assume you set your own goals here, too? Out of curiosity, what was our actual delivery rate last week?" asks Junior.

He looks in a big binder: "89 percent."

"Well, I guess you know my recommendation," says Junior.

"Constantine, the new lines that we'll launch this year have a high cost of delay, and it's critically important to have every sample produced by the plant ship on or before needed so we can get the testing done," reminds Ricardo.

"I second that," says Joe.

"So what was the delivery performance of prototypes, Constantine?" asks Junior.

Another look at the binder and Constantine replies: "We've never tracked those, but I know that we had a line down for two weeks, and we had to skip some prototypes to meet our production targets."

"Can we have a separate chart that shows our on-time delivery of prototypes, too?" asks Junior. Constantine obliges and sits, happy to be out of the spotlight as Stephano walks over to report the metrics on cost, for which he has always been responsible.

"I assume all indicators are green," says Junior before Stephano utters a word. "But let's at least see what cost metric merits a green."

The cost metric chart is all green, and Junior has had enough: "I see a pattern here. Have we no room for improvement? This meeting is about getting better and meeting corporate goals. It's not about personal performance or targets that would affect your bonus. How can we improve if we don't even know what to improve? I was looking forward to seeing red and a root cause to explain why it's red. And then I wanted to know how I or somebody else in this room could help, maybe by removing a roadblock, approving resources. If we can't even see the problems, how can we fix them? Isn't that what this meeting is supposed to be about, Sofia?"

Claudia jumps in before Sofia gets to answer. "Don't expect me to be the first person showing a red chart here if everybody else has green."

"Is there a reason for that Claudia?" asks Sofia.

"Sure. It makes me look bad. I'd feel like I'd be the only one who screwed up. You'd ask embarrassing questions, and I'd have to defend myself and my department. I know how to run my business, and I don't need help. And if I do, it's between me and Junior. I'm not going to air my department's dirty laundry in front of you all."

Junior stares at the ceiling. He's red in the face, and it's been months since he's been this upset. "Claudia, it can't work that way anymore," says Junior, wanting to scream but holding it together. "Period."

Sofia takes a different tack to diffuse the situation: "Let's summarize for today: We need trend charts with weekly averages and targets. We need rules on every chart for when they turn red or green. Giovanni and I will work with all of you, and then let's try this again next week."

Junior moves in front of the door before anyone can leave. "One last comment: nobody will get fired for a red metric. In fact, I think recognizing a problem is the first step toward fixing the problem. I will applaud anyone who does that. In fact, if I wanted to discipline somebody, I think it should be for complacency and inability to see opportunities for improvement and not having the courage to ask for help." He then turns and leaves the room.

Nobody says a word as they leave the room.

***

Mo and Luca had asked Constantine if they could borrow a resource from the Taiwan plant for a few weeks to help implement lean manufacturing principles in Fumane's prototype shop and test lab. Constantine was principally in agreement, but he wanted to avoid any questions later and decided to let Junior know. He asks Mo to come along when they meet.

"Our Volta team is looking for quick and easy implementations of lean principles that will bring significant results," says Mo to Junior. "Lean manufacturing principles are not new to Davanti, as you know, and they can likely be transferred to the prototype and test operations with a similar effect that they had in manufacturing. They could also generate early results to help keep people motivated in the initiative."

"Yes, I can see why that would work," agrees Junior.

"But we don't want to reinvent known best practices for those processes," continues Mo. "So we'd like to invite one of the folks who implemented lean in the Taiwanese plant to help with our effort."

"Of course, I support that," says Junior "But I have to ask a question. A few years ago when we had transformed the Taiwan plant, I asked if the changes there would apply here in Fumane. The decision was made not to replicate in Italy what was done in Taiwan."

"That's correct, Junior," says Constantine.

"So who made that decision—wait a minute," says Junior, pausing. "Let me rephrase the question: what prevented us at that time from implementing lean here in the prototype shop?"

"I think most of us involved were convinced that implementing lean in the R&D organization, even the labs and shops, would kill creativity," says Constantine. "I'm sorry, but we never gave your question the right consideration."

"Kill creativity? We didn't have much anyway. Sorry for my frustration. It's a different time, and we're a different company. Please move ahead with your suggestion, and let me know if I can be of any further help."

***

Mo is on his way back from lunch when he gets a text from Marie: "I'll be in Caprino Veronese for training this weekend. Care to join me on Saturday?"

"Sure," responds Mo.

"Great. I hope you're up to it. I need to ride the mountains."

"Good location. I'll be ready."

"Meet me at Santa Maria Maggiore at 10:00 am. Ciao."

Mo had plans to go to his parents—a back-to-school shower of sorts with the grandkids—but Marie caused him to quickly forget about that. Now remembering his commitment to the party, he calls his sister, hoping she'll understand. He sort of explains why he can't make it but says as little as possible about Marie. His sister wants to know more and guesses it has something to do with a woman. Catherine is a little upset that he would change plans, but since she's the one who keeps bugging Mo about a girlfriend, she lets him off the hook.

Mo hangs up and calls his parents, explaining that he has to change plans. They are completely accommodating—more looking forward to the seeing the grandchildren than Mo. His mind then jumps to the lean effort in the prototype shop and the idea to bring a Taiwan engineer to Italy. He realizes the work in store and heads quickly to Luca's desk to get the wheels in motion.

***

Caprino Veronese sits in a valley south of the Monte Baldo mountain range in the Italian Alps. The town offers access to a number of high-elevation cycling routes. The Saturday morning drive to the church in Caprino Veronese is less than 30 minutes, and Mo arrives precisely at 10:00 am as Marie pulls her bike off her car.

"Mo! You've made it."

"Yes. Wouldn't miss it. How's your bike?" Mo immediately asks, and then gives her ride a quick lookover.

"You see, I've been keeping it oiled. Does that surprise you?"

"No, no," says Mo, although he is surprised that it looks to be in good condition. After getting on his bike, he advises her to lead the way.

Together they bike north, and after more than three hours they've reached the northern end of the mountain range and decide to head back after a short break for a light lunch that each has packed for themselves. Mo is exhausted; Marie has worn him out again. A few times she would wait at the top of the hills for him but would give him no time to recover once he caught up.

"It looks like you're still working too hard and not riding enough," says Marie jokingly as she admires the beautiful valley below.

"Yes. You are correct. And you are clearly in racing shape. Good for you."

"Thank you for noticing. . . . It's good to see you again."

"Thank you for the invitation, Marie. Despite the beating I'm taking, I really enjoy our rides."

They both sit and stare at the puffy clouds and green hills.

"Do you have time for a drink and a bite when we get back to town?" asks Marie.

"Absolutely."

The ride back to town, with more downhill, goes faster than the northerly route. They change clothes in their cars and stop at a local pizzeria with outdoor seating and, to their pleasure, a decent beer list. Exhausted, they sit, order, but don't talk much. When their food and beers arrive, they devour them. This day they enjoy the pizza and lagers almost as much as each other's company and the late summer sounds and breezes.

"This has been nice," says Marie.

"It has. But next time, I pick the place. And maybe no bikes."

"Whatever you'd like, Mo. I hope it's soon. I do. I hope it's soon."

***

La Vuelta is the last important multistage race of the pro season, held during three weeks from late August into September. Most riders prepare their racing season to peak for the Tour de France and then recover at the beach for a while after the gruesome event. Some who do well in the Tour will skip La Vuelta, but it's an opportunity for others to end their season on a high note and secure positions for next year. The race is also a stage for Spanish riders to shine in front of millions in their homeland.

Most of the Davanti riders are participating this year, including Rossa. They are, however, obviously worn out and usually hang back in the peloton. Nevertheless, this is an important showing for Davanti the company because Spain is a significant sales territory.

The race also is an opportunity for Davanti engineers to keep an eye on the cracks first experienced in the Tour. Davanti competitors wonder why so many Davanti engineers are hanging out with the Davanti mechanics at the start and finish of stages. On the final day of La Vuelta, as riders make their way to Madrid, a Spanish rider holds a commanding lead throughout and is eventually atop the podium wearing the "Jersey de Oro." While the Davanti team put in a good effort, it's bad news and good news: no team member on the podium, but no cracks on the bikes.

***

When the second weekly metrics meeting starts, everyone is tense. Despite what Junior said, nobody wants to discuss their problems in the open. They've been used to hiding them and fixing them quietly on their own—often with a bandage. Only when a problem could not be contained would they go to Junior—blaming somebody else, describing circumstances out of their control, and asking for resources to fix it. This meeting continues the major cultural change for everybody, and culture takes time to change. Sofia is well aware of the challenge, and she realized after the first meeting that she needs to help Junior transform the group and offer more coaching.

Junior recognizes the anxiety and attempts to lighten the mood. "I'll go over the La Vuelta metrics first—all red." The group chuckles. "See, that was easy."

Sofia and Giovanni had held individual and group meetings in the conference room for several days with everyone to clarify the targets of the metrics. Some preferred to talk to Junior directly before providing their input, and there were constant quests by most to have targets set as low as possible so they could easily be achieved. Junior would have none of it: "If I ask for 10 percent, I might get 10 percent. But if I ask for 30 percent, I might get 20 percent. I'm 10 points ahead," he told everyone repeatedly. "We didn't win the Tour by shooting for a top 10 finish. We raced for perfection and first place."

"Before we get started, I have a question," says Gina, who is only an observer in the meeting. "Traffic lights have red, green, and yellow. Why don't we have yellow?"

"So what do you do when the traffic light turns yellow?" asks Sofia.

"Sometimes I stop, sometimes I don't; it depends," says Gina, puzzled.

"So many times you consider the yellow light to be a red and act as if it is. You stop. Other times you treat it like it's green, and don't change your speed."

"Yeah, pretty much," says Gina, smiling. "I still don't follow?"

"That's the behavior we want to avoid at Davanti," explains Sofia. "Yellow adds a level of complexity, but offers no real, clear action associated with it. So people wait until it goes away or turns red. And those companies that try to associate action with yellow usually find that the action is the same one they'd take if it was red. So in our system, if it's yellow or questionable, we color it red. . . . Thanks for the question, Gina. Who's first?"

Carolina starts with a review of the safety metrics. The incident metric is still green. The target of zero was achieved.

"What would happen if we had an incident?" asks Junior.

"Then I would present our root-cause analysis and the countermeasures we took," says Carolina.

The safety coordinator also shows near misses, and that chart is red. "We had a near miss in the lab. A technician tripped over a hose without injury, a number of colleagues saw the accident almost happen and reported it, and corrective action was taken. This indicator will go back to green unless we find another near miss in the coming days."

"Will we all be happy if we don't find a near miss?" asks Sofia.

Carolina thinks for a moment: "I think we should work hard at finding near misses. I think we need a target that shows how good we are at looking for and finding near misses."

"Remember, when it comes to showing respect, there is nothing more important than to care for employees' safety," counsels Sofia. "But should our care for safety be limited to the workplace?"

"Another good point," says Carolina. "I like that idea. We'll come up with something." She steps aside and makes room for Constantine.

The plant quality metric is red this time. Constantine shows a trend chart, and, indeed, the chart shows a drop in quality for three consecutive weeks. Constantine explains that if they are below target or had two consecutive weeks of decline, he will present the root cause and corrective action. In this case, the problem was overlapping paint lines; the root cause was insufficient training with a new paint machine. The equipment manufacturer has completed the necessary training, and the problem has not recurred.

Constantine also shows trend charts for warranty returns, customer complaints, and mistakes caught by dealers. Some indicators are red, and Constantine explains that root-cause analysis has started.

The delivery metric for regular production bikes is green. However, delivery of samples that need to arrive in Fumane for the production release of the upcoming bike lines is red. Constantine says all equipment is working again, and he sees no reason why they won't catch up in the coming week.

Ricardo also added a chart showing on-time delivery for both local prototype building and testing, and both of those are red and still far off their targets.

"This is largely due to the recent process changes," says Ricardo, "but if we aren't seeing improvement in the next two weeks, I will create a task force to help get us on target." Several people, including Junior, offer their help; Ricardo thanks them, but says no assistance is needed as of yet. Ricardo also presents new charts for meeting technical release and launch dates on time, and they, too, are red due to late delivery of samples from the plant. "Here, too, process changes have contributed to these problems, but I'm still confident that we'll release the products needed by the end of the year as scheduled."

"I would like to make a point here," says Sofia. "One that applies to Ricardo's metrics as well as others. Late R&D release can escalate to a huge problem with launch and sales later. So if we catch that problem early, we can help Ricardo make up the lost time and still have an on-time launch. That is the reason why we review these metrics weekly and prefer leading indicators. The same applies to all other metrics: we want to catch a problem early and fix it before it escalates into a major problem later on."

The sales and marketing metrics cover traditional metrics like sales and results of ads/promotions, but now also include missed sales due to unavailability of goods in the stores and key process measures, such as shipment delays, customs delays, and dealer complaints. Claudia can't argue about the numbers—they are appropriate and accurate—but she's not happy that everything is red. She complains that it will be a while until she even knows the profits generated and points her head toward Stephano. Nevertheless, she lays out the need for root-cause analysis and planned countermeasures should the red trend continue.

Stephano shows cost metrics that he would have previously shown in his monthly finance review—factory cost and cost of goods purchased. They are green and cause no concern; he makes it clear that Constantine and Diana are responsible for the numbers behind those charts and that they had reviewed them ahead of time. Then he shows overhead cost (red), which he explains is partially due to the use of temporary labor during the summer. Everybody knew why that happened, but they argue over Stephano's new chart that shows overhead allocated by function. Each function head suggests a different calculation, Stephano defends his numbers, and Junior eventually intercedes.

"Stephano explained his calculations and, while they differ from what you might prefer, they are an accurate portrayal of overhead. You understand how he calculated the overhead, so you can figure out how and where to help to meet the targets. If not, I'm happy to help you."

Anika steps forward and points to charts on employee engagement: "We never had a metric like this. We will rely on internal and third-party data. We'll have an independent employee engagement survey soon, which also will provide a benchmark with comparable companies in our area. Meanwhile, we're starting our internal metrics by tracking the number of people engaged in improvement activities, multidisciplinary teams, hackathons, and idea-generation initiatives. They're not perfect, but they easily show a trend. I've also tried to quantify events like the recent t-shirt initiative. We were flooded with volunteers after that. And I've been thinking about another new metric that I want your opinion on: people going home on time and happy."

"I go home happier, but what is on time?" asks Junior.

"I let people decide the time they go home for themselves," says Carolina. "But I'd like to know how many have to stay later than they would like. And just like you, Junior, many of my staff leave happier now because they see every day what they accomplished and know they'll not be asked the next day to do it over."

Anika returns the group's attention to a few remaining HR charts: "And, of course, I'm tracking the traditional metrics like turnover, job acceptance, employee complaints." She points to data for each component.

"So why the uptick in turnover?" asks Constantine.

"Ah, you noticed that. That's unusual. It would be very easy to blame it on all the changes underway, but at the moment I can't say that. We've not completed all the exit interviews yet. I hope they will shed some light on this. I will communicate the root cause as soon as I know it."

Everyone looks relieved that the display of metrics is over and somewhat proud of their contribution to Davanti's cultural change.

Junior steps forward: "Nice work, all of you. I'm really pleased. I don't mind the red. It tells me that we're finding problems, making them transparent, and working to prevent them. This will help us collectively solve any issues that stand in our way of improvement."

Chapter 23

New Ideas and New Revenues

As the end-of-summer days get shorter, the start time for the Wednesday ride has been moved up by a half hour. Nobody wants to carry a bike light. Most people still like to wear the yellow jerseys they've received, including Junior and Mo, although they wear a long sleeve layer under it now. And many are still trialing competitor bicycles. About two dozen people this day are on their bikes and ready to go. Mo turns to Marco and asks, "Where's Vinnie? He never misses a ride."

Just as Marco begins to respond, Vinnie rides in the front of group. "Hey, Vinnie, it's about time," someone yells. Vinnie gets off his bike and proceeds to let the air out of both tires.

"Vinnie, what are you doing?" asks Junior. "What the . . ."

Vinnie—in his typical style—says nothing. When it's clear that all air has been released, he gets back on the bike and rides. Everyone thinks he's crazy. Or maybe they're crazy and can't believe what they've seen. They're concerned about keeping air in the tires, and Vinnie just let it out.

The bikers soon follow after Vinnie, and most are in front of him by the first turn out of the parking lot. As they ride, he quickly falls far behind.

Vinnie rides slowly for about a half hour and takes a shortcut back. When he gets to the parking lot, he pumps the tires back up and sits on the bench waiting for the other riders to get back. His tires appear to be holding air.

The first one to get back is Junior.

"You OK, boss?" asks Vinnie, surprised to see the CEO and certain he took a shortcut as well.

"Oh, sure, just a little sore today," says Junior. "My back was acting up, so I cut the ride short. Could be my bike setup. I'll be fine. Have a good night." Junior leaves quickly, and Vinnie waits as the rest of the riders gradually arrive back and talk about the ride.

"Just what was that about?" asks Marco, pedaling his bike up next to Vinnie.

"I just rode 15 kilometers on two flat tires. Stop by the lab tomorrow, and I'll show you how I did it."

Everyone stares at Vinnie, his tires, and then back at Vinnie.

"Tomorrow. You'll see."

***

Thursday morning after the ride, Mo, Marco, and others show up in the lab just as Vinnie suggested. Vinnie pulls the tire off the rim; it appears to those in the room to be a standard tubeless tire, but it's been stuffed with a stiff yet very light material that resembles an open mesh of spun fiber and some bike grease.

DOI: 10.4324/9781003231837-23

"It's stiff enough to prevent the tire from collapsing when it's deflated," Vinnie explains. He also shows how he put a wider, softer flange on the rim so it would reduce the pinching of the flat tire against the road. "I still had to ride rather slow. I'm thinking they could spin this material right into a new tire and maybe in an organized pattern. It should still be possible to mount the tire easily enough."

"With all this stuff in the tire, how was the ride when you inflated it?" asks Marco. "The tire must have felt like it's made of wood."

"At the high-inflation pressure of bicycle tires—8 bar (110 psi)—who would notice the difference?" says Vinnie.

Seeing the crowd around Vinnie, Ricardo has been listening in and is truly impressed. "We are really making progress with innovation," he thinks. Vinnie would have been the last person he would have expected to develop something like this and then make a show of it.

"Your stunt proved the most critical question to everybody yesterday," says Ricardo. "You may have found the holy grail of bike tires—maybe any kind of tires. Chains and tires are the Achilles heels of today's bicycles. This could be huge."

Vinnie appreciates the high praise for the idea, but senses something else is coming.

"You know, we're lucky none of our lawyers saw it," says Ricardo.

"What do you mean?"

"You and me would be in Junior's office right now trying to explain why we're giving away Davanti innovations. I don't know who would be in deeper trouble, you or me. Although I enjoyed your stunt, it could have ruined our opportunities to patent your idea."

"So do the lawyers know?" asks Vinnie.

"I doubt it."

"So let's leave it at that."

"OK, but we'll need to confess when we start filing for patents. I've got your back this time, but please, no more such tricks outside the Davanti walls."

"Yes, boss," says Vinnie with a sly grin.

"I almost believe you."

***

Due to some scheduling issues for Junior, the third metrics meeting was pushed back to Thursday afternoon. The leadership group goes through the essential metrics without interruption, and, since no one's root-cause analysis points to a single person, many constructive recommendations are made.

"I'm curious to see how we're doing toward our new corporate goals," says Junior.

"They must all be red; we've not met one yet," says Claudia.

"Yes, Claudia, that's correct," says Sofia. "But remember, we didn't expect to hit them the first month. If we had, it would probably mean we didn't set them high enough."

Giovanni refocuses the group's attention and shows the proposal that Sofia helped him draft: He suggests that Claudia could report on sales from new products and services, including the sales from the new non-bike products. Sofia will help Joe develop a metric to assess how Davanti is "delighting our customers," specifically those who are not pro racers. Stephano will start regularly reporting on net profit margin for all products, existing or new. All agree with the proposal.

The group then discusses more fuzzy goals, like respect for people. Anika volunteers to enlist a team to work on defining a metric for respect. She'll include it in the people metrics that she already reports.

Given her role, Sofia promises to look at measuring the change in culture, the effects of continuous improvement, and the progress of the innovation excellence transformation.

Constructive suggestions are made regarding the existing and proposed metrics, but eventually they all conclude the same thing: the initiative must soon show results to the top and the bottom lines—without that, nothing else really matters. But unlike in meetings past, everyone is optimistic about the path forward and believes that if they get the process right and achieve a meaningful culture change, the results will follow.

"Please keep in mind that it's the leading indicators that warn us about upcoming problems," advises Sofia. "Let's make sure we have enough of those in the mix. And I hope that as we learn more, we can drop less relevant ones as time progresses. I'll also work some more with Giovanni on measuring speed to market and efficiency in addition to setting appropriate milestone targets for the new metrics. Giovanni, I'd also like you to work on a standard process for this meeting, so we can transfer the responsibility for the meeting to a staff member and you can get back to your regular job."

"Sure, will do, Sofia," says Giovanni, clearly in agreement with that plan.

Junior quietly has been watching the report outs and metrics proposals, but he's clearly got something on his mind: "Nice work, everyone. New things always take time at Davanti, and I want to personally thank you for sticking with this and collaborating as a team. You've showed a lot of respect for each other and clearly put the objectives of the customer and the company ahead of departmental or personal goals. But before we take a short break, I have an important comment I need to make: All the metrics we're talking about must be accomplished with the utmost integrity and by following all rules and guidelines. If you feel like you have to cheat, lie, or violate any laws or standards, please talk to me. In addition, I don't want anybody to do anything that would make another associate, especially one of your peers, feel uncomfortable or degraded in any way. And I'm looking forward to attending your functional huddles, and in those I expect you to voice the same concerns to your associates: functional metrics should be accomplished the right way and not at the expense of another function or by trading off another corporate metric."

Junior pauses for a moment, waiting for comments. No one says anything, afraid they'll trigger another speech about Fausto Sr.

"When we reconvene, Stephano will report on traditional financial metrics," concludes Junior. "See you in 10 minutes."

When the executives return to the conference room, Stephano starts to present his finance report. He would normally have stated the financials in Junior's staff meeting near the end of the month, but Junior asked him to move it to this meeting instead. "We closed the books yesterday, and I'm happy to share last month's results with you today."

Before Stephano can proceed, Junior interrupts him: "Talk about a lagging indicator. Why does it take three weeks to close the books? If we had a problem in early August, we'd find out about it seven weeks later."

Stephano mumbles something about general accounting practices, before Junior interrupts him again.

"Why can't we close the books every day?"

"That would be a huge change in the process," says Stephano, visibly shaken by the suggestion. "We don't get data until well into the following month."

"Did you ever ask for that data on a daily basis? We really don't need everything, just the leading indicators."

Stephano again begins to mumble about general accounting practices, when Sofia comes to his rescue: "I can help you Stephano. We'll take it one step at a time. Maybe we start with closing the books weekly."

The disillusioned Stephano nods, and then goes through the business metrics with which everybody is familiar and in the traditional format of the monthly updates—except they are now posted on the wall and not within a PowerPoint presentation. He covers sales, revenues, profit, cash flow, and cost. Junior asks his typical questions, and some people make the usual comments.

"I'm looking forward to weekly financials," says Junior. "Can you also build in trends with targets and red and green lights?"

Stephano looks at Sofia with a helpless face.

"Will all this information stay on the walls in this room? Will we lock the doors? What if others come in here and look at this?" asks a concerned Joe.

"Is there anything they should not be allowed to see?" responds Junior.

"We never shared information like this with our staff," says Stephano with a concerned face.

"Well, everybody is engaged in the effort that these metrics describe, why would they not be allowed to see the results?" asserts Junior. "Anika, maybe you could organize a few tours to help everybody better understand the metrics that are posted here."

"Our lower-level huddles will be working toward these metrics, so it makes sense they should see them here if need be," adds Sofia.

"Sofia, remind me again how tiered huddles work," says Diana.

"We're setting the example here with the weekly corporate huddle. We expect everybody in this room to have similar meetings with their staffs, maybe a day earlier to review their own functional metrics and discuss problems in their areas. With that information, we can appropriately update the corporate metrics for this meeting and bring up issues where help is needed. And, of course, we expect supervisors or first-level managers to do the same thing so that results can roll up from the frontline to the functional huddle, and issues can rise to the next level if help is needed for their resolution."

"I like the idea of rolling things up, eventually to our level, with everybody engaged," says Junior.

"Hopefully, most issues get resolved before they ever get to your level, Junior," says Sofia. "But I want to stress that things don't only roll up. Help, recommendations, questions must also roll down to make this effective."

"So are we all responsible for this roll-down process?" asks Diana.

"Of course, and it follows the same channels," concludes Sofia. "It's not only how we manage down to the frontline, but also how we exhibit support and respect for everyone along the way. You'll be surprised how much easier some aspects of your job will become when you've got the support and engagement of people both above and below you."

***

The t-shirt initiative had enthused more volunteers than needed for development of the R&D product creation process (PCP), so to leverage everybody that wished to be involved, several teams were formed to detail out and make initial improvements to the subprocesses. Representatives from each team integrated all the PCP subprocesses and summarized their work in a value-stream map (VSM) of the entire PCP. Today the same representatives meet with some project managers and Volta team members around the VSM, which is posted on the wall of Emilio's old office. Together they intend to take the work on the PCP to the next level. Ricardo starts the meeting by summarizing the progress to date.

"The Volta team initially made a high-level map of the PCP that we used to match business needs with capacity and to make sure that work is sufficiently staggered to avoid pileups. The team set a cadence based on the business need and boosted the capacity of our bottleneck process (prototype) to meet the cadence. Now we must ensure that the upstream process—*engineering*—can also meet the cadence. But before we look at resource needs for engineering, we want to improve the process—no need to assign more staff to produce waste. I think we've gathered enough input and details to attempt to improve this process."

"We're looking for 100 percent on-time delivery and a 50 percent reduction in cycle time, right?" asks Gina. "So what comes first: speed or on-time delivery?"

"What do you think?" replies Ricardo.

"Hmmm. I remember from the training that if you don't deliver, it doesn't matter how efficient you are. I'm guessing that also applies to speed."

"Correct again, Gina. But this doesn't mean that we first optimize the process solely for delivery—some of the principles apply to both delivery and speed. When we say delivery comes first, it means that we won't trade off delivery for speed."

"Since we're starting with delivery, what principles are most likely to help?" asks Bart.

"Two good examples are scheduling to capacity and loading every process at only 70 percent of its capacity to accommodate surprises," offers Ricardo.

"It also helps to set up and follow a standard process that is very predictable," adds Sofia, who has joined the meeting.

"Thanks, Sofia," says Ricardo. "And as you can see, I've also invited Giaccomo Quercia to give you all a refresher on the principles that likely apply to the work at hand today."

"What are examples of principles then to achieve our speed targets?" asks Serfino.

"I actually wanted this team, after today's training, to come up with your own list of principles that apply, but, since you've asked, let me share a very simple roadmap I've used before," says Ricardo, walking over to the whiteboard and starting to draw. "First, we should overlap all activities as much as possible; I understand we can't start drawings before we are finished with calculations, but we don't need to wait until all calculations are finished."

Serfino and the others nod, recognizing the practicality of that.

"After we overlap, we need to recreate the critical path and apply the principles of TOC[1] to the critical path, just as we applied it to our bottleneck before."

Ricardo waits for everyone to digest the information, then points to the VSM and the activities on the critical path: "First, we remove all waste and constraints from the critical path. After that, we make sure that everything is delivered to the critical path when it's needed. The critical path should never wait. And then we should look at investments and improvements to make the critical path even faster."

"That's easy: we just double the staff," says Johnny Torto.

"That would be one way to do it," confirms Ricardo with a look of dissatisfaction. "But before we invest, I challenge you to first apply what you learned or will learn again from the lean training."

"But even when we do all of this, something else could turn into the critical path, right?" comments Alexandra. "Something currently not on the critical path."

"You paid good attention in the class, Alexandra. Yes, if we see that happen, we deal with that new path the same way. And once we are happy with the critical path, I want you to think about the process as a relay race. The project is the baton, and the runners are the engineers or other contributors."

"We would surely drop that baton," chuckles Serfino.

"Maybe, and there may be times when the runner with the baton has to wait at the handover because the next runner is busy doing other things. Although you shouldn't run a 1,500-meter race while simultaneously competing in a relay event."

Everybody laughs at Ricardo's illustration.

"So I challenge you to think about getting the process to where there are no stoppages, nice continuous flow, and good handovers."

"Can one runner carry two or three batons and hand them off in succession?" asks Johnny.

"No. One project per person. Single-piece flow," interjects Gina.

"I understand that we make projects wait if we multitask," says Bart. "But single-piece flow will never happen. As long as I've worked here, we always worked on at least four projects at the same time to make sure everybody is busy."

"If we had to have waiting, I'd prefer to have the engineer wait. Rather than move to a new project, we can keep the engineer busy with filler tasks that can be parked as soon as new critical project work arrives," says Ricardo. "The cost of an engineer waiting is likely to be much less than the cost of delay for a project. Single-piece flow is the fastest way to execute tasks. It will take some effort to get there."

"It's Little's Law," states Giacomo. "Cycle time is equal to work-in-process divided by throughput. Cycle time will always be minimized by minimum WIP. The WIP is one if we apply it to an individual; it should be the minimum possible if we apply it to a process or a system."[2]

"And to keep WIP low for a process, we only start a new iteration when another one has been finished," says Stella. "It's called 'pull.'"

"Wait a moment," interrupts Giovanni. "That's not how we pull in the plant. We don't start a new bike when another one comes off the assembly line. We have a separate pull kanban between every step in the process, and we have a small inventory buffer between the steps, so nobody ever runs out of work."

Ricardo watches the discussion, pleased with the level of engagement: "What you describe, Giovanni, is like running a relay race and stacking batons between the runners in case the one baton to arrive is delayed. It's a popular pull method and widely used. But I prefer that we 'flow when we can, pull when we must.' And I challenge you to design the process for smooth flow at the handoffs between all subprocesses. Then we only need one pull signal—to start a new iteration."

"Why do we need a pull at all—why not just start eight new PCP iterations every week?" asks Serfino.

"That would only keep the work in process at a minimum if there are no fluctuations," replies Ricardo. "Our approach deals with reality: if the process that sets the pace—in our case the bottleneck prototype shop—slows down for some reason, we throttle the start of new work, and if prototype speeds up, we start more."

"But we have short and long iterations," says Gina. "When one finishes, which one starts next? The long ones first?"

"I can help with that," says Sofia. "It's always the one with a 'need-to-start date' that is the closest to the planned date. Of course, assuming a long and short iteration have the same finish dates, the longer iteration will have a much earlier start date. It's like what occurs in a well-run restaurant kitchen. Some dishes for a table are intentionally started as late as possible so it can go warm on the plate with dishes that take longer. If five people order five different dishes, the fastest dish doesn't come to the table early. The kitchen starts the fastest one the latest so that all dishes come out together."

"And how do we actually know when it's time to start a new iteration?" questions Johnny. "Will a bell ring?"

"That's what kanbans are for," says Alexandra, annoyed. "You must have missed that in the class. And I assume whenever a new iteration needs to start the kanban is given to the first engineer in the process."

Johnny gives her an apologetic look. "I'm sorry, but a lot of this is new to me." A few others give Johnny an empathetic look since they, too, appear challenged by the concept.

"Giacomo will go over kanbans a bit today, and we'll discuss them more when we begin to apply them," says Sofia, sensing the anxiety.

"But how does this make us faster?" questions Alexandra. "We used fixed amounts of time to calculate the start of the iterations. So if I work faster and finish the work ahead of time, I sit on my thumbs and the project waits until the next person is ready. What's so lean about that?"

"Alexandra, if you or any of your colleagues finish work early, please bring it to the attention of your managers and help them reduce the iteration times. And maybe you can help the team to create a formal process for continuous cycle-time reduction."

"I see another problem with single-piece flow," comments Bart. "A particular engineer always has to be free when it's time to start a new iteration. It's not as if everybody can do any kind of work."

"Why is that?" asks Sofia.

"We know *our* work—we all work differently," says Johnny. "I couldn't do the work of Serfino. If I could, I could jump in when he gets overloaded. But there is some work that only a very few engineers know how to do, and they're unlikely to share their secrets with anybody else."

Ricardo sits up straight, looks around the room at everyone, and speaks clearly and sternly: "This is where we have to talk about standard work. Granted, there are rare special tasks. But except for those, we should establish the best methods and have everybody follow those standards. That way many engineers are able to do the same task. It creates predictability, flexibility, quality, and speed."

Many engineers try to avoid Ricardo's gaze.

"And most importantly, standard work helps us identify deviations and problems so we can make improvements. I understand the concerns about creativity and wanting to hold tight to your special skills, but I trust that going forward this is a non-issue for this team."

Bart holds up both arms as if to say, "I surrender." Others nod, signaling that they'll get on board.

"Thanks for a lot of good questions and comments," says Ricardo in a more casual tone. "It's time to get to work now. But before I turn it over to Giacomo, I want to note that Caroline will chair this effort. She may split you up in small groups to work on details and schedule regular integration meetings where your suggestions are aligned so that they work together to create a smooth flow. She'll also remind you to look at the activities behind the bottleneck—testing and analysis. Any questions?"

"What are we going to do with all the time we'll save?" asks Gina.

"I'll let the team answer that question," says Ricardo with a grin, pleased with the optimism.

***

Because Rebecca Sabrese came to Davanti with a strong background in retail bicycle sales, Marco asked her to take the lead on the Toricelli project, which is exploring options to rent, lease, and finance bikes as well as market used racing bikes. For a few weeks she's been looking into sales ideas and pricing models. Charles from finance has offered to verify her numbers once they're drafted and assist with banks.

Today Rebecca sits with Marco to go over what's she's learned and where she may need assistance.

She immediately jumps to a lack of data, specifically marketing research: "What kind of resources do we have for marketing studies?"

Marco explains how Davanti has traditionally done market research: "We develop bikes for the best riders in the world, and then we sell them to anybody who can spend the money to buy them. People want to ride what the pros ride. And we develop our bikes with the pros. They provide the input, test the bikes, etc. But for our consumer products, we commission the market research if needed. Or we use our own associates: Most people who work here are bike enthusiasts. They ride their bikes on weekends, even to work, and they have access to the shops to do bike development on their own rides. They're developers and consumers like me. We also *try* to stay close to the dealers who know quite well what they can sell. But I have to admit that when it comes to getting in the heads of dealers and observing consumer preferences, we may have a gap. So what do you suggest that we do?"

Rebecca concedes that Davanti is probably doing appropriate research with the pros for their racing lines, but her retail expertise tells her that Davanti needs closer contact with all of its customers. "At my old job, I would personally call recent buyers and ask about their experiences with their bikes purchases," she tells Marco. "I'd then try to make improvements to their purchase experience and pass the information about the bikes to the manufacturers. Here, I'd probably pass it on to you or Joe, and you can share it where needed. I'd like to formalize the entire process."

"We do have a call-in and online support line for feedback and complaints, and we take those discussions very seriously, but I like your idea of calling the new owners after a few weeks and asking for feedback. It's proactive and isn't slanted toward those with bad experiences. Keep pursuing the idea. What else have you discovered?"

"It's what I haven't discovered: There isn't much history or knowledge at Davanti about the Toricelli opportunities. There were a few rough-draft agreements with dealers from years ago, but those never went anywhere. Others in the market have made these services work, but that doesn't necessarily mean the ideas are good for Davanti."

"So, Rebecca, what's the most critical question you need answered?" asks Marco, now very comfortable with the innovation excellence approach and how to communicate it.

"I initially thought there was a critical volume of sales that we needed, but with such little overhead and fixed cost, the expense is likely proportional to the revenue. I think we could find customers, but I wonder how much they're willing to pay for each option. And I also have no idea what options customers would prefer: rent, lease, finance, or buy used."

"So why don't we ask them?"

"I could try to set up an experiment at the store of my former employer, but I'm not sure they would go for that."

"Or I could take you to one of our Davanti dealers in town. You have enough sales experience that when a customer walks in the door, you can engage them in a discussion on renting, leasing, financing, and buying used bikes—you start learning and tell us what you find out."

"The dealer would kill me if I started selling only our own bikes in their store."

"On the contrary," responded Marco. "We explain to the dealer that you are there only to learn about new business models and that they would be the first to get a crack at that new offering. It can also enhance their standing as having a tighter relationship with Davanti."

"OK. I'll give that a try. Get me in contact with the dealers, and I'll set it up."

Notes

1. Theory of constraints.
2. J.D.C. Little, *A Proof for the Queuing Formula: L = λW*, Operations Research, Massachusetts Institute of Technology, Cambridge, MA, 1961.

Chapter 24

New Ways of Leading and Managing

Just like half a year ago, Junior parks his Camry behind Marcel's Maserati Quattroporte in front of Trattoria di Giorgio. On this early autumn evening, he's reminded of how difficult work seemed last spring. He walks inside the restaurant and is directed to the veranda where Marcel sits at the same small table overlooking hills and vineyards.

"Hello, Fausto," greets Marcel. "I hope this table is OK. It's still plenty warm and beautiful out here."

"It's fine," says Junior. "Good to see you."

"I'm sorry that Martina could not join us. It's been a while since I've seen her. But since Luci had to take care of business in Milano, we'll have to do."

"Martina sends her best. She wanted to be here, but she's teaching a ceramic workshop tonight. One of those classes for tourists. You know, they make something that will remind them of their time in Italy while they have wine, cheese, and salumi during the class."

"That sounds interesting. But isn't that dangerous with the kiln and all?"

"No, not at all. They don't get to fire their pieces; Martina does that for them once they've been completed."

"Well, give her my best. Maybe next time."

The waitress had approached, waiting for an opportunity to take a drink order. She senses a pause in their conversation, steps forward, and asks, "Signore Ricco, Signore Davanti. Welcome. It's good to see you both again. Can I get you a drink or appetizer?"

"It's good to see you, Giada," says Marcel. "For now, I'll have an Aperol."

"The same, please," says Junior, raising two fingers.

"I'll be back with them shortly. Sorry to interrupt."

"It really is nice to be back here with you. . . . So how are you, Fausto? You look a little weary tonight. Life is supposed to be easier for you now."

"Just a little tired today."

"Maybe it's all that excitement from the Tour de France. I saw you on TV shaking hands with the French president. You're courting the right people these days."

"I didn't see that."

"It was on France 2. You and the president were in the background when the camera panned to show some of the bikefest activities. But anyway, congratulations on such a great win. You can take that to the bank."

DOI: 10.4324/9781003231837-24

"Nothing really to take to the bank. The Tour takes more cash than it delivers."

"I doubt that. You can't buy that kind of publicity. Think of the value it adds to your company, my friend. Remember the big picture."

"I don't see that in any of my metrics, Marcel. Sofia didn't tell me about that one."

"You've got me, there," says Marcel, laughing. "How was your vacation in Sicily? I hope you haven't settled on a villa yet. Your options get bigger and better by the day with the progress you are making at Davanti."

"It was wonderful. The girls and their families joined us for a week. I wanted to just stay there. And if things continue at Davanti the way they're going now, I may be able to retire on the job soon."

"What do you mean?"

"The new organization and the way we seem to work with huddles and standup meetings have reduced my workload so much that I feel idle half of the time. I've been hanging out in the training classes, which I really enjoy by the way."

"So you've learned my secret. How do you think I can manage several companies at the same time?"

"Sofia says she's going to put me to work again. What do you think that's about?"

"I'm sure she was talking about the stuff good lean leaders do: stay current while showing humility and respect for people."

"Yes, I know the terms."

Giada returns with two Aperol, a basket of bread, and a bowl of giardiniera, and sets them on the table. "Here you are, gentlemen. Please let me know when you'd like to order. I'll be nearby."

Junior and Marcel thank the waitress, take their glasses, and jointly say, "Saluti."

"I'm surprised you've so quickly reached the point at Davanti where you feel as if you have time on your hands," says Marcel. "Some companies try and never get there. It has a lot to do with the person at the top. You. I assume that assigning crossfunctional or value-stream responsibilities worked out well. You've pushed technical and operational responsibility down to the level of the highest competency—but you still have the right to know what's going on, and you still hold the power over important decisions. The money and the liabilities are still yours."

"Yes, we're getting there, but that's also been tricky, and I can't quite get my head around how to proceed. Do I wait for people to tell me what I have the right to know? If I probe, does it look like I don't trust them."

"And if you asked, you'd get a long report or PowerPoint presentation that fails to capture what you really need to know, and it wouldn't make things any easier. If I want to know what's really going on, I do gemba walks, one-on-one meetings, skip-level discussions. I go see for myself. I talk to the people who do the work and get the facts that I need. And I do it with humility and respect for the frontline employees and their superiors."

"Wouldn't managers think I'm second-guessing them? Inquiring behind their backs?"

"It all depends on how you do it. If you rarely go out or act like you're on a witch hunt or an inquisition, they probably will think that. But if you *regularly* go with humility, curiously observe, and assume everybody acts with integrity and with the right intent, that will not happen."

"So how do you make time for that?"

"Well, you've already told me that you've got half your day open."

"I was being a bit facetious."

"OK. I have my standard work laid out for every day. In the morning, I like to do gemba walks and attend huddles on the floor. Then I have my own huddles. After lunch, I have one-on-one meetings with direct reports. Later in the afternoon, I have my calls with the leadership of the different companies. And at least one half-day a week, I meet with a larger group in one of my companies where I engage them in how we can improve the business, the company, work on succession planning, things like that. If you don't make it a standard for yourself, you'll quickly get absorbed again by all the details that you shouldn't be involved in. And I always keep 20 percent of my time open for unforeseen things that require my attention, like it or not."

"That sounds easy, but I'm sure it takes a different kind of discipline."

"It does, but it's easy to get used to."

"But how do I not lose control through all of this. My right to know only goes so far."

"Good point, Fausto. You still hold people accountable. Empowerment with accountability. If somebody proposed a course of action to you, and you both agreed that is the way to do it, that person is accountable to deliver as you agreed."

"But things happen, right? Unforeseen events?"

"Then the person is responsible to let you know. They may suggest a different course of action, or you both may agree on a different deliverable for that person. But remember, you may still have to coach the person or help when needed. And even the best make mistakes. But enough with coaching and accountability, how is my favorite product going?"

"I don't know much about Maseratis," says Junior with a grin.

"You know what I'm talking about: the ski bike. Where's it at?"

"Oh, that one. I'm told it will soon be ready for the gate at which we decide to invest money for technology development."

"That's good news, Fausto. I'm pleased to hear that."

"Do you want to come by and see it, or I can send you a report?"

"Fausto, you guys are the experts. I trust you on this. Today, I just want to congratulate you on how quickly you're pulling this Davanti transformation off. You know, in a successful transformation, leaders have to change first—and you deserve a perfect score of 10 for that, my friend."

"Thank you, Marcel. That means a lot coming from you," replies Junior seriously. He then grabs a piece of bread, smears some giardiniera on it, and takes a bite. "You know, in the spring I would have thought six months was like an eternity. But the time has gone by so fast. . . . Let's call Giada over; I'm starved. I've been thinking about their orecchiette with sausage and broccoli all day."

***

Carolina Petrale has handled the administration of the visual planning room—called "Bike Operation Management" or "BOM" within Davanti. Since she took the assignment, Joe and the PMs (Mo, Gina, Stella, Roberto Rapa, Pablo Norte, and William Chen) have spent a lot of time there with her as they got organized. Carolina enlisted Gina's help for the room's administration for the first couple of months, and plans are to transfer that role to a technician from the prototype shop once the room is beyond its growing pains. Gina also is documenting the process and the lessons learned for a playbook that she will write.

The BOM is a reflection of the new bike portfolio and the resulting product roadmap. Although it took a long time to get them right, Joe is happy with the outcome. "Nobody knows how long our Italian sculptors took to create their masterpieces," he likes to say. "All that matters is that the final product looks perfect."

The new portfolio is theoretically capable of delivering according to the corporate goals and with optimum results. Joe is proud that every new product is projected to generate significant revenue and that the total value of the portfolio has doubled under his tenure. His confidence is not subdued by the fact that some of his colleagues still wait for the proof. To date, there is nothing tangible, only the portfolio translated by Joe and his team into the new product roadmap for the next three years out with the estimated number of iterations required to deliver the goods.

Taking their input from the roadmap, the PMs put a tag on the planning board for every needed iteration as far out as practical. Gina encouraged them to reserve the space early, but everybody understands that things may still change significantly before the prototypes are built, and that the iteration estimates may be on the high side. But Gina insists that once a project is through the PCP gate, the dates and the need for prototypes should be very well defined and few if any last-minute changes will be needed. She holds everybody strictly to the rule that when work has started in engineering, no change to the timeline or targets can be made.

The new board not only shows the iterations needed from the prototype shop but also the ones needed from the manufacturing plant in Taiwan. The plant board looks identical to the prototype board, except that there is no fixed capacity limit for the plant. Due to the upcoming launch of two new bike lines, the teams expect five sets of prototypes per week from the plant. The Davanti product release standard requires that a representative sample of the new bikes—in each size and type with final paint and components—is sent from Taiwan to Fumane for inspection, final testing, and assessment of appearance. The plant has more than enough capacity to provide the samples, but prototype orders often get pushed back in favor of regular production tickets.

Luca has hired a few temps and scheduled overtime, but the project managers still have been scrambling to fit all tags in the space available for the prototype plant. Since the process is still relatively new, Gina makes sure that for at least the first two months all tags are appropriately staffed to ensure on-time delivery of the prototypes from both the plant and the local shop.

For today's meeting—the first companywide session—project managers have made all problems visible on the board. A large arrow indicates the current week. The tags to the left of the arrow (past weeks) are marked with a red "X" when the delivery date was missed and a green "√" for those that were delivered on time. The tags in the future do not have marks yet, but some are turned 45 degrees to indicate that there is a problem to be discussed in the meeting. All tags show the name of the project, name of the project manager, reason for prototypes, and both start and delivery dates; many also have handwritten notes.

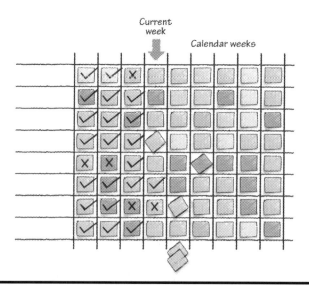

Figure 24.1   Prototype Visual Planning Board.

Joe leads the BOM meetings, attended by the PMs as well as most functional managers and even some directors; since this is the first such event at Davanti, many want to become familiar with the process. Some managers have also brought staff. Ricardo comes with staff members Bart, Carolina, and Luca.

Gina reminds the group that every problem is clearly visible and that eventually it should not take more than 10 seconds to see all the problems on the board. But, she warns, it may take a little longer to resolve them because "today I can see a lot of them."

Joe suggests starting with the missed deliveries. "I want to know how I or somebody else in this room can help to get those back on track. When will they ship?"

Constantine apologizes for the delay and says they all now have revised dates. As he reads the new delivery dates, Gina writes them on the tags and moves the tags to the appropriate week. "I have authorized overtime until we catch up," he says.

"Will all be shipped express delivery?" Marco asks.

Matteo, the new supply-chain manager, confirms that they will, "but I hope as this process matures, we can ship through regular channels."

Joe wonders what would have happened if they did not have this meeting and the visibility it created. In the past he would have found out three weeks from now, and the problem would have been solved in Junior's office by Junior. Today, Junior isn't even in the meeting. Joe grasps the importance of this meeting and the opportunity it offers to catch all problems early when there is still time to fix them before larger consequences occur.

"Thanks, Constantine and Matteo," says Joe. "Please tell the PMs immediately if any further delays occur. So let's look at the prototype shop."

The board has a few red X marks for missed deliveries in the prototype shop.

"We had some late shipments of components from the US and Japan," reports Luca. "That's why I assigned one of our foremen to find the root cause of the problem. It may just be a temporary problem in customs. But we need to be certain."

"Good, what is next Gina?" presses Joe.

"We should now discuss all the tags for the coming weeks that are turned 45 degrees on the board and see if anybody here can help with the issues," advises Gina. "Let's start with the samples we need from the plant."

Constantine promises to use overtime as long as needed to get all samples shipped, but the discussion about the bikes from the prototype shop takes longer to resolve. Several PMs want their prototypes all in the same week, and there simply is not enough capacity. In one case, Luca promises additional overtime, and for another they agree to move a less-critical tag to an open spot a few weeks out.

"Any other problems we must discuss today?" asks Joe.

A few PMs bring up issues, all of which can be handled with the help of somebody present in the meeting.

"Claudia, any concerns on your side?" questions Joe.

"I can only sell bikes when they are in the store, and I'll let you know when sales are affected," she says matter-of-factly.

"I'm sure you will," replies Joe.

Marco helps out: "We are working with stores and dealers. They're already making room for the new bikes. I think we've never been more ready to sell than we are now. All advertisements—print and online—are ready for distribution, and I'll release them in the coming weeks as Ricardo confirms the product release dates."

"We'll also be adding visibility in this room of the technical release schedule of future products," says Bart. "That will alert us to potential problems much earlier in the process."

"Very good," says Joe. "I'm really impressed with this meeting today. I've been at Davanti for more than 15 years. We've never had so many early indicators of potential problems, and, more important, the confidence that we have the right countermeasures in place to resolve them. Without this meeting today, we'd all be arguing in Junior's office when the complaints from dealers and customers started to roll in. This is a great start."

"I see how this process can help us avoid big problems in the coming weeks," admits Claudia. "But I'm not celebrating until the right bikes are in the right stores at the right time with the right price tags on them. It would be the first time that's happened—in my time at Davanti, anyway—and I'm still holding my breath today."

***

Mo and his team—Sergio, Serfino, and Alexandra—meet in the obeya room that they had created for the Leonardo project. Every day they meet for 10 minutes as they did during the first phase of the project. Tony Donatello, an engineer, recently joined the team because of the extended scope. Tony had checked out some of the hydraulic-drive options after the first hackathon. Bolaji joins as an observer.

The obeyas at Davanti are not full rooms, but rather areas defined by large whiteboard walls that surround a table and a shelf. The walls are covered inside and outside with data, sketches, drawings, and writings. The shelf contains samples the team needs to discuss. The small table in the middle is covered with other aids, such as technical papers, markers, and additional samples. The team continues using the sprint boards that track the status of activities—work to be done, in progress, and completed—only now there are a lot more tags.

Walking to the meeting, Mo considers all the project had been through in recent weeks:

Mo had started his new PM assignment with a lot of motivation and excitement. He spent more than a week educating himself about the new scope of the project. He knew a lot about gears already, but he had to catch up on hydraulics and the means to transfer power from the gear box to the rear wheel. He talked to Tony, the new guy, and some of Tony's colleagues who worked on the hydraulic power transmission and was impressed with all the work they had done. They had explored options with key hydraulic component manufacturers that supply a variety of industries, including the air and space industry where weight also is a big concern. Hydraulic-powered bicycles were not new to them—they had explored hydraulic drives on and off, but they had never looked at pro racing bicycles. They contributed many good ideas, one of which caught Mo's attention: a two-wheel-drive option for time-trial and off-road bikes. He also was fascinated with the concept of a hydraulic accumulator: on a rider's descent, the hydraulic motor would help with braking, and energy would be stored in a pressure vessel (accumulator) and could be reused for a boost on a rider's next climb. Mo had also come to appreciate what Sergio had learned about the medical shafts, and he was happy Ricardo had prevented him from scrapping the idea.

After Mo's project passed the TCP gate, he spent an extra day making sure that sufficient prototype shop capacity was available for the technology creation process of the project. Ricardo had just added that requirement to the gate checklist. But when Mo showed his development plan to Ricardo, his excitement was dampened. Mo wanted to split the development tasks into hydraulic and mechanical and vary one component at a time as he had learned in school. He intended to test a couple of gears with every transmission option from the hackathon and see what works the best. Ricardo took him a step back.

"Mo, what do we, our suppliers, universities already know about what you are suggesting to develop here? And where is the knowledge gap?"

Ricardo also had suggested that Mo talk to the knowledge manager Bolaji. The two later identified what knowledge was available, mostly in the head of Davanti employees, and what gaps had to be closed. Mo and his team concluded that the biggest knowledge gaps were around the gear mechanisms. They were much larger than the gaps surfaced about the drive mechanisms.

After Mo had reviewed the knowledge gaps with Ricardo, he had new confidence to propose a significantly reduced number of experiments.

"Mo, I like your diligence identifying the knowledge gaps, but how do you know that the best option is already among those you have at the moment? Maybe there are better gears and shafts out there. And could mixing hydraulic and mechanical components be a better solution?" When Ricardo saw Mo's helpless expression, he suggested that he talk to Stella, who had just finished set-based concurrent engineering training.

Mo quickly followed up with Stella, who explained that Mo might want to consider a much bigger design space to start—a larger slate of options and concurrent experiments to see how they interact together. Mo recognized the approach as design of experiments (DOE), which he also had learned in school. With DOE, he could even establish correlation equations and draw tradeoff curves. He was certain that Ricardo would be pleased.

When Mo showed Ricardo his comprehensive DOE plan—with many more options and the plans for all possible permutations—his mentor again frowned: "There are more than 3,000 experiments here, Mo. How long will this take, and how many resources will it require?"

"I thought we wanted to explore many options and their interactions," explained Mo. "They don't all need an experiment; we can do some of them by modeling and calculations, and maybe we can do a simplified Taguchi experiment.[1]"

"I appreciate that you considered modeling and calculations. But do you think all the options you considered will be in the final product?"

"Certainly not."

"Then do we need to carry inferior options all the way through all permutations of a DOE?"

"We don't know enough yet to eliminate them."

"Correct. But can we find out which ones we can eliminate fast and with minimum effort? Maybe some options are prohibitively expensive; others may have issues with weight or fit. Maybe some could be eliminated based on other constraints using calculations or modeling. And can we plan the experiments so that a lot of options will drop out in the first round."

"That makes total sense," agreed Mo, "just like we did when we started the project with critical questions. But how do we learn about interactions without the full DOE? And I also want to get correlation equations or knowledge curves out of the DOE."

"As for the interactions, we don't need to know all interactions—the important ones can be worked out in integration events where we build bikes or subassemblies from the most promising options and test the assemblies. But if you need more data about interactions or if you want to generate a knowledge curve to close a gap, by all means, run the experiments you need for that. And remember, even if you don't need the interactions, running experiments in parallel is a lot faster than running them concurrently."

"But in the first phase, we ran things in sequence to manage the risk—highest risk first, and stop early if needed."

"Good point. There is a time for each. At this time, what do you think is the highest risk piece of this project?"

"Sergio received some good data on the drive cable. A lot of knowledge is available on the other power transmission concepts. So that leaves the gear mechanism as the highest risk. We probably even need the gears with the hydraulic-drive options."

"I agree, Mo. So how can we make sure the gears get enough attention in the first set of experiments? Maybe you can bring along just a few transmission options to make sure you have something to test the gears with."

"Sure, I can see that helping," concluded Mo.

After his meeting with Ricardo, Mo proceeded to work with the team and Diana's staff in procurement to identify as many good gear-mechanism suppliers as possible. They identified the best partners to work with (eight in total) and sent functional specs to them as well as a request for the vendors to submit samples and data. Diana insisted they include at least one current component supplier to keep them interested in Davanti innovation.

The team was convinced they had enough drive-mechanism options to test the gears in the first set of experiments, and also determined the internal hub, rear-gear mechanism (used by Vinnie) was adequate at this time. They parked other good ideas that had come out of the hackathon to focus on the gear mechanisms.

Mo developed the plan for the testing of the gear mechanisms—including torque, strength, durability, friction—made drawings for fixtures, and set minimum performance criteria. He ran the plan by the team, and they agreed with his approach. Mo then spent considerable time on a comprehensive plan for the first set of experiments, applying project management software and assigning a person to every task. Mo told his team and boss, Bolaji, he'd review the plan for experiments at the next team meeting.

At today's Leonardo meeting, Mo projects his Gantt charts on the flat screen and goes through the tasks with the team. He has already created the sprint boards for the first few weeks and asks his team to create the tags according to his plan. "Every morning at 8:30, we'll move the tags. This way, I'll see if we make sufficient progress or if I need to change the plans." Despite leaving soon for Lausanne and lean workshops at the École Polytechnique Fédérale, Mo takes his share of tasks. He plans to work in the evenings, and he hopes his schedule will permit him to call into the daily meetings.

Alexandra and Serfino accept their assignments without much enthusiasm but have no comments. Their tasks are largely a continuation of the work they did before on this project. Sergio, however, does not look happy when he sees his assignments; he'd never worked on a project team, and he did not know what to expect. Tony asks a lot of questions about the plan and his tasks, but Mo confidently addresses all the issues. It's unclear to Mo if Tony agrees with his plans. Bolaji says little during the meeting, which Mo takes as an endorsement of his plans.

"So why don't you get your tags organized on the scrum boards," instructs Mo, "and we'll discuss them tomorrow."

***

Ricardo had formally assigned Gina to oversee the work on the crack problems discovered in the Tour de France. Several of her projects (like Darvin) had been discontinued when the project portfolio was revised. She was looking forward to the assignment, in addition to her work on the ski bike and other continuous-improvement (CI) projects.

With Ricardo's coaching, Gina follows a standard process and developed an A3, which Ricardo reviews with her on a regular basis. This typically takes only 15 minutes given the ability of the A3 to communicate details rapidly, so Gina (like others) just walk up to Ricardo's desk when they see him there, which is usually after 4:00 pm, unless he's at soccer practice with his kids.

Most have embraced the A3 process, thanks in part to Anika conducting a solid A3 problem-solving training program for the office (similar to the training used in the plant). The training is based upon *Managing to Learn*,[2] but Davanti added a few important parts like control plans and formal sharing and documenting of new knowledge. After the initial classroom session, the A3 training is reinforced by coaching people as they actually use the process on a real problem. Ricardo always makes time for the A3 reviews because, for him, an A3 is not only about solving problems but also about coaching and developing people. He uses a catchball process to get agreement on deliverables. In this process, Ricardo tosses his expectations to the associate who either runs with the ball or tosses it back if adjustments or help are needed. When the associate keeps the ball, Ricardo holds the associate accountable to either meet the deliverables or to indicate when more adjustments are needed.

Ricardo already had several A3 reviews with Gina, who has done a great job documenting the background and the current state of the problem. Her team confirmed with calculations and finite element modeling that the bike design is sound, so the team has documented all the changes made since the bike design was released. It looks like the problem is isolated to bikes made in Taiwan, and the cracks were so far only found in bikes used in the Tour de France. Her A3 problem statement reads: "Small cracks occurred in the mounting area of the front derailleur in the Tour de France on bikes made in Taiwan."

With the help of team member Dong Chen, a manufacturing engineer in Taiwan, the team has used a fishbone diagram to list all possible causes related to materials, machine, manpower, and methods. For every main cause, they ask "Why" as many times as needed to dig down to root causes, which are recorded on the diagram.

Recent discussions between Ricardo and Gina were mostly about the targets of the project, not so much about the root causes. Gina and the team had initially proposed a completion date of late November, but Ricardo could not agree with that date: bikes were supposed to arrive in the stores by then. After the team narrowed the problem down, Gina proposed a November 1 completion date. Ricardo had asked if there was anything he could do to further move up the date, and the team requested more lab time and additional resources in the plant. Ricardo complied. ("I'll do my part; now the ball is back in your court.") Gina then committed to an October 15 completion date. ("Yes, I know you'll hold me and the team accountable to meet that October date, and I think we can do that.")

For today's A3 review, Gina comes with fresh information from the team: Taiwan had to change suppliers for an accelerator they use in the carbon-fiber resin, and tests in the Fumane lab determined that the new resin needs more time to cure than the current Davanti spec requires. The team believes the cracks are caused by material weakness due to under-cure combined with the high torque in the mountain stages of the professional races.

"We've asked the plant to run experiments with an updated cure," explains Gina. "They'll airfreight the samples and the bikes tomorrow."

"Great, but I hope you didn't put all your eggs into that one basket."

"Of course not. We're pursuing several other potential countermeasures, including reducing the age limit on the carbon fibers used in the bottom bracket and increasing the fabric tension during the winding."

"Very good. How will you test the fixed bikes?"

"We'll run the standard test protocol in the lab. We noticed that most cracked bikes came from one rider: Pasquale Barto. The team knows the tour riders switch gears under much higher torque than average riders or even amateur racers, but Pasquale seems to be the strongest on the team. Johan contacted Pasquale already, and he'll be available to test a couple of the fixed bikes in the Pyrenees during his regular training for the end-of-the-season races. One of our team members will be in the Pyrenees with Pasquale in a few days."

"Gina, that's a great plan. Please see me as soon as you have the results and let me know if anything unexpected happens. Have you thought about the last part of the A3—implementation, control plans, knowledge sharing, and documentation?"

"I'll pencil those in the A3 for our next review."

"I'm looking forward to it. I'll see you in a few days."

***

Junior welcomes Joe, the bicycle product director, into his office for his first one-on-one meeting. Sofia had encouraged Junior to start having the meetings after he complained that he was only seeing staff in huddles or standups or if they had a grievance. She advised him to, first and foremost, explain the purpose of the meetings; listen; learn; let staff guide the agenda; encourage transparency; and offer help as needed. She thinks he should also, at least for a while, ask how strategy deployment is progressing.

"Things are going well," Joe explains. "But I'm guessing you could tell that because I haven't been in your office arguing with my colleagues. And when the bikes are in the stores before Christmas, even Claudia will be happy."

"How do you run a product value stream? You know, you're the first Davanti person tasked with that, and we need to learn from you. We may have more Joe's in Davanti one day."

"I had a very good teacher. Sofia helped me a lot, and I had more than one discussion with the product directors from Fusilli. They shared their standard work for how they manage their value streams."

"So what was your biggest challenge so far?"

"Getting the portfolio right. Making money starts right there. There is no bigger waste than developing the wrong things. But you made things easier for us with the vision of creating value for the customer *and* growing the value of the company. No more of this trying to accommodate all those people with different opinions of what we should do."

"How are you getting along with everybody? I don't hear any complaints."

"You know, that's an interesting question. In the old organization, we always fought because we could never agree; we had to blame somebody when something went wrong. Now we can only blame ourselves. It's very clear to me and all my team that we own this thing, and we get direct feedback for our actions. We make mistakes, but we learn the lessons and move on. But there is something else that I realized: I was always wondering why a small company like Davanti had so many layers and such a complicated decision-making process. I always thought some control was appropriate, but now we're so much faster and make better decisions without the controls."

"No wonder you got better after you stopped bringing every conflict to me. What do I know about many of those issues anyway? I felt like the judge who rules based on the best plaidoyer," jokes Junior. "So how can I help you now?"

"Well, you certainly helped me by hiring Horst. Is it your plan to create a second value stream?"

"That certainly is the plan," notes Junior, "but we need a little more experience first, and I want to see how things develop with Horst? But for now, how do you think the strategy deployment is going?"

"Everybody understands the direct line of sight of their actions to objectives, goals, and our product strategy. They can't forget—we posted them above our visual planning board. And the customer has, indeed, replaced you as the referee. All in all, things are going well. But if you really want to help, please keep Claudia out of my hair for another few months?"

"OK, but I can't promise you much with that. Can I attend your huddles a few times, so I can learn? I will stand in the back."

"Sure, you're welcome any time. And if you have a question, don't hesitate to ask."

"I will do that."

"So, Junior, do you really think we'll get into mountain bikes and electric bikes one day?"

"That's an excellent question. Those are good opportunities for expansion, but there are others: there are many countries where you can't even buy a Davanti racing bike, and our online sales are barely noticeable."

"You're right about both. We should stick our heads together and see how we can explore those opportunities."

"Maybe it's time for another off-site meeting," suggests Junior. "I will have Anna take a look at that."

The meeting ends after 30 minutes as planned on a friendly and cordial tone. Junior is pleased with how it went and looks forward to updating Sofia. He can't remember the last time an important meeting has gone so well.

***

Mo arrives at the École Polytechnique Fédérale de Lausanne (EPFL) on Sunday early afternoon. His workshops, including Lean Project Management, Leading a Lean Transformation, and a few traditional innovation management courses—begin on Monday morning. He stays in a small hotel within walking distance of the EPFL campus. From the hotel, he gets a glimpse of Lake Geneva and the mountains on the other shore. In only a few weeks, fresh snow will begin to bring white caps back to the Alps. The trees are changing, and the colors are brilliant, especially at this time of day as the late sun washes over the mountains.

Mo has been looking forward to the classes and to exploring the beautiful city of Lausanne and its surroundings. He's equally excited about seeing Marie, who is currently working in Montreux—only a half-hour train ride away.

On Sunday late afternoon, he picks up Marie at the train station in downtown Lausanne. They walk along the lake admiring the expensive villas and the mountain range. They dine at a restaurant along the lake shore before Mo walks Marie back to catch her train around 10:00 pm. They share a kiss and make plans to meet in Montreux on Wednesday after Mo's last class of the day.

Mo enjoys his workshops during the day, after which he spends an hour or two on Monday and Tuesday walking to a different section of town and then catches up on work until midnight. Each day, an early morning fog is replaced by crisp late-summer air and blue skies. Wednesday, after his class, Mo drives to Montreux. He meets Marie at a jazz club, where they take in a set and then grab sushi at a nearby restaurant. Marie asks Mo about his classes; she seems genuinely interested, so Mo describes them in great detail. Mo drives her to her hotel; they again share a kiss, and then make plans to meet on Friday at noon back in Lausanne. Mo's classes end on Friday morning, and Marie will take time off.

Meeting near the train station on Friday, they head to the harbor—Le Port d'Ouchy—and nearby park. They have an afternoon cocktail and then take the train up to the old town, where they climb the steps of a 12th-century cathedral for a sunset view over the lake, the French Alps, and the city of Lausanne. They have dinner in old town, and, to Mo's surprise, learns that Marie plans to stay overnight in Lausanne. She had booked a hotel near the train station and checked a bag before Mo showed up. They walk to her hotel and make plans for them both to check out early the following day, hike in the Alps, and spend the evening in Zermatt. When Mo offers to book them rooms, he's advised that "one will do."

Mo picks up Marie, and Saturday morning they park on the outskirts of Zermatt. The town is free of combustion-engine vehicles to protect the mountain views. An electric shuttle takes them to their hotel, where they drop their bags and get a shuttle to the trails. Saturday's hike is breathtaking, with both getting their first view of the Matterhorn. They eat a light lunch of fruit and nuts on the trail, and when they get back to town at sunset they're starved. They find a classic Swiss restaurant near the hotel and share a bottle of wine and fondue. Despite a long day of hiking, they walk through town after dinner, saying little but thinking a lot about the evening ahead.

"You OK if we go back to the hotel?" asks Mo.

"Never been more OK," replies Marie.

Sunday morning, the weather has changed to fog and rain. They sleep in, order breakfast delivered to the room, and try not to think about the week ahead without each other.

Notes

1. A simpler and shorter version of a DOE—originally developed for quality but also popular for product design. Named after Dr. Genichi Taguchi, the Japanese scientist who developed the methodology.
2. John Shook, *Managing to Learn*, Lean Enterprise Institute, Cambridge, MA, 2008.

Chapter 25

Davanti Starts to Look Lean

"Muda, muri, mura" seemed to be the only three words Lee Cheng, the lean expert from Davanti's Taiwan plant, knew. He repeated them constantly, while pointing everywhere in the prototype shop with an angry look on his face. As his tour of the shop continued, he got increasingly angry and said "muda" much louder; sometimes he drew a circle in the air with his hand and said, "All muda; too much muda." Luca quickly understood that Lee had found many opportunities for improvement. When Lee couldn't take it any longer, they sat down.

"So where do we start, Mr. Cheng?" asked Luca.

"Everywhere. We will start Saturday at 6:00 am when nobody is here. You bring a large dump truck, and we take everything out of here that is not absolutely needed for the work. Then we wipe the floor and polish the equipment. Bring buckets and cleaner. On Sunday we will move equipment and create cells. Then . . ."

"Wait a minute, Mr. Cheng. Is this how you did the transformation in the Taiwan plant?"

"Taiwan and many others."

"I'm sure that is a very efficient method, and I recognize that you could do this type of work with your eyes closed, but do we have to do it that way here? Can we do it a little different?"

"How different?"

"I would like to first teach the employees the principles of 5S and waste and make sure they understand why we're doing this. And then *they* can clean *their* workstations, throw away the stuff that is not needed, and shine *their* equipment and so on."

"Too long. That takes much too long."

"But we learned so much about employee engagement in our training. We can't ignore that."

"Workers can get engaged later. Your way will take too long."

Luca imagined what would happen on Monday when Vinnie finds out they threw away half of his stuff and he is now part of a cell. "Mr. Cheng, I'm sorry, but that's not how we do things here in Italy."

"How do you do things?"

"I just explained how: train and engage and then change. And I'm OK if it takes a little longer here because it will also last a lot longer if we do as I suggested."

"OK. You are the boss. And you should call me 'Lee.'"

***

That Saturday, instead of throwing things away, they made plans to engage the employees in the shop initiative. On Monday, they explained the concepts of 5S to several employees and coached them through the steps—sort, straighten, shine, standardize, and sustain.[1]

DOI: 10.4324/9781003231837-25

"Why must a machine shine?" Lee asked everybody. And when there was no answer, he explained: "So you can see when something is wrong. How could you see when your press leaks oil if it is already covered with grease?"

Some technicians stopped by the freshly cleaned workstations and asked questions, and some followed the example right away. After more training and assistance from Lee, technicians set up the frame prototype operation as a cell layout. They moved core-making equipment, cutting tables, assembly stands, the winding machine, and polishing and painting equipment in a U-shape around the perimeter of the curing area and created an operation that resembles an assembly line in a factory. Lee coached the technicians in workflow and related concepts and worked alongside them for improvements every day.

Luca also formed a team to create a replenishing system so they only keep the materials they need in the next 30 minutes at their workstations; the technicians involved taught their colleagues and even appointed an associate to do milk runs a few times a day. The associate walks by all the workstations every 30 minutes, makes a list of what needs to be restocked, and then picks up and delivers all needed supplies so that each person doesn't have to run to the supply room for themselves.

Lee had delayed his return to Taiwan twice—not because the Davanti shop technicians were slow learners, but because he fell in love with Italy. He pronounced every Italian food and wine without accent and continued to expand his vocabulary with every breakfast, lunch, and dinner. He actually grew very fond of his Italian colleagues. He called them "cavalletta" (grasshopper) and made rubbing motions when seeing an associate who needed more learning, saying "wax on, wax off," reminiscent of the movie *The Karate Kid*.[2] Many of the technicians got the joke, and others did not; but they all enjoyed his company and called him "sensei" (teacher).

Lee could not believe how many friends he made in his short time in Fumane. Every evening somebody new would take him home for dinner or to a local restaurant or winery. Lee told them about China, and they taught him about Italy—its history, customs, and food. He was having the time of his life and told everyone he met. He eventually headed back to Taiwan, with all the foods and wines he could get through customs and wonderful memories.

A week after Lee left, Luca was able to stop the overtime and temporary resources in the prototype shop because they could meet the ticket with their existing resources. Soon after that, he told Joe that he would soon have enough capacity for two more iterations, and the PMs looked forward to getting the new capacity filled. They also filled the capacity for iterations of the technology creation process (TCP) and for work of the idea creative process (ICP).

After Lee's departure, Zing Frang, an expert of lean in the lab, arrived from Taiwan. He had led the lean implementation in the Taiwan plant's quality assurance lab and did the same with the test lab in Fumane. He stayed for a week, helping Davanti staff to mimic the improvements that had occurred overseas. He, too, spent time with Davanti staff in the off hours, but he was more homesick than Lee and happy to depart.

Despite the rapid and sometimes dramatic changes in the shop and lab, few engineers and technicians objected. They were engaged and recognized that the improvements made their jobs easier and were keen to keep up the systems that their new friends had helped them install.

***

Although Junior prefers huddles now to manage the day-to-day business, he still holds a 30-minute staff meeting on Mondays to ensure ongoing communication with his team and to discuss strategy and issues that may need the involvement of all his staff. Many see it as an opportunity to discuss recent racing activities—race results during the season and team changes in the offseason. On this day, Junior asks Sofia to kick off the discussion.

"Thanks for all the help establishing the corporate metrics," begins Sofia. "We'll review those at our regular standup, but we have two more important tasks related to them: As we start to measure our improvement, we must remember where we started. Many companies forget to record their starting point, and down the road when leadership asks about how much improvement was made, they must painfully recreate those numbers with little buy-in. That's not too hard to do for financial metrics and cost data, where we have a long history, but it will be difficult for new metrics like people engagement, speed, and delivery. I'm asking all who are responsible for corporate metrics to show the starting point on every chart. Likewise, it's equally important to record the starting point for your functional metrics, too."

The executive team recognizes the rationale of what she is asking, and no one objects.

"What's the other message, Sofia?" asks an impatient Leandro. "You said there were two tasks."

"Change in processes can easily be measured. But the change in behaviors, which I am starting to see, is harder to quantify but certainly no less important. When it comes to behaviors, consistency creates new habits. And remember, behaviors will not change unless leadership consistently demonstrates the new behaviors. And we're not only talking about respect and humility but also good practices, like identifying problems, always looking for root causes, practicing PDCA, etc. I may coach some of you from time to time, but don't wait for me: set the example, coach each other and your associates, and remember to reinforce the right behaviors you see with a 'thank you.'"

"Sofia, I agree that we're on our way to inculcating good, lean behaviors," says Junior. "I'd like for Davanti to be known as much for that as our racing success. Thanks for keeping this front and center. . . . So let's now switch subjects. Ricardo, why don't you go next."

"We are on track with the launch of the two products later this year," reports Ricardo. "We had the design release meeting of the new Primo Veloce amateur line, and the production release for the different PV bikes is underway. Everything about the upgraded Primo Sempre pro line is signed off, except for a problem with the front derailleur mount. I'll give an update when that is released. All new bikes will be released to production in small batches and in the order specified by marketing, a few every week, so we can start production as soon as a model or size clears. We won't wait any more until every single model is tested and inspected. I'm confident that we'll have sufficient inventory for the Christmas selling season."

Everybody looks at Claudia, and when she has no comment, Junior gives the floor to Anika. She reports that three people, two from engineering, had accepted jobs at other companies. She did the exit interviews and found out that all three were recruited for their knowledge about innovation excellence by two noncompeting companies nearby in the province of Verona.

"How's that for a return on our training investment?" ridicules Claudia. "I'm glad I didn't spend my time teaching them."

"You can educate your staff with a chance that you might lose them, or you don't educate them and keep them as they are," says Anika, sharply, weary of Claudia's negativity. "In years past, we had many exit interviews during which people complained about the lack of training and opportunities for advancement."

"I agree with Anika, and if they're worth more to another company than they are to us, then shame on us for letting them get away," says Sofia. "Sure, this can happen in a good transformation, but we're good to report on it, and we can try to get in front of it."

Ricardo comments that one engineer said the new job could better accommodate his family schedule, but also admitted that the lean skills he'd acquired were valued by his new employer. Ricardo adds that none of them actively looked for another job.

"I'll keep a close eye on salary and benefits benchmarks in the area," continues Anika. "I believe we're competitive, but we may need to adjust salary for key employees. What concerns me the most is that all three associates were recruited by agencies, and I hear that calls from headhunters have really increased recently. We get that from time to time, but generally it's one recruiting company working for one of our competitors. This is different. These are different agencies all looking for talent in innovation excellence, and I only found one company in the area who advertises hiring of people with that background. And keep in mind that most of what's known about Davanti's innovation excellence is word of mouth. We've not had any grand announcements or press releases."

"Can we do something about it?" asks Diana. "Is it legal to swipe our employees like that?"

"Where do they get the names?" asks Constantine.

"These days headhunters often get the contacts through social media, but I checked and none of the people who left Davanti had updated their profiles with their skills related to innovation excellence."

"I had a case once where a disgruntled employee gave the name of his boss to a headhunter," says Sofia. "And it's not unusual for one employee to get contacted and then, if they're not interested in a move, mention other employees that might be."

"I got a call from a headhunter," admits Leandro. "I replied to the questions that the recruiter asked me, and then I asked some questions of my own about the legitimacy of the recruiting organization. She said they only call people when they have *validation*—whatever that means. She claims it's when the recruiting company and the target's company both identify an appropriate candidate. She confirmed that someone within Davanti said I fit the profile that she was looking for."

"Maybe Sofia is right," says Anika. "Somebody here could be feeding names to headhunters because they don't like what's going on."

"How can we find that person?" asks Stephano.

"That would only be possible if a headhunter would slip up with the name, but they're professionals; they're not likely to disclose their sources," says Anika.

"We knew there would be some resistance to this initiative," explains Sofia. "Some people still think what we're building here at Davanti is the wrong thing to do, and they believe they do the company and themselves a favor by fighting it with any means at their disposal. I can deal with cases of open resistance, but it's difficult to combat covert resistance. If we're lucky, this person or persons will reveal themselves in other ways. We could then talk to them about their concerns."

"I'm not happy about losing good people for any reason," interjects Junior. "Yet in some ways, it's proof that we're doing the right things here. How much should I be concerned?"

"It's often just an annoyance," says Sofia, "as long as it's not covert resistance from a leadership position—a much bigger problem. That almost derailed an initiative for me. Fortunately, I had a determined internal champion who saved the transformation."

"So what will we do about the calls?" asks Constantine.

"Please don't ask our associates to report the calls," advises Sofia. "The best we can do is to treat our folks right, communicate with them regularly, listen intently, and encourage them to voice all concerns. Maybe the headhunter calls will decline, but don't count on it. Even without anyone leaking information, the word about Davanti's innovation capabilities will get out. Just wait until dealers start getting new bikes and other products on time and their sales start to rise. They'll know we've changed, and people will talk. Consider it a good casualty of innovation excellence."

***

After some coaching, Sofia had suggested that Junior begin his foray into solo gemba walks by parking in the rear of the building, entering though the lab or through the prototype shop, and then walking back to his office. (Junior's office is in the front of the building, and he would typically park at the front entrance and immediately head to his office.) The lab and shop shifts start at 7:00 am, which is about the time Junior comes to work. For the week, he's left his dedicated parking spot empty and parked in the rear. Each day as Junior walked through the test lab or prototype shop, he took a different route and talked with anyone he met along the way.

Today in the lab, he walks by the workstation of Penelope Dicomo. She is around 50 years old, and he watches her tie her apron and put the first bike of the day on her work stand.

"Good morning, Penelope," says Junior, grateful that he remembered her name.

She turns and is stunned: "Good morning, Mr. Davanti. What brings you out here this early. We must have a serious problem. Who screwed up?"

"Nobody screwed up. I'm just taking a different route to my office."

"I heard about that. Some have complained that you're taking their parking spots. You know, we've only seen office people here when there's something wrong. Since you're here personally, it must be really bad."

"Didn't your father work here, Penelope?"

"Yes, he started to work for Mr. Davanti Sr. He's retired now."

"I remember him. How's he doing?"

"His health isn't the greatest, but he's happy. And every time I see him, he tells me stories about when he worked at Davanti. Only good ones; he must have forgotten the bad ones."

"Sorry to hear about his health. How are you doing?"

"Just working. You know, same grind every day."

"I know what your dad used to do here, but what are you doing?"

"I'm the last one to see the bikes that we make or modify, and I make sure everything works perfectly. Then I tune the bike. But I rarely get a good one; most need fixes like this one."

"Fixes? What's wrong? Isn't this a new bike that we just assembled here?"

"It is, but the shifter cable is routed incorrectly, so I need to correct that before I can tune the derailleur."

"How many bikes need adjustment?"

"Too many. You know, the folks here know that Penelope will catch it and fix it. So many don't bother to get it right themselves."

"Looks like many customers would be unhappy without Penelope's magic touch."

"The Davanti team racers, for sure."

"Oh, what do you do for the racers?"

"Same. I'm the last one who gets to see their race bikes. We used to send some bikes to a German tuner, but now we tune them all here. I adjust the brakes, the derailleurs, grease the chains. I adjust the seat, handlebars, and pedals for every rider. Johan sends me this chart," she says, pointing to the wall. "And he calls me every time a rider complains."

"I see Rossa's name there. But it looks like something is crossed out and changed. Is that what Johan called about?"

"No, Johan gave me the original settings, but when I saw Rossa in the Giro on TV, I noticed that he worked awfully hard on the ascents. It looked like his seat was placed too far forward, so I moved it back for the Tour de France. A then when I saw him on TV again in the Tour, he looked so much better."

"Did you tell Johan?"

"No, I'm not looking for trouble. But I discussed it with my supervisor. He said, 'Just do what you think is right, nobody will notice anyway.'"

"So how long have you done this kind of work, Penelope?"

"About 10 years now. I started tuning *all* derailleurs after the Giro incident, and nobody has thrown a bike in a ditch since. I know how to avoid what caused Rossa's problem in the Giro."

"So you've personally been tuning every bike for every pro rider? Did anybody ever call you and thank you for what you're doing?"

"Are you kidding? I only get a call when they think I messed up. Johan is polite about it, but I know his prima donnas threaten to switch brands every time something isn't perfect."

Junior watches Penelope as she fixes and then tunes the bike she has on her stand, asking a few more questions and saying often, "I didn't know that." After a while he thanks her. "Next time I come here, I want to learn how you adjust the derailleurs for the pros so they never malfunction."

"Thanks, Mr. Davanti, for stopping by and showing interest in my work. Sorry I was not too friendly with you at the beginning. I look forward to talking again."

"It was my pleasure, Penelope. Have a good day."

Junior is late for his 8:00 am meeting, and he has at least five phone messages waiting for a reply. Right after the meeting, he calls Johan, who answers on the first ring. The season is winding down, and Johan recognizes Junior's number.

Junior runs an idea by Johan: "Anna can print 'Thank you' notes with the names of every technician who helped prepare the bikes for the Davanti team this season. What do you think about having all the riders sign the cards and send them back?"

"That's a great idea, Junior. Not sure why we didn't think of this earlier. Those folks in the lab do an awesome job, and I'm glad we finally found a small way to thank them. I'll see most of the riders next week, and I'll ship the cards right back to Anna."

Then Junior tells Johan what Penelope did for Rossa's bike in the Tour. "What was her name?" asks Johan.

"It is Penelope Dicomo."

"Thanks, Junior. And thanks for the idea."

"Good luck this week, Johan. I'll let you get back to work."

Junior hangs up and then discusses his plan with Anna. He asks that "when you get the cards back, please give them to me. I will personally pass them out."

***

In the obeya room for the Marconi project are Stella, her team members (Vijay, Gino Latieri, Mariano Disota, and Veronika Albero), Ricardo and his R&D managers, reps from manufacturing and supply chain, and some of the Volta team members who are there to observe and learn. Bolaji also watches with interest as this event presents opportunities to inject or collect knowledge.

"Welcome to our first integration meeting," starts Stella. "Except for Ricardo, this is new to all of us, so we're going to learn as we go. I, for one, am excited to pilot the technology creation process."

Everyone else seems just as curious for how things will proceed.

"These integration meetings will keep everybody appraised of progress, review the latest test results, and gather suggestions. We'll also show you samples and the data for assemblies that were made by integrating the best components and assembly processes. Like Toyota and a few other manufacturers that have successfully conducted integration events, we'll use our meetings to keep everybody working on or interested in the different facets of the technology. The meetings also will keep everybody updated on the progress of the technology and informed of the next steps of the project."

Stella explains to the group that they wanted to stick with the inventor theme used by their colleagues for the other projects, thus the "Marconi" name, and describes the scope of the project:

"We're developing the technology to make a low-cost, carbon-fiber frame inspired by the way welded aluminum frames are made. The technology could, for example, be used on an inexpensive but high-quality sports bike. At this time the scope is still a little fluid, and it may change as we learn more. Some of our colleagues, Fabian and Gino, had reduced the risk of this idea to the point where Davanti decided to invest in the development of the technology."

All in the room nod, indicating that they've kept up so far.

"But before we get to the technology itself, I'd like to walk you through the process that we're pioneering to close our knowledge gaps: it's inspired by what is known as *set-based concurrent engineering* or *SBCE*. SBCE was discovered at Toyota, and it has worked perfectly for the development of new cars. Many of the same principles apply to what we do here at Davanti, but we have to be flexible as we adapt the process to bicycle technology development. I went to SBCE training a month ago, and I'm anxious to coach the team in applying what I learned. Ricardo also asked me to write the initial SBCE playbook based on our experience with this project and the next few to follow, like Mo's Leonardo project. With that, I'll turn it over to Gino."

"We started the project by identifying what knowledge we had at Davanti about this technology," begins Gino as he stands. "Most of the knowledge was in people's heads, including my own. So we brought together a group of seasoned and experienced engineers, including our retired friend Fabian Tuzzi; technicians; and manufacturing experts and got all their input. We made graphs, like knowledge curves and sketches, to visualize knowledge within Davanti. We then gave all the knowledge summaries to Bolaji, who is heading up the R&D knowledge management initiative. You can see some of the graphs on the walls here." Gino walks over to nearby charts.

"After we documented what we know, we asked the same group to help us identify what we did not know about this technology—the knowledge gaps we had." Gino shows a list of those gaps in order of importance. "Although we feel that all gaps need to be closed eventually, we know that if we cannot address the first three on the list, we may not succeed. First, we must find the right tubes, learn how to connect the tubes to the bottom bracket and steering column, and then learn how to taper the tubes or put some kind of a stiffness gradient in them. So the initial focus will be on closing those three gaps—they're all needed, they affect each other, and there is no hierarchy among them. We'll develop them concurrently, hence, SBCE. Only after that will we attack further gaps, like making steering columns or bottom brackets out of tubes. For now, we're cutting those pieces out of existing bikes."

The attendees are fixed on Gino, waiting anxiously to see where this goes.

Gino points to a table on the wall: "As you can see, we defined the following three sets:

Tubes

■ These are mostly commercially available, extruded, short-fiber-reinforced tubes that we can cut to the right length and angle. We included tubes of different diameters and wall thicknesses.

Stiffness Gradient

■ Partially filled tubes with stiff foam were used.
■ We inserted a smaller diameter tube into a larger diameter one, like you would do in plumbing.
■ We also sliced a section open at the end of the tube, cut out triangular pieces, and closed the tube up again, like you would taper metal tubes.

Connection Methods

- We tried a variety of glues.
- We also experimented with several welding methods, like friction welding.
- And we looked at various taping methods."

Gino explains that they started with a large number of options in each set—about 800 possible combinations because they did not want to miss anything as they began. Some of the ideas came from a hackathon that Sofia had organized. Gino then shows samples of some options that were considered initially and eliminated. He then sits to make room for Veronika.

"After we identified all possibilities, we tried to eliminate the lesser options in a very efficient manner," says Veronika. "For example, we asked our engineers to perform calculations and modeling to determine the minimum strength, stiffness, durability, and adhesion required and the costs to achieve these critical areas. As you can see, there are some red areas on these tradeoff curves." She points at a graph showing stiffness as a function of thickness with an area shaded in red. "We must avoid the red area because it would create cracks in the frame."

"What was the purpose of this analysis?" asks Giovanni from manufacturing.

"This exercise allowed us to eliminate more than one-third of the options. We also eliminated other options because of the high price of the materials or because they were unsuitable for welding. And we only retained two methods to taper the tubes or produce a stiffness gradient. After the exercise, we had about 100 combinations left. When all predictions were exhausted, we proceeded to other methods to develop the missing knowledge—you know, things like experiments, working with suppliers, consulting with universities. . . . You can see a summary here on this chart."

Mo is surprised to see only a handful of experiments done at Davanti and asks why.

"Good observation, Mo," replies Veronika. "With help from procurement, we consulted with a company in the area that designs and makes plastic parts and composites for the automotive and aerospace industry. They are not a competitor, and we may be able to purchase a lot of the welding knowledge from them. They ran a lot of the experiments for us. They have the welding equipment, the glues, the tape, etc., but they had to get used to the stiffness of our carbon-fiber assemblies."

Mo gives an understanding nod.

"After we determined the most suitable tubes, methods to create a stiffness gradient, and connection methods, we combined the most promising ones and created subassemblies," continues Veronika. "And as Gino explained to you earlier, we used existing technology to make bottom brackets and steering columns." She passes around several subassemblies as she explains the test results.

"I'm glad to have something I can touch, bend, and poke," notes Marco. "That tells more of a story to me than all the numbers on the board?"

After answering many questions, Veronika nods toward Stella, who walks over to a whiteboard.

"Now that brings us to the next purpose of this meeting: feedback and input," says Stella. "Is there anything the team may have overlooked? Do you think we missed anything, any ideas to make the experiments faster, cheaper?"

The group offers a few suggestions, which Stella writes on a whiteboard so that they can be considered in the next round of experiments.

"We've obviously been highly focused on our project and objectives," comments team member Mariano. "Can you see anything here that could be used right now, in an existing product, in a new product, anywhere else? Anyone? Giovanni, you seem to be in deep thought."

"I just had an idea: If we could build frames in two or more pieces and then put them together like you do here, we could increase our manufacturing capacity by at least 30 percent because our large winding and assembly robots are the bottleneck; we could put the splices in an area of low stress. I think I'll cut up a few frames and see if your contractor can put them back together."

"That's a great idea, Giovanni. We may be able to help you with that."

"I see that you already made a complete frame," says Ricardo, pointing to a rugged bike in the corner.

"That was in the creative phase of the project," comments Gino. "It consists of pieces cut from existing bikes. It was more of a minimum viable prototype. But we rode it on the road."

"So where exactly are you today?" asks Ricardo. "Can we build a complete bike with the best knowledge and thinking you have today? Is what you have already good enough for at least some generic cycling application?"

Stella and Gino look at each other; they have given the question a lot of thought and expected it to be asked: "We did the subassemblies because we did not want to jump to a full product right away. But a very generic bike that could be ridden makes sense to manage the risk. It would not be good enough to win the Tour de France, but the integrated product would establish a benchmark for where we are today. It also gives us a chance to see how everything we learned so far works together, and maybe it will identify gaps that we don't yet know about."

"How long will it take to get a few bikes made between the plastics company and the shop?" asks Ricardo.

"We can do the frames in less than a week," replies Gino confidently. "And we can use wheels, drivetrains and other components from the storeroom to save time."

"Please let me know when they're done," says Ricardo.

"So if we can already make a bike, why not skip all the other stuff there—focus on that bike and perfect it?" asks Matteo. "We badly need a cheap sports bike in our portfolio."

"That only *sounds* like a good idea," cautions Ricardo. "But it would violate some innovation excellence principles critical for this phase of development: First, this bike is in the portfolio for the season a year from now, so we have time to get it right. Second, a key lean principle I learned from Toyota is to leave all options open as long as possible; you never know what may happen, good or bad. Third, if we focus on one bike, the best outcome is one bike if we're lucky. But if we leave all options open and focus on knowledge and the technology, who knows how many bikes or other projects we may be able to spin out of this?"

"I guess I never saw it that way," says Matteo. "I'm learning something new every day."

"Unless somebody sees a reason to stop or redirect this project, I would like Vijay to go over the plans for the next set of experiments and give you an estimate for when we have the next integration meeting," concludes Stella.

Vijay starts with the remaining knowledge gaps and the targets for the next set and shows what work has been planned. He gets many questions and suggestions and updates the plans accordingly.

"Of course, we also need to wait for the evaluation of the subassemblies and the bikes because that will reveal more knowledge gaps," he explains.

Everyone in the room appears pleased with the outcome of the meeting, and it clearly shows on their faces. Rarely had such a look been seen within Davanti.

Before they begin scheduling the next meeting, Sofia asks, "What do you think of this approach? Did you find the integration meeting helpful?"

"This was excellent," says Giovanni. "It keeps all of us up to date and give us an opportunity to identify our own knowledge gaps and offer help where we can."

"Thanks, Giovanni," says Stella. "So if there are no objections, I assume we have everybody's support to continue with the plan we have laid out. I'm looking forward to our next integration meeting in about a month."

***

Horst Havenstein, the non-bike project manager, has been a real ball of fire. He's used to much shorter timelines than the Davanti folks. Coming from the fashion industry and a retail giant, he brought a different concept of the cost of delay than that held by Davanti personnel. "If you miss the first good weather day in the spring, you've lost a month worth of sales," Horst lectured his Davanti colleagues, who realize their new bikes rarely made that cutoff in the past.

To get the Davanti bike and street apparel line started, Horst ordered a large variety of samples from some of the best casual clothing brands, and he had the Davanti race logo printed or embroidered on the merchandise in various patterns. Horst made arrangements with stores in different regions to put the merchandise up for sale—one rack per store—but with a different mix of merchandise in every store. He asked the stores to try different price tags on different days, and told the stores that Davanti wanted no money back from the sale—just some data: what they sold every day in what region and at what price.

"This will prime the dealers for these types of products and tell me within two weeks what sells and what does not," Horst told Junior. "Once I have that data, we'll place the first large order and scale up from there to be ready for the Christmas season. And then we'll start collecting revenues on the sales."

In addition to his apparel experiment, Horst put the Davanti logo on air pumps, bike tools, and specialty clothing, such as bike shoes and gloves. Diana the procurement manager helped him to find the right partners—all top-of-the-line suppliers. And Horst uncovered another gap at Davanti: There really isn't a good dealer program that can help dealers succeed. Davanti never had a broad enough line of product to see the need for that, leaving many opportunities to build profitable dealer relationships to the competition. He believes that if Davanti can offer some non-bike goods and a few more attractive finance options before the next selling season, Davanti can lay the groundwork for and experiment with a much better dealer program.

Horst also started work with Diana on bike components—chains, pedals, seats, derailleurs, rims, and tires. But that foray is a little more delicate than bike clothing. They could easily step on the turf of their suppliers, like Coppimechanica. But on the other hand, Davanti is not planning to manufacture the components; they'd still buy them from a supplier and collect royalty for the Davanti name and maybe Davanti designs (in the past, they'd typically give all component ideas and work away, which was the case with the Darvin project and Coppimechanica). Horst and Diana also have suggested that Davanti manage the distribution of components and other merchandise, moving those goods along with their bikes. Coppimechanica would be a welcome partner if they made an appropriate offer to manufacture the components.

Horst, who knows the bike retail market well, also has suggested to Joe and Ricardo that a joint-venture agreement with the right partner could offer a quick entry into off-road or city-bicycle markets. There are challenges involved with that idea, too, since Davanti would only partner with a manufacturer of top-of-the-line bicycles, which could be a competitor in existing markets.

On the product promotion side, Horst has been working with Marco on merchandising ideas; exploring advertisement synergies (e.g., promoting non-bicycling merchandise on the pro racing tours); and boosting the Davanti brand in underrepresented areas of the world: "We have two riders from Columbia on our Davanti team," he says, "but their fans can't buy a Davanti bike in Columbia."

Horst also challenged Marco to take a good look at the Davanti bicycle names: "Names like 'Davanti Nella Gara PS' and "Davanti Nella Gara PV' don't have the marketing effect that those products deserve. I understand how the names evolved from Fausto Sr.'s first product, but they no longer appeal to today's customers." Marco is thrilled to finally have the support for something that, in his opinion, has been long overdue. His mind is jumping to the names of cars, motorcycles, sport articles, and even food.

When Junior hears about Horst's experiments in their one-on-one meeting, he immediately goes to see Ricardo. It's a little after 4:00 pm, and Ricardo is at his desk doing an A3 review and has another associate waiting for a review. Ricardo acknowledges Junior, who politely sits, listens, and humbly waits for his turn. Junior thanks those with A3s as they leave, and then tells Ricardo how much he's liked watching the A3 process and Ricardo's coaching.

"But that's not the reason you came here," guesses Ricardo.

"Correct. I just talked to Horst about the business experiments he's running. At first, I was taken aback. He's trying so many ideas so quickly. Without a lot of effort and resources, it looks superficial. But then I thought, couldn't we use this method to speed up bike innovation: try hundreds of things and know within a few days what works?"

"Junior, we studied the fashion industry in business school, and I use their model for the innovation process right now at Davanti. My goal is to get us as close to the fashion industry process as possible. We've already explored close to a hundred new ideas based on that model, and we've identified about a dozen for further investments. In fact, Mo's project was the first that followed our version of that process, and a few more have quickly followed. With every new project, we learn and get better. And I'll watch Horst closely—I'm sure he can teach us a few more things."

"Come to think of it—you didn't ask for any money for all those experiments. I'm very impressed," says Junior. "Let me know if I can help. Well, forget about that. Maybe I can help the most by getting out of your way."

"No, Junior, we always need your leadership. None of this would be happening without you."

***

Mo had asked Bolaji for a 15-minute meeting to go over an issue with the Leandro project. Bolaji is a seasoned Davanti engineer and a good leader. He is a patient listener, who often does not answer right away because he likes to carefully consider his response. The innovation excellence training was new to him as was Ricardo's coaching; he quickly embraced both because he was convinced they made him a better leader.

"That was quite a plan you shared with the team in the Leandro sprint meeting the other day, Mo. So how are things going? What can I do to help you *today*?"

"Thanks Bolaji. Things are moving, but I don't think I have the right engineers on the team."

"Please explain."

"Alexandra and Serfino are pretty good. I give them instructions, and they go off and do what I've told them. Same with Sergio, although he's not comfortable working on the gears yet, so I assigned him to mostly testing activities because of his background. But I'm not sure Tony listens to my instructions. And when he does, he comes back trying to tell me that my suggestions won't work. I end up arguing for hours with him. Then he's slow to deliver, dragging his feet because he doesn't like my recommendation. He's spent a whole week just trying to prove me wrong."

"Did he succeed?"

"He thinks he did."

"Besides these attitude problems, do you think he has the competencies the team needs?"

"Hard to find out. He's so stubborn. I don't know if it's a personality or skills problem. There's so much to do on this project, and I can't waste my time trying to win arguments."

"Maybe I can help. Who is responsible if you tell people what to do?"

"They are. I told them what I want done. They're responsible to do it."

"But what if they prove what you told them was wrong?"

"I guess, then I'm responsible and we need another round of arguments."

"Do you think they'd know what to do without you telling them?"

"Maybe. But how would I know for sure?"

"Could you ask them?"

"I guess I could. And if they have the same idea as I have, they'll consider it as their idea and be happy to run with it. I'd eliminate a lot of arguments. I get it."

"And who do you think is responsible now?"

"Well, now it's clearly the engineer. It's technically their idea. But what if they give me the wrong answer?"

"Could you help them? Maybe ask questions to understand what they know and don't know that prevents them from having the right answer."

"I could ask them questions, educate them, and ask questions until I get my answer. Is that what you want me to do? It will take time. Of course, I might learn something in the process as well."

"I'm not telling you what to do, Mo, I'm just trying to help you solve a problem. Your idea isn't bad. They may find your answer and accept it as their own. And it may take less time than the arguing you do now."

"I should give this a try. I'll lay out the cookie trail until they find the answer that I like."

"So, Mo, now you found a way to help them find *your* answer. What if your answer is not the best one? These engineers develop new knowledge very fast on their projects. Isn't it possible that *they* have better answers than you?"

"That could happen. I certainly don't have all the answers. I guess I could ask them before I even lay out my ideas. If I like their solution, we don't need a discussion. But what if their suggestion is terrible? It's possible that could happen. Some of them have very little experience. What then?"

"What do you think?"

"Well, then I ask clarifying questions until I find out where they need help. And if neither of us has a good answer, maybe we can figure it out together."

"Great idea, Mo. Telling people outright what to do is very disrespectful—it ignores their knowledge and capabilities. What you're proposing is highly respectful and engaging. Do you think you could practice this for a while? You'll make mistakes. It's not easy. Just be sincere in your search for the *best* answer, and don't get hung up on whether it's the answer you want or they want. Reflect on mistakes when they happen, adjust, and move on."

"Yes, I want this to be natural, not forced. They'll see right through that."

"Is it OK if I attend some of your meetings at the beginning? It will be an opportunity to coach you. And by all means, if you run into a problem, talk to me."

"Please attend if you'd like. I can't wait to try this out. I might find I have the right engineers after all. And this could be the key for managing such a large project. What have I got to lose?"

Notes

1. *Lean Lexicon Fifth Edition*, compiled by the Lean Enterprise Institute and edited by Chet Marchwinski, Lean Enterprise Institute, Cambridge, MA, 2014.
2. *The Karate Kid*, directed by John G. Avildsen, Delphi II Productions, 1984, film.

Chapter 26

Davanti Innovations Pick Up Speed

In the weeks after her meeting with Marco about the Toricelli project, Rebecca was a whirlwind of activity: she set up discussions with nearby dealers and potential customers. She gathered enough insights to create a web page within the Davanti URL where customers can explore bike-purchasing options and reserve a spot on a waiting list for a bike. She also posted videos on YouTube, which generated a lot of buzz on social media. From the internet experiments, she learned that:

- Renting bikes is attractive to racers, but only for certain races.
- Most recreational riders like a finance option.
- Leasing is attractive to amateur racers because they could get a new bike every season.
- Leasing has huge potential with bike clubs, which could lease a new pool of bikes every season and make them available to members on demand.
- Cost-conscious customers are anxious to buy used pro bikes or bikes that exhausted their leasing capability.

In no time, she had a variety of selling experiments going with local dealers, bike clubs, and even a small sports-store chain. Leftover bikes from the pro races and Davanti's non-confidential excess test inventory were made available. Luca's technicians check the used bikes out and retune them as necessary per instruction from Davanti's legal counsel; the used bikes are labeled and sold as "Certified by Davanti Nella Gara."

Rebecca experimented with price, service, payment terms, and delivery options for the various sales venues to find a sweet spot that satisfies Davanti, dealers, and customers. The dealers start to like her because she gives them some lucrative new options with the "Davanti" name on them. With the help of a local bank, Charles from finance set up a service to manage the transactions, much like an automaker-financing company, with all its advantages (e.g., the bank is responsible for the finance administration and will repossess bikes if customers default on their payments).

Rebecca is having a blast. She always wanted to be a small business owner, and now she feels like one. It is easy to sign up additional dealers for the project, and many wonder why it took Davanti so long to come up with the idea. Not only is the business fun for Rebecca, but it immediately started generating income. She rented storage space in town, and a former lab technician

DOI: 10.4324/9781003231837-26

helps her with administrative tasks. Her biggest bottleneck is becoming the availability of used bikes. "Give me the new ones," joked Marco. "I'll turn them into used bikes for you."

Mo and Marco also enlisted Rebecca's help to use the dealer network to pass out test bikes to amateur racers. She found out that the dealers want to be involved with that option. They want to give the bikes to the best and most reliable racers who frequent their stores. They're sure the amateurs will love to participate in the testing and feedback of the bikes. Racers will have to bring the bikes back to the stores at regular intervals for Davanti engineers to inspect them and gather feedback, and the increased foot traffic pleases the dealers.

***

Just as quickly as Rebecca's initiative took off, so too did the work of Gina's team on the ski bike. After legal filed initial patents, the team answered the first critical question (customer interest) by setting up a web-based survey in coordination with a popular skiing magazine to gauge interest, which was overwhelmingly positive. Their second critical question (manufacturability) was then answered by building a few bikes in Fumane with the help of a French ski manufacturer that Marcel had recommended. For the third critical question (rideability), the bikes were tested near Zermatt by a tester working for the ski company that made the blades; early results confirmed the desired handling characteristics. The team shared the test results with a few ski resorts in Italy and Switzerland to rouse interest in the new sport. And, of course, Junior gave regular updates to Marcel.

After the success of the ICP, Gina and her team then worked to close knowledge gaps identified after passing the project's technology gate, engaging experts inside and outside Davanti. Gina and her team meet today with the Marconi team; she had attended the first Marconi integration meeting and was intrigued by the new technology, and she wants her team to learn more about it. They gather in the obeya, look at samples the Marconi team has created, and get an update on the knowledge created so far.

"I bet we could make a complete ski bike with the technology you're developing," concludes Mimi Positivo, an engineer on Gina's team. "Although I think it's a bit early to make that decision."

"So why not include a set of experiments in your project's TCP?" suggests Stella from the Marconi team.

"We've got too many ideas and experiments planned for the technology process as it is," counters Johnny Torto, who had joined Gina's team. "I fear we're already falling behind. It would take far too long to get up to speed on the welding technology."

"You don't have to repeat what our team already knows," says Stella. "My team can take your best design and build a few prototypes with what we have learned to date."

"That's a great and generous idea, Stella," says Gina, surprised by the level of cooperation rather than the competitiveness that had existed among the Davanti employees in the past. "We'll send the drawings over to get you started."

***

After the new PCP got up and running, Carolina, Gina, and the PMs kept a close eye on the process and manually assigned all resources. After the process stabilized, however, Carolina worked with the team of volunteers who had designed the PCP process details to:

- Optimize the process for flow and speed.
- Manage variability.
- Standardize the process.
- Make problems visible.

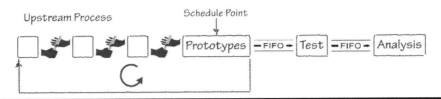

Figure 26.1 PCP Kanban System.

It was easy for Carolina and the others to understand Little's Law and single-piece flow when applied to one engineer (i.e., WIP of one). But applying a WIP of one to a process with many contributors was more challenging because most engineers would sit idle while one works, and, thus, the throughput would be very low. After discussions with Sofia, Carolina now understands that Little's Law also applies to a whole process. However, they'll need to experiment a little to find the right balance between WIP and throughput to achieve minimum cycle time while at the same time managing the variability of the process. The trainer Giacomo had also re-educated the team on kanban systems and their benefits: automate the process, make invisible engineering work visible, and highlight problems.

The team printed all active kanban cards from Gina's spreadsheet: i.e., every product iteration tag (PIT) on the visual planning board has a kanban with a title and expected start and finish dates. The iteration kanbans cover the upstream critical-path activities from the start of the iteration to the building of prototypes; after prototype the iteration moves first-in first-out (FIFO) to test and then analysis. They also formalized the position of a "design engineer" who would have overall responsibility for the iteration, including outcome and documentation, and who could help coordinate the support work. They decided to add the design engineers' names to the kanbans.

They handed out the cards that were at or past the expected start date to the design engineer whose name was on the card; the design engineer either performed the upstream work or passed the card to a colleague for that work. The team decided that when an iteration finished in the prototype stage, they would begin a new iteration, thus aligning the new work with the performance of the prototype operation.

To no one's surprise, the engineers were suspicious when the kanbans were first introduced: many wondered if this new tool would be used to measure their productivity. Ricardo briefed them in the engineering area, explaining the purpose of the cards and reassuring everybody that there was no hidden purpose. Some engineers then started to visually display the cards at their desk.

After a while the kanban process crystallized: When it is time to start a new iteration, the project manager has a short kickoff meeting with the design engineer and representatives from the appropriate downstream resources and support groups, like modeling, drawing, styling, etc. The R&D staff has done many iterations over the years—although not in such an organized fashion—and the design engineers know the staff that will be involved depending on the work content of the iteration. Together they discuss the work at hand and make detailed plans. For example, if only a small frame modification is needed, the design engineer may decide to make the drawing modification. But if the iteration calls for an entirely new frame, the drawing group will get involved. The plans and handoff dates necessary to hit the finish date are agreed upon and noted on the kanban. Occasionally downstream staffs make a copy of the kanban and keep it at their desks as a reminder of what's coming. With this much clarity and communication, nobody is surprised when the kanban is passed on to them.

The same iteration team also meets at the end of the iteration when all test results are analyzed to reflect on two things: did they accomplish the goals of the iteration and, if not, what needs to be done in the next iteration? They also determine if any new knowledge was created and, if so, how will it be communicated and documented. The other subject of the reflection is the process itself: did the process work as expected, and, if not, what improvements are needed and to whom do they need to be communicated?

As the kanbans made their way through the relay, Carolina walked through the engineering area every day, looking at the posted cards and asking questions to learn about the workflow. Sometimes she had to manage a situation where an engineer had several cards at the same time. As Carolina discussed the work with the engineers, she learned that the engineers thought they had plenty of time to finish the work by the time specified on the kanban. She also found out that after work had progressed to the prototype shop and subsequent testing, the engineers were done with their work on the iteration for all practical purposes. They might occasionally be called to the shop for followup and also were involved in the analysis of data after testing, but both activities were so minor they did not need any special planning.

Carolina also noticed that some engineers had no cards. Since nobody wanted to be seen sitting idle, they found themselves work to keep busy. Some went through their test results for a third or fourth time; some worked on their discontinued projects (just in case), thinking the new leaders might change their minds; some helped colleagues; and some volunteered for CI work. She also noticed that some PMs started engineers on an iteration without waiting for a kanban to be released.

The kanbans had finally made the invisible engineering work visible. Since the visual planning board worked so well for iteration planning, Carolina asked the PCP team to create a board to make the resource assignments—from the start of an iteration through prototype—visible in one place. After a few experiments, the team converged on a board with a column for every engineer and rows for work that is either overdue, active, or next. There also was a row for parked cards (i.e., work that had been interrupted) and a row to signal that an engineer needs work. Besides the critical kanbans for the PCP, the team handwrote cards to visualize non-critical path work, such as some support tasks and work on the TCP or ICP. On the right of the board, they placed upcoming and completed cards.

When the team started to populate the board with kanbans, the expectation was to see a lot of overload and imbalance. Yet when all cards were posted, Carolina was surprised to see neither—just a lot of empty space on the board. Instead of jumping to conclusions, she decided to watch the board for a week.

As the board evolved and a similar board was implemented in the test lab, Carolina noticed that iteration work was still performed as if everything was in an express lane, and the relay-race process seemed to work well. And to no surprise, the problems caused by variability (different length of

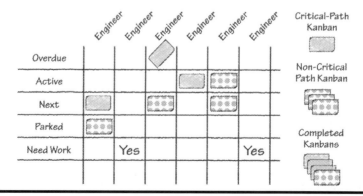

Figure 26.2 Resource Assignments Board.

tasks, availability, varying difficulty, occasional setbacks, etc.,) became visible and could be dealt with expediently. And the best part was that the iterations were delivered on time or close to it.

But puzzled by the continued excess capacity, she verified all cards vs. the master spreadsheet: everything checked out perfect. "Do we have too many engineers? What is going on?" she thought.

Carolina shared her findings with Ricardo, who was just as surprised and confused as she was. "How could years of late deliveries have happened with too many resources?" he asked. "Maybe Sofia can shed some light on this."

***

Standing in front of the resource assignments board, Carolina reflects on what they learned about engineering capacity. Sofia, Ricardo, Gina, Leandro, and Bart listen carefully as she expresses her and Ricardo's surprise about the lack of pileups and the seemingly excess resource availability.

"I've seen this before," says Sofia. "In a push process, everything is started upfront and *pushed* through the system. Everybody gets overloaded because there is no attention to the real need and no alignment with the capacity. Every new project, scope change, or other activity that anybody wants gets started, and things quickly queue up in front of the bottleneck and get sorted out with a priority system. And as more projects and requests come in, the natural reaction by the R&D director is to use the conditions to argue for more resources, and the spiral continues."

"Why does that happen?" asks Carolina.

"Within Davanti, there really were no companywide goals for R&D," explains Sofia. "No strategy, no product planning, and no means to assess value for what was undertaken. Everybody fought for their own projects, even Emilio, who should have been sorting this out."

"And neither were there standards for how many iterations to run or what other work to do within an iteration, so people cut corners when busy and stretched work otherwise," adds Ricardo. "And Junior knew that he didn't know R&D well enough to interfere, so he was only called in to settle disputes after a lot of time and money was wasted. But in Emilio's defense, R&D was always staffed for the worst-case scenario so that every panic could be handled whenever it surfaced."

"So why did everybody accept any work, knowing they couldn't deliver it?" asks Gina.

"I think that Davanti has a strong 'never say no' culture," notes Sofia. "Junior, the charismatic leader, set the example. The leaders, including Emilio, rarely said 'no' to Junior or anybody who had Junior's ear. But that did not mean that the accepted work got done. When an engineer or project manager was asked by a superior to do something, they accepted the assignment, put it on the pile, and worked on everything on-and-off to keep everybody somewhat happy. Saying 'no' was culturally unacceptable, and questioning a boss or superior doesn't fly in a command-and-control environment."

"Where did the money come from to keep all this going?" asks Leandro.

"R&D was a pit from which everybody drew with very little visibility or accountability," replies Ricardo. "The pit was filled or refilled based on Emilio's pleas to Junior. The only thing Junior had visibility over was new hires, capital investments, and maybe some discretionary spending for things like training or travel."

"It's interesting you mentioned capital investments or lack thereof," says Bart. "Is that why we never upgraded the bottleneck to handle all the work we pushed into the process?"

"Correct," replies Sofia. "The bottleneck is normally the most capital-intensive step of the process. Chances are the bottleneck produced enough not to warrant the investment. You actually may have had something resembling *pull*. Although it was messy and too late in the process, marketing pulled the projects they needed most from the large queue in front of the prototype shop by putting them on the top of the priority list and relegating everything else to linger or die. But, as we saw, you can only sell so many top-of-the-line bikes. Maybe they got what they really needed after all—at a price—but who really knows what was invested in projects that never made it or what value could have been derived from them."

"We wasted so much engineering resources on canceled, abandoned, and changed projects. But now that we schedule to available capacity, reduced stop and go, and minimized changes with late start, how can we be sure that *we* have the *right* capacity now?" asks Carolina.

"You'll only get the truest sense of capacity when you set the takt to customer demand and assign resources in every step of the process to meet the takt," says Sofia. "I believe we have that now for the eight iterations in engineering, and I think we have a visual of it in front of us."

"What do we do with all those engineers?" wonders Carolina, pointing to the empty spaces on the board.

"That's a good problem to have, especially since Davanti has a lot of versatile R&D talent," says Sofia. "We now have capacity to staff the growing ICP and the TCP as well as work on the processes and continuous improvement. It's an envious position."

"We can add a few people to the knowledge projects that just got underway," adds Ricardo.

"Can we make that work visible, too?" asks Gina.

"I've also seen companies create a 'job jar' for work that doesn't have critical delivery dates, like knowledge documentation," says Sofia. "Engineers draw from the jar when they're waiting for their next kanban."

"I'll work with our team to create a job jar," says Carolina.

"You know, we might even have enough engineers if we increase the capacity in the prototype shop and take on more business," reasons Bart. "Our friends Lee and Zing from Taiwan created more than 20 percent extra capacity in the prototype shop and in testing, and somebody will find ways to use it."

"For now, you'll be happy to have a resource buffer, especially in engineering and the shops," says Sofia. "And with attrition, things may balance out over a year or two. Meanwhile Junior won't complain if you keep the engineering budget flat."

"Should we adjust the process times we originally estimated?" asks Bart. "The engineers think we gave them more than enough time. That, too, will create more capacity."

"I think you may want to let the kanbans mature a little more," adds Sofia, "then I'll coach you through some lean tools that companies use to gain additional speed and efficiency."

"I really thought I had seen it all, but I learned a lot these past weeks," says Ricardo, smiling. "I guess that's what this initiative is all about."

"So, Carolina, how are you planning to use this board?" asks Sofia.

"We've started to use it for huddles every other day. There is a lot of variability in the work and the assignment process, but we're making problems visible with flags for late, waiting for something, etc. And engineers who need help turn their cards 45 degrees. So far we made improvements in every huddle, but I assume more systemic problems will surface soon, indicating where we need to take a more systemic problem-solving approach, like our A3 process. We also pay good attention to 'parked cards' because they signal work stoppage. If we cannot solve the problem in the huddle, we ask for help or form a team to address the situation. And then we're planning to optimize WIP as we make improvements to cycle time and throughput."

"And what do the engineers say?"

"This is *their* board. This is how they communicate with us about status and their need for help. They assess the work, and they tell us when they need more time or what help they need. And I also noticed that whenever somebody falls behind, we immediately find volunteers to pitch in. I think they trust the process and realize there is no hidden agenda. But the biggest challenge for me still is to have engineers raise their hand when they need work. And it's obvious that the kanbans not only represent pieces of work—they represent real people, and real people make their desires known. For example, engineers like to stay with the same project until it's finished, so they want to be assigned to all iterations of a project. They feel as soon as they invested time in a project, they want to see it all the way through. And this is a great tool to make that possible without too much shuffling."

"Just wondering what marketing will do when they see that we have open capacity?" asks Gina. "Those guys will have no problem coming up with new products to fill that capacity."

"I'm sure you're right," replies Ricardo. "We want them to come up with ideas. But I think Marco will temper their enthusiasm. He understands that not everything marketing wants is worth doing, even if we have capacity."

***

When Marie's assignment in Montreux finished, she was pulled on to an engagement in Verona, which is only 30 minutes from Fumane. Being so close to Mo, they now see each other frequently, even during the week. They also FaceTime frequently, going over their day and making plans for the weekend. The racing season ended for Marie, so they just hang out in either city.

Saturday evening Mo heads to his parents after spending the morning and afternoon with Marie; she will be entertaining her parents in Verona. He walks into the villa with a bottle of wine and a bouquet of sunflowers for his mom, and the Pensatores easily notice his good mood. Catherine and husband Eric look at Mo and glance at each other as if to say, "There's no mistaking that look."

"Maurice, the flowers are beautiful, but don't you like my cooking anymore," chides his mom. "I mean, we don't see you so much. You used to come every weekend—sometimes for the entire weekend."

"You're cooking is better than ever. And it smells fabulous tonight. I'm guessing pasta, rapini, and pesto. The garlic is everywhere."

"I don't get to hear as much about your work," says his dad somewhat sadly. "You seem to be doing so much interesting stuff. I'd like to know more. I hope that's still going well."

"Dad, it couldn't be better. Of course, I couldn't be busier as well. After the workshops in Lausanne, I've been running from one R&D meeting to the next. If it's not my bike project, it's CI projects. But I don't mind. It's been great, and time flies."

"Well, maybe you can come out for fishing one day, and we'll talk all about it. You've not been on the lake all fall, and there's only so much time left before I'll have to lift the boat."

"Sure, I'd like that," says Mo earnestly, noticing that his sister and brother-in-law have not stopped staring at him. He stares back at them: "What? What's with the smiles and looks?"

"So my internet dating idea worked, didn't it?" concludes his sister.

"Wrong. I never used it and don't have any plans to."

"But . . ."

"But none of your business."

Mo's mom interrupts the two: "Mo, I'm glad if you've found somebody. I don't care how you did it. I can see how happy you are. A mother knows these things. And I bet you're hungry."

"Mom, you're right, so let's open this wine, and I'll help you get dinner on the table."

***

Junior invited his leadership team plus Marco and Horst to an off-site meeting at a nearby boutique hotel. The facility has a large, contemporary conference room and offers meeting guests plenty of privacy and light refreshments—perfect for the morning's meeting. Junior asked Marco to bring Rebecca and a few of the less-tenured employees in the company, wanting more diversity and a few millennials in the mix.

Junior starts the meeting by discussing the new business initiatives that Horst and Rebecca are leading. "Both are doing surprisingly well and have uncovered a wealth of new opportunities for Davanti. This makes me wonder what else we're missing. And if there is something—which I'm pretty sure there is—how do we move quickly on it? Some of you made suggestions in one-on-one meetings, and I made a list of those for us to start."

Junior reads from a card the suggestions he's gathered, which include more bike offerings, geographic expansion, retail stores, selling Davanti technology, online sales, and acquisitions or partnerships.

"What's missing?"

"I thought we'd also be looking at bike services as a new opportunity," comments Constantine.

"Let's add that to the list. I would like to pick one or two new opportunities today and create teams to investigate them and come back with a proposal. I know we don't have a lot of information to make the right decision as we sit here. In fact, we should approach this with the same methodology that Ricardo and Horst have taught us: instead of getting bogged down in a lot of market research studies, let's determine the most critical questions and then run quick, small business experiments. And remember, we don't have to develop these business opportunities by ourselves; we can partner, acquire companies, buy or sell licenses. As long as it's consistent with our objectives and goals, I'm wide open for how to get it done."

Junior and the group discuss the opportunities, concluding:

- *Recreational and city bikes*—Davanti should pursue innovation and breakthrough technology with the knowledge already in the company.
- *Davanti technology*—Get more aggressive in leveraging Davanti technologies in other areas, like bike helmets and other sports articles. Davanti should consider licensing the technology rather than manufacturing the products. Ricardo will make a proposal at the next meeting.
- *MTBs*—Everyone agrees that MTBs (mountain bikes) are an attractive area for expansion, but since Davanti has very little knowledge in this area, they form a team with Ricardo, Marco, Horst, and Diana to explore options (e.g., develop the technology internally, find an appropriate partner, buy licenses, acquire another company). Diana will lead the team.
- *Services*—All believe that getting into services beyond race support would interfere too much with the dealers; dealers make a significant income on bike service, and they are the best positioned geographically to perform the service. They would likely drop Davanti bikes the minute Davanti competes on service.
- *Retail stores*—Junior and his team conclude that if Davanti has its own stores, it would again interfere with the interests of dealers. But they do decide to experiment with one store in a large retail complex where there are no Davanti dealers in the vicinity. That would also be a great opportunity for marketing experiments. Marco, Horst, and Rebecca will work on that initiative.
- *Serve the dealers*—"I'd like us to think of the dealers as customers, too," says Junior. "What do they need, and how can we help them be more successful?" The group explores options such as education, dealer councils, more flexible credit for dealers, and becoming an exclusive supplier so dealers would not need to sell competitor bikes anymore. Junior asks Claudia to head up that team and work with Marco, Joe, Rebecca, and Horst.

The group also discusses the regions in which Davanti bikes are not currently sold, aware of the many missed opportunities for Davanti to expand in other countries: "Our pro race team participates in the Tour Down Under in Australia and the Tour of Qatar every year, yet our sales in those bike hotspots have been almost zero," says Joe. "People there can't even buy a Davanti bike unless they order one online. I'd never consider buying a bike through our antiquated website, especially for what we charge. And I'm pretty sure we couldn't price the shipping to Qatar anyway."

"It's not just the far corners of the globe," says Claudia. "We have huge holes in the United States. We also have the Tour of California. Maybe we start there."

"Good point" says Joe. "Let's you and me put a team together to explore the expansion options, starting with the US. With this group's approval, I'd also like to engage Marco's team and a few IT experts in creating a better website and kickstarting online sales. I think we need to start a truly global web business and maybe join forces with web giants like Amazon and Alibaba. Remember, we're selling stuff other than bikes now, and we need exposure."

Everyone tells Joe and Claudia to go for it, including Junior, who then starts to wind down the meeting. "I trust you know full well how to go about these new assignments. And if you deployed the innovation excellence processes in your areas, you should have eliminated so much waste from your own schedules that you're glad to have something new to keep you busy. I don't want to have status meetings on these initiatives. Just drop me a note from time to time, give us a briefing in the communications meeting, or we can discuss in the one-on-one meetings. But if you need my help, then you *must* come see me right away."

To Junior's amazement, no one objects to anything, not even Claudia. His staff ask only a few clarifying questions about their assignments.

"Really, that's it?" asks Junior. "No arguments? What happened? We've always had arguments and fights—in every meeting, on every subject."

"What's to argue with, Junior," says Stephano. "This all makes sense, for us and for Davanti. It aligns perfectly with our objectives and strategy."

"I'm just a little surprised, that's all."

"You know, Junior, I'd rather work on expanding our global network than arguing in your office about problems that we should never had had in the first place," adds Diana. "My new project is certainly more challenging, but a lot more rewarding, too. I have the feeling my team will succeed and have a lot of fun. I think we all feel that way."

Junior looks at the ceiling and smiles, thinking of how far they've come in a relatively short time. And the meeting is going to end by 11:00 am. "Thank you for a productive meeting. You're all welcome to have your first team meetings here if you'd like. We have the room until 1:30 pm, and lunch will arrive at noon. I'm heading back to do a few gemba walks."

***

Bolaji waits to speak with Mo after a Leonardo sprint meeting. During the meeting, Mo had tried to apply some of Bolaji's coaching tips. The meeting went well until Tony made a suggestion that Mo didn't like. Tony wanted to test a cooling device that a hydraulic supplier sent him, convinced that it would reduce the temperature of the hydraulic oil. Mo argued that the device would add too much weight and friction and take up unnecessary testing time and resources. Tony was visually frustrated but eventually stopped arguing as the meeting closed.

"Mo, let's sit and talk." The two grab chairs at a nearby table. "I can see how you're applying what we discussed. How's it working for you?"

"Thanks again, Bolaji. I appreciate your coaching. I think some of it has worked, but I've got a lot yet to learn about management and leadership."

"Mo, I took many leadership classes in my career at Davanti and at my former employer, but nothing had the impact that the lean leadership training has had. I wish I had learned that earlier in my career. I would have been a so much better leader and person. That's why I love the opportunity to coach folks like you now, so you don't have to learn the hard lessons like I did. So what do you think about Tony's reaction in the meeting today?"

"His idea isn't in our plan and has a very low chance for success. We have a pretty full slate; he should understand that."

Bolaji pokes his head over a partition and sees Ricardo at his desk. "Let me get Ricardo. I may learn something as well."

Bolaji gets up and returns with Ricardo. Mo explains what happened in the meeting.

"What would be the worst that could happen if you let him try it?" asks Ricardo.

"We would waste money and time, and it wouldn't work."

"So no safety or technical issues. Why not just let him try it?"

Mo is surprised. "We waste time and money, learn nothing, and promote poor engineering judgement."

"We may not learn much technically, but maybe *he'll* learn something. And, then again, maybe he'll surprise you and it spins off another idea."

"And you'd both support me if I did that?" asks Mo.

"It's an important part in people development. First of all, we want people to come up with new ideas and take reasonable risks. Second, it shows respect to let him learn from his mistakes, even if it costs an experiment. Failures are part of learning, and people development requires a little investment and patience sometimes."

"But I'm not sure he has the right motivation, either, and I even doubt he'll learn from this effort."

"Respect for people also means to always assume positive intent. Remember, you have the right to know what he's planning to do so can you keep up a good dialogue, ask the right questions, and coach him through this."

"So where does it stop? Do I let anybody try anything?"

"Use good judgement, Mo. You might be surprised what works and what doesn't. And please talk to one of us if you're unsure. We'll help you."

***

The Wednesday after-work riders now gather dressed in long pants and shirts. Although the ride starts earlier now, some brought lights. Mo shows up with a competitor bike he picked up the week before. Rolling the bike toward Ricardo, he says, "If this continues, I won't need to buy a new bike. I'll just pick one up every Wednesday. Then you can keep my old clunker; I won't miss it."

"Oh, you'll get your clunker back," says Ricardo, "but today you have a different choice."

Mo had hoped to choose another competitor bike, but sees mostly a bunch of black bikes, some with a terrible finish and all identified by a number on them.

"Ricardo, what are these?"

"We want you to try these today. We'll only bring out the competitor bikes if all these are taken."

"I'll take one," says Junior, who stands behind Mo. Vinnie hands Junior a black bike.

"Sure, me too," says Mo, following the boss' example.

"Make sure you sign the waiver and fill out the evaluation form when you come back. And one more thing; you can't take these bikes home. That means, Mo, you'll be united with your clunker again very soon." Mo groans.

No one takes the time to read the entire waiver; it includes something about "experimental nature" and asks the signee to stop riding and call as soon as they notice anything unusual. It also has a half page of legal jargon that Davanti's lawyer charged two hours to compile.

Most riders don't like the look of some of the bikes, and wonder who could possibly sell something like that; Davanti would never make a bike like that. As the riders exit the lot, Ricardo gives Vinnie a wink.

About two hours later, as the early autumn sun is close to setting, all of the riders have made it back to Davanti and returned their black bikes and feedback forms. No problems occurred with the bikes and no complaints, except for unanimous dislike of the appearance.

Junior and others ask for something better looking next time. "We got some odd looks from riders out there and the people we passed. What if someone recognizes me riding this? They'll think it's a Davanti bike."

As Ricardo looks at the feedback, he notices that it's mostly positive. The Davanti engineers and staff obviously like the softer ride of the black bike. That doesn't surprise Ricardo: Davanti engineers design the top-of-the-line bikes based on the feedback from pros, not based on personal preference. Ricardo is especially curious about Junior's comments: he also praised the soft ride of the bike, thought it was fun to ride downhill, and wrote in the comment section, "And will you tell me what was under the paint?"

What Ricardo will tell him and the other riders is that he'd asked Vinnie to paint some of the Marconi bikes black along with a few standard Davanti bikes to make this somewhat of a blind test. Ricardo is encouraged with this first evaluation of the bikes and glad they all came back in one piece.

Vinnie looks over the feedback as well and smiles: "This is certainly a quick and cheap test for experimental bikes. And to think that these were the bikes from the project's first integration event. Imagine if we'd done more testing and refinement."

"Yes, this is all good news," says Ricardo. "Maybe we can learn enough soon to extend the experiments to amateur riders in town. Of course, we must do a little more testing first to keep the lawyers happy."

Even if they don't know it yet, the day's ride will familiarize Davanti engineers and staff with the newest products. The company has always hired bike enthusiasts and racers and given them access to tools and workbenches. It's why Monday at 4:00 pm is a busy time in the Davanti shop, with engineers and technicians returning after weekend rides or races and improving their equipment from what they learned days before. With the black-bike experiment, Ricardo started to engage a larger group of experts in the innovation creation process.

But it's not the only subjective test the R&D team has planned. Davanti has several resident "ride" engineers, experts at evaluating bikes for subjective criteria like ride comfort, downhill handling, stability, etc. They evaluate new frame designs and handlebars, but also combinations of components like wheels, seats, and brake handles. They mostly ride routes around Fumane, but sometimes take the bikes to velodromes, higher mountains, or southern Italy if they need warmer weather. Davanti also has a couple of former pros under contract who join the Davanti test engineers when needed.

Subjective testing is still just that—subjective—but over the years Davanti learned to make it as scientific as possible. They minimize outside influences like wind, weather, routes, and road surface. They'll often instrument the bikes with devices like accelerometers, GPS, altimeters, and strain gauges. The most important part of testing is the dialogue between the tester and the design engineers before, during, and after a test. Plans are to extend the Marconi testing to this group of engineers and riders, and then get the bikes to some amateur racers. Then the engineers will really get a sense of what the Marconi technology can achieve.

Chapter 27

R&D Strategy, Metrics, and Huddles

Ricardo gathered around a corner table in the engineering area the members of his department that were working on the knowledge management project. For a project update, he also invited the R&D managers and project managers so they can start becoming familiar with this important part of the new R&D initiative.

Bolaji, the technology manager, had worked hard through late summer and early autumn to get the knowledge initiative organized. For that, he had teamed up with senior engineer Enzo Scarpitti and new hire Peter Hendrikson.

"I'm going to ask Bolaji, Enzo, and Peter to walk us through their activities of late with knowledge management," says Ricardo. "Ask questions or comment as we go."

Enzo talks first about how they started by interviewing engineers, beginning with the most experienced, to document what they know about bicycles and Davanti technology and how they use that knowledge in the design of new bicycles. He explains that although most of what they shared was verbal and anecdotal, he began to see relationships and correlations, and his colleagues sometimes confirmed what he already knew. He then summarized the interviews and considered how to make it all visible, easy to understand, teach, and reuse.

Enzo had enlisted two of his buddies, Giuseppe Perche and Pietro Metallo, to form the first Davanti knowledge council, which Bolaji had nicknamed "The Commilitones" (comrades in arms). They like to meet in the cafeteria, slurping espressos for hours and sometimes moving to an outside picnic table for a smoke. Enzo says that Ricardo has agreed to consult them for all important technical decisions and has asked them to be involved with engineer training and the writing of the Davanti design and test standards.

Peter talks about his work at knowledge mining. He uses the Davanti bike-construction database (which contains virtually all design details of Davanti prototypes and production bikes for more than 10 years back) and the Davanti test-results database, which share a common identifier. Enzo helped him initially focus on a few critical areas, such as the intersection of tubes (e.g., bottom brackets, steering tubes). He also looked at front-wheel forks and handlebars to find correlations between construction features and test results. Using a statistical software package and a spreadsheet, he plotted curves that show the mathematical relationships, such as the fatigue resistance in function of the material thickness or the dynamic spring rate of the front-wheel fork in function of its curvature.

DOI: 10.4324/9781003231837-27

"In school, we called these graphs 'tradeoff curves,' but I prefer the term 'knowledge curves' because we will use them for a lot more than to assess tradeoffs," Peter explains.

Enzo adds that he knows many of those relationships empirically, but he appreciates that somebody finally put them into a mathematical formula and represented them graphically. "This will be easy to teach to new engineers because it's visible," he says, adding that "the equations can also be used in our prediction models and simulations. We can even use them to validate our finite element models. I wish I had them when I designed bikes."

"You've got them now," says Ricardo, "and your designer days aren't over Enzo."

"The correlations may not be perfect," adds Peter, "but they beat empirical knowledge and opinions by an order of magnitude."

"One goal of this initiative," says Bolaji, "is that we make it easy to find and reuse all this knowledge. If engineers can predict the performance of the bike from the knowledge that we already have, they don't have to reinvent things. This also helps them to find knowledge gaps and focus on the right experiments needed to close those gaps. And, of course, if they learn something new, we include the new learning in our knowledge repertoire."

Enzo explains that he has been able to validate and supplement Peter's curves with information obtained during the interviews with experienced designers. He also used anecdotes and stories to give Peter guidance on what relationships to look for. He says that he hopes that one day Davanti can combine all the mathematical relationships in a single computer simulation that can help engineers design bikes without prototypes and testing.

When he and his friends are done compiling their anecdotal and empirical knowledge, adds Enzo, Peter will use language-processing software to see what facts can be extracted from that dataset; he may not find scientific relationships, but there may be clues for what to look for in the test and construction databases.

"This is excellent work," says Ricardo. "You're going from test data, reports, and anecdotes to mathematical relationships and, maybe, one day white papers, theories, models, and simulations. I assume you've given some thought to my questions from our prior meeting: How can the knowledge that we have and any new knowledge be shared quickly and effectively across the organization? And how can we assure that everybody first looks at all the knowledge that we have before embarking on a new design and experiments?"

"Maybe I can help here," suggests Peter. "When I did an internship during my college days, I learned about design standards at a car company. We can put the knowledge we're gathering into Davanti design standards."

Bolaji likes the suggestion: "They taught that in my knowledge management class as well. Even modeling or simulation tools and knowledge curves are wasted if the knowledge doesn't consistently and efficiently find its way into products. In my class, they suggested that your best product is a reflection of your best knowledge. All knowledge must be embedded in design and product standards. And all new bikes should be designed according to the standards. And every time new knowledge is created, the standards are updated, and all engineers are informed of the updates."

"I agree that we should have design standards, but how do we allow engineers to experiment outside the design standards?" cautions Ricardo. "If everybody designs only according to the standards, how can we ever really innovate?"

"Good point, Ricardo," says Bolaji. "We had some case studies in our seminar where they suggested that since the design standards are based on the best and most current knowledge, the test results could be predicted from the knowledge curves or models. They waived some testing for designs that were within the standards, but they allowed designs outside the standards if appropriate testing was performed."

"That has been my experience, too," says Ricardo. "But I'll always insist that every design gets tested for safety and basic quality."

Enzo thinks that his crew could quickly come up with a first set of design standards: "Let's start with the best designs in each category and see from the knowledge curves how tight or wide the freedom would be before affecting safety, performance, and quality."

"Engineers should be thrilled about the standards," interjects Bolaji. "Think of all the prototypes and testing they can skip. Now they can focus on innovation, and we'd get so much faster."

"Standards are necessary and a good place to start," notes Ricardo, "but they should not replace thinking. There's always new knowledge that's not in the standards yet, especially if you push the technology envelope. We may find it from our own research or from suppliers, the internet, customers, universities, technical papers. We'll still need to encourage engineers to go look for knowledge beyond the standards. It's never quite black and white with standards or creating new knowledge. Remember, engineers tend to trust their own knowledge the most and tend to verify everything that comes from other folks or even the standards. And for some engineers, it's certainly more exciting to start drawing, constructing, or experimenting right away than to follow standards and look for knowledge."

"We could overcome some of that reluctance by enforcing the standards or the reuse of knowledge with checklists; we may have to do that," says Bolaji. "But we want to start by engaging all engineers in the knowledge management process—not forcing compliance out of the gate. I believe we need to make it easy for them to find and understand knowledge, and then their acceptance will follow. Training will be vital, and leadership and the PMs can play a big role by asking engineers the right questions and providing the appropriate coaching."

"How can we encourage engineers to make knowledge management their own?" asks Ricardo.

"Above all, we want senior engineers or subject matter experts to *own*, teach, and update pieces of the knowledge," says Bolaji. "Their teaching will allow suspicious engineers to ask questions and gain confidence. I'll also enlist a team to create a Wikipedia-like internal website. As people put new knowledge in, everybody can ask questions, suggest additions, make comments, and criticize or validate. All entries will have names with them—to credit people who contributed and allow readers to find the experts for discussions and questions."

Bolaji pauses briefly to allow the group to grasp the scope of the undertaking.

"Lastly, we want *engineers* to write, validate, and update the standards. Any addition to the standards will have the engineering background and names of the folks who contributed them. This way our standards will be correctly perceived as an engineering catalogue of knowledge rather than a book of laws."

"Great ideas," says Giuseppe. "I love the Wikipedia idea, but I'm not sure what the lawyers will say about that. All that knowledge in one place—hope nobody hacks into our server. And what would prevent a disgruntled engineer from feeding it to the wrong people?"

"That's a very valid concern, Giuseppe, and it certainly needs discussions with the legal team to ensure confidentiality," says Peter. "But the same can be said of how we store our knowledge now. If people want to break the law, they'll do it."

"I suppose that's true," says Giuseppe.

"We know that we have spies all around the test circuits trying to get a glimpse of new designs and features," continues Pietro. "But let me share some experience from my previous employer. We had a merger with another company that had independently developed knowledge about similar products. I was on the team charged with combining both companies' knowledge. It turned out that about 80 percent of our basic knowledge was the same. Beyond that, neither company could use much of the other's knowledge. The remainder was only of value within a specific context of our own manufacturing processes, R&D capabilities, prototyping capabilities, processes, etc. Again, we should always be conscious of potential knowledge theft, but we shouldn't let that stop us. So I think the Wikipedia idea has a lot of merit, and I would love to contribute to it as the effort gets traction."

Bolaji briefly goes over future plans for the Davanti knowledge management system, including new knowledge identification and capture. He then looks to Ricardo to wrap up the meeting.

"So let me give this team a few new challenges: How can we make the learning from experiments more effective?" asks Ricardo. "Can we operate in a more scientific manner, like formulating a formal hypothesis before every experiment and documenting if we confirmed or refuted it? New knowledge occurs if there is a surprise in the results. At my former employer, we made an A3 for every large experiment and also used that in the documentation and sharing process."

The Commilitones look at each other, giving the question serious consideration. "We'll work on that," says Guiseppe. "We can start with the meetings the engineers have before and after every iteration."

"Finally, I want to thank this team for its excellent work and great progress toward a KM system," concludes Ricardo. "And I especially like how you're planning to engage the engineers around the process. Now here is another challenge for this team: how can we get our engineers to think like the Wright brothers—use all available knowledge and run all needed experiments *before* we design and build? So let's talk about this again in a month or two, and please let me know if I can help or remove obstacles for you."

***

Mo gathers his notes and sets off to update Sofia and the Volta team on his quick-wins project. As he walks toward the conference room, he recalls the nervousness he felt when addressing Junior and the executive team in the spring. Today he has no such feelings, only positive news that he's anxious to share.

After he was assigned to lead the quick-wins project, Mo formed a few subteams, which did gemba walks and talked to many people. The team members initially focused on the eight traditional wastes, which they had remembered from their lean training, and also were mindful of Sofia's list of the usual suspects. They found a lot of opportunities, but also noticed that some wasteful activities already had improvement initiatives underway—those would still make their list even though Mo's team wouldn't claim credit for any of those savings.

When Mo enters the room, the Volta team and Sofia are already there. He walks to a whiteboard, which has a list of categories: "Me and the subteam leaders are going to walk through each category of what we believe are our biggest wins:

"*Prototypes and testing:* After Lee and Zing completed their work in the prototype shop and the test labs, capacity increased between 20 and 30 percent, and those areas are still working on additional improvements. The immediate consequence of the improvements was the elimination of overtime and temporary resources. Luca further agreed to transfer several technicians to other areas in engineering where they will help out engineers with administrative work. They also decided to not replace the folks who will start retirement at the end of the year.

"A subteam set up a visual planning board in the test lab. The work of the prototype shop is scheduled on the BOM board, which has helped to make problems with workflow visible, and daily huddles keep staff focused on the most urgent issues on the boards. Large savings also came from efficiency improvements, 5S, flow, pull, and the creation of work cells. The 5S initiative created so much space they were able to close a warehouse they had rented in town for test-bike storage.

"Before the reorganization, all prototyping and testing costs came out of a big, shared pool, and the goal was to get as much out of that pool as possible. Now that the test cost is reassigned to the projects and PMs control their own budgets, the PMs encourage the engineers to only build and test what is absolutely needed.

"All prototypes used to get new components (rims, derailleurs, chains, etc.). But nobody really remembers who made that rule, and the components usually weren't stressed in the testing. A technician has been assigned to recover and catalogue the components once they're removed from the prototypes. And since Lee had reorganized the supply store, there was plenty of space there.

"*Shipping:* Before lean, virtually all plant bikes needed for testing were expedited to save time. Now that shipping time is part of standard timing, expediting is limited to rare cases. However, here we found a negative consequence of the new organization: PMs are no longer bundling their shipments with their colleagues because they don't want to pay for somebody else's freight. Stephano's people are trying to work that out.

"*Engineering:* The engineering department was adequately staffed, and the only personnel reductions came through attrition. Nonetheless, engineers can do a lot more iterations now, and they also picked up a fair amount of new work, like technology development, idea assessments, and CI initiatives. A lot of that has been made possible because several engineers who recently retired were replaced by technicians. The technicians help the engineers with tasks such as compiling test data, writing requests, ordering components, and arranging shipments, which allows engineers to focus on more important tasks and has resulted in a noticeable drop in engineering costs.

"Lastly, across all the areas, the Volta teams found a lot of small improvements, from office supplies to paint usage in the shop, travel cost, etc. Although individual savings were small, they added up to quite a large total.

"Now a drumroll: Charles is going to show the cost-saving numbers," concludes Mo.

Charles illuminates a spreadsheet on the flat screen that reveals *monthly* savings had reached 100,000 euros. "This is a conservative estimate, and the numbers will increase in the coming months," he explains.

"This is incredible," says Sofia. "I expected immediate savings, but not this much."

"I participated in many gemba walks, and I was able to see it firsthand," says Anika. "These numbers are accurate and will be visible in the next financial report."

"How should we communicate this?" asks Sofia.

"The finance report will come out next week, and I think that's a good time for a communication," says Charles. "Should the communication come from Junior?"

"Why not have a celebration?" suggest Mo.

"A celebration is a great idea," says Anika. "Everyone has contributed to this in some way. If you have ideas for what we should do, let me know, and I'll discuss this with Junior."

"This is only the beginning," explains Sofia. "In a couple of months, we should have the first visibility of the business impact from innovation excellence—sales, revenue, and costs. And we probably have enough data and other metrics, like on-time delivery and cycle time, that we can communicate at that time. Of course, it will be a while until people understand the impact of OTD and cycle time on the business, but it's a good idea to get people used to the measures. But let's plan this celebration first; we'll talk about the next celebration when we have the data."

***

"Good morning, everyone," greets Junior at the weekly communications meeting. The gathering continues to allow directors and others to keep him and each other apprised of the daily business and the transformation's progress; share information that should be passed on to associates; and, for Junior, it's another opportunity to see where his help is needed. "I hope you've had a good weekend, despite the sudden chill that seems to have taken over. . . . I'd like to add another component to our meeting: Let's start with a message about respect and care for people. It could be a message about safety, engagement, recognition, or ethics. I'll start us off today and hope that you will follow, both here and in your own meetings."

"I like that idea," affirms Anika.

"Today I'd like to thank Ricardo for setting an example for all of us. And I'm not only talking about how he moved his desk to the middle of the engineering room. I've noticed an enormous change in the whole engineering area: People are happy, they perform well, they help each other. The engineers reorganized their work area—it's clean, organized, and quiet. It's obvious that people not only respect each other but they also respect their work area. What a difference from only a year ago! Soon I'll walk in there and every problem—if there are any—will be visible. I won't even have to ask where I can help."

"Thanks, Junior," says Ricardo humbly. "I appreciate your reaction to the R&D changes. I'll start us off with some findings from the Wednesday tests of competitor bikes. After several weeks of blind testing, our riders rated the two closest competitors equal to Davanti. This confirms what we are seeing out in the market, and I assume nobody here will argue with those results."

"Did we benchmark our competitors before this?" asks Joe.

"Yes, we did the routine bike analysis and testing, but I don't believe it was enough," replies Ricardo. "So we now created a benchmark obeya, where everybody, engineers or not, can explore competitor products, cutaways, test data, manufacturing processes, market share, and prices at any time. And if you want to personally ride competitor cycles, you know where to find them."

"Could we do blind tests with the pros?" questions Leandro. "You know, slip a competitor bike in with Davanti paint?"

"Don't even think about it," says Ricardo, reflecting back to Mo's meeting with them. "Unless they know exactly what it is, they won't put their butts on it. And we want to keep them convinced Davanti bikes are still far ahead. Just imagine if a rider likes the competitor bike better, and we have to explain what it is."

Junior asks about the black bikes with the poor finish—the one he rode and how his rating compared with the rest of the riders. Ricardo explains that those were bikes from the Marconi integration event and briefly describes the project and the purpose of the integration event, from which the bikes evolved. "And, Junior, your assessment aligned with most others. Our engineers are not pros—they all like the softer ride."

"When will those bikes be ready for sale?" asks Claudia, and everyone looks to Joe, the product director, wanting to hear the same thing. Joe says the project is on the radar, and that it will be moved up in the next portfolio update. Ricardo explains that lab testing confirmed the positive results from the Wednesday ride, and they are looking at some amateur race testing in the southern hemisphere in the winter. But he also raises concerns over confidentiality: "If the word gets out, we'll soon have spies along the roads on Wednesdays. So please, keep this in this room."

Diana talks about a supplier development initiative they started in procurement. It includes supplier training, collaboration projects, and faster deliveries. "First of all, 90 percent of our purchases come from a handful of suppliers. We can drastically minimize the remainder of our supply base. We can build long-term relationships with the larger suppliers around collaboration, service, quality, and performance improvement instead of negotiating on price alone. This also will cut down on bureaucracy and make us much faster and more agile. And over the long term this should reduce supplier costs."

Everybody in the room applauds Diana for this long-overdue initiative.

Stephano talks next about work to calculate cost of delay or just the cost of waiting. He said they are making progress. He explains that it is actually a very simple formula, but that it's difficult to get accurate assumptions. "Here's our big takeaway so far. The cost of delay is generally huge compared to what it costs to avoid the delay, at least for everything we've attempted to calculate so far. And that is why we don't need perfect accuracy to make most of these decisions. For example, if working overtime or securing extra resources costs 50,000 euros to avoid a 500,000 COD, who cares if the COD is 500,000 or 520,000?"

"Nice work, Stephano," says Junior impressed. "Anika, how's your work with succession planning going?"

"Yes, well, I've been working with some of you on this," Anika says. "I want to remind everybody that I still need your input by the end of the week. Early next year we'll have an off-site meeting to finalize the plan. Please don't only think about successors for yourself—we need plans for everybody. And that includes positions like knowledge management, dual-ladder positions, councils, and CI work."

"Thanks for the update on succession planning, Anika," says Junior. "How are we doing on the dual ladder?"

"We've created the first positions: three in R&D, two in manufacturing, one in finance, and one in sales and marketing. The first appointments were made by senior leadership, and we asked the nominees to write typical position descriptions that can be used for future nominations. The first nominees also formed a team with a few other associates to develop the nomination process and the career plans. I'm heading up that team personally."

"Why wasn't a project manager appointed to a dual-ladder position?" asks Diana. "We have a lot of very talented project managers."

"I made a career plan with every project manager," says Leandro. "Project management positions have traditionally been entry positions into corporate management and leadership positions, and most project managers prefer that career track. But as soon as we're done with the succession planning, I'll revisit the career plans with some of our project managers. I certainly would like to find a senior candidate for a dual-ladder position who would spend time on standards and playbooks."

"OK, good," concludes Junior. "Anything else before we wrap up?"

"Yes, Junior," says Ricardo. "We identified the root cause for the problems with the Tour de France bikes, and countermeasures have been implemented and verified. All new Primo Sempre bikes are now made with a new process, and design standards were updated to ensure that the problem will not reoccur."

"Design standards?" says Constantine, surprised. "I didn't know we had those. I'm glad to hear that."

"We do now," responds Ricardo. "We completed the design release of the product, and the incremental production release is progressing very fast."

"And I can confirm that the first Primo Veloce bikes have started showing up in the stores, and they'll soon be followed by the PS models," says Joe. "I want to take this opportunity to thank Constantine, Ricardo, Claudia, and their staffs for an excellent job in pulling this off despite some of the recent obstacles."

"Likewise," adds Junior. "Well done, everybody. Keep transforming. And if you see somebody do something exceptional, please thank that person. And let all of us know. I may want to stop by and express my gratitude, too."

***

Monday afternoon Ricardo posts a new version of the R&D strategy next to the department's vision and the goals on the wall outside Emilio's old office. Ricardo developed the strategy with his team, and, whenever improvements are suggested, he updates the postings.

The R&D strategy has remained essentially the same as when Ricardo and his team developed it:

- Provide constant flow of the right innovative products at the right time.
- Leverage innovation excellence principles to become more agile, faster, and efficient.
- Build a world-class technical organization (talent, knowledge, and processes).
- Create a culture based on safety, quality, innovation, respect, and collaboration.

The board also reinforces R&D philosophies—flat and responsive; flexible and agile; focused; collaborative; and engaged, empowered, respected, and trusted associates—by identifying recent actions and individuals illustrative of the philosophies.

Ricardo also posted a simple x-matrix to create a visual representation of the strategy deployment: It starts with the four strategic items that are then broken down into single activities and deliverables. The matrix also includes the responsibilities and support resources.

The R&D metric charts are posted to the right of the strategy and grouped by:

- *Safety:* In addition to the traditional safety metrics, Carolina, who is responsible for corporate safety, started a 24/7 metric that also includes safety at home. She often likes to pilot new initiatives in R&D.
- *Quality:* The first R&D quality metric is "right the first time" and tracks the need for correction and rework in some key areas. Another quality metric, still in development, tracks the cost of problems that could have been avoided by a better design. Input for that metric comes from recalls (which Davanti fortunately has not experienced in recent history), warranty claims (for problems like cracks, poor ride, failed components, etc.), and feedback from customers and dealers.
- *Delivery:* The delivery metrics include OTD of prototypes, tests, drawings, calculations, styling, and other critical subjects. The delivery-need dates are identified on the kanban cards, and the actual delivery dates are filled in by the engineer when the kanban is closed out. Since Davanti R&D does not have a computerized kanban system yet, Carolina asked one of the lab technicians to key the information into a spreadsheet for analysis. (He took that job over from Gina who got it started.) Total cycle time and cycle times for individual tasks are extracted from that spreadsheet as well as total work in process (WIP) and throughput. Graphs and trend charts are reprinted every week. Since Ricardo knows that efficiency correlates with speed, he did not ask for another efficiency metric at this time, but he keeps a close eye on total WIP because he knows that is the best leading indicator for cycle time.
- *Innovation outcomes:* A few metrics that gauge the effectiveness of the new innovation process also have been added to the wall: how many new ideas were investigated, how many made it to the technology creation process, how many went to the product creation process, and how many spinoffs were created. They plan to add a few more as the transformation continues. Ricardo wants to see at least 10 times more ideas started than make it into products, and he wants to see more than one new product—which he calls "spinoffs"—from every idea that is pursued. Gina had suggested that R&D also measure the total amount of new ideas that are generated. Ricardo, however, chose not to include such a metric, explaining, "That is like measuring success by how many people have been trained. If you want ideas, you get ideas, same for patents—but that says nothing about the market success of those ideas and patents."

- *Employee engagement:* Anika—who also likes to pilot HR metrics in R&D, especially those aimed at engagement, happiness, respect, etc.—contributed metrics related to people. She has started some experiments to find the right metrics, including the use of simple online surveys, counting the number of people who volunteer for crossfunctional activities, and the number of times employees received notes of gratitude or thanks from a leader. Anika even figured out a way to gauge how many people formally help others, practice knowledge sharing, and accept responsibility beyond their jobs.

The R&D metrics follow good reporting standards: All metrics show the starting point, the desired trend, and the targets. They also show the intervals for updating and the individuals responsible for the updates. Ricardo plans to have his team look at additional metrics soon, especially those that track how R&D contributes to other corporate goals (e.g., driving the innovation excellence transformation).

Next to the metrics is the schedule of tiered huddles that recently started to take place in R&D. After Ricardo's encouragement and with his coaching, all the suborganizations in R&D started huddles on a regular schedule. Some huddles evolved fast and through the sharing of best practices, and others caught up quickly. Today all R&D associates, from the technicians in the lab to the leadership, are involved in some form of regular huddles, and the problems roll up daily from the lower tier to the leadership huddles. Although the R&D huddles are still evolving, they serve as a pilot for the other Davanti organizations:

- *Associate huddles:* Associate huddles start every day at 7:15 am when the prototype shop and test lab supervisors meet with their teams for 10 to 15 minutes in front of their huddle boards. They look at attendance and the prior day metrics for safety, quality, delivery, cycle time, and people engagement. Any deviation from the standard or expectation for the recent day is marked in red and quickly addressed. Then they discuss the challenges of the upcoming day and what help is needed and where. They also use the huddle to make important announcements and recognitions. Everybody is encouraged to call out people who helped them or excelled at work or in the community. Then they discuss employee concerns, and, as a group, pick one area where everybody will try to improve that day.
- *Supervisor huddle:* At 8:15 am each day, Luca meets for 15 minutes with the supervisors, and their huddle follows a similar pattern to that of the lower-tier huddle. Supervisors bring up problems and items that need Luca's help. Luca notes items that need to be communicated upward and enlists the help of Carolina, his manager, if needed.
- *Operations huddle:* Three times a week, Carolina has a huddle at 10:00 am with Luca and the other members of her team, including a finance rep and an HR person. They follow a similar standard as the lower-level meetings, and Carolina collects information for the huddle with Ricardo.
- *Project manager huddle:* Bart, the R&D programs manager, and all PMs convene a daily 15-minute huddle at 11:00 am in the BOM room, where they discuss the help the PMs need from R&D to keep their projects on track. Bart also attends Joe's weekly huddle and notes all issues that need to be brought to the R&D huddles.
- *Technology huddle:* Bolaji, the technology manager, meets with a different engineering group every day for 30 minutes at 9:00 am: designers on Monday, stylists on Tuesday, TCP project managers on Wednesday, etc. They either meet in front of the kanban board or in the work area, and they discuss challenges with delivery, staffing, tools, training, and the like.

The three R&D managers (Bart, Carolina, and Bolaji) have a lot to discuss all week, but since they sit as a group, they talk through problems—e.g., sharing resources, addressing common technical problems, solving organizational issues—as they pop up.

As Ricardo completes his posting of the updated materials, Stella and Mo walk past and look at the new strategy documents on the wall.

"I wonder what Emilio would say if he saw this?" asks Stella.

"He'd probably think we're going to get nothing done because we're in meetings every day," jokes Mo.

"Well, he'd be right about meeting every day," says Ricardo, turning around and acknowledging that he'd heard them. "But he'd be surprised by how much we do get done. And not just how much, but also how fast the important stuff gets addressed."

***

Ricardo starts his R&D leadership huddle at noon on Wednesday in front of the metrics board on "Emilio's wall," as it's come to be known. He also has a similar huddle scheduled for Mondays and Fridays. He is joined by the three R&D managers and the R&D project managers. Anika represents HR, Giovanni represents manufacturing, and Charles speaks for finance; occasionally engineers will be asked to attend.

The problems are so clearly marked on the metrics board that it takes less than 10 seconds to identify them. The group examines those problems that need their attention or awareness. But the main focus is on those problems that need help from Ricardo or somebody else in the room.

Today there are no issues with safety, but there are problems with first-time-through quality in R&D. It's suggested that the standards are not good enough and need to be updated. Bolaji will form a team to work on that. There are still OTD issues with the plant (other than the newly released products), and Ricardo promises to join Giovanni in talking with Constantine about getting resources to catch up. Paint issues with prototypes from the plant don't seem to be under control either; although the Fumane shop corrected the urgent samples, the less-urgent samples were sent back to the plant at the plant's expense. Anika draws everybody's attention to the open positions and the need to move some more associates from the lab to the engineering area. Carolina volunteers to help her expedite that process.

Other issues identified via the metrics or flagged with tags are discussed and mostly resolved in a consistent sequence:

■ Is there a standard process?
■ Was the standard process followed?
■ Is the standard good enough?
■ Has the issue been resolved, and, if not, what help is needed to get it resolved?
■ Is the fix permanent, and, if not, has the root cause been identified and is a team working on countermeasures?
■ If the problem is complex and systemic, has an A3 been assigned to an individual or a team?

After the metric charts are reviewed, the attention switches to issues escalated from the lower-tier meetings, like a capacity issue in the lab:

■ Although there is more than enough total capacity, some people still occasionally get overloaded when special knowledge or testing is required. For example, the Primo Sempre line requires one specific test that now is in high demand because of the upcoming launch of that line and the recent problems. Carolina will head up a small team to attempt to better stagger those requirements.

■ The knowledge management mining effort has stressed the Davanti computers, and Bolaji is getting frustrated with long computing times and jobs that get hung up and need to be resubmitted. Bolaji will prepare a work order for Ricardo's signature to release resources from the IT department to remedy the issue.

■ Anika still needs a list of candidates to work with her on the dual-ladder nominating process, and the managers promise to respond this week.

The team moves over to the R&D kanban board and looks at issues that could not get resolved in lower-level huddles. Kanbans that need to be discussed are turned 45 degrees so they can easily be spotted, but today there are no such issues.

At the end of the meeting, Ricardo goes over information that needs to be passed down to the lower huddles, such as communication from Junior's meeting or organizational changes, and he opens the floor for news, recognitions, celebrations, etc. This "shout-out" portion of the huddle has become popular in lower huddles, and Ricardo's group appears to like it as well: they publicly recognize colleagues or associates who excelled at work, in sports, in school, and in the community; people also recognize associates who helped them or who did something exceptional. All folks that are recognized are invited to the huddle: today it's the team that worked on the crack problems in the Tour de France; their final A3 is posted on the wall. They enjoy the gratitude and respect of the R&D leaders, and they stay for questions and comments about their project. After about 30 minutes, Ricardo adjourns the huddle.

Ricardo had invited the other Davanti directors and managers to audit the R&D tiered meeting process, and, after his group leaves, he spends some time coaching the directors and managers with the setup of their own huddles and describes how to encourage the escalation of information from tier to tier. Ricardo and the other directors will soon participate in a "pinnacle" huddle—Junior's weekly metrics review and his communication meeting will eventually morph into the pinnacle meeting, and the CEO will chair it.

***

Diana from procurement calls Mo: "Hello, Mo, I have Tim Albright on the phone. He's the CTO from ACE, our US component supplier, and he would like to talk to you if you have a few minutes."

"I know who he is; I specified their components for many years. Please put him through."

"Very good. Here he is."

Diana connects Mo with the CTO of ACE Inc., one of the largest bicycle component manufacturers in the world. The company, which is bigger than Davanti, is headquartered in Colorado Springs, Colorado. Tim's company has several large plants in the Far East and smaller plants in many other countries. They make components for virtually every bike in the world, from race bikes to commuters. The company grew mostly by acquisitions, and today they make everything from derailleurs and chains to rims, brakes, and even bike apparel. One of the few areas they've yet to enter are electric-bike components.

"Hello, Mr. Albright, to what do I owe this pleasure?"

"Hi, Mr. Pensatore. First, I need to apologize. We tried to bid on those gear motors for your project, but we had to decline because we saw no hope to meet your time frame. This is just too new and fast for us."

"That's OK. I think we're covered."

"We certainly don't like to miss out on any new bike idea in the world. We studied your patent applications and concluded that you may be working on a chainless bike. To make a long story short, although we can't bid on a gear mechanism, we have something that might work for you."

The CTO describes a very simple gear mechanism, made from molded, short, fiber composites. Since the gear size is so small—less than two centimeters for the smallest wheel—they achieve a very large step up when going from gear to gear, so they need only a small number of gears to cover the range of today's derailleurs. For that reason, the mechanism only weighs a fraction of what Mo is used to, and it has very low friction.

"Why can't you put it on a bike, Mr. Albright?"

"If we combine it with a chain, there are no real advantages. You still have a chain. But if you ever figure out how to get rid of the chain, we might have a gear mechanism for you."

"There must be another catch," says Mo. "Something tells me there's more."

"There is. We've never been able to make it work with rigid, power-transfer mechanisms like a drive shaft. It could work, but the adjustments to connect a mechanical rod or other fixed devices become prohibitively complicated."

Mo asks a few more questions and totally surprises the CTO by saying, "I'd like to test a few of your mechanisms. When can I have them?"

"When do you need them?"

"Can I have them next week?"

The CTO chokes and then laughs. "You're kidding, right?"

"I don't need perfect mechanisms; they're not for race bikes yet. And don't bother buying molds for the gears, either. You can machine them or even 3D-print them. We're not doing final durability testing at this time."

"I'm sorry for my surprise, Mr. Pensatore. We seem to have a totally different conception of development time at ACE than you have at Davanti. But I will pull out all stops to get you something, maybe not next week but very soon."

"Thanks, Mr. Albright. I appreciate the effort. I'm sorry to put you under a time pressure, but we're moving as fast as possible here."

"I understand."

"I look forward to testing your mechanisms and talking again soon."

***

Rebecca's success with the Toricelli initiative has turned into a headache for Marco. Rebecca and Marco have been called this morning to Junior's office. Marco has kept the Davanti leadership well appraised of the status of the new venture, and Stephano reported the finance numbers along with the other Davanti revenue streams. But no one has paid much attention to the effort because they knew it was an experiment, and they wanted to give it enough time before discussing how to integrate it within Davanti—if at all.

Marco and Rebecca walk into Junior's office, where Claudia is already seated at the boss' small conference table. Then it dawns on Marco: Rebecca's business must have affected new bike sales, which are Claudia's responsibility.

"Hello, Junior, Claudia," greets Marco tentatively.

Before Junior can speak, Claudia bursts out: "I knew this innovation stuff would ruin the company! Why couldn't you all see this coming?"

Junior tries to calm her concerns: "It's still an experiment, Claudia. Although we may have lost some direct sales of new bikes, we gained sales overall, and we certainly increased our revenues. And if you've been talking with the dealers involved, you know they like it."

"Do you even know where this little operation's money is going?" accuses Claudia. "How much money falls between the cracks or ends up in the dealers' pockets? Since all expenses come out of my overhead, there's no way to track this."

"Claudia, all of the financial tracking has been vetted by Charles and Stephano, and the corporate setup has been blessed by legal," says Rebecca calmly. "We've got every euro accounted for. . . . I regret the impact on new bike sales; we should have discussed that more with you and your group. But it took off so fast; even you must realize, it's turned into a real business and a moneymaker."

Marco, fearing the worst, suggests they collaborate: "When this was an experiment, it made sense to set it up as a separate, self-sustaining operation. If it didn't work out, it wouldn't negatively affect Davanti day-to-day sales activities. But this should no longer be an experiment. I think we should integrate the Toricelli business into Davanti's sales and marketing operation. Claudia, you could then work directly with Rebecca. I think you both will make a great team and can learn a lot from each other. I bet you can come up with an aggressive plan for expansion that would actually lead to *more* new-bike sales. Once we get people hooked on riding a Davanti, many will want to own one. This also will give us the synergy to deal with an upcoming problem: how do we convert used-bike sales to new-bike sales? There is a very high demand for certified used bikes, and we want to make sure that a used-bike sale leads to a future new-bike sale."

Marco's idea puts the Toricelli responsibility under Claudia, which appeals to her, as he knew it would. Junior seems to like it. Claudia has had no problems working with Rebecca; since the marketing department joined sales, they've found ways to get along. "I'm fine with that if Junior and leadership sign off," says Claudia. "There should be ways that both Toricelli and new sales can benefit from this, and I'd like input into those decisions. I want to be involved, but I don't necessarily need to direct the unit myself. I'm happy with Rebecca continuing to run the show."

Rebecca looks apprehensive but relieved that she's still in charge. Marco is happy that he weathered the storm. Junior is pleased he didn't have to referee an outcome. "I like the plan, Claudia and Marco. I'll get leadership behind this. Let's sell a lot of everything Davanti."

Chapter 28

Results to Celebrate

Huddles, one-on-one meetings, and gemba walks are now part of Junior's standard work. This morning he again parks in the back of the building—but in a parking spot far from the entrance to the prototype shop, where no one can be upset that he took a prime spot. He grabs his backpack off the passenger seat, makes the long walk to the door, and then slowly enters, surprised by how tired he feels. "I really need to get in better shape," he thinks.

Inside he sees Penelope, who must have seen him park. She's in the aisle waving at him as he enters: "Hello, Mr. Davanti, you've got to see what Rossa sent me. I just know that you had something to do with this."

On a previous gemba walk, Junior had passed out some of the "Thank you" notes from Johan and the pros to the technicians who had prepared their bikes for the racing season. Penelope was off that day, so he left her note on her workstation.

"Hello, Penelope."

"Please come back to my work area!"

Junior follows her, and she points to a large poster of Rossa on the podium in Paris. It is signed by Rossa and dedicated, "To the Best Bike Tuner in the World." In a handwritten note that Penelope has attached to the poster, Rossa thanks her for going beyond the call of duty to tune his bike. "I noticed the difference," he wrote. "Thanks for helping me win the Tour!"

"The guys around here are so jealous. Nobody ever got a letter from the Tour de France winner. My dad was beside himself when I showed it to him. Here, look at this!" She shows Junior a selfie she took with her dad and the poster. "My dad doesn't grasp everything anymore, but this one he perfectly understood. He would have been no less proud if I had won the Tour myself. I cried for half an hour when I got this."

Penelope tells Junior how everybody in the shop stopped by and looked at her poster. They've also given her the nickname, "World's Best Bike Tuner." She says, "Some of those guys finish the bikes now before sending them to me for tuning."

"Looks like you got their respect, too," says Junior. "You certainly deserve it."

"So what should I do when I get a bad bike again?"

"What would be appropriate?"

"I could send it back, but on what authority can I do that?"

"Tell them that is *your* new rule. And congratulations again, best bike tuner in the world."

Junior walks around the shop and hands out the remaining notes and asks the technicians about their current undertakings. He calls each by name, and is genuinely interested in the details

DOI: 10.4324/9781003231837-28

of their work. Occasionally he pulls a pad out of his pocket and writes down a note. He stops by one of the daily huddles and stands in the back observing for 10 minutes. Gradually he makes his way to the door that leads back to the main building and his office.

He stops in the cafeteria, grabs an espresso from a new machine that's been installed, and continues to address everyone he meets by name. Back in his office, he sits, clicks on his email, and types Johan a note: "Please make sure that Rossa gets this: 'Augustine, I want to thank you for sending the nice note and poster to Penelope Dicomo. She cried for half an hour when she got it. You have a fan for life now, and you will be assured of having the best-tuned bikes in the world. And if you ever come to this area, please stop by. I'll introduce you to her and all the other folks who work so hard for you and your teammates,' Fausto Davanti Jr.'"

The next day Junior gets a reply from Rossa: "Mr. Davanti, thank you for the kind remarks. Please give my regards and thanks to all those in the company who support us through the season. To an even better season next year."

***

As more capacity in the bottleneck area—the prototype shop—became available, Carolina added more space on the visual planning board. She had verified that testing had increased capacity after their lean initiative, and she was confident that the upstream engineering processes were adequately staffed to deliver sufficient work to the prototype shop. But she also noticed that whenever she added capacity, it was filled immediately. However, it was not earmarked for new products; the capacity was being filled with more iterations for existing projects.

Puzzled, she asked Bart why there weren't more new products coming to prototype. "We had a discussion in the last business huddle about the portfolio," Bart answered. "Currently there are no short-term plans to add new traditional products to the Davanti lineup because the market is saturated. We're trying to grow that business short-term with better dealer incentives, new financing, leasing options, and a few more face lifts." Bart confirmed that the added tags were all for more iterations on existing projects, but, since Joe's business pays for the R&D operation, Joe is not happy about adding iterations just because there is capacity for them.

Bart also filled Carolina in on the new strategic initiatives that were being considered: expanding the market in more countries, diverse bike offerings like recreational or city bikes, and possibly the development of mountain bikes: "Those new initiatives, which are about to start, have their own budgets, and they will certainly need R&D capacity once they show up in the portfolio. But at the rate you've been creating new capacity, I think we can handle the additional workload."

Carolina, Bart, and Ricardo meet in front of the visual planning board to discuss the capacity situation, and decide to show only the eight iterations per week that the current business portfolio needs. "We need to continue to promote more idea generation," says Ricardo. "That, in turn, will lead to more need for prototype capacity as well as more technology development."

"But what do we do until then?" asks Bart, aware that some shop and lab technicians are currently underleveraged.

"We can engage the technicians in more improvement activities and continue to move some to open positions in other areas on a temporary basis," says Carolina. "We want to remain flexible, so we can quickly scale up as soon as the new products appear in the portfolio."

"I like this flexible approach," responds Bart. "I don't think it will be long before new projects begin to hit prototyping, and then we'll reshuffle the engineers."

"I'm good with that as well," adds Ricardo. "It's lean, and that's what we're all about."

***

Junior has asked Sofia to join him in the cafeteria for lunch. But since it's an unseasonably warm December afternoon, they take their trays of food outside to the courtyard. Like Davanti, the cafeteria has also transformed (with a generous "subsidy" granted by Junior). It's become more like the food courts at Fusilli. Instead of a few, stale offerings each day, there are stations for salads, soups, sandwiches, and a few entrees every day, ranging from international fare, like sushi and tacos, to more local offerings of pastas.

Sitting across from each other at a picnic table, Junior asks, "Sofia, how can I be sure that Davanti quality won't suffer from all this lean stuff? You know, we were always obsessed with quality. It worries me that with so much else on everyone's minds, they might neglect the basics."

"Well, Junior, you could just trust me on this. It's worked before."

"Touché, but please indulge my concerns. Tell me what you know and why you know it."

"When I came here to Davanti, quality was clearly one of the strengths. So for me it wasn't an immediate concern, which is not always the case in my work. But I also noticed how Davanti achieves good quality—through inspections."

"Yes, so? It works. What's wrong with that? That's how my dad taught me. It's hard to argue with success."

"Your dad did what virtually every company in the world does: inspect. But inspection or even quality incentives are not the best methods to assure quality. Toyota legend Shigeo Shingo, who started his career as a quality inspector at a train manufacturer, learned that inspection was an inferior method when it came to achieving good quality. Everybody knew there was an inspection downstream of their work, and they were confident the inspector would catch their mistakes. And when the final inspector in production missed too much, they added another level of inspection or came up with better incentives. Eventually more scientific methods, like six sigma, emerged to improve but not eliminate inspection."

"I'm with you so far."

"Shingo learned that the best method to achieve quality was to engage all workers and make everyone responsible for their own quality. Later he introduced the methods at Toyota, where nobody accepts bad quality, nobody makes bad quality, and nobody passes on bad quality. And all workers are empowered to stop the production line if they see anything wrong that might eventually be passed on to a customer."

"Ah, yes, the famous andon cord."

"Exactly. But Shingo also learned to engage workers in designing processes and methods that made it impossible to make mistakes or poor quality—you've heard about poka yoke."

Junior nods.

"Shingo's approach was perfected by Toyota and other companies and proved to be superior to traditional inspection and control methods and also proved many Western business schools wrong," continues Sofia. "His methods work as well for invisible office work, where inspection can be tricky at times. It works very well in R&D."

"So how can you change that in our culture?"

"You start by having everybody send anything back that is not perfect, and you ask associates to keep records of what gets sent back."

"Making it visible—wouldn't that embarrass people?"

"It depends on how you present it. People don't make mistakes on purpose, and individual mistakes can be corrected in private. But if an individual is unable to deliver perfect quality, the individual is empowered to stop production and ask for help."

"And then production is resumed when the problem is fixed. And that by itself will assure perfect quality?"

"It helps. Most often it's not a person who's making a mistake, but the process they're trying to work in is inadequate. When you make problems visible to everyone, you engage people in developing solutions to improve the quality of the work they do, including improving processes. That's when you see a lot of quality improvements. And there are many other lean principles that complement this approach and help create better quality."

"Such as?"

"Give people enough time to do good work (i.e., avoid overloading). Single-piece flow (focus on one thing at a time). Empowerment to stop work if something is not perfect. Standard work. Design the product for quality in the first place. You know about these, Junior. But in many companies, they're just sprinkled here and there. To change the culture, we need to educate everyone. Every Davanti employee can understand these concepts. They're not challenging to grasp or to implement."

"Yes, I agree. But, as you point out, given our good quality results to date, there's never been the impetus to change. So why change a good thing now?"

"Good is the enemy of better."

"OK. I believe that as well."

"One facet of quality here does seem unusual to me, Junior. Why is manufacturing responsible for Davanti quality?"

"That position held the responsibility under my dad, and it stayed that way. It makes sense to me. Constantine's responsible for the plant. Isn't that where quality occurs? He's done a good job, has he not?"

"First, Constantine strikes me as a good executive whom you're lucky to have. I've seen this type of arrangement where it's like the fox guarding the henhouse; a plant manager cuts corners to meet production targets and keeps relaxing the tolerances to improve yields. My comment has nothing to do with Constantine. But quality is not only done in the plant. It's done everywhere, and if a product is poorly designed, there's little the plant could do to change that."

"So what do you suggest?"

"Could you put the R&D director position in charge of quality, and let the plant quality managers report to both R&D and manufacturing?"

"I can, but won't Constantine complain?"

"Very likely, especially since he won't be setting his own quality targets anymore. But we can explain to him that quality is hard to achieve in the plant after the product is designed—quality starts when the product is first discussed. Plus, Constantine needs more time to get familiar with his new responsibility of the supply chain and just may welcome the change."

"I just don't want to be a referee again, with Ricardo in one ear and Constantine in the other."

"The customer is the referee, and a new quality culture must be designed around the customer. It starts in R&D and follows the complete value stream all the way to the counting of the money."

"Once again, I ask an innocent question and get a head full of stuff to think about."

"Junior, your questions are never so innocent. You may not recognize some problems in detail, but you know enough to ask the right questions."

"I suppose you're right. . . . Say, the lunch offerings are quite good. For a simple salad, it's delicious. I rarely eat in the cafeteria, but that may change."

"I agree. Another positive change at Davanti. Thanks for making it possible. I'm sure the associates wholeheartedly endorse how you've transformed the cafeteria. Who wouldn't?"

***

With Christmas less than two weeks away, most Davanti employees are in a good mood and looking forward to the upcoming holiday break. A few remember the Christmas celebrations that

Fausto Sr. would organize for the associates every year. The first ones were at his house around a huge Christmas tree. When the party got too big, it was moved to a restaurant and eventually ended up at the plant. Junior was encouraged many years ago by finance and legal to discontinue the tradition because the dinner bill and the liability became too big. This year, however, he's missing those times and believes he's struck a balance of festive with professional caution: all employees are gathered either inside the prototype shop or just outside around a pizza truck in the yard. A large, garage-like door has been raised so everyone feels together. The weather is cool, but the sun and comradery have everyone feeling warm. And nearly everyone is wondering why they're celebrating. Junior's email invitation referred to something about the first successes of the innovation excellence initiative.

After Junior saw the latest financial results—Stephano now closes the books weekly—he was ecstatic. Even though Stephano cautioned that "these are only preliminary results," Junior was blown away by the numbers and wanted to do something special. Anika suggested the celebration: "People will feel rewarded, and those who are still on the fence will get closer to buying in."

"With the money we saved, I can invite the whole town and, with the increased revenues, maybe the next town over as well," said Junior.

Since they were celebrating the first successes of the initiative, Junior did not want the celebration to be confused with a Christmas party; there are no Christmas decorations, other than a modestly decorated tree in the corner of the yard near the "Manno's Pizza Camion." The Manno staff has rolled out dough for dozens of pizzas, and Davanti employees can select toppings from a large bar with ingredients attached to the side of the food truck. Most people make their own pizzas, and then hand them to the "pizzaioli" who bake them in a woodburning oven in less than three minutes. (Many employees are hanging out next to the oven to stay warm.) In addition to the pizza line, Manno has brought an expansive salad and antipasto bar. To top it all off, "Batto's Gelatos," the best gelato shop in town, serves dessert.

After much eating, laughing, and fun, the crowd grows quiet as Junior walks to the center of the yard. He takes a microphone and explains that he had received several unexpected Christmas presents this year: "The first present is that we now have the two new bike lines in the stores and they are selling well. I am most proud that it took less than six months to develop them. A year ago, nobody would have thought that was possible."

The employees politely applaud, waiting to hear about the next gift.

"The second present was given to me in the form of the last financial report. Our innovation excellence initiative has already netted total cost savings of a quarter-million euros."

This news brings more applause accompanied by shouts and cheers.

"And the third present comes in the form of our new business initiatives," Junior continues. "The clothing and accessories are a hit this holiday season; I see that some of you are wearing Davanti-branded jackets today. We've also been able to put together finance and leasing options in just a matter of a few months, allowing customers to use them for their Christmas shopping. And we did all of this without an increase in the budget. I'm looking forward to seeing these new businesses and initiatives grow in the coming months. I think this is only the start of exciting things for Davanti."

The employees cheer loudly and long, and Junior has to raise his palm to quiet them down. "My dad taught me that when you get something, you must give something in return. That's why you all have been invited to this celebration today and why you'll find a small, monetary 'thank you' in your next check."

The employees again cheer loudly.

"All this is a result of a lot of change at Davanti. And if I look around, I still see the same people. I am most proud that you all changed and made this possible. So I want to publicly recognize a few of the many individuals who contributed way beyond my expectations." Junior calls up two lab technicians who led the 5S initiative and cell setup in the prototype shop, a technician who improved the safety of a test machine, and a finance specialist who worked countless extra hours to make weekly finance reports possible. In addition, he calls up the entire Volta team for their well-known CI contributions. Junior hands everybody a small token of appreciation to the applause of the whole company.

"If anyone is not convinced that we're doing the right thing, please come see me right away. I promise you that this is just the beginning. There will be more milestones we reach and more celebrations. I wish you all a very merry holiday season and a happy new year. . . . And please, eat up. We've got lots of delicious pizzas and gelato left!"

Junior steps back into the crowd and joins a group of employees in line for gelato. "This is too good to pass up," he says as he shakes hands and personally thanks everyone for what they do for the company. Across the yard, he sees Vinnie, who he's known since they were children running around the office, and wonders what their fathers would think of Davanti today.

***

With Christmas falling on a Saturday, Mo leaves work on Thursday and heads directly to his parents' villa, where he'll stay through the weekend. For the Pensatores, Christmas is the absolute best time of year and features the most amazing foods.

On Christmas Eve, the entire family—Mo's parents and his sister and brother and their families—as well as a few close friends celebrate the Feast of the Seven Fishes. Catholic Italians have eaten fish for centuries on Christmas Eve, and in recent decades some have adopted the more Western habit of celebrating the meal as a "feast" featuring seven types of fish and seafood. Some are grilled by Mo's father (shrimp and calamari), some fried (smelts), and some baked or steamed (such as baccala, a dried and salted cod that his mom rehydrates and serves in a tomato sauce with chickpeas, garlic, and basil). On Christmas Eve, Babbo Natale (Father Christmas) has a gift for all the children; the adults, like many Italians, will exchange modest gifts on January 6 (the Epiphany).

On Christmas day, Mo's mom serves a huge roasted pork loin with pears, wine, and prosciutto along with gnocchi in a mushroom cream sauce. For weeks, Mrs. Pensatore has been baking treats—pizzelles, biscotti, and pignoli cookies (Mo's favorite)—and all seem to be nibbling the sweets constantly. His parents' villa is large enough to accommodate all the family for the weekend (albeit with each family stuffed into a single bedroom, and Mo sleeping on a couch in his father's den), which keeps everyone off the roads and the cappuccino and wine flowing.

Come Monday morning, Mo hardly wants to look at any more food, but his mom entices him with warm, freshly baked bread, butter, jam, and espresso. While his siblings scurry around, packing their suitcases and loading their cars, Mo spends a quiet moment with his mom. "This has been wonderful, mom. You've always made the holiday so special. I wish I could do more to show how thankful I am."

"Mo, you being here and sharing Christmas with us is all I want. It's all we've ever wanted. I'm so happy you were here. Now, drink your espresso before it gets cold."

"I'll need it to stay awake."

"Maybe next year you'll be here with someone special. No?"

"One never knows, mom. Which reminds me; I've got to get going. Thank you again, mom. And happy new year." Mo gets up from the table and gives his mom a kiss. "I'll say bye to pop on the way out. It looks like he's helping Catherine get the kids together."

"Happy new year, Mo. You be safe."

Leaving his parents and Lake Garda, Mo heads east to Geneva where he'll meet Marie at the airport. He's packed a second suitcase suitable for their destination. They'll catch a flight to Tenerife, the largest of the Canary Islands, and then grab a ferry to La Gomera.

They wanted to take a ski trip between Christmas and New Year, but resorts are horribly crowded during that time of year, and lift tickets are expensive. They've instead opted to take the ski trip in late January to Chamonix, Marie's favorite place—where France, Switzerland, and Italy meet. Some of Marie's coworkers rent a chalet there every year, and they're happy to accommodate both Marie and Mo. For the holiday, however, they both just wanted to get away to a quiet, exotic place. The sleepy, small, subtropical island of La Gomera, one of the Canary Islands, was Christopher Columbus' last stop before heading west. They're planning to hike through the volcanic mountains, walk the black-sand beaches, and enjoy Spanish food and drink as they welcome in the new year. On January 2, they'll fly back to Geneva and be back at work the next day.

As Mo drives and listens to holiday music through the radio, his phone rings and the music is replaced by Marie's voice: "Hello, Mo?"

"Yes, it's me," says Mo into his car speaker. "Hi Marie. I can't wait to see you."

"Me too. That's all I wanted to say. I'm really looking forward to La Gomera. Well, I don't want to distract you. Be safe."

"I will. I'll see you soon. I look to be about two hours away from starting a wonderful week."

Chapter 29

New Year for a New Davanti

Junior starts the January communications meeting by wishing everybody a happy and prosperous new year. For many, the second Monday of the month is their first day back in the office after the holiday break. Some look happy to be back, and others are missing the relaxed days of family, friends, and good food.

"I have a feeling that we're going to have a year like Davanti has never seen before," Junior says, "and I'm glad you all are leading the way." Junior then recognizes Stephano and his organization for all the work they've done to reduce the reporting cycle times and turns the floor over to Stephano.

"Thanks, Junior, and, as you know, we closed the books early for December and last year, but the results must still be checked and verified a few more times," Stephano says as a disclaimer. "But as Junior announced before the holidays, the savings from the innovation excellence transformation have been substantial, and we're pulling a significant increase in revenue due to the new bikes and merchandise sold over the Christmas season. And I expect another peak later this month after the Eurobike show."

Everyone looks pleased by the news, except Claudia, who fidgets in her chair. She then clears her throat as if she was getting ready to read a prepared statement: "You know, Junior and Sofia, when this whole thing started, I was very pessimistic. I'd seen many initiatives at Davanti that fizzled without results, but I must admit now this one has been different. I apologize, Sofia. I underestimated you and the power of innovation excellence. I don't fully know how you did it, but please keep doing it. You have my full support from now on."

"Thank you, Claudia," responds Sofia. "It took a lot of courage to say that. I really appreciate it as well as the work you've put in to get us to this point."

There is an awkward silence, which Marco finally breaks. "OK, let me tell you why Stephano is optimistic about Eurobike. In addition to the new products, we have our new merchandise and incentives, including financing and leasing, which Horst and Rebecca will help promote. We also have a lot of small business experiments planned for this year, and we'll get quick feedback from both dealers and bikers at the show. I'm really excited about Eurobike this year, as is Claudia. We think we'll sell like never before."

When Marco is finished, Anika announces new leadership training: "Johan Leffe will be in town next week. He'll teach a class on 'Leadership Lessons from Racing.' He will be joined by Junior, who will teach 'Lean Leadership and Gemba Walks.' The classes are mandatory for all Davanti leaders, but they're open to other associates who are interested."

Anika also mentions a couple new experiments that she has planned: The first one is to make the Volta team a permanent working group, and maybe collocate the members. She suggests

DOI: 10.4324/9781003231837-29

rotating membership and leadership and using the team for needs beyond innovation excellence. She also considers membership or leadership with Volta an important part of corporate leadership development. Another experiment, called "pairing," will collocate key people—leaders or associates—who must work closely together to succeed, such as design and manufacturing staff or accounting and procurement personnel. "I'd also like to experiment pairing professionals for certain difficult tasks," she adds. "They'll work together on one drawing, one calculation, etc. and share responsibility for an aggressive goal. I not only expect synergy and better results but also knowledge sharing and relationship building. I'm convinced that there is hidden developmental and human potential that might come out of that experiment."

"Thank you, Anika," says Junior. "Pairing sounds like a wonderful opportunity to improve collaboration within Davanti. . . . Joe, tell us about the new portfolio and the new products for the coming year. We're all anxious to hear what's coming."

"I know we have open R&D capacity now, which puts us in a nice position," responds Joe. "But we haven't yet made the final decisions on what we'll launch this year. We'll continue the development of several great products, including a new top-of-the-line platform. But we don't have to make the decision for the new launches yet. We are fast enough now that we can wait a few more months to assess the market, get more feedback from the Eurobike show, and wait until all dealer orders are in. We have enough in the works that we can quickly pull the right ones as soon we learn a little more. I'm a big believer in making no decision until it's absolutely necessary."

"We're planning to use the open capacity for new projects, like the mountain bikes, and we have a lot of CI work going on," adds Ricardo. "We've also begun some crosstraining to create flexibility and better serve Joe's team and accommodate late decisions. And I'm glad we have time to rigorously develop modules and platforms—that will become particularly important as we expand into other lines and add more speed. We really don't need a new bottom bracket or steering tube for every new bike. We can have modules that we know work well, designers pick the module that works the best for their application, and we only design a new module if the current ones can't meet the performance requirements. In addition to the modules, I'd like to design several of the future bike lines as platforms."

"Don't we have platforms already?" asks Matteo. "Like our PS and PV lines, for example? We're spinning new products off of them, no?"

"Our new products are designed by improving the current ones. If we keep doing that, we'll limit our innovation to that one product, with only limited changes to those designs," explains Ricardo. "We need to make *versatile* platforms that are flexible and robust so that we can derive many new products off of them. We'll start to develop them in a set-based mode: begin as broad as possible and narrow them down by eliminating lesser options. I learned that at my former company. The broader platforms will give us the ability to adapt to changing market conditions, customer requirements, and competition. We've started the redesign of the new PS line with that approach. It's not just an improvement of the current design, but a broader design space that will give us the bikes needed to expand geographically, a variety of price options, and maybe even special designs for certain races."

"Who knows; maybe one day we'll win the elusive Paris-Roubaix,[1]" wonders Joe.

"Maybe," says Ricardo, "or we derive a better-riding bike for that race from the Marconi platform, which not only gives us a more efficient way of producing bikes but turns into a great platform from which to derive better riding bikes for rough terrain."

"Anything else, Ricardo?" asks Junior.

"Yes, I'd like to discuss the design and test standards that we're implementing in R&D. The standards help us with quality, delivery, and speed. And—before you ask—we're making sure they don't kill creativity. We also added standards for the scientific and statistical interpretation of test results, especially the results of subjective tests. In the past, we left a little too much up to the individual interpretation of the engineers."

"Glad to hear that," says Marco. "We in marketing were often accused of *steering* decisions our way with insufficient facts and fictitious stories. But I've seen that happen with test data, too. I didn't have the courage to ask the right questions."

"I fully support all those initiatives, especially the last one," says Junior.

"The folks in R&D also set an example for everybody by developing standard processes for a lot of their work, like the kanban process for the PCP work," adds Sofia. "If you want to see the improvements in quality, delivery, and speed for yourself, please join Ricardo, Junior, or their staff on a gemba walk."

"OK, I'll wrap us up," says Junior, who proceeds to tell them about discussions regarding the quality director role. He explains his recommendation to put Ricardo in charge of corporate quality and the reasons behind that decision. "But, I'll be honest. Ricardo is doing great things, and I'm concerned about overloading him. We should consider an additional manager position in R&D. And Constantine will assist Ricardo for a while."

"Frankly, I'm happy to relinquish the quality director role," says Constantine, who had discussed the change with Junior prior to the meeting. "I've got enough on my plate dealing with the many manufacturing and supply-chain opportunities that are arising. I also believe that Ricardo will really move our already excellent quality efforts forward. He's the right person to take this on."

"Thank you, both," says Ricardo, "and for the confidence expressed by all of you. I know I have big shoes to fill and a lot to learn, especially when I make my first trip to the Taiwan plant."

***

Mo spent most of the two weeks after the holidays grinding away in his office. He visited his parents on the Epiphany to exchange gifts with family, and then caught up enough on his projects to head out for a week of skiing with Marie. He drove from work directly to Chamonix on Friday evening and joined Marie and her colleagues at a chalet they rent every year. Late January is a good time in the Alps: ample snow has arrived, the crowds are smaller, and the prices—albeit still high given the fantastic skiing and gorgeous views—are lower than the Christmas holiday and the warmer days to come in February and March.

The weather has been cloudy and snowy all week, but he and Marie have had a great time. They are both expert skiers and enjoyed the slopes at every skill level and under all conditions, and the beautiful, fresh powder seems to never stop coming down. Mo immediately hit it off with Marie's friends and, despite long days of skiing hard, they all had abundant energy for "après ski" in and around the town, which is an easy walk from the chalet. For Mo and a few others in the group, tonight is their last night. They've stretched their budgets by dining casually, and tonight isn't much different: pizza and drinks at Chamonix Pub and Pizzeria.

"I'm sorry this trip is coming to an end," Mo tells Marie, having to nearly yell over the laughing and shouts of all the diners in the packed little pizza parlor.

"Me, too. But we'll be back, right?"

"Absolutely. And there is plenty of ski season remaining. We can get out somewhere for a day or so."

"Yes. But I'll miss you. It's been wonderful being with you every day."

A waitress arrives with their custom pizza—anchovies, onions, and hot peppers on a bianco pizza—as well as another round of drinks. Marie is drinking Cosmopolitans, because she says they warm her up, and Mo is drinking a Belgian IPA tripel. They thank the waitress, touch their glasses, and then take a drink.

"I have a feeling that I won't have any trouble sleeping tonight," says Mo of his high-alcohol ale.

"You and me both," responds Marie, taking another drink of her martini. "But who wants to sleep? It's our last night here together."

***

Junior parks his Camry, but he does not see Marcel's Quattropole yet. He gets out of the car and, with a heavy snow falling, heads into Il Macellaio e Il Fornaio. He's quickly seated and handed a menu. He doesn't need it: he looked at the menu online and knows exactly what he wants, starting with an appetizer of salami, ricotta, and fig crostini, which he orders for them both along with aperitifs: two Biciclettas (white wine, Campari, soda water, and an orange slice). Moments after placing the order, Marcel comes bounding into the restaurant.

"Fausto, happy new year!" exclaims Marcel, giving Junior a firm hug as he stands to greet him.

"You as well, my friend. I've taken the liberty of getting us started."

"Great. Anything is fine. So tell me about your holiday. Where did you go?"

"We enjoyed the holiday at home with the kids. It was good to relax. It was a long, tiring year."

"How is Martina?"

"She's good. She sends her best. . . . I can guess where you were: Val d'Isère. Am I right?"

"No. Luci and I were in Austria with a couple of friends this year for the first time in many years. Kitzbühel and St. Anton am Alberg were crowded, but Saalbach and Hippach were great. And we even stopped in Lichtenstein. It was wonderful. And how are things at Davanti?"

"We're starting to see results, and even our strongest critics are beginning to change their minds."

"I am glad to hear that, Fausto. The speed of your racing teams must have rubbed off on the folks in your offices."

"We had savings with lean manufacturing in the plants, but I never realized the same thinking applied everywhere."

"If you get savings in manufacturing, you can put those in the bank. But I've not seen many companies achieve prosperity by just eliminating waste in manufacturing. I'm sure you had big gains in efficiency and capacity in the plant, and now I hope you can leverage innovation excellence to create the products and opportunities to fill that capacity and grow the company without additional investment."

"I believe we'll see that," says Junior. "After the departments understood that they have to work together and not compete against each other, everything started to come together."

"That is an important observation. Achieving excellence in one department may help save a little money, but, as you've seen, the benefits grow almost exponentially when you create systems that extend the excellence over the whole corporation."

"I'm starting to understand the engagement of all parts of the organization, but what do you mean by creating systems?"

"A system is a group of processes working in harmony, supporting each other, and often creating synergy and extraordinary results. Based on what I hear from Sofia, your innovation creation system in R&D is on track for creating the right products at the right time. Align that with your sales, financial, and HR systems, and Davanti will soon win more than bike races."

"I wish I'd known this many years ago."

"I have another secret to share with you: I like to buy companies like Davanti—good competent companies who just did not develop their full potential. I help them realize that potential using the principles we taught you. But don't be alarmed. Davanti is not on my radar. But as I reflect on how I was able to help you folks at Davanti, I realize that I may have missed a great business opportunity."

"Ah, now comes the bill."

Marcel laughs: "No, Fausto, I learned a thing or two from you and Davanti. You taught me that we don't always have to buy the companies. I think we've missed opportunities to advise larger companies—and share the results rather than buying them. Believe me, they have the same issues as small companies—or worse. And sharing in the results from an initiative could be very lucrative given the modest investment on our end."

"But I'm sure there's going to be a bill for the advice to Davanti. When is it coming?"

"I've got something better than a bill."

"Two bills?"

"I don't have a bill. I have a business proposal."

The waiter arrives with the appetizers and drinks. "Excuse me, gentlemen. Your crostini and Biciclettas."

"Thank you," says Junior quickly, anxious to hear Marcel's idea. When the waiter leaves, he turns back to Marcel: "Please, continue."

"I'm inviting you to join the board of my newest company."

"Me?"

"The new company has the generic name of 'Ski Bike Adventures,' but we'll likely change that. You'll be joined on the board by the CEO of a French ski manufacturer and the CEO of one of the largest European ski resort conglomerates. I've secured venture capital for the new enterprise, and the CEO of the venture company also will be on the board."

"And how much do I have to kick in?"

"We expect Davanti to develop and manufacture the bike frame and do the final assembly of the product. There will be venture capital to subsidize the R&D effort."

"You forgot that I plan to retire soon."

"This will give you something to do in retirement, and you'll receive stock in the venture to pay the mortgage on that new villa. While Davanti produces the frames and assembles the bikes, our friends from the ski company will make the blades, and the ski resorts will promote the sport. Initially, the resorts will loan ski bikes for free to some of their members and local clubs. Then they'll start renting at all their locations and offer lessons. They'll also organize competitions, demos, etc. . . . What do you say?"

Junior is speechless, but then mumbles, "I know nothing about skiing, but I trust you—I'm in!"

"I thought you would be. You'll be a real asset for the board, and I'm pleased you accepted. Over the next weeks, my lawyers will meet with you to go over the contracts, but today we toast to the new year and the new enterprise."

***

Johan Leffe has led the Davanti team for eight years. Junior values Johan's professionalism and ethics, and he's happy that he can trust Johan with the full team operation; he rarely interferes in team affairs.

After Johan impressed Junior with how he managed Rossa in the last racing season, Junior invited him to share his leadership experience with the Davanti staff.

Johan—who essentially lives in the team car and in hotels with the team most of the racing season—is not particularly comfortable with conference rooms. He hasn't prepared PowerPoint slides, preferring to share stories and explain cases. Anika will take notes during his seminar, hoping to capture and document his knowledge.

Everyone attending the seminar—Junior's staff, project managers, and others selected by their department leaders or requesting to attend   are anxious to hear Johan speak. Most have never had an opportunity to meet him.

After a quick introduction, Johan begins with the tenets of his leadership style:

- His job is to help riders excel—he works for the riders—and is part of a team of soigneurs, mechanics, drivers, etc. whose focus is on the racers.
- He develops riders, and winning is a consequence of developing good riders.
- He respects all his riders and staff—he knows they all do the best they can.
- He makes a point to thank and appreciate people every day, from the riders to all the support staff, and talks to everyone every day.
- When they have breakfast or dinner as a team in the hotel, he mostly sits with staff members, not the riders—the riders must have time to talk without him around.

He says he likes to engage riders and helpers, frequently asking them for their input on everything from race strategy to nutrition: "We do this as a team every day. I listen to them first. The same is true for an individual rider. I usually get their ideas first—for daily strategy, season preparation, and career development. This is contrary to most people's impression of a coach or director. Most people think of the coach as a drill leader, the one with the whistle, who calls the plays and tells players what to do. I don't operate like that."

Johan's audience is glued to his every word.

"I ask for input from the entire team, including support staff, to set a race strategy that allows us to challenge for or defend the leader jersey. From that collaborative framework, the riders are empowered and encouraged to make their own decisions. I can't be on the radio to discuss opportunities that require split-second decisions during the race. And this is a critical component: I support the riders even if their initiatives fail—that is how they learn."

He stresses the importance of coaching and developing athletes: "We have some of the best racers, and we did this without paying release fees to other teams. I saw their potential as young riders and worked with them and developed them. Their potential was not only in their muscles, but also in their heads. There is so much more to racing than simply pounding your legs up and down. We want riders who understand the sport, team dynamics, how to train, and how to win."

Johan says the success and well-being of the riders and staff are *his responsibility* and that he cares for them as if they were his own family. "Some riders leave the team for financial reasons and better deals, but, nonetheless, they remain my friends for life. Others would never leave the team regardless of what anybody else offers them. The reason for that is that we really care about their safety, their happiness, and their development, which goes far beyond physical abilities."

Johan takes a brief break and asks if there are any questions.

Gina raises her hand and asks, "Are there riders that you have a hard time getting along with? You know, the prima donnas, those riders who know they're the best and want to be treated differently."

"Make no doubt about it—the prima donnas make the team what it is. They often have the respect of their teammates, and the domestiques know very well that they work for them. But they, too, must earn that respect. I spend a lot of energy getting everyone on the team to respect each other. Sometimes you get a prima donna who is natural team player and fits right in, but, as you know, this year was a particularly big challenge."

"So how did you work through it?" asks Gina.

"You build on strengths. Then you identify the weaknesses, both as a cyclist and a teammate. You work with them to improve the weaknesses. You take it in small steps, one day at a time. You give daily feedback, and you help them formulate a plan for the next day. You need to find the right coaching moments. Of course, sometimes you must let them hit a wall before you make any progress. You all remember this season's wall."

The attendees acknowledge that they know who and what Johan is talking about.

"The small steps worked well with Rossa, regardless of if it was a training day or race. We focused first on earning respect by appreciating domestiques, by listening to teammates, by appreciating coaching advice. . . . And every day we reflected on the day before: How did it go? How did everybody feel? What can we do better next time? I helped Rossa recognize the results of his changed behavior or the lack thereof." Some attendees shake their heads, imagining what it would be like to be on the receiving end of Johan's critiques. Everyone is obviously impressed with Johan's approach and results.

"Mind you, any good coach would do the same," says Johan humbly. "It's not about me being extraordinary. Every good leader or manager should be doing this for their own development. I learned as much from Rossa as he learned from me. A good leader is always learning, and this difficult season and experience helped me become a better manager, and I thank him for that."

"Johan, does this approach work with everyone on your team?" asks Anika.

"Oh, yes. I use the same approach for athletic development: Engage the athletes in setting goals, coach them in small steps, provide plenty of feedback and praise. It works for all types of behaviors, and it works with anyone. And I believe it works in any environment, which, I guess, is why I'm talking with you today."

Marco wants to know how Johan picks the leader on the team and how other riders accept his decision.

"The leader position is earned by demonstrated performance and the respect of the rest of the riders. There is certainly competition for that role, but there cannot be rivalry within the team. Good communication with all the riders keeps me informed of riders who aspire for the leadership position, and I give them every opportunity to develop and prove themselves. But we have had situations where we were unable to accommodate an aspiring leader, and I helped him find another team where he could excel—and we remained friends ever after."

Junior sits in the back of the room and takes notes, fascinated with what Johan has to say. Johan finishes his portion by taking more questions. Some have to do with his leadership style, and others ask questions about the pro circuit, such as his favorite race and expectations for the coming season. Johan thanks Junior for inviting him to share his knowledge, and then takes a seat as Junior rises to share his experiences with lean leadership and gemba walks.

"Johan, thank you for the leadership insights today," says Junior, shaking Johan's hand as they pass. "I'm grateful that you are not only our head coach but a role model and valuable member of the Davanti organization."

Junior's staff is aware of his gemba walks. In fact, most people at Davanti have heard about the walks or seen him on them: A few think they are a way for Junior to stick his nose into other people's work. Some think it's something that Sofia told him to do, believing they'll soon end. Others believe that gemba walks are something that only owners do. Many of Junior's directors know, however, he wants them to follow his lead and set an example with their own gemba walks.

Junior wants to tell the group the real reasons behind the walks, and starts off with a personal remembrance of how he used to manage the company: make all decisions, do as much work as possible single-handedly, delegate what you are not able to do, give precise instructions, and have a good control and followup system. With this approach, he says, he had no idea what happened in 80 percent of his own company. People lined up in front of his office for advice or a decision, and the only time he left his office was to go to a conference room or somebody else's office.

"I was the first to complain about innovation at Davanti, yet I did little to change that. Among many other things, I learned to let people try something—it costs very little—and if it's done the right way, it can be very effective and lead to unbelievable results. I tried things, too. But along the way, I also had a big problem with innovation excellence. I thought everybody else in the company had to change, but soon found out that I had to change first and set the example."

He describes the transformation of his leadership style and the lessons he learned—the difference between delegating and engaging and how to help others take ownership, responsibility, and accountability. "Now decisions are made or proposed by the people who are the best positioned to make them—the people who do the work. They must be engaged in changing the way they work because they're the only ones who know the work. They must be empowered to make suggestions or improve things. It's these people, the frontline associates—the workers, mechanics, engineers, accountants—who create value. Leaders and middle management add no value unless they help those who create value be successful.

"I understood that I should refrain from telling people what to do, but I felt I had the right to know what's going on. Before innovation excellence, people used to bring all problems, complaints, and questions into my office along with long PowerPoint presentations to make their arguments. The information system at Davanti was like a distillery. At the bottom was a messy melt. As stuff evaporated, the more refined substance rose higher up the distillation column. Same with the news at Davanti: the higher you were in the organization, the more refined the information. The sticky stuff and the messy details stayed down, and when the time came to clean it up, it ended up in my office. So eventually I went out to see for myself and help people avoid the mess in the first place. I could talk about many leadership aspects today, but I chose gemba walks because the walks should embody many lean leadership behaviors."

Junior pauses and pours a glass of water. "One of the best parts of innovation excellence is that now I have time to do what I should have done a long time ago. And one of those things is to go and see what actually happens in Davanti."

Junior explains how he parks in the back of the building and walks through the labs on his way to his office. He also uses other itineraries, like following a project, a purchase order, or a finance transaction. Staff or other leaders have recently begun to accompany him, and he asks those who have to raise their hands.

"Gemba walks are not the only way I get to see and hear about what's actually happening in the company: to my standard work schedule I've added huddles, one-on-one meetings, and, since I saw Ricardo use A3s, I started coaching people through A3s. The key in all of these activities is that you show interest in the work people do, you show respect, you learn, and you find out where your help is needed. This all tells me what's *really* going on. You know, it's easy to get hooked on metrics and think you can lead by looking at metrics in your office. But metrics—like the work that produces them—are best studied where they occur, together with the people who produce and keep them. And if there is a problem, that's where it's solved, where the work is done. . . . Any questions?"

"Are you expecting all of us to begin gemba walks?" asks Diana. "We've already got a lot on our plates."

"I am," says Junior. "What you see and learn on a gemba walk, in huddles, or other quick feedback events in your department can prevent the sticky mess from landing on your desk days or weeks later, when it will be much more difficult to solve and take far more time. Gemba walks can help you clean your plate, while showing that you respect your associates."

"Junior, you frequently talk about respect these days. Can you define respect?" asks Claudia.

"Good question, Claudia. Experts may have a better definition, but here is mine: People come to work every day to do a good job—and they do the best they can, and leaders should respect that. But employees don't always succeed. And if something goes wrong, it's almost always because they work with inadequate tools, they have the wrong process, maybe they never were trained adequately, or they need help. So I always assume that people have the right intent. I also learned that people know so much more about their jobs than I do, so I always ask them for their suggestions, which is another great way to show respect."

Then Junior walks through a list of suggestions for conducting gemba walks and showing respect:

- Leave your position at the door.
- Speak the local language. "That is the language that the people understand."
- People are often concerned, and you must put them at ease by explaining why you are there.
- Employees will compliment you and tell you how great everything is, but don't go to the gemba to boost your own ego.
- People are humans first, then they are workers; show interest in their lives and their work.
- Ask what they struggle with and show empathy. Ask how you can help them to make their work easier.
- Thank people for the work they do.
- Ask questions—but only questions to genuinely learn. Employees know when they're on trial.
- Don't blame or entertain blame.
- Make people feel important and respect them for their knowledge and skills.

"Although I go out to see problems, I don't go out to solve them myself. People try to show me where they struggle, and they often assume I have the power to make all problems go away. I can't fall for that. I need to remember to engage people in solving their problems—especially when I think I know the solution—and then I help with coaching, removing roadblocks, sometimes even facilitating."

"Junior, I walked with you in the prototype shop the other morning, and I noticed that you encouraged an associate to do better," says Carolina. "Might they think you're challenging their current level of effort?"

"They might, but I make sure they understand they're empowered to make improvements, and I can help them if needed. I ask, 'What can you do just a little better, a little faster today than you did yesterday? What prevents that from happening?' My challenge for them to get better is focused on how they do what they do, not on their effort. Maybe I can motivate them to question what they do every day and the process by which they do it? I want them to understand the theoretical limits of improvements; nothing is out of reach. That is how I hope they take it. And on the next walk I'll thank them for their effort and, ideally, compliment them on what they've been able to accomplish."

"Can you explain the process you use to conduct a gemba walk?" asks Stephano. "I understand the respect part, but I'd like some details on how to get started."

"Sure, I was just about to go through some tips for the process:

■ Identify where you're going in advance, and define and follow a trail, a roadmap. And for your first few walks in an area, let people know why you're coming.
■ Look at metrics, displays, or what people show you. Ask questions and look for areas where problems are made visible.
■ Help people understand how their work relates to the corporate objectives and goals.
■ Ask people how they contribute to safety and quality and how they contributed today.
■ Ask what improvement they made today or what they're planning to do.
■ Listen, show empathy, but make no commitments.
■ And if you engage an associate in making an improvement or solving a problem, it's imperative to make a note and follow up with them later. You are also allowed to hold people accountable. If an associate accepts responsibility to do something, it's OK to follow up and expect a delivery.

"Sometimes I like to follow the trail of a project or a process and invite the people responsible for the different areas to walk with me. It's amazing how much they learn about the work that is done in an area adjacent to theirs. They discover where they can do better to help the downstream department and often stop things they've been doing for years that the downstream department didn't need."

"Junior, I'll be honest. I'm uncomfortable with this, both doing a walk myself and you or others walking in my department," says Claudia. "I manage my own people, and I want them to come to me if they have a problem. I feel like you're stepping between me and my reports."

"That's a fair point, Claudia. I wrestled with that a lot in the beginning. So did an associate ever complain to you about my observations, or did I ever follow up with you for something that I found out during a gemba walk?"

"Not yet, but I'm expecting it to happen."

"It won't happen. If I conducted my walks in ways that interfered with your management, it would be disrespectful to you. Of course, I notice things that could be done better by management in pretty much all departments, but I'm convinced that you and the other directors, managers, and supervisors will notice the same things during your huddles and on your own gemba walks. And if I found something urgent or related to safety, I'd come directly to you in a respectful manner. As for you and others doing gemba walks, I understand your discomfort. I was the same way when Sofia asked me to start. And like me, you may need help, which can be provided if you ask for it. Frankly, Claudia, I think you're ready for gemba walks. I think you'll quickly recognize how beneficial they are. And I think you'll enjoy them."

"When you put it that way, we can't really say 'no' now can we," says Stephano.

"You could, but you'd be doing yourself and Davanti a disfavor. . . . People in the company have had a traditional opinion of hierarchy in Davanti, one that was built upon command and control. We have to get people used to a different hierarchy. We have to turn the traditional pyramid upside down. When you're walking and talking with associates, you're one of them, not above them. You're supporting and helping them, not judging them. I work for all of you, and you work for those who report to you, and they work for our customers."

"So how would you define your job or even my job as a leader now?" asks Anika.

"Create the right environment, remove obstacles, and set direction. Then help people be successful and develop future leaders. And if you think about it, this can't be something you do in addition to what you're already doing—this should be all that you're doing."

Junior continues to answer a few more questions and, as he does, he shares a few stories, including Penelope's experience. As he wraps up, he offers help and coaching to anybody who wants it. "And you can walk with me any time or invite me to walk with you. That will show everyone that we're all in this together."

Note

1. The Paris-Roubaix race—from Paris to Roubaix near the Belgian border—began in 1896 and is famous for its difficult terrain and the damage it does to bikes, which over the years has prompted the development of specialized frames and cycling components.

Chapter 30

Calling 118

Ricardo and Sofia are scheduled to attend the regular Volta team meeting, and they've asked Horst to accompany them. Horst has some catching up to do with the Davanti innovation excellence lingo, but he's clearly familiar with and used many of the principles for years.

Before the Volta team gets started, Ricardo voices his appreciation: "You folks have done an excellent job defining the R&D processes so far, and your work on the quick wins has been communicated to and appreciated by the whole company. I'm hoping you're ready for the next challenge. So what do you think it should be?"

"From our training, I'd say that since we've already focused on safety, quality, and delivery, maybe efficiency and people engagement should be next," offers Mo. "Although we've been doing people engagement all along."

"That's correct about people engagement, Mo," says Ricardo. "As for efficiency, I don't like to work on it." The Volta team looks surprised. "Do you remember me saying that if you work on speed, you get the efficiency for free. The gains from speed are normally higher, and it's a lot easier to engage people in speed improvements than efficiency."

"You are so right, Ricardo," notes Anika. "Every time we talked about efficiency at Davanti, budgets and positions were cut. That engages no one."

"So why do we want to be fast in R&D?" asks Sofia. "Give me your thoughts." She stands to write the team's responses on a whiteboard:

- Beat competition—first mouse gets the cheese
- Better cash flow and ROI
- Faster learning
- Creates agility to react to the market
- Capture opportunities

"I think it will be easy to engage associates behind those reasons," says Marco. "And as my marketing professor used to say, 'Even if you're on the right track, you can still get run over if you don't move fast enough.'"

"You got that right," says Horst. "I can show you the scars."

"So how can we leverage innovation excellence principles to get faster—faster than we already are—and, of course, without losing safety, quality, and on-time delivery?" asks Ricardo.

DOI: 10.4324/9781003231837-30

"Well, if I'm thinking about speed, I'd look at the flow of materials, or, in our case, the flow of work as represented by the kanban cards," suggests Giovanni. "I'd also look at the flow of information beyond what's on the kanban."

"Correct," answers Ricardo. "And as you may remember from your lean training, it's the principles that we're looking for. We're not concerned yet with the tools we'll use—lean or other kinds. Those may come later in deployment."

"This should be similar to what we did with the product creation process," suggests Gina.

"For those of you on the PCP improvement team, that will serve as a good pilot. But PCP is just one process in our chain, and I encourage you to look at the whole chain. The effect of innovation excellence grows rapidly if you can take a system approach or stretch the initiative over many processes and organizations that are aligned and work together. When we looked at waste elimination for quick wins, we could get by with looking at just one function, like the labs. But for speed, a system or at least a broader look may be in order. If you only speed up one member of the chain, and the speed is not replicated at upstream or downstream activities, you won't gain much. Remember the relay race—everybody has to train and be fast, and everybody has to be ready when the baton arrives."

"I still have a hard time with the single-piece flow," says Alexandra. "When you cook breakfast, you don't put the toast in the toaster and wait for it to be done before starting the coffee machine."

"Of course not," counters Sofia. "But would you interrupt your work to put coffee on just to get the eggs started?"

"No. I'd sequence things better. I would get the eggs going when the coffee is dripping, and work on the toast when the eggs are cooking. So I assume we're allowed to split up tasks and start the tasks in the right order, but we wouldn't interrupt a task until we get to a logical break point."

Stella laughs at Alexandra's example and continues: "I now understand how to cook breakfast, but I don't understand how we can innovate faster if we have set times for iterations in the kanban system."

"Then we should reduce those times and string the iterations closer together," Mo suggests.

"Agreed on the way to cook breakfast and the iterations," says Sofia. "Iteration times could certainly be something for this team to tackle, but before we get too deep into the details, let's have a little fun. Let's create teams of three, and every team should make their list of the top 10 speed principles to rely on. List them from the most beneficial to the least. Think back to the innovation excellence training. We'll see who comes closest to my list. I've done this exercise many times—I know the wisdom of a large crowd."

While the teams, including Ricardo, work on their lists, Sofia hears a lot of comments about the traditional methods to increase speed: drop everything else, spend more money, fast-track items, buy new technology, hire more people. After about 10 minutes, the teams have lists of their top 10, and then Sofia reveals her top 10 in reverse order.

"As we reveal Sofia's list, let's see if we can assign a volunteer to every item to document improvements already made and find new opportunities," suggests Ricardo.

The teams compare their lists to Sofia's as she starts with the 10th most important principle:

#10 Create flexibility: "We should cross-train people in all areas so they can move to where the work is and avoid the potential for a bottleneck," says Sofia. Anika volunteers to head up a subteam and work on that subject, reminding all that "we have laid the groundwork already with standard work."

#9 Overlap activities: "How can we overlap activities?" questions Stella when Sofia reveals the second principle. "We can't test before we have prototypes."

"That's correct, Stella, but today we collect all prototypes and only when we have the complete batch do we start the tests," notes Ricardo.

"I get it," says Stella. "We could start the longest test when the first prototype is available, and a week later when we get the last prototype, we start the shortest test."

"Excellent idea," says Gina. "Even where we can't work completely in parallel, we can overlap to a very large extent. I'd be happy to lead that subteam."

#8 Apply TOC principles to the critical path: "This came up a few weeks ago when we discussed the engineering portion of the PCP," says Giovanni. "I'm on that team. I'll take this one and see how we can expand on what we learned on the PCP."

#7 Adhere to late start: "Getting 'a jump' on projects leads to changes, corrections, and rework, all of which are a waste of time and the enemy of speed," says Sofia. "We've done a lot of standardizing to late start already, and we probably don't need to give it much more attention right now." Mo volunteers to document the savings already achieved and expand the initiative beyond R&D.

#6 Apply buffers and schedule at 70 percent of capacity: "This takes discipline," warns Ricardo. "We've already implemented this to some extent, but it needs more tuning. It's always tempting to dip into that 30 percent."

#5 Relentlessly eliminate waste: "This is another item that has already seen a lot of effort, but our work here never ends," says Sofia. Mo volunteers to monitor waste elimination activities and look for more opportunities.

#4 Institute standard work: "This work also has already begun in R&D, but it's a big item when you consider all of the work and work components that every position does, and we need to expand standard work beyond R&D," says Sofia. Rene from procurement agrees to create a small team and see how they can promote the idea of standard work through all office processes.

#3 Reuse knowledge: "Our initiative for this in R&D is well on its way and starting to bear fruit," says Bolaji. "I'll ask my team to incorporate some goals specific to speed. And we need to extend the KM training to the complete value stream."

#2 Follow lean project management: As the No. 2 item is revealed, Gina explains that Leandro, the PMO director, has some of Davanti's most experienced PMs working on the PM playbook, and she will make sure that enough attention is placed on speed.

#1 Create single-piece flow: "This is the foundation of the kanban process—from cadence to pull—that was recently implemented in the PCP," says Stella. "I like that process, and I'm happy to help expand the ideas to areas adjacent to the PCP."

"So let's score—please count how many matches you have," requests Sofia.

Mo's team wins the competition, and the team members give each other high fives.

"This reminds me," adds Sofia, "that with all the fun, I forgot to announce that Mo will head up the speed initiative. He just finished the quick-win project; the functions are now responsible for the initiatives you helped Mo get started. In this assignment, Mo will keep an eye on the subteams we created today, and he'll find a few more volunteers, if needed. Mo will work with all of you to take existing initiatives to the next level and make sure that all the learning is integrated and leveled across as many processes as possible. And then, of course, he'll enlist all of you in creating an effective relay race from an idea to collecting the cash. And since we need to free some of Ricardo's time to learn his new quality assignment, I'll coach Mo on this project."

Mo's colleagues appear surprised that he's been tapped to lead two initiatives in a row. But no one questions Sofia's choice, especially since some of the Volta members, like Gina and Stella, have already volunteered for many other projects.

"And just as we did with the cost savings, we should focus first on the areas that promise the best return. And remember to benchmark where we were before innovation excellence and where we are today. And then, Mo, please engage the team in setting a monthly goal for improvement."

Mo nods, confirming the direction offered by Ricardo.

"So, Horst, what do you think?" asks Ricardo.

Horst has thoughtfully taken in the proceedings. "It's impressive. Let me sit through another meeting or two to get familiar with the current initiatives. Then I'd like to share some practices from my former company that may help. Our design times were measured in days; we manufactured and shipped within a couple of weeks; and our planning and logistics processes were world-class. I'm sure there will be opportunities to apply principles that we used."

"Well, I think we can wrap up Volta for today," suggests Mo.

"Oh, wait," urges Stella. "Let's call our speed project 'Ferrari.'" Everybody likes the idea, and Ferrari is off to the races.

***

Junior periodically meets with Sofia over lunch in the corporate cafeteria. Months ago, they'd be one of only a handful of employees there. With the new food stations, seats are at a premium. They find a spot in a corner where they can talk freely and enjoy their meals: salad for Sofia, and Junior has a panini made with salami, capicola, and mozzarella.

"The Fusilli visit has helped in many ways," says Junior as he scans the room. "When should we visit another company?"

"We're still digesting what we learned at Fusilli," says Sofia. "No pun intended. But we have had several video followup calls with Fusilli, and Anika took a few people to a friend's company to learn about their dual-ladder system."

"Excellent. I'm always surprised by how much more there is to learn. But, I guess, that's an attitude we should all embrace."

"You're right, Junior. At Davanti we've had our classroom training, and that helped us get going with the learning as well as engage associates to help set up the right processes. We also got our leaders started on the right behaviors by engaging them in delivering the training. Ideal behaviors really sustain new ways of working and improve the culture. People must learn those on the job, and that is especially important for leaders. They must set the example and help everybody else."

"How would that occur? Will you follow them all day and correct them when needed?"

"That would be one way of doing it. Behaviors are hard to measure but easy to observe. Coaching after direct observation is effective, and I try to find coaching moments whenever possible. But primers are a better overall approach. A primer creates a situation where people can practice, make mistakes, reflect, and learn on their own. It works especially well with managers and leaders, and, quite frankly, Junior, you are our best student."

Junior grins: "I didn't know I was I being taught."

"We've set up some primers already, like the huddles and gemba walks, and we're adding a few more—A3 coaching and one-on-one meetings. Primers are based on what I call the magic triangle:

■ Go see and show respect
■ Find out where people struggle
■ Engage/coach people in making improvements

"During the primers, people get feedback, they can learn if changes in their behavior are required, and they can experiment. Some catch it quickly, others improve with reminders by associates or leaders, and, for the hard core, you need to be patient and find a coaching moment. But the key is that primers must have a safe environment—professionally and emotionally—that gives people the opportunity to practice, learn, and seek advice without inhibitions or consequences. And you can also offer coaching to those who may not notice they need it."

"Well, I experienced that myself."

"When you shared your experience with gemba walks, that was an excellent form of coaching. In fact, gemba walks are one of the best primers we have at Davanti."

"Other than me, who else have you coached on gemba walks?"

"Leandro asked me recently to do a walk with him."

"How did that go?"

"Leandro is getting the hang of it. Not everybody learns as fast as you, Junior."

"Give me an example."

Sofia tells Junior about her walk with Leandro and how she was able to assist him:

> Sofia had explained the magic triangle to Leandro prior to the gemba walk. He had picked the Primo Sempre project, and they walked the steps of the project in reverse order, starting with the production release. The first area they visited was the engineering area where they talked to the engineers who made the final paint and assembly drawings and who wrote the manufacturing specifications. The engineers had followed the visual planning schedule and used the kanban cards to start their work. They also had positive comments about the new process.
>
> Sofia and Leandro then reviewed the results from the design-release meeting with Bolaji and Bart, and then continued upstream, talking to the engineers who did the design and testing that leads up to the design release. Everything seemed fine, but one engineer complained about the new process and how he felt he was working on an assembly line. The engineer said he didn't get enough of a break between iterations: "When I finish one kanban, I have the next waiting." Leandro explained to the young engineer the need to work fast and efficiently to meet all release dates, and promised to speak with other engineers to see if they have similar problems. The young man was not impressed with the response.
>
> They continued the project trail into the engineering phase until they stopped at the point where the project started.
>
> At the end of the walk, Sofia had asked, "So how do you feel about the walk, Leandro?"
>
> "Everything seemed to be working smoothly, and everybody seemed pleased, except the one engineer. I'll have to look into the concern he raised. But I'm not sure everything is as perfect out there as it looked. And I didn't see many visuals to confirm how the process is working."
>
> "Great observations, Leandro," replied Sofia. "What can we do about the absence of visuals?"
>
> "I guess I need to ask Carolina why we don't have them yet."
>
> "Could you maybe walk the process together with Carolina and engage the engineers in creating the visuals?"
>
> "I guess that would be a better way to do it."
>
> Sofia also had recognized a few coaching moments in the walk with Leandro:

"Let's discuss behaviors," she said. "Although you're a leader, you can't appear that way on a walk. When the engineer complained about the process, you lectured him on having to work faster and promised to further look into his complaint. Could you have shown interest in his work by asking more questions and empathy for his struggles, and then asked *him* for suggestions and how you can help *him* improve the situation?"

"Maybe I could also have started explaining why it's important for the work—not the engineer—to be faster and more efficient, and described it in language he could relate to? And maybe explain what he personally can gain from faster work."

"Excellent. And you also noted that everything seemed to go well out there."

"Is that because nobody wants to admit that they struggle?"

"Exactly. And if there was a big problem, they sure don't want to be associated with it. But if you show interest in their work, ask humble questions, and develop trust, you eventually can find out what's really going on and motivate people to make suggestions for how they can improve the work they're doing."

"So why didn't you stop me and correct me?" Leonardo humbly asked.

"You mean like a youth soccer coach who yells instructions to the players on the field? That would not be appropriate. But I'm glad you understand what we're talking about. I'm sure you'll reflect on how to change your behaviors and try new things next time. And if you have a question, please come and ask."

"But how do I know what to improve if you or others don't point it out to me?"

"If you show genuine interest in the work people do, why they do it, and how they feel about it, many things will reveal themselves. You can get your best feedback when you ask them what you can do to help them. And then you can reflect about what they tell you and, maybe, what they don't tell you. And when you ask people what they expect from you, please ask them for suggestions on how you can improve what you do for them—not just critiques of your performance or behavior. People may not give criticism to your face, but they might give you suggestions. This feedback is your ticket to becoming a better and more successful leader—you won't get anything like it in a yearly performance review. And remember to thank the associates and make them feel important. It will take a little time, but I'm sure you'll master it."

Leandro appeared as if scales had fallen from his eyes: "I can't wait to put this to use on my next gemba walk."

"Leandro grasped all that I explained," Sofia tells Junior. "Think about it. He'd never been trained to lead in that way or maybe any way. Few people are."

"I'm pleased that Leandro wants to learn this," says Junior. "Has he done any walks since then to test your ideas?"

"He's set to do another walk later today. I'm confident he'll get a lot out of it."

***

Leandro has selected to walk the Primo Veloce development project, and he invited Bart to join him. As they start their walk, they ask the people they meet a few questions, such as what they do at work and how they feel about it. They ask how their work relates to the company goals, and, after asking, take a look at some visuals the engineers prepared. In one area, they learn about the number of jobs that were returned by the downstream operation because there was something missing.

"We created a checklist, and we now make sure no job leaves this area before we checked everything off," explains a young engineer pointing out the improvement that was made.

Both Leandro and Bart ask followup questions to better understand the system that was created. With a clear understanding, they thank the engineers in the area and move on to another location where a stylist goes through the process she uses to create the look of a bike.

"Many people don't see or even experience all the performance hidden in this bike," she explains. "I try to make that visually apparent."

"I had no idea we're doing all this stuff in a project," says Bart. "So how do you feel about what you do?"

"You know, I'm coming up with all this stuff, but I never hear back from anyone," she says. "Sometimes I get complaints, but I never learn if my work is adding value. And I have no idea if what I do is appreciated or even noticed by customers?"

"So how can we help you with that?"

"I don't know. I'll think about it. I'll come up with something."

"Thanks for sharing all of this. We'll check back with you next week to hear your suggestions. How about same time next week?"

"Sure. Thanks for stopping by."

As they continue their walk upstream, they talk to a couple of engineers who do the modeling and calculations for all new bikes and hear about some of the more complex aspects of engineering: "Not everybody knows how to do the structural calculations and run FEA[1] models," explains an engineer, "and why bother all engineers to learn all that, including sophisticated software, and only use it once every couple of months? We do this all the time, and we're very good and efficient at it."

Leandro and Bart show a lot of interest in the advanced technical work, which the engineers appreciate. However, the engineers also show a visual board that is covered with red: "This is the time we wait for the stuff we need to do our work. When we get the kanban, we usually have to contact various engineers many times, begging for drawings, material properties, gauges, tolerances, etc. We waste a lot of time waiting and following up."

"Wouldn't this be noticed because the kanbans are late?"

"Some of the work is not on the critical path—thus, less noticeable—and sometimes they close the kanban, despite missing information from us."

"Why do you think that happens?"

By this time, a number of engineers have joined the conversation. They offer assumptions, ranging from upstream steps not knowing the engineers need the information to an absence of standards.

"This problem seems a little complex," says Leandro. "But you folks seem to understand the process well. I'd be happy to sponsor an A3 if one of you would like to take a look at the root causes and propose countermeasures."

One of the engineers, who says he's taken the problem-solving/A3 training, volunteers, and Leandro thanks him for that.

"So what do you think we as leaders can do better to support you?" Leonardo asks.

"I'm glad you've taken the time to ask about what we're doing here," says one of the engineers, "but why this sudden interest? And what's this got to do with innovation excellence?"

Leandro reflects on Junior's recent gemba walk training and explains the reasons for their gemba walk.

"OK, now I understand," replies the engineer. "I wish you had told us that at the beginning when you came here. I think it would have put us all a bit more at ease."

Before leaving, Leandro thanks the engineers for their feedback and wraps up the gemba walk. He's pleased that it went well and that he acted on Sofia's input. As he reflects on the walk, he finds several things that he'll do differently next time, like gaining associates' trust by better explaining the purpose of the gemba walks, setting expectations upfront, and asking deeper questions and maybe "why" from time to time to display more genuine interest and more empathy for their problems.

While Leandro and Bart did their walk, other walks were occurring within Davanti: Diana walked the purchase-order process. Anika walked the hiring process. Finance leaders walked the path of their payment transaction, from the reception of the goods and services to where the funds were received by the supplier.

Sitting down to write up his observations, Leandro considers how far he's ventured out of his comfort zone with gemba walks, surprised by how much easier the second was than the first, and already looking forward to his next walk.

***

Junior completes a one-on-one meeting with Constantine, and thanks him for the conversation and for helping Ricardo take over quality control. "My pleasure, Junior. Have a good day," says the manufacturing director as he leaves the office.

Constantine had said nothing to upset the CEO, but Junior suddenly looks uncomfortable after the manufacturing director leaves his office. He buzzes Anna and asks for a Pellegrino.

"Here you go," says Anna, walking in and lowering a glass of the sparkling water on to Junior's desk.

"Thank you."

"Are you feeling OK? You look like you're in some discomfort."

"My back and neck are killing me. I don't understand it. Constantine and I had a good meeting, and then suddenly I'm feeling this upper back pain. I don't understand it. . . . Well, I have felt it before, but never quite like this."

"Are you sure you're OK, boss? You clearly look to be in pain."

Junior stands and tries stretching to relieve the pain. "My shoulders and arms are tight as well. This is not good. Anna, please call 118 and Dr. Meglio. I think I'm having a heart attack."

Anna grabs the phone on Junior's desk and reaches the 118 dispatcher. She gives their location and the nature of the emergency, and then puts the call on speaker phone so Junior can hear as well.

"If you can, quickly give him four aspirin," says the dispatcher. Anna runs from the room into her office; she rummages through her desk and runs back to Junior with the aspirin. He chews one and puts it under his tongue, as the dispatcher instructs, and washes the others down with the Pellegrino. "Please stay on the line with me until you hear the sirens," advises the dispatcher.

With her cell phone, Anna punches in the number of Junior's doctor, but gets his voicemail. She leaves a message: "Fausto Davanti may be having a heart attack. He's taken aspirin, and emergency is on the way." She then calls Gus at the security desk and tells him what to expect.

Junior tries to sit, but the pain is now greater and he stands and paces around, waving his arms and trying to relieve the vice around his upper body: "Oh mio Dio! What is taking them?"

After what seems an eternity—but is less than five minutes—they hear the sound of sirens approaching. Anna tells the dispatcher that they are near and hangs up. Junior looks pale and lies down on the floor. "Relax, Fausto, they're very close," comforts Anna.

She soon hears a commotion in the lobby and then people running down the hall. Two EMTs rush into the room, followed closely by Dr. Meglio.

"Junior, how are you feeling?" asks Dr. Meglio.

"I'm tight everywhere. Back. Arms. Chest."

"Is your pain worsening?"

"No. I don't think so. It's not great, but it's a bit better than it was a few minutes ago."

"That's the aspirin working, Junior. It may have saved your life."

Junior begins to sit up. "Junior, just lie back. We're going to get you out to the ambulance now."

"I think I can walk out."

"No. Just lay back and relax."

Anna is on the phone calling Junior's wife Martina, explaining what's going on and that he's in good hands with the doctor and the medics. Outside in the hall, dozens of employees have gathered, having seen and heard the ambulance and anxious to know what's happened. In less than a minute, the EMTs have Junior on a gurney and are wheeling him into the hall. Junior can see the scared faces of his employees as he rolls past them, and holds up his palm as if to say, "I'll be fine."

In a moment, Junior's view has changed to that of the interior of the ambulance. The doctor has torn open Junior's shirt; one EMT attaches EKG leads to Junior, which will monitor his heart activity, and the other takes his blood pressure, checks his oxygen, and gets a blood sample.

"I'm feeling much better, Doc. Is this really necessary?"

"Junior, you're feeling better because you're probably coming out of your heart attack already. But we need to know for certain what's going on, and something is, indeed, going on. Your blood pressure is 180 over 120. Please just stay calm. We're almost to the hospital."

The ambulance stops, and Junior is wheeled out and toward the emergency room doors. Martina is standing at the doors and grabs Junior's hand as they wheel him in. The EMTs get ready to object, but Dr. Meglio signals that it's OK. "Il mio amore, you'll be fine," she says. "You're in good hands."

Junior is quickly sent to an ER room, Martina at his side, and staff begin taking his vitals. He's completely alert, but still in some pain. After about 10 minutes, Dr. Meglio enters the room.

"Junior, you're going to have a cardiac catherization in a few minutes," says Dr. Meglio. "The EKG info points to a heart attack, and the blood test already shows elevated levels of troponin, which also indicates myocardial infarction."

"What's the catherization? What will they do?"

"The cardiologist will tell you more prior to your procedure, but here is what will happen: They'll first insert a catheter, ideally in your wrist, and they'll move that up to your heart to look for blockages."

"And?"

"Well, one of three things: One, there are few or no blockages and we treat you with medicine. That is unlikely. Two, they find blockages. In that case, they open them if possible with an angioplasty procedure and, if necessary, insert a stent or stents to keep them open. And three, if there are major or multiple blockages, you'll have surgery to repair them. But there is no reason to expect the worse."

"Thank you," says Junior, shaking his head in disbelief. "I just don't believe any of this is happening."

"You'll be OK," says Martina. "There are many, many people praying for you. Your daughters are on their way, and you'll see them soon."

A hospital transport tech and RN walk into Junior's ER room. "They're ready for you in cath, Mr. Davanti, so we're going to move you. Mrs. Davanti, you can come along until they actually take him in."

Back at Davanti headquarters, Anna receives a text from Martina and then sends an email to all the Davanti employees: "Fausto Davanti was taken to the hospital today by emergency services. Mrs. Davanti wants you to know that he appears to have suffered a heart attack; he is alert and undergoing treatment. Please keep him in your thoughts and prayers. I will provide more information as it becomes available."

Note

1. Finite element analysis.

Chapter 31

Do the Right Thing

During Junior's cardiac catheterization, doctors found a 99-percent blockage in his left anterior descending artery (a massive heart attack also known as "the widow maker"). They opened the blockage with angioplasty, and then inserted a 30-millimeter stent to keep it open. Unlike what Junior had heard from friends who have had a similar procedure, he was not suddenly feeling better with blood flowing more freely. He had a lot of pain in his chest due to the extensiveness of the cath procedure and size of the stent, and was given morphine to relieve the pain.

He spent a sleepless evening under observation in the hospital and was told that if everything checks out, he could be discharged the following day. Junior's daughters and Martina sat with him until nearly midnight, and then he insisted they go home and get some rest.

Martina arrives back at the hospital early morning, and finds Junior sitting up in bed. "Good morning, my love, how are you today?"

"I'm feeling a bit better. No longer any pain in my chest."

"Did you get any sleep?"

"Not a wink. A hospital is no place to sleep. Every time I'd start to doze off, another alert would sound or they'd come in with meds or to check something."

"I'm so sorry. . . . Have you spoken to your doctor?"

"Yes, he was here at the crack of dawn. He ordered an echocardiogram, which they just completed, and said he'd get the discharge rolling after he sees those results."

"That all sounds good."

"Yes, I guess. I wish I was never here, and the sooner I leave the better—with or without a discharge. . . . Did you bring my phone?"

"Yes," says Martina, reaching into her bag and handing her husband his phone. "I also brought you a change of clothes."

"Thank you." Junior looks at his phone, and sees dozens of text messages from friends, colleagues, and employees, all expressing their concern. He reads through many as tears well up in his eyes.

"What is it, my love?"

"Everyone is so kind. I didn't know people cared so much."

"Of course they care. You are like a brother or father to many of them."

"I should let Anna know what's going on."

"There will be plenty of time for that. Why don't you put that phone down and try to rest? Discharges never go fast; you could be here a while. I'll call Anna for you and let her know what is going on so that she can keep the folks at Davanti up to date."

***

DOI: 10.4324/9781003231837-31

When Mo wakes in the morning, he puts on coffee and checks his phone to see if there's any news on Junior. Nothing.

After breakfast as he's getting ready to head to work, he looks again and sees a corporate email from Anna: "Fausto Davanti is resting comfortably after undergoing a catherization procedure to open a blocked artery. Martina Davanti thanks you all for your support and will pass on new information when it is available."

***

It's not until early afternoon that Junior's case manager and a cardiologist from the cath team arrive. He's slept most of the morning and through lunch. Martina has been sitting and reading in a chair next to him. Junior awakes when he hears his name called.

"Mr. Davanti, we're going to go over your summary, and then make sure you're ready to get out of here," says the case manager. "How does that sound?"

"Very good. I'm ready."

"First things first, Mr. Davanti," says the cardiologist, who goes over details of the cath procedure and what they found, including a number of smaller blockages that were not addressed. "We also got your echo results back. They help us to see how your heart muscles are pumping and moving blood to and from your heart."

"Yes, and how is that?"

"It could be better. A normal-functioning heart has an ejection fraction of about 55–75 percent—the percentage of blood pumped from the left ventricle on each contraction. Your heart is pumping at about 30–35 percent. There is more information about the cardiomyopathy in your take-home packet, and we'll discuss it more when we get you in for your first office visit."

"The percentage will go back up, though, right?"

"I can't say. I wish I could. At this point, we don't know if you permanently damaged the muscles on the left side of your heart. Meds, cardiac rehab, and diet and nutrition can help improve the blood flow and the ejection fraction, but it's impossible to predict at this moment."

"Is there any reason why I should expect the worst? And what is the worst? What if it doesn't improve?"

"There's no reason to presume the worst. Just follow your rehab instructions, which will put you in a good position for a positive outcome. When we do a followup echocardiogram in a few weeks, we'll know more."

The cardiologist goes over Junior's prescriptions and his near-term physical limitations: walks of no more than 5 minutes for the first week, 5–10 minutes the second week, and then 10-minute additions each week thereafter. ("So much for gemba walks for a while," he thinks.) His cardiac rehab is scheduled to start in two weeks. He's not allowed to drive or lift anything for five days so as to not open the wound on his wrist where the cath entered. Other restrictions and instructions follow, and Junior, dazed, just shakes his head in disbelief.

The cardiologist wishes Junior the best and leaves, followed in by a case manager, who goes over a numbing number of hospital details. Martina takes notes as best she can. Junior signs a few documents, and then he's allowed to get dressed, sits in a wheelchair, and is ready to be rolled back into society.

***

Junior and Martina are greeted at the door by their housekeeper.

"Fausto, I'm so glad to see you walk in," says Silvia. "I've been praying for you."

"Thank you, Silvia. Every prayer helps. I appreciate your concern."

When Junior walks through the foray and into the main living area of the house, he's overwhelmed to tears. Every spot imaginable is packed with flowers. "I've never seen anything like this," says the housekeeper. "You are an incredibly popular man!"

Junior, with Martina at his side, walks around the room and begins to look at each vase in detail and reads the cards that are attached. There are flowers from every department, from the race team, and from many individuals, from Sofia and Marcel to Penelope and Mo. Tears stream down his cheeks.

"Junior, you should sit for a while. We'll look at the rest a few at a time. I asked Silvia to set up your study with everything you'll want close at hand, and she's had a recliner brought in so that you can easily rest throughout the day. Is that OK?"

"Yes, yes," says Junior, overwhelmed by the incredible expression of sympathy for him from the Davanti folks and others. He knows popularity has nothing to do with this; he realizes that people are genuinely concerned about him.

He and Martina walk back to the study, passing flowers and plants along the way, and into the study. Martina helps him to the recliner and acquiesces to his request for his laptop.

He opens the computer and finds more than a hundred emails titled "Get Well!" or similar. They've come from staff in Taiwan, suppliers around the globe, and seemingly every employee who works or has ever worked at Davanti. He begins reading them and replying with a simple "Thank you," and then it dawns on him: People are clearly worried about him and maybe even scared. He is, literally, Davanti Nella Gara. As much as he depends on them, they also depend on him and the company.

"Those folks are under my care," he realizes. "Davanti provides for them and their families." Some worked for his dad, and some are the second-generation Davanti employees. What would happen to all those individuals and their families if he had not survived the heart attack? And what will happen to them if he sells the company now? And what's happened to them every day until today, when he never fully grasped the profound impact he could have on so many lives?

Junior suddenly feels uncomfortable for not realizing all of this earlier. How could he have led Davanti all these years and not recognized the people for whom they were and what the company meant to them? Surely his father had known; why didn't he understand that as well? In hindsight, he can see why some of his staff challenged him when he came up with the goal to increase the value of the company. People are smart—they can understand what is said and interpret what is not said. Maybe he should have been upfront and told them the full story. How was not doing that showing them respect? Seeing all the sympathy now, maybe he should have done this differently. He's pleased with the transformation and how he's guided and supported it, but not with how and why he's orchestrated it. Davanti employees deserve better.

"It's certainly not too late to do it right," he thinks. "We've not even put the company up for sale yet. What would a compassionate and caring leader have done to this point? What should a compassionate and caring leader do now? How can I remove their fear?"

Junior replies to a few more emails, and then leans back and nods off in the recliner. When he wakes an hour later, he's still thinking about his behavior as CEO—past and future. "Everyone in Davanti has helped me increase the value of the company. I can't just indiscriminately sell to the highest bidder. The buyer could initially honor my dad's wishes but then one day drop the racing team and move HQ to a location with much lower labor costs. If I'm no longer around, what could I do to prevent that?"

Junior wonders how Marcel and Sofia would react to his thoughts, and then realizes it doesn't matter: he needs to do the right thing for the company and for the employees, and he's got plenty of time to think this through and do it right.

***

Junior worked a few hours per day from home, while Stephano—who filled in for Junior previously when the CEO was traveling or on vacation—ran the day-to-day operations within Davanti. Junior also did a few video meetings, and warned everyone that he'd be back before long. Everyone asked how he was doing, and he told them that he felt fine, and left it at that. There will be plenty of time to discuss the big lifestyle changes he had begun, including a plant-based diet and what would be considered heresy in Italy—omitting oils and fats from his meals. A friend had told him about a US doctor, Caldwell B. Esselstyn Jr., whose research showed that such a diet could not only prevent heart disease but reverse it in those who had it.[1] Fortunately, the diet does not eliminate wine, so he enjoys a glass with the dietary-compliant meals that he and Martina dream up.

This afternoon, Junior joins a video call with Stephano and Johan Leffe to hear about the Davanti race team's contracts and budgets for the upcoming season.

"Junior, you look good," says Johan. "I'm glad to see your face. You really scared all of us. We thought you would leave us orphans. I'm so happy to see that you are recovering well."

"Yes, Johan, I'm fine. Thank you all again for your outpouring of good wishes. They are much appreciated. I followed the team's effort in the Tour Down Under and the Tour of Qatar. No wins, but better than in past years."

"Junior, you are correct. No one on the podium, but our riders won a number of stages in the two events."

"So maybe we should let Domingo Pucci run the team more often," jokes Junior. Leffe usually does not travel to the southern locations; he lets his assistant cover both races while he spends time with his family in the winter, focuses on recruiting, and catches up with business in the office.

"He'll make a great directeur sportif one day, but not quite yet," says Leffe. "It helped that Rossa took part in both races. He's embraced the publicity commitments and responsibilities that come with being famous now, and he's really spreading the Davanti name. Some of the Australian and Middle East papers and TV stations interviewed him; we see his picture everywhere now."

"There has been a Rossa effect in sales as well as the races," says Stephano. "Maybe we should rename the PS bike 'La Bici Vincente di Augustine Rossa.'[2] Although currently only online orders are possible, we definitely saw a spike from Australia and the Middle East this past month. Claudia thinks that if we can extend our dealer network this year to include those regions and others, we'll get comparable sales as to what we get outside of Italy, France, and Spain."

"That would be excellent," says Junior. "I'd love to see Davanti bikes around the globe."

"And not just bikes," adds Stephano. "The clothing is really selling well in Australia."

"Now if we can only race as well as we sell," says Johan. "I'm betting our effort on the circuit will directly affect sales."

"So what do you think about the upcoming season, Johan?" asks Junior.

"The winter races were a good preparation for the upcoming season, and I was pleased with the performances of some of our younger riders. This week, we'll get everyone back together at the training camps in Spain and begin the push to race well in the Classiques. I'm expecting nothing but great things from Rossa and the team this year."

"Well, on that note, I think I'm going to call it a day," says Junior. "If you and Stephano have race-budget issues to work on, please continue. I'm going to dream about Davanti wins for an hour or so."

***

While Junior works in his study, Martina is nearby, reading in a chair. The doorbell sounds, and she gets up to answer it. Junior hears the conversation as the door opens.

"Luci, Marcel, it's so nice to see you. Please come in. Junior will be so happy to see you."

Martina leads Marcel and Luci to the study, which he enters with a large, expensive basket of gorgeous fruit. "I wasn't so sure of your diet these days, Fausto, and I did not want to set a bad example."

"That's perfect, Marcel," says Junior as he sets the basket on his desk. "Thank you both so much. I can eat everything in that, and I probably will." Junior and Martina give them both a generous embrace.

Martina pulls a few strawberries out of the basket, hands Junior one and keeps the rest. "Oh my, these are wonderful. . . . Can I get either of you anything? An expresso, cappuccino, water, wine?"

"No, we're fine," says Luci. "We just want to see the two of you."

"OK, but let me know if you do."

"And how are the both of you?" asks Luci. "You look good, Fausto. Martina must be taking good care of you."

"We are both doing well," replies Martina. "Our life is only a little different, and we're both grateful for that."

"As are we," says Marcel.

"Luci, would you like to see what I've been working on? We can let the boys talk. But don't get him too excited, Marcel," she says jokingly. "You have a way of doing that."

"If you don't mind, I'll catch up with Martina."

"Please do," says Junior. "Marcel will keep me occupied, I'm sure."

"So how do you feel today?" asks Marcel.

"I feel very good. Stronger every day. I'm nearly up to a full workday."

"And the heart?"

"I have to believe that the meds, my diet, and the rehab will take care of any lingering effects."

"Such as?"

"My heart was not pumping as much as it should, and there are still some blockages. But I really believe that won't be the case when I'm checked again."

"I'm glad to hear your optimism. You seem to be in great spirits."

"I'm alive, and that's a happy place to start. And I've always believed that things happen for a reason. And when things happen and life changes, you have to adapt."

"I like that you want to adapt, Fausto. What are you planning?"

"I'm thinking about moving up the sale of the company. The heart attack convinced me that I'm not immortal. I need to spend time relaxing with Martina and the girls while I can. The next time I'm wheeled out of my office, it may not be in an ambulance."

"I think that's a good idea, Fausto. It's an appropriate time. Not everything at Davanti is ripe yet, but potential buyers will see the fruit developing and have an idea of what it will be when it matures. And I'd be very happy to help you with that process."

"Are you making me an offer?"

"No, Fausto, I would have made that offer a year ago. The company is too expensive for me now. Remember, I buy ailing companies and repair them. Yours is on the mend."

"Yes, with your help we came a long way, and I've been thinking a lot about that lately. I've been thinking about a lot of things lately, both about me and about Davanti Nella Gara."

"For instance?"

"Well, besides the sale, here is a Davanti question that bugs me: what comes after excellence?"

"*Wow*, what a difficult question. You've had too much time to think, my friend. I'm not sure I have the right answer. There certainly is not a name for it yet, and I've not reached that point with any of my businesses. If you look at world history, there has always been decay after excellence or at least significant change for the worse. And often excellence was achieved at the expense of others and resulted in unmanageable growth. In business, we've seen similar things happen, but on a much smaller scale, of course."

"Mind you, we're nowhere near excellent, Marcel. But I'd like to think we'll get there and have to answer that question one day."

"I think the biggest problems companies have with excellence is that they're so focused on becoming excellent that they forget about how to sustain it. Even with the systems in place to monitor and manage the day-to-day, they slip into autopilot. But Davanti looks to be on the right track. You're building the systems and culture to get the company where it needs to be. And those also will help you sustain your success."

"I believe we're getting there, but we've got a ways to go."

"Just remember that excellence doesn't sustain itself, and it has an inherent danger: companies work to perfection and believe that perfection will solidify their future. And that is not true. First of all, after some time the curve of achievement flattens and the returns from excellence get smaller and smaller. And second, things change around them: the economy, the political systems, the competition. And some fail to adapt both to internal needs and external pressures. And history has taught us that decay often begins with a succession."

"That's what worries me."

"But I've also noticed that *truly* excellent companies are remarkably robust, and change is part of their DNA, allowing them to easily figure out the sustainability piece and evolve. I believe that all elements of innovation excellence—from strategic thinking to agility and respect for people— are tremendous assets when it comes to sustainability. So to finally answer your question: maybe it's agility, the willingness to change, and the realization that you never can stop improving that comes after excellence."

"I sort of came to the same conclusion, Marcel, but how do I sustain the company in the short term, like after the upcoming sale?"

"I think your dad had the foresight to ensure his wishes remained intact, and your commitment to them can help sustain Davanti when you're not in charge. And you can certainly negotiate that and trade some sustainability commitments for cash."

"Good point. But that brings up another question that has been bugging me recently. Along with the outpouring of compassion after my heart attack, I sensed fear among Davanti associates— fear for my health, but also fear of the unknown. You know, what happens if Junior isn't in charge. I think I know how to remove the fear, but what do I replace it with?"

"Dr. Deming recognized that good leadership starts with driving out fear. It's the first thing I try to do when I acquire a new company—calm people's fear about changes to come. So what are your plans?"

"I want to, first, be honest with everybody and tell them everything this time. I must prove how much I've always cared about them. I also want to reassure them that they'll be cared for in the future, regardless of what happens to me."

"Based on the respect and care you've already shown them, with your gemba walks and other activities, I believe they'll trust you and whatever you plan for them. I'm still learning a lot about this myself. A friend of mine says genuine care and love turned his company around; the level of engagement it created was beyond his dreams. I've seen similar things in a few of my companies. Fusilli, for instance. Treating people right isn't that difficult and pays huge dividends. People who feel loved and cared for give you just so much more."

"I'm glad you're validating my thoughts, Marcel. I'd like to engage our associates in the sale of the company. What do you think?"

"That can work, but it likely comes at a price to you. If they want a piece of the company, that will have to come from somewhere. Unfortunately, I'm not an expert on employee ownership or similar programs, but I can get you in contact with some good advisors who can help you with those questions—and maybe I can learn something from you. For now, I'm happy we're talking, that you are here, and that you are on the path of recovery. You even get to pick the restaurant for our next get together."

"Thanks, Marcel. I'll keep you posted on the sale and how I involve the associates."

***

The Leonardo team had been inspired by the Wright brothers' approach: Test and learn before you design and build. They had written a test protocol for testing all gear mechanisms they received from suppliers. They weren't interested in how they function on a bike—i.e., they did not attach them to a bike to see which ones work the best—they were more interested in learning about the mechanisms and visualizing that knowledge. They measured gear ratios, friction, strength, durability, weight, volume, inertia, and many other parameters. They plotted some characteristics against others and made knowledge curves, which now cover the walls of the obeya room. For example, they documented durability as a function of weight and friction as a function of gear ratio, and learned that heavier devices also have high inertia, as expected, but not higher friction, and that strength is not correlated with weight.

They summarized all the data on a radar chart, which included baseline values for a chain and derailleur drive. For every critical performance measure (like friction, weight, cost, strength) on the radar chart there is a red zone that defines the *entry-level target*: if a device has one or more critical values below the entry level, it will be eliminated in this round. Since the devices are not made for use on bicycles, Mo and his colleagues expect that they will have to work with the manufacturers to optimize the devices, but they feel that if a device has a value below the entry level, it is highly unlikely that the manufacturer would be able to reach an acceptable level of bike performance in a reasonable amount of time.

As more than 90 percent of the test results are tabulated, the radar chart shows a disturbing picture: every device has at least one value below the entry-level target. Mo is quite discouraged by these results.

"During our first phase of testing when we looked at the data and knowledge curves from suppliers, we were convinced that we would find a solution," exclaims Mo. "What happened?"

"Back then, our only concern was that the major performance areas like friction and weight would be in the ballpark," says Serfino, "and they still are." He points at some of the curves from the initial exploration that are still on the wall. "And we confirmed some of those curves with our own testing. The problem is that we added more minimum requirements in this phase, and there isn't one device that can meet them all."

For Mo's team members, this is a project like any other: you run experiments, you generate data, you analyze the data, you visualize the knowledge, and you determine the next step. As such, they won't hesitate to recommend freezing a project if that is what the data tells them. For Mo this is a different story: this is his baby. He invented it and invested a lot of time and thought into this idea. For Mo, this project has enormous emotional value, and he's thought about it day and night—he believes it just cannot fail.

The only bright spot in the data is that almost every device has a different weakness; this could be a glimmer of hope, and Mo encourages his colleagues to consider this option: "We can work with several suppliers and have them pool their technologies, which might give us a chance to eliminate the entry-level problems," reasons Mo.

"I don't think that's a long-term option," says Serfino. "You're asking Davanti to fund a risk option: it would take a lot of small experiments to reduce the risk and the willingness of competing companies to work together."

"But we've got a lot of promising mechanisms to transfer the power to the rear wheel," argues Mo.

"Yes, but without a gear box, those mechanisms don't have value," counters Alexandra.

Mo nods. He cannot argue with that point, and he sees where this is headed. "OK. We have no choice but to accept your suggestions and freeze the development of the gear and the transmission mechanism. For the time being, this is the last Leonardo meeting," concludes Mo, not quite believing it's come to an end.

"Mo, I know you're not happy about this," says Serfino. "But we should all be pleased with the rigor of our process and approach. Just imagine if we had started to build bikes right away—as we used to do—and arrived at this conclusion a year from now."

"Yeah, I get it," says Mo with a heavy heart as he helps his teammates document the results. Sergio also is disappointed the development of his cable drive will not progress, but he's got another idea in mind; he plans to propose that the drive replace the cables for derailleurs and brakes on a bike.

As Mo works on the documentation, he begins to imagine not working on the project. His only hope is that in a year or two from now, the gear mechanisms have improved to the point that one may be suitable for the bike application. He also worries how his colleagues will perceive this failure. What will he tell Ricardo? What will Sofia think? What will Junior say? Will his failure be a topic at lunch meetings and Wednesday rides? "Maybe this is why inventors like to keep their projects under the radar," he thinks, "to avoid embarrassment."

***

Junior has been spending a few days a week in the office, usually working from home on days when he has cardiac rehab—not so much because it wears him out, but because the timing of the workouts and getting cleaned up afterward makes it more convenient to be at home on those days. He was, however, able to set his rehab schedule so it doesn't interfere with his Monday meetings.

Junior starts the meeting, his first since the heart attack, by thanking everybody for their dedication and concern while he was gone, and thanks Stephano for running the day-to-day that he could not cover. The staff press him for details, and he tells them a bit about the heart attack, but doesn't want to dominate the meeting with talk of his health. He quickly shifts gears: "This incident has certainly affected my plans for the future. As you know, no one in my family is interested in taking over the company. I always planned to sell the company one of these days, but that timeline now has been moved up."

All around the room, eyes are bright and mouths open. Claudia breaks the silence: "Will we be working for Marcel and Sofia?"

"No, certainly not. I'll let everyone know what's going to happen next week in a town hall meeting. My priorities are adhering to my dad's wishes—as always—as well as caring for the people of Davanti and the sustainability of the Fumane site. These mean more to me than getting optimum cash for the company. Of course, I'll get a sufficient amount, so please don't be concerned about that. In the meantime, I would like to announce that Stephano will lead the sale and transfer process. We'll make sure it's transparent to you and everybody else in the company. And I want you to tell me or Stephano what concerns or suggestions you have. Please put your minds at ease; your lives won't be any different, I assure you. But, for now, it must be business as usual. Potential buyers will want to visit the company, and who knows how long the process will take or if it will even succeed in finding the right buyer."

After dropping his bombshell, Junior opens the meeting for questions and the regular news and communications. The sale of the company is on everybody's mind—most thought that Davanti was done with change for a while. After many concerns about the sale were discussed, they finally get back to regular business.

Ricardo talks about the office andon he is introducing in his new function as a quality director. He reminds everybody what the andon cord is and how it is used in the plant: "Quality is not achieved by inspection; it is achieved by engaging and empowering everybody in the process of making perfect quality, and it starts in the design of the product, the purchasing of the components, the financial estimates, the marketing predictions. What would you do if you saw water on the floor? You would fence off the area and get it cleaned up as fast as possible so nobody would slip and fall. Right? We need to take the same stand on anything else we see that is not perfect."

"Please explain how that works here," suggests Claudia.

"While visiting our plant in Taiwan, I saw how everybody embraced andon. It's certainly not the only quality tool, but it's a good one to start with. There they use an andon cord to stop production processes. Of course, we won't have a cord dangling through the halls. We will, however, halt projects and processes if somebody sees something that could lead to less than perfect quality, and then we'll address the root causes before we continue. This will be covered in andon training that I'll introduce for the office."

"Is this like what companies use to anonymously report legal or ethics violations?" asks Diana.

"I don't think quality concerns need to be anonymous. In fact, they should be publicly acknowledged. But just like with ethics, I would like to teach our folks the reasons why we need to do this, the basic principles, and then let them suggest the best means to make this successful. And maybe one day associates coach their colleagues when they see less-than-perfect quality or behaviors rather than using the andon or a reporting line."

When Ricardo finishes, Leandro gives an update on some of the main projects:

- A second integration meeting for the Marconi project has resulted in a second set of bikes that are being tested on the road and in the lab.
- Two new technology creation projects have passed the TCP gate.
- New corporate initiatives, like the mountain bike development and the business expansion, are making progress.
- Two new PMs have been onboarded for projects recently created by Horst. They report to Horst and Leandro.

Anika is next and talks about personal performance management at Davanti. "We usually get only bad feedback on our performance management system because we only hear from the people who are rated low. But it's becoming more and more obvious that some of our cultural problems are rooted in our assessment system, which we use for pay raises and promotions: only one person assessing an individual's performance, each person using a different measuring stick, forcing a single ranking. Over the years this has caused a lot of internal competition and mistrust. So I pulled together a team that suggested the following:

- People are assessed by a functional manager and a project manager according to standardized criteria, including collaboration, innovation, seeking out existing knowledge, practicing PDCA, etc. Each employee will receive a formal feedback report that identifies precise opportunities for improvement.

- We'll also gather scores from the following process: Everybody in the company will get to vote for who they want to work for them, who they would like to work for, and who they would like to work with. And they also identify those with whom they would rather not be associated. In addition to the votes, people must give reasons why they made their choices. That will be important feedback for improvement.
- Everybody, including leaders, will be assigned a mentor. The mentor could even be a peer or subordinate. Mentors will discuss the feedback and comments with the people being assessed and coach them (in small steps) toward improving behaviors and performance. The mentor's assessment of the mentee's effort to improve also has a weight in the overall performance rating."

Anika pauses and then concludes: "I'd like to get your feedback on these ideas. We don't have time in this meeting, but please offer your thoughts the next time we get together or stop by my office."

"Excellent, Anika," says Junior. "Well overdue but better late than never."

Claudia reports next that she engaged Horst and Rebecca in developing a comprehensive Davanti dealer program. Although Junior didn't formally assign the dealer responsibility to Claudia, he's happy she took the initiative, and nobody seems to have a problem with her managing the program.

"Horst has a lot of experience from his previous job," Claudia explains, "and Rebecca has earned respect from the dealers with the Toricelli initiative. She also knows how to leverage internet tools and deserves a new challenge. This will help immensely as we create the dealer network and council—before long we'll be identifying gaps and opportunities as voiced by the dealers. We'll also leverage Davanti's current offerings combined with training, financial support, and incentives to engage more dealers and expand the program. We must help our dealers to be successful, and I sincerely believe this will be a huge benefit to both dealers and Davanti, and it will help drive the new Davanti corporate initiatives and open new markets. Lastly, I want to call out the groundbreaking work that Rebecca did to get dealers communicating with Davanti and set the stage for this program. She's also blended her efforts seamlessly into sales and marketing and shared many good ideas for upping conventional sales, and I'm grateful to have her on my team."

Everyone is a bit surprised and amused at Claudia's enthusiasm and positivity. "Excellent, Claudia," says Junior. "I will stop by Rebecca's desk to thank her for starting the initiative and congratulate her for what it has turned into. And lastly, I'm amazed about what I heard today. Those are fantastic new initiatives. Given that they all were developed while I wasn't even here makes me all the more comfortable when I think about my retirement."

Stephano is the last to speak and thanks everybody for supporting him in Junior's absence. He announces that a Swiss finance company that specializes in mergers and acquisitions has been retained to start the sale process. "And please bring your concerns and suggestions regarding the sale to me or Junior at any time. This is a momentous event for Davanti and us, and, if we do this right, we all stand to prosper."

Notes

1. Caldwell B. Esselstyn Jr., *Prevent and Reverse Heart Disease*, Avery, New York, 2008.
2. Augustine Rossa's Winning Bike.

Chapter 32

Features of Failure

After the last Leandro meeting in the obeya room, during which his team recommended to freeze the project, Mo spent the next day staring at his computer and going over all the results one more time. He eventually summoned the courage to set up a meeting with Ricardo for the end of the day.

They meet in the obeya room in front of all the data, and Mo summarizes the results. Ricardo asks him a few questions, but Mo is surprised that Ricardo expresses no concern or disappointment.

"What does the team say?" Ricardo asks.

Mo explains the team's recommendation, and, in doing so, shows his disappointment.

"And what do you think, Mo?"

Mo tries to be factual and not question the team's recommendation, but he's clearly distressed.

"First of all, I give you very high marks for the management of this project," comforts Ricardo. "You followed the right protocol, and you showed exceptional leadership. And you accepted the team's recommendation, despite your personal disappointment. That takes courage, and I thank you for that. Remember what we discussed and what was stressed in the innovation training: at least nine out of 10 new ideas that are explored in the creative phase will not progress into a product. You ideally want to freeze them after the first small experiments, but sometimes they fail a little later—like in your case where everything hinged around the gears. Ideally you could have included a low-risk option in your experimental sets that would have allowed you to learn a little more about the power-transfer mechanisms, like Sergio's cable. Devices like that might be used in other bike applications. But that's something to consider for a new project. We certainly didn't invest a lot in the development of this idea. I'm happy with the outcome of this project and ready to move on. How about you?"

"How can I be happy? We failed," exclaims Mo, and then catches himself and calms down. "Maybe one day I'll understand, but I'm not quite there yet."

"I understand how you're feeling, Mo. I've been there. People get emotionally attached to projects. That is one reason why so many bad projects drag on for so long. But you should have no regrets: you managed the project well, and if you continue like that you'll certainly succeed—with another idea and another project. Regrets are justified if you think you missed something, could have tried harder, made a mistake, or used poor judgement—but none of that is the case here. It's time now to document everything that you and your team learned, and then I'll talk to you soon about other opportunities."

"Ricardo, so many people knew about this project. What will they think? What will Junior think? He rode the early prototype."

DOI: 10.4324/9781003231837-32

"Mo, I see your concern, but you shouldn't worry about that. Your project was our pilot for a new process—a process by which we try to bring revolutionary technology to Davanti, and it had high visibility. At Davanti everybody has been used to R&D projects that mostly ended up in a product. The Davanti culture hasn't celebrated problems and certainly hasn't celebrated frozen or discontinued projects. That's got to change. Think of the information you gathered that will benefit other engineers and other projects. I'll talk to Sofia and make sure that everyone knows the value of what has occurred, including Junior. He'll be happy to see that the process worked as it was intended. He's seen dozens of projects drag on for months before failing, consuming cash day by day. The new process that you spearheaded minimizes that and we've proven it works."

"Thank you, Ricardo. I appreciate your frankness and encouragement."

Ricardo gives Mo a pat on the back as he gets up and leaves the obeya. Only one or two engineers are still at their desks; most have left for the day.

In the hall, Mo feels his phone vibrate in his pocket. It's a text from Marco. "Marianne is tapping a new keg of IPA. Join me?"

Mo is encouraged enough by his meeting with Ricardo that he quickly decides to join Marco for a beer and snacks. "On my way."

***

After dashing back to his office and grabbing his laptop and jacket, Mo makes a beeline to Bruno's Birreria-Ristorante. It seems like months since he's stopped in. More time with Marie has meant less time with Marco for a beer, but Marie is cramming for a new client engagement, and Mo is on his own.

Mo walks through Bruno's front door, and sees Marco, laughing and engaged in conversation with Marianne, who is waving her hands wildly. He sees Mo and calls him over. "Mo, you're just in time. The first of the new IPA," says Marco, handing him one of two glasses on the bar. "But you've missed Marianne's story. Maybe she'll tell it again."

"I'll be telling it all night," says Marianne. "Welcome back, stranger. . . . Hey, why the long face?"

"It's nice to see you, Marianne," says Mo sincerely. "Sorry, I just need a beer to cheer me up."

Mo and Marco touch glasses, nod to each other, and take a sip.

"Yeah, Mo, you look pretty down; it's either about Marie or Leonardo, right?"

"Well, I'm actually glad you put it that way. It's not Marie, and I'm glad of that. It's Leonardo   frozen."

"Looks like you learned your first lesson about innovation, Mo. Let me share a few things I've learned about innovation. It's one of my favorite subjects, and I've been doing a lot of reading. I've been waiting to confirm some of what I've read with what's going on at Davanti, and it looks like I just got my first sighting: innovators must learn to deal with failures—a hundred failures for one success, they say. Failures are part of experiments."

"It's not that easy," says Mo.

"Believe me, I know. Wallace Carothers, who is credited with inventing nylon, never saw it produced and had given up on the project. He also suffered from depression and committed suicide."

"I'm not that depressed. And I know of Carothers. It wasn't just the failure of his innovation that led to his death."

"Yes, that's true. But my point is: Successful innovators get right back up when they fall, and they keep going sometimes with a modification of the idea or a new one. How many failures do you think Edison had in his career? It looks like it takes a certain toughness to be an innovator.

Fortunately for you the failure came early—just imagine if you would have spent three years on this project."

"Ricardo said the same thing. I get it," says Mo, taking another sip from his beer.

"Another thing I read is that the really good ideas never seem to die—they just take breaks. At one point, Carothers actually gave up on his work with polymers that led to nylon. Maybe you, maybe somebody else at Davanti, or maybe a competitor will make this direct drive work one day, with a twist, with new technology, or something else. And I could talk to you for hours how real innovators always have many irons in the fire. One thing that never seems to die is their passion to invent. I see that in you, too, Mo."

"I'm sorry to be a downer, but how can you and Ricardo be so OK about this? I failed at the first real chance I ever had at innovation."

"Did Ricardo say that?"

"No. He convinced me that I should only have regrets if we missed something. I don't think we missed anything."

"I'll send you some links to articles about great and not-so-great innovators and their failures—people like Walt Disney, Stephen King, Soichiro Honda—as well as those who had big regrets, like the fifth Beatle, Kodak, Blockbuster, Yahoo. That may help you put things in perspective and feel a little better. Trust me, Mo, you are in great company when it comes to innovation and failure. And you've got a lot of inventing ahead of you; I'm sure Ricardo and Sofia have the next opportunity planned for you."

Mo takes another sip and gets Marianne's attention. "Thanks, Marco. Send me the links. I'll give them a look. I'm not doing anything else this weekend, except watching a little football. . . . How about we order a couple burgers. We got to eat if we want to drink."

"Good idea. Two burgers with the usual," says Marco to Marianne.

"Tomato, mozzarella, prosciutto, and onions? Am I right?"

"You got it. And two more IPAs, please."

Mo nods in agreement.

"It looks like the weather may be breaking soon," notes Marco. "Maybe a ride soon?"

"Yeah, I'd like that. I'm thinking I'll ride to work on Monday if it's warm enough. It will be a nice distraction. I have no idea what to expect come next week."

"We never do. We only think we do."

***

As Mo rides his bike through the company gate on Monday morning, he immediately notices her: she steps out of an open convertible (although it's only 10°C) on to the Davanti visitor lot, wearing a cowboy hat, denim jacket, country-style blouse, tight jeans, and cowboy boots. A mountain bike, like nothing that anyone at Davanti has ever seen, sticks out from the back seat. Jennifer Stone's long dark hair flows from her hat, and Mo imagines he's stepped into the old American West.

Jennifer is a former mountain bike world champion and now, in her early 40s, she looks like she can still compete. She and her bike flew in from Salt Lake City the previous day. Jennifer is a senior partner at Redlands Raptors, a small mountain bike company in Moab, Utah. Two former mountain bike pros founded the company 13 years ago, and Jennifer bought into the company a few years later when her pro career ended.

Jennifer, her two colleagues, and a handful of MTB enthusiasts have designed some of the best and most expensive mountain bikes on the market. But due to intense competition, they only operate in niche markets and in custom designs. They design the bikes by "trial and error" and promote the ultimate customer engagement in their designs: They customize bikes for their customers and get to see what they like and don't like. They also let experienced racers and fans use their facilities to experiment with their own bikes and bike components, and Redlands learns a lot from those no-cost experiments. The company owners and customers bike together on Utah trails and in races, and when they come upon something that gets riders excited, they adopt it in their bike designs.

Redlands Raptors has about 15 employees in their small plant near Moab. They buy carbon-fiber frames, including prototypes from China, and components from Japan and domestically. The company makes about 50 bikes a day—half of them custom-made for dealers, racers, and enthusiasts. They sell most of their bikes in two stores: one in Moab and one in Leadville, Colorado, which are hot spots for mountain bikers in the summer. They also sell through a couple of multibrand dealers in the US and one in Germany. Most of the company's other sales are through a well-designed internet site that allows customers to specify their own bikes.

Despite Redlands Raptors' bike performance, business has declined. The leadership team has tried many things to stop the slide, but without success. When Davanti put their team together to look at a mountain bike line for Davanti, Horst, who was aware of the Utah company through his former employer, suggested they talk to Redlands. Ricardo and Marco visited the company and were amazed at the technology and quality. Ricardo had summarized his assessment: "I would put 'Davanti' on those bikes right away."

For Redlands Raptors, Davanti is a good partner. It gives them access to a high-quality manufacturing operation and distribution—at least in Europe—and the opportunity to expand their networks. Stephano and the lawyers had prepared a contract by which no cash would be exchanged to get the partnership underway. Redlands gives Davanti unlimited use of their technology, and Davanti agreed to invest in manufacturing and distribution of Redlands Raptor bikes. They consented on a formula to share the revenues and agreed on a manufacturing strategy: standard mountain bikes would be produced in the Davanti Taiwan plant, and custom bikes would be manufactured in the Moab plant and the Fumane shop.

Jennifer plans to spend the next four weeks at the Davanti headquarters to finalize the details of the joint venture. She'll also educate Davanti engineers about MTBs and work at integrating Davanti bike knowledge into the Redlands designs, which will help to make the bikes manufacturing-friendly for the Davanti plant. She'll also work with Davanti procurement to leverage the Davanti component prices for the MTBs, which will be a significant cost reduction for Redlands Raptors. And she'll inspire Davanti IT to create a better website for Davanti.

Once inside Davanti headquarters, she's greeted by Marco. These two will come up with a marketing strategy for the "Davanti Della Montagna" line, and along with Matteo they'll design a distribution network.

"My goodness, Marco, it's beautiful here," says Jennifer with a drawl. "I thought I'd miss Utah, but now I wonder."

"It's good to see you again, Jennifer. Let me get you set up in an office, and then I'll give you the quick tour of what's been happening here. Would you like an espresso or cappuccino?"

"No caffeine for me; I've had too much already. Coffee is so good here."

"Is there any place where you'd like to start?"

"Yes. I would like to see the prototype shop. I'm looking forward to building prototype frames here, and I'd like to see some of those things we discussed during your visit to Utah, like your hydraulic and cable-drive ideas. They'd help us develop my dream bike: a two-wheel-drive MTB that would finally eliminate the rear wheel skidding on steep climbs and difficult turns."

"Yeah, I thought you'd like that. . . . I'm glad to see you brought your bike."

"I plan to check out the MTB trails nearby as soon as possible. Thanks for the contacts of your MTB friends. They said they'd be delighted to introduce me to Italian mountain biking, food, wine, and other wonderful things this country has to offer."

"They're thrilled. You're Jennifer Stone, after all, and they know your reputation. Just take it easy on them."

***

Mo has put all his work energy into the Ferrari project, and the team's first meeting to improve R&D speed kicks off in Emilio's old office. The team cleaned up remnants from previous projects in the room, removing old information from the walls and giving them enough space for regular standup meetings. Today, however, they've gathered around a table to collect facts, take inventory of the activities that are already going on, and plan new improvement work.

Mo asks the team to report on the 10 highest-impact items that Sofia had laid out in the order of importance:

Single-Piece Flow/Kanban Process

Carolina reports that they have implemented the shorter iteration times in R&D and moved the iterations closer together. She further reports that the number of iterations has declined, but she is not sure yet why. She also talks about a few improvements that were made to the resource visibility board that will alert everybody earlier if an engineer has more than one critical-path task at the same time. "And we're starting to optimize adjacent processes like plant release with single-piece-flow principles," she concludes.

Lean Project Management

Gina reports on the progress of the playbook, which she is helping to write. Together with Bolaji, they are trying to standardize the need for iterations and have already started to make a list of iterations and tests that can be replaced by computer simulations. She also talks about the project templates they're creating for the routine work. "This makes the work of the project managers and engineers easier, a lot faster, and more efficient," she says.

Knowledge Reuse

Bolaji describes knowledge reuse initiatives underway and the knowledge curves and equations that his colleagues have put together. "That knowledge is now finding its way into design and modeling tools," he explains. "We're teaching the knowledge reuse process in a workshop, and we're engaging all engineers in the process. And we're inviting all other functions to the workshop."

Standard Work

Mo split standard work in to two categories: design standards and work standards.

"Our most experienced engineers have now started to document what designs we know to work best for what bikes and what designs should be avoided," explains Bolaji. "The best possible design rules are reflected in our design standards. If we design a new bike, we encourage engineers to start with the standards; if they can meet the performance requirements with the standards, we'll only require safety and validation testing, which will save us a lot of time. And get this: The bikes we're launching this year, for example, are within the design standards and serve as our pilot. Our standards team is now writing test protocols for *new* designs—those that are outside the standards. For example, a drastic change to the front fork will require a lot of safety testing, and a change in the bottom bracket will require a lot of durability testing. But as we gain field experience with those new designs, they'll be included in the design standards and we won't retest further designs except for safety and quality."

"I like that idea," says Stella. "I've always wondered why we did so much testing on bikes when we've already made thousands of them."

"In the absence of test standards, engineers had no choice but to test everything for fear of being second-guessed," says Bolaji. "Now they follow the standard, and if the standard isn't good enough, we change the standard."

Carolina explains the work standards: "We documented the best way to do engineering work, and we teach everybody accordingly. The standards, of course, are different for the different phases: more creative freedom upfront, more discipline at the end. Although the main driver for the standards were safety, quality, and delivery, we expect a significant gain in speed and efficiency, especially from the PCP.

"And in the shops, we upgraded standards that were already in place, and there is a major initiative to close the gaps where standards didn't exist. Standards also make it easy to see deviations—look for more visuals in the shops and in the engineering area. And I want to remind you all of an important point that both Bolaji and I adhered to: all standards were written by the people who do the work. As we mentioned before, standards are not rules enforced by a 'standards police.' They simply document the safest, best, easiest, and fastest way to do work. So since the engineers or technicians who do the work wrote the standards, we expect a very high level of adoption and compliance."

"That sound great, Carolina," congratulates Mo. "Anything else."

"Yes, with standard work, many people can now do the same work, which creates flexibility. We can move the people where the work is and reduce waiting time. Anika started a crosstraining program in R&D and an incentive for people to take training and learn new tasks."

"Flexibility will be tied to salary and opportunity for advancement," adds Anika.

"Thanks, Anika," says Mo. "What complaints do you hear about stifling creativity with standard work?"

"I think we've given associates enough opportunity to use their creativity for product innovation. And, of course, if they find better ways to do the work, they're encouraged to suggest a change in the standards."

Waste Elimination

This item gets tabled, since most of this work has been completed and Mo wants to focus on the newer items on the agenda.

Time Buffers

Carolina explains that *time buffers* originally had been added to guarantee on-time delivery during the start of the lean initiative, and that she and her team are working to gradually reduce or remove them. "But we've started to systematically add resource buffers where we didn't already have them." She comments that scheduling to 70 percent of capacity is still a hard sell, and that it doesn't matter how often you draw the Kingman equation.[1] "But we learned that people usually agree to at least run an experiment with a capacity buffer. And if you document the performance before the experiment, it's easy to prove that the principle works—after all, the Kingman equation is a law of physics and operations, and you know it will work every time."

Late Start

Late start had been implemented in engineering and project management with the kanban system. Carolina had been tracking changes, reworks, and canceled iterations. "It was hard to establish a baseline for late start," she says, "but we all knew there was a ton of changes. Our records now show no recent cancelations and virtually no late changes. Charles and I are working on a decent estimate for the savings in time and money from late start, and we're stunned by the amount. Does that make sense, Sofia?"

"It does," Sofia confirms. "I've seen this before. The savings from the late start can surprise you, especially if changes to hardware, such as molds, are involved."

"Me and my marketing colleagues were responsible for a lot of the late changes in the past, but now, with the speed of iterations, we have less time to request changes. We had to develop the discipline to get all our ducks in a row before the work is started, and, for the most part, we're doing that," comments Marco.

Critical Path

The application of theory of constraint principles to the critical path of processes beyond the PCP has not progressed much. Several team members volunteer to help Giovanni with this initiative.

Overlapping Activities

Gina shows data for several processes where they started testing when the first prototype became available and started modeling and simulations once the first drawing was complete. She also talks about test jigs and fixtures that are now ordered at the same time the prototypes are ordered. "Our bike designs have been so similar for so many years that we can safely order the raw materials for molds or dies when the design starts, then the mold and die makers are ready to machine when the first drawings are completed. But we still need to work with procurement on some paradigms—in the past they've waited until a full stack of approved drawings has piled up before the lengthy bidding process began. And the bidding process itself is worth another improvement project."

"We didn't expect this all to go well or quickly," counsels Mo. "Keep working with them."

"Since we combined *flexibility* with *standards*, which makes sense, that's our list of the 10 biggest hitters," says Mo. "I'm happy with our progress, even though we don't have a lot of data yet. . . . So how much total cycle time reduction can we achieve over the next six months with all the activities we discussed today?"

"We have a good idea about the PCP process, but we haven't looked much at the TCP and the ICP yet," comments Giovanni.

"Why not set the target for the PCP, then, first?" says Gina. "I suggest a 40-percent improvement to PCP speed."

Most of the team members think they can do better, and agree to 50 percent in the next six months. But they also agree to keep the target among the team members for now, and only publish it when they can confirm the feasibility of the projection at the next meeting.

"I really don't care so much about the target," says Marco to everybody's surprise. "The most important gain for me is not even measurable right now."

"And what would that be?" questions Gina.

"It's February, and we haven't had to make a decision yet what we launch this year. You can't believe how much money Davanti wasted by making product decisions too early and without the right data and information. We got it wrong almost every season. This year, because we're fast enough, we can wait for more feedback from the Eurobike, we can survey the spring market, we can watch the competitors, we can talk with the dealers—and then we can pull forward what we need. We'll get this 100-percent right this year for the first time since I've been here. Speed is contributing to that."

"And when we introduce a new bike, we'll have the next generation launched before anybody figures out how to copy us," adds Gina.

"Maybe this is true for all important decisions" says Mo. "We're all trained to make decisions as early as possible to speed things up, but do they really make us faster? Maybe there's an optimum time for all things: when we have ample information and we can still capitalize on speed."

"Remember that the increase in speed also helps with internal customers," reminds Charles from finance. "For example, closing the books on the last day of the month and providing bike cost information within a day helps everybody make better and faster decisions."

"Good point, Charles, and that reminds me of another important item—the flow of information," points out Mo. "Information needs to keep pace with the process. We mapped the flow of information in our first VSM, but I'm not sure that we looked at it since then."

"I'll take another look at the information flow and speed," says Stella.

"Thank you, Stella."

Rene from procurement has an important announcement: "We reviewed our purchasing policies and were able to establish longer-term, collaborative contracts with our larger suppliers. The deals also mean that we no longer need to get quotes on small quantities or special orders. This will really help with items we need quickly." Then he gives a summary of the new process to the applause of the whole team.

"Mo, before you ask, I'm happy to tell you that I've heard virtually no reaction from the engineers regarding our speed initiatives," says Anika. "I rarely get good feedback, so take the absence of complaints as good news."

"When I've talked about speed on gemba walks, everyone starts to understand it as a process improvement and doesn't see it as a personal burden," says Bolaji.

"Likewise," adds Carolina. "They get it. Their work is more productive and not any harder. And I think we removed a lot of hassles and frustration and actually made their work easier, too. They can see the results of their work every day now. I really think the engineers and technicians are starting to provide the momentum. They're making this go, and we're just pointing the direction."

"Horst, you've been with us for a while now; what's your take on this?" asks Mo.

"This is a much more complicated process than I am used to, but I like the way you go about it," says Horst. "Speed and agility are your biggest assets. I'm just wondering when you will extend the speed thinking to observing the market, customers, and getting dealer or customer feedback. For example, we should be riding with the first two people who buy the newest bike at a local dealer."

The Ferrari team members recognize this omission with a collective nod.

"Please look at the whole system," he continues. "All the upfront folks, but especially those in R&D, hold the keys to making the process faster for procurement, manufacturing, and supply chain. The easier you make their jobs, the more speed you will gain."

The Volta team members are fascinated by other ideas that Horst shares with them—e.g., development of user stories and rider personas; launch of quick, micro-marketing experiments; expanded use of business analytics with dealer, customer, and web data—and they take good notes, anxious to try some of his suggestions.

"Lastly, I think Sofia got you started on some good principles and suggestions," says Horst. "But your competitors know about them, too, or at least will soon when they notice your success. Your competitive edge will lie in what you can do beyond those classic principles. I'll try to arrange a tour at one of the fashion companies in Milan. That will give you some new ideas for the next level of innovation and speed."

***

Anna had originally scheduled Junior's town hall meeting for 4:00 pm in the cafeteria, but a sunny and warm break in the late February weather has brought everyone to the outdoor commons area to hear the CEO. Junior starts by thanking everybody for their concerns, thoughts, and prayers following his heart attack.

"First off, let me say that I'm feeling well and healthy, thanks to modern medicine, a good diet, and more exercise than I care for. I would like to stand here today and tell you that I'm as good as new, but I'm not and probably never will be. That's just the nature of heart disease, and I've learned to live with that. Learning to live with it has forced me to consider how I will live with it day by day. Do I want to continue working 10- to 12-hour days, or is it time to retire and relax? I believe it's time to retire."

The employees look at each other, some surprised and some nodding as if they saw this coming.

"Retirement presents two issues: As you know, I don't have a Fausto III to groom for my role. And, of course, I need to finance my retirement. I've been thinking about my exit for some time, and I know how the uncertainty around my retirement affects everybody. But you should not be worried. I've had a lot of time to think about how to take care of all of you. In fact, I was so overwhelmed by the sympathy you all have shown since my heart attack that I learned a few things I should have known, which caused me to change my priorities. I regret not sharing my priorities or plans sooner, but that ends now: first, I promised my dad to make sure the 'Davanti' name stays on bikes for as long as possible and that they keep winning races."

Employees politely applaud their CEO.

"My second priority was my wellbeing in retirement, but I came to the conclusion that I want to put *your* wellbeing and your future ahead of mine."

Junior pauses, and the employees aren't quite sure how to react.

"You helped build this company, and in the past year you've worked incredibly hard to increase the value of the company. I used to say that nothing had changed at Davanti since my dad's time. That is no longer the case. Davanti is an innovative, vibrant, and growing company, thanks to you. And your future depends on what happens to Davanti next, and that's why I decided to make sure you are all taken care of first."

Now comes the applause, but not like the applause given to a race winner. It is humble tribute that shows gratitude and respect.

"I am here today to ask *you* how we can best take care of all of *you* when the company changes ownership. How can we assure *your future* and the future of this site? How can we get that accomplished so this big change makes us all big winners? You've been pretty good sharing your concerns and desires with me during gemba walks, and I expect to hear more from you personally about this. I'd also like you to nominate colleagues in your departments who will speak for all the associates, including those at the plant in Taiwan, and make formal recommendations for how you'd like to see the company transition upon my retirement. The folks you appoint will work with Stephano, who's overseeing the sale. He'll make sure that you are represented adequately during the change of ownership. Anika will help you get started."

More polite applause as Junior pauses, wipes his eyes, and struggles to gather his emotions: "I love you all, and that will not change when I retire."

As Junior steps away from the microphone, people line up to shake his hand, wish him well, and thank him. Some, like Penelope and even Vinnie, give Junior a warm embrace. Some people go back to work and come back later as the line shortens, but all want to speak with Junior, who spends a couple hours talking to individuals. Tired of standing, he eventually puts on a jacket and sits at one of the picnic tables. As his employees speak with him, he has a good idea how he can take care of them after he retires.

Mo eventually makes his way to Junior, wishes him all the best, and thanks him for his concern for the employees.

"Mo, you've been part of this change since the beginning. I still remember your presentation and riding your prototype. Thank you. . . . So how is your direct-drive project going?"

"We've learned a lot. I can fill you in at another time. I just want you to know how much I appreciate all the changes at Davanti and our pursuit of innovation excellence. I've never been busier, but it's been good and a lot more fun."

"I'm glad to hear that. Please let me know if I can do anything for you."

Mo says goodbye to Junior and rushes back to work, forgetting to respond to Marie's texts that had come in during the town hall.

Note

1. Simon Elias, "The Equation of Lean," Lean Competency System, February 2016: The Kingman equation states that three variables—arrival variation, process variation, and utilization—influence the length of the queue.

Chapter 33

Mo, Marie, and Leonardo

As February winter gradually gave way to the hope of spring in Italy, Mo and Marie played a game of hit and miss. Without a permanent client commitment, Marie was moved around Western Europe to wherever her firm needed her help: one week in Spain, the next in the UK, and then back to Switzerland. On the few weekends when she was available to see Mo, he had been visiting family or had made plans to spend time on the slopes with his college chums. Even texting and calling between the two was sporadic, but they'd eventually connect and spend most of their conversation discussing how much they miss each other.

But today, Mo senses an urgency in Marie's text that he's never seen before:

"In town. Need to see you ASAP. I'm stopping by at 7."

"OK. I'll grab us some takeout before you get here."

Marie arrives promptly at 7:00 pm, and knocks on Mo's apartment door. He opens the door and gives her a big hug.

"I've been waiting weeks for this."

"Me, too, Mo. It's been too long."

"Come in. Give me your coat and bag."

Mo has set the table with takeout—paninis, chips, and cold beer—along with some pickled vegetables that he'd brought back from his parents. Marie walks to the table and scrolls on her phone.

"I need to show you something," she says, pulling up a picture and showing it to Mo with a smile. "Do you know what this is?"

"It looks like an exam report from a doctor."

"It's a pregnancy report from my gynecologist."

"Are you saying . . ."

"Yes. I'm in the third month. I knew something was up, but I didn't have the courage to do the test myself or see my doctor. I finally did."

"How did this happen? I thought we took the necessary precautions." Mo looks at Marie and takes a few nervous steps that take him nowhere.

"Not only bike chains malfunction," says Marie calmly. "I hadn't planned for this to happen, but it did."

"So what will we do? What options do we have?"

"There is only one option for me. I did not have to think long or hard about this. I'm planning to have the baby. I want children, I love you, and, although I would have preferred to wait a little longer, I'm not unhappy about this."

DOI: 10.4324/9781003231837-33

Mo is in a state of shock. "But your bike career? Your professional career. You should think about your priorities."

"I know my priorities, and having the child is No 1. I can get back on the bike later, and my company has a great pregnancy program. . . . I gotta say, I was hoping for a different reaction from you. You don't look happy."

Mo stares with his mouth open, saying nothing.

"Can I have something to drink?" asks Marie. Mo brings her a water.

Marie sips the water and remains quiet as they stand for what seems like an hour. Mo eventually suggests they sit down and eat, which they do in near silence.

"I know this is all new to you, Mo. I've had a lot of time to think about it and get my head around it—both the responsibility and the joy of what's to come. You deserve some time as well. Just remember that the daddy job is yours if you want it."

She had hoped for a happy moment with Mo, but now sees that may have been unrealistic, and it certainly won't happen tonight. Her hope turns to sadness, and a tear rolls down her cheeks. They continue to eat quietly. Marie eventually gets up, puts her dish and glass in the sink, and grabs her phone, coat, and bag. She kisses Mo on the cheek and leaves. Mo sits at the table, staring at his beer but not drinking it.

***

The next day Mo calls in sick, not wanting to talk or see anyone. He works on Ferrari at home as well as the odd and end tasks to finish his old assignments. But he does not get a lot done in his apartment because his mind is constantly wandering. He gets a few texts from Marie throughout the day:

- "I know this must be difficult for you. It's difficult for both of us."
- "I wish you could imagine the possibilities."
- "Let me know when you'd like to talk."

Mo does not answer them.

The following day Mo rides his bike to work. He's glad he doesn't have any meetings set for the day. (He rescheduled a Ferrari team meeting to the end of the week "to give people a little more time to work on their assignments," or so he claims.) Once at work, he tries to concentrate. He hides in the obeya room and pretends to document the frozen Leonardo project.

Marco looks for him in the cafeteria at lunch, but Mo is eating at the desk in the empty obeya room. Marco sends him a text: "What's up, Mo? Where you hiding?"

"Not hiding. Just busy. I'm in the obeya room."

Marco walks down to the obeya room after finishing his lunch, and immediately notices that there is something wrong. He thinks Mo is still upset about Leonardo.

"Are you OK, man? I see you missed work yesterday."

"Just a cold or something. You know how it is in the spring."

"Well, if you're feeling better today, how about pizza at 6:00? I'll buy."

"Sure. I'll see you there. Domenico's, right?"

"You got it."

As Marco leaves the room, Mo gets another text from Marie: "Take your time. The dad job is still open. It's yours whenever you decide to take it."

***

Domenico's looks to be a throwback Italian bar. It's a long, dark-wood room with a bar that runs end to end. Until a decade or so ago, it would have only been filled with middle- and old-aged men. That quickly changed when the owner hired a cook that could knock out incredible pizzas of all styles. Five years ago, the owner installed a sophisticated wood-fired oven, and now Domenico's is crowded with people of all types. Marco is sitting at the bar next to two young women, one with bright purple hair and the other with green hair (not their natural colors). Marco waves Mo over to an open seat next to him.

Mo doesn't wait to be asked what's going on, and tells Marco as soon as he's seated: "Marie is pregnant."

"Wow, congratulations. So when is the wedding?"

Mo looks past Marco to the bartender, and asks for a glass of house Chianti.

"You know how conservative my parents are. They'll ban me from the house for life. This has never happened to a Pensatore. I'm not happy about this."

"There is always a first in every family. And it doesn't really matter if you're happy or not."

"And what will people at Davanti say?"

"Who cares what the people in the company say? It's your life, live it how you want. Wedding then kid, kid then wedding, it doesn't matter. The main thing is that you have the right girl, that you love her, and that you have a healthy kid. Right?"

"You don't get it. We were going to travel the world: skiing, biking, wineries. Now she's messed it up!"

"I think you had something to do with that, pal. And how can you say that? She's carrying your child. You'd better put on some big-boy pants and get ready for different travel plans."

"This wasn't supposed to happen. I've only just begun to even think about getting married." The bartender sets down Mo's wine, and asks if they're ready to order. Marco politely waves him off, and Mo takes a large gulp of wine.

"Marco, I have no idea how to handle a baby. Feeding, diapers, bathing."

"Just feed them powdered milk, and you can clean them with a vacuum." Marco thinks his joke is hilarious, but Mo just stares at him.

"So what do you hear from Marie? This must be equally hard or even harder on her."

"She said she's not unhappy. She's been texting me a lot. I think she's looking forward to the baby. And she says she's keeping the dad job open for me."

"Then you better take that job as long as it's still there. You don't want to screw that up."

"I can't even answer her texts."

"Mo, you might be the only one besides Marie and her doctor who knows right now what's going on. She needs your support. Her parents probably don't even know. You not communicating with her is probably breaking her heart. That's not like you, Mo. What would your parents think of that type of behavior? And there's only so long that Marie will put up with it."

Mo finishes his Chianti and tells Marco that he's tired and going to pass on pizza.

Marco sees that Mo needs more time to get through this difficult situation, and tries to change the subject: "How are things at work? Looks like you have another great project. I'm really impressed with the plans for the Ferrari project. That alone was worth Sofia coming to Davanti."

"Ferrari is moving fast. Pun intended. It's a good distraction right now—from Leonardo, from everything."

"Sure, I understand. Hey, I'm going to get a thin crust with anchovies and hot peppers. Why don't you get another glass and help me with that? Not eating won't solve your problem."

***

Mo spends the rest of the week ignoring Marie's texts and not even listening to her voicemails. At work, it's obvious to those who talk with him that he's not happy; he claims to be under the weather. He avoids every meeting that he can, and spends a lot of time in the obeya room—still documenting (much slower than necessary and many times over) the Leonardo project. Mo does not join his friends in the cafeteria, who tell him that they miss him and his mom's leftovers.

On Thursday evening, his phone rings, thinking it's Marie again. He looks and sees that it's his mom. Mo cannot ignore a call from his mom, although that is exactly what he'd prefer to do.

"Hello, mom. How are you?"

"I'm fine, Maurice. How are you? It's been a couple weeks since we've seen you, and we're hoping you might come this weekend."

"Just busy, mom. You know, work and stuff."

"Is everything OK? You don't sound like yourself."

"Just a lot of work, mom, and a lot of problems right now."

"I understand. Your dad had days like that. Maybe he could help you. Why don't you come over . . ."

"I will think about it, mom. I'll let you know on Saturday morning."

***

Come Saturday morning, Mo calls his mom and tells her he can't make it to Lake Garda, but he will try during the week ahead. He puts on long pants and a thick layer of clothes and heads out in the valley for a ride. His ride is short—not because of the cold weather—but because his head swims with thoughts about Marie. It's almost worse when he's alone on the road.

He thinks that if Marie would just show up with the baby and move in, everything could be worked out. But he does not call her or text her to tell her that. Why? Then he visualizes visiting his parents with Marie and the baby. What would his sister say? How would his mom react? Would she talk to him? His dad would probably leave the house and go fishing. His brother would say nothing and play with his kids. As he rides back to his apartment, he thinks about meeting Marie on this same road and wonders what she's doing. He really should call her. But what will he say? How does he proceed? Doing nothing can't go on forever.

Once back at his apartment and warming up after his ride, Mo boots up his laptop and checks his email. He finds a long email from Marie and sits down to read it: She tells him that she's had a rough time since she's seen him. Just eight months ago, she was getting over a former boyfriend, but this is much harder. She told her parents about the pregnancy, and they're thrilled to be awaiting their first grandchild. Marie says she spends considerable time every day on the phone with her mom. Of course Marie's mom wants to know who the father is, but she's said nothing for now. She's tells Mo that she's been busy at work, sees her OB-GYN on a regular basis, and spends all of her spare time concentrating on the baby. Her company has helped her plan her pregnancy leave and has promised to schedule her for local assignments, especially as the pregnancy progresses. At the end she writes: "I love you as much as I ever have. I can't make you love me or this baby, but I wish you'd think about the joy this can bring to our lives. Yours, Marie."

Mo closes his laptop and feels like a jerk.

***

Mo is typing away at his laptop and staring at tradeoff curves on the obeya wall when he gets a text from Marie: "I was at the doctor today. I am expecting a girl. I would like to name her Chiara. What do you think?"

Mo starts typing—"That's my mother's . . ."—and then stops typing when Luca shows up at his desk.

"Mo, I've been looking everywhere for you. You've got to see this," exclaims Luca.

Mo hits the "send" button on his phone by mistake.

"What's so urgent, Luca?"

"Why aren't you eating with us anymore? We miss your mom's food."

"Just under the weather, I guess. You know, the test results from Leonardo and closing out the project."

"Maybe you should hold off on that." Luca puts a printout with test results on Mo's desk.

"What's this? I thought we finished all testing."

"This device came in late from the US. I thought you'd want it tested, so we ran the same tests on it as we did with the others."

"Oh yeah, the ACE device. I remember now. How did that end up in the lab? I thought they would send it to my office. They must have had the lab address in their system. I didn't even know it arrived. So how'd it do?"

"I liked it the minute I saw it. The folks who made it obviously know bikes."

Mo scans the test report and his eyes light up: "Luca, this is what we're looking for."

Mo feels like hugging Luca, who helps him quickly add the data points to a spider chart that is still on the wall. "Look, this one is better in almost every area, and nothing is in the red," says Mo.

"But in the lab, we were wondering how you would connect this ACE gear to a rigid shaft or any other rigid, power-transmission devices. The whole device moves when you switch gears. We had to make a special fixture to run some of the tests."

"I think Tim Albright, the ACE CTO, mentioned this when he called me. They stopped the project when they couldn't solve that connection problem. I thought back then, if nothing else, we could connect it to a hydraulic pump and run a flex hose back to a hydraulic motor."

"Yeah, a hydraulic pump would work," agrees Luca.

"Wait a minute—Sergio's cable," yells Mo. "That thing is flexible. We may have saved the Leonardo project!"

Mo rushes away from his desk and to the engineering area, where he catches Ricardo at his desk and shares the news with him.

"Aren't you glad you had so many options in your plan?" asks Ricardo rhetorically. "That's the secret for success in this phase of innovation—the more options you include, the higher your chances for success. So what do you suggest now?"

"Let me talk to the team, and we'll come up with a plan."

"I look forward to seeing it. And as you develop your plan, please think about the following: You looked at a large number of gear mechanisms from hand tools, and you found a promising one outside of that area. Could there be other promising mechanisms to learn from, like the gears on my lawn tractor or mechanisms hidden in other machines?"

"Good point once again! Thanks, Ricardo."

***

Mo quickly reassembled the Leonardo team and shared the results of the ACE device. His teammates were surprised and also wondered how Mo forgot about the device and never mentioned it. Mo wondered the same thing himself. Nonetheless, they were pleased to have a chance to get the project up and running again. They called ACE and asked for a whole set of derivatives of the device they just tested, but were told it may take a few months to get them. Mo is convinced that after he tells Tim Albright about the plans for the project, they'll pull out all stops to send the new devices sooner.

Then the team put together a new set of experiments for concurrent engineering. They included four variants of the ACE gear, but this time they also added a "safe" option. For this option they selected the internal gear hub that Vinnie used on the rear wheel of the first prototype. It was Serfino who had the idea to "turn that mechanism around" and use it as the front gear box. When Serfino learned that ACE has been making those internal gear hubs for a long time, he suggested that the team enlist ACE's help mounting the gear box right between the pedal arms. The safe option, although technically not the most exciting, will give Mo's team a chance to create a complete drivetrain that can be used on a real bike in the next integration event, enabling them to learn how the different drive mechanisms (like Sergio's cable) interact with the gear mechanism. And Sergio was pleased with the safe option because it's the first chance to test his shaft on a real bike.

Mo told the team of his most recent discussion with Ricardo, which opened his eyes to other gears in other machines or industries.

"I was wondering about that," says Serfino. "I also wondered why we never looked at worm or helix gears. If you don't mind, I would like to explore those areas—without slowing down my current assignments, of course."

The rest of the team approves and expresses their desire to follow Serfino's lead.

"Thanks, Serfino," says Mo, "and if you find something, please run some simple experiments like we did in the first phase of the project. Meanwhile, let's continue with our plans for the ACE gear."

After more discussion, the Leonardo team plans to explore the following sets in their next experiments and tests:

Gears

- Four new gear options based on the experimental ACE device
- Two traditional hub gears with different gear ratios based on ACE's existing technology

Shafts

- Two sets of Sergio's flexible cable
- A solid-drive shaft with universal joints that could be connected to the moving ACE gear. They also made the shaft telescopic so it can expand and contract as the gear moves.
- Two hydraulic options, attaching a pump to the ACE gear and running a flexible hose to a hydraulic motor on the rear wheel

Power Transmission on the Rear Wheel

- Notching the brake disk (the Chainbuster idea)
- Reuse the conical gear from the first prototype
- Putting gear teeth on the side of the tire rim (Alexandra's favorite—from the hackathon)

The team also started to explore two brand new ideas: First, Sergio found low-friction universal joints for his cable. He learned that bending the cable by more than 30 degrees at a tight radius causes too much friction. The universal joints would allow longer cables and more flexibility and open the door to front-wheel drives for bicycles.

The second new idea is based on the fact that chain bikes need a very strong fork between the pedal axle and the rear wheel (chainstay), one that is strong enough to support the high tension and torque of the chain. But now that all options are to flexibly connect the pedal forces to the rear wheel, that fork can be significantly modified. It can be made lighter to save weight and thinner to create a softer ride. The three Commilitones (the Davanti knowledge council) suggested that the team try replacing the fork with a single, stronger leg on just one side of the bike, which would be revolutionary and improve the ride of the bike tremendously. Ricardo had suggested that Mo give them a tour of the project to see if they could contribute some of their knowledge and experience, and they were quick to offer the idea.

The Leonardo team doesn't plan to include the fork modifications into their experiments just yet. They can now, however, use Davanti knowledge curves, computer simulations, and design tools to explore those modifications. A structural engineer was added to Mo's team to integrate the new design ideas with the drive options.

Since computer simulations are faster than building prototypes, Mo is hopeful that whenever they build their first bike, they can include a version of the new fork. As Mo is setting up visuals to document the new experiments and ideas, he reflects on what Marco had told him when the Leonardo project was frozen a few weeks ago: "Good ideas rarely die, but they sometimes take a break." He also remembers what Ricardo kept pointing out: "The broader the design space that you start with, the higher the chances for success." And he comes to understand that the team didn't need design of experiments (DOE) to eliminate all the weak options: all of the gear mechanisms (except for the late arrival ACE) were eliminated in the first experiment. Mo now understands what Ricardo told him about his original DOE. "We would have wasted a lot of time and resources testing the unfit mechanisms with all the other variables, like drive shafts and rear-wheel drives."

Mo is surprised and exhilarated to be working on Leonardo again. But despite all the data and diagrams flooding his brain, his thoughts keep racing back to Marie and the baby.

Chapter 34

Davanti for Sale

Davanti associates met a few times after work in the cafeteria to discuss their interests in the sale of the company. Anika made arrangements to have coffee, espresso, and snacks freely available for everybody. It was a wild mix of people from department leaders to custodians. Some employees from the Taiwan plant participated via video conferencing.

Initially everyone talked randomly, but they respected each other enough not to interrupt. Then a shop foreman suggested that the group appoint a volunteer to make a speaker list, and each speaker would be given five minutes. The foreman called for volunteers to lead the discussion, and the group applauded the first hand that went up: a woman who works in procurement took on the role and made a list of speakers. Each was called and given their time to speak. By the second meeting, after many had spoken, the assembly's desires became clearer.

Some people promoted the idea to ask Davanti for cash out of the sale, prorated to years of service. The Taiwan reps were interested in guaranteeing hourly wages and work conditions. Others wanted some form of employee-stock ownership as part of the deal. As the talks continued, the consensus crystallized around guarantees for employees in Taiwan and assuring that jobs remain in Fumane rather than a cash outlay for employees. Many wanted jobs guaranteed in a sale agreement and believed that with the right conditions attached, it was worth pursuing and in line with the vision of Fausto Sr.

Most in the group also wanted the right to veto a contract due to a potential buyer's history: reputation for treating employees, environmental records, workplace safety violations, etc. A few thought that such a requirement would be difficult to sell, but the majority wanted to try. So the assembly appointed four representatives—a shop technician, an engineer, an administrative assistant, and an assembly-line worker from Taiwan—to draft a proposal that focused on the guarantees for Taiwan, keeping jobs in Fumane, an employee stake, and the right to reject a potential buyer. To their surprise, both Junior and Stephano agreed to give it a try. Junior promised to invite the representatives to the table when negotiations for the sale begin.

Delatour Global, the Swiss accounting firm retained by Davanti to prepare the sale, had listed the company on the day of Junior's town hall meeting. As soon as they sent out a company profile, about a dozen potential buyers came forward with questions. Delatour vetted the buyers' interests and capabilities to follow through on an acquisition, and then Junior and Stephano held meetings with the most attractive suitors at the accounting firm's Milan office.

Junior and Stephano invited a few potential buyers to tour Davanti headquarters and interview some of the associates. The German company Borges GMBH, a global supplier to the auto industry and other sectors, asked for more extensive interviews with key personnel in Fumane and Taiwan:

DOI: 10.4324/9781003231837-34

technical staff, including Ricardo, some of his managers, and PMs; several engineers; and technicians. An NDA had already been signed and the individuals to be interviewed—which included Mo and Sergio—were briefed by the Davanti lawyers; they were allowed to answer any questions, but when it came to sharing documents or drawings, the lawyers would have the final say.

***

Sofia has scheduled a meeting with Mo, Ricardo, and Anika in Sofia's office on succession planning. Ricardo and Anika walk in together, chatting and laughing about a reality show they'd seen on RAI the night before. Mo follows right behind, unsure why he's been asked to attend. With both the Leonardo and Ferrari projects going full bore, as well as his day-to-day work, he's afraid to land any more special assignments.

Sofia starts the meeting by talking about her plans. "Junior's recent problems caused an unexpected change in Davanti that I now must prepare for. As the sale progresses, we need to make plans for sustaining the innovation excellence transformation at Davanti."

"No buyer would want to stop it," suggests Anika.

"That's right. But we'll need someone in charge of it. I've been on loan, and who knows when my time with Davanti will be coming to an end. Not to mention that Davanti needs a complete org chart, including my position."

Mo is wondering what any of this has to do with him, that is until Sofia drops the bomb: "We'd like to groom you as my successor—a crash course of coaching, if you will. Mo, I'm sorry I did not talk to you first, but we came to this decision as a team and wanted to present the offer together."

"What about my projects?" asks Mo.

"You can work on those as time allows and certainly finish them after the coaching. Of course, they may be affected by the future developments of the company, too."

"I'll provide the help you need," says Ricardo. "We're not removing you from your projects. That wouldn't be fair to you. And we need them to continue."

"But I like what I'm doing now, and I feel like I'm in over my head as it is. And I saw the challenges that you faced, Sofia. I'm so impressed with your people skills—I'm not sure that I can handle anything even close to that, certainly not now and maybe never. I'm only a small cog in this machine with no power and certainly very little authority."

"First off, you've gained a lot of respect from everybody in the company in the time I've known you," counters Sofia. "And, Mo, I didn't start out as the person I am today. I was the worst at managing people, having grown up in a total command-and-control environment earlier in my career. My people-management skills only started to improve when I first experienced lean. I learned all by trial and error, and the more I learned about lean people management, the more successful I became in my work, and the more engaged and happier I became. My exposure to innovation excellence came when Marcel bought a company that I was working for, and, I have to say, it added another level to my people skills. I wish I had an opportunity to learn all of this when I was as young as you, Mo."

"I echo that," says Ricardo. "I think you have the potential, but people are not born with leadership skills. They have to be learned, and I think you have a great environment and exceptional coaching here at Davanti, especially if you can learn from Sofia."

Anika also encourages Mo's acceptance of the role: "The good things at Davanti are not based on the changes Sofia made. They're the results of the changes *people* have made under her influence—that's a skill they don't teach in college, Mo. You're getting a huge opportunity here."

"I understand. It's just a lot of balls to juggle right now. I don't want to get burned out or screw up."

Mo reiterates that he likes what he's doing now and being an engineer, and he wonders if he is even the right candidate for the job. Ricardo reminds Mo he's proven his technical ability, he's shown great leadership potential, and it's time to expand his leadership abilities by taking advantage of this unique opportunity: "We'd prefer to give you more time to ease into this, but we don't have any control of that. You're the right person within Davanti—maybe the only person—for this role right now."

"I'd be available at any time to assist," reassures Sofia. "Even after I leave the company. You have my cell number."

Anika talks about raising his status in the company and the pay raise that would accompany the role. Mo is glad to hear that offered, but he still refuses to commit. They all finally agree to give him a few days to think about it, although Sofia says they need to finalize the position soon due to the company sale and would need time to find somebody else if Mo declines.

"I promise you that I'll give this serious thought," says Mo, who stands, leaves the meeting, and heads back to the obeya room. "What would be my most critical question here?" he wonders. Try as he might to think rationally about this, as an engineer would, he's overcome by many thoughts and emotions: "What would dad think? There is nothing wrong with a higher position and more money, and who knows if I'll ever get another chance if I let this one go? I like the people at Davanti; it's the only company I've known, and I want to do what's best for my friends. But I'd rather just hunker down in the obeya room and become a better engineer. Maybe things will fall into place on their own." Before he knows it, he's in the obeya room, alone again. "Is this really what I want?"

***

Paul Haupt introduces himself as the executive director of the value stream for non-automotive drivetrains at Borges GMBH. He oversees the development, marketing, sales, and manufacturing of those products. He tells Mo and Sergio that his company started as a producer of electric equipment, including hand tools, industrial controllers, and factory automation equipment. They also have a small division of automotive components for combustion engines and controls. After they acquired a company specializing in electric-car components, they rapidly expanded that business. Electric drives for non-automotive applications are Borges' latest venture: drives for cycles, scooters, Segway-like devices, skateboards, and anything else that could zoom around with battery power and computer controls. Paul explains that he'd recently added hybrid drives to the division's lineup. These drives, like in hybrid cars, recover energy during braking and turning.

"You may wonder why I'm talking to you personally," he says to the two who have puzzled looks on their faces. "We toured Davanti, studied patent applications, looked at samples and prototypes, talked to your leadership, and concluded that Davanti holds many pieces of the puzzle we're trying to complete. Both of you work on some critical pieces."

Sergio gives Mo a look of "I get it," and Mo returns the gesture.

"To make a long story short," continues Paul, "we studied transportation needs around the world—from urban to rural areas, from business to recreational, and from moving people to delivering food and packages. We concluded that the product best suited to address the current gaps is a bicycle that is very light-weight, maybe foldable, so it can be carried easily on public transportation, elevators, and into apartments. It must be totally maintenance-free, sharable, both human- and battery-powered, and with a USB-charged battery that's so small that it can be carried in a purse or a briefcase and charged up while a rider drinks a coffee. We currently make about a third of the global e-bike drives, but today's e-bikes look more like electric motorcycles; they're not sustainable because they're heavy, need a lot of maintenance, and require large charging/docking stations to be sharable. We need a revolutionary approach, a redesign of the complete bike."

"Light weight and no chain," says Mo. "I understand how those puzzle pieces would work for you, but you also mentioned 'hybrid' drives."

"Hybrids are needed to minimize the battery size. Light-weight bikes are still easy enough to pedal, which of course extends battery life, and we need to recover as much energy as possible on downhills and during braking in the city. We like the gears you are developing because they would allow us to integrate the motor, the gears, and the recovery system in one small unit. And with the help of Davanti, we might house it all in the bottom V between the pedals."

"Would I be able to ride a bike while I read texts or surf the web?" asks Sergio. "In other words, will they be autonomous?"

"We make many of the controls for autonomous cars, and that technology is scalable. But at this time, I wouldn't dive into a traffic jam and count on the bike to meander around cars and pedestrians. And by the way, since we produce drives for sharable scooters, we have the technology to make these bicycles sharable and theft proof. When we incorporate a wheeled stand under the pedals, we can even make the bike come to the rider when called."

Mo wants to know if a gear box is still needed or if sufficient torque can be generated by the electric motor alone. Paul is convinced the gear box is indispensable, and the more gears with low friction it features, the better it is for energy efficiency—just like with cars. "We can certainly boost the torque for starts and small uphill rides, but that takes a heavy toll on the battery and on the durability of the motor."

Paul asks Sergio and Mo many detailed technical questions to better assess the status of their projects, and he seems pleased with their answers before he proceeds: "Your projects and knowledge are critical for the advancement of our technology. I have a rather large team that works on these concepts, and I would really like the two of you to join that team after the sale, which I believe will go through. I'm also intrigued with the innovation process you use here at Davanti. I never heard about such an approach, and I'm anxious to learn more about it."

"Would this require relocation?" asks Mo.

"My complete operation is currently in our headquarters in southern Germany. But since we're all bound to secrecy, I can tell you that we're negotiating to place all bicycle development and engineering here in Fumane."

"That's a relief," says Mo. "It's the right thing to do. This is where the bike knowledge is."

"I understand where you're going with electric bikes, but Davanti's main business is racing bikes. What will happen to our race team and our race bike technology?" asks Sergio.

"Davanti has been a profitable business, and there are no plans to change anything in the current business model. We want Davanti racing to stay strong or even better than it has been. Racing will remain synonymous with the Davanti name."

"I'm glad to hear that as well," states Mo.

"There's so much to like about Davanti. We are tremendously impressed with how the company has been growing in the last year, and we see potential for more rapid growth with the initiatives currently underway. I assume that my company will run Davanti as an independent subsidiary and keep it on the path it has embarked on. That would also be best for my company to learn bicycle technology. Motors and controls can be scaled down from what we learned in the automotive industry, but we feel we need to get involved in the design and manufacture of a complete bicycle. And we also need light-weight materials and economies of scale. So we jumped on the opportunity when Davanti went up for sale."

"What other Davanti technologies can advance your cause?" asks Sergio.

"We want to look at Davanti's run-flat tire options. Tires are the second biggest maintenance issue for bikes after the chain drives. Although the Davanti idea might get a rider to a safe place, it still needs a lot more development. We'd likely work with a tire company in that effort."

As Paul talks, Mo imagines that Borges could be a good fit for Davanti. He also thinks that none of this would have occurred without the innovation excellence initiative: "We are the race-bike experts, and, although we had the right talent and some great technologies, none of these opportunities are currently in our grasp. Davanti would have been challenged to develop a market presence with any city or electric bikes."

As the meeting adjourns, Paul says, "I'm super impressed with what you folks have accomplished here at Davanti in such a short time. It would have taken us years and a lot more people to get that much done. I hope that we can work together in the near future and, if that doesn't happen, I wish you the best of luck for Davanti and your careers."

"Thank you, Paul," says Mo. "It's been an enlightening meeting, and we're excited about the opportunity. We hope for the best outcome, and, in any case, wish you the same good luck."

***

Mo accepts an invitation from Marco to hit the roads the Saturday following the Borges meeting. The weather is warm in the valley, but too chilly to head up into the mountains, so they ride on flat roads at a recreational pace and talk a lot.

Marco talks about the Eurobike show and regional expansion, but he's most excited about the MTB project and his time hanging out with "cowgirl Jennifer." He's looking forward to a lot more traveling, especially another trip to Utah. "They're letting me choose from their MTB lineup, and I'll have a dozen guides to some of the best MTB terrain in the world. Jennifer promised to make an MTB rider out of me. Who thought a year ago that something like this could ever happen at Davanti?"

"Looks like I'm not the only busy guy these days."

They also talk about the pending sale, and Mo briefs Marco about his meeting with Paul Haupt.

"Looks like they want you more than the company."

"They want Davanti and Davanti's innovations."

"I thought I knew everything about innovation. But what surprises me is how your idea has evolved. I'm sure you weren't the first one to have the idea to eliminate the chain, and when I saw your first prototype, I was supportive but not overly impressed."

"Well, now the truth comes out," says Mo jokingly.

"That's not what I'm getting at. I can't believe what happened to your idea in a very short amount of time. And then out of the blue comes Borges, and they want the technology for something nobody at Davanti imagined. I think the secret to a lot of successful innovation is not the idea itself, but the processes that enable it to morph into something else, allowing others to find it and synergize it. I think we're up to something big here. I wonder what's next?"

"Yes, I agree. In the right environment, a good idea is like a caterpillar—one day it's just a caterpillar, then it's a chrysalis, and suddenly it transformed into a beautiful butterfly. There's no telling what you'll get out of a good idea."

"Can you imagine working for Borges?"

"Sure. But it's all happening a bit fast for me."

"Speaking of fast, how is Marie doing?"

"Very funny."

"I couldn't resist. How do you think she's feeling? I mean, she still doesn't know if she'll have the father in the delivery room."

"There's a lot going on, Marco, and that is one of many things. I'm processing them all. I once read about not making any decisions until you absolutely have to."

"Yes, but . . ."

Mo quickly bikes ahead of Marco to end the conversation. Marco, who's in better riding shape, eventually catches him and changes the subject to the renaissance of the Leonardo project, which seems to re-engage Mo.

"So what do you think will happen to Sofia if they sell the company?" asks Marco.

"Funny you should ask. That's another one of my problems. They want me to be her successor."

"Wow, Mo! That's wonderful. Congratulations. I wish they'd offer me a shot like that. I hope you accepted."

"I'm still thinking about it."

"Mo, you're thinking way too much. Some decisions need no thinking. And who knows how long those opportunities will be there? You can't turn that job down. Man, you're not thinking straight. Maybe a beer and pizza will help."

"It won't hurt—loser buys." Mo tries his best to beat Marco back to town, but Marco is standing next to his bike at Bruno's when Mo pedals up.

"So I beat you again. But you know what, my friend, this is the only thing that hasn't gone your way of late. You'll see that one day."

***

The following week Mo continues to juggle his projects, his emotions, and his stories—i.e., who knows what and who doesn't. He told his family about the pending sale of Davanti, how his project plays a big role in that sale, and the many requests from the buyer for information that he's required to answer. His dad is especially excited for him and said it's a harbinger of good things to come. Mo also discussed his new speed project with his dad. "I don't think I could have handled the load you've got right now," replied his dad. "I'm proud of you, Mo."

"You don't know the half of it," Mo would have liked to say. In addition to the baby, he's not told his family about the new job offer as Sofia's replacement. His family wishes they could see more of him, but they understand that he is incredibly busy and needs to work some evenings and weekends to catch up. As long as Mo calls his mom frequently and keeps her informed, all is good.

He still gets texts from Marie, though not as frequently as before, which has Mo concerned. She updates him on her doctor visits and sends pictures of the baby room that she has started to create in her apartment. She also told Mo that she talks to her mom and dad every day and how blessed she feels by their support. "But they want to know about the dad."

Mo now occasionally answers her texts, usually nothing more than a polite, short reply and reminds Marie of how busy he is. At least Marie knows that he's still reading her texts, he thinks, all the while realizing that he should be doing something more. He senses that the time is coming to make up his mind.

It's been about a week since Ricardo and Sofia approached Mo about the innovation excellence position, and he's sure they want an answer when Ricardo takes him outside to talk. The weather is chilly but sunny, and spring flowers are beginning to emerge. They sit at a picnic table.

"Can we help you, Mo? Is something bothering you? You've not been yourself the last few weeks. I can't give you advice about your personal life, but I care about you and I'm getting concerned."

"There is a lot going on, Ricardo, and not all of it has to do with work. A few weeks ago, my girlfriend informed me that she's pregnant. I was stunned. I'm still stunned. It changes all my plans. I'm not sure what to do, and I've been trying to sort everything out."

"I'm excited for you, and I understand your confusion. It happens. But there are no blessings as great as having family and kids. I would exchange nothing in the world for that. Yes, I had other plans, too, but nothing can replace my family."

Mo talks about his personal situation, his family, and how he's afraid this won't end well. "And what will everyone here think when they hear about this?"

"Mo, you shouldn't care what others think. It's your life. Your friends will support you and congratulate you—others likely won't even notice or care. And does it really matter to anyone if you're married or not? I don't think so."

"Maybe you're right."

"I know I'm right. I don't like to tell anyone what to do, as you know. But this time I'm telling you to think about you, your girlfriend, and the baby, and forget about what anyone—your family, friends, colleagues—thinks. And if it could help, we've got counseling available at Davanti."

"No, I'm fine. Thank you for listening. I appreciate it."

Ricardo and Mo sit without talking for a few minutes, each enjoying the view of town and the distant hills above nearby buildings. Ricardo then breaks the silence: "Mo, I don't mean to pressure you, but we've got to make a decision for Sofia's replacement soon. Even if you had more time, I don't think your decision would be any easier."

"Yes, you're probably right."

"Why not just try the job? Ease into it at your own pace. Sofia is willing to work with you on the timing. We can even announce this as a temporary assignment until you decide to make it permanent. We will, however, list you on the org chart that the buyer sees."

"Will Junior and Anika be OK with that approach?"

"Mo, we're just giving you some time to get comfortable with the role. If you find it's not your thing, then we've all been upfront about it from the start. You take care of your personal situation, and we'll take care of things for you here at Davanti. You're the right person for this job, and it will help you in many, many ways. What do you say?"

Mo senses a weight coming off his shoulders as he makes the decision to try the new job: "Maybe I could ease into the dad position, too, and try it out first," he thinks. But then it hits him that he will be a dad even if he doesn't take on the day-to-day responsibility. Mo knows what he should do and *wants* to do. "I guess I will be a dad and an innovation excellence leader," he tells Ricardo.

"I'll let Sofia and Anika know about the job. I'm sure you'll make the right decision with your girlfriend."

Chapter 35

Ever After

Junior had looked for Mo a few times in the engineering area, but could not locate him. Eventually he asked Ricardo where he could be found, and Ricardo took him to Mo's hideout in the obeya.

"Mo, I've been looking for you."

"Good morning, Junior. I'm sorry you had to search for me. I've been spending time in here as we get the Leonardo project on a new track."

"Great to hear that. Maybe you and your team can share the progress with me one day. But I need to talk to you about a different subject today. Would you please follow me to my office?"

Mo stands quickly and, with wobbly legs, walks next to Junior. He has no idea what this is about, and can't imagine it's good news; he's never been summoned to the CEO's office like this. He wonders if Sofia has shared her succession plans with him.

The two walk past Anna, who smiles, which gives Mo no relief, and into Junior's office. Junior closes the door and asks Mo to take a seat. Now Mo is completely unsettled.

"Mo, please relax; it's not bad news. On Friday afternoon, Stephano and I will meet with Borges, our potential new partner. We hope that Friday will be the last of our meetings, but we left Saturday open just in case. The meeting will be in Switzerland at the accounting firm that handles the negotiations and transaction. One of the participants in our meeting, the potential buyer's VP of operations, Petra Hoff, would like to meet with you Friday morning. We're hoping you could accommodate that."

"Why would she want to see me?" asks Mo. "Are you able to tell me what we'll be discussing. Any details?"

"She and other executives have asked to talk to several of our associates before finalizing the deal, and I granted all the permissions, including yours. I believe you've already spoken with Paul Haupt about technical details. But I'm afraid I have to defer to Petra for the subject of this upcoming meeting."

Junior just added another weight on top of Mo's already overloaded brain, but Mo also believes that Junior would never ask him for anything that would not be in Mo's best interest. He's started to expect detours to his comfortable life, and this is just one more.

"Please tell her that I'll be happy to meet on Friday morning. Where is it that we'll meet?"

"Thank you, Mo. The meeting is in a little town close to Geneva in one of the firm's field offices. Please keep the plan quiet for now. Anna has the details for you. And after the meeting, let's talk about how it went."

***

DOI: 10.4324/9781003231837-35

Mo travels to Switzerland by train Thursday night and checks into the same hotel he stayed when he attended Marie's race in the area. On Friday morning, he gets up early, but he's too nervous to eat breakfast. He stops for an expresso at a street café and arrives in an Uber about . minutes early at the address Anna had given him. He walks into the lobby of a large office build ing and sees the security desk, which makes him think all the more about the need for secrecy. He signs in as instructed by a burly guard and then hears, "Hi, Mo."

The voice is unmistakable. When he turns, he sees familiar bright eyes staring at him. "Marie. What are you doing here?"

"I work here. You've forgotten the name of my company?"

Mo is speechless.

"It's Delatour Global. My company was retained to manage your deal. When I saw Davanti on the list of new projects, I applied for that team. I was hoping our paths might cross again one of these days."

Mo still only stares at her. It's obvious now that she is pregnant, but she looks great. She seems happy and appears to have adapted very well to the changes in her life. Mo never saw Marie in work clothes, and he is surprised how professional she looks in her blue suit, white blouse, and attractive jewelry. "You look great, Marie. It's so good to see you."

"Really? I hear so little from you. I wasn't sure what you'd say."

Marie reaches out and grabs Mo's hand. Mo is hoping that nobody sees them. She pulls him over to a small sofa in the lobby, and they sit down. Marie is glad Mo showed up early for his meeting. "I saw your name on the list of visitors today, and I was hoping I could catch you before your meeting."

"Sorry, Marie, I'm under so much pressure right now. I really should . . ."

"Yes. I understand. There's a lot of pressure everywhere. . . . I'm pretty sure the meeting today won't reduce your stress; it may even add to the decisions you'll have to make. But I want to wish you the best of luck for whatever brought you here today."

"Thank you," replies Mo genuinely. He's pleased to see Marie but confused by the pieces of his life colliding. "How are you doing?"

"Getting by. Is there any chance you could carve out a little time for me today? Maybe lunch?"

"I just don't know how long . . ."

"Your host and her brass are lunching with your CEO and director at noon. Your meeting will be over well before then. But you're listed for the whole day, so they may need you again in the afternoon. What do you say? I meet you here at noon."

"Yes, fine," he says reluctantly. His head is really swimming as they stand up and Marie takes him to the security desk.

"Bonjour, Marie," says the guard. "Looks like you folks know each other."

"Bonjour, Louis. We're good friends."

Marie waves as she heads back to her office, and the guard takes Mo to an elevator and then to his meeting room. He offers Mo a chair in the small conference room and leaves. Moments later a friendly woman enters and asks Mo if he would like a coffee. Mo is ready to ask for breakfast, but he's happy to accept coffee and the few cookies she brings.

Petra shows up as Mo is getting ready to taste the coffee—he's already eaten the cookies. Petra is in her mid-50s and, based on her demeanor, has been a business executive for some time. She introduces herself and tells Mo that she joined Borges only a few years ago as VP for new ventures. She now runs Borges' global operations and explains that she is on the negotiating team because of her current and past responsibilities. She gets right to business with German efficiency.

"So tell me a little about yourself, Herr Pensatore."

Mo talks about his love for bikes and his career as an engineer at Davanti.

"But you must have done other things recently."

"Oh, yes, I manage the first project that was picked for Davanti's new innovation excellence process."

"I heard about that project. I understand that you discussed it with Paul Haupt. What else are you working on?"

"I picked up a few continuous improvement projects, and I'm leading a project to improve innovation speed. I think I've played an important part in the innovation excellence transformation at Davanti. I wasn't sure you were interested in that today."

"Very much so."

"Well, in that case, I recently took a new assignment to lead the transformation."

"That's impressive. Borges is merging with Davanti largely because of Davanti's technology, but that's only one reason. When we toured Davanti and learned more about the company, we discovered a few things that we not aware of. We consider them of equal if not of higher value than the technology: The first thing we noticed is the exceptional engagement of the associates. Me and my colleagues were equally impressed with how fast Davanti transformed. We had looked at Davanti two years ago as a possible partner; we see a very different company today. Davanti has leveraged its strengths and is closing its business gaps in an impressive manner. Your recent initiatives have not matured where the results are visible in the financial reports yet, but we know a good thing when we see it and other suitors are likely to see it soon as well. So I want to talk to you about Davanti's transformation and how you can help us embark on a similar culture change."

"I'm confused. I thought . . . I guess . . . I'm curious: assuming this deal is completed, what will happen to my project?"

"Your project will be a key piece of Paul Haupt' s puzzle. And we have plenty of engineers at Borges and Davanti that you can train and coach to continue your good work. It needs to continue."

Mo is now totally flabbergasted, and looks like Junior looked when the CEO first met Sofia.

"I'm here because I want you to join Borges as our innovation excellence leader. We've had small successes with lean in our factories, but we had no idea how to extend the initiative to the rest of the company. Furthermore, we did not understand that innovation excellence could have such a profound impact on the associates and the culture. I understand you have limited leadership experience, but the folks at Davanti talk very highly of you and your leadership potential. You'll join a team at Borges that knows how to integrate new talent."

"How do you see my initial role? I know virtually no one at Borges and will have little to no real credibility with your staff."

"We'd expect you to take the Borges leaders and associates to Davanti for them to learn—there is no better place to learn than where you can see the work for yourselves, right? They'd learn from you, your colleagues, Davanti leaders. . . . Davanti has an impressive people management model, and I have great visions of what that can do for all of Borges' operations. But don't get worried; we won't throw you in over your head. Although we'll give you a significant promotion, we'll use you more as a coach and advisor at the beginning, and then ease you into positions with more direct leadership responsibilities. And in our new organization you'll find many opportunities for advancement, if you are interested. I assume you could even go back to an engineering job one day if that would be your desire."

Mo still sits there with his mouth open and dry. He quicky takes a gulp of his lukewarm coffee as Petra continues.

"I wanted to talk with you personally to show how important this innovation excellence tra[n]s formation is for me, and how impressed I am with the impact it has had on the people at Davan[ti]. I don't expect a decision from you today, but here's my business card. I've added my personal c[ell] phone on the back. You'll meet with our HR director and a couple more folks this morning, and [if] anybody fails to give you an answer you need, please call. Any other questions for me right now?"

"I learned what I know from Ricardo Capace and Sofia Saggio. What will happen to them?"

"We have big plans for Herrn Capace. We'll need him at Davanti during the transition, and I am sure he'll move to bigger opportunities soon after that. We may actually move all bike operations to Italy. Frau Saggio doesn't work for Davanti, as you know, and it will be entirely up to her and her company if we can collaborate. I have great regard for what she's done with Davanti, and hope to talk with her one day."

"I love my work at Davanti, but I especially like the people and the way Davanti has evolved in engaging everyone in the company. Will I be in for a surprise at Borges?"

"You may, but rarely is there much buyers' remorse when we bring staff on board. We've worked hard to develop trust and respect throughout the company. With that said, Davanti is unique. But you'll have the freedom and influence here to make the changes necessary. And you can count on me to support you and help you with that. Oh, I almost forgot—what we discuss today must stay in this room. OK?"

Mo nods.

"Then I'll also tell you that Herr Davanti will take a position on the board of the joint venture and remain accessible to you at any time—he promised me that."

"That's good to know. I have so much respect for him. We've all come a long way at Davanti, and it started with Fausto Davanti Jr. Without his leadership, we'd not be talking today."

After fielding a few more questions from Mo about the company's organizational chart and access to admin personnel, Petra rises and shakes his hand. She opens the meeting door, and calls in and introduces Klaus Blum, who comes in to go over the HR details with Mo. Klaus is a young HR director, and just like Petra gets right to business. He talks about salary, benefits, and the answer to Mo's most important question: relocation. Mo's position would be south of Munich near the borders of Germany, Switzerland, and Austria. "It could be worse," thinks Mo, "at least I will have mountains to bike and ski." He's concerned, however, by the four-hour drive to his parents. And he can't yet fathom how Marie would fit into this picture, if at all.

When Klaus finishes, he makes room for Sabine, a relocation specialist, who carries stacks of information about living and working in southern Germany. She also talks about language classes that are available to him and his family, relocation arrangements, life at Borges, and activities, schools, universities, parks, etc., in Germany. Mo is surprised to see it's 11:50 am. He thanks Sabine, who leaves a card with him along with a pile of information and brochures.

Mo sits alone in the room for a moment, trying to process all that he's heard. He is a bit overwhelmed but also flattered by Borges' interest and aggressive move to secure his position. "What will Marie think?"

***

Marie is in the lobby when Louis the guard brings Mo down, and she waves to him. Mo walks over to Marie and takes her hand.

"Where are we going for lunch?" asks Mo.

Most of the Delatour staff are out on assignments Monday through Thursday, with only principals, admin staff, and those working with clients in the region in the office. On Fridays, however, they all ascend on the building and local restaurants become crowded. The office has no cafeteria,

: there is a little sandwich place across the street. Marie suggests they go there because the food
ast and good. They make the short walk, get in line, order, and then take sandwiches and drinks
a small table that has just opened up.

"How was your meeting, Mo?"

"They're offering me a significant promotion at Borges."

"Congratulations. I knew something big was up when I saw Petra's name on the schedule. Did
you expect this? You don't seem happy."

Mo scratches his head. "It's a lot to take in, I'll tell you that. All of this comes after my project
failed and then got resurrected, after I started a major new project at Davanti, and then after they
offered me the position of the transformation leader at Davanti."

"And on top of that, your girlfriend is expecting your baby."

Mo stares at his sandwich for a minute. "Yes, there is that, too."

Marie is very composed and continues eating. When she finishes her sandwich, she says, "I
have a mammoth appetite these days. Eating for two, you know."

Mo nods.

"Maybe we can talk later about your priorities. Since it's Friday, Mo, why don't you come over
tonight? It's about time for you to experience my cooking."

Mo thinks really hard but cannot come up with a reasonable excuse not to go. He just says,
"OK."

"Great. I'll pick you up in the lobby at 5:00. I assume you left your bag with the guard."

"I did. Five will be fine." Despite being so hungry earlier, Mo leaves half his sandwich uneaten,
and Marie asks if she can have it. "I'd better get back in case they ask for me."

"It was nice of you to come, Mo. I've missed you. I've missed being with you. I've missed talking with you. Maybe you'll have more to say tonight. Maybe you'll say that you missed me as well."

The two get up and quietly walk out of the restaurant and back to the Delatour office.

***

Marie left work early to buy groceries. Mo was not called back in for another meeting, and spent
the afternoon working from a small guest office, wondering how the negotiations were going and
questioning his priorities about everything. He's happy when Marie sticks her head into the office
and asks if he's ready to leave.

"Absolutely," says Mo, who rises, puts his laptop away, and grabs his bag. "Let's go. It will be
nice to get some air."

Marie is surprised to see Mo smile and without the look of confusion on his face. They walk
outside and take Marie's car to her nearby apartment, which is on the second floor of a modern
complex of small apartments.

"You've never been here," says Marie as she parks in an underground garage. She points at a
wire cage in the corner where she keeps her bike and skis.

When they get upstairs, she shows Mo around the apartment, including Chiara's room that
Marie has decorated for their little daughter. She obviously had a lot of fun with the decor, and
admits that she got carried away. Mo smiles at the whimsical decorations and vibrant colors.

"You know my mother's name is . . ." Mo stops his sentence when Marie suddenly takes a call,
signaling that it's important. "My mom. She calls me every day around this time."

Marie has a short, happy talk with her mom while Mo looks around. Eventually he hears
Marie say, "Mom, I have to run, I have a guest."

Mo had wandered into the kitchen, and Marie catches up with him to resume the tour. The
apartment is organized and bright, with many large windows. They return to the kitchen, which

overlooks a central courtyard for five other buildings, and Mo helps Marie prepare dinner: sc
lops, pilaf, and a large salad. While they cook, they talk about Mo's work, Marie's work, a
quickly get back to Mo's meeting with Borges. "Tell me more about it," begs Marie. "You rea
said nothing at lunch."

"To make a long story short, I think they will merge with Davanti sooner than later. They'r
not only interested in our technology; they're just as interested in our innovation excellence
transformation."

"So did Petra recruit you for your engineering knowledge and product ideas?"

"She offered me a promotion, but it's not in engineering."

Marie is surprised.

"They want me to help them transform their company like our consultant Sofia helped transform Davanti."

Mo describes what he's done recently at Davanti, explaining that, even with that experience,
he feels underqualified. "They didn't seem to care and offered to support me in any way possible.
They put together a great package; the compensation is more than appropriate."

"That's amazing, Mo. That's a big step up. And where is the job?"

"That's the bad part. It's in southern Germany."

"That's wonderful, Mo. I'd love to move there if I had an opportunity."

As if Mo did not have enough surprises today. Marie tells him that she spent a lot of time working in the area as part of her job and loves the region. "It's close to the mountains, many lakes,
great skiing, and Germany is a great place to live and raise a child," she says as if she was ready to
move to Germany regardless of Mo joining her or not.

"But to get back to your job interview. You know that Chiara and I have an open position, too.
I was wondering if you'd like to interview for that one as well?"

Mo is speechless again.

"Let me know when you're ready, if and when that day ever comes." Marie wants Mo to step
up and commit, but she's determined to live and enjoy her life regardless of his decision.

Their conversation over dinner turns light and carefree, talking about cycling, food, and the
coming of good weather. Mo feels relaxed for the first time in weeks, and he realizes how much
he's really missed Marie. They talk into the night, and she asks Mo to stay. He suggests he sleep on
the couch so that Marie can get a good night's rest, but she will have none of that, and they spend
a wonderful night together. In the morning, Mo rises early and has coffee and croissants ready for
Marie when she gets up.

"Thank you, Mo, for this, for everything," says Marie as she pours a cup of decaf and sits across
from him.

"I think I'll take the dad job," Mo says bluntly, breaking open a croissant and staring into
Marie's eyes. "That is, if it's still available."

Marie chokes on the coffee, jumps up and throws her arms around him as if she would never
let him go again. "I won't make you interview. You're hired."

The two embrace for minutes, then Mo takes a step back and looks seriously into Marie's eyes.
He starts to speak, then stops, and then quietly says, "I'm sorry I took so long to make the right
decision. And I know I've acted like a jerk at times."

"Mo, it's OK. I'd rather wait and have you be all in with me and Chiara than you make a hasty
decision that you'd regret."

"Thank you, Marie. I am all in. . . . Maybe you can help me with my other decisions."

"What other decisions? We're moving to Germany, right?"

"*Wow.* That was fast. Are you sure? Are we sure?"

"I'm sure we're sure. Mo, you'll do great at whatever you set your mind to. This job and the [lo]ve is just what you need—just what the three of us need."

Marie tells Mo that she thinks her company would move her to their German unit ("Weißt du, [ic]h spreche fließend Deutsch"[1]) and she could be assigned to clients in the region after the baby arrives to limit her travel.

"I'm glad you've got this figured out. . . . Maybe we should spend the weekend talking about our plans. I don't need to leave until tomorrow afternoon. I'll just need to pick up a few things."

"I think that's a great idea, Mo. And maybe we can spend a little time this afternoon shopping for Chiara as well. There's still a lot I'd like to get for her."

"There's a lot that *we'll* get her. . . . And I'd like to get you something as well."

"Oh, what would that be?"

"A ring. Will you marry me, Marie?"

Marie gives Mo a huge embrace. "Yes. Absolutely."

***

Mo called Marie early Monday morning when he arrived at work in Fumane. At 7:00 am, he was the only person in the building. With the excitement of the weekend, he couldn't sleep and decided to get a jump on the week.

"Hi Marie. I just had to call you. I figured you'd be up."

"Yes. About ready to head into the office. It will be a busy one today. We have an 8:30 briefing to go over the Friday meetings."

"Well, have a good day and a good week. I love you, Marie."

"I love you, Mo. I'm so excited for us."

"Yeah, me too."

At noon that day, Mo got a text from Marie: "Deal is finalized in principle. I will be in Fumane later this week to work on financial details and agreements. Can I stay with you?"

"Absolutely. It will be wonderful to see you."

Wednesday evening, Mo picked Marie up at the train station. As they drove to Mo's apartment, she talked about the details of the sale, knowing that he had signed a non-disclosure and that all the information would soon be public knowledge.

On Thursday they drove to work together. Marie found her two colleagues and got to work on the deal. But they took a break before lunch and Mo took Marie around the building, introducing her to his friends, starting with Marco. They both work until about 6:30 pm, then Mo gets a chance to show Marie the town. They stop at Bruno's for dinner; out of habit, Mo's grabs a seat at the bar.

"Hey there, stranger," says the bartender Marianne. "Where have you been?"

"Marianne. Hello. I'd like you to meet my girlfriend . . . uh, my fiancée. Marie, this is Marianne."

"Hello, Marie. So you're who's been keeping him away."

"It's nice to meet you, Marianne. . . . So Mo is a regular, I take it."

"Yeah, he and his buddy Marco keep my tip jar full. He's a good guy. You'll want to keep him."

"That's my plan," says Marie, playfully pulling on Mo's ear.

"So what will you two have?"

"I'd like an IPA."

"And I'll have a Pellegrino."

"Coming right up."

They receive their drinks, order a large pizza with mushrooms, cheese, and pancetta, and as they eat, Mo tells Marie everything she'd ever want to know about Fumane and more.

"Will you miss Fumane, Mo?"

"I'm sure I will. But that would be nothing compared to how I'd miss you if I decided to st[...] here and go on being a self-centered engineer. This is starting to feel so right to me. I'm excited [...] start a new chapter in life."

***

On Friday afternoon, Junior has a town hall meeting to bring everybody up to speed on the future of Davanti. Anna is recording and livestreaming a video of the event for the folks in Taiwan so that those who could not attend in person get to hear the news as well. Everyone gathers in the courtyard outside the headquarters. It's a warm spring day, and the crowd is buzzing. They know a deal has been struck, but most don't know what it is or with whom.

Junior walks to a microphone and waves to get the employees to settle down. In a moment, you can hear a pin drop.

"Thank you. This is a big day for Davanti and for you. But before I get to the business at hand, I have to share some personal good news with you." Junior looks at all the faces before him, moving from one to the next and the next. "After some recent tests, my cardiologist was able to tell me my heart is almost back to normal. I'm going to be around for a while—like it or not!"

The employees give Junior an emotional applause, cheering him as never before.

Junior waves his arms and eventually gets them to quiet down again: "Now more good news for all of you. Although Davanti changes owners, it still remains Davanti; I look at the transaction as more of a merger. The German company Borges GMBH wants to invest in electric bikes, and they like our technology. And I think they bring as much to us as we bring to them. As a joint entity, we are both stronger organizations. We have signed an agreement in principle, but there are many details to be taken care of. Davanti will continue as an independent company just as it has been since my dad founded the company. The transformation that we've embarked on will go on. Nothing will change, especially Davanti's commitment to racing. The new operation will have a Davanti president, who we'll name in the near future."

Most employees applaud, glad to know that Davanti will remain "Davanti."

Junior then announces that Borges will be bringing their bike operations to Italy: "I hope we have enough room here in Fumane; it's possible we may have to expand this facility or find another place nearby. We've spoken with city officials about opportunities. And it looks like there will be a bright future for our friends in Taiwan also."

The growth of headquarters brings louder and longer cheers.

"You may be wondering what will happen to me?" asks Junior.

An employee in the crowd yells back, "What will happen to you, Junior?" The crowd laughs.

"I'm glad you asked," says Junior, laughing as well. "So I can make sure you all are being properly cared for, I'll be joining the board of Borges. I will always have your interests front and center."

Junior then gives a brief summary of the negotiations, including an employee stock option plan, and tells them that their designated representatives on the sales team will provide more detailed information to the various organizations: "You will have your say in the future of Davanti and conditions in Fumane."

The ownership news brings loud applause and cheers. Some employees are visibly moved by the news.

"I want to thank Stephano and the Davanti representatives who were engaged in the negotiations. They've put together an excellent deal for both Davanti and Borges. I thank the Borges executives for bargaining so openly and honestly. But you are the ones who truly need to be thanked. Borges leadership was incredibly impressed with the commitment and value each of you e to Davanti on a daily basis—I knew it, and it's apparent to those looking from the outside They're also envious of what we've accomplished with innovation excellence and want to make at the model for their entire operation. Some of our folks, like Mo Pensatore, have been invited help them in that regard; you'll see a lot of their staff come here to learn. And we have much to earn from them as well. Collaboration works both ways: Borges is a leader in digital technology— they even have autonomous bikes. They've excelled at using digital technology in their plants and offices, including R&D, and they'll help Davanti do the same. Expect more change as we jointly create synergy with all those initiatives."

Junior asks everybody to collaborate with the Borges and Delatour personnel, who are in Fumane to work on the final details, and discusses likely timing for the closing. "Of course, we need to get approval from the authorities, but we think we'll have everything wrapped up before the Tour de France is over this year."

Hearing their CEO mention the Tour, the employees start to repeatedly chant—"Da-van-ti, Da-van-ti . . ."—and even Junior joins in, pumping his fist to the rhythm of their voices. Finally, he raises his hands to quiet the crowd. "I'm proud of you all. My father would be proud of you all. Thank you. I love you all." He then walks away from the microphone and mills about in the crowd, saying hello by name to the employees he greets, answering a few questions that are posed to him, but mostly accepting congratulations from grateful associates. This time, he thinks, he's finally treated them right.

Mo asks Marie to join him among those waiting to see Junior. After about 15 minutes they congratulate him, and Mo expresses his thanks for all that the CEO has done for him. He also introduces Marie as his fiancée, "who is here because she happens to work for Delatour. She's also a great bike racer and kicks my butt every time we ride." Marie blushes and says, "It's nice to see you, Mr. Davanti."

"Welcome to Fumane, Marie. I saw you at a meeting in Switzerland. Congratulations and good luck to you both. I'm happy for you."

Mo and Marie say goodbye to Junior, and then walk back into the building. "Stop by my desk, Marie, when you're finished for the day, then we'll get some dinner."

"I can't wait. I'm already starving."

***

At 6:30 pm, Mo looks up to see Marie walking with her backpack toward his desk. He quickly closes down his work and jumps up. Since no one else is in the office, he gives her a hug and kiss. "I've picked a special spot for us tonight. We haven't properly celebrated our engagement."

"Engagement—that sounds wonderful."

They walk to Mo's car in the nearly empty Davanti lot, and head to Gusto, an intimate restaurant that many consider the finest in Fumane. Mo has to park a few blocks away because the town is crowded on a beautiful Friday night. As they walk among the crowd, they pass a popular casual restaurant as the door opens and a group of women pour out. They look like they've had plenty of fun and are getting ready for some more. Mo did not notice them until he hears his sister Catherine: "Hey, Mo," she yells, happy to see him.

"Uh, Catherine, hello," stammers Mo.

"Nice to see you," says Catherine as she rushes closer to talk. "Is this your date."

"This is . . ."

Catherine takes a step back and looks at the two of them together. "Do I see what I think I'm seeing?"

Marie smiles, and Mo fumbles for words, finally saying, "This is Marie. My fiancée."

"Mo, I think you got the order wrong. Didn't you pay attention when mom lectured us about such things?"

Marie laughs, but Mo is not pleased: "Really? That's what you say?"

"Oh, I'm just kidding, Mo. You two look wonderful together. Congratulations on the engagement and the baby!"

"Marie, this is my sister Catherine."

"Nice to meet you, Catherine."

"It's a pleasure to meet you, Marie. . . . Have you told mom you're getting married and having a baby, Mo? Do you know if it's a boy or girl?"

"Girl," says Marie politely.

"I can't wait to talk with mom about this!"

"I've not talked to mom yet, so please don't mention it. I'm afraid she may have a reaction like yours," giving Catherine a frown.

"Oh, you shouldn't be worried. She'll be so excited. So will dad."

"But you just said . . ."

"Oh, please. That kind of thinking went out years ago. Mom will be thrilled. Let me handle this—just show up with Marie on Sunday for lunch, and we'll celebrate. It will be great. Trust me."

"Is this OK with you, Marie?" asks Mo.

"Absolutely. I'd love to meet your family."

"Then I guess it's set," says Mo nervously.

"See you then. I should catch up to my friends from the bank. We like to go out every couple of weeks—leave the kids with the husbands, you know."

"Well, have fun, and be careful."

Catherine rushes off, and Mo and Marie continue walking toward Gusto.

"Is everybody like that in your family?"

"No. Don't worry. I don't know who she got it from."

***

Since he had not seen Sofia at work for more than a week and had not heard from her, Mo gives her a call on Saturday morning while Marie talks to her parents: "Sofia. Hi. It's Mo. How are you?"

"I've been busy, Mo," she says. "And with everybody at Davanti focused on the merger now, for the time being my energy is better spent elsewhere. How have you been?"

Mo tells Sofia about the meetings he had with Borges and their job offer.

"Congratulations, Mo. I was aware of their plans, and I hope you accepted the offer. Marcel and I advised Junior and Stephano throughout the negotiations. I am convinced the deal will work out very well, and I'm really happy they recognized the right person to take the Davanti knowledge to Borges. It's really just an extension of what Ricardo and I envisioned for you. Since you're pulled into Borges, I offered to stay on in my current role a little longer and coach someone to continue Davanti's transformation."

"And then?"

"Well, just between you and me for now, after I set up my replacement in Davanti, I'll head up Marcel's new consulting company. Our plan is to consult with small to large companies that want to pursue innovation excellence. We'll get paid a percent of the increase in client revenue, and Marcel has challenged me to come up with the appropriate financial models. And since I will be the president of the new venture, I need to recruit the right staff and train them . . . Care to come work for me?"

Mo is flattered but declines, and talks about his own plans, including his plans together with Marie.

"I am so excited for you and Marie. I hope I can meet her one of these days."

"So maybe your new company will consult for Borges one day."

"Well, that is entirely up to them and you. Marcel is telling me that we won't lack for customers. But I'd certainly enjoy working with them one day. But even if I don't, you and all my friends at Davanti should call at any time for any reason. Davanti is my baby, and it will always be my baby."

"I'm excited for you Sofia. And I'm sure you'll hear from me sooner than later. There's so much I have to learn."

***

Leading up to the Sunday meal at his parents, Mo tells Marie everything imaginable about his family. She understands how close he is to them all, and she doesn't intend to break that apart. But she also wants Mo to focus on growing his own family. Mo agrees.

On a foggy Sunday morning they drive to Mo's parents' villa. Marie brings a bouquet of flowers, and Mo has a special bottle of Brunello for his dad. Mo's mom greets them on the front porch.

Mo parks the car and jumps out to get the door for Marie, yelling to his mom. "Hello!"

They walk up to the porch, and Marie presents the flowers to Mo's mom. "These are for you, Mrs. Pensatore."

"Thank you, and please call me Chiara."

"Mo!" says Marie. "You never told me!" She covers her mouth with both hands and looks like she is in shock. "I didn't know your mom's name was Chiara," she finally says.

"I had tried to tell you, and then I forgot about it."

"You only wrote 'my mom's . . .'"

"This is all my fault, Marie. I didn't want you to be surprised."

Mo's mom is confused, and, as the rest of the family gathers behind her, she asks, "Surprised by what? That I have a name?"

"No, mom," says Mo, shaking his head. "Marie picked the name 'Chiara' for our baby without even knowing it was your first name."

Mrs. Pensatore's eyes widen.

Mo realizes that he's blurted out the real surprise: "And I guess you now know our real surprise. We're having a baby girl."

Mo's mom gives Marie such a big hug that Marie cries tears of joy.

"You've chosen a wonderful name for your baby, Marie. I'm so glad you did."

They walk into the house, and Mo's dad, sister, and brother and their spouses and children introduce themselves to Marie. Everyone gives her a cautious hug, and she smiles and wipes away tears after each. "It's so nice to meet you all."

Benito pours aperitifs for the adults (except for Marie), and Catherine brings out a large antipasti tray. They all sit in the living room, getting to know each other, and then Mo announces that they are engaged.

"That would be surprise No. 2," says Catherine, "but who's counting? And where's the ring?"

"I'm working on that," explains Mo. "Things have been going pretty fast."

"He'll find one," says Marie. "If he knows what's good for him."

As they move to the dining table, looking forward to pasta carbonara with a side of roasted spring vegetables, Mrs. Pensatore turns to Mo and Marie: "Have you set a date for the wedding? I would love to help organize it with you?"

"I'd certainly appreciate your help, Chiara. Thank you so much. I think you and my mom will work well together. I want you to meet her and my dad soon."

"Yes, yes, definitely."

"But we've got time to plan the wedding. It's not our first priority right now. One thing a time: the baby, the new jobs, the move . . ."

"The move—what move?" asks Mrs. Pensatore, who looks around for a seat. Catherine quickly leads her to a chair to gather herself, and says, "Surprise #3."

Marie looks at Mo with a brow raised.

"I haven't had a chance to talk to my parents about any of this yet," says Mo sheepishly.

"I'm so sorry," says Marie apologetically.

"So will you tell us now?" asks Mo's dad. All eyes are on Mo again. His sister just shakes her head, wondering what Mo's been thinking of late.

"I mentioned a potential sale or merger involving Davanti. It's going to happen with Borges GMBH from Germany."

"They're my favorite supplier," yells Benito. "That's great that you'll be working for them! Congratulations, Mo."

"They offered me an excellent position. It's a big promotion. I'll be working in continuous improvement, not in engineering."

"That is fantastic," says Mo's dad. "They were a good supplier even when I was working. I understand they grew a lot, but why would they hook up with Davanti?"

Mo gives a short summary of the pending deal and starts to talk about their technologies when his mother, tired of the business discussion, cuts him off. "So what about *the move*, Mo? Please tell me about *the move*. What's going on."

"I would start my new career at the Borges headquarters in southern Germany, just across the Alps from here. It's not too far. Only about four or five hours. And if we don't have enough time to come here, maybe you can visit us in Germany."

"Of course we will," says Mo's dad. "You may regret you said that. I'd love to get out of here once in a while."

"If that is where my grandchild is, then that's where I'm going to be—a lot," threatens Mo's mom. "That's a promise."

"Mo, please tell me that we're now done with surprises for today," begs Marie.

"Yes, Mo, please say there are no more surprises," repeats Mrs. Pensatore.

"No more surprises. I promise. That is unless we're not going to eat. That would be a surprise."

Catherine and Benito bring in lunch as they all talk more about the move to Germany and the baby. Marie can feel the love of Mo's family and enjoys their company. Benito and Catherine's kids tell her all about their school and sports activities, and she imagines her daughter doing the same one day. After dinner, Mo helps to pass out pieces of Italian cheese cream cake, giving Marie a plate and kissing her on the cheek. He feels like he now has two families, and he likes how that feels.

Even though they all are likely to see each other soon again, they all say long goodbyes to each other when it's time to leave. Catherine talks for minutes with Marie at the car, offering her any kind of assistance at any time. Benito offers to help Mo with the move. Mo's parents hold hands on the porch and wave goodbye as Mo and Marie eventually drive away.

When they arrive back at Mo's apartment, they're both exhausted. They just hang out on the couch and talk about their stressful day and Mo's many surprises.

"You know, I must be the luckiest girl in the world. Just imagine if I hadn't broken my chain that day in the mountains."

"It's been a roller-coaster ride since."

"It sure has been. I hope it gets smoother now. I know it will. But what a story: There's a fair maiden in distress on a mountain, and a handsome prince rides to her rescue," she jokes. "They in love, get married, start a large family—maybe not quite in that order—and live happily ever er. This would be great material for a cheap romance, you know, the kind of dime novels they l in the train stations."

"I've never read those."

"Oh, I do. I enjoy them on my train trips."

"Maybe one day somebody writes *our* story," says Mo. "That I'd love to read."

Note

1. "You know, I speak German fluently."

Index

Note: Page locators in *italics* represent a figure

3M, 139, 150n2

Printed in the United States
by Baker & Taylor Publisher Services